THE **GREEN** GUIDE

Wine Regions of France

Pinot Noir grap harvest in Burgundy , S. Sauvignier/MICHELIN

MICHELIN

General Manager	Cynthia Clayton Ochterbeck

THEGREENGUIDE WINE REGIONS OF FRANCE

Editors	Jonathan P. Gilbert, Rachel Mills
Contributing Writer	Jane Anson
Production Manager	Natasha G. George
Cartography	Stephane Anton
Photo Editor	Yoshimi Kanazawa
Photo Researcher	Claudia Tate
Interior Design	Chris Bell
Layout	Michelin APA Publications Ltd.
Cover Design	Chris Bell, Christelle Le Déan
Cover Layout	Michelin Apa Publications Ltd.

Contact Us

The Green Guide
Michelin Maps and Guides
One Parkway South
Greenville, SC 29615
USA
www.michelintravel.com

Michelin Maps and Guides
Hannay House
39 Clarendon Road
Watford, Herts WD17 1JA
UK
✆01923 205240
www.ViaMichelin.com
travelpubsales@uk.michelin.com

Special Sales

For information regarding bulk sales, customized editions and premium sales, please contact our Customer Service Departments:

USA 1-800-432-6277
UK 01923 205240
Canada 1-800-361-8236

HOW TO USE THIS GUIDE

PLANNING YOUR TRIP

The blue-tabbed PLANNING YOUR TRIP section at the front of the guide gives you the information you need to organise a **wine tour in France**. You'll find ideas, practical information, a host of wine buff activities, a calendar of events, as well as information on shopping and sightseeing.

INTRODUCTION

The orange-tabbed INTRODUCTION section explores the wine growing regions' **Terroir** and geology. The **History** section spans from early wine harvesting to the modern day. The **Wine Production** section delves into modern appellations, while **Enjoying Wine** explores tasting, serving and, of course, drinking.

DISCOVERING

The green-tabbed DISCOVERING section features the principal **wine growing areas by region**, with plenty of wine-related attractions, **driving tours** and **walking tours**, as well as activities for when you just want to stroll around town or put your feet up. Admission prices shown are normally for a single adult.

ADDRESSES

We've selected the best hotels, restaurants, cafes shops, nightlife and entertainment to fit all budgets. The Legend on the cover flap explains the price categories. See the back of the guide for an index of hotels and restaurants.

Sidebars

Throughout the guide you will find blue, orange and green-colored text boxes with lively anecdotes, detailed history and background information.

A Bit of Advice

Green advice boxes found in this guide contain practical tips and handy information relevant to the sight in the Discovering section.

STAR RATINGS★★★

Michelin has given star ratings for more than 100 years. If you're pressed for time, we recommend you visit the ★★★, or ★★ sights first:

★★★ **Highly recommended**
★★ **Recommended**
★ **Interesting**

MAPS

- National Wine Regions map.
- Local Wine Regions maps.
- Local tour maps.

All maps in this guide are oriented north, unless otherwise indicated by a directional arrow. The term "Local Map" refers to a map within the chapter or Tourism Region. A complete list of the maps found in the guide appears at the back of this book.

© AVTG/iStockphoto

PLANNING YOUR TRIP

INTRODUCTION TO THE WINE REGIONS OF FRANCE

DISCOVERING THE WINE REGIONS OF FRANCE

Welcome to the Wine Regions of France

Few things say France better than a freshly baked baguette, a wedge of cheese, and a glass of wine to wash them down. Getting to know the regions and the people where the wine is produced brings you closer to the heart of the country; with each region offering its own distinct pleasures.

Andlau and its vineyards, Alsace
© Fotokate/Dreamstime.com

ALSACE *(p84–115)*

One of the best organised and most picturesque wine routes in France, this easy to navigate road winds through flower-filled villages and vine-covered slopes. From Strasbourg to Colmar, you can visit wineries for more than 170 kilometres along the eastern foothills of the Vosges mountains.

BEAUJOLAIS *(p116-133)*

As you head south of Lyon, the rolling hills of the Beaujolais region offer a taste of the good life in France; with regular festivals, dynamic winemakers and uncomplicated food-friendly wines. Attractions include the regional capital of Villefranche-sur-Saône and the wine cultural centre of Le Hameau-en -Beaujolais.

BORDEAUX *(p134–175)*

Recent years have seen Bordeaux transformed; with spectacular renovations in the city itself, rewarded by a new UNESCO World Heritage status for its 18th century centre. As the region throws off its stuffy image, more and more wineries in iconic villages such as Margaux, Saint Émilion and Pauillac have opened up to visitors.

BURGUNDY *(p176–215)*

Understanding the secrets of the mythical names of this region, from Chablis and Pouilly Fuissé to Gevry Chambertin and Romanée Conti, becomes a little easier once you have driven through the wine roads here, passing tiny villages with low stone walls, church spires and vines on every side. Many vignerons are happy to spend hours in the cellars talking you through the nuances of the terroir.

CHAMPAGNE *(p216–253)*

With its two main centres of Reims and Epernay, a weekend in Champagne is a rewarding experience. Many of the famous houses offer well-organised, impressive tour facilities to visitors, while discovering the smaller properties that bottle their own Champagne offers the perfect contrast.

COGNAC *(p254–262)*

Another region where there is a fascinating contrast between the big, internationally-recognised names and the smaller family-run houses. The town of Cognac is charming and romantic, with a large central park and an attractive river.

CORSICA *(p263–275)*

The "ile de la beauté" makes an excellent destination for a longer break, where you can divide your time between the beaches, the rocky interior, and getting to know the many wineries that are dotted around the coastal strip.

JURA *(p276–295)*

A lesser-known part of the country with beautiful scenery, where you can discover unusual grape varieties and fascinating wine-making traditions, including the production of the distinctive Vin Jaune.

LANGUEDOC-ROUSSILLON *(p296–334)*

This large and varied region covers ever-changing landscapes from the walled city of Carcassonne down to the beaches and cliffs of the Mediterranean. The reds of the region tend to be rich and robust, from the heat-loving grapes of Syrah and Mourvèdre.

LOIRE VALLEY *(p335–369)*

Fairy-tale castles, Renaissance chateaux and the stately Loire river somehow seem to fit the delicacy and freshness of the wine, often from Cabernet Franc or Sauvignon Blanc grapes.

PROVENCE *(p370–391)*

One of the most seductive and popular regions in France, the vineyards are often tucked away from the bustling coastal resorts, but still benefit from the same blue skies, hot summers and relaxed approach to life. A glass of Provençal rosé, with its faint blush of delicate pink, is the perfect accompaniment to the climate.

RHÔNE VALLEY *(p392–421)*

Divided into two highly distinct parts, the northern Rhône offers stunning landscapes with the near vertical vineyard slopes of Côte Rotie and Crozes-Hermitage, in complete

Vineyards and the village of Oingt, Beaujolais

J. Damase / MICHELIN

contrast to the more gentle southern Mediterranean landscapes around Avignon and Orange, containing the famous names of Gigondas and Châteauneuf-du-Pape.

SAVOIE AND BUGEY *(p422–433)*

Located on the sunny slopes of the Alps, from Lake Geneva to Lake du Bourget, and along the Rhône river down through the Ain, this region is known for its spectacular scenery, skiing and its many thermal spa resorts, but also offers fascinating discoveries of little known wine.

SOUTH WEST *(p434–465)*

From the mountains of the French Pyrénées, and up past Toulouse and Cahors through Gascony and Bergerac, this rewarding, diverse area is full of indigenous grape varieties, each making distinct wines that can be hard to find outside of the region, making cellar door visits all the more special.

Cucugnan, Languedoc-Roussillon

E. Larribère/MICHELIN

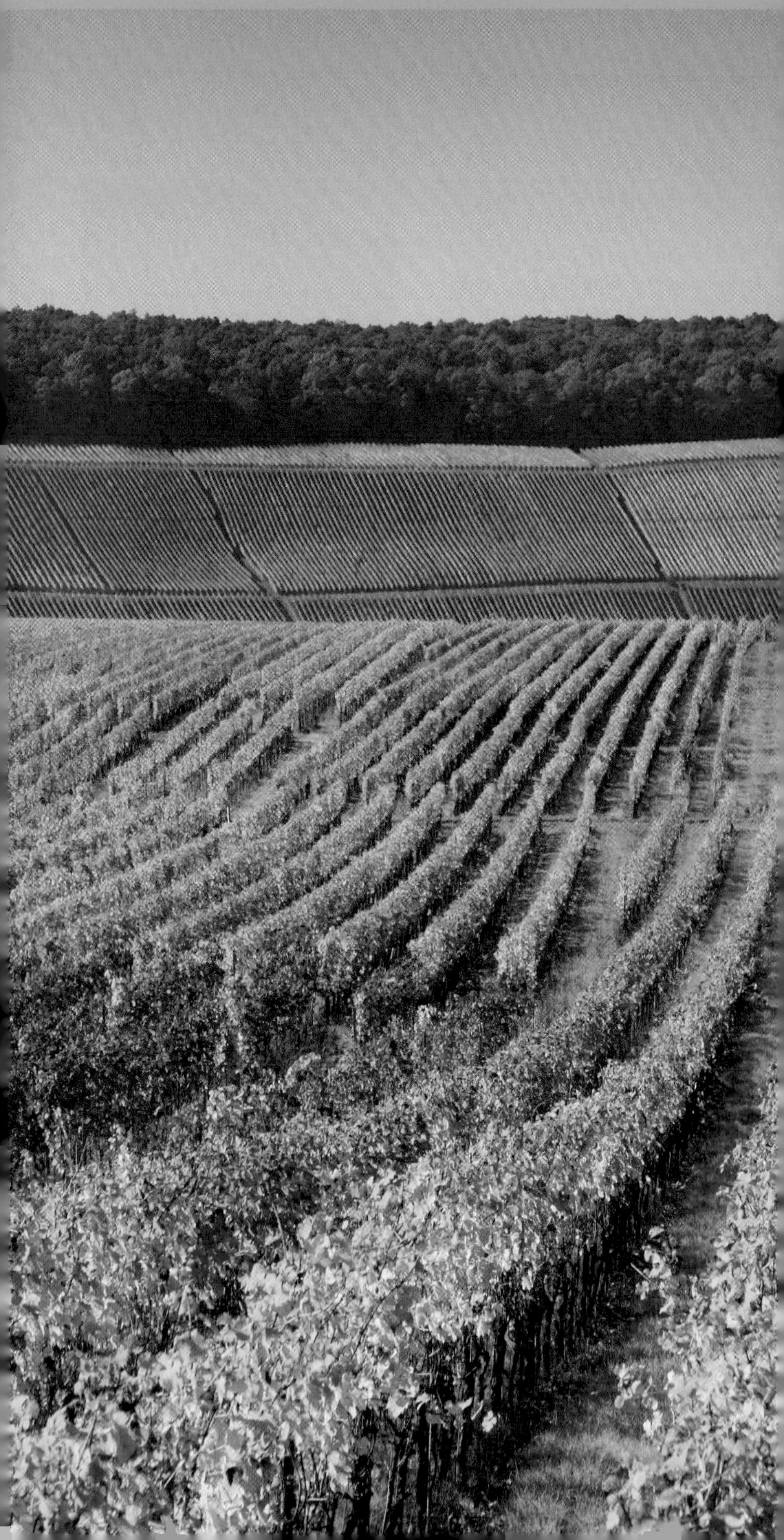

PLANNING YOUR TRIP

Bordeaux vineyards in autumn
© AVTG/istockphoto

When and Where to Go

WHEN TO GO

SEASONS

Spring, summer and autumn are the best seasons to visit France but there is a region for every season.

Summer in France is a lovely time, but be forewarned that most of the French population seems to go on holiday in August, so prepare for crowds in resort and coastal areas, and busy roads to the main tourist areas. Things are quieter in June and September, when French children are still at school. You'll also find that some restaurants and shops close for all or part of August. In the wine growing regions, summer is a time of selective pruning, tending and watchful waiting as the grapes slowly ripen to perfection and *veraison* occurs. Harvesting generally begins in early September; you may find that the wine trails through the vineyards and even some wineries themselves are closed to visitors while the grapes are being gathered, although more and more wineries are realising that visitors enjoy seeing this process, and some now offer the chance to get involved for a few hours.

Autumn brings a return (*la rentrée*) to routine. You'll find bountiful produce in the markets; burnished colours sweeping mountain and countryside; and comfortable daytime temperatures. The vineyards, after a busy period of being emptied of their precious bounty, turn yellow, gold and red before shedding their leaves. In the cellars, the winegrowers turn to the various tasks and stages of transforming grape juice into wine.

Winter can be a quiet time in the countryside and coastal areas, but snowfall draws skiers and other winter sports-lovers to the mountains. Christmas markets flourish in many of the wine regions; the ones in Alsace are famous, but you'll find them in Champagne, Burgundy, Jura, Languedoc, Rhone and Provence as well. In the vineyards, the winegrowers prune back the dormant vines and repair posts and supports; malolactic fermentation begins in the cellars.

Springtime brings rain and warmer temperatures to many inland areas. Provence's infamous wind, the mistral, lowers temperatures but clears away haze to reveal distant views. New vines are planted in the vineyards around March, while new growth brings a haze of green to the established and older vines, as the life cycle of the vine begins again, and winemakers watch out for any spring frosts that could damage emerging vines.

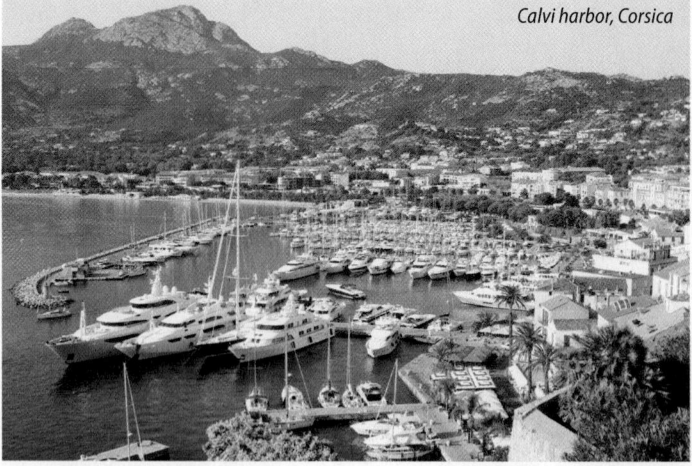
Calvi harbor, Corsica

CLIMATE

For an overview of a specific region of the country, see the Michelin Green Guide series, which cover 24 regions of France (13 of the guides are in English), such as Normandy, Brittany, the French Riviera and Provence). In general the French climate is a moderate one; extremes of either heat or cold are rare for the most part, so that outdoor activity of some kind is almost always possible. Inland the winters are chilly and darkness comes early, especially in the northern latitudes. As spring turns to summer, the days become long and warm and by June the sun lingers well into the evening. Spring and autumn provide opportunities to explore the outdoors and enjoy the lovely countryside and coastal areas of France. In winter, snowfall throughout much of the interior of the country, as well as in the mountainous regions near Italy, permits a wide array of winter sports, such as downhill skiing and snowboarding. However, gray skies in this period are not unusual for much of the country, especially in Paris.

WEATHER FORECAST

National Forecast: ✆32 50. Information about the weather is also available online at www.meteofrance.com.

WHERE TO GO

CITY BREAKS

Exploring vineyards doesn't have to mean ignoring the many vibrant, culturally-rich cities of France. Most wine areas have large cities at their centre, such as Bordeaux, Reims for Champagne, Lyons for Beaujolais, Dijon and Beaune for Burgundy, Toulouse for southwest France and Montpellier for the Languedoc. These cities are often filled with wine bars, wine boutiques and many have wineries within their city limits that can be easily visited on foot or public transport. Even Paris and the Île de France has its own vines and an interesting wine museum (www.museeduvinparis.com).

Bordeaux vineyards in autumn

© Hattiney/Fotolia.com

ESCAPE TO THE COUNTRYSIDE

One of the many attractions of spending a few days or longer around the vineyards of France is that vines tend to grow in some of the most beautiful parts of the world - most usually in gently rolling countryside such as Beaujolais or the Loire, or the more dramastic craggy landscapes of the northern Rhone or the Savoie. Visiting wine regions naturally lends itself to combining winery visits with outdoor activities such as walking or cycling, and every wine region in France is accessible by rivers that also offer the possibility of getting out on boats. A trip down the Canal du Midi, for example, offers a relaxed and leisurely trip through the countryside of southwest France and the Languedoc.

BY THE SEA

A cooling sea breeze can have a beneficial effect on the quality of tihe wines, giving the grapes a chance to cool down and gain delicacy over their growth cycle, and a number of wine regions offer the chance to combine visits with trips to the coast. The vineyards of Bordeaux are within easy striking distance of the Atlantic coast, and the chic resort of Arcachon, while Cassis and Bandol in Provence offers a continual backdrop of the sparkling blue Mediterranean sea. A few islands also have their own vineyards with views directly over water - Corsica being the largest, but also the Ile de Poquerolle and the Ile des Embiez on the Cote d'Azur, and the Ile de Ré in Cognac country.

What to See and Do

SIGHTSEEING

The wine regions offer visitors more than endless visits to chateaux. All of these regions have outstanding natural beauty, and can be enjoyed by non wine-lovers just as much, combining visits to wine properties with a range of other activities, from trips to the beach in Provence, the Languedoc and Bordeaux, to mountaineering or skiing in the Savoie or Jura. All tourist offices offer organised sightseeing tours, while individual tour companies are suggested throughout this guide.

GASTRONOMIC TOURS

One of the great joys of wine is how it enhances the experience of local foods, and in most cases regional wines and foods have evolved in parrallel, such as the hearty duck dishes and rich red wines that are traditional in Madiran in southwest France (*p450*), or the delicate red and white wines of the Loire that go so perfectly with a freshwater river fish from the local rivers, or a gentle 'Sainte Maure de Touraine' goat's cheese (*p341*). Each region has its specialities, and local restaurants often offer tasting menus where the chef will suggest the best local food and wine pairings. L'**Atelier des Chefs** in Paris, Lyon, Bordeaux and Nantes is a cookery school that regularly offers food-and-wine matching courses (www.atelierdeschefs.com), and many of the regional wine schools and generic wine bodies offer similar courses.

CULTURAL SIGHTS

Most wine regions in France have long histories, meaning there are cultural sites to discover at the same time as the wines. These many be historic, or religious, such as the monolithic cathedral in Saint-Émilion (*p147*), and the Gothic cathedral in Reims (*p218*). Increasingly, the chateaux themselves offer cultural activities, from music concerts in the grounds during summer months, to art exhibitions in the winery throughout the year. Some combine culture and entertainment - Château du Clos Luce in the Loire (*p343*) has a "cultural theme" park dedicated to the life of da Vinci.

SPORTING ACTIVITIES

You will find plenty of ways to get outside and active when touring the French wine regions. Many of the wine routes are best viewed from two wheels, and there is currently a project underway in Burgundy to compete an 800 kilometre-long circular cycle route through all the major tourist attractions of the region. In the meantime, companies such as DuVine offers tours

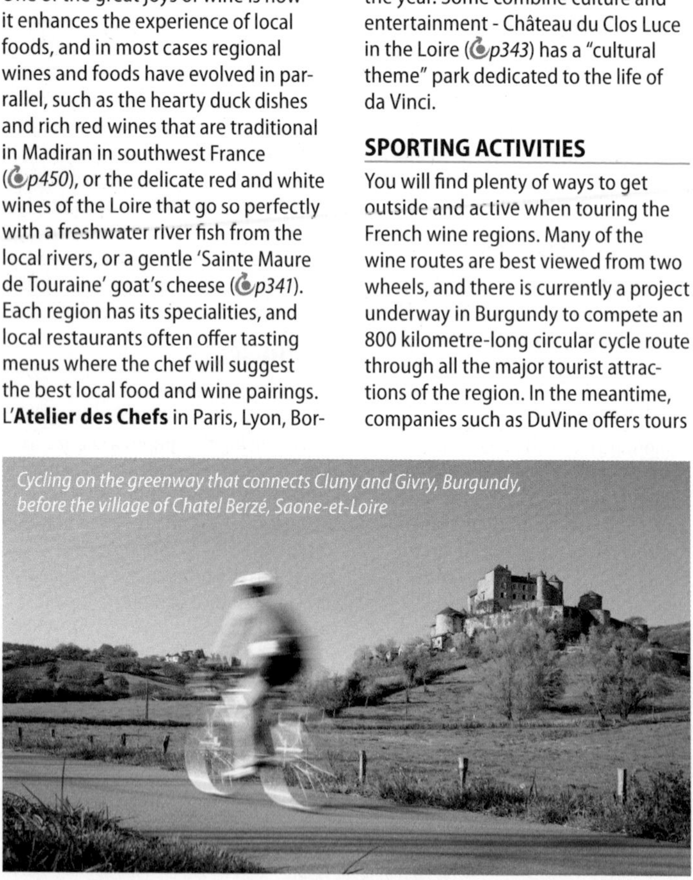

Cycling on the greenway that connects Cluny and Givry, Burgundy, before the village of Chatel Berzé, Saone-et-Loire

through Burgundy (www.duvine.com). Alsace's Route des Vins offers walking alternatives at every point, taking you further up into the higher vineyards and off the beaten track (*p88*). Golf courses are dotted all over the Bordeaux, the Loire and Champagne regions. Pretty much every region offers opportunities for water sports, horse-riding, or tennis. For more extreme sports such as abseiling or mountain biking, head to Corsica, the Jura or the Pyrenees.

St-Vincent procession, Champlitte, Haute-Saône
M. Paygnard/MICHELIN

STUNNING VIEWS

It goes without saying that there are few views more attractive than a vineyard in Autumn, heavy with grapes, or with its leaves just turning gently yellow and orange. But there are also plenty of other stunning views to be had in the wine regions. Among the most dramatic are the sharp inclines of the slopes in Côte Rotie in the northern Rhone, and the stunning gorges and grottos of Cahors in the Lot and the Bergerac region of southwest France. Vineyards with views over the blue seas of the Mediterranean can be found easily in Provence, while Alsace vines are accompanied by the stunning Vosges mountains at every point.

Fêtes du Vin

SAINT VINCENT

Quite how Vincent came to be the patron saint of wine-producers, no-one really knows: perhaps it was because he has the word "vin" in his name. Over the centuries, however, the saint has become the figurehead of France's proud culture of wine, and given his name to the *sociétés de saint Vincent*, which began as mutual aid groups, uniting fellow *vignerons* long before the age of beneficent, or "friendly", societies.

The feast of St Vincent is celebrated in many wine producing regions, either on 22 January, the *"fête"* itself, or on the nearest weekend. The day is usually marked by the procession of the saint, a church service, and a wine tasting and meal for the wine-growers.

In **Burgundy**, between Dijon and Beaune, the St Vincent's day celebrations are *"tournant"*: held in a different wine growing village from year to year. The same is true of events in **Savoie**, in the **Côte Chalonnaise**, around **Auxerre**, in the **Chablis** region, in the **Bourgeuil** appellation, in the vineyards around **Nantes**, and in **Champagne**. Other regions always hold their festivities in the same place.

"Les Saint-Vincent fixes" are annual highlights in **Arlay** and **Champlitte** (Jura), **Villié-Morgon** and **Visan** (Rhône Valley), **Savignac-de-Duras** (South West), **Puy-Notre-Dame** (Loire Valley), **St-Amour** (Beaujolais), and **Assignan** and **Villespassans** (St-Chinian/Languedoc).

OTHER CELEBRATIONS

JANUARY

weekend before St Vincent: **Fête des amis des vins de Chitry** – Chitry (Burgundy). ✆03 86 41 41 28.

nearest Sun to St Vincent: **Les Ampélofolies du Cabardès** – Moussoulens (Languedoc). Wine, truffle and foie gras festival. ✆04 68 24 92 46.

FEBRUARY

1st Sun: **Wine and Truffle Festival** – Carpentras (Rhone Valley).

1st weekend: **Percée du vin jaune** – Jura (location varies). Tapping of the first barrel of *vin jaune* after six years and three months of maturation. www.jura-vins.com.
St Vincent's day: **Fête du Gosier Secs** "dry throats festival" – Vaux-en-Beaujolais (Beaujolais).

MARCH
Sun before Palm Sun: **Nuit de la Blanquette** – Limoux (Languedoc). Marks the end of a week-long *Carnaval*. ✆04 68 31 11 82. www.limoux.fr
last weekend: **Vignoble en fête** – Saint-Mont (Southwest). ✆05 62 69 62 87.
3rd Sat: **Fête des vins de Bourgueil** – Tours (Loire Valley). ✆02 47 97 92 20. www.vinbourgueil.com.
around Mar 20: **Concours des vins** – Villefranche-sur-Saone (Beaujolais) Public tasting Sat & Sun. ✆04 74 02 22 20.

APRIL
1st & 2nd weekends: **Printemps des Châteaux du Médoc** – Médoc (Bordeaux region). ✆05 56 73 30 50. www.pauillac-medoc.com.
Apr-May: **National Book and Wine Days** – Saumur (Loire Valley). ✆02 41 40 20 60. www.bouvet-ladubay.fr
Easter: **Les Vinées tonnerroises** – Tonnerre (Burgundy). ✆03 86 55 14 48. www.tonnerre.fr
last weekend: **Fête de Saint-Marc** – Villeneuve-lèz-Avignon (Rhone Valley). ✆04 90 25 61 33; www.villeneuvelesavignon.fr.
late Apr/early May: **Fête des crus du Beaujolais** – Beaujolais.

MAY
May 1: **Randonnée des cadoles Les Riceys** (Champagne) – Country walk and picnic. Admission fee. ✆03 25 29 15 38.
Sat after Ascension: **"Le Bon Aire est dans les Caves"** – Albas (Southwest). Music and wines. ✆05 65 22 19 10.
late May/early June: **Fête de la Fleur de Vigne** – Angers (Loire Valley)
May 1: **Vins et rigottes en fête** – Condrieu (Rhone Valley). ✆04 74 56 62 83.
Whitsun (Pentecote): **Festival de Rablay-sur-Layon** – Rablay-sur-Layon (Loire Valley). ✆02 41 78 32 74; www.rablaysurlayon.com.
mid-May: **Fête du clairet** – Quinsac (Bordeaux). ✆05 56 61 82 73
Ascension Thu: **Rondes en Sauternais** – Sauternes (Bordeaux region). Bike and walking tours. Admission fee. ✆05 56 63 68 00
3rd weekend: **Vitiloire** – Tours. ✆02 47 21 61 95. www.tours.fr.
late May: **Fête des vins des coteaux d'Aix** – Rognes (Provence). ✆04 42 16 11 61.
La Médocaine de VTT bike rally through the vines of Margaux; www.medocainevtt.com

JUNE
end Jun in even-numbered years(2010, 2012): **Fête du vin** – Bordeaux. Tastings and concerts. ✆05 56 00 66 00. www.bordeaux-fete-le-vin.com.
June 1: **Procession of the flasks** – Boulbon (Provence). Hymn to Saint Marcellinus, blessing of the wine.
2nd weekend: **Balade gourmande** – Igé (Burgundy). ✆03 85 33 33 56. www.domaine-fichet.com.
last weekend: **Fête des vins du Roussillon** – Perpignan (Roussillon). ✆04 68 66 30 30
3rd Sun: **Jurade** (spring festival) – Saint-Émilion (Bordeaux region). Ceremonies, processions and music✆05 57 55 50 50. www.vins-saint-emilion.com.

JULY
1st weekend, even-numbered years): **Fêtes Henri IV** – Ay (Champagne). Open days at estates; gastronomy; fireworks; parade; sound & light show. ✆03 26 56 92 10.
1st weekend: **Les Petites fêtes de Dionysos** – Arbois (Jura). ✆03 84 66 55 50.

mid-Jul, even-numbered years: **Les Tables de Cyrano et Roxane** – Bergerac (Southwest). Wines, gastronomy, concerts.
4th Sun: **Fête du vin** – Cairanne (Rhone Valley). ✆04 90 30 86 53. www.vignerons.cairanne.com.
2nd Sat: **Fête vigneronne du Grand St-Jean** – Faugères (Languedoc). Procession of wine brotherhoods, auctions. ✆04 67 23 47 42.
15 Jul: **Festival du muscat** – Frontignan (Languedoc). ✆04 67 18 50 04. www.tourisme-frontignan.com.
3rd Sat: **Les Vignades** – Hyères (Provence). ✆04 94 01 84 50
1st Sun: **Balade gourmande** – Ladoix-Serrigny (Burgundy). Vineyard walks, picnic and music. Admission charge. ✆03 80 26 41 74.
last weekend: **Fête du vin** – Mittelbergheim (Alsace). ✆03 88 08 01 66.
1st Sat: **Wine-growers pilgrimage** to Brouilly chapel – Mont Brouilly (Beaujolais). ✆04 74 66 82 19.
2nd weekend: **Fête des vins** – Pfaffenheim (Alsace). ✆03 89 49 60 22.
1st weekend: **Fête du vin et du champignon** – Le Puy-Notre-Dame (Loire Valley) ✆ 02 41 38 87 30.
3rd weekend: **Fête des peintres de vignes en caves** – Saint-Bris-le-Vineux (Burgundy). ✆03 86 53 31 79. www.saint-bris.com.
1st Sun after July 14: **Fête du cru Saint-Chinian** – Saint-Chinian (Languedoc) ✆04 67 38 02 67.
2nd Sun: **Fête des vins et de l'andouillete** – Saint-Lambert-du-Lattay (Loire Valley). Tastings, footrace. ✆02 41 78 30 46.
1st weekend: **Fête de la fontaine** – Wangen (Alsace). Village fountain flow with wine (11am–12.30pm). ✆03 88 87 50 02.
last weekend: **Fête du vin** – Wettolsheim (Alsace). ✆03 89 22 90 30.

JULY–AUGUST

Les Grandes Heures de Cluny – Cluny (Burgundy). Concerts followed by tastings in the cellars.
La Grande Tablée du Saumur-Champigny – Saumur (Loire Valley). ✆02 41 50 00 22.
Estivales du Musique au Coeur du Medoc ✆06 69 32 48 19; www.estivales-musique-medoc.com

JULY–SEPTEMBER

Festival musical des Grands Crus de Bourgogne – Burgundy (various locations)

AUGUST

1st weekend: **Fête du vin au pays du Brand** – Andlau (Alsace)
1st weekend: **Fête médiévale de la véraison** – Chateauneuf-du-Pape (Rhone Valley). ✆04 90 83 71 08.
2nd weekend: **Fête des vins de Duras** – Duras (Southwest). Hot-air ballon flights. ✆05 93 94 13 48. www.cotesdeduras.com.
last week: **Fête des vignerons** – Eguisheim (Alsace). ✆03 89 41 21 78.
1st weekend: **Fête du raisin** – Fréjus (Provence). Celebration of the first grapes; wine tasting, dances, Mass. ✆04 94 51 83 83.
1st weekend: **Fête des vins** – Gaillac (Southwest). ✆05 63 57 15 40.
3rd weekend: **Fête du vin et de l'amitié** – Gueberschwihr (Alsace). Open days.
weekend of Aug 15: **Fête du klevener**– Heiligenstein (Alsace). ✆03 88 08 26 54.
Aug 14–15: **Fête du vin de Madiran** – Madiran (Southwest)
1st 15 days: **Jazz in Marciac** – Marciac (Southwest). Wine events coincide with the jazz festival; www.jazzin-marciac.com
1st weekend: **Fête du vin de Jurançon** – Monein (Southwest). ✆05 59 21 30 06.
3rd weekend, every other year: **Fête du trousseau** – Montigny-lès Arsures (Jura). Open days in the cellars, gastronomy.

2nd weekend: **Fête du vin de Buzet et de la gastronomie** – Nérac (Southwest). ✆05 53 65 23 24.
3rd Fri: **Festival des vins de Savoie** – Notre-Dame-de-Bellecombe (Savoie). ✆04 79 31 61 40.
3rd Fri: **Jazz and Wine** – Pauillac (Bordeaux region). ✆05 56 59 03 08. www.pauillac-medoc.com.
3rd weekend, off-years of the Fête du trousseau: **Fête du Poulsard** – Pupillin (Jura). ✆03 84 66 55 50.
last weekend: **Journée de l'Océan** – Quncy (Loire Valley) ✆02 48 51 30 12.
last Sat: **Fête des amis de Brouilly** – Saint-Lager (Beaujolais). Picnic on the slopes of Mont Brouilly. ✆04 74 66 82 19.
last Sun: **Festival provençal et fêt vigneronne** – Séguret (Rhone Valley). ✆04 90 46 91 06.
1st weekend: **Fête du vin** – Turckheim (Alsace). ✆03 89 27 38 44.

SEPTEMBER
1st weekend: **Fête du Biou Arbois** (Jura) – Procession of a giant bunch of grapes through the village, ✆03 84 66 55 50; www.arbois.com.
2nd Sun of Sept: **Vendanges à l'ancienne** – Arbois (Jura). Procession in traditional dress. ✆03 84 66 55 50.
1st Sun: **Fête du vin de Cassis** – Cassis (Provence). ✆08 92 25 98 92.
last Sun or 1st Sun in Oct: **Fête du pressurage** – Champvallon (Burgundy). Grape pressing using the antique pressoir. 03 86 91
Odd-numbered years: **Fête des vendanges** – Cognac region. ✆05 45 82 48 14.
early Sept: **Marathon des Chateaux du Médoc et des Graves** – Médoc (Bordeaux region). ✆05 56 59 01 91. www.marathondumedoc.com.
3rd Sun: **Fête du Biou** – Pupillin (Jura). *See Arbois above.*
1st Sun: **Fête des ménétriers or Pfifferdaj** – Ribeauvillé (Alsace). Historical parade, tastiings
3rd Sat & Sun: **Fête des vendanges** – Saint-Émilion (Bordeaux region). Weekend festival with music and fireworks on Saturday night, procession and swearing in of new intronisees into the Jurade on Sunday. ✆05 57 55 50 51. www.vins-saint-emilion.com.
2nd weekend: **Foué Avaloue** – Saint-Père (Loire Valley). ✆ 03 86 28 00 40.
2nd Sun: **Les Foulées du Saumur-Champigny** – Saumur (Loire Valley). ✆02 41 52 97 41. www.saumur-champigny.com.
1st Sun: **Sentier gourmand** – Scherwiller (Alsace). A series of tastings on a vineyard walk. 03 88 92 25 62.
2nd or 3rd weekend: **Fête des vendanges** – Tain-l'Hermitage (Rhone Valley). ✆04 75 07 78 96.
4th Sun: **Fête du Biou** – Vadans (Jura). *See Arbois above.* ✆03 84 66 20 01.
1st weekend: **Ban des vendanges** – Vinsobres (Rhone Valley).

OCTOBER
mid Oct: **Fête des vendanges** – Banyuls-sur-Mer (Languedoc). ✆04 68 88 31 58.
1st weekend: **Fête des vendanges** – Barr (Alsace) ✆03 88 08 66 65.
3rd Thu: **Fête du vin nouveau** – Beziers (Languedoc). Dance of the vines and blessing of new wine. ✆04 67 31 27 23.
3rd Sun: **Paulée de la côte chalonnaise** – Côte chalonnaise (Burgundy). ✆03 85 45 22 99.
last day of harvest: **Grand cochelet des vendanges** – Épernay (Champagne). Wine-growers feast. ✆03 26 55 27 49.
2nd weekend **Molsheim Grape Festival**, Alsace. ✆03 88 38 11 61
3rd Sun: **Fête des vendanges** – Joigny (Burgundy). ✆03 86 62 11 05
2nd Sun: **Fête du vin nouveau** – Jullié (Beaujolais). ✆04 74 69 22 88

2nd weekend: **Fête des vendanges à l'ancienne** – Marcillac (Bordeaux region). ✆05 57 32 41 03.

3rd Sun: **Fête des vendanges** – Marlenheim (Alsace).

2nd weekend: **Fête du raisin** – Molsheim (Alsace). Cellar open days, music and folklore. ✆03 88 49 58 37.

1st Sat: **Vendanges à l'ancienne at Domaine de Carcher** – Montfort-en-Chalosse (Southwest). ✆05 58 98 69 27.

last weekend: **Fête du vin bourru** – Nuits-Saint-Georges (Burgundy). ✆03 80 62 11 17.

3rd Sun: **Fête des vendanges** – Obernai (Alsace).

1st weekend: **Fête du paradis** – Odenas (Beaujolais). Tasting, outdoor activities. ✆04 74 02 22 10, www.beaujolais.com.

3rd weekend: **Auction of Grands Vins of Languedoc Rouissillon** – Saint-Jean-de-Cuculles (Languedoc). Vineyard walks, tastings. ✆04 67 06 23 35. www.vin-encheres-france.com.

3rd weekend, odd-numbered years: **Vendanges à l'ancienne** –Massif de Saint-Thierry (Champagne). ✆03 26 03 12 62.

3rd week: **Fête des vendanges** – Sauternes (Bordeaux region). ✆05 56 76 69 13.

last weekend: **Fête des vins de Chablis** – Chablis (Burgundy). ✆03 86 42 80 80 (tourism office).

NOVEMBER

3rd week: **Les Sarmentelles de Beaujeu** – Beaujeu (Beaujolais). Beaujolais-Nouveau festival. ✆04 74 69 55 44.

3rd Thu, midnight: **Tapping of the first Beaujolais Nouveau** – Belleville (Beaujolais). In the cellars of the town hall. ✆04 74 66 44 67.

3rd week: **Gaillac Primeur** – Gaillac (Southwest). ✆05 63 57 15 40.

3rd Thu: **Presentation of the Beaujolais-Nouveau** – Pommiers (Beaujolais). Tastings starting at 6pm; open days at the cellars following weekend.

weekend before Nov 11: **Fêtes des vins de l'Auxerrois** – Saint-Bris-le-Vineaux (Burgundy). ✆03 86 53 66 76. Admission fee.

3rd Wed: **Fête du Beaujolais Nouveau** – Tarare (Beaujolais).

DECEMBER

1st Sun: **Fête du millésime** – Badol (Provence). ✆04 94 90 29 59.

ist weekend: **St Nicholas** procession in Molsheim, ✆03 88 38 11 61

last 2 weekends: **Les Bonnes Chauffes of December** – Cognac and Jonzac, various events surrounding the start of distillation. ✆05 45 36 47 35. www.abc-cognac.com.

Vendanges du pacherenc de la St-Sylvestre – Viella (Southwest). Midnight harvest of dried grapes. ✆05 62 69 62 87.

SALES, FAIRS AND MARKETS

Events are listed by month and arranged by venue in alphabetical order.

FEBRUARY

last weekend: **Tain-l'Hermitage** – (vallée du Rhône). Salon des vins. ✆04 75 08 06 81.

MARCH

3rd weekend: **Blaye** (Bordeaux region) – Marché aux vins. ✆05 57 42 91 19. www.aoc-blaye-com.

3rd week: **Bourgueil, Saint-Nicolas-de-Bourgueil** (Loire Valley) – Foire aux vins. ✆02 47 97 92 20. www.vinbourgueil.com

3rd weekend: **Loudon** (Loire Valley) – Foire aux vins. ✆05 49 98 18 41.

2nd weekend: **Montlouis-sur-Loire** (Loire Valley) – Salon des vins de La Bourdaisière. ✆02 47 45 00 16.

3rd weekend: **Nuits-Saint-Georges** (Burgundy) – Hospices de Nuits-St-Georges sale. ✆03 80 62 67 00; www.hospicesdenuits.com.

mid-Mar: **Vallet** (Loire Valley) – Expo-Vall. ✆02 40 33 92 97.

S. Sauvignier / MICHELIN

2nd weekend: **Vouvray** (Loire Valley) – Saveurs et vins de Vouvray. ℘02 47 52 71 07.

EASTER

Reuilly (Loire Valley) – Foire aux vins. www.vins-centre-loire.com.

Thu before Easter: **Les Riceys** (Champagne) – **La Foire du Grand Jeudi**: Large sale where you can find things covering every aspect of wine culture and cultivation under one roof. ℘03 25 29 15 38.

APRIL

last Sun: **Beaujolais –** Fête des crus du Beaujolais. ℘03 85 23 98 60.

3rd Sat: **Brignoles** (Provence) – Foire-exposition des vins du Var et de Provence. ℘04 94 69 10 88. www.foiredebrignoles.fr.

last 2 weeks: **Chinon** (Loire Valley) – Foire aux vins de Chinon. ℘02 47 93 30 44.

3rd weekend: **Lalande-de-Pomerol** (Bordeaux region) –Open days at the châteaux. ℘05 57 25 21 60. www.lalande-pomerol.com.

3rd week: **Mâcon** (Burgundy) Salon des vins. ℘03 85 21 30 00. www.leparcmacon.com.

15 days after Easter: **Onzain** (Loire Valley) –Salon des vins d'Onzain. ℘02 54 70 25 47.

MAY

2nd weekend: **Beujeu** (Beaujolais) – Vente des Hospices de Beaujeu at the municipal theater; the world's oldest charity sale, dating to 1797. ℘04 74 04 31 05. www.hospices-de-beaujeu.com.

2nd weekend: **Bourg-sur-Gironde** (Bordeaux region) – Open days at the châteaus of Côtes de Bourg. ℘05 57 94 80 80. www.cotes-de-bourg.com.

Ascension weekend: **Colmar** (Alsace) – Foire du pain, du vin et du fromage écobiologiques. ℘03 89 47 67 54.

Ascension Thursday: **Guebwiller** (Alsace) – Foire aux vins.

1st weekend: **Saint-Émilion** (Bordeaux region) – Open days at the châteaux of Saint-Émilion. ℘05 57 55 50 55. www.vins-saint-emilion.com.

WHITSUN *(Pentecôte)*

Cadillac (Bordeaux region) – Open days at Premières Cotes de Bordeaux and Cadillac. ℘05 57 98 19 20.

Mailly-Champage (Champagne) – Foire aux vins et la gastronomie. ℘03 26 49 81 66.

Sancerre (Loire Valley) – Foire aux vins de Sancerre. ℘02 48 54 11 35. www.maison-des-sancerre.com.

JULY

approx. Jul 14: **Barr** (Alsace) – Foire aux vins.

1st or 2nd weekend: **Luir** (Corsica) – Foire du vin. ℘04 95 35 06 44. www.acunfraternita.com

weekend after Jul 14: **Ribeauvillé** (Alsace) – Foire aux vins.

1st Sat: **Sancerre** (Loire Valley) – Musique aux caves. ℘02 48 79 08 12.

last weekend: **Sauveterre-de-Guyenne** (Bordeaux Region) – Fête de la vigne et de la gastronomie. www.sauveterre-de-guyenne.com. ℘05 56 71 53 45

AUGUST

week after 2nd Fri: **Colmar** (Alsace) – Foire aux vins d'Alsace. ✆03 90 50 50 50.

Aug 14–15: **Duravel** (Southwest) – Foire aux vins et aux produits régionaux. ✆05 64 24 65 50.

around Aug 10: **La Chartre-sur-le-Loir** (Loire Valley) – Foire aux vins.

Aug 14–15: **Madiran** (Southwest) – Fête du vin. ✆05 62 31 90 67.

weekend before Aug 15: **Menetou-Salon** (Loire Valley) –Cellar open days. www.vins-centre-loire.com.

weekend of Aug 15: **Obernai** (Alsace) Foire aux vins.

Aug 15: **Pouilly-sur-Loire** (Loire Valley) – Foire aux vins et aux produits du terroir. ✆03 86 39 03 75.

SEPTEMBER

1st weekend: **Bar-sur-Aube** (Champagne) – Foire aux vins de Champagne. ✆03 25 27 14 75.

1st & 2nd weekend: **Belfort** (Jura) – Foire aux vins de France et gastronomie. ✆03 84 55 90 90.

1st weekend: **Langon** (Bordeaux region) – Foire aux vins, fromages et pains. ✆05 56 63 68 00 www.federation-langon.fr

1st weekend: **La Sauve** (Bordeaux region) – La Sauve open days. www.lasauvemajeure.com. ✆05 61 11 02 22

OCTOBER

1st weekend: **Barr** (Alsace) – Fête des vendanges. ✆03 88 08 66 55.

3rd weekend: **Cérons et Graves** (Bordeaux) – Open days.

3rd weekend: **Fronsac** (Bordeaux region) – Open days at the châteaux.

NOVEMBER

3rd weekend: **Clos de Vougeot, Beaune, Mersault** (Burgundy) – "Les Trois Glorieuses" auction of Hospices de Beaune wines. The largest and most famous wine auction in France.

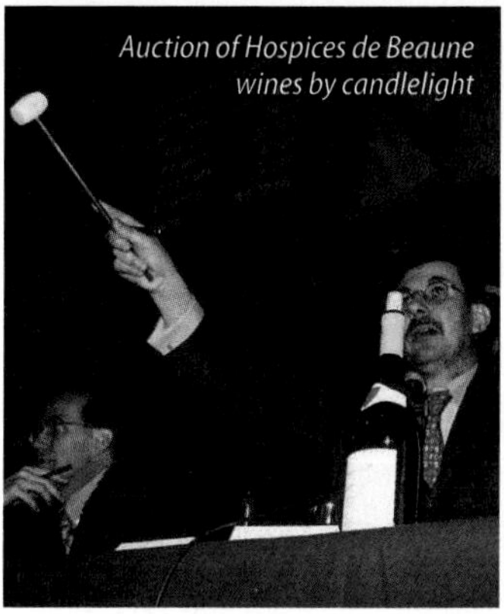

Auction of Hospices de Beaune wines by candlelight

S. Sauvignier / MICHELIN

✆03 80 26 21 30. www.hospices-de-beaune.tm.fr

3rd Fri: **Eauze** (Southwest) – Foire des eaux-de-vie, with large range of local Armagnacs and Floc de Gascogne. ✆05 62 08 11 00.

last weekend: **Loupiac** (Bordeaux region) – Open days, understandikng the process of making this noble rot wine, plus food matching. ✆05 56 62 92 22. www.vins-loupiac.com.

3rd weekend: **Saint-Paul-Trois-Châteaux** (Rhone Valley) – Salon des vins du Tricastin.

3rd weekend: **Fête des vins Grand public**, Beaujeu (Beaujolais), concentrating on the new wines of the year. 04 74 69 22 88; www.aucoeurdubeaujolais.fr

DECEMBER

1st weekend: **Pessac-Léongnan** (Bordeaux region) – Open days. ✆05 56 78 47 72. www.otmontesquieu.com.

Saint-Bris-le-Vineux (Burgundy) – Marché du réveillon at the Caves de Bailly. ✆03 86 53 77 77. www.caves-bailly.com.

Couronne d'Or Wine Tasting Exhibition, Strasbourg, Alsace. ✆03 88 87 75 80

Christmas Fair, All ées de Tourny, Bordeaux. Christmas presents, plus food and wine from the region. ✆05 56 00 66 00; www.bordeaux-tourisme.com

BOOKS

WINE GUIDES

Hugh Johnson's Pocket Wine Book 2009 (32nd edition). Hugh Johnson. Traditional annual pocket reference, with maps, charts, recommendations and star ratings.

Wine Report. Tom Stevenson (2009). Pocket-sized annual guide with insider tips from local experts on new vintages, harvest forecasts and trends.

The Wine Buyer's Guide. Robert Parker (2008). Sixth edition features tasting notes, ratings and prices organised by producer and vintage.

REFERENCE

The Art and Science of Wine. James Halliday, Hugh Johnson (2007). The winemaking process demystified, with detailed descriptions of each stage, plus recent developments and new technology.

The World Atlas of Wine. Hugh Johnson and Jancis Robinson (2007). Fifth edition, with region maps, vintage charts and authoritative, entertaining descriptions by two of the wine world's most respected writers.

The Oxford Companion to Wine. Jancis Robinson (3rd ed, 2006). More than 3,000 entries, essays and articles by more than 70 contributors on all facets of wine and winemaking around the world.

Terroir: Role of Geology, Climate and Culture in the Making of French Wines. James Wilson (1999). A scientific, social and historical study of France's terroirs, including maps, drawings, glossary and other helpful information.

The Wine Lover's Guide (series). Michael Busselle. Series of books covering winegrowing regions of France.

The Wines and Winelands of France: Geological Journeys. Charles Pomerol (1989). An explanation of the relationship between geology and wine.

WINE TASTING

How to Taste: A Guide to Enjoying Wine. Jancis Robinson (2008). A clear and comprehensive process for tasting, including tasting theory and specific exercises, organised by major wine types.

Essential Winetasting: The Complete Practical Winetasting Course. Michael Schuster (2005). Step-by-step method for tasting and assessing wines including sensory descriptions, vocabulary, and information on grape varieties and winemaking.

The Art of Wine Tasting: An Illustrated Guidebook. Richard Kinssies (2004). Guidebook includes notes, flavor wheels, notepads and instructions for hosting a tasting party.

The Taste of Wine: Art and Science of Wine Appreciation. Emile Peynaud (1991). Geared toward professionals and wine buffs, this guide to evaluating wines includes sections on theory, physiology and vocabulary.

WINE AND CUISINE

Richard Olney's French Wine & Food: A Wine Lover's Cookbook. Richard Olney (1997). Menus and recipes organised by French winegrowing regions.

An Omelette and a Glass of Wine. Elizabeth David (1997). Collection of 62 articles and essays on French cuisine and culinary history.

Recipes from the French Wine Harvest: Vintage Feasts from the Vineyards. Rosi Hanson (1996). Recipes and descriptions of generations-old traditions from winemakers throughout France.

Food, Wine and Friends (Fiona Beckette, 2007). A cookbook that suggests wines and other drinks to go with a range of recipes.

PERIODICALS

Decanter Magazine. Available from selected wine shops and online at *www.decanter.com.*

Food and Wine.
Available from selected wine shops, on subscription and online at *www.foodandwine.com*.

The Wine Advocate.
Robert Parker's newsletter, available on subscription and online at *www.erobertparker.com*.

Wine Spectator.
Available from selected wine shops, on subscription and online at *www.winespectator.com*.

TRAVELOGUE

Vine Garden: a Life-Changing Summer in the Gardens, Vineyards and Châteaux of the Heart of France. Alex Dingwall-Main (2006).
An affecting memoir of a summer travelling through several wine-growing regions.

In the Vine Country. Edith Somerville and Martin Ross (1893; reprint 2001).
Wondrous and witty tale of two cousins from Ireland on a tour of the 19C Médoc.

BIOGRAPHY

The Ripening Sun: One Woman and the Creation of a Vineyard. Patricia Atkinson (2003).
Emotion-driven story of the author's first year establishing a vineyard in Bergerac.

Virgile's Vineyard: A Year in the Languedoc Wine Country by Patrick Moon (2004).
History and culture in the entertaining tale of one man's move to his inherited Languedoc property.

Long Ago in France. MFK Fisher (reprint 1992).
Nostalgic and beautifully written account of the author's years as a graduate student in Dijon in 1929.

Chateau Monty, Monty Waldin (2008)
From the TV series of the same name, journalist Waldin recounts his experiences as he converts a vineyard in the Roussillon to Biodynamic farming.

BOOKSHOPS

- **Books for Cooks**
4 Blenheim Crescent, London, W11 1NN.
✆020 7221 1992.
www.booksforcooks.com.

- **Librairie Gourmande**
4 r. Dante, 75005 Paris.
✆01 43 54 37 27.
www.librairie-gourmande.fr.

- **Kitchen Arts & Letters**
435 Lexington Ave., New York, NY 10128. ✆212 876 5550.
www.kitchenartsandletters.com.

FILMS

Mondovino. Jonathon Nossiter, 2004 (subtitled).
Iconoclastic documentary of terroir that critiques trends and personalities behind the globalization of the wine industry.

Babette's Feast. Gabriel Axel (1987; subtitled).
A Parisian chef and political refugee creates an epicurean feast for two sisters of a religious sect, and their congregation in Denmark.

Sideways. Alexander Payne. (2004).
Compassionate, comical story of a middle-aged oenophile and his soon-to-be-married buddy on a bachelor weekend in California.

A Good Year. Ridley Scott (2006).
Lush Provençal scenery backdrops the tale of a British executive reluctantly inheriting a chateau.

Bottle Shock. Randall Miller (2008).
The story of the 1976 Judgement of Paris, when Californian wines beat their illustrious French counterparts for the first time.

Know Your Cellar

CHOOSING WINE CLASSIFICATIONS

Vins de Table

The first and most general of the categories of wine is the "vin de table", which takes in all wines described as "vin de pays" or "vin de table".
A vin de pays comes from a specific geographic area, frequently a *département* or region. With the new EU wine regulations that came into force in July 2009, these are now protected by IGPs (Indication Geographique Protegée) An IGP must meet strict standards which govern the planting of grape varieties, the yield per hectare and the wine's alcohol content; once the classification has been given, the wine must be of a consistent quality level. The label on the bottle usually shows the grape variety used. *Vins de pays (IGPs)* are widely available and very affordable.
Vins de table, in contrast, are most usually sold under a brand name. For the most part, they are produced by mixing wines from France or other European Union countries. Producers are not required to use the term "vin de table" on the label.

Vins de Qualité Produits dans une Région Déterminée

This category, usually abbreviated to **VQPRD**, covers wines described as appellations d'origine vins de qualité supérieure (AOVDQS) and the **appellations d'origine contrôlée** (AOC). With the new EU wine regulations, these classifications have an added protection, the AOP (Appellation d'Origin Protegée).

The AOVDQS classification

In terms of quality, these wines are between the vins de table and the AOPs, and have to pass an official analysis and tasting. AOVDQS status is often short-lived, as the best wines in the category are developed into AOPs.

The AOCs

Particularly rigorous monitoring surrounds the production of the AOC wines. The grape varieties grown and the percentage of each variety must be approved by the Comité national des vins et des eaux-de-vie, part of the Institut national des appellations d'origine, or INAO. There is a minimum and maximum yield and a minimum alcohol content, measured as the minimum sugar content of the wine before its ageing begins. Standards are also set for cultivation methods, the size of the vines and the vinification process. A tasting must also take place before AOC status can be confirmed: such careful control ensures that the AOC label is a mark of quality. As of 2009, there were 394 appellations d'origine contrôlée (wines, eaux-de-vie, ciders and rum).

AOCs in detail

An **appellation** is a defined geographical area of France which produces wine; the word, and particularly the phrase "appellation protegée", is sometimes also used to mean a

New EU Wine Regulations

In August 2009, the EU finally brought in the new regulations that had been discussed for a number of years. These include a phasing-out of distillation schemes, carefully-protected grubbing up of vines, environmental protection of wine-growing areas, and simpler labelling rules. This is aimed at protecting the interests of producers and consumers, and intends to ensure quality will be based on protected geographical indications and designations of origin. EU wines will be labelled for grape variety and vintage.

standard of wine, or the actual wine itself. The appellation name may refer to a region (Bordeaux or Burgundy), a sub-region (Entre-deux-mers) or a smaller district or commune (Volnay). However, four regions of France classify their wines in a particular way, in addition to the AOC:

Wines from **Alsace** always show the grape variety on the label: only Riesling, Gewürztraminer, Muscat and Tokay-Pinot Gris grapes can be used to make an Alsace Grand Cru. This term signifies a wine from one of 50 terroirs that have a particularly strong reputation, among the most famous being Bruderthal, Hatschbourg and Rosacker.

In the **Bordeaux** region, the oldest official classification, based on the ranking of the wine estates, dates back to 1855, and recognises 61 Médocs, one Graves red wine (Haut-Brion) and 26 Sauternes. The 1855 Grand Crus are divided into five categories, while today there are also classification systems in Graves and Saint-Emilion (where there are three categories that undergo a ten-yearly revision). Of the prestigious appellations, only Pomerol wines are not classified in any way.

In **Burgundy**, the term "climat" is used to refer to the best plots of vines, named after a part of a locality or group of localities.

In Burgundy there are:

- 23 regional appellations, which indicate that the wine is from the region;
- 44 appellations communales (or village appellations). These are labelled with the name of the place where they are produced;
- 635 Village Appellations, plus Premiers Crus: a further distinction awarded to localities or climats within a village;
- 33 appellations Grands Crus designate exceptional wine from a single climat, which gives its name to the wine.

Beaujolais-Villages, Bourgogne-Aligoté and Crémant de Bourgogne are examples of regional AOCs.
Pommard, Meursault and Fixin belong to the category of appellations communales.
Chablis 1er Cru Fourchaumes and Pommard 1er Cru Les Rugiens are appellations communales for which the climats are classified as Premier Cru.
A Montrachet is a grand cru from the communes Puligny-Montrachet and Chassagne-Montrachet.

In the **Champagne** region, the appellation is applied to 319 communes (with potential to rise to 357 by 2014) which are listed in a "scale of Crus" ranking from 80 to 100%. The 17 highest, ranked at 100%, are designated as "Grands Crus". The "Premiers Crus" from 50 communes are given a percentage score from 90 to 99%. This information may appear on a Champagne label, but producers are not obliged to use the term AOC on their bottles. In the case of good vintages, you may find bottles of champagne marked with a year, indicating all the grapes came from this one year.

Vins de Garage

This term was first used in the 1990s in the Bordeaux region: it refers to wines produced in small quantities, blended in new barrels and stored in a garage because the producer has no storehouse and only a small plot of land. Vinification techniques count for more than the inherent quality of the terroir, but the dense, concentrated wines produced in this way can fetch high prices. They are increasingly less fashionable, however, as questions are raised over how well the wines age.

MARKS OF EXCELLENCE

The Prize Winners

When you buy a bottle of wine, you may see that it has won prizes or medals at tasting competitions. Some of these competitions are very prestigious, like the Concours general agricole, held at the Salon international de l'agriculture in Paris. Another name you may see or hear is Les Citadelles du Vin, held in the Bordeaux region each year and endorsed by the OIV (Organisation Internationale de la Vigne et du Vin).

At these *concours*, the wines are presented in identical bottles, marked only with numbers: the range of wines is tasted "blind" by professional tasters who, judging by taste, smell and sight, mark the elements of the wines according to a scorecard agreed in advance. A gold, silver or bronze medal at these events gives a wine prestige and a commercial edge in a competitive market. Since 2000, an award for excellence has been given to producers in recognition of their results at the previous five events: a list of these producers can be found at www.concours-agricole.com or www.citadellesduvin.com.

The Great Vintages

A wine's vintage, or *millésime* in French, is the year it was produced. The key to a great vintage is the weather: a hot, dry, sunny end of May and early June to give good, early flowering, then a warm spell from mid-August to harvest-time. But good years differ from region to region and the quality will vary even within a region: a storm, or an over-hasty harvest can change everything. Among the best years were 1900, 1921, 1929, 1937, 1945, 1947, 1949, 1955, 1959, 1961 (regarded as the vintage of the century), 1964, 1966, 1967, 1970, 1985, 1989, 1990, 1996, 1999, 2000, and 2005. 2003 was exceptionally hot, giving fruit-filled, high alcohol wines.

For quick reference, consult the table of vintages on the inside back cover.

BUYING WINE

WHERE

From the Producers

A visit to a *vigneron récoltant* – a wine-grower who produces his own wine – is a good way to try wines and buy a few bottles, or even a case or two, but but be sure to make an appointment first. The grower will take the time to talk you through a tasting, from most modest wines to the best. As you would expect, the prices follow the same upward curve, but are always lower than you would expect from a retailer.

There are a few points to remember on a first visit. The tasting itself is usually free, so make sure you don't abuse your host's hospitality. Even at the risk of seeming impolite, decline any nuts or cheese, both of which can flatter a poor wine and mislead your taste buds. Spit out the wines you try: you'll need a clear head when it's time to talk about prices! Even if you don't find any huge bargains, you'll still save money on transport costs, and the pleasure of the experience is worthwhile in itself. Many estates also ship wine to retailers in the UK and the USA. It can be worth asking the producer if their wine is exported abroad as it may be more economical and convenient to buy in bulk at home than to take it back with you.

Producers' addresses are listed in the Shopping Guide section in each chapter.

From a Cave Cooperative

There are around 850 of these wine cooperatives in France, producing wine for their 111,000 members and selling it by the bottle or in bulk. On the whole, their production techniques are steadily improving.

The addresses of these cooperatives can be found in the Shopping Guide section in each chapter.

From a Wine Merchant

A good wine merchant should be willing and able to offer personalised advice to the customer, particularly when it comes to the pairing of food and wine. Wine merchants need to know the characteristics of the wine region and the specific appellation, and be able to buy and sell at the right price. Their wine tastings are a chance to introduce customers to new wines and bring together clients and producers.

There are 450 members of the Fédération nationale des cavistes independents, which is well-known in the world of wine for its choice and good value for money. The national chains Nicolas and Repaire de Bacchus also have a good reputation.
Wine merchants' addresses can be found in the Shopping Guide section in each chapter.

From a Supermarket Wine Event

Special wine sales, or "foires aux vins", are organised by major supermarket chains such as Auchan, Carrefour, Leclerc, Intermarché, usually in September, with a smaller version in Spring. The choice, or at least the quantity, is enormous, even if the discounts may be less generous than you might expect. If you get there early on opening day, however, you may chance upon some interesting wines, especially from the Bordeaux region. Be sure to do your research first: study the catalogues, prices, vintages and appellations, and check that the wine on the shelf is the one you're after.

From a Regional Wine Event

Regional wine fairs give you the chance to try wines sold by the producers, while sampling local delicacies. You may find regional arts and crafts on display too. It's a pleasant way to learn more about local wine, and the people who make and drink it!

From a Wine Club

The idea is simple and, to many people, very appealing: members receive a monthly choice of wines chosen by sommeliers, chefs and other wine experts, as well as invitations to wine events. And if you don't like the wine you've bought, you can send it back. Before joining one of the many wine clubs, it's worth comparing the terms of membership and the savings offered.

At a Wine Auction

In the heady excitement of the auction rooms, the prices paid for wine range from the reasonable to the extravagant. You'll be bidding against professionals – wine brokers and restaurateurs – as well as amateur wine-lovers, for lots from restaurant cellars, private owners or groups of investors. The greatest wine auctions take place at Christie's, Sotheby's and Drouot, and in Burgundy, at the famous Hospices de Beaune wine sale which takes place on the 3rd Sunday of November every year. If you're tempted, take a copy of one of the French-language reference books: *La Cote des grands vins de France* or the *Guide Bettane & Desseauve*. During the viewing, find out as much as you can on the provenance of the bottles and how they have been stored. Check the corks and the level of the wine, and ask to see inside unopened crates. Remember that there is a fee to pay for every lot sold, for the buyer as well as the seller.
Find out more on the internet: www.idealwine.com; www.iencheres.com.

In bulk from the barrel

You can buy wine "on tap" from the producer, at a cooperative and from some wine merchants, and there is a saving to be made: wine costs 25% less from the barrel than in the bottle. But there are drawbacks, too. You'll generally be buying *vin ordinaire*: make sure you check where it's come from. Wine in plastic containers is very susceptible to heat, so bottle it as soon as you can, and remember to take the price of bottles and corks into account.

Vins Primeurs

Combining a knowledge of wine with an instinct for the futures market, buyers of new "vin primeur" pay in theory half the price of their wine before it has been aged and bottled: acquiring 2005 vintage wine in Spring 2006, for example, and receiving shipment of the wine itself in 2007 or even 2008. This method of buying wine is most common in Bordeaux, but vins primeurs are also sold in Burgundy and the Rhone, on a smaller scale.

The dealers' prices when the subscription opens in April gives buyers a fair idea of the prospects of the year's vintage: the balance of the cost is paid either a few months later, or on delivery for particularly good deals. Wine traders, growers and wine clubs may all offer the chance to buy wine this way, but remember that not every year can be a *grande année*, and what you are actually doing is speculating on future value - not always a safe bet, as recent price fluctuations during 2009 have once again demonstrated. Because of the increasing value of many of these wines, they often remain very expensive even at "en primeur" time, but there is still the thrill to be had of receiving your allocation of the most sought after bottles.

On the Internet

Once again, take time to research and compare. Keep an eye out for special offers and you'll find that there are some good deals to be had. Vins primeurs are purchased directly, so these wines will be the same price everywhere, but prices for older wines depend on demand, supply and the reputation of the vintage. Here are a few Internet sites you may wish to try:
www.lawinery.fr
www.chateauonline.com
www.millesima.com
www.chateauinternet.com
www.chateaunet.com (French only)
For tracking down bottles and comparing prices across merchants, **www.wine-searcher.com** is a useful site.

Transport and Taxes

The bottles of wine or spirits you buy should have a metallic sticker over the cork, stamped with the image of a woman's head: the Marianne logo. This disc (known as a *capsule representative des droits*) is proof of your right to transport the wine within France and is obligatory by order of the French tax and excise service. It is green for AOC and AOVDQS, blue for IGPs (vins de pays), orange for unfortified sweet wines and yellow for Cognac and Armagnac. If you buy the wine in a bulk container, you should instead be given a paper authorisation called a "congé". This transport document, issued by the French customs authorities, is the equivalent of the *capsule*. The regulations surrounding the importation of wine for personal consumption or as a gift to Canada and the USA can seem confusing at first sight. Both nations' border authorities classify wine as a restricted import: you may bring in a limited quantity – 1 litre to the USA, 1.5 litres into Canada – in accompanied baggage as part of your personal exemption (currently valued at US$800 and CAN$750). Duty (3% of the value) must be paid for higher volumes, but customs officials can, and do, decide to impound large quantities if they suspect the wine is for resale. If you plan to bring a significant quantity of alcohol back with you, you are strongly advised to find out about taxes and limitations on unlicensed imports in your home state or province, contact the relevant government authority *(www.customs.ustreas.gov; www.cbsa-asfc.gc.ca)* and make arrangements in advance at the port of entry. Alternatively international shipping agents may be able to undertake some of these arrangements for you. Alcohol may not be sent by mail.

STORING YOUR WINE

Any lover of fine wine dreams of having their own cellar; a store of carefully chosen bottles, slowly taking on their full character and kept in perfect condition. The pleasure of a wine cellar blends memory and personal taste with a sense of anticipation and discovery.

THE PERFECT CELLAR

Wine Cabinets

Mini-cellars – or wine cabinets – may be expensive and most take up space, but they do provide an ideal storage environment. Make sure that the model you buy keeps out UV light, and that there is no noise or vibration from its motor to disturb the wine. A good cabinet will store wine at different temperatures and be fitted with anti-odour and anti-mould filters. Leading brand names include Electrolux, EuroCave, Tastvin, Liebherr, Vinosafe and Climadiff.

An Underground Cellar

The ultimate way to stock young wines and allow them to develop to a flavourful maturity: wine is a fragile, living product which needs to be handled carefully, and there really is an art to cellaring it well. The first rule is that the cellar should be clean and should be used for storing wine and nothing else. Don't keep household cleaning products, cheese, vinegar, paints or solvents in the cellar, as all of these can affect the flavour of the wine.
If you want to build yourself an underground cellar, companies like Côté Cave will sell you a prefabricated cellar which is quick and easy to install. When planning the size of your cellar, you should allow 1.5m^3 per 100 bottles.

Temperature

White wines are more sensitive to changes in temperature than reds, but wines of any kind are best stored at a constant temperature of 10-14C: within this, 11-12C is ideal. If the room is too warm, the wine ages too quickly; too cold an environment slows the process and can lead to tartrate crystals forming. Below -4C, the wine will freeze.
The cellar is best located where it will not be affected by changes of temperature. If possible, it should face northeast and be ventilated by ducts at the foot of the north wall and the top of the east wall. Air conditioning is another option. At the very least, it is worth investing in a **thermometer**.

Humidity

Ideally, a cellar should have white-washed walls, a dry solid floor covered with gravel, and a steady humidity of between 70 and 80%. Wines prefer moist rather than dry air, which may dry out the corks and lead to leaks.
The only disadvantage of the damp atmosphere of a cellar is that wine labels may peel off: you can protect them using cling film or clear adhesive plastic. If the humidity of the cellar falls below 50%, either water the gravel or place a basin filled with water and charcoal in a corner of the room.
To make sure your wine is being kept in the best conditions, you should consider buying a **hygrometer**.

Light

Over-exposure to light affects the tannins in wine and disturbs the ageing process. Neon lights are far too harsh for a cellar – choose lighting which is muted and, if possible, indirect. Your third purchase should be a supply of **40W bulbs**.

Vibrations and Noise

Passing trucks and trains cause vibrations which unsettle the molecules of the wine and prevent it from ageing as it should. A simple way around the problem is to place anti-vibration rubber pads or "feet" at the base of the racks, if they are not fitted with these already.

WHEN TO DRINK

Do keep a track of what wine is in your cellar, and ensure that you drink your wine while it is still in its prime - it is a shame to spend so much time storing it and not be able to enjoy it in the end! And remember that not all wines are meant to age; there are plenty of wonderful wines that give great pleasure when young, such as a Beaujolais Village, or a Chinon. And from regions such as Bordeaux, the generic appellation wines are also best to be drunk within ten years - not everything rewards long cellaring.
You should also be aware of your own preferences; if you prefer a very fruit-filled, powerful wine, then ensure you are drinking wines on the young rather than old side of their ageing process. Enjoying wine is all a personal process of discovery.

ORGANISING YOUR CELLAR

Wine Racks

Storage racks come in a wide range of materials, including metal, wood, lava rock, reinforced concrete or conglomerate: stability should be your first priority.

Metal racks which hold bottles on wavy metal bars are affordable, easy to fit and are a very economical use of cellar space. Wine racks with compartments made out of wood, bricks or plywood make it easier to arrange your wine in batches, according to age or type, which in turn simplifies the job of managing a larger cellar. If you opt for wooden construction, make sure that the wood has been given a water-resistant finish and reject any structure made from timber that has been sprayed with a chlorophenol-based pesticide.

Standing or in the Rack?

The bottles should be laid flat, as this keeps the wine in contact with the cork and stops the cork from drying out. You will notice that, in most cellars, the bottles are stored with their necks facing the wall, which makes it easier to read their labels.

Spirits and sweet wines should be stored standing up, to prevent the alcohol from damaging the cork.

Arranging the Bottles

There are two reasons why bottles of wine should be left in cardboard boxes for as little time as possible. You should unpack them at the earliest opportunity to check that they are in the correct condition and, unlikely as it sounds, storing wine in the box may affect the flavour. Wine delivered in a wooden case, on the other hand, is best left in its original packaging,. Even wines which are meant to be drunk young will be much better after "resting" for two weeks or even for a month, and distinguished vintages need to be left for a few months at least if they are to be enjoyed at their best.

The temperature in your cellar will be slightly lower near the floor, because hot air rises, so Champagnes should be placed at the bottom level, with other white wines above them. Next should be the bottles of rosé, followed by reds which require only a short storage, and finally the reds to be laid down for long maturation.

Managing your Cellar

The best way to stay on top of your wines is to buy a **cellar book**, sold in some stationers and specialist bookshops. Alternatively you can make your own. Each page should have a space for the name of the wine, its appellation, its region, its colour, its vintage, the year before which it should be drunk, the time and place of purchase, the price and the details of the producer and supplier. You can then note down the number of bottles in stock and tick them off as they leave the cellar. Finally, jot down your own notes on the wine after the tasting or meal. A number of internet sites, including www.idealwine.com, offer an online cellar-management facility.

Insurance

Unfortunately, few insurers offer a policy insuring your wines against theft. It may be safer to trust to discretion rather than advertising a valuable cellar by fitting reinforced doors. In the case of your most jealously guarded wines, consider removing the labels and identifying them by code instead.

Renting Cellar Space

A number of storage companies and wine merchants now offer specialised cellarage. If you need to store large stocks of wine in the Paris region, two of the many cellars providing this service are:

- **La Cave** – *7 impasse Charles-Petit, 75011 Paris; www.lacave-web.com*
- **Les Crayères des Montquartiers** – *5 chemin des Montquartiers, 92130 Issy-les Moulineaux; www.crayeres-montquartiers.com*

LEARNING MORE
TASTINGS, COURSES AND HOLIDAYS

If you've always wanted to find out more about the ideal blend of fine food and drink, or just put a love of wine into words, France is the place to perfect your appreciation and knowledge, and find out more about what you like. Courses for beginners and experts take place around the country. The best way to learn, though, is hands-on: comparing a series of wines chosen to bring out the variation between, or within, one or more regions, grape varieties or vine-yards. You'll be tasting them "blind", just like the experts do. On averge, expect to pay 50€ for a 2-3 hour course, while a wine weekend in Burgundy, including food and accommodation will cost about 380€.

WINE TOURS

Arblaster & Clarke
℘01730 263 111; www.winetours.co.uk – Wine tours specialist, with various tours available.

Gourmet Touring
℘00 33 6 32 80 04 74; www.gourmet-touring.com – Based in the Gironde,this company offers a selection of options based around food, and wine.

Grape Escapes
℘0870 766 7617, www.grapeescapes.net – Self-drive wine holidays in the Loire and Burgundy.

Outside France

The American Wine Society – *www.americanwinesociety.com* – Accreditation, awards and competi-tions, wine events, travel, publications and much more.

International Food and Wine Society – *www.iwfs.org* – Promoting a "knowledge and understanding of wine and food", the IWFS has branches in 40 countries.

The Wine Society – *www.thewinesociety.com* – Organises tastings and offers buying advice to its members. Sales by phone and online.

The Wine & Spirit Education Trust
℘20 7089 3800; www.wset.co.uk – This UK-based charity oversees qualifications and runs courses for wine enthusiasts and professionals.

Around France

Prodegustation *℘0820 82 10 20 – www.prodegustation.com* – A training organisation that aims to reduce Tasting sessions, wine weekends and vineyard tours.

Savour Club *℘0820 72 03 33 – www.lesavourclub.fr* – Tasting sessions of six wines, in a gastronomic setting.

In Paris

École du vin de Paris – *25 r. de la Félicité, 17e arr. ℘01 43 41 33 94. www.ecoleduvin.fr.* Founded by Olivier Thiénot, the School of Wine is open to professionals and individuals.

Grains Nobles – *5 r. Laplace, 5e arr. ℘01 43 54 93 54. www.grainsnobles.fr.* – A team of young wine enthusiasts organises introductory courses at this Parisian wine cellar.

Union des oenologues de France – *21-23 r. Croulebarbe, 13e arr. ℘01 58 52 20 20. www.oenologuesdefrance.fr.* Introductions to wine tasting and more.

At the wine merchant's

Many wine merchants organise tastings as a way of introducing the wines they sell, often enlisting the help of the producers or even bringing along an *oenologue* to conduct the event. Every autumn, the **Fédération nationale des cavistes independents** organises tastings to coincide with the Fête du vin. *177 ave. Charles-de-Gaulle, 92200 Neuilly-sur-Seine. ℘01 46 37 88 45.* **Lavinia** – *3-5 blvd. de la Madeleine, 1e arr. ℘01 42 97 20 20. www.lavinia.fr.*

Know Before You Go

USEFUL WEBSITES

www.ambafrance-us.org
The site of the French Embassy in the USA provides basic information, a news digest and business-related information, with special pages for children, and pages devoted to culture, language study and travel. Links to selected French sites (regions, cities, ministries).

www.franceguide.com
The French Government Tourist Office/ Maison de la France site is packed with practical information for travellers to France. The home page has links to more specific guidance, for American or Canadian travellers for example.

www.FranceKeys.com
This sight has plenty of practical information for visiting France. It covers all the regions, with links to tourist offices and related sites. Very useful for planning the details of your tour in France.

www.fr-holidaystore.co.uk
The French Travel Centre in London has gone on-line with this service, providing information on all of the regions of France, including updated special travel offers and details on available accommodation.

www.visiteurope.com
The European Travel Commission provides useful information on travelling to, and around, 36 European countries, and includes links to some commercial booking services (ie vehicle hire), rail schedules, weather reports and more.

www.wines-france.com
Official website of Viniflhor, a public agency concerned with regulation and marketing of wines and other horticultural products. A good general site for learning about French wines, with links to regional organisations.

TOURIST OFFICES

For information, brochures, maps and assistance in planning a trip to France travellers can apply to the French Tourist Office in their own country.

Australia and New Zealand
Level 13, 25 Bligh Street, **Sydney**, New South Wales 2000
℘(02) 9231 5244; Fax (02) 9221 8682; info.au@franceguide.com

Canada
1800 Avenue McGill College, Suite 1010, **Montreal**, PQ H3A 3J6
℘(514) 288-2026; Fax (514) 845 4868; canada@franceguide.com

Ireland
℘(15) 60 235 235;
info.ie@franceguide.com

South Africa
P.O. Box 41022, **Craighall** 2024
℘(27) 11 523 8292;
Fax (27) 11 523 8299

United Kingdom
178 Piccadilly, **London**, W1J 9AL
℘0906 8244 123 (60p per minute)
Fax 020 7493 6594 ;
info.uk@franceguide.com

United States

New York
444 Madison Avenue, 16th Floor, NY 10022;℘(212) 838-7800,
Fax (212) 838-7855;
info.us@franceguide.com

Chicago
205 North
Michigan Avenue, Suite 3770, Chicago, IL 60601; ℘(514) 288-1904, Fax (312) 337-6339;
info.chicago@franceguide.com

Los Angeles
9454 Wilshire Boulevard, Suite 210, Beverly Hills, CA 90212; ℘(310) 271-6665, Fax (310) 276-2835;
info.losangeles@franceguide.com

The French Tourist Office also offers information, ℘(514) 288-1904.

EMBASSIES AND CONSULATES			
COUNTRY	**ADDRESS**	**TEL**	**FAX**
Australia	4 rue Jean-Rey, 75724 Paris	01 40 59 33 00	01 40 59 33 10
		www.france.embassy.gov.au	
Canada	35 avenue Montaigne, 75008 Paris	01 44 43 29 00	01 44 43 29 99
		www.amb-canada.fr	
Ireland	12 avenue Foch, 75116 Paris	01 44 17 67 00	01 44 17 67 50
		www.embassyofirelandparis.com	
New Zealand	7 ter run Léonard-de-Vinci, 75116 Paris	01 45 01 43 43	01 45 01 43 44
		www.nzembassy.com	
South Africa	59 quai d'Orsay, 75343 Paris	01 53 59 23 23	01 53 59 23 68
		www.afriquesud.net	
UK	Embassy – 35 rue du Faubourg St-Honoré, 75383 Paris Cedex 08	01 44 51 31 00	01 44 51 32 34
	Consulate – 16 rue d'Anjou, 75008 Paris	01 44 51 31 01	(visas)
		www.britishembassy.gov.uk	
USA	Embassy – 2 avenue Gabriel, 75382 Paris	01 43 12 22 22	01 42 66 97 83
	Consulate – 15 ave. d'Alsace, 67082 Strasbourg	03 88 35 31 04	03 88 24 06 95
		www.amb-usa.fr	

INTERNATIONAL VISITORS ENTRY REQUIREMENTS

PASSPORT

Nationals of countries within the European Union entering France need only a national identity card (or in the case of the British a passport). Nationals of other countries must be in possession of a valid national **passport**. In case of loss or theft, report to your embassy or consulate and the local police.

VISA

No entry visa is required for Canadian, US or Australian citizens travelling as tourists and staying less than 90 days, except for students planning to study in France. If you think you may need a visa, apply to your local French Consulate. US citizens should obtain the booklet *Safe Trip Abroad* (US$2.75), which provides useful information on visa requirements, customs regulations, medical care etc for international travellers. The booklet can be ordered by phone (℘202-512-1800) or online (http://bookstore.gpo.gov) or consulted on-line (www.gpoaccess.gov). General passport information is available by phone from the Federal Information Center (item 2 on the automated menu), ℘800-688-9889. US passport application forms can be downloaded from http://travel.state.gov.

CUSTOMS REGULATIONS

The Customs Office (UK) publishes a leaflet on customs regulations and the full range of duty-free allowances; available from HM Revenue and Customs, ℘08450 109 000, or download it at http://customs/hmrc.gov.uk. The US Customs Service offers a publication *Know Before You Go* for US citizens: order it from the customs office nearest you, download it or view it online from the Know Before You Go section at www.cbp.gov/xp/cgov/travel/vacation/kbyg.

There are no customs formalities for travellers bringing their caravans into France for a stay of less than six months. No customs document is necessary for pleasure boats and outboard motors for a stay of less than six months but the registration certificate should be kept on board.

Americans can take home, tax-free, up to US$800 worth of goods (limited quantities of alcohol and tobacco products); Canadians up to CAN$400; Australians up to AUS$900 and New Zealanders up to NZ$700.

Residents from a member state of the European Union are not restricted with regard to purchasing goods for private use, but the recommended allowances for alcoholic beverages and tobacco are as follows :

- **Spirits** (whisky, gin, etc) - 10 litres
- **Cigarettes** - 3200
- **Fortified wines** (port etc) - 20 litres
- **Cigars** - 200
- **Wine** - 90 litres
- **Smoking Tobacco** - 3 kg
- **Beer** - 110 litres

HEALTH

First aid, medical advice and chemists' night service rotas are available from chemists and drugstores *(pharmacie)* identified by the green cross sign. All prescription drugs should be clearly labelled; it is recommended that you carry a copy of the prescription.

It is advisable to take out comprehensive insurance coverage as the recipient of medical treatment in French hospitals or clinics must pay the bill before reimbursement.

Nationals of non-EU countries should check with their insurance companies about policy limitations. You can then negotiate reimbursement with your insurance company according to your policy.

Citizens of EU countries should apply to the relevant Department of Health and Social Security before travelling for the European Health Insurance Card (valid three to five years), which entitles the holder to urgent treatment for accident or unexpected illness in EU countries. Applications are available at post offices or online at www.eehic.org.uk. A refund of part of the costs of treatment can be obtained on application in person or by post to local Social Security Offices *(Caisse Primaire d'Assurance Maladie)*.

Americans concerned about travel and health can contact the International Association for Medical Assistance to Travelers, for details of English-speaking doctors in different parts of France: ✆(716) 754-4883.

The American Hospital of Paris is open 24hr for emergencies and consultations with English-speaking staff, at 63 boulevard Victor-Hugo, 92200 Neuilly-sur-Seine, ✆ 01 46 41 25 25. Accredited by insurance companies.

The British Hospital is just outside Paris in Levallois-Perret, 3 rue Barbès, ✆01 46 39 22 22; http://hertford-british-hospital.org.

DRIVING IN FRANCE

Driving Licence –Travellers from other European Union countries and North America can drive in France with a valid national or home-state driving licence. An international driving permit is useful because the information on it appears in nine languages (keep in mind that traffic officers are empowered to fine motorists). A permit is available (US$10) from the National Automobile Club, 1151 East Hillsdale Blvd., Foster City, CA 94404, ✆800-622-2136 or www.nationalautoclub.com; or contact your local branch of the American Automobile Association.

Registration papers and safety jackets –If you are taking your own vehicle to France, it is necessary to have the registration papers (log-book) and a nationality plate of the approved size. All vehicles must also be equipped with a warning triangle and reflective safety jackets in case of break-downs. Non-possession of these may incur a fine of 135 euros.

Vehicle Insurance – Certain motoring organisations (AAA, AA, RAC) offer accident insurance and breakdown service schemes for members. Check with your current insurance company in regard to coverage while abroad. If you plan to hire a car using your credit card, check with the company, which may provide liability insurance automatically (and thus save you having to pay the cost for optimum coverage).

ACCESSIBILITY

Many of the sights described in this guide are accessible to people with special needs. Sights marked with the ♿ symbol offer access for wheelchairs. However, it is advisable to check beforehand by telephone.
On TGV and Corail trains operated by the national railway (SNCF), there are special wheelchair slots in 1st class carriages available for a special rate. On Eurostar and Thalys, special rates are available for accompanying adults. All airports are equipped to receive physically disabled passengers.

Additional information is available from the Royal Association for Disability and Rehabilitation (RADAR), 12 City Forum, 250 City Road, London, EC1V 8AF, ✆020 7250 3222, www.radar.org.uk; or from the French Government Tourist Office, 444 Madison Ave., 16th floor, New York, NY, 10022, ✆212-838-7800, www.franceguide.com. Web-surfers can find information for slow walkers, mature travellers and others with special needs at www.access-able.com.
The red-cover **Michelin Guide France** and the Michelin **Camping France** guide indicate hotels and camp sites with facilities suitable for those with physical disabilities.

Getting There

BY PLANE

The various national and other independent airlines offer services to one of Paris' two airports (Roissy-Charles-de-Gaulle, CDG, to the north, and Orly, ORY, to the south), Bordeaux, Lyon, Mulhouse, Toulouse, Marseille, Nice, Montpellier and Perpignan. North American airlines usually operate flights to Paris. Regional airports are well connected to both Parisian airports. Contact airline companies and travel agents for details of package tour flights with a rail or coach link-up as well as Fly-Drive schemes.

MAJOR AIRLINE COMPANIES:

Air France
✆36 54 (0.34 €/mn), daily 6.30am-10pm
www.airfrance.com

British Airways
✆0825 892 892 (0.15€/mn) Mon-Fri 2-5pm; www.britishairways.com

United Airlines
✆0810 72 72 72, Mon-Fri 8am-8pm, Sat-Sun 9.30am-6pm
www.united.fr (French site)

KLM
✆089 270 2608, (0.34 €/mn), www.klm.com

Easyjet
✆0871 244 2366
www.easyjet.com

BY SHIP

From the UK or Ireland. There are numerous cross-Channel services (passenger and car ferries) from the United Kingdom and Ireland.
To choose the most suitable route between your port of arrival and your destination use the Michelin Tourist and Motoring Atlas France, Michelin map 726 (which gives travel times and mileages) or Michelin maps from the LOCAL series (with the yellow cover).

For details apply to travel agencies or to:
Norfolkline – In the UK: ✆0870 1642 114; In France: ✆03 28 59 01 01; www.norfolkline.com.

Brittany Ferries – In the UK: ✆0870 9 076 103; In France: ✆0825 828 828; www.brittany-ferries.com.

Irish Ferries – In the UK: ✆08705 17 17 17; In Ireland: ✆0818 300 400;

In France: ✆02 33 23 44 44; In the US: ✆(772) 563 2856; www.irishferries.com

Seafrance – In the UK: ✆0871 663 2546; In France: ✆03 21 46 80 00; www.seafrance.com

P&O Ferries – In the UK: ✆08705 980 333; in France: ✆0825 120 156; www.poferries.com.

LD Lines – In the UK: ✆0870 428 4335; in France: ✆0825 304 304; www.ldlines.co.uk.

BY COACH/BUS

Eurolines (London), 4 Cardiff Road, Luton, Bedfordshire, LU1 1PP, ✆ 08705 143219.
Eurolines (Paris), 22 rue Malmaison, 93177 Bagnolet, ✆0892 8990 91.
www.eurolines.com is the international web site with information about travelling all over Europe by coach (bus).

BY TRAIN

Eurostar runs via the Channel Tunnel between London (King's cross St Pancras) and Paris (Gare du Nord) in under 2hr30 (bookings and information ✆0870 518 6186 in the UK; ✆1-888-EUROSTAR in the US; www.eurostar.com). In Paris it links to the high-speed rail network (TGV). Eurailpass, Flexipass, Eurailpass Youth, EurailDrive Pass and Saverpass are three of the travel passes which may be purchased by residents of countries outside the European Union. Contact your travel agent or, in the US, Rail Europe 2100 Central Ave, Boulder, CO, 80301; ✆800-848-7245; www.raileurope.com.
If you are a European resident, you can buy an individual country pass, if you are not a resident of the country where you plan to use it. In the UK, call Rail Europe, ✆08708 371 371. Information on schedules can be obtained on web sites for these agencies and the SNCF, respectively: www.raileurope.com, www.europrail.net, www.raileurope.co.uk, www.sncf.fr.

At the SNCF site, you can book ahead, pay with a credit card, and receive your ticket at home. There are numerous discounts available when you purchase your tickets in France, from 25-50% below the regular rate. These include discounts for using senior cards and youth cards (cards with a photograph must be purchased – 53€ and 49€, respectively), and lower rates for 2-9 people travelling together (no card required, advance purchase necessary). There are a limited number of discount seats available during peak travel times, and the best discounts are available for travel during off-peak periods. The TGV also runs a service aimed at families, called iDTGV (www.idtgv.com) where you can choose cheaper train fares by travelling in carriages that are equipped for families with children. You can choose between the quiet iDZen, or the livelier iDZap, where entertainment includes the hire of portable DVD players and you don't need to worry about children disturbing other passengers.
Tickets must be validated *(composter)* by using the orange automatic date-stamping machines at the platform entrance (failure to do so may result in a fine).
The French railway company SNCF operates a telephone information, reservation and prepayment service in English from 7am to 10pm (French time). In France call ✆08 36 35 35 39 (when calling from outside France, drop the initial 0).

BY CAR

Drivers from the British Isles can easily take their car to France via the cross-Channel services (*see above*) or via the Eurotunnel. Contact Eurotunnel, P.O. Box 2000, Folkestone, Kent CT18 8XY; ✆08705 35 35 35 (reservations); ✆08000 969 992 (customer information). www.eurotunnel.com. *See also Getting Around By Car.*

Getting Around

BY TRAIN

SNCF, the French rail network, offers service throughout France. Trains are punctual, well-maintained and comfortable, and rail lines access all but the smallest towns and villages. High-speed **TGV** (*trains à grande vitesse*) trains are among the fastest in the world, whisking passengers among larger cities at speeds of up to 300km/hr. TGV trains offer first- and second-class service and buffet/bar cars; the "new look" trains include onboard restaurants, family facilities, plug points for lap-tops and many other amenities for comfort and convenience. As the TGV network expands, **Corail** trains are being transferred to regional and intercity lines. Speedy and comfortable, Corail trains are a good option for regional travel. Local service to smaller towns is provided by the **TER** network; trains are a bit less luxurious, travel at slower speeds and make more stops.

Some points to remember when travelling by train in France:

While optional on regional and local lines, reservations (additional charge) are always advisable. Reservations are required on TGV trains.

Be sure to stamp (*composter*) your ticket in the orange validation machines prior to entering the boarding platform; if you fail to do this, you could be fined for travelling without a validated ticket.

The price of train travel in France varies depending on the class of service and the time and date of travel. In general, it's wise to book in advance for the best deals as well as options on reduced-fare passes.

Online ticket sources include:

Rail Europe: www.raileurope.co.uk in the United Kingdom or www.raileurope.com/.us in the US.

SNCF: www.voyages-sncf.com.

BY COACH/BUS

In France, bus or coach travel is rarely seen as an easy way to get around the country, and trains are used fare more regularly, mainly due to the large distances across the country and the regularity of the train service. But in some of the less easily accessible areas, such as into the mountains in Provence-Alpes, there are good routes operated, and many of France's departments run their own rural bus services. The larger cities all have regular local bus services, and trams are being reintroduced in many cities, such as Bordeaux, Montpellier and Lille. Other major cities, such as Paris, Toulouse and Lyon, have efficient Metro systems of underground trains. To travel further afield, a hop-on, hop-off bus service run along the same principles of a Eurailpass is run by Ze Bus (☎05 59 85 26 60, www.ze-bus.com) where a bus pass with accommodation and breakfast starts from 35 euros per day and can take you all over the country.

Larger coach operators such as **Eurolines** also link major destinations in France with other European cities. ☎0892 89 90 91 (0,34€/min), Mon-Sat 8am-9pm,www.eurolines.fr.

> **Caution**
>
> Due to the ongoing renumbering of the French highway system, some road numbers mentioned throughout the guide may not correspond to posted signage. Please consult the Michelin Atlas France for further reference.

BY CAR

DRIVING REGULATIONS

Highway code

The minimum driving age is 18. Traffic drives on the right. All passengers must wear seat belts. Children under the age of 10 must ride in the back seat. Headlights must be switched on in poor visibility and at night; use side-lights only when the vehicle is stationary.

In the case of a breakdown, a red warning triangle or hazard warning lights are obligatory, and safety vests must be worn. In the absence of stop signs at intersections, cars must yield to the right. Traffic on main roads outside built-up areas (priority indicated by a yellow diamond sign) and on roundabouts has right of way. Vehicles must stop when the lights turn red at road junctions and may filter to the right only when indicated by an amber arrow.

Speed Limits

Speeding regulations are rigorously enforced – usually by an on-the-spot fine and/or confiscation of the vehicle. Although liable to modification, these are as follows:

- **toll motorways** *(autoroutes)* 130kph/80mph (110kph/68mph when raining);
- **dual carriageways and motorways** without tolls 110kph/68mph (100kph/62mph when raining);
- **other roads** 90kph/56mph (80kph/50mph when raining) and in towns 50kph/31mph;
- **outside lane on motorways** during daylight, on level ground and with good visibility – minimum speed limit of 80kph/50mph.

PARKING REGULATIONS

In town there are zones where parking is either restricted or subject to a fee; tickets should be obtained from the ticket machines (*horodateurs* – small change necessary) and displayed inside the windscreen on the driver's side; failure to display may result in a fine, or towing and impoundment. Other parking areas in town may require you to take a ticket when passing through a barrier. To exit, you must pay the parking fee (usually there is a machine located by the exit – *sortie*) and insert the paid-up card in another machine which will lift the exit gate.

TOLLS

In France, most motorway sections are subject to a toll *(péage)*. You can pay in cash or with a credit card (Visa, MasterCard).

PETROL/GAS

French service stations dispense: *sans plomb 98* (super unleaded 98), *sans plomb 95* (super unleaded 95), *diesel/gazole* (diesel) and *GPL* (LPG). Petrol is considerably more expensive in France than in the USA, although less expensive than in the UK. Prices are listed on signboards on the motorways; it is usually cheaper to fill up after leaving the motorway.

RENTAL CARS

There are car rental agencies at airports, railway stations and in all large towns throughout France. European cars usually have manual transmission; automatic cars are available in larger cities only if an advance reservation is made. Drivers must be over 21; between ages 21-25, drivers are required to pay an extra daily fee; some companies allow drivers under 23 only if the reservation has been made through a travel agent. It is relatively expensive to hire a car in France; Americans in particular will notice the difference and should make arrangements before leaving; take advantage of fly-drive offers when you buy your ticket, or seek advice from a travel agent. Nova can be contacted at www.rentacar-europe.com or ☏0800 018 6682 (freephone UK) or ☏44 28 4272 8189 (calling from outside the UK). All of the firms listed below have internet sites for reservations and information. In France, you can call the following numbers:

- **Avis**
  ☏08 20 05 05 05
- **Europcar**
  ☏08 25 35 23 52
- **Budget France**
  ☏08 25 00 35 64
- **Hertz France**
  ☏01 42 05 50 43
- **SIXT-Eurorent**
  ☏08 20 00 74 98
- **National-CITER**
  ☏0825 16 12 20
- **Baron's Limousine**
  ☏01 45 30 21 21 provides cars and drivers. (English-speaking drivers available.)

Where to Stay and Eat

Individual hotels and restaurants are described in the Address Books within the *Discovering the Wine Regions of France* section of the guide. *For coin ranges, see the Legend on the cover flap.*

MICHELIN GUIDE

Don't forget the red-cover **Michelin Guide France**, with its famously reliable star-rating system and descriptions of hundreds of establishments all over France. The **Michelin Charming Places to Stay** guide contains a selection of some 1,000 hotels and guesthouses at reasonable prices.

WHERE TO STAY

CHAMBRES D'HÔTE

The French counterpart to a Bed & Breakfast, this type of lodging describes rooms in the private homes of owners who can share their knowledge of the region (and often the wines). It's a good choice for stays in small villages or out in the country. Nightly rates normally include a substantial breakfast; some establishments also serve dinner for residents only for an additional fee *(table d'hôte)*. Always reserve in advance.
Gîtes de France – www.gites-de-france.com.

BOUTIQUE HOTELS

Often located in converted historic properties, wine chateaux, or run by families who place their own individual stamp on the décor and service, these hotels offer a warm welcome and a characterful lodging experience. Breakfast is often included in the nightly rate.

INDEPENDENT HOTELS

These full-service hotels are located in larger towns and cities, but are not affiliated with a chain.
Arcantis – a network of independent hotels throughout France: www.arcantis-hotels.com.

CHAIN HOTELS

Offering convenience and predictability, chain hotels in France include: **Louvre Hotels** – (including the **Kyriad**, **Campanile** and **Concorde** chains): www.louvrehotels.com.
BandB hotels (www.hotel-bb.com).
Accor Hotels – (including the **Ibis**, **Sofitel** and **Novotel** chains): www.accorhotels.com.

WHERE TO EAT

Your dining experiences in France could range from a simple meal in a casual bistro to an elaborate, multi-course affair in an upscale establishment. Regardless of the type of restaurant, you'll discover the national passion for good food made with fresh ingredients often gathered the same day at the local market, bakery, fishmonger and butcher shop.
Fine dining restaurants typically serve elaborately prepared classical dishes, often updated for contemporary tastes, in elegant surroundings featuring designer furnishings and decor.
There are many small restaurants, sometimes run by families, serving well-prepared traditional or regional specialities in comfortable (often historic) surroundings, all with a warm welcome and friendly service. Many such places set tables outside in nice weather.
Traditional French meals include a starter course (*l'entrée*), a main dish (*le plat*), a cheese and salad course and dessert. Traditional dishes such as quiche, *steak au poivre* (pepper steak) or *coq au vin* (chicken simmered in red wine) are simply prepared with the freshest ingredients.
Rich (and often expensive), **classical** French cuisine describes an elaborate style of cooking and food presentation that makes use of cream-based sauces, precisely cut vegetables and the finest cuts of meat and fish.
France's broad range of climates and landscapes makes for a remarkably diverse array of locally produced food products and **regional specialties** that go excellently with local wines.

Useful Words and Phrases

TALKING ABOUT WINE

Acidity – *Fr.: Acidité.* Lends freshness and a vigorous quality called "nervosité" in French. If too acidic, a wine is aggressively sharp; if lacking in acidity, it tastes "flat".

Alcoholic Content – *Fr.: Titre alcoométrique.* Percentage of alcohol in a volume of wine at 20°C. This must be stated on the label.

Ampelography – The science of grape varieties.

Appellation – Name of a region or district, denoting a wine which is typical of the area and reflects the local geographic and human factors of production.

Aroma – Scent of a wine at the moment of tasting. In young wines, the primary aromas – flowery, fruity or vegetal – reflect the grape variety. Secondary aromas develop during fermentation; the wine may take on undertones of banana, boiled sweets or candy, wax or butter. Tertiary aromas, linked to the wine's ageing, may suggest smoke, wood or game: they make up a wine's "bouquet".

Assemblage – A blend of grape varieties, producing a better wine than the sum of its parts.

Astringency – The quality of a wine that gives the sensation of the drying of the mucous membranes. Linked to high tannin content; most noticeable in younger wines.

Ban des vendanges – Official proclamation of the date on which the harvest starts.

Biodynamic – Method of farming that respects the environment by taking into account the characteristics and cycles of nature.

Botrytis cinerea – A type of fungus which, in wet weather, can lead to grey rot *(pourriture grise)* – a disaster for the grower – but in dry, sunny conditions causes noble rot *(pourriture noble)*. This latter concentrates the grape sugars and is a vital element in the production of certain sweet wines.

Bouquet – The combination of aromas developed by ageing.

Cépage – The type of vine which produces the grapes. The French term for grape variety.

Chai – A wine storehouse, above ground, as opposed to the *cave*, or cellar.

Chaptalisation – The adding of sugar to the wine must.

Château – Word often used to designate a wine-producing property, even if it does not have a château in its grounds. The term may only be used of an AOC or AOVDQS.

(vin) Crémant – A sparkling wine.

Cru – Literally "growth": a wine's geographical origin.

Encepagement – Planting with (a particular variety of) vines. The overall varietal composition of a wine-making area.

Egrappage – Removal of the grape stalks during the wine-making process.

Lees – *Fr.: Lie.* Solid deposit in wine, left by the yeast, which appears after fermentation. Leaving the wine "on the lees" can enhance the aroma of white wines and lend them extra character. When a Muscadet is produced this way, its label will say "mise en bouteille sur lie".

Liquoreux – Sweet wine with sugars at a concentration of over 40g/l, produced from a harvest affected by noble rot, such as Sauternes, Gewürztraminer, Coteaux-du-Layon.

Lutte raisonnée – Environmentally friendly farming using non-chemical treatments.

Moelleux – A full, mellow wine, not usually as sweet as a *vin liquoreux*. It contains 12-45g/l of unfermented sugars.

Mousseux – Effervescent wine under 3-6 bar pressure at 20°C.

Oenology / Enology – *Fr.: Oenologie, un oenologue.* The science of wine, as studied by an oenologist.

Passerillage – Process in which grapes are sun-dried at the foot of the vine or on a bed of straw *(paille)*. This increases the sugar content of the grape. The method is used to make wines known as *vin de paille*.

Perlant – A very lightly sparkling wine, made so by the natural presence of carbon dioxide, is said to be "pearling" when poured: a few fine bubbles stick to the side of the glass.

Pétillant – This describes wines which are less effervescent than a *vin mousseux*, with a gas pressure of between 1 and 2.5 bar.

Phylloxera – A plant-louse that devastated Europe's vineyards from the 1860s, attacking the roots and leaves of the vine.

Polyphenol – A type of chemical compound that gives wine its colour and includes tannins.

Primeur – Wine from the last harvest sold from 3rd Thursday in November. To be drunk very young. All such wines must be labelled "vin nouveau" or "vin primeur".

Récoltant – Literally "harvester" – a grower, either one who sells his grapes or makes his own wine.

Robe – The colour of a wine.

Sommelier – More than just a wine-waiter: a sommelier is also responsible for the choice, purchase and storage of wines.

Storage – *Fr.: Garde.* Over time, a fine wine meant for long storage – a *vin de garde* – develops the mature qualities of a great wine.

Surmaturation – Literally "over-ripening" – this makes for a concentration of sugars in the grapes, a necessary element in the production of *vins doux naturels, vins de paille,* and *vendages tardives*, fine wines from Alsace made from late-picked grapes.

Tannins – Organic substances found in the pips, skins and stems of the grape: they play an important part in the ageing of red wines and the development of their bouquet. A tannin-rich wine often has a strongly astringent quality.

Terroir – The combination of a vineyard's natural elements; soil, subsoil, climate, exposure… and the grower's input that makes the most of them.

Vendanges vertes – Literally, "green harvests": the trimming-off of leaves and picking of unripe grapes to encourage the remaining crop to ripen.

Véraison – The final stage of grape-ripening, when the colour changes.

Vigneron – A wine-grower who cultivates vines and produces wine.

Vin Doux Naturel – Sweet fortified wine.

Vintage – *Fr.: Millésime.* The year of the grape harvest

Basic Information

BANKS

Although business hours vary from branch to branch, banks are usually open from 9am to noon and 2pm to 5pm and are closed either on Mondays or Saturdays. Banks close early on the day before a bank holiday. A passport is necessary as identification when cashing travellers cheques in banks. Commission charges vary and hotels usually charge more than banks for cashing cheques.

COMMUNICATIONS

NATIONAL CALLS

French telephone numbers have 10 digits. Paris and Paris region numbers begin with 01; 02 in Northwest France; 03 in Northeast France; 04 in Southeast France and Corsica; 05 in Southwest France.

INTERNATIONAL CALLS

To call France from abroad, dial the country code (33) + 9-digit number (omit the initial 0). When calling abroad from France dial 00, then dial the country code followed by the area code (minus the initial 0) and number of your correspondent.

INTERNATIONAL DIALLING CODES

(00 + code):
Australia – ✆**61**
Canada – ✆**1**
Ireland – ✆**353**
United Kingdom – ✆**44**
United States – ✆**1**

PUBLIC PHONES

Most public phones in France use pre-paid phone cards *(télécartes)*, rather than coins. Some telephone booths accept credit cards (Visa, MasterCard/Eurocard). *Télécartes* (50 or 120 units) can be bought in post offices, branches of France Télécom, bureaux de tabac (cafés that sell cigarettes) and newsagents, and can be used to make calls in France and abroad. Calls can be received at phone booths where the blue bell sign is shown; the phone will not ring, so keep your eye on the digital screen.

MOBILE PHONES

Most mobile phones built for North American wireless networks do not function in France, which uses GSM (Global Service for Mobile) technology operating on different frequencies than are used in North America. If your phone does not support GSM technology (check with your provider), you can rent or buy a GSM phone for use during your stay. In general, renting a phone is advisable for shorter stays while buying is probably cost-effective for longer visits, but be sure to shop around and compare price schemes carefully. Good places to start include www.telestial.com, www.mobal.com and www.internationalcellular.com.

ELECTRICITY

The electric current is 220 volts. Circular two-pin plugs are the rule. Adapters and converters for small appliances should be bought before you leave home; they are on sale in most airports. If you have a rechargeable device (video camera, portable computer, battery recharger), read the instructions carefully or contact the manufacturer or shop. Sometimes these items only require a plug adapter, in other cases you must use a voltage converter as well or risk ruining your appliance.

EMERGENCIES

EMERGENCY NUMBERS	
Police:	**17**
SAMU (Paramedics):	**15**
Fire (Pompiers):	**18**

MONEY

VALUE-ADDED TAX (VAT)

In France a sales tax (TVA or VAT) is added to most purchases. For non-Europeans, this tax can be refunded as long as you have bought more and

€175 worth of goods on the same day in the same shop. This fixed amount may vary, so it is advisable to check with the VAT-refund counter (*service de détaxe*). Collect the appropriate forms at the time of purchase and present to Customs officials on leaving France for processing. Customs Information Centre: ✆ 08 25 30 82 60 (€0.15/min) or www.douane.gouv.fr.

CREDIT CARDS

Visa is the most widely accepted credit card, followed by MasterCard. Both companies charge a 1% transaction fee on credit card purchases in a foreign currency. Other cards (Diners Club, Plus, Cirrus etc) are also accepted in some cash machines. American Express is more often accepted in premium establishments.

Most places post signs indicating which card they accept. Cards are widely accepted in shops, hypermarkets, hotels and restaurants, at tollbooths and in petrol stations.

Be sure to remember your PIN number; you will need it to use ATMs and to pay with your card in shops, restaurants etc. PIN numbers have 4 digits in France; inquire with the issuing company or bank if the code you usually use is longer.

Before you leave home, check with the bank that issued your card for emergency replacement procedures. Carry your card number and emergency phone numbers separate from your wallet and handbag; leave a copy of this information with someone you can easily reach. If your card is lost or stolen while you are in France, call one of the following 24-hour hotlines:

- **American Express**: ✆ 0800 832 820
- **Mastercard/Eurocard**: ✆ 0 800 901 387
- **Visa**: ✆ 0 800 90 11 79
- **Diners Club**: ✆ 0 810 314 159

These numbers are subject to change, but you can also check at **ATM machines**, where they are usually listed. You must report any loss or theft of credit cards or travellers cheques to the local police

CURRENCY EXCHANGE

Since 2002, **euros** have been the only currency accepted as a means of payment in France.

There are no restrictions on the amount of currency visitors can take into France. Visitors carrying a lot of cash are advised to complete a currency declaration form on arrival, because there are restrictions on currency export. If you plan to arrive in France outside of business hours, it's wise to have a few euros with you; check with your local bank about exchanging before you leave, but for better rates, do most of your currency exchange in France.

To exchange currency, look for a "Bureau de Change" desk in banks, travel agencies, airports and train stations. Transaction fees vary from place to place, and must be posted. When in doubt, simply ask (before proceeding) how many euros you'll receive for the currency you're exchanging. You'll need your passport or other proof of identity for most transactions, particulary when cashing travellers cheques.

You can also exchange currency by using your credit card (4-digit PIN required) at ATMs to get a cash advance or to withdraw directly from your bank account (debit card).

Be aware that Visa and Mastercard both charge a 1% fee to convert a foreign currency withdrawal.

Also ATMs and home institutions both usually charge a transaction fee, so try to avoid multiple withdrawals of small amounts.

EXCHANGE RATE

At press time, the exchange rate for one euro (1€) was: US$1.35; GB£0.68; CAN$1.48; AUS$1.64.

For up-to-the-minute rates, consult www.xe.com.

POST / MAIL

Main post offices open Monday to Friday 8am to 7pm, Saturday 8am to noon. Smaller branch post offices generally close at lunchtime between noon and 2pm and at 4pm.

Postage via air mail:

UK	Letter	(20g) 0.70€
North America	Letter	(20g) 85€
	Postcard	0.85€
Australia New Zealand	Letter	(20g) 85€

Stamps are also available from newsagents and *bureaux de tabac*. Stamp collectors should ask for *timbres de collection* in any post office.

PUBLIC HOLIDAYS

Public services, museums and vineyards may be closed or may vary their hours of admission on the following public holidays: **Note:** *Much of France goes on holiday for nearly all of the month of August; many businesses, attractions, hotels and restaurants may be closed. Phone or check online in advance to confirm.*

1 January	New Years Day (*Jour de l'An*)
13 April	Easter Monday *(Pâques)*
1 May	May Day (*Fête du Travail*)
8 May	VE Day (*Anniversaire 1945*)
Thurs 40 days after Easter	Ascension Day *(Ascension)*
7th Sun-Mon after Easter	Whit Sunday and Monday (Pentecôte)
1 June	Whit Monday *(Pentecôte)*
14 July	*Fête* **National** France's National Day **(or Bastille Day)**
15 August	Assumption *(Assomption)*
1 November	All Saints' Day *(Toussaint)*
11 November	Armistice Day *(Armistice 1918)*
25 December	Christmas Day *(Noël)*

SMOKING

France officially banned smoking in public places in February 2007. The ban prohibits smoking in offices and schools, and was extended to restaurants, dance clubs and most bars in 2008.

TIME ZONE

France is 1hr ahead of Greenwich Mean Time (GMT). France goes on daylight-saving time from the last Sunday in March to the last Sunday in October.

PRICES AND TIPS

Since a service charge is automatically included in the prices of meals and accommodation in France, it is not necessary to tip in restaurants and hotels. However, if the service in a restaurant is especially good or if you have enjoyed a fine meal, an extra tip (this is the *pourboire*, rather than the *service*) will be appreciated. Usually 1.50€ to 3.50€ is enough, but if the bill is big (a large party or a luxury restaurant), it is not uncommon to leave 7€ to 8€ or more.

As a rule, the cost of staying in a hotel and eating in restaurants is significantly higher in Paris than in the French regions. However, by reserving a hotel room well in advance and taking advantage of the wide choice of restaurants, you can enjoy your trip without breaking the bank.

Restaurants usually charge for meals in two ways: a *menu*, that is a fixed price menu with 2 or 3 courses, sometimes a small pitcher of wine, all for a stated price, or *à la carte*, the more expensive way, with each course ordered separately.

Cafés have very different prices, depending on where they are located. The price of a drink or a coffee is cheaper if you stand at the counter *(comptoir)* than if you sit down *(salle)* and sometimes it is even more expensive if you sit outdoors *(terrasse)*.

CONVERSION TABLES

Weights and Measures

1 kilogram (kg)	**2.2 pounds (lb)**	**2.2 pounds**	*To convert kilograms to pounds, multiply by 2.2*
6.35 kilograms	14 pounds	1 stone (st)	
0.45 kilograms	16 ounces (oz)	16 ounces	
1 metric ton (tn)	**1.1 tons**	**1.1 tons**	
1 litre (l)	**2.11 pints (pt)**	**1.76 pints**	*To convert litres to gallons, multiply by 0.26 (US) or 0.22 (UK)*
3.79 litres	1 gallon (gal)	0.83 gallon	
4.55 litres	1.20 gallon	1 gallon	
1 hectare (ha)	**2.47 acres**	**2.47 acres**	*To convert hectares to acres, multiply by 2.4*
1 sq. kilometre (km²)	**0.38 sq. miles (sq.mi.)**	**0.38 sq. miles**	
1 centimetre (cm)	**0.39 inches (in)**	**0.39 inches**	*To convert metres to feet, multiply by 3.28; for kilometres to miles, multiply by 0.6*
1 metre (m)	**3.28 feet (ft) or 39.37 inches or 1.09 yards (yd)**		
1 kilometre (km)	**0.62 miles (mi)**	**0.62 miles**	

Clothing

Women			
Shoes	35	4	2½
	36	5	3½
	37	6	4½
	38	7	5½
	39	8	6½
	40	9	7½
	41	10	8½
Dresses & suits	36	6	8
	38	8	10
	40	10	12
	42	12	14
	44	14	16
	46	16	18
Blouses & sweaters	36	06	30
	38	08	32
	40	10	34
	42	12	36
	44	14	38
	46	16	40

Men			
Shoes	40	7½	7
	41	8½	8
	42	9½	9
	43	10½	10
	44	11½	11
	45	12½	12
	46	13½	13
Suits	46	36	36
	48	38	38
	50	40	40
	52	42	42
	54	44	44
	56	46	48
Shirts	37	14½	14½
	38	15	15
	39	15½	15½
	40	15¾	15¾
	41	16	16
	42	16½	16½

Sizes often vary depending on the designer. These equivalents are given for guidance only.

Speed

KPH	10	30	50	70	80	90	100	110	120	130
MPH	6	19	31	43	50	56	62	68	75	81

Temperature

Celsius (°C)	0°	5°	10°	15°	20°	25°	30°	40°	60°	80°	100°
Fahrenheit (°F)	32°	41°	50°	59°	68°	77°	86°	104°	140°	176°	212°

To convert Celsius into Fahrenheit, multiply °C by 9, divide by 5, and add 32.
To convert Fahrenheit into Celsius, subtract 32 from °F, multiply by 5, and divide by 9.

NB: Conversion factors on this page are approximate.

Turning Champagne bottles in the cellars of Pommery, Reims

INTRODUCTION TO THE WINE REGIONS OF FRANCE

Wine Production

"What is there in this bottle, Babette?" she asked in a low voice. "Not wine?" "Wine, Madame!" Babette answered. "No, Madame, it is a Clos Vougeot 1846!" Martine had never suspected that wines could have names to them.
Karen Blixen, *Babette's Feast*

VARIETIES AND APPELLATIONS

THE SCIENCE OF VARIETY

Ampelography

From the Greek word *ampelos*, or vine, ampelography is the study of grape varieties. These varieties, referred to in French as *cépages*, can be identified by sight by their different shoots, flowers, early and mature leaves and the shapes of their grape-bunches, as well as their development through the year – the emergence of their buds, their flowering, and the colouring of their leaves in autumn. Varieties also differ in their ability to resist an attack of oidium, mildew or grey rot, or a parasite like phylloxera. One characteristic shared by all varieties, however, is the fivefold nervation of the leaves: the patterning is clearest on the underside of the leaf.

We know from Pliny the Elder's writings that descriptions of grape varieties played a part of Roman cultivation, but although Olivier de Serres's *Théâtre d'Agriculture*, published in 1600, does mention various *cépages*, it was not until the mid-18C that the great Swedish botanist Carl von Linné, better known as Carolus Linnaeus, published precise taxonomic descriptions of the different types of vine. By the end of the 1780s, botanical collections had been planted in Béziers, Dijon and Pessac-Léognan and, in the century that followed, the study of ampelography was to spread from Spain to Russia. In 1951, the Office International de la Vigne et du Vin produced a standardised code for assessing grape varieties which is still the recognised guide.

The last 25 years have seen great changes in the distribution of varieties around France. The viticultural map has been redrawn in the Languedoc, where growers have planted Syrah and Mourvedre alongside their traditional Grenache and Carignan. Some varieties, Cinsault and Folle Blanche among them, have fallen out of favour, while others, such as Chardonnay, Sauvignon, Merlot and Syrah, are grown in greater quantities than ever before.

Not all grape varieties have the potential to make great wines: growers make a formal distinction between poor, medium-quality or so-called "noble" grapes. Only the last of these are used for wines today, and these are classed in one of two further groups. Those termed "cépages universels" adapt to different growing conditions with relative ease and produce wines with consistent and identifiable character wherever they are grown. Cabernet-Sauvignon, Cabernet Franc, Gamay, Syrah and Merlot all belong to this category, as do white wine varieties like Chardonnay, Gewürztraminer, Muscat, Sauvignon and Riesling. Other

Varietal or Cuvée?

Varietal wines, or "vins de cépage", are made from a single kind of grape; famous examples include Muscadet, Beaujolais, Sancerre, Montlouis and Meursault. Blended wines, on the other hand, are made by mixing together different grapevarieties; they include Bandols, Saint-Chinians and Pomerols. Châteauneuf-du-Pape can be made with thirteen different types. Traditionally, varieties are only named on the label in Alsace though Bourgogne-Aligoté from Burgundy and Muscadet, from the Nantes region are two notable exceptions. Increasingly, producers from all regions are indicating grape variety or varieties in the label.

cépages, including Chenin, Mourvèdre and Pinot Noir, will only grow well in particular areas, but these too may be considered "noble" varieties.

Matching Variety and Terroir

The growers' and oenologists' choice of vines is in part made for them by the INAO's legislation, which determines which varieties are to be grown in the appellation region. Beyond this, all the factors of the terroir, and the quality of wine to be produced are crucial considerations. Early-ripening varieties can be grown in colder areas, while later ones need a long, hot growing season.

To get an idea of the range of *encépagement*, imagine a cross drawn over a map of France, from the Pas-de-Calais to the eastern Pyrenees, and from the north of Charente-Maritime, on the Atlantic coast, to Haute Savoie in the Alps. In the northwest quarter, which includes the Loire Valley vineyards, Gamay and Cabernet Franc are grown for red wines and Muscadet, Pineau de la Loire and Sauvignon supply the white. To the Southwest, reds are made from Cabernet-Franc too, but also Cabernet-Sauvignon, Merlot and Malbec, while the trio of Sauvignon, Semillon and Muscadelle dominate white wine production.

The northeast quarter, covering the great vineyards of Champagne, Burgundy and Alsace, grows Pinot Noir and Gamay for varietal reds. Burgundy's whites are made from Chardonnay and Aligoté, while an Alsatian white may be produced from Riesling, Gewürztraminer, Tokay-Pinot Gris, Sylvaner, Muscat, Pinot Blanc or Pinot Noir.

Finally, the reds of Southeast France are made from Syrah, Grenache, Mourvèdre, Cinsault and Carignan and the region's whites from Roussanne, Marsanne and Ugni Blanc.

But how many more varieties could you name? The studies of the great ampelographer Pierre Galet cover some 9,600 grape types, making up 99% of the world's grapes, yet only 20 varieties account for around 87% of France's viticulture.

S. Sauvignier / MICHELIN

RED VARIETIES

Cabernet Franc

Well represented in the vineyards of the Southwest, Dordogne and around Bordeaux, where it is grown at St-Emilion and Pomerol, Cabernet Franc can also be found in Languedoc and in the Loire Valley, notably in AOC Bourgueil, Saint-Nicolas-de-Bourgueil and Chinon.

Cabernet Franc likes hot, sandy, gravelly soil. Its little bunches are made up of round, blue-black grapes.

The young wine's cherry-red robe deepens with age; a strongly aromatic nose combines the red-fruit aromas of strawberry and cherry with liquorice or pepper; it sometimes has a little acidity to it, but its tannic character is invariably smooth and fine.

Cabernet-Sauvignon

The classic Médoc grape, Cabernet-Sauvignon is also cultivated in Languedoc and the Loire Valley. A late-ripening variety, the vine gives of its best in hot, dry soil like the gravelly mix of the Graves appellation: its little, deep-violet grapes produce wines with good ageing potential.

Its intense colour may range from dark ruby to deep garnet shades, and when under-matured can be recognised by its unmistakeable peppery aroma. A well-aged example, however, combines blackberry with tertiary notes of smoke

White and Red

Vines which have white grapes produce white wines, known as *blancs de blancs*. Grapes with darker skins can also be used to make white wine – *blancs de noirs* – if the skins are not left in contact with the juice, a process known as maceration. If they are, the result is a red or a rosé.

and leather. Rich in tannins, these wines reward longer cellarage.

Gamay

The 36,000 hectares of Gamay grown in France include 99% of the Beaujolais vineyards. In Burgundy it is combined with Pinot Noir to make Bourgogne-Passetoutgrain, and is also grown on the Loir around Vendôme, on the Côte Roannaise, in Savoie and in the Estaing, Entraygues and Fel appellations. An early variety, most at home in granitic soils, the Gamay vine produces blackish-violet grapes. Its light robe is a brilliant red with a blueish-purple tint. A strongly fruity nose, full of red fruit, combines with a lively, faintly acidic taste without noticeable tannins.

Grenache

Grenache covers almost 100,000ha of Provence, the Rhône Valley (Gigondas, Lirac) and Languedoc-Roussillon (Banyuls, Rivesaltes, Maury). It is often blended with Syrah and Mourvèdre. Resistant to dry and windy weather, it thrives on steep, shale-rich terrain and hot, dry, stony soil. Its black grapes grow in tight-packed bunches.

The intense red of younger wines tends towards dark brick or mahogany in older vintages and *vins doux naturels*. A ripe, red-fruit nose also has notes of spice, and a taste reveals a robust, round wine, rich in alcohol, which echoes the fruity, spicy character of the bouquet.

Merlot

The third most common red grape after Carignan and Grenache. It is most common in its area of origin, the Bordeaux region, and is particularly associated with Saint-Emilion, Médoc and Pomerol (Pétrus), but can also be found in Languedoc-Roussillon. This sturdy early-ripening variety is usually planted in areas of clay and chalk. Merlot grapes are blue-black.

Look for a garnet red robe and a bouquet which combines violets, red fruit, and spices, sometimes a hint of prunes or plums. Smooth and supple in the mouth, it is more structured when blended with Cabernet-Sauvignon.

Mourvèdre

Provence (Bandol), the Rhône Valley and Languedoc-Roussillon all produce

Merlot grapes

Mourvèdre's close clutches of little, late-maturing black grapes. It lends structure to heady *vins de garde* which will improve with age for up to a decade. Mourvèdre is recognisable by its deep, dense colour, between crimson and dark purple. An intense, spicy aroma of forest fruit, blackberry and liquorice sets off a refined tannic quality, spicy fruit and a good, long finish in well-aged wines.

Pinot Noir

A noted Burgundian grape, it is also used, on its own or in a blend, to make Alsatian wine, Champagne, Rosé-des-Riceys and Loire wines from the Menetou-Salon and Sancerre appellations. Jura and Savoie also produce Pinot Noir. Its "personality" varies from one terroir to another, but the grapes are always the same in appearance: blueish black, in very tight bunches. The vine prefers chalky soil. Whatever Pinot Noir may lack in vibrancy of colour, it more than makes up for with its perfumed aroma and good cellaring potential. A frequently powerful nose, where strawberry, blackcurrant and cherry scents predominate, is matched by a rich fruit flavour; after a few years of storage, the tannins mellow pleasantly.

Syrah

A fine variety with strong links to the upper Rhône valley, where its varietals and cuvées include Grand Crus (Côte-rôtie, Hermitage, Cornas). Saint-Chinian and Faugères are the names most associated with it in Languedoc-Roussillon. Like Gamay, it grows well in granitic soil, but it flowers and fruits late: the grapes are oval in shape, with a blue-black colour. Syrah wines have a strong, dark colour and, being rich in tannins, are generally powerful. Their initial aroma is marked by spicy red fruit, with violet and pepper notes coming through.

WHITE GRAPES

Aligoté

A Burgundian grape, much admired in varietal wines from the Bourgogne-Aligoté and Bouzeron appellations, and in cuvées including the well-known Crémant de Bourgogne. Planted over 1,700ha in Burgundy, Jura, Savoie and around Die, the early-flowering vine should be grown on chalk. Its little round grapes are off-white with an orange tone, and flecked with brown. Its dry, fresh, light white wines should be drunk young. Poured over a measure of crème de cassis, it makes a typically Burgundian aperitif. Its robe, pale gold or sometimes a light straw-yellow, has a fine green tint to it. Its floral bouquet of acacia or honeysuckle mixed with apple also has a mineral note to it. It tastes fruity, round and slightly dry.

Chardonnay

In its native Burgundy, Chardonnay makes refined *vins de garde* including Corton-Charlemagne, Montrachet, Meursault and Chablis, while in Champagne it is used to make blanc des blancs. It is also cultivated in the Loire Valley, Savoie, Jura and Limoux. At home on lime-rich or clay soil, as well as the chalky Côte des Blancs south of Épernay, it buds early, making it vulnerable to spring frosts, and bears little bunches of golden yellow or amber grapes. The typical result is a nicely balanced wine which ages well and combines a brilliant, subtly green-tinted colour with acidity, intense, complex aromas and an all-round elegance. Tasters catch the scent of nuts, almonds, lime tea, toast and a faint aroma of butter, sometimes accompanied by honey or citrus notes. Depending on the nature of the terroir, Chardonnay may take on a mineral character, as at Sancerre or Chablis, a more fruity quality in a Meursault, or even suggest a hint of woodland undergrowth in wines from the slopes of Corton.

Chasselas

A white variety grown in the Crépy and Pouilly-sur-Loire appellations, but is best known as a table grape called "Chasselas de Moissac". It is grown less and less in France, increasingly replaced by the Sauvignon grape, and now covers no more than 450ha, but produces enjoyable wine in the Valais and Vaud cantons of Switzerland, where it is known as Fendant and Dorin respectively. It is

Chardonnay grapes

© felinda/iStockphoto

an early, delicate variety; its round, pale green grapes with russet speckles are used to make a dry white.

The wine's robe is very light yellow, almost transparent, with a hint of green. Depending on the terroir from which it comes, the lightly *perlant* young wine may have a slightly more floral or mineral balance, or a fruity or spicy quality.

Chenin

Also known as *pineau de la Loire*, it is the Anjou region's foremost variety, grown at Saumur, Vouvray and Montlouis. The whites produced may be dry, *moelleux*, *liquoreux* or sparkling: Coteaux-de-Layon, Quarts-de-Chaume, Bonnezeaux and Savennières number among the most popular Chenin wines. This characterful variety will flower and fruit early, and flourishes in pebbly schist soil. Noble rot develops easily on its closely grouped golden grapes.

Dry Chenin wines are round and lively, and some will improve with age for up to ten years, by which time its pale yellow robe will have turned a rich golden shade. A very floral wine, with acacia notes to the fore and a suggestion of honey or quinces, it is known for its delicate and well-balanced flavours.

The sweeter wines are meant to be stored: their green-gold colour sometimes deepening to a warm amber. The fruit-and-flower tones of pear and may-blossom are joined by the aroma of polished wood. Expect an ample, developed flavour with the taste of exotic fruits in the finish.

Gewürztraminer

The celebrated *cépage noble* of Alsace produces comparable, strongly characteristic dry or sweet wines in the Moselle region. A hardy vine, early to flower, it comes into its own in clay soil, producing bunches of little, oval grapes in a pretty shade of pink.

Given time, golden Gewürztraminer wines take on a richer amber robe. The smooth, round taste is matched by an intense and elegant nose, and it is here that the variety lives up to its name, combining *Gewürz*, or spice, with lychee scents.

Marsanne

Marsanne is much cultivated in the northern Rhône valley where, blended with Roussanne, it makes some very fine wines: Hermitage, Crozes-Hermitage, Saint-Joseph and Saint-Péray. Many terroirs of Languedoc are also to its liking, and it is grown successfully in the Cassis appellation of Provence. It is vigorous and late-growing, but oxidises easily. Happiest in a mixture of silt and pebbles, it bears round, white grapes with a touch of gold.

The colour of a Marsanne varies from pale and faintly green to a mid-gold. The unmistakeable may-blossom in the nose of an early wine gives way to spice and honey notes and the scent of wax. It is marked by a sense of vivacity and "roundness" and, in certain well-aged vintages, a delightfully long finish.

Muscadet

Originally from Burgundy, the Muscadet or melon grape was introduced to the area around Nantes at the beginning of the 18C, where it is now found in the appellations Muscadet-de-Sèvre-et-Maine, Muscadet-Côteaux-de-la-Loire and Muscadet-Côtes-de-Grand-Lieu. Here, its iodine character shows the influence of the shale soil and the Atlantic Ocean. As an early variety, it is vulnerable to a late frost, and it is also susceptible to disease. Its little grapes are a golden yellow.

When matured on its lees, Muscadet develops a slightly *perlant* character. It is conspicuously pale, with an iodine nose. The mineral quality of a young wine is joined by a bouquet of floral scents after a few years. Its taste is pleasantly light and lively.

Muscat blanc à petits grains

This is the variety which makes the sparkling Clairette-de-Die and sweet Muscats from Frontignan, Saint-Jean-de-Minervois, Lunel, Mireval, Beaumes-de-Venise, le cap Corse and Rivesaltes: it is an early grape which is best grown in pebbly soil and likes a hot terroir.

For the production of *vins doux naturels*, the yield is limited to 28 hl/ha. The amber yellow grapes are closely clustered in long bunches.

Muscat wines are recognisable by their pale gold colour and a bouquet which combines roses, citronella, a touch of citrus fruit and a slight menthol note.

Petit Manseng

This variety is most at home among the round stones of Béarn, where it yields only 20 hl/ha but lends a mellow tone to Juraçon whites, and is part of the blend in wines of the Béarn, Irouléguy and Pacherenc-du-Vic-Bilh appellations. A vigorous and early vine, it may nonetheless fall victim to oidium and mildew. The thick-skinned little grapes are harvested by sorting or by *passerillage*.

Petit Manseng produces rich and expressive wines, which may rise from 12% to 16% in strength. They have a golden robe, a nose of honey and cinnamon with ripe, peachy fruit, and a delicate quality on the tongue.

Riesling

The noble grape of Alsace par excellence. It accounts for almost a quarter of the region's viticulture. This late variety grows well on exposed slopes and is equally well suited to sandstone or granitic sand. The Riesling grape, a spherical, speckled fruit, may be anything from light green to yellow-gold, and grows in distinctive cylindrical bunches.

A good Riesling can be stored for ten years, or even longer, in which case its brilliant pale yellow colour, tinctured with green, will have had time to darken to a deep gold. Flowers, peaches, citronella and mineral notes predominate in a lively bouquet. A very aromatic wine, it has good balanced acidity and the vivacious keenness the French refer to as "nervosité".

Sauvignon Blanc

Although it originates in Bordeaux, Sauvignon is now far more widespread, grown for blends or varietals in South-west France, the Loire Valley (AOC Sancerre), Provence and Languedoc as well as the Entre-deux-mers appellation. Vigorous and adaptable, the vine grows with equanimity in flinty clay, limestone and calcareous marl, bearing golden-yellow oval grapes in small bunches.

Sauvignon makes pale-coloured wines with a faint green glint to them. Though quick to take on the character of the terroir, which determines their robust or softer body, most have traces of blackcurrant and boxwood in their bouquet, often accompanied by a smoky character and sometimes with an accent of gunflint.

Semillon

Another Bordeaux *cépage*, it makes both fine sweet wines (Sauternes, Loupiac, Monbazillac), and notable dry whites

(Graves): usually in combination with Sauvignon and/or Muscadelle. A robust variety with a preference for *graves* and calcareous clay, Semillon is France's second most common white variety after Ugni Blanc (Cognac and Armagnac). Its round, whitish gold grapes grow pinker as they ripen.
Semillon makes a straw-coloured wine with a golden edge to it, and a discreet scent of dried fruit and honey, the latter being reflected on the palate. A big, powerful wine.

A sweet Semillon is opulence itself: brilliant gold in colour with a bouquet of honey and citrus, round and well-defined to the taste.

A LOOK AT THE LABEL

Even before you open the bottle, you can tell a lot about a wine's provenance and style. French and European law requires six types of information on the label. Most important is the name of the appellation followed, as the case may be, by the words "appellation d'origine con-

UNDERSTANDING THE LABEL

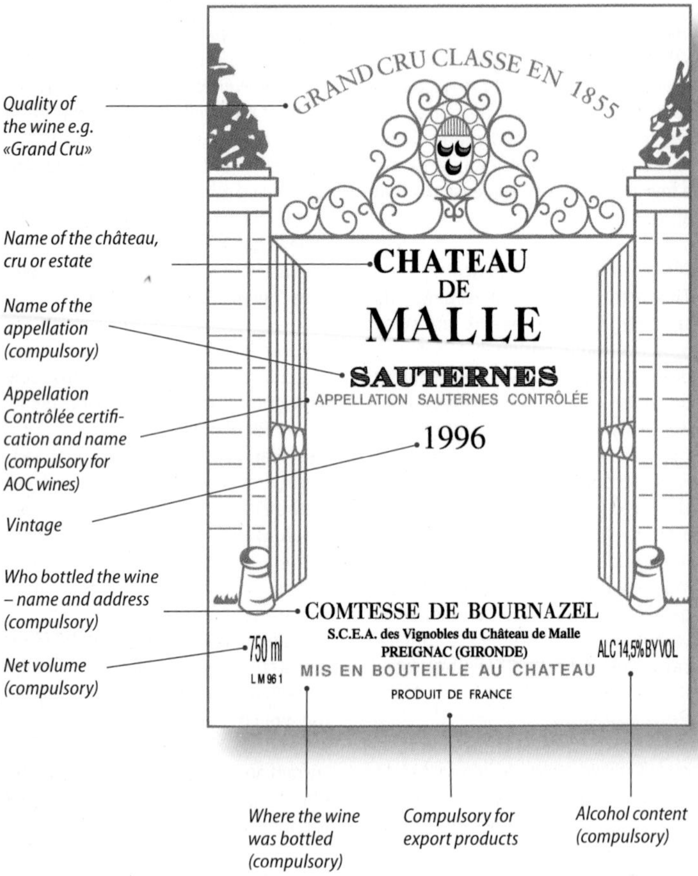

trôlée", "appellation d'origine, vin délimité de qualité supérieure" (AOVDQS) or the classification "vin de pays". Then comes the name and address of the bottler, the alcohol content, the net volume, country of origin and a batch number. Optional information includes the name of the vineyard, Cru or Château, a brand name, the vintage, grape variety, the colour of the wine, and any medals awarded at professional tastings. The label on the back gives advice on serving temperature, storage, suggested dishes to accompany the wine, and more about the grapes

LEGENDARY WINES

The making of wine entails a sort of alchemy: this thick, sticky juice extracted from simple fruit is reborn as nectar, bestowing moments of pleasure on those who consume it. When the wine happens to be a Romanée-Conti, a Petrus or a Chateau d'Yquem... the pleasure is infinite.

ROMANÉE-CONTI

Grown in a single vineyard of 1.8ha, Romanée-Conti is one of six Grands Crus thriving in the Côte de Nuits commune of Vosne-Romanée. It falls entirely within the Domaine de la Romanée-Conti, which therefore has the right to include the word "monopole" on the wine label, indicating that the appellation is controlled by a single estate.

Owned by the monks of the Saint-Vivant monastery, the terroir was known during the late Middle Ages as "Cloux des Cinq-Journaux," then as "Romanée." In 1760, the Prince of Conti acquired the vineyard (for a relative fortune), and bestowed his name upon it. The estate changed hands several times after the Revolution, and was enlarged through the acquisiton of the Échézeaux, Richebourg, La Tâche and Romanée-Saint-Vivant properties. At present it is owned by Aubert de Vilaine and the Leroy family.

The Pinot Noir grapes grown on this terroir of lime trees and calcareous soil are transformed into a wine ranking in the stratosphere of excellence. With low yields (just 25 hectolitres per hectare), vines more than 40 years old, biodynamic cultivation methods, rigourous sorting, malolactic fermentation and maturation in new oak barrels, the appellation produces 6,000 bottles each year of richly coloured wine, fine and powerful in the mouth with a spicy, floral bouquet.

The vineyard was entirely replanted in 1947; production resumed five years later, hence the lack of vintages from 1946–1951. Wines from this estate are sold by the case, each containing 11 bottles of other Burgundy Grand Cru wines and a single bottle of Romanée-Conti.

PETRUS

Unlike Romanée-Conti, Pétrus is named for the surrounding area, and has a relatively short history. Madame Loubat, the vineyard's owner from 1925–1961, hit upon the idea of promoting her wine by sending several bottles to Queen Elizabeth of England on the occasion of her 1953 coronation. The idea succeeded beautifully. In 1964, one of Mme Loubat's heirs sold a portion to Jean-Pierre Moueix; his successors today entirely manage the Pétrus vineyard.

Situated on the highest point in the Pomerol appellation, this 11.8ha estate maintains its yields at low levels, making for a somewhat rare (and expensive) wine. Its excellence results from a happy marriage of a fine grape variety (Merlot), the terroir (a hint of clay in the soil), a favourable vineyard exposure and the careful work of the winegrower to preserve the vines, now more than 40 years old.

Harvesting occurs here in the late afternoon, and winemaker Olivier Berrouet supervises the short fermentation period. Afterward, the wine is aged for 21 months in new barrels. Petrus achieves the height of perfection after a long storage period. If you are lucky enough to drink it, you will be struck by the rich, dark robe; the fragrances of truffle and dark-skinned fruits; the roundness, finesse and amplitude in the mouth.

CHATEAU D'YQUEM

In 1993, the Chateau d'Yquem celebrated four centuries of ownership within the same family. In 2001, two-thirds of the buisiness was acquired by the LVMH group. June 2004 brought the sudden retirement of Count Alexandre-de Lur-Saluces, the last descendant of Françoise Joséphine de Sauvage d'Yquem, the "Lady of Yquem", who led the vineyard and the estate to their early status in the rankings of French wines in the late 18C. Today the estate is managed by Pierre Lurton.

The stately château rises amid the vineyards on the highest hill in the Sauternes region. The 100ha are planted with 80% Sémillon and 20% Sauvignon vines. Wines produced here are meant to be stored, some for 50 years. They owe their quality to the estate's gravelly soil underlaid with a clay subsoil; a sophisticated drainage system; and the presence of the Ciron, a tributary of the Garonne, which creates morning mists favourable to the growth of the beneficial mold *Botrytis cinerea* (noble rot). Grapes here are painstakingly picked, one by one, over three or four harvesting waves, a practice that was introduced by Lady d'Yquem. The wines age over three years in new oak barrels; only the finest are kept after bottling. All this makes for extremely limited production; a bottle of Chateau d'Yquem is rare and expensive.

The precious nectar, with its lovely golden robe, is suffused with the fragrances of apricot, peach, honey and toasted almonds. It's large, rich and unctuous, with an incomparably long finish in the mouth.

THE PRICE OF FAME

At public sales, excitement mounts at the appearance of these legendary wines. In 2009, a bottle of 2001 Romanée-Conti brought 3,670 euros; a 1989 Petrus 1,900 euros; and a 1990 Château-d'Yquem 400 euros.

To guard against the inevitable counterfeiting, the estates have had to create anti-fraud labelling schemes. A watermark is used in the label at Château d'Yquem, for example. The ochre-yellow label at Petrus, which shows a drawing of St. Peter holding the keys to heaven, the vintage year and the Petrus-Pomerol appellation name, incorporates a hologram. Beware if you see "Château Petrus", sign of a fake (they do exist!), and be aware as well that there is no 1991 Petrus vintage, owing to a poor harvest. For the same reason, there were no bottles produced at Château d'Yquem for the vintage years 1964, 1972 and 1974.

WINE CRAFTS AND PROFESSIONS

From grafting the vine to pouring the first glass, dedicated experts ensure our enjoyment of wine. Each of them needs a knowledge and love of their craft, whether they are making a local vin de pays or a Grand Cru.

THE PEOPLE

Viticulteurs and Vignerons

The distinction between a viticulteur – traditionally a cultivator of vines – and the vigneron, who turns the juice into wine, has never been as simple as these definitions suggest. Modern-day vignerons need to play a part in the whole of the process, tending the plants, taking charge of the vinification and putting the wine on the wholesale or retail market. Most of their working day is spent in the open air, but they must put in long hours in the chais or the cellars. To do the job well, a vigneron needs to understand the soil and climate, and take the responsibility of being an owner, manager and his own boss. A 21C viticulteur needs at least a professional school certificate in agriculture and farm management, and many study for a further technical degree.

A typical example would be Nadia Bourgne, who plays a full part in her husband Cyril's job as a wine grower, achieving professional qualifications in wine production and sales and marketing. Since the couple acquired La Madura estate in the Saint-Chinian appellation of the Languedoc back in 1998, Nadia's job has been to orches-

A New Breed of Owner

The length of ownership of vineyards and estates in France runs the gamut. Some are passed down from generation to generation within the same family for decades, even centuries. Others change hands frequently. In recent years, some noteworthy figures from the world of industry have taken the reins at well-known winegrowing estates. Concerning themselves with quality, respect for the environment and the viability of the business, these industrialists-turned-winegrowers are revitalising a sector of the wine industry that was showing signs of deterioration. For example, the Domaine du Mas Amiel, located at the foot of the Corbières mountains, was acquired in 1999 by Olivier Decelle, former president of Picard Surgelés. Similarly, Chantal and Gérard Perse, former owners of a chain of hypermarkets, purchased several prestigious Crus in Saint-Émilion in the 1990s, including Chateau Pavie. In the Cahors region, Alain-Dominique Perrin, former president of Cartier, acquired the Domaine de Lagrézette. And lastly, the Chateau Smith-Haut-Lafitte in Pessac Leognan is today owned by Daniel and Florence Cathiard, former ski champions and owners of the Go Sport chain; the chateau recently added Les Sources de Caudalie, a luxurious vinotherapy spa.

trate their accounts and financial affairs, and the orders and shipping, to organise tastings and to keep up their working relationship with wine merchants, restaurateurs and other customers. As if that were not enough, she also lends a hand with the harvest, like everyone else.

The Oenologist

Official qualifications in oenology have been recognised in French law since 1955, defining its graduates as "scientists of wine" from its production to its storage. The Universities of Dijon, Montpellier, Reims, Bordeaux and Toulouse offer four-year degree courses which are renowned for their teaching of scientific and technical expertise.
The oenologist is far more than just a taster: he or she advises the viticulteur on the choice of grape varieties and the cultivation of vines, takes part in the vinification process itself, conducts chemical and bacteriological analyses of the grapes, both in their raw and fermenting states and passes on his or her knowledge to wine brokers and sommeliers.

The Sommelier

A sommelier is in charge of the wine at a gastronomic restaurant, a wine bar or even a specialist delicatessen and wine shop, where tasks include not only choosing which wines to buy, but also monitoring stock and purchases, taking delivery of the bottles and maintaining ideal storage conditions in the cellar. In a restaurant, it is the sommelier's responsibility to keep the cellar book and discuss the best food and wine combinations with the head chef. All of this is done with one eye on value for money for the customer, who is the focal point of the sommelier's profession. Knowing how best to serve the wine – at the correct temperature, in the right shape and size of glass – may seem simple, but these skills require a knowledge of Crus, vintages and varieties, an acute nose and palate, and an ability to be discreetly helpful and on hand.
The profession has come a long way from the status of the nobleman's *échanson*, the cupbearer or steward who had charge of his lord's linen and plate as well as his bread and wine. These days, a sommelier will have taken a formal qualification from a catering college. In 2000, the job joined the list of trades recognised in the Meilleur Ouvrier de France awards, given to top professionals in their fields, but competitions to find the best sommelier in France, Europe and the world have existed for much longer, as have the keenly contested regional titles. Among those to

have made a name for themselves in the world of wine are Philippe Faure-Brac, Olivier Poussier, Éric Baumard, David Biraud, Arnaud Chambost and Enrico Bernardo. Although the roll of honour may suggest otherwise, the profession is by no means a male preserve.

Nor even a French one: the master of the cellars at the Michelin-starred restaurant La Tour d'Argent in Paris is an Englishman, David Ridgway. Most modern-day sommeliers would recognise his description of a fascinating and seemingly limitless professional world, a day-to-day life spent keeping track of wine legislation, balancing the budget, updating the list, working out a long-term buying plan for *vins de garde*, discovering new Crus and making weekly visits to the vineyards. Most, too, would agree that sommeliers and their wine-drinkers 'have never had it so good!' Contrary to the old stereotype, David comes across as modest and cultivated, a sound judge of character in the matter of customers as well as wines. He trains his juniors and advises his diners, dealing patiently with the occasional 'buveurs d'étiquettes', "label drinkers" who would rather have a status symbol on their table than appreciate the wine in their glass. Since 1986, he has held the keys to a treasure-trove of around 500,000 bottles, of which the oldest date back to the mid-19C!

The merchant

The professional privileges of a medieval Bordeaux wine merchant were generous: exemption from excise and the king's taxes, the right to form guilds and even mint money. From the 17C onwards, the wine trader was at the head of a new mercantile class, distinguished by the prestige of massive international trade. Nowadays, wine traders buy wine from independent producers, which they bottle when they judge the time is right. Some even produce their own wines.

FROM CASK TO GLASS

The barrel

The wooden barrel began to replace the heavier, more fragile terracotta amphorae and flasks of the Ancient World in the 3C AD. Modern day production may involve more precision engineering alongside the traditional work of the craftsman, but the design and principle of the wooden cask have remained almost totally unchanged. A boost for the industry came in 2004, when five workers from the Rousseau cooperage in the Côte des Nuits region were awarded the title of Meilleur Ouvrier de France. Between 1995 and 2000, the industry grew by 250% in France, as oenologists and vignerons began to rediscover the added quality of the wooden barrel compared to metallic containers.

Barrel-makers have been using the sessile oaks *(quercus petraea)* from the forests of Tronçais, Loche and Jupille, in the Centre region, for as long as anyone can remember. The slow-growing, fine-grained trees are much sought-after, and have more suitable aromatic and tannic properties than the common oak *(quercus pedunculata)*, but this latter variety is considered a good choice for the more naturally robust wines from the southwest corner of France.

To ensure that they work only with the best materials, most cooperages make the barrel from start to finish, beginning with the choosing and felling of the tree. The staves are split, shaped and dried outside for up to two or three years before the machine tool stage. They are then assembled and given a first firing while the cooper checks the curve of the barrel. The second firing, the *'contre-chauffe'*, 'torrefies' the barrel, conditioning it for either red, white or rosé wines. Finally, the bases, or heads, are fitted, a bung-hole is cut and water-tightness is checked.

Among the many different names for a wine barrel are those that describe its contents – *muid, demi-muid or foudre* – and others that vary with the regions. *Barrique* is originally a Bordeaux term, while a Burgundian barrel is a *pièce* or *feuillette*.

The bottles and the box

When it first appeared in the 13C, the word "bouteille" meant a leather wine-

Cork-oak bark

S. Sauvignier / MICHELIN

skin. Unlikely as it seems, the credit for the first long-necked, cork-sealed bottles goes to the English craftsmen of the 17C. By 1730, glass bottles strong enough to store champagne were in common use and by 1735, the French royal court was issuing royal edicts announcing the correct shape of the champagne bottle and the official method of sealing the cork. The familiar model, with rounded shoulders and long neck, quickly became the standard before different regions began to diversify their shapes by the end of the century: Alsace developed the *flûte*, Anjou the *fillette*, Burgundy its *pot* and Jura the distinctive *clavecin*, not to mention the magnum and jeroboam in Champagne. The Saint-Gobain glassworks now produces around 4,000 million bottles a year.

Most bottles contain 75cl, but other sizes are half (37.5cl), magnum (2 bottles), jeroboams (4 bottles), methuselah (8 bottles), salmanazar (12 bottles), Balthazar (16 bottles) and Nebuchadnezzar (20 bottles). The sizes influence the development of the wines in the bottles: it is quicker in halves, and slower in a magnum and other larger sizes.

The new arrival, the wine box, is often referred to as a "Bib" in French. The vacuum-sealed plastic bag stops the wine from oxidising for several weeks and typically holds 3 to 20 litres. Wine boxes are unbreakable, recyclable and easy to transport.

Corks

Drinkers, producers and professional appreciators are all divided on the subject of natural corks. Perhaps the only undisputed argument in favour of a "real" cork is an environmental one: only commercial cork-oak cultivation will preserve the rich natural habitat of the oak forests

A cork-oak can live for two hundred years or more, but cork can only be harvested after 25 years: bark grows by 1 to 1.5mm per year. Every nine years, in spring, a piece of oak is carefully taken from the tree. The area around Céret, in the Pyrenees, is France's main cork-producing region, but 52% of the world's corks come from Portugal.

Synthetic corks and screw-caps may eliminate the problem of "corked" wine (although this fault comes from an organism known as TcA; or 2,4,6-Trichloroanisole), but many producers insist that these solutions are more suited to young-drinking wines than *vins de garde*. The traditional wisdom is that only a natural cork allows for the transfer of gases which is a vital part of the wine's maturation, but increasingly quality producers are experimenting with alternatives.

Glass and crystal

"It is difficult to enjoy a good wine in a bad glass." **Evelyn Waugh**

The technique of blowing glass is almost two thousand years old. Drinking glasses were a rarity until the 13C (though fine examples of Roman glass survive to this day) when returning crusaders brought them home from Damascus. The wars and political divisions of 16C Italy made the country unsafe and unprofitable for peacetime crafts, however, and soon the French court imported not only precious Venetian glassware, but the glassblowers themselves, who set up workshops in Nevers. Fashions changed again a century later, when only pewter, gold and silver vessels were thought fit for a noble table, but Louis XIV's sumptuary laws brought glass back again.

In 1764, the Bishop of Montmorency-Laval petitioned Louis XV for the right to build a glassworks to compete with the glassware imported from Bohemia. By 1816 it employed 3 000 people and had installed the first crystal kiln; crystal production was to be one of the industrial successes of post-Napoleonic France.

For wine-lovers, however, the most famous name in crystal is that of a 19C Austrian manufacturer, Riedel. Today the firm makes over 80 different styles of glass: evocative names include "Bourgogne Grand Cru", "Champagne millésimé" and "Sauvignon Blanc". Each one is designed, with the help of oenologists and viticulteurs, to bring the best out of a particular wine, in the nose and on the palate.

VINE TO BOTTLE

Tending the vine demands care and effort in every season, but late summer's long ripening is the making of the vintage: the grapes, laden with scents and rich in sugars, are ready for their transformation to begin.

THE DOMESTICATED VINE

Left to develop naturally, the vine grows as a creeper, like the lianas of the rainforest and other members of the Vitaceae family. When pruned, its growth is brought under control, but vines trained up a wall can reach impressive sizes. The "treille du Roy" in the gardens of the Château de Fontainebleau covered 1.5km: the espalier-trained vine was a Chasselas.

During the growing season, the viticulteur trains the vine, and in winter he prunes it: the vine grows in diameter and becomes more knotty with age. In spring, buds appear on the vine-branches (or *sarments* in French), and from these grow the stems, their tendrils, leaves and flowers. Only 10% of these will be pollinated and turn into fruit. In August, the stems undergo a change; they in turn become branches, developing a bark. The spiralling tendrils wrap around anything that will support them.

THE VIGNERON'S CALENDAR		
Winter	No vegetable growth between November and February	Trimming the branches Clearing the stones from the foot of the vine *(épierrage)* and protecting the base of the plant from frost with a covering of earth
Spring	Sap rises, growth of buds in March-April. Blossoming May-June	Uncovering the foot of the vine Trimming and training the branches Trimming off the buds to concentrate production Ploughing to aerate the soil Harrowing out weeds
Summer	First development of the fruit *(nouaison)* in July Final ripening stage *(véraison)*	*Vendange verte*: cutting off some of the unripe bunches to limit the yield Cutting off leaves to give the grapes more sun Disease and pest treatments
Autumn	Harvest time in September-October	

Vineyard in Vézeley, Burgundy

S. Sauvignier / MICHELIN

A truly Mediterranean plant, the vine survives happily on only 500-600mm of rain per year, and needs this water most during the period of growth from April to July. A vine may live for between 40 and 60 years: younger plants produce large volumes of light, acidic wine, while older ones give a lower yield of more concentrated grapes.

In colder regions, early-fruiting varieties can be picked before the first frosts of autumn. The northern vineyards are more suitable for white grape production: black grapes need too much calorific energy, and therefore sunshine, to take on their full colour.

PLANTING THE VINEYARD

New vines are always planted in springtime; but deciding "when" is easier than answering the questions "what?" and "why?" In both cases, the viticulteur is limited by regulations from **Viniflhor** *(www.viniflhor.fr)*, an organisation which ultimately answers to the French Ministry of Agriculture. New planting is only allowed during the restructuring of a vineyard, to improve production, for example, or to replace vines which have become too old and unproductive. Only the varieties authorised for local use may be planted and, in every case, the number of plants per hectare is regulated too.

Ever since the phylloxera crisis of the 19C, almost all plants are the result of grafting and varieties propagated by taking cuttings, which preserves their individual characteristics.

The size of the vine influences the quality and quantity of the yield: vines are cut high or low, depending on the risk of frost and the richness of the soil. They may be pruned and trained to fit a steel-wire trellis, either "en cordon de Royat" with two equal branches running horizontally along the wire or "en Guyot", with one long and one short, or grown "en gobelet", with five or six branches without a wire support. This last method, more common in the Mediterranean, is less suited to mechanised farming and more work must be done by hand.

When harvest-time comes, the harvesters pick off the whole bunch of grapes (although not with some sweet wines, that may need part of the bunch left behind due to staggered ripening times of the individual berries). The bunch is made up of a stalk and the grapes themselves. The stalk is fibrous and contains, among other things, water, tannins and naturally occurring organic acids. The fruit itself is surrounded by an outer skin which is itself covered by a kind of waxy powder or dust. This substance, known as "bloom", or *"pruine"* in French, forms a water-resistant layer on the fruit and keeps in its yeasts. The skin contains elements which lend colour and aroma to the wine, the pips are rich in oil and tannins and the grape pulp gives a colourless juice made up of water, sugar and more organic acids. The percentage of sugars in the grape rises as summer draws on. When the grapes are becoming ripe, they change colour: this final stage of ripening is called "*la véraison*".

SEPTEMBER: THE MOMENT OF TRUTH

Between the flowering of the vine, one hundred days before the harvest, and the *vendange* itself, important chemical changes take place inside the plant. These can make a big difference to the fruit it produces. A cold spring usually means a smaller crop. Too much heat will "burn off" the aroma of the grape by speeding up its growth. Old vines show greater resistance in hot weather whereas the grapes of a younger vine dry out, but wines gain in concentration when the grapes are subjected to a strong heat. The ideal recipe for aromatic grapes is sun, heat and a little humidity, but ice, storms and drought can be devastating. The correct temperature is most vital in August and September, just before the harvest, but even if these months go according to plan, it is vital to check the sugar content – and thus the ripeness – of the grapes before picking.

THE ORGANIC ESTATE

The last few years have brought changing attitudes to both producers and consumers of wines, who are becoming more interested in provenance. The demand for locally-grown, authentic products is on the upswing, as is trend towards sustainable farming, healthier food and drink and a healthier environment. France and the French wine industry are no exception.

Biodynamic farming

This approach to farming was first given a name and a systematic philosophy by Rudolf Steiner who, in 1924, published what was to be a prescient and influential work explaining his ecological system of thought. Stressing the importance of the soil and the natural environment, he recommended treating the cultivated plant with products from animal, vegetable and mineral sources at particular times in the annual growth cycle, and stressed the importance of tilling and preparing the ground.
Since the 1970s several ecologically-minded agricultural movements (biodynamic, organic) have taken root, following Steiner's precepts. As demonstrated by the Syndicat international des vignerons en culture biodynamique, the use of chemical herbicides, pesticides, miticides and other systemic affectors wreak havoc on the natural environment by destroying insects and other natural predators, inhibiting beneficial plants and poisoning the groundwater. The application of liquid herbal preparations, animal and vegetable composts and rock crystals in place of chemical herbicides and pesticides is current practice on many estates around France, and the positive effects of this "gentler" approach to the soil is reflected in insect populations, the local flora and the purity of the ground water.
The goal of biodynamic viticulture is to produce high-quality wines, each reflecting the individual characteristics of its terroir as a direct result of respect for the environment. Biodynamic farming is practised by some of the major winegrowers in Burgundy (Leroy, Leflaive, Lavon), Champagne (Fleury), the Rhone Valley (Chapoutier, Beaucastel), the Loire Valley (Nicolas Pinguet, Nicolas Joly), the Jura (Pierre Overnoy, Stéphane Tissot), Bordeaux (Alain Moueix), and others.

Organic farming

Organic farming is similarly concerned with respecting the environment and protecting the quality of the land. Its mode of production is based on managing the microbiotic activity and balance of the soil, the recycling of organic waste and the protection of natural vegetation, like hedgerows and the uncultivated land around a plot. Chemical herbicides, fungicides, insecticides and fertilisers are not used: instead vegetable extracts and treatments derived from copper and sulphur are used to dispel pests and ward off diseases. The vinification process should involve as few preserving and stabilising elements as possible and limit the use of sulphur. However, far from being an invitation to "let nature take its course", organic farming means a greater investment in human effort as well as organic products and materials.

To be marketed as "organic", agricultural products must be monitored and given a certificate by one of the independent, state-approved organisations set up for the purpose. European Union legislation covers many aspects of food production, but the vinification process is not yet one of them. Wines may therefore only be described as "produced from organic grapes".

Most organic vineyards are currently located in the south of France (Languedoc-Rouissillon, Provence, Aquitaine).

Visitors to an environmentally conscious French estate are almost certain to hear the term *"lutte raisonnée"*. The words literally mean something like "considered, measured struggle" in defence of the vine and sum up a move away from heavy-handed chemical cure-alls for blights and parasites. This ecologically responsible approach to cultivation prefers natural, biological solutions for pest and disease control. Vines are not routinely dosed: the grower only treats them when help is really needed.

THE "VENDANGE"

The harvest is an exciting but anxious time for everyone involved with wine: until the grapes are safely gathered in, the year's vintage is still at risk from a sudden hailstorm or a torrential downpour out of the blue.

Although an institution of ancient origin, the "ban des vendanges", or official declaration of the start of the harvest, was for many years more than just a quaint old tradition: it was aimed at stopping over-eager viticulteurs from picking their crop before it was ripe. Although since 2008 with new regulations, the "harvest bans" are no longer enforced, there are often still processions in traditional costumes in September, to be

Manual harvesting, Beaujolais

© Katja Kodba/iStockphoto

Vin Doux Naturel

In the 17C, a Catalan physician called Arnau de Vilanova discovered a way of halting the fermentation of wine, but still retaining the aromas of the grape, by an admixture of liqueur. The method, known as mutage to oenologists, is used to make wines known as *vins doux naturels*, produced from over-ripe Muscat, Grenache or Malvoisie grapes. The grape juice, or "must" should contain more than 252g of sugar per litre. During fermentation, the wine is enriched with alcohol of 95º or more, in a quantity equal to 5%-10% percent of the grape must. Against all usual wine wisdom, these *vins doux naturels* are normally exposed to the air and, in the case of Banyuls or Maury, are even left out in the sun in glass containers. In fact, this unusual treatment lends them an interesting oxidised character and a wonderful colour with a hint of deep amber-brown.

Harvest Time

© Kevin Miller/iStockphoto

seen at Saint-Étienne in Alsace, during the Jurade festival in Saint-Émilion, and in Burgundy, performed by the Chevaliers du Tastevin. This latter and other fraternal associations, also celebrate on January 22, the feast of Saint Vincent, patron saint of winegrowers.
When the crop is gathered by hand, the bunches are cut by the harvesters using secateurs, placed in a solid plastic carrying-box or a bucket worn on their backs, then transferred to a big grape-pannier called a *benne*. Harvesting machines shake the vines and gather the grapes while leaving the stalks. This method costs between a half and two-thirds the price of a manual harvest, but not all areas are accessible to machines, and some regions, including Champagne and Beaujolais, do not allow them to be used.

Grapes on their way to the wine press

© Rachell Coe/Dreamstime.com

THE WINEMAKING PROCESS

From harvest to fermentation

Once the grapes are picked, the stems are removed from red varieties. This process, known as *égrappage*, is common practice in almost every vineyard, except those in Beaujolais and Champagne. This method is used to make "softer", less tannic wines, but varieties which are naturally low in tannins, such as Pinot Noir, are all the better for being fermented with a part of their stalk.
Red grapes may also be pressed in a machine which bursts the grape without crushing the pips or stalk: the pressing mixes up the grape skins, juice and natural yeasts and aids maceration.
Vinification consists in the fermentation of fresh grapes, grape must and grape juice. During this natural process, the yeast in the grape skins makes the sugars in the juice turn to alcohol and causes the mixture to release carbonic gas.

Making a red wine

In the case of nearly all of the grape varieties, the juice of the fruit is almost completely colourless. A longer or shorter maceration allows red or rosé wines to take on colour from the pigment in the skins of red grape varieties. Once the grapes are de-stalked or pressed, the pips, skins and in some cases the stalks are put in the fermenting vat with the juice. Sulphur dioxide is added to prevent oxidisation and act on the fermenting yeast. Fermentation and maceration take place simultaneously. As maceration goes on, the percentage of juice in the mixture rises to up to 70% of the volume. Hours of maceration will produce a rosé and a few days will make a light red for drinking young, but *vins de garde* need two to three weeks of this treatment to take on the necessary tannic character. During fermentation it may be necessary to displace the must which has settled at the bottom of the vat in order to dissolve more of the materials at the top, which will give the wine its colour and aroma. During this *remontage*, the must is run off into another vat and the solids are put into the press. The *vin de presse* obtained in this way may or may not then be blended back in, and the wine continues its malolactic fermentation which softens the wine by reducing its acidity.

Making a rosé

The only French rosé made by mixing red and white wines is pink Champagne, and attempts to loosen these rules across other areas were denied in 2009. All of the others are produced in one of two ways. The first, called "pressurage", makes very pale *vins gris*; the red or pink tint of the grape skins colour the wine in the press, but there is no extra maceration and grapes are picked specifically to make rosé wine, so keeping higher levels of acidity.

The more common *"saignée"* method follows the procedure for red wine, but requires the wine-maker to draw off the juice after a few hours of maceration and separate the juice from the solid matter. The juice then continues to ferment at a low temperature, and the resulting wine is deeper in colour than *vin gris*. This is usually a by-product, intended at concentrating the red wine, but makes a very pleasant drink in itself.

Making a white wine

White wine starts with particularly careful harvesting. The vinification process is the same as for red wine, except that no (or very little) maceration takes place. The grapes are put straight into the winepress where they are crushed, drained and pressed. The grape juice is then separated from the solids – a process known as *débourbage* in French – and sulphur dioxide added to destroy the yeasts which do not play a part in the fermentation. Fermentation takes place at a low temperature, which protects the fresh, delicate flavours.

Ph. Gajic / MICHELIN

Mosaics showing the art of making Champagne, No. 6 Rue de Mars, Reims

Bottle filling line

© Manuel Ribeiro/iStockphoto

Sparkling wine and the "méthode traditionnelle"

Until recently this process was known as "méthode champenoise" or the "Champagne method". Although there are now geographical restrictions which determine which wines may be referred to by this name, the technique is used in other parts of France as well. The grapes are picked with particular care and transported immediately to the pressoir before they have a chance to oxidise. The initial stage is identical to the standard white wine method. Then sugar and yeast are added to a blend of still white wines, and a second fermentation takes place inside the bottle: sugar turns to alcohol and carbon dioxide is produced. This development, which gives champagne its fizz, traditionally takes place in A-frame racks called *pupitres*, in which the bottles are held with their necks tilted downwards. Every day, for up to two months, they are "riddled" or given a quarter-turn and moved further towards the upside-down vertical. Finally it is time for the *dégorgement*: by freezing the neck of the bottle then removing its cap, the wine-maker can extract the yeast solids which have collected in the neck without losing the pressure in the bottle. After a top up of champagne and sugar, called *liqueur d'expedition*, the bottle can be sealed with a cork and wrapped with all its distinctive trimmings at the neck. After bottling, the wine may only be sold after a minimum of 15 months in the cellars.

MATURATION AND BOTTLING

Once the maceration has taken place, the wine is stored in barrels or vats which must be kept full to prevent their contents from oxidising. The amount of liquid lost by evaporation is known as ullage and the process of topping-up is referred to in French as *ouillage*, supposedly from the *oeil*, the "eye" or bunghole of the barrel. Wine is added once or twice a week.

The next task is to clarify the wine by removing any undesirable particles in it; this may involve the use of a filter or the addition of substances known as finings. The latter method dates back to Roman times and involves adding gelatine, egg-white or a substance called isinglass, taken from a fish's swim bladder, to the wine in the barrel. The impurities gather at the bottom of the barrel and the wine should then be racked, or drawn off, to avoid the risk of contaminating tastes or smells. A second racking takes place in spring and the third in the September after harvest.

Now the wine can undergo one last, delicate operation: the bottling process. The wine is drawn by gravity into a bottling machine and the filled bottles are given their label and sealed with a cork. Once the wine has rested for a while, it's time to taste it.

Enjoying Wine

WINE TASTING

"First, one takes the glass in the hollow of the hand, to warm it, then one swirls it with a circular motion, so that the alcohol may release its scent. Then one raises the glass to one's nose and gently breathes in. Then one places the glass back down and talks about it."
(Charles-Maurice de Talleyrand, statesman and gourmet, 1754-1838)

THE RIGHT APPROACH

What is wine tasting? Who can do it? And how do you start?

Wine tasting is a bit like a game; one that stimulates the senses, demands awareness and concentration, tests your memory, and can be taken more or less seriously. For a professional, tasting means judging in some way: appraising a wine's quality, evaluating its potential in a blend or ranking it among others as part of a competition. For an amateur, it can be a way of learning to notice more about what you're drinking, doing justice to a good wine by appreciating what is good about it, and analysing it purely for the enjoyment of doing so. David Ridgway, chief sommelier at La Tour d'Argent, is a real believer in the "convivial, relaxing side of wine; you shouldn't have to try too hard to enjoy it, or forget the pleasure of wine": a philosophy to which we can all raise a glass.

Putting it into words

Finding the best way to express a wine's impression and sensations is a question of taste in itself. A description of a wine, or the idea of describing it at all, might discourage or confuse one person, while another is enthusiastic and intrigued. Some wine talk comes across as over-scientific, too remote from our sociable experience of wine round the table; other tasters' free-associations sound exaggerated or too far-fetched. Taste is subjective, individual, and yet the experts seem to understand each other, know what to look for, and recognise the same sensations that their fellow experts find.

The taste experiences which oenologists draw on to express themselves are really no different from everyone else's, and are based on comparisons with things we have all experienced ourselves: the way our senses respond to fruits, plants, spices, materials or even places.

The four basic kinds of taste are the starting point. Sweetness is detected by the tip of the tongue, and acidity just behind and underneath the tip. The salt receptors are on the sides of the tongue, and at the back is where we sense astringency or bitterness. This is why it is important to taste from the right kind

Oenologists at work

S. Sauvignier / MICHELIN

of glass, one which will guide the wine on to the tongue.
The recognition of scents, like that of tastes, is something we use in every-day life: the first step to improving your skill is simply to be more aware of it. Practice your ability to recall different aromas. Try thinking about the smell of fresh bread in a bakery, flowers in a garden, fruit or herbs in the kitchen, or coffee and chocolate. Practice at home with jars of spices. You can even train your senses with wine tasting scent kits, although these are only synthetic approximations, and tend to fade over time.

Organising a tasting

The best time to taste wine is before a meal (ideally before lunch), when the taste buds are best able to sense the wine's different qualities. Choose a room which is around 20°C and lit by natural light, or at least a light which will not distort colours. The tasting room needs to be free from the smell of cigarettes, flowers, perfume or food.
You should have a spittoon ready if you are planning to taste a large number of wines, but most tasters will not rinse their mouth out if tasting a series of similar wines. This said, some people find it helps to have some bread and water during the tasting. On a plain white tablecloth, set out transparent, non-coloured glasses, ideally ones with a tulip-shaped bowl and a long stem. Glasses this shape will allow the aroma to concentrate and will prevent the wine from being heated by the warmth of the taster's hand. Remember that too small a glass leaves too little of the wine in contact with the air and makes it harder to smell it properly. Once you have practised a little, try tasting the same wine in different-shaped glasses; you'll find the experience, to the nose and on the palate, is not quite the same. Young wines should be opened one hour before tasting and left to stand upright, but an older wine should ideally be in a wine basket, in the same position in which it was stored in the cellar.

Judging a wine by its "robe": an important first step in the tasting process

S. Sauvignier / MICHELIN

TASTING IN THREE STEPS

Looking at wine

At a "blind" wine tasting, the label and sometimes even the shape of the bottle are concealed, so your first sight of the wine will be in the glass. Pour out a third of a glass and look at the wine. How would you describe its "robe": its intensity and brilliance of its colour? These first observations can tell you something about the vinification and storage of the wine as well as its age and its alcohol content.
Tilt the glass, at eye level, hold a sheet of plain white paper behind it and observe the wine's clarity. A wine should always be clear, but it may occasionally be opaque or cloudy.
Look at the wine at the top of the glass: a brilliant colour is a good sign, particularly in a white wine, when it is indicative of a wine's acidity, but wine can also be lustreless and dull.
What can you discover about its age? A white wine is pale, lemon- or straw-yellow when young and becomes more golden with age. If it is brown or brownish with age it is said to be maderized. Young reds frequently have an off-blue note to their cerise, garnet or ruby colour, but they may take on a hint of brown, orange or even mahogany.

Wine-tasting session in a cellar in Beaune

Ph. Gajic / MICHELIN

Rosés can range from pale *vin gris* – the lightest rosés with only a hint of colour to them – to a tint of peony red, but develop an orange, salmon or apricot shade over time.

A fine wine with concentrated flavours clings to the side of the glass when lightly swirled and then runs back down in fine drops: it is said to have "legs" (also an indication of alcohol content). Intense colour extending all the way to the intersection with the glass is one indicator of quality, but also of youth.

The aroma in the glass

Take the glass by the base and smell the wine while moving it as little as possible in the glass. Then lightly swirl it to aerate it and smell it again: some people close their eyes to concentrate better. Now swing the wine round the glass more vigorously before stopping it sharply with a reverse twist, thus "breaking" it. This releases new aromas from the wine, perhaps including some, like the scent of sulphur, which do not belong there.

Not all wines are strongly aromatic. Oenologists refer to primary aromas, characteristic of the grape type, and secondary ones, which vary in character according to the manner of fermentation. Tertiary aromas, those arising from the ageing in the barrel or bottle are known collectively as the "bouquet".

Some varieties have distinctive aromas: Cabernet Sauvignon smells of blackcurrants, Pinot Noir is suggestive of strawberries, cherries and blackberries. In white wines these primary aromas usually fall into three categories: floral scents, recalling acacia, honeysuckle or fruit-blossom, fresh fruits such as apple, peach, pear or lemon, and mineral scents like flint.

Reds and rosés are often reminiscent of violets, roses, orange-blossom or peonies. Their scents may also call to mind a whole basketful of fruit and vegetable associations including figs, apricots, peppers, mushrooms or truffles as well as red fruits like cherry, strawberry, blackcurrants or mulberries, and spicy tones like pepper.

Secondary aromas are produced by the action of the yeast: tasters might identify

Different types of tasting

Describing a wine is easier when you have something to compare it to.
A paired tasting means comparing wines in twos. Are they the same? If not, how are they different? For a triangular tasting, three glasses are poured: two contain the same wine. The three are tasted in random order, with no going back to re-taste.
A vertical tasting means trying a number of different vintages from the same appellation and noting the way the wines change with age.

Men and Women: two different approaches to wine?

One of the many things to discuss about wine is whether there truly is a male and female approach to tasting. "Typically, women like 'vins flatteurs', which are subtle and aromatic and bursting with bouquet, have silky, smoothly dissolved tannins, and are gentle on the tongue. Men, on the other hand, tend to like a more powerful sensation on the palate and punchy tannins." (Isabelle Forêt, www.femivin.com). While comparing experiences, you can decide for yourself if this is true.

banana, candy or boiled-sweet flavours, butter, candle wax, beeswax or wheat. The bouquet of white wines is characterised by the scent of wood, honey and dried fruit and flowers. Red wine bouquets may have a touch of red fruit or preserved fruit, wood, game, spice (clove or cinnamon) as well as "balsamic" scents like pine resin, cedar and juniper, and roasted or burnt aromas of coffee, tobacco, cocoa, smoke, or toast.
Analysing these aromas is not easy, particularly at first. Sometimes it is hard to pick out any particular smell; at other times the scent "jumps out at you" and the identification is clear and immediate: Burgundy strawberries, or a flinty Sancerre.

Tasting the wine

Take a sip of wine and move it around your mouth, then open your lips, take a "sip" of air and inhale it into your nose, amplifying the aromas.

Glass of Champagne

Y. Kanazawa/MICHELIN

What are the flavours in your mouth? First sweetness, then acidity, then astringency. The qualities of the wine? Structure, balance, harmony and "length", the word used to describe the quality of a lingering but undistorted aftertaste. The taste should confirm the impression in the nose. It should allow you to gauge the alcoholic content of the wine, the smoothness of a wine, related to the presence of glycerine, sugar and alcohol, which can make it seem pleasantly substantial and well-tempered or else too thick and heavy in the mouth. A red wine is thin or robust. A white is dry, medium or sweet, these last two definitions being more general approximations of the French *moelleux* and *liquoreux*. The right degree of acidity is very important. When the balance is just right, the acidity makes a wine lively; too much makes it tart and piquant, but too little leaves it tasting flat and uninteresting.
Finally, consider the wine's finish after spitting or swallowing. If the exact flavour persists pleasantly in the mouth, that is an indication of a fine wine... if the finish lasts 10 seconds or more, it is said to have a "peacock's tail"!

CHAMPAGNE: A SPECIAL KIND OF TASTING

Much of this tasting technique applies to champagne, but there are certain special things to look out for. Do not fill the flute completely. Take time to observe the colour of the champagne: is it pale straw-yellow or a deeper shade? Does it have a greenish edge to it? It may even be pink. Look at the size of the bubbles. The smaller they are, and the more slowly they rise up the glass, the better the champagne. Smell the champagne, then give it the lightest of swirls and gauge the aroma again. Can you pick out vanilla, rose petals, peach, citrus, honey or spices? Now taste it, holding it in your mouth but without rolling it around your tongue. Now swallow. Elegant, delicate, floral? You decide…

SERVING WINE

The beauty of the bottle and its label, the crystal glasses, the smooth white tablecloth, fine food and the company of good friends: all of these things add to the convivial enjoyment of wine.

AN ART IN ITSELF

Opening the bottle

Wine may improve with age, but it does not become any less fragile after long storage: quite the reverse. The older the wine is, the more care must be taken when bringing it out of the cellar.

The next task is to open the bottle without disturbing the contents. The corkscrew, an invention for which the English wine-lovers of the mid 17C can take the credit, has been designed and redesigned in thousands of different ways, but nearly all have a 'queue de cochon', the "pigtail" spiral, and a handle. Some also have a knife or capsule cutter and a lever. Pulltap, Kalao and the famous cutler, Château Laguiole, are among the brand names favoured by some French sommeliers.

Cut the capsule just below the ring, remove it and wipe the top of the neck with a clean cloth, and screw into the middle of the cork without putting the screw right through the cork. Only *vins de garde* have a long cork. If you are right-handed, hold the lever of the corkscrew to the edge of the neck with your left index finger as you ease the cork out in a slow, continuous movement.

If you detect an unpleasant odour of must, the wine is corked: this is caused by fungus which has survived the sterilisation of the cork. If the wine does not smell bad, wipe the neck of the bottle again and, to prevent drops of wine staining your tablecloth, insert a non-drip pourer into it.

If the cork gets stuck in the bottle and breaks off, try to reinsert the corkscrew at an angle and then pull carefully. If this doesn't work, push the cork down into the bottle, but make sure you don't spray wine over yourself, or anyone else. This method of opening a wine doesn't alter its flavour, but it is one more reason to have a decanter at the ready. If sealed with a vacuum-sealing cork, any leftover wine in a bottle will keep for at least 48 hours.

Champagne

Of course, if you find yourself without a corkscrew, you may have no choice but to drink champagne! The most theatrical and dangerous way to open a bottle of champagne is with a cavalry sabre, slicing through the cork where its mushroom bulb meets the mouth of the bottle and allowing the pressure of the wine to push out the base. Expensive and hazardous to practice, this party-piece should only be attempted by the experienced.

The more conventional method involves tearing off the capsule, unwrapping the cork from the iron wire *"muselet"* holding it in place, holding the cork with your thumb and turning the bottle, not the cork, with your left hand. Always make sure that the bottle is pointing towards the wall, at an angle of 45 degrees. Serve the champagne immediately, holding the bottle at the bottom and filling each glass gradually, with two or three pours, so that they do not overflow. A special kind of cork, which compresses the air, can be used to reseal a bottle of champagne and keep in its effervescence.

Decanting wine

Over many years, the question of whether or not it is necessary to decant wine has become confused by questions of status and etiquette. Decanting is only really necessary when there are deposits in the bottle. These may form in older wines, particularly those reds which are particularly rich in tannins. Decanting oxygenates a tannic red wine by exposing it to the air as much as possible. As white wines are usually free of these deposits, with the exception of some in which tartar crystals may form

Wine thermometer

© Chiyacat/Dreamstime.com

during storage in the refrigerator, and whites are not tannic, it seems unnecessary to decant them.

Decant your bottle by pouring the wine slowly but steadily into a carafe held at an angle, stopping as the sediment reaches the neck. A lighted candle or a torch may be held under the neck to illuminate it and help the pourer see more clearly. Some sommeliers use a funnel and a piece of muslin to filter the wine. The wide base of the carafe allows the wine to breathe, its long neck holds the aromas and the glass, or crystal, sets off the colour of the wine.

A young *grand vin* (two to four years) will benefit from being decanted two to three hours before the meal: during this time, the tannins will soften and the bouquet will become fuller and more enjoyable. On the other hand, an older vintage, particularly a burgundy, may lose some of its bouquet: it's much better to leave it in the bottle, which should be opened only a few minutes before serving.

Wine Temperatures

These are given as a guide only. It is not uncommon for reds to be served too warm and whites too cold, which does not show them at their best.

16 to 18°C Mature, tannic reds
14 to 16°C Younger reds
13 to 15°C Red *vins doux naturels*
12 to 14°C Young, light reds
11 to 13°C Dry white wines, champagne, rosé, red *primeurs*
8 to 9°C *Vins moelleux*; light, dry whites; sparking wines
8°C White *vins doux naturels*
6°C *Vins liquoreux*

The perfect temperature

Serving wine at the correct temperature is not just a point of wine etiquette, it's a vital part of appreciating the delicate components of a wine. If it is too cold, it will be harder to appreciate the bouquet in all its breadth and character and the acidity will seem disproportionately strong. Too warm, and the alcoholic taste of the wine tends to drown out the other flavours. In any case, your bottles should leave the cellar some hours before they are due to be served and should be kept as still as possible during that time.

It is worth remembering that, once at the table, the wine will increase in temperature by one or two degrees, or more in summer.

If you want to be sure of serving wines at precisely the right temperature, you might consider investing in a wine thermometer. Whites and rosés should be kept in a champagne bucket filled with cold water rather than packed with ice. You should never put champagne, or any other wine, in the freezer compartment, and once a bottle has been put in the refrigerator, it is best to leave it there until the day it is to be opened.

As a guide, remember that young wines are served colder than old ones: to chill a young red, place the bottle in a bucket of cold water. A wine is said to be "chambré" – at room temperature – at 18°C.

FINE GLASSES FOR FINE WINES

For those who could afford them, wine glasses began to be widely used in the 17C. Two hundred years later, they had become part of the formal dinner service, and it was this grand era of social etiquette which originated the custom of arranging different glasses by size according to the drink, from water by way of red wine to liqueurs. During the 20C, different shapes of glass became increasingly associated with different regions: a long green stem and a round bowl in Alsace, a generously rounded bowl narrowing at the top in Burgundy, the classic tulip form of Bordeaux and the narrow Champagne flute.

A brilliant, perfectly transparent crystal glass seems literally to cast new light on the wine, magnifying all the nuances of its colour. The shape and finesse of the glass can alter the way we experience the combination of bouquet, flavours, acidity and tannins.

The bowl of the glass should be wide and round enough to allow the aromas to open up properly when you swirl the wine in it. The glass also needs to be large enough for you to be able to smell the wine as your lips touch it. And for the wine purist, an elegant, slender stem is all part of the aesthetic appreciation!

Baccarat, Saint-Louis, Cristalleries royals de Champagne, Cristal de Sèvres, Daum, Lalique and Riedel are among the major glassmakers who produce superb, mouth-blown wine glasses. When investing in fine wine glasses, it is a good idea to test them, so far as you can in a shop: lift them up, turn them around in your hand and go through the motions of drinking with them. Test several, and you'll probably find that one or two styles feel less stable, too heavy or too narrow.

The best way to look after your glasses and carafes is to wash them by hand, in very hot water but without any liquid soap or other cleaning products. As soon as they have dripped dry, wave them gently to and fro through the steam from a pan or kettle: this helps to keep them shiny. Then wipe them with a canvas cloth washed in boiling water and used only for wiping glassware. The best way to store glasses is hanging upside down, to stop them retaining dust or odour.

Chavignol goat's cheese and a glass of Sancerre make a perfect combination

S. Sauvignier / MICHELIN

FOOD AND WINE

A time and place for everything

If you are serving more than one wine with a meal, there are a few practical things to remember if you want to avoid overpowering your taste buds. A young red or a lighter Grand Cru should be served before a richer one. In general, younger wines come before older ones, dry wines before sweet ones and whites before reds. If you're serving fish, white wines are usually a sound choice; reds traditionally accompany red meat. If all of these rules have their own flavourful and successful exceptions, there is one other which you should always keep to: each new wine should be a delicious improvement on the last.

Simple food and sumptuous wines

A cook can plan a meal in one of two ways, choosing wines which will go well with the cuisine or preparing dishes which will suit the wines. One way of planning a menu is to pair simple wines with more complex dishes and vice versa. Another, an even more sure-fire success, is to compose a meal by region.

A region in harmony

Wines and food from the same area – from the same terroir – nearly always

What to drink with…

Shellfish: a dry white wine like a Sylvaner, a Riesling, an Entre-deux-mers, a Chablis, a Mâcon-Villages, St-Joseph, Cassis, Palette, Picpoul-de-Pinet, Muscadet or Montlouis.

Fish: again, a dry white, perhaps a Riesling, a Pessac-Léognan, a Graves, Meursault, Chassagne-Montrachet, Hermitage, Condrieu, Bellet, Bandol, Patrimonio, Coteaux-du-Languedoc, Sancerre, Menetou-Salon.

Poultry or charcuterie: red or a light white. Try a Tokay-Pinot Gris, Pinot Noir d'Alsace, Coteaux-Champenois, Côtes-de-Bourg, Côtes-de-Blaye, Côtes-de-Castillon, Mâcon, Beaujolais-Villages, St-Romain, Tavel (a rosé), Côtes-du-Ventoux, Fau-gères, Coteaux-d'Aix-en-Provence, Ajaccio, Corse-Porto-Vecchio, Anjou or Vouvray.

Red meat: Médoc, St-Emilion, Buzet, Volnay, Hautes-Côtes-de-Beaune, Moulin-à-Vent, Morgon, Vacqueyras, Gigondas, Bandol, Côtes-de-Provence, Fitou, Minervois, Bourgueil or Saumur.

Game: a full-bodied red such as a Pauillac, St-Estèphe, Madiran, Pommard, Gevrey-Chambertin, Côte-Rôtie, Cornas, Corbières, Collioure or Chinon.

Salad: traditionally wines are not served with dressed salads, as the conflicting tastes of wine and vinaigrette disagree with one another. As with all such rules, there are exceptions, but most sommeliers would recommend a fine (French!) mineral water.

Cheese: a white or a red wine, but avoid heavily tannic reds, as the combination of full-fat cheese and tannins can be unpleasant to the taste. Try a Gewürztraminer (with Munster cheese), St-Julien, Pomerol, Margaux, Pouilly-Fuissé, Santenay, St-Amour, Fleurie, Hermitage, Châteauneuf-du-Pape, St-Chinian, a *vin jaune* from the Jura (with a Comté cheese from the same region), Pouilly-Fumé or a Valençay. In a rare example of the influence of British taste, you may well be offered a port or Banyuls with blue cheese. Dry white wines, on the other hand, are generally excellent with goat's cheese.

Desserts can only be improved by a good dessert wine: try a Muscat-d'Alsace, Crémant-d'Alsace, white or rosé champagne, Sauternes, Monbazillac, Jurançon, Crémant-de-Bourgogne, a vin de paille, Cerdon, Muscat-de-Beaumes-de-Venise, Banyuls, Maury, any Muscat, a Limoux, Coteaux-du-Layon or Bonnezeaux. Red *vins doux naturels* such as Maury or Banyuls go deliciously with chocolate.

When **cooking** with wine, the golden rule is to serve the wine that was used in preparing the dish. If you are planning to serve a Grand Cru, then use a less distinguished wine of the same region in the recipe. Once you have finished cooking, add a little drop of the wine to the dish: you'll find it brings out the flavours superbly.

bring the best out of each other. Try a cassoulet with a Madiran or Fitou, foie gras with Gewürztraminer, Sauternes or Jurançon, *magret de canard* with a Tursan, oysters and Picpoul-de-Pinet, entrecote bordelaise with St-Emilion, *boeuf bourguignon* and a Volnay, chicken à la basquaise with an Irouléguy, grilled andouillette with Chablis, bouillabaisse and a white from Cassis, Alsatian *choucroute* with a Pinot Blanc, a crottin de Chavignol goat's cheese with a Sancerre, Sainte-Maure, a Touraine goat's cheese, with a Cour-Cheverny, tarte Tatin and a Saumur-Champigny, and strawberries with a red Bergerac.

The perfect menu

As these examples show, it would be easy to plan a meal with a different glass of wine accompanying each course, moving from light, acidic wines to rich, tannic ones, and even finishing off with an Armagnac, a Calvados or an eau-de-vie. Although this would be difficult to do at home, many French restaurants make this sort of culinary *tour de force* a point of gastronomic pride.

GREAT DINNERS AND EVERYDAY PLEASURES

"A drink for the king!"

In the days of the French monarchy, high fashions in food, wine and etiquette, as in everything else, often followed the king and court, although royal tastes were often surprisingly frugal. When King Louis XIV dined in company, his cupbearer would fetch his plate, cutlery and carafe of wine and water from the buffet. It was not until the reign of his successor, Louis XV, that bottles, in individual buckets, appeared before the royal diners. The custom was novel enough for a courtier at the King's château in Choisy to record that "the King was graciously pleased to serve several glasses of wine to Monseigneur the Archbishop of Paris, as the bottles were on the table". The wine buckets also allowed the diners to rinse out their glasses between drinks.

At Louis XVI's *grand souper*, the King would be presented with a single bottle of still wine from Champagne, on ice, followed by a bottle of Clos-Vougeot. This selection never varied, from one meal and season to the next, and nor did the manner of service: the king would pour himself a single glass and then pass the bottle to the other diners at table, and would take a small glass of Madeira with dessert.

Napoleon was no lover of leisurely gastronomy, regarding time at the table as wasted. The Emperor would take lunch alone and dine with the Empress Josephine, yet even he kept up the form and grandeur of the Ancien Régime banquet. Little record survives of the dishes served at these Imperial dinners, but we know that the guest of honour was fond of a glass of Chambertin.

The glory days of gastronomy

The Exposition Universelle, held in Paris in 1867, drew many of the crowned heads of Europe to the French capital. In June, Wilhelm I, King of Prussia and later the German Kaiser, invited Alexander II, Tsar of all the Russias, the Tsarevich Alexander, the future Alexander III, and Bismarck to dinner at the Café Anglais. The meal was to be a truly memorable one, later to go down in culinary history as The Dinner of the Three Emperors.

The chef of the Café Anglais, Adolphe Dugléré, had trained under the great

Dining Room, Napoléon III Apartments, The Louvre

Antonin Carême, who had been the head of many royal kitchens, including the Prince Regent's. Acclaimed as "The Mozart of cuisine", the Bordeaux-born Dugléré was in fact no *enfant terrible*. Described by one contemporary as "a taciturn artist who revelled in contemplative isolation", he nonetheless composed menus on a typically splendid Second Empire scale.

Dugléré's kitchen prepared a rich potage à l'Impératrice and a potage Fontanges, made with consommée, peas and sorrel; a soufflé à la reine, sole à la vénetienne – in a white sauce with tarragon and other herbs; a saddle of lamb à la bretonne – with a bean purée; poulet à la portugaise; a warm quail terrine; a cold truffled lobster "parisienne" and Champagne sorbets. These were followed by duck à la rouennaise, canapés of ortolan (bunting) with aubergine, asparagus and a cassolette princesse. They finished with bombes glacées.

Claudius Burdel's selection of wines earned the *maître de cave* the patronage of all three of the royal diners, who made him their buyer by appointment. The wines served included an 1810 Madeira, an 1821 sherry, an 1846 Chambertin, the 1847 vintages of Châteaux Margaux, Yquem and Latour and a Châteaux Lafite from 1848.

Sadly, we will never know exactly how the Emperors' wines must have tasted. The list is a snapshot in time. It not only confirms the pedigree of some of the most enduringly famous names in the world of wine but also reminds us of how much that world has changed since the days before phylloxera. In 1867 that destroyer of traditional wine-growing, still unidentified, had not spread beyond the lower Rhône, and the wealth and

Wine Therapy

Among the vineyards of Chateau Smith-Haut-Lafitte, the Spa de Vinotherapie Caudalie offers beauty treatments based on the health benefits of wine. Here you can enjoy red wine baths, a "Sauvignon" massage, or a honey and wine body wrap while sipping on a red wine infusion. The antioxidant properties of the polyphenols found in wine, together with the benefits of the local spring water – which is rich in iron, fluoride and sulphur – combine to help fight against the effects of free radicals, responsible for 80% of the ageing of the skin. Wine polyphenols and resveratrol, a compound found largely in the skins of red grapes and recognised for its effect on the elasticity of the skin, are used in Caudalie's range of beauty products (p145).

© Daniel Cathiard/Chateau Smith-Haut-Lafitte

patience of the wine market had yet to be depleted by the social cataclysm of the World Wars, before it was in turn transformed and reinvigorated by the world wine revolution of the last decades.
Exceptional dinners, their menus the stuff of dreams, have been organised since then, of course, but one in particular merits a mention. In 2003, the Grands Vins de Bordeaux celebrated St. Petersburg in the following manner: a 1999 Domaine de Chevalier white Pessac-Léognan with the appetisers; a 1996 Chateau Haut-Brion white Pessac-Léognan along with the carpaccio St-Jacques; a 1986 Château Cos-d'Estournel Saint-Estèphe followed by a 1983 Château Canon Saint-Émilion accompanying the quail tart; another Saint-Émilion, this time a 1975 Château Figeac, and a 1975 Château Pichon-Longueville Comtesse de Lalande Pauillac with the beef filet in red wine sauce; and a Chateau d'Yquem with the Roquefort.

"À VOTRE SANTÉ!"

"If wine were to disappear from human production, I believe it would cause an absence, a breakdown in health and intellect, a void much more dreadful than all the excesses and deviations for which wine is thought to be responsible." – Charles Baudelaire.
Wine has been used for the treatment of a variety of ills since Ancient times. More recently, numerous scientific studies have pointed to the health benefits of regular (moderate) consumption of good quality wine.

"Wine is the most healthful and most hygienic of beverages"

Louis Pasteur (1822-1895)

The Ancient Egyptians recognised the medicinal and antiseptic virtues of wine: the Edwin Smith papyrus explains how to heal an open wound using a balm prepared with wine and honey. In Ancient Greece, Hippocrates (c 460-c 375 BC) prescribed white wine for the treatment of diuretic conditions and red wine for the treatment of diarrhoea. Claudius Galen (c AD 130-c 200), physician to the Roman Emperor Marcus Aurelius, treated gladiators' injuries by washing them with wine.
In the Middle Ages, wine was used as a disinfectant and in the preparation of numerous remedies. A 13C herbalist advised that those wishing to eliminate body odour should wash with wine and rosewater. Aniseed and sage wines were recommended to aid the digestion. The famous Medical School of Salerno pronounced: "[Who] would not be sea-sick when seas do rage, Sage-water drink with wine before he goes". This preparation was also recommended for the treatment of anxiety, trembling hands and fever.
In the 17C, Guy Patin, Professor at the Royal College of Pharmacy and Anatomy, regarded consumption of *vin cuit* as the ideal way to settle the stomach. Under Louis XV, the Duke of Richelieu drank a glass of Bordeaux with each meal to prevent intestinal troubles. In recent years, scientific studies conducted the world over point to the benefits of regular consumption (in moderation) of good wines. Results of these studies can be explored at the "Vin et Sante" website *(www.vinetsante.com)*, and the authoritative trade publication *La Journée Viticole*.

> **The Joy of Wine**
>
> With all the technical specificity, even mystery, surrounding the growing, making, tasting and serving of wine, it's important to remember that true enjoyment of the fruit of the vine is often a function of time, place and company. With friends or family, in convivial gatherings or quiet moments, a good wine increases pleasure, adds eloquence and heightens joy, making a celebration of every occasion.

THE FRENCH PARADOX

In 1990 an article appeared in *Health* magazine which put forward the baffling observation that the French, while famous for their rich cuisine (foie gras, cassoulet, confit de canard) and good wine, experienced very low levels of

Wine has been used for the treatment of a variety of ills since Ancient times

© PhotoDisc, Inc

cardiovascular disease. Research by the American cardiologist Arthur Klatsky revealed that those who consumed a moderate amount (2-3 glasses a day) of tannic red wine (Bordeaux and other wines from southwest France) had a lower incidence of cardiovascular disease than those who drank no wine at all. He reported that this was due to the remarkable antioxidant action of the polyphenols present in the wine. More recently, Dr Roger Corder, Professor of Experimental Therapeutics at the William Harvey Research Institute in London, published a book entitled *The Wine Diet* (2006) that further backed up these findings. He looked at the links between one to two glasses of wine per day and vascular health and his research again found that certain wines of France where the grape skins were particularly high in polyphenols, such as the Tannat grape from Madiran in southwest France, seemed to offer particular health benefits when taken in moderation and with food.

The physiological effects of alcohol

Alcohol…
…narrows the field of vision
…can cause dizziness
…alters judgement of distances
…affects the reflexes
…reduces concentration levels
…reduces inhibitions.

Someone in good health metabolises 0.1g-0.15g of alcohol per hour.

What's in wine?

Wine contains 80-90% water and around 1,000 other components, including alcohol, polyphenols (tannin, anthocyanin and flavonoids), acids, minerals (including potassium and sodium), vitamins and trace elements (including copper, zinc and manganese). In fact, the composition of wine has been found to be similar to that of the gastric juices thus promoting digestion of proteins and fat. The presence of resveratrol – known to stimulate cell multiplication – may also protect the body against certain cancers. Studies have indicated that moderate consumption of wine increases good cholesterol and lowers blood-clotting levels and, for people over 65, a regular glass of wine has been shown to reduce the onset of senile dementia and Alzheimer's disease. And as the physicians of Antiquity suspected, wine has powerful anti-bacterial properties.

Wine and Weight Loss

For more than thirty years, the French cordon bleu chef Michel Guérard has advocated that gastronomy and dietetics should go hand in hand. At his restaurant in Eugénie-Les-Bains, southwest France, diners are encouraged to enjoy a single glass (10cl) of wine as part of the "slimmers" menu". The chef at the Sources de Caudalie Spa uses Bordeaux to bring rich flavour to dishes which are still low in calories. According to a Danish study, wine drinkers suffer far fewer obesity-related health problems than do those who drink beer and spirits. The calorie content of wine compares well with beer and spirits: a 10cl glass of red wine at 12% contains 89.5 kilocalories, a glass of rosé 86.8 kilocalories, a glass of white wine 86.4 kilocalories and a flute of champagne 80.8 kilocalories. It is said that when Marlene Dietrich wanted to lose a little weight, she took to a diet of yoghurt and champagne!

DRINKING AND DRIVING

Driving under the influence of alcohol is a serious offence in France. The police have the right to check the level of alcohol in the blood of anyone driving a vehicle, either by conducting a blood test or by using a breathalyser - with 0.5g per litre of alcohol in the blood being the maximum allowed, or 0.25mg per litre of expired air. Note that there is as much alcohol in a 10cl glass of wine at 12% volume as there is in a 25cl glass of beer at 5% volume or a 2cl measure of spirits. Each "glass" increases the level of alcohol by 0.2g per litre of blood. Drivers who refuse to give a breath test are treated in the same way as would be a driver with a level equivalent to or higher than 0.8g per litre of alcohol in the blood. Drink driving offences are usually punishable by a fine (135 euros for between 0.5mg-0.8mg, and up to a maximum of 4,500 euros for over 0.8mg), disqualification from driving for up to three years and up to two years' imprisonment.

THE NEW FRENCH PARADOX

Despite wine playing such a crucial role in the identity of France both at home and abroad, and its economic importance to the country, recent years have seen increasing threats to wine producers from health lobbies, and from the French government, who have threatened to make the free tasting of wine at chateaux illegal, and have backed several high profile cases where newspapers and websites have been sued for writing about wine without displaying clear health warnings about the dangers of alcohol. The French lobbying group for the wine industry, Vin et Societe (www.vinetsociete.fr), was been instrumental in clarifying the rules governing the promotion of wine through the Evin Law; the French alcohol and tobacco policy law passed in 1991 that is intended to regulate alcohol advertising. In June 2009, after months of heated discussions on both sides of the argument, the Senate in Paris ratified an amendment to the Evin Law, ensuring that the internet was included among the list of allowable media for wine companies. The main beneficiaries of this were wine producers, and online wine merchants who were threatened with having to close down their sites. At the same time, the minimum age for buying alcohol was raised from 16 to 18, and drink-as-much-as-you-like bars were forbidden, as was the sale of alcohol in service stations after 6pm. However professional tastings continue to be allowed.

Terroir

When wine-producers in France, or anywhere else, want to talk about all the natural elements of the vineyard, they use the word "terroir". It means the sum total of an area's climate, geology, geography and ecology, and the special character it brings to the wine produced in that locality. To make the best of a good terroir, the grower must understand its soil and subsoil, the exposure of its slopes and the particular grape varieties that will flourish there.

SOIL TYPES

The history of the terroir begins with the ancient Egyptians and Romans, who marked the origin of their wines on the side of their jars and amphorae. The monks of the Middle Ages also noticed that the quality of the grapes they grew varied from one plot of the vineyard to another. In modern times, geographers and geologists have confirmed what the monks long suspected: the defining quality of good wine-producing land is its hydrology, the way it supplies water to the vine. Of course, there is no single, ideal type of soil: many different types can all produce Grand Crus. A single grape variety can also produce many subtly different styles of wine, depending on soil type and ageing method. The character of a Chardonnay grape comes out very differently in a Corton-Charlemagne, a Chablis and an Arbois.

Even an overview of France gives some idea of the great variation of soils and rock from region to region. Alsace's vineyards, for instance, are on a geological mosaic of schist, red sandstone and igneous rocks like granite and gneiss. Champagne's soil is chalky, whereas Burgundy's calcareous rock is intermixed with clay. Chinon and Bourgueil are particularly chalk-rich, while Beaujolais is mostly granite and shale. In the Rhône valley, the vines grow on shale and rounded, cobble-like stones, or *galets*, which are also characteristic of Languedoc, and Saint-Chinian and Faugères in particular. Médoc wines are produced from vines grown in a distinctive gravelly combination of pebbles, sand, flint and quartz which is known as *"graves"*. St-Emilion wines come from limestone land, whereas the famous Petrus vineyard is on a weald of clay, which retains water extremely well.

FAVOURED GROUND

A grape variety will only reveal its full potential in a place that suits it: marl and chalk for Chardonnay or Pinot, *graves* for Cabernet-Sauvignon and clay for Merlot.

S. Sauvignier / MICHELIN

Soil type is crucial to the quality of the wine

Gamay and Syrah call for granite, and Grenache prefers shale. Two wines from the same grape, but grown in different soil, may reveal discernible differences in colour and aroma. Wines from chalky ground stand out as mellow, smooth and "round"; clay, on the other hand instils a depth and strength of colour, and strong tannic character. The finesse and lightness derived from silica soil is as distinctive in its way as the bold character of a wine from iron-rich ground. The pebbly, alluvial *graves* brings out the rich fruit flavours of a wine: if aged well, its rugged, emphatic tannins will mellow into a broad and aromatic palette of greater complexity.

Climate, prevailing winds and the bioculture of the area also affect the vines. The plants of the surrounding area, be they oaks, mimosas, pines or cypress trees, add and take away different soil nutrients. Dark-coloured soils, which absorb more solar radiation, are particularly suitable for red-wine varieties, which need plenty of sunlight to encourage the assimilation of chlorophyll and boost the production of tannins. Pale-coloured earth is better for whites. Sauvignon, for example, flourishes in the chalky marl of Sancerre whereas in Corbières the Grenache grape enjoys the shale-rich earth and makes excellent, dark-red *vins doux naturels*.

WATER

The grapevine is a Mediterranean plant and copes well with dry conditions; in fact, the traditional wisdom of the grower holds that vines need to suffer a little if they are to give good results. As the vine grows, it absorbs water through its roots and expels it through the leaves, a process known as evapotranspiration. The level of groundwater below the vineyard's soil will vary from one year to the next, and the lower it is, the better the harvest will be, as it is the shortage of water that stops the plant's growth and allows the grapes to start absorbing sugars. As the vines grow older, the roots push deeper into the well-drained ground in their search for water and nutrients, and as a consequence the plant becomes less vulnerable to hard drought or sustained downpours. Young vines, on the other hand, have shallow root formations; they are more likely to rot in an exceptionally wet year, or struggle for moisture in a long, dry season.

Terraced vineyard near Cassis, Provence

S. Sauvignier / MICHELIN

EXPOSURE

Wine-growers dread the hazards of extreme weather. Hail shreds the vine leaves and damages the bunches of grapes beneath them. An icy winter may kill off the plant completely, while a sudden rainstorm just before harvest can be the ruin of a good crop. Even a less dramatic change can have an effect. A year with lower than average sunshine means unripe grapes; a cold growing season results in a more astringent wine.

Growers tend to plant their vines on hillsides, usually facing southeast: if it rains heavily, the water runs away down the slope. Of course growers can optimise the conditions of the terroir by improving its drainage. A good example of the complementary elements of a good terroir is the Bandol-producing Château de Pibarnon estate, planted on chalky land with blue marl beneath. Its southeast-facing slope curves round the inside of a cirque, which protects it from the force of the mistral. The grapes ripen slowly and the chalky soil gives them great tannic finesse in the bottle.

Wine History

The origins of the vine are lost in the mists of time. Wine production is an ancient science, though, and well recorded in literature. Perhaps the most recognizable of these recounts the Biblical account of how Noah cultivated the ground and planted vines after the Flood – and then drank on the wine…

IN THE BEGINNING

EARLY WINE HARVESTS

In 2000 BC vines were a common sight in many of the gardens of **Egypt**. They were grown for their black fruit and also for their red wine, which was drunk at feasts and celebrations. The best wines came from west of the Nile Delta, Memphis and Fayoum. Tomb paintings show each step in the wine-making process: bunches of grapes being picked, the grapes being pressed by foot in large vats, fermentation of the wine in earthenware jars and finally consumption of the wine at a celebratory feast.

In Ancient Egypt, wine was aged in pottery jars with a straw stopper sealed with clay. The jars were each identified by an inscription on the neck which indicated the content, origin, quantity, year and names of the wine-maker and proprietor – the same information, in fact, that is shown on many modern-day wine labels.

FROM EGYPT TO GREECE

The Egyptians taught the arts of viticulture and fermentation to the Greeks. As Phoenician trading posts sprang up throughout the Mediterranean – from Asia Minor to Gaul, Southern Italy and Sicily – so this knowledge spread. The best wines came from the Greek islands of Chios, Thrace and Samos, as well as from Capua and Falerna in Italy. The wine was transported by sea throughout the Phoenician Empire in amphorae similar to the Egyptian jars, but with two handles and a rounded base. Wine made from ripe grapes dried on straw was fermented in *pithoi*, large earthenware jars which were buried underground; this wine was diluted with sea water, flavoured with herbs, honey and spices and served at banquets.

ROMAN TIMES

In around 200 BC, the Romans began to take an interest in viticulture and wine, even describing wine from Falerna, which took on a golden hue as it aged, as a Grand Cru.

The works of Pliny the Elder, Cato the Elder, Columella and Galen contain a mine of information on Roman viticulture, with opinions on vine varieties, vineyard locations, wine presses, how best to announce the start of the grape harvest, fining using egg white, fermentation and aging the wine in amphorae and *dolia* (large earthenware jars). The Romans enthusiastically built up huge cellars and Pliny recounts that a certain Hortensius left no less than 10,000 amphorae of wine on his death. Pompeii was a great wine-trading town and counted no less than 200 taverns. It was from here that amphorae were exported to Narbonne, Toulouse and Bordeaux to be filled. It was the Romans who, tired of the

Under the aegis of Bacchus

At Mas des Tourelles in Beaucaire, Diane and Hervé Durant produce Roman wine with the help of specialists from the French National Scientific Research Centre (Centre National de la Recherche Scientifique, CNRS). Inspired by Pliny the Elder, Cato the Elder and Columella, they have reconstructed a Gallo-Roman cellar and produce wines such as *turriculæ* (to the recipe of the Roman agriculturist Columella), *mulsum* (made with honey) and *carenum* (a sweet white wine). The grapes are trodden by foot, squeezed in presses similar to those used in Ancient times, then the juice is left ferment in *dolia*. As 2,000 years ago, they stabilise and flavour the wine with plants, aromatics, spices, sea water and honey.

amphorae's tendency to shatter, started using barrels to transport the wine.

FRENCH WINE

The Greeks, who established a colony at Marseille (Massalia), taught the Gauls the art of wine-making in around 600 BC. But it wasn't until the 1C AD, that Gaul passed from being mainly an importer of wine to being the largest exporter of wine in the Roman Empire. During the Pax Romana, wines from the Narbonnaise (Languedoc), Bordeaux and Rhône valley developed formidable reputations. Gaulish domination of the wine trade led Emperor Domitian in 82 AD to forbid the creation of new vineyards and to decree that half the vineyards of the Roman provinces be uprooted. In spite of this, the French vineyards prospered and extended along the Rhone Valley, to Burgundy and the Moselle. In 280 AD vine cultivation was again legitimised by Emperor Probus.

Archaeological excavations of Roman settlements in France have uncovered scores of earthenware jars, sarcophagi and mosaics decorated with scenes of the grape harvest. Pruning knives, amphorae and barrels (which were invented by the Gauls) have also been discovered. Many of these items are on show in the archaeological museums of Lyon, St-Romian-en-Gal, Narbonne, Istres, Nîmes and Cap-d'Agde. During construction work in Marseille in 1947 the remains of a commercial Roman warehouse used for storing *dolia* were uncovered. Some examples are display in the Musée des Docks Romains in the city. Archaeologists have carried out excavations in some of the great French wine *domaines*, including Molard in Donzère in the Drôme, the villa of Sauvian near Béziers and the Mas des Tourelles villa in the Beaucaire region.

Wine and Religion

The aphrodisiac qualities of wine are associated with fertility and rebirth and as such the vine has always been an important religious symbol. Ancient religions each had their wine God: the Egyptians had Osiris, the Greeks Dionysos and the Romans Bacchus. In the 1C AD, wine was adopted as a symbol by Christianity; Jesus turns water into wine at a Jewish wedding in Cana and shares bread and wine with the disciples at the Last Supper.

S. Sauvignier / MICHELIN

Mosaic of Infant with Grapes, Musée de l'Arles et de la Provence antiques

FROM THE 11C TO THE 18C

The fall of the Roman Empire led to the decline of many vineyards. But wine production continued in the monasteries, where it was an indispensable part of everyday life, used in the celebration of Mass and for consumption at meal times. After the Norman invasions, peace returned, towns grew and churches and vineyards were established throughout France. The Church played an important part in the propagation of the vine and the advancement of wine-making techniques. From the 12C, Cistercian monks were responsible for the creation of renowned vineyards at Beaune, Pommard, Vosne and Le Clos de Vougeot. The Cistercians observed how the vines grew, pruning them, taking cuttings and grafting, and noticed how the colour and aroma of the wines were influenced by the soil, location and aspect.

By the Middle Ages, wine was a feature of everyday life: on the tables of the rich and poor, on the shelves of the apothecary and next to the sick-bed, in the Church and the Synagogue. Wine became a valuable economic commodity which could be sent further than ever before because of advances in transport. La Rochelle became famous for the export of wine and salt to England and Holland. At the beginning of the 13C, the region of Bordeaux was exempted by King John Lackland (1167-1216) from taxes on exported wines and the English quickly developed a taste for that region's wine.

The end of the Middle Ages and the Renaissance saw land reform which put vineyards into the hands of city-dwelling aristocrats and the bourgeoisie. The growth in the towns and cities – where the water was not always safe to drink – led to unprecedented demand for *vin ordinaire*. Cabarets and open-air cafés serving wine sprang up, to cater for the common people.

The extraordinarily cold temperatures during the winter of 1709 caused vines everywhere to freeze. Agricultural and oenological advances made during the 18C form the basis of modern-day viticulture techniques: grape varieties and soil types were defined and the procedure for making champagne was established. The English opened important trading houses at the gates of Bordeaux for the export of red wine to Great Britain and white to Holland. After the French Revolution (1789), the largely aristocratic and ecclesiastically-owned vineyards fell into the hands of the peasants and middle classes and the *vignobles* took on something of the appearance they have today. The quality of the wine also improved.

D. Hée/MICHELIN

Spectacular winepress at Champvallon, Yonne.
The design dates from the 12C and it was built in the early 14C.

SCIENCE ENTERS THE WORLD OF WINE

The 19C saw the publication of numerous treatises on vines and grape varieties. Increasing industrialisation of the wine-making process led to vineyards being set up and expanded in the Languedoc, Bordeaux and the French colony of Algeria, where large quantities of cheap, poor-quality wine were produced. The advent of the railway meant that wine barrels could be easily transported.

Disastrously, the fungal disease oidium appeared in 1851 in Bordeaux, having come to France from America. This was followed by severe bouts of phylloxera (vine louse) and mildew, culminating in the destruction of almost the whole of the French vine stock in the late 19C. The scientists Pasteur, Planchon and Gayon, as well as explaining the science behind fermentation, recommended the grafting of French vines on to phylloxera-resistant New World rootstock.

The 20C was dominated by legislation: the government outlawed fraudulent labelling and laws were passed regulating viticulture with the aim of improving wine quality and limiting production levels. The *appellation contrôlées* were established by decree in 1935.

In the last hundred years, increasing mechanisation of wine-making has made it much more of a scientific process. The use of heating cables, aromatic compound chemical fertilisers, biochemical processes and the advent of cloning techniques has radically changed the way the industry operates.

Unfortunately the 20C also brought troubles to the French wine trade. French domestic spending on alcoholic beverages dropped from 12.4% in 1960 to 9.6% in 2002 and at the same time the consumption of alcohol went down by more than a third. There has been a huge increase in wine-growing regions throughout the world; vineyards now take up nearly 8 million ha. The New World vineyards of Australia, New Zealand, South Africa, Chile and California are producing more and more first-class wines.

Mechanical harvesting

S. Sauvignier / MICHELIN

In the face of this unprecedented international competition and the domestic slump in sales, the French wine industry is undoubtedly feeling the pinch.

In spring 2004, the then-president of the INAO, René Renou, proposed reforms of the AOCs to respond to the crisis in the French wine trade. He proposed the creation of an *Appellation d'origine contrôlée d'excellence* (AOCE) which would be reserved for "luxury wines to long for and dream about". The *Appellation d'origine contrôlée* would be used on "easy-drinking, reasonably priced wines" and labels would indicate the grape type. These proposals would require a complete revision of all the appellations, backed up by a rigorous system of controls, and although not followed to the letter, did usher in tighter quality controls across France from 2008.

Despite these upheavals, wine-making is the second largest agricultural industry in France, with an annual turnover of 9€ billion and wine continues to be the country's principal foodstuff export. France maintains its position as number one wine producer in the world, just ahead of Italy.

DISCOVERING THE WINE REGIONS OF FRANCE

Vineyards and the Chapelle de la Madone in Fleurie, Beaujola

1 - ALSACE

Alsace enjoys a position at the heart of modern-day Europe, while remaining true to its time-honoured traditions. The Alsatian wine-producing region is remarkable for the diversity of its varieties of grape vines, which produce highly distinctive wines. Its delightful flower-decked villages and row upon row of vineyards cloaking the foothills of the Vosges mountains enhance a long-standing tradition of hospitality, which its wine-growers are keen to uphold. Here, the cellar is much more than just a place to store or buy wine; it is a place where enthusiastic wine-growers take the time to explain the distinctive character of each individual wine.
Alsace's vineyards, which date back to Roman times, owe much to the loving care of the region's monasteries, but it was not until after the Second World War that today's quality regulations were applied across the board. The systematic planting of noble varieties of vines was recognised in 1962 by the creation of an Alsace AOC, after which time it became mandatory to bottle wine in the region in which it was grown. The distinctive qualities of Alsatian wines were rewarded in 1975 with the creation of an Alsace Grand Cru AOC awarded to fifty or so terroirs with precise geological and climatic characteristics, and then AOC Cremant d'Alsace in 1976. Alsace also differs from other wine regions in France by systematically putting the grape variety on the label, and so making it easy for first-time visitors and also worldwide wine drinkers to appreciate and understand the wines.

Highlights

1 Take a boat ride down a canal in **Colmar** (p99)
2 Get close to over 300 Barbary Macaques at **Monkey Mountain** (p93)
3 Step back to the MIddle Ages in **Kientzheim** (p96)
4 Go hiking in the **Vosges Mountains** (pp88, 140)
5 Experience a **Christmas market** (pp94, 97)

The Alsace Wine Road winds from north to south for over 170km, following the foothills of the Vosges mountains, and from many spots walks are easily followed through the vineyards themselves. Remember that during the harvest period, access to the vineyard trails can be restricted The description of the route in this chapter is organised from north to south, but you can do it in either direction. Colmar, the largest city, lies roughly midway. The A35 motorway skirts this scenic route to the east, so you can speedily access different sections if pressed for time

Village and vineyards of Blienschwiller

R. Mattes/MICHELIN

OVERVIEW

The Terroir

Michelin Local Map 315 – Bas-Rhin (67) and Haut-Rhin (68)

Surface area: 15,535 hectares stretching from north to south along a strip of land 120km long and 2 to 5km wide, 40% of which is in Bas-Rhin and 60% of which is in Haut-Rhin. It also comprises an enclave in the northernmost tip of Alsace around Wissembourg.

Production: approximately 1.15 million hectolitres per year. (150 million bottles). The vineyards are planted in terraces extending from the Vosges foothills down to the plain at altitudes from 150 to 400m.

The climate is semi-continental with rainy springs, cold winters and very sunny summers and autumns. Geologically, the soil is varied including limestone-marl, loess, sandstone, schist, volcanic sediment and numerous conglomerates of marl.

The Wines

Alsatian wines are defined primarily in terms of the variety of grape (90% white). **Alsace AOC**: Chasselas, Gewürztraminer, Muscat, Pinot Blanc, Pinot Gris, Riesling, Sylvaner for white wines and Pinot noir for red and rosé.

Alsace Grand Cru AOC: Gewürztraminer, Muscat, Pinot Gris, Pinot Noir and Riesling.

Crémant-d'alsace AOC: Auxerrois, Pinot Blanc, Pinot Noir, Chardonnay, Pinot gris and Riesling.

"Vendanges tardives" and "Sélection de grains nobles": since 1984, *"Vendange tardive"* (late harvest) or *"Sélection de grains nobles"* can be found on wine labels to designate grapes affected by noble rot, meaning that they have a sugar content of over 14° in late harvests and over 18.3° in *"grains nobles"*. The production of such wines is carefully controlled; single grape variety only and chaptalisation (the addition of sugar to increase alcohol) is forbidden.

Wissembourg and Cleebourg

The tiny vineyards of Wissembourg, at the northernmost tip of Alsace, are exceptional both by their distance from the rest of Alsace's vineyards and because the majority of the grapes harvested in the area are vinified in Germany, where they are used in the making of Baden wines (an exception to strict EU regulations). The vineyards of Cleebourg, on the other hand, have remained French.

- **Michelin Map:** Michelin Local Map 315 - Bas Rhin (67).
- **Info:** www.vinsalsace.com.
- **Location:** Northeastern France, by the border with Germany.
- **Timing:** Two days, or day trip from Strasbourg.
- **Don't Miss:** A taste of Gertwiller gingerbread.
- **Kids:** The local stork sanctuary.

WISSEMBOURG VINEYARDS

17km N of Haguenau on the D 263. Michelin Local Map 315, L2.

Despite a troubled past, the border town of **Wissembourg**★★ has retained a great deal of its rich heritage and a stroll through its appealing streets and lanes is most enjoyable. The Protestant **Eglise St-Jean** dates back to the 15C although the belfry is 13C. The **Eglise St-Pierre et St-Paul**★, built in sandstone, is 13C Gothic. Inside, the enormous 15C fresco depicting Saint Christopher is the largest painted statue in France; it measures 11m in height.

Those interested in the history of everyday life in Alsace should make a point of visiting the **Westercamp Museum**, located in a 14C Medieval building that was once a chancery, displaying traditional costumes of northern Alsace. There is also an interesting collection of art from the 17C and 18C *(Place Joseph Thierry; Open Mon-Fri 9am-noon & 1.30-5.30pm, Sat-Sun 2-5pm; t03 88 73 30 41).*
The bridge over the Lauter river is a good spot for views of the historic **Bruch district**, and a walk around the old **ramparts** offers views of the old town's weather-worn roofs.

CLEEBOURG VINEYARDS

7km S of Wissembourg on the D 77. Michelin Local Map 315, L2.
Unlike Wissembourg, Cleebourg's vineyards have remained French and a cooperative cellar handles nearly all the production of the 190 hectares of vineyards spread over the towns Wissembourg, Cleebourg, Rott, Steinseltz and Riedseltz. Peter Jülg in Seebach is the only independent wine producer in the area. The hospitable **wine cellar of Cleebourg**, near a stork sanctuary, offers a good selection of attractively priced wines and some excellent Pinot Gris *(see Shopping Guide).*

Alsace Wine Road

In addition to being one of France's most famous wine routes, the Alsace Wine Road is without doubt its most attractive. It zigzags for 180km from Wissembourg to Thann offering delights for the eye and the palate, including vineyards, flower-decked villages, old castles, wine cellars, excellent restaurants and wine-growing festivals. The region deserves its reputation for its *Gemütlichkeit*, a delightful, if untranslatable, sense of warm conviviality.

- **Michelin Map:** Michelin Local Map 315 - Bas Rhin (67). Map p91.
- **Info:** www.vinsalsace.com.
- **Location:** From Strasbourg down to Mulhouse, close to the Swiss border. 180km itinerary. Allow two days taking your time.
- **Timing:** Two to three days minimum.
- **Don't Miss:** The brightly coloured market sqaure in Obernai.
- **Kids:** Naides Aquarium; Otter Park.

DRIVING TOURS

1 FROM MARLENHEIM TO CHÂTENOIS

68km. Marlenheim is 21km NW of Strasbourg via A 35 & N 4. Map p91.
As far as Rosheim, the route skirts the Vosges foothills.

Marlenheim

The welcoming town of Marlenheim is a well-known wine-producing centre boasting a vast choice of restaurants. The vineyards date back to 5C. The Steinklotz Grand Cru is produced here from Pinot Gris, Riesling and Gewürztraminer on steep limestone slopes.
The imposing wine merchant **Artur Metz** is open to visitors with a good-choice of regional wines, plus there is a wine school *(102, r. du Général-de-Gaulle, 03 88 59 28 60; open Mon–Fri 10am–12.30pm and 2–6.30pm, Sat 10am–12.30, 2–6pm; www.gcfplanet.com).*

Wangen

The twisting lanes lined with handsome old houses and arched porches make Wangen a typical wine-growing village. Don't miss the medieval fortifications including two towers, one of which is called the "Niederturm". A good producer here is Thierry Martin (see Shopping Guide).

Westhoffen

This wine-growing village, also famed for its cherries, still boasts a number of 16C and 17C houses as well as a Renaissance fountain. In Eglise St-Martin, look for the 14C chancel and stained-glass windows. An unusual 19C oriental-style synagogue can also be seen. In the heart of the village, wedged in between two churches, the **Etienne Loew Estate** sells sought-after wines including a Grand Cru Altenberg *(28 r. Birris, 67310 Westhoffen, 03 88 50 59 19; Open by appt. 8am–noon & 2–6pm).*

The surrounding vineyards reach as far as the towns of **Bergbieten** and **Traenheim.** At Bergbieten, the **Roland Schmitt** organic wine-growing estate, produces extremely subtle wines *(see Shopping Guide).* The equally well-known **Frédéric Mochel** estate in Traenheim possesses an old 17C wine press and is open to the public *(56 r. Principale, 67310 Traenheim, open by appt. Mon–Sat 8am–noon & 1.30–6pm; 03 88 50 38 67; www.mochel.net).*

Avolsheim

Chapelle St-Ulrich, adorned with handsome 13C **frescoes**★, is thought to be one of the oldest chapels in Alsace. This village is also a good place to pick up the cycle track along the Bruche canal. The neighbouring village of **Wolxheim**, whose terroir is particularly suited to Riesling, produces the Grand Cru Altenberg of Wolxheim that was one of Napoleon's favourites. For a good example, try the Clément Lissner estate (20 rue Principale, 67120 Wolxheim, t03 88 30 10 31; Open Mon-Sat 8am-noon & 1-7pm www.lissner.fr).

Molsheim★

Forced to leave the Protestant states, Benedictine, Carthusian, Capuchin and Jesuit monks fled to Molsheim, making it the capital of the Counter-Reformation in Alsace. Although dating from the early 17C, the **Jesuit Church**★ was built in the Gothic style; its graceful interior proportions are remarkable. As was often the case elsewhere, the region's vineyards flourished under the care and attention lavished by these religious communities. Molsheim boasts a Grand Cru classé, Bruderthal, where Riesling and Gewürztraminer do particularly well. It can be tasted at the **Gérard Neumeyer** estate *(see Shopping Guide).*

Another of Molsheim's claims to fame is the presence in the 1920s of the factory of the legendary Italian car manufacturer, **Ettore Bugatti.** As a result, every year in early September the town hosts a parade of vintage automobiles during the Bugatti Festival. The **Musée de la Chartreuse**, on the site of a former Charterhouse (1598-1792), exhibits several of the models built in the town between the two World Wars *(open May–mid-Oct Wed–Mon 10am-noon & 2-6pm; Sat 2-5pm; 3€; 03 88 49 59 38; www.chartreuse-molsheim.info).*

Rosheim★

The tourist office has created a historic walk around the town.

It begins on a **wine trail** offering a splendid panorama of the vineyards. **Eglise St-Pierre-et-St-Paul**★, built in yellow sandstone in the 12C, features an octagonal belfry; the gable on the west front depicts humans being devoured by lions. The **Romanesque house**, located on Rue du Général-de-Gaulle between n°21 and n°23, is Alsace's oldest stone edifice dating from the second half of the 12C.

Leave Rosheim

From here on, the route becomes much hillier, rising to reveal a view of the plain of Alsace where the ruins of numerous castles, such as Ottrott, Ortenbourg, Ramstein and Landsberg, can be seen perched on hilltops.

Boersch

Three old gates provide access to the town of Boersch. The Porte du bas (lower gate) leads into a **square**★ lined with old houses, the most remarkable of which is the 16C town hall. Leave Boersch through the Porte du Haut (upper gate). Stop at the **Spindler marquetry workshop** to see an exhibition and a video presentation of its history - now with its third generation of Spindler artists (*open 10am–noon & 2–6pm; Aug Tue-Sat 10am–noon & 2–6pm; 03 88 95 80 17; www.spindler.tm.fr*).

Ottrott

This characterful village stands on a steep slope at the foot of Mount Ste-Odile and is famed for its Pinot noir wine (known locally as Rouge d'Ottrott). Its two châteaux are worth exploring; Lutzelbourg (12C) with a square building and round tower and the larger and more elaborate 13C Rathsamhausen castle.

Further on the road towards Klingenthal, the huge **Naïades aquarium** is home to over 3,200 fish from all over the world. (*open daily 10am–6.30pm (last entrance 1hr prior to closing); Dec 24 & 31 10am-4pm; Dec 25 & Jan 1 1.30-6.30pm. 10€; 03 88 95 90 32; www.parclesnaides.com*).

Obernai★★

Visitors run no risk of thirst in Obernai; in addition to being in the heart of wine-growing country, it is also home to the famous Kronenbourg beer brewery. Obernai has everything you would expect to find in Alsace: storks, old houses with multicoloured roofs, flower-decked lanes... and legions of tourists. **Place du Marché**★★ is lined with houses whose gold-coloured hues sometimes border on crimson, bathing the streets of Obernai in a distinctive luminosity. The former covered market of the **Halle aux Blés**★ dates from 1554. The 13C **Tour de la Chapelle**★ belfry is home to a chancel which is all that remains of the former chapel; the 16C Gothic spire rises to a height of 60m. The **town hall**★ was rebuilt in 1848, but retains a number of architectural elements (14C-17C) such as an oriel window and a beautifully carved balcony, both added to the façade in 1604. Countless **old houses**★ add charm to the area between the market square and Place des Etoiles, particularly on Ruelle des Juifs. Look out for the 13C three-storey stone house on Rue des Pèlerins. The regularly rebuilt **ramparts** (the best conserved section is the Maréchal-Foch) offer tourists and residents the opportunity of a pleasant stroll.

The 3.6km **Schenkenberg wine trail** (*1hr 30min*) enables walkers to discover some 250 hectares of vineyards, with views over the Vosges mountains. Park your car at the ADEIF memorial, a 12m cross commemorating those who were conscripted into the German army during WW2. In summer, weekly guided tours are organised on Wednesday mornings at 9.30am, followed by a visit to a cellar. Enquire at the tourist office. If you do not have time to do the whole trail, visit Domaine Seilly, (30 rue du General Leclrec; t03 88 95 55 80; Open Mon-Sat 9am-noon & 1-5pm; www.seilly.com).

Return to the D 35 via Bernardswiller.

Heiligenstein

This village is famed for its Klevener, a dry white wine made from a pink-skinned variety of Traminer similar to the Savagnin grape that is used to make Jura wines.

Jean and Hubert Heywang's wine estate is an excellent place to discover this wine (*see Shopping Guide*).

Barr

Barr is famous for both its tanneries and its wines, particularly the Kirchberg Grand Cru. The Gewürztraminer, Riesling and Pinot Gris varieties produce heady wines. Sample them at the **Alsace Willm estate** (*see Shopping Guide*). The **Klipfel estate** is open to the public, offering wine-tasting sessions in their atmospheric old cellars (*6 av. de la Gare, 67140 Barr; open daily 10am-noon and 2-6pm; by appointment; 03 88 58 59 00; www.klipfel.com*).

Take the time to venture into the courtyard of the 17C **town hall**, adorned with a carved loggia and balcony, to admire the rear section.

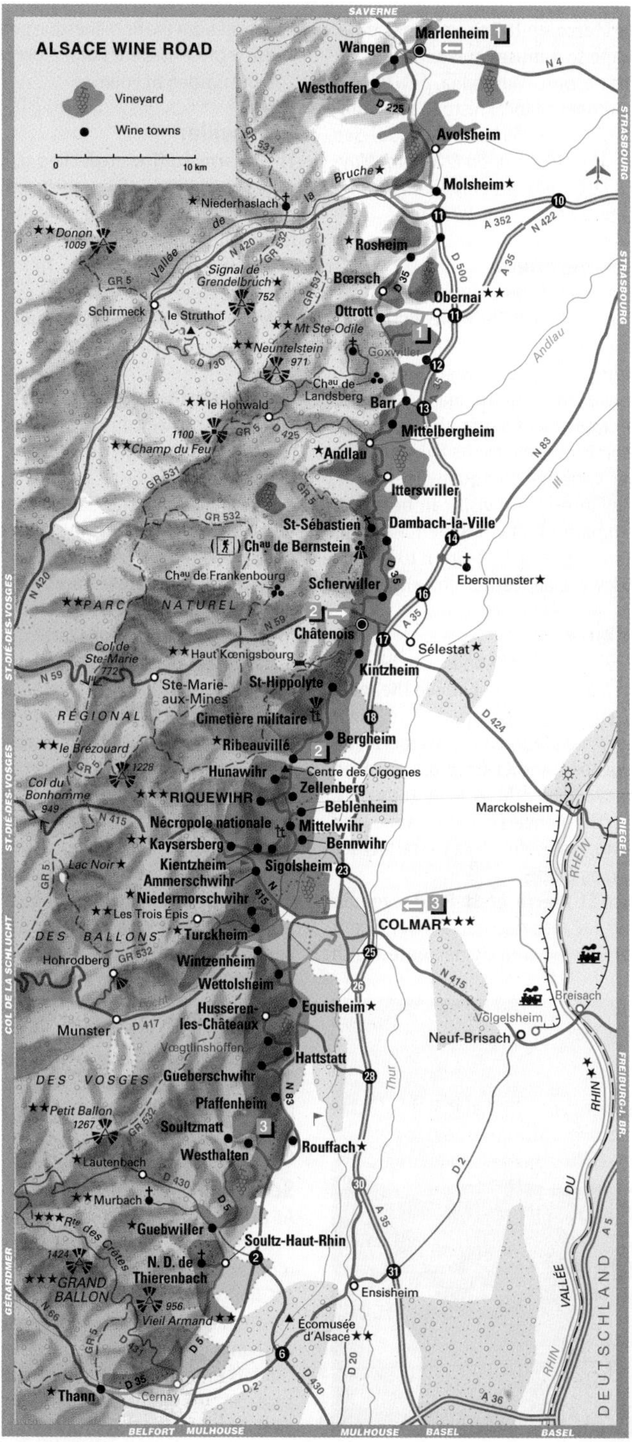
ALSACE WINE ROAD
Vineyard
Wine towns
0
10 km
SAVERNE
Marlenheim
Wangen
Westhoffen
Avolsheim
Molsheim
Rosheim
Bœrsch
Obernai
Ottrott
Mt Ste-Odile
Neuntelstein
Goxwiller
Chau de Landsberg
Barr
Mittelbergheim
le Hohwald
Champ du Feu
Andlau
Itterswiller
St-Sébastien
Dambach-la-Ville
Chau de Bernstein
Chau de Frankenbourg
Scherwiller
Ebersmunster
PARC NATUREL RÉGIONAL DES BALLONS DES VOSGES
Châtenois
Sélestat
Haut Kœnigsbourg
Kintzheim
St-Hippolyte
Ste-Marie-aux-Mines
Col de Ste-Marie
Cimetière militaire
Bergheim
Ribeauvillé
le Brézouard
Hunawihr
Centre des Cigognes
Col du Bonhomme
RIQUEWIHR
Zellenberg
Beblenheim
Nécropole nationale
Mittelwihr
Bennwihr
Kaysersberg
Lac Noir
Kientzheim
Sigolsheim
Ammerschwihr
Niedermorschwihr
Les Trois Épis
Turckheim
COLMAR
Marckolsheim
Hohrodberg
Wintzenheim
Wettolsheim
Eguisheim
Husseren-les-Châteaux
Munster
Vœgtlinshoffen
Hattstatt
Breisach
Volgelsheim
Neuf-Brisach
Gueberschwihr
Pfaffenheim
Petit Ballon
Soultzmatt
Westhalten
Rouffach
Lautenbach
Murbach
Rte des Crêtes
Guebwiller
Soultz-Haut-Rhin
N. D. de Thierenbach
GRAND BALLON
Vieil Armand
Ensisheim
Écomusée d'Alsace
Thann
Cernay
Niederhaslach
Donon
Schirmeck
le Struthof
Signal de Grendelbruch
Vallée de la Bruche
STRASBOURG
ST-DIÉ-DES-VOSGES
COL DE LA SCHLUCHT
GÉRARDMER
RIEGEL
FREIBURG-I.-BR.
BELFORT
MULHOUSE
BASEL
DEUTSCHLAND
VALLÉE DU RHIN
RHEIN
Thur
Ill
Andlau

Folie Marco, an 18C nobleman's house, is home to a museum where 17C-19C furniture, porcelain, china, pewter and mementoes of local history are exhibited *(30 rue Sultzer; Open Jul-Sep Wed–Mon 10am-noon & 2-6pm; May-Jun & Oct weekends only 10am-noon & 2-6pm; 4€; 03 88 08 66 65).*

Mittelbergheim

The houses of this delightful town are built on a hillside. The town hall square is lined with handsome Renaissance buildings. The Zotzenberg Grand Cru vineyard (on limestone-marl soil) stands at an altitude of 320m above the village. It is reputed for its Sylvaner, but other varieties do equally well here. A very interesting visit can be found at Domaine Rietsch (Open Mon-Sat 8.30am-noon & 1.30-6pm; t03 88 08 00 63; www.alsace-rietsch.eu).

Andlau★

The two belfries of Andlau can be seen from a distance rising above the roofs and surrounding forest. The town boasts three Grands Crus, Wiebelsberg, Muenchberg and Kastelberg. If you need to know more, **Marc Kreydenweiss**, one of the pioneers of biodynamic wine making, is a useful place to start *(see Shopping Guide).*

Eglise St-Pierre-et-St-Paul★, rebuilt in the 12C, has retained a magnificent **doorway**★★ entirely decorated with bas-relief from the Romanesque period. These represent scenes of the Creation and the Garden of Eden.

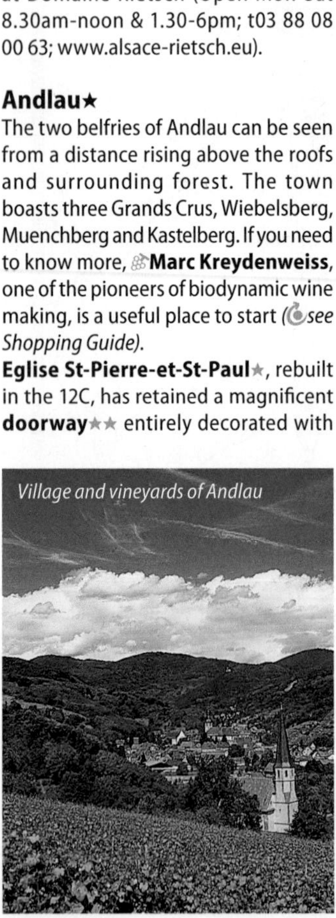

R. Mattes / MICHELIN

Itterswiller

This charming flower-decked village clings to a hillside of vineyards, with a pretty church containing a 14C mural. Itterswiller does not possess a Grand Cru, but the locality of Fruhemes is noted for its Riesling.

A **wine and gastronomy trail** *(1hr)* leads to a splendid viewpoint.

Dambach-la-Ville

The historic town centre, encircled by ramparts, is stunningly picturesque. The Frankstein Grand Cru is famous for its excellent Rieslings and Gewürztraminers, and the town is a thriving wine-producing centre.

The **Ruhlman estate** offers a visit of the cellars, the vineyards and a tour of the medieval city in a small train. Wine tasting takes place in a 17C cellar *(34 r. du Maréchal-Foch, 67650 Dambach-la-Ville; open daily by appt. 8am-noon & 2–6pm; 03 88 92 41 86; www.ruhlmann-schutz.fr).*

For a splendid view of the Alsace plain and the vineyards, turn left 400m past the Porte Haute (upper gate). At the top of the road, turn right onto a trail which goes as far as Chapelle St-Sébastien. Inside the chapel is an ornate late 17C Baroque altar caved in wood.

Continue along the trail *(2hr there and back)* to the **ruins of the castle of Bernstein**. Built in the 12C and 13C on a granite ridge, all that remain today are the main building and a pentagonal keep. It commands a wonderful panorama of the plain.

Scherwiller

At the foot of the fortified castles of Ortenbourg and Ramstein, an old guardroom with an oriel and a number of fine 18C houses can still be seen in the town, as can some former wash-houses along the banks of the Aubach.

Guided tours of the **wine trail** are available over Jul and Aug every Thurs at 5pm. The **André Dussourt Estate**, at the foot of Ortenbourg castle, has opened its 18C cellars, which boast hundred-year-old barrels among other curiosities, to the public. *(2 r. de Dambach, 67750 Scherwiller; open Mon-Sat 8am-noon and 1-6.30pm; Sun & holidays by appt.; admission charge; 03 88 92 10 27; www.domainedussourt.com).*

Châtenois

An unusual Romanesque belfry with a spire and four timber watchtowers is one of the more eye-catching sights of this town. A **wine trail** leading up to the summit of the Hahnenberg *(3hr there and back)* also gives information about local bee-keeping and honey.

2 FROM CHÂTENOIS TO COLMAR

54km. Châtenois is located 5km W of Sélestat on the N 59. Map p91.

As far as Ribeauvillé, the road is dominated by countless castles, among them the ruins of Kintzheim, Frankenbourg, St-Ulrich, Girsberg and Haut-Ribeaupierre, and the imposing mass of Haut-Koenigsbourg. This is definitely worth a tour, particularly a walk around the castle keep and the Medieval gardens (*for full details, plus contact and opening times, see Stepping Back In Time*).

Further along the same road is Hohlandsbourg castle.

Kintzheim

At the foot of Haut-Koenigsbourg Castle, Kintzheim (not to be confused with Kientzheim in Haut-Rhin) is a major tourist centre with two animal parks.

The **Volerie des Aigles** (Eagle Aviary) is located in the courtyard of the old feudal castle where awnings provide shelter to some 80 birds of prey *(20min walk there and back; open daily, mid-Jul to Aug 10am-noon & 1.30–6pm; Apr–mid–Jul & Sept-Nov 2–5pm; closed mid-Nov–late Mar; 40min show, enquire as to times; 9€; 03 88 92 84 33; www.voleriedesaigles.com).*

Continue driving along the forest road then on the D 159. Turn left after 2km onto a lane leading to the electrified fence encircling Monkey Mountain.

On 20 hectares of parkland planted with pine trees, **Montagne des Singes** (Monkey Mountain) is home to 300 barbary apes from the Atlas mountains who live wild in the park and have apparently had no difficulty adapting to the Alsatian climate. (*open Jul–Aug 10am–6pm, May–Jun & Sep 10am–noon and 1-6pm; Mar-Apr & Oct–Nov 10am–noon & 1-5pm; closed Dec-Feb; 8€; 03 88 92 11 09, www.montagnedessinges.com).*

Straddling the neighbouring town of Orschwiller, the **Praelatenberg Grand Cru**, formerly the property of the monks of Ebermunster Abbey, is planted with Riesling, Gewürztraminer, Muscat and Pinot Gris varieties and its siliceous soil produces very full-bodied wines.

Saint-Hippolyte

Fountains adorned with flowers in summer and a handsome Gothic church add to the appeal of Saint-Hippolyte which is renowned for its pinot noir and gewurztraminer wines. A good example of the local Gloeckelberg Grand Cru can be found at Domaine Bott Freres (t03 89 73 22 50, www.bott-freres.fr). Just outside Saint Hippolyte, in Rorschwihr is Domaine Fernand Engel (see Shopping Guide).

Bergheim

The lime tree said to date back to 1300 and the 14C Porte Haute (upper gate) bear witness to the history of this wine-growing town. Inside the medieval wall, flanked by three slender round towers, a large number of fine old houses can be seen. Look out for the fountain in the market square and an imposing 19C synagogue.

The 18C **church**, built out of red sandstone like the town hall, still retains a number of 14C architectural features. (*open daily Jul–Aug; rest of the year enquire at the presbytery, 1 r. de l'Eglise; 03 89 73 63 20).*

The Altenberg vineyards of Bergheim dominate the town below, producing Gewürztraminers and Rieslings. You can sample them at the **Gustave Lorentz estate** *(see Shopping Guide)*.

Ribeauvillé★

The ancient towers of Ribeauvillé, dominated by the three Ribeaupierre castles (12C-13C), are topped by several stork nests. This pleasant stop along the Wine Road boasts three Grands Crus: Osterberg, Kirchberg and Geisberg. Many reputable wine-growing estates are located in Ribeauvillé, among them **Trimbach** *(see Shopping Guide)*.
The semi-pedestrian **Grand'Rue**★★, extending the length of the town, is lined with timber-framed houses, their window boxes laden with geraniums. The **Halle au blé** (corn exchange) and **Tour des Bouchers**★ (Butchers' Tower) are particularly worthy of note.
Beyond Ribeauvillé, the road rises half way up the hillside, offering a panorama of the Alsatian plain. Between Ribeauvillé and Colmar, you are in the heart of Alsace's vineyards, whose plentiful hillsides are dotted with famous wine-growing villages and towns.

Hunawihr

Hunawihr is one of the gems of the Wine Road, hidden away in the foothills of the Vosges but well worth discovering. The atmosphere of this peaceful, welcoming village is summed up by its 16C church, which alternates between Protestant and Catholic ceremonies.
The Rosacker Grand Cru vineyard, which you can walk through on a **wine trail**, is planted mainly with Riesling, but Gewürztraminer does equally well in this soil. The **Mittnacht Frères** wine estate is well worth a trip *(see Shopping Guide)*. One hectare of the Rosacker Grand Cru is also the site of Trimbach's Clos Ste Hune, one of the great white wines of France.

Centre de réintroduction des cigognes et des loutres (Stork and Otter Park)

Open Jun 10am–6pm; July 10am-6.30pm; Aug 10am-7pm; rest of year times vary. 8.50€; 03 89 73 72 62. www.cigogne-loutre.com.

Since 1976, the centre has been trying to suppress the migratory instinct of Alsace's storks which was endangering them. The reintroduction centre allows visitors to get a closer look at the nesting process and observe several couples as they raise their newly-hatched fledglings during the spring and summer season. Over 200 storks are raised here. In 1991 an otter reintroduction centre was added to the site and the otter, which had disappeared from French rivers, is gradually returning to the region as are beavers and salmon.

Zellenberg

A tour of this high-perched village, which commands a superb view of Riquewihr and its vineyards, will take you about 40min on foot (enquire at the town hall or tourist offices of Ribeauvillé or Riquewihr).

On leaving the village, a **wine trail** leads through the Froehn Grand Cru vineyards.

Riquewihr★★★

Where the warring invaders of yesteryear failed to take Riquewihr by force, the peaceful hordes of tourists have succeeded and each year its ramparts are stormed by some two million visitors. Spared by the many wars which ravaged the region, the town looks just as it did in the 16C. Since the Middle Ages, wine has been the backbone of Riquewihr's prosperity and the town has two Grands Crus, Sporen, suited to Gewürztraminer and Pinot gris, and Schoenenbourg, devoted primarily to Riesling. Riquewihr is home to a number of renowned wine firms including **Dopff et Irion** and **Hugel et Fils** *(see Shopping Guide)*.
The mullioned windows, gables crowned with antlers and turreted staircase of **Wurtemberg Ducal Palace** is home to the **Musée de la Communication en Alsace**, highlighting the different means of communication used throughout the region over the centuries *(open Apr–Oct and during the Christmas market, 10am–5.30pm; 4.50€; 03 89 47 93 80; www.shpta.com)*.

Riquewihr, surrounded by vineyards

JACASS/MICHELIN

Liebrich House★ (cour des Cigognes) dates from 1535 with a picturesque courtyard with balustraded wooden galleries (mid-17C), a well dating from 1603 and an immense wine press (1817). **Hansi Museum** is reached through a souvenir shop. Upstairs are watercolours, lithographs, decorated ceramics and posters by the talented Colmar-born artist and caricaturist Jean-Jacques Waltz, known as Hansi *(open Jul–Aug daily 10am–6pm; Apr–Jun & Sep–Dec Tue–Sun 10am–6pm; Jan weekends 2–6pm; Feb–Mar Tue–Sun 2–6pm; closed Jan 1 & 25 Dec; 2€; 03 89 47 97 00).*

Preiss-Zimmer House★ is Riquewihr's best known sight. After crossing over several successive courtyards, you will reach this house that belonged to a wine-makers guild.

Farther on to the left is the former **Cour Dimière** (tithe court) of the lords of Ribeaupierre. At the end of Rue du Général-de-Gaulle, on Place de la Sinn, admire the lovely **Sinnbrunnen fountain** dating from 1580.

The tiny **Rue des Juifs** leads into the unusual Jewish courtyard, a former ghetto, at the end of which is a narrow passage and a wooden staircase which leads up to the ramparts and the Musée de la **Tour des Voleurs** (Thieves' Tower) with a torture chamber, dungeon, guardroom and living quarters of the warden of this former prison *(Open 10.30am–1pm & 2–6.30pm; closed early Nov–Easter; 2.50€, combined ticket with Dolder Museum 4€; 03 89 86 00 92).*

Built in 1291, **Dolder Door**★ was reinforced in the 15C and 16C and the portcullis and position of the old drawbridge (1600) can still be seen. To the left are the ramparts of the Cour des Bergers (shepherds' courtyard). The staircase to the left of Dolder Door leads to the **Dolder Museum** which contains engravings, weapons and artefacts relating to local history *(open daily Jul–Aug 1.45–6.30pm (weekends only rest of year); 03 89 86 00 92).*

At n°2 Rue du Cerf, note the semi-circular door of **Kiener House**★ *(not open to the public)* built at an angle to make it easier for vehicles to enter. The traditional courtyard features a spiral staircase, corbelled storeys and a well dating from 1576. Opposite, the former Stag Inn dates from 1566. Continue along Rue du Cerf and left into Rue Latérale, where you can admire some fine houses among which n°6, the house of the merchant Tobie Berger, still has an original 1551 oriel and in the courtyard a fine Renaissance doorway.

At n°16 Rue de la Première Armée, **Bouton d'Or House** dates back to 1566. At the corner of the house, a cul-de-sac leads to what is known as **Cour de Strasbourg** (1597), which was formerly the tithe court of the chapter of Strasbourg Cathedral.

Opposite **Jung House** (1683) on Rue de la Couronne is an old well called the **Kuhlebrunnen** (cool fountain).

Beblenheim

This village, which boasts a late 15C Gothic fountain, stands on the hillside of the vineyards of the Sonnenglantz Grand Cru whose 35 hectares are planted with Pinot gris, Muscat and Gewürztraminer. Wine trail, where you will learn about Chrétien Oberlin, who was born in this village and whose research contributed greatly to the improved quality of Alsace wines.

The **Bott-Geyl** biodynamic wine estate produces excellent wines *(see Shopping Guide)*. The **Espace Alsace Coopération** is also worth a visit: Made up of 17 cooperative cellars on the Alsace Wine Road, it offers a wide range of Alsatian wines and local specialities *(68980 Beblenheim; open 10am–7pm; closed Jan–Feb; 03 89 47 91 33.*

Mittelwihr

At the southern exit of the village stands the Mur des Fleurs Martyres (destroyed in 1944) which was planted with blue, white and red flowers during the Occupation in token of Alsace's loyalty to France. The area's mild climate explains the presence of almond trees.

A **wine trail** winds its way through the Mandelberg vineyard that Mittelwihr shares with Bennwihr. Primarily devoted to Riesling and Gewürztraminer, it is known for its particularly fruity wines.

Bennwihr

This village, in the heart of which is a monumental fountain devoted to Saint Odile, was destroyed in 1944 and later rebuilt in keeping with local architectural traditions. Bennwihr shares the Marckrain Grand Cru vineyards with Sigolsheim, whose joint micro-climate particularly favours Gewürztraminer and Pinot gris.

Sigolsheim

This village was also badly damaged during the fighting around Colmar between 1944 and 1945, although the 12C **Eglise St-Pierre-et-St-Paul** still remains. Sigolsheim is proud to possess three Grands Crus: part of Marckrain, part of Furstentum, shared with Kientzheim, and Mambourg, renowned for its strong Gewürztraminer. The **Domaine Schillé Pierre et Fils** estate offers a fine selection of Grands Crus and other local wines *(see Shopping Guide)*.

Go down Rue de la Première Armée to the national necropolis, 2km northeast past the Capuchin Convent.

National necropolis

From the car park, 5min walk there and back. 124 steps. A great many soldiers of the First French Army are buried here, alongside their comrades from North-Africa, also killed in 1944. A central platform commands a **panoramic view★** of the neighbouring peaks and châteaux, as well as of Colmar and the Alsatian plain.

Kientzheim

The profusion of timber-framed houses, old wells and sun dials in Kientzheim is such that visitors often feel they've stepped back in time to the Middle Ages. Schlossberg, Alsace's first Grand Cru vineyard created in 1975, culminates at an altitude of 350m to the northwest of Kientzheim and is characterised by its rich floral Riesling. The **Cave Vinicole de Kientzheim** represents some 150 producers and offers excellent-value wines, including Grands Crus; we also recommend the **Paul Blanck** wine estate *(see Shopping Guide)*.

Originally built in the Middle Ages, the **old castle** was transformed in the 16C. Today it is the headquarters of the **Confrérie St-Etienne**, the official body in charge of controlling the quality of Alsace wines awarding them a seal-style label. The three-storey **Museum of Alsatian Wine and Vineyards** possesses a well-stocked wine library and interesting pieces such as an immense wine press and countless rare tools.

open daily Jun–Oct, 10am–noon & 2–6pm; 4€; 03 89 78 21 36; www.musee-du-vignoble-alsace.fr).

As you pass through **Porte Basse** (lower gate), known as the Lalli, look up and admire the carved head poking his tongue out at passers-by. It is believed that his defiant grin was intended to mock assailants who had broken through the first wall of defence.

Kaysersberg★★

The small town remains fiercely proud of one of its sons, **Albert Schweitzer** (1875-1965), Nobel Peace Prize winner in 1952. Missionary surgeon, organist and writer, he is above all remembered for his tireless fight in Africa against under-development and illness. He died in September 1965 in Lambaréné, Gabon. The **Albert-Schweitzer Museum**, next door to his birthplace, displays documents, photos, personal items and souvenirs which retrace his life. *(open daily Apr–Dec 9am–noon & 2–6pm; 2€; 03 89 47 36 55; www.schweitzer.org).*

The town's medieval character is still strong, making its Christmas market one of the most famous of Alsace. The **Weinbach estate**, located in the former Capuchin vineyard, is also one of the best known in Alsace *(see Shopping Guide).*

The square in front of **Eglise Ste-Croix**★ is adorned with a fountain dating from 1521, restored in the 18C, representing Emperor Constantine. Look out for the mermaids and pelicans around the church's Romanesque doorway. In the chancel is a magnificent **altarpiece**★★ (1518) by Master Jean Bongartz of Colmar.

Rue de l'Eglise, Rue de l'Ancien-Hôpital and Rue de l'Ancienne Gendarmerie all boast ornately carved timber-framed **houses**★, one of the town's main architectural attractions in addition to those of Grand'Rue.

The **fortified bridge**★ possesses a crenellated parapet and even a small chapel. As soon as you reach the other side, look for **Brief House**★, also known as the "Maison du Gourmet" and admire its richly sculpted and painted wood panels and covered gallery.

Fortified bridge of Kaysersberg

JACASS / MICHELIN

The **Musée Communal** is located in a Renaissance house with turreted staircase. On display are religious artefacts (a rare 14C statue of the Virgin, a 15C Christ with branches of palms), traditional arts and crafts and archaeological finds from Bennwihr. *(open Jul–Aug Wed–Mon 10am–noon & 2–6pm; 2€; 03 89 78 11 11).*

Ammerschwihr

After being destroyed by fire following bombing in December 1944 and January 1945, the town was entirely rebuilt in keeping with regional traditions. Eglise St-Martin, whose chancel is lit by modern stained-glass windows, the Renaissance façade of the old town hall, Porte Haute (upper gate) and two fortified towers (Thieves' Tower and Bourgeois Tower) are the only relics of the town's past.

A number of high quality local wines are produced, such as that made by the **Sibler estate** *(see Shopping Guide).*

Niedermorschwihr★

The modern church of this charming village tucked away in a landscape of vineyards has retained its 13C corkscrew belfry, the only one in Alsace. The oriel windows and wooden balconies of the old houses which line the main street set the scene. The jam and confection-

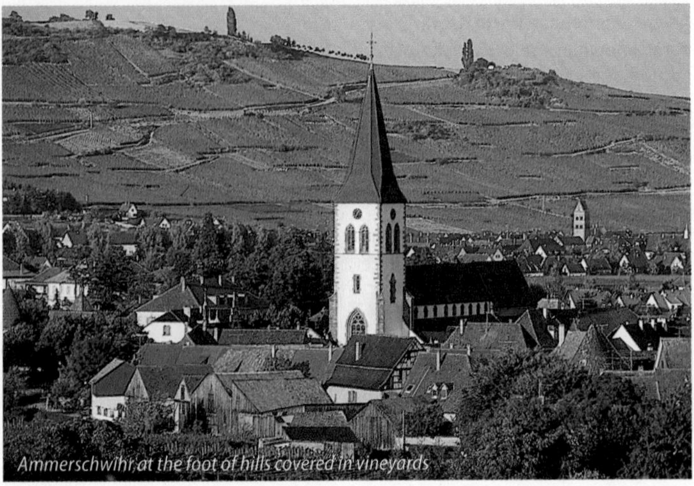
Ammerschwihr at the foot of hills covered in vineyards

R. Mattes/MICHELIN

ery shop of Catherine Ferber, known as the 'Jam Fairy' and increasingly internationally-renowned, is not to be missed (Maison Ferber, 18 rue des 3 épis), t03 89 27 05 69). The Sommerberg Grand Cru, which lies to the north of the village on a very steep granite slope, produces Rieslings which are ideal for laying down. We recommend **Albert Boxler's** wine estate *(see Shopping Guide)*.

Turckheim★

The road out of Niedermorschwihr winds its way through acres of vineyards until the ramparts of the picturesque town of Turckheim come into view. Old roofs, the multi-coloured tiles of its belfry and nests of storks complete the picture of this town that enjoys upholding ancient traditions; from May 22 to October, a night-watchman in traditional dress patrols the town every evening.

The Brand Grand Cru, overlooking the town, produces Riesling, Pinot gris and Gewürztraminer on its granite soil. The **Zind-Humbrecht estate** is one of the best in Alsace *(see Shopping Guide)*.

For a pleasant walk through the vineyards *(1hr there and back)*, leave the town through the Porte du Brand to the **wine trail** which bears right after 30m, level with a small chapel. This 2km stroll through vines has signposted explanations of local wine-growing,

Opposite Quai de la Fecht, **Porte de France** leads through a massive 14C quadrangular tower complete with stork's nest. **Porte de Munster** is typical of the town's three other gates. **Place Turenne** is lined with old houses. On the right stands the guardroom with a fountain in front, while the gabled Renaissance town hall is to the rear. **Grand'Rue** is flanked by countless old houses which date back to the late 16C and early 17C.

Wintzenheim

Nestling in the heart of vineyards which include the Hengst Grand Cru, this village located at the start of the Munster Valley has old fortifications (1275), a number of old houses on Rue des Laboureurs, a lovely 18C fountain depicting the Virgin Mary and the former manor-house of the Order of the Knights of Malta, now the town hall.

The Hengst Grand Cru is famed for its Gewürztraminer which acquires rich spicy aromas on ageing. Sample it at the **Josmeyer estate**; the proprietor, Jean Meyer, is an art afficionado who commissions artists to design the estate's wine labels. Works by Alsatian sculptor Michel Wolfhart are on view in the paved courtyard, beneath a lime tree planted during the Liberation. *(see Shopping Guide)*.

3 FROM COLMAR TO THANN

59km. Michelin Local Map 315, G-I 8-10.
See itinerary 3 on map p91.
Leave Colmar on the D 417.

Colmar★★★

Whether you visit on foot or by boat along the canals of Little Venice, the profusion of fountains, storks, half-timbered houses and window boxes overflowing with brightly coloured geraniums leaves no doubt as to the town's Alsatian heritage.

Neither war nor time seems to have left even a wrinkle on the town. Undisputed capital of Alsatian wine, Colmar not only hosts a magnificent wine fair every year, it is also home to the headquarters of the **Maison des vins d'Alsace** (*see Shopping Guide*).

If interested in buying wines, make a beeline for **Robert Karcher's cellar** (*see Shopping Guide*).

A tour of the **historic town**★★ is the perfect way to discover its many sights *(the tour leaves from Place d'Unterlinden, near the tourist office)*. As you go down Rue des Clefs, admire the beautiful pink sandstone tiles on the 18C town hall.

At Place Jeanne d'Arc, turn right into Grand'Rue. The **Protestant church** is in a former Franciscan church (13C-14C), which has been restored to its former beauty after several years of work. Further on, the lovely Renaissance-style **Maison des Arcades**★ is flanked on each corner by two octagonal turrets.

You now reach **Place de l'Ancienne-Douane**. The former Customs square is one of the most picturesque of Colmar, lined with countless timber-framed houses such as the **Maison au Fer rouge**. The former **Customs House**★ (or Koifhus) is an impressive building whose roof is covered in colourful tiles. Merchandise subject to town taxes was stocked on the ground-floor of the main building (1480) while the members of the league of ten free cities met upstairs.

Continue down Rue des Marchands. **Pfister House**★★, a gem of local architecture, was built in 1357 for a hatter from Besançon: painted façade, a corner oriel on the first floor cleverly built into ornately carved and decorated second floor gallery. In the same street, look out for the 15C **Schongauer or Viola House**, which belonged to the painter's family and the **Cygne (Swan) House**, where he is said to have lived; at n°9 a wooden sculpture depicts a 17C merchant.

The downstairs floors of the birthplace of sculptor **Auguste Bartholdi** (1834-1904) are now a **Local History Museum**. It traces the life and work of the sculptor of the Lion of Belfort, Clermont-Ferrand's Vercingétorix and the Statue of Liberty in New York. One of the rooms is devoted to a collection of Jewish art (*open Mar–Dec Wed–Mon 10am-noon and 2-6pm, last entrance 1hr before closing; closed May 1, Nov 1 & Dec 25; 4.10€; 03 89 41 90 60; www.musee-bartholdi.com*).

An arcaded passage opposite the Bartholdi Museum will take you to Place de la Cathédrale. It is on this square that Colmar's oldest house, **Adolphe House** (1350), stands, as does the **town's former guardroom**★ (1575). The latter boasts a superb loggia from where the magistrates took their oath and proclaimed infamous sentences. The **collegiate church of St-Martin**★, commonly referred to as the "cathedral", is built out of red sandstone and its main door is flanked by two towers. A sundial can be seen on the south tower. St-Nicolas' Door, the work of Master Humbret, depicts the legend of St Nicolas. Good quality furnishings inside (18C organ by Silbermann).

Leave Place de la Cathédrale along Rue des Serruriers. The **Dominican church** is a slender building whose tall capital-free pillars and 14C and 15C **stained-glass windows**★ provide the setting for the famous painting by Schongauer, **The Virgin of the Rose Bower**★★ (*open daily Apr–Dec 10am–1pm & 3–6pm; 1.50€*).

Now walk along Rue des Boulangers and turn right into Rue des Têtes. The street's name and that of the **Maison des Têtes** (House of Heads) come from the numerous carved heads that adorn the façade of this fine Renaissance building. Continue on to **Place d'Unterlinden**. The Logelbach (Canal des Moulins) cuts

Little Venice in Colmar

R. Mattes / MICHELIN

Place d'Unterlinden, which literally means "square under the lime trees", in half. The **Musée d'Unterlinden**★★★ is housed in a former Dominican convent founded in the 13C. Its 13C **cloisters**★ built out of pink sandstone from the Vosges, are lined with rooms devoted to Rhenish art (primitive Rhine painters: Holbein the Elder, Cranach the Elder, Gaspard Isenmann and Martin Schongauer). The museum's pride and joy is however the world-famous **Isenheim altarpiece**★★★ which can be found in the chapel next to works by Schongauer and members of his school (24-panel **altarpiece depicting the Passion**★★). The Isenheim altarpiece was painted by Matthias Grünewald from 1500-15 for St Anthony's Convent of Isenheim. The altarpiece was exhibited in the church according to a complicated calendar, whereby the statues of the central panel were only visible on St Anthony's Day. The realistic detail, expressionist style, and a vivid use of light and colour make it an undisputed masterpiece of the period (*open May–Oct 9am–6pm; Nov–Apr Wed–Mon 9am–noon & 2–5pm; closed Jan 1, May 1, Nov 1 & Dec 25; 7€ with audioguide; 03 89 20 15 50; www.musee-unterlinden.com).*

Finally, make sure you have time to explore **Little Venice**★, a neighbourhood bordered by the Colmar and Lauch canals. It is home to several districts including the Tanners' district, whose tall narrow timber-framed houses have lofts where the skins were dried. The **Krutenau**★ district on the opposite bank of the Lauch was once a fortified town inhabited by produce-mongers who plied the waters in flat-bottomed boats. From the quay leading to the St-Pierre bridge, a lovely viewpoint overlooks Little Venice and old Colmar. If mood strikes and weather permits, a boat ride *(30min)* along the canals is a lovely way to visit the area (*Apr–Sept boat rides depart 10am–12.30pm & 1.30–7pm; Oct & Mar weekends only 10am–12.30pm & 1.30–7pm; 5€; 03 89 41 01 94).*

Leave Colmar by the D 417

Wettolsheim

This small town claims the honour of being the birthplace of Alsatian wine. Wine-growing was introduced here in Roman times, later spreading to the rest of the region. The 13C Hagueneck castle stands 2km to the west of the town. The Steingrubler Grand Cru, also to the west, enjoys an excellent southwest aspect and a sandy, gravelly soil ideally suited to Riesling and Gewürztraminer. The biodynamic **Barmès-Buecher wine estate** produces wines noted for their body and subtlety (*see Shopping Guide).*

Eguisheim★

A wine-growing centre, Eguisheim boasts Alsace's largest **cooperative cellar** (*see Shopping Guide).*

The Eichberg and Pfersigberg Grands Crus produce Rieslings, Gewürztraminers and Pinots gris. The **Albert Hertz estate** and **Léon Beyer firm** both offer a fine selection *(see Shopping Guide)*.
Surrounded by vineyards, Eguisheim spirals out in concentric circles around a 13C octagonal castle. Even though its three famous towers which used to serve as sundials for the workers toiling in the plain below, are now in ruins, the town's lanes and old houses around **Grand'Rue** and a **walk around the ramparts★** offer a charming picture.
You can also embark on a **wine trail**, complete with guided tour and tasting *(approx. 2hr; open mid-Jun–mid-Sept Sat 3.30pm, Aug Tue and Sat 3.30pm, rest of the year, by appt. with the wine-growers listed with the tourist office)*.

Husseren-les-Châteaux

At 390m, the village of Husseren is the highest point of the Wine Road and commands a splendid view. The ruins of the three castles of Eguisheim loom over the village and the Five Castle Route *(see Stepping Back in Time)* starts from Husseren. The **Kuentz-Bas Domaine**, one of the best known in the region, is open to the public. The wine-tasting cellar is decorated with old tools and objects used in cellars and vineyards *(14 rte. des Vins, 68420 Husseren-les-Châteaux; open Apr–Nov Mon–Sat 9am–noon & 1–6pm, Fri 5pm; admission charge; 03 89 49 30 24; www.kuentz-bas.fr)*.

Voetlingshoffen

The church possesses an altar from the Capuchin Convent of Colmar. The reputation of the village's excellent Muscat is in part due to the presence of the Hatschbourg Grand Cru.

Obermorschwihr

Dominated by its half-timbered belfry, this traditional village produces Muscat and Pinot Noir wines.

Hattstatt

The origins of the formerly fortified town can be traced back over many centuries. The church (first half of the 11C) possesses a 15C wall and a stone altar from the same period. Note the lovely Renaissance calvary on the left in the nave. The handsome 16C town hall is flanked by old houses. Hattstatt produces part of the Hatschbourg Grand Cru suited to Gewürztraminer, Pinot Gris and Riesling.

Gueberschwihr

Camped on a vine-covered hillside, this village is proud of its magnificent three-storey Romanesque belfry. Next to the church are some Merovingian tombstones. The Goldert Grand Cru, the same golden colour of the vines, is renowned for the quality of its Pinot Gris, Gewürztraminer and Muscat.

Pfaffenheim

Many original old wine-growers' houses are still visible in this wine-growing village, whose origins date to the 9C. The 13C apse decorated with floral motifs of the **church** is well worth a look.
Pfaffenheim shares the Steinert Grand Cru with the town of Westhalten. Its Gewürztraminer, Pinot gris and Riesling are reputed to age particularly well. The **Pierre Frick biodynamic estate** produces full-bodied wines *(see Shopping Guide)*.

Rouffach★

The historic town of Rouffach is famed throughout France for its annual fair of organic produce. The town is also well known among all those interested in taking up wine-growing as a profession for its **wine school** which has its own vineyard. The **René Muré estate** (Clos St-Landelin) offers a particularly fine selection of wines *(see Shopping Guide)*.
The structure of **Notre-Dame de l'Assomption** church dates from the 12C and 13C, but the north and south towers, unfinished due to the 1870 war, are 19C. The **Tour des Sorcières** (Witches' Tower, 13C and 15C) is machicolated and crowned with a four-sided roof complete with stork's nest. Up until the 18C, it was used to imprison women accused of witchcraft. On the same square as the Witches' Tower are the Gothic Maison

Church tower and spire and Tour des Sorcières, Rouffach

de l'Oeuvre Notre-Dame and the old town hall whose Renaissance façade is surmounted by a twin gable.

Westhalten

At the start of the Vallée noble, this village surrounded by orchards and vineyards, is proud of its two fountains and a number of ancient houses. The vineyards extend over the slopes of the Grands Crus Zinnkoeplfé, Vorbourg and Steinert particularly suited to Gewürztraminer, Pinot Gris and Riesling wines, as you'll note at the **Eric Rominger estate** (*see Shopping Guide*).

Soultzmatt

On the banks of the Ohmbach and at the foot of the upper section of the Zinnkoepflé Grand Cru, the highest of Alsace (420m), since the 13C Soultzmatt has tempered its passion for wine with the production of mineral water, sold today under the Lizbeth brand. The Nessel mineral spring is recommended for those with liver disorders, an interesting complement to the Wine Road! Wagenbourg Castle dominates the landscape. **Paul Kubler's estate** provides an excellent opportunity for wine tasting (*see Shopping Guide*).

Guebwiller★

Since the Middle Ages, wine has been the town's main source of income, with the brief exception of the 19C when the Schlumberger Empire and its textile mills provided employment for the whole town. Guebwiller boasts four Grands Crus: Kitterlé, Kessler, Saering and Spiegel, which produce Riesling, Gewürztraminer, Muscat and Pinot gris wines. Compare them at the **Schlumberger estate** which, at 140 hectares, is exceptionally large for the region (*see Shopping Guide*).

The handsome **Neoclassical collegiate church of Notre-Dame**★ was built from 1760 to 1785; the rich **interior decoration**★★ is strongly Baroque in style. **Eglise St-Léger**★ is a fine example of the Late Romanesque Rhenish style.

The five floors of **Florival Museum**★, located in an 18C residence, are devoted to collections of minerals and objects which depict the town's wine-growing, craft and industrial past. However its pride and joy is a substantial collection of works by **Théodore Deck** (1823-1891) a ceramicist who succeeded in recreating the gorgeous deep turquoise blue glazing known as "bleu de Deck". (*open Mon, Wed–Fri 2–6pm, weekends & public holidays 10am–noon & 2–6pm; closed Jan 1 & Dec 25; 2.30€; 03 89 74 22 89*).

Soultz-Haut-Rhin

Soultz, a town of mineral springs and storks nesting in chimney stacks, is home to some lovely old houses such

as the one occupied by the tourist office (1575). Take a walk along the ramparts past the "witches' tower" and pause at **Eglise St-Maurice** to admire its colourful 15C wooden low-relief, Silbermann organ (1750) and immense mural.
The former headquarters of the Knights of the Order of Malta is now home to the **Nef aux Jouets** (Toy Museum) with exhibits of dolls, rocking horses and other toys from around the world, and also several play areas for young children. *(12, rue Jean Jaurès, 68360 Soultz; open Apr–Dec Wed–Mon 2–6pm; closed public holidays; 4.60€, 6-16 1.50€; 03 89 74 30 92).*
On the road out of Soultz, the **Cave vinicole du Vieil-Armand** centralises the wine production of 150 hectares of vineyards belonging to 130 wine-growers. It produces two Grands Crus: Ollwiller, from Wuenheim and Rangen from Thann. The basement is devoted to a Wine Museum (1, route de Cernay 68360 Soultz, *open Mon–Sat 8am–noon & 2–6pm, Sun 10am–noon; 03 89 76 73 75; cavevieilarmand.free.fr).*

Thann★

Thann is the last stage of the Alsace Wine Road, ending in a blaze of glory with the Rangen Grand Cru.

The vineyards can be reached by Chemin Montaigne and Rue du Vignoble *(open to walkers only, restricted access late Sep–late Oct)*; by the Rue du Vignoble (bicycle path and path to Chemin Montaigne); and by Rue du Kattenbachy (at the rear of the small valley to the right at the start of Chemin Montaigne).
The **collegiate Gothic church of St-Thiébaut**★★ (14C-early 16C) illustrates the transition towards the Late Gothic style. A stunning **doorway**★★ adds interest to the west front. Inside notice the pentagonal chapel and polychrome wooden statue of the wine-growers' Virgin, sculpted around 1510, and the intricate sculpture on the 15C oak **stalls**★★ reworked in the 19C. Look out for the foliage, gnomes and comic characters with their impressively lifelike features. From the bridge across the Thur, admire the view of the 15C Tour des Sorcieres (Witches Tower), crowned by an onion-shaped dome, which is all that remains of the former fortifications.

Finally those with energy to spare can walk *(1hr)* up to the ruined castle of Engelbourg, whose keep collapsed leaving part of the lower wall intact around an empty centre. Local folklore has dubbed this unusual shaped ruin the **"witch's eye"**. The remaining ruins are preserved and partially restored each summer by an ongoing international project that attracts people from a wide range of countries. Several low stone walls have been rebuilt, and the area is maintained to ensure the beautiful view back over the city of Thann is cleared of vegetation.

STEPPING BACK IN TIME

Château du Haut-Koenigsbourg★★

8km SW of Châtenois by the D 35 and the D 159. Open Jun–Aug 9.30am–6.30pm (last admission 30min before closing); Apr–May & Sep 9.30am–5.30pm; Mar & Oct 9.45am–5pm; Nov–Feb 9.45am–noon & 1–5pm. Closed Jan 1, May 1 & Dec 25. 7.50€, no admission charge 1st Sun of the month (Oct–Mar). 03 88 82 50 60; www.haut-koenigsbourg.net.
The sight of this immense fortress, 300m long and perched at a height of almost 800m, rising out of the early morning mist is truly unforgettable. No wonder then that Jean Renoir chose it as the location for the prison camp in his anti-war masterpiece, *La Grande Illusion*, filmed in 1937. Built by the Hohenstaufens in the 12C, it fell into the hands of highway robbers for a time before being claimed back by the Habsburgs in the 15C.
It was then abandoned for several centuries, subjected to pillaging and fire, until the town of Sélestat finally gave it to Kaiser Wilhelm II, a great lover of romantic castles, who had it restored by architect Bodo Ebhardt. After visiting the various buildings, enjoy the panoramic **view**★★ over all the wine, corn and salt toures from Lorraine through Alsace.

Route des Cinq Châteaux (Five Castle Route)★

17km tour starting from Husseren-les-Châteaux, plus a 2hr (there and back) walk. Take the road out of Husseren and bear right onto the signposted "Cinq Châteaux" forest road. 1km farther on, park your car (car park) and walk to the "three keeps" of Eguisheim (5min climb).
Weckmund, Wahlenbourg and Dagsbourg are the names of the three red sandstone **keeps of Eguisheim** perched on the hilltop. After the demise of the Eguisheim family, the three castles became the property of the bishops of Strasbourg in 1230. *From here you can either walk (1hr) to the castle of Hohlandsbourg, or return to your car, and carry on the Five Castle Route.*
On your left, 6km beyond the keeps of Eguisheim rises the imposing **castle of Hohlandsbourg** built from 1279. Unlike its sandstone neighbours, this castle is built out of granite. Destroyed during the Thirty Years War, it was rebuilt and adapted to artillery warfare, which explains the numerous holes for firearms. The local towns have decided to turn it into a "historic and cultural centre" recreating a medieval garden and staging shows of knightly pageantry. *(open Jul–Aug 10am–7pm, 45min guided tours; rest of year times vary; 4.20€, couples 4€, admission charges vary during shows; 03 89 30 10 20; www.chateau-hohlandsbourg.com).*
The keep of Pflixbourg can be reached on foot along a path 2km further on, to the east of the castle. The Ribeaupierre family acquired the keep, the former residence of the representative of the Holy Roman Emperor in Alsace, in the 15C. A vaulted water tank stands next to the keep. From here, enjoy the excellent views of the Fecht Valley and the plain of Alsace.

OUTDOOR ACTIVITIES IN THE VOSGES

Mountain views

The **Grand Ballon**★★★ *(30km SW of Guebwiller on the D 430 and the D 431 from Markstein; leave your car at the hotel and take the path to the left; 30min walk there and back)* or the Ballon de Guebwiller is the highest point of the Vosges at 1 424m. As you would expect, it commands a stunning **view**★★★ of the southern Vosges mountains, the Black Forest and in fine weather as far as the Jura and the Alps. Don't forget your binoculars.
From the **Petit Ballon**★★ *(16km NW of Guebwiller on the D 430; at Lautenbach head north on the forest road to the Pass of Boenlesgrab and then onto the Petit Ballon; from the Kahler Wasen farmhouse-restaurant, 1hr 15min walk there and back)* a view extends over the plain of Alsace, the hills of Kaiserstuhl and the Black Forest to the east. To the south is the Grand Ballon range while to the west and north lies the Fecht Valley. The altitude at this point is 1,267m.

Para-gliding

At the **Ecole de Parapente Grand Vol** qualified instructors run courses and train beginners in the basics of paragliding. A special beginner's course is available. Paragliding can be practised from age 14 upwards *(18km SW of Andlau on the D 425; Niedermatten farm, 67220 Breitenbach, school open Apr-Nov Sat-Sun; paragliding site open year-round; 03 88 57 11 42; www.grandvol.com).*

Skiing over the Field of Fire

The **Stade de neige du Champ du Feu** *(12km NW of Chatenois on the D 424 then the D425; Le Hohwald, 03 88 97 35 05; ww.lechampdufeu.com)* lies in the heart of the medium altitude Vosges mountains, between 900 and 1,100m. The immense plateau has 90km of ski slopes, 18 Alpine ski trails and ten ski lifts. At under an hour from Strasbourg, it unsurprisingly attracts large numbers of snowboarders, downhill and cross-country skiers, as well as snowshoe hikers.
The resort also boasts 17 ski-lifts, a number of restaurants and hotels, and is a Certified French School of Skiing. In summer, the mountains here are also the starting point for many trails maintained by the Club Vosgien (www.club-vosgien.com).

LIFE IN ALSACE

Ecomusée d'Alsace★★

22km NE of Thann by the N 66, the N 83, the D 2 and the D 430. Open Jul–Aug 10am–6pm. Apr–Jun and Sep–Oct Wed-Sun 10am–7pm. Mar-Apr and Nov call for times. 12€; 03 89 74 44 74. www.ecomusee-alsace.com.

This open-air museum has been created on almost 20 hectares of land, and easily rewards at least a half-day visit. Most of the events and shows depicting life in Alsace are held in the evenings in the summertime, but there are things to do here throughout the year.

The wish to preserve the rich regional heritage was at the origin of this open-air musuem devoted to the region. The tour invites you to step inside peasant homes, grouped by region, offering an insight into 19C and 20C society.

The musuem calls upon all five senses; you can taste the bread baked in old ovens, touch the warm flanks of the shire horses and the potter's cold clay, and witness at first hand the many traditions and know-how that have made Alsace such an interesting and distinctive region in France.

Colourful façade of an Alsatian house, Écomusée d'Alsace

R. Mattes/MICHELIN

There are also lots of outside activities to do that are fun for adults as well as children. An apple orchard is devoted to ancient varieties that are available for sampling either as juice or fruit, plus there is a bee-hive with local honey to try, and a petting zoo of farmyard animals. Finally the presence of Alsace's emblematic storks nesting on the weathered roofs remind visitors that Alsace is their natural habitat.

WINE BUYING GUIDE

INFORMATION

Maison des vins d'Alsace (Civa) – *12 av. de la Foire-aux-Vins, BP 1217, 68000 Colmar. 03 89 20 16 20. www.vinsalsace.com. Open Mon–Fri 9am–noon & 2–5pm. Closed Dec 25–Jan 1.*

A major centre devoted to Alsace wines comprised of 5 regional wine-growing bodies. You will find relief maps showing villages and Grands Crus, interactive screens explaining the wine-grower's work and the wines of Alsace, brochures, posters, souvenirs. An answer to all your questions about Alsatian wines.

Useful Tips 2005 brought noteworthy late-harvest wines, although rain in October meant there is some inconsistency in quality. Overall, yields were down 8% on 2004, to 1.15 million hl. 2006 proved a difficult year for wine growers, but the best made wonderful wines, with great delicacy and freshness in the dry whites. Harvest conditions meant there are very few late harvest wines in this vintage. Yields were down again to just over 1 million hl. 2007 in contrast is seen as one of the best vintages of recent years; ideal growing and harvest conditions, and yields back up slightly to 1.1 million hl. For 2008, expect to find fresh fruit-driven dry white wines with a great ageing potential.

CHARACTERISTICS

White wines –Powerful aroma. They can be dry, sweet or liquoreux. Riesling: exuberant, with floral notes and hints of menthol and citrus fruits when young; on ageing, takes on a distinctive "kerosene" note. Tokay-Pinot Gris: full-bodied, often sweet with linden, exotic fruit and smoked notes. Sylvaner: exuberant, slightly dry and fruity. Pinot Blanc:

fruity and tender. Gewürztraminer: very aromatic, with hints of rose, violet and exotic fruits, particularly in the late harvest vintages. Muscat: generally dry, very fruity, with lemon notes.

Red wines – *The P*inot Noir can range from a light near-rosé to a dark, ruby-red colour; a fruity, generally low in tannin, wine.

Sparkling wines – The exuberant Crémant-d'Alsace has lasting bubbles and notes of hawthorn blossom and sometimes ripe grapes.

STORAGE

White wines – Excellent cellar life with the exception of *Sylvaner* and *Pinot Gris* which should be drunk within three to five years. Good Rieslings can be kept for twenty years and more, most of the other wines for ten years. **Red wines** – Most of the *Pinot Noir* should be drunk within three to five years.

PRICES

After a period of sharp price increases, most of the prices have steadied out, and generally speaking these wines offer excellent value for money, and go well with a large variety of foods.

Alsace AOC– 3€ to 8€ (white); 5€ to 25€ (red).

Alsace Grand Cru AOC – 5€ to 75€ (white); 20€ to 45€ (red).

Vendanges tardives and Sélection de grains nobles and some special vintages – 10€ to 75€.

Crémant-d'Alsace – 5€ to 10€.

WINE MERCHANTS AND COOPERATIVES

Cave vinicole de Cleebourg – *Rte. du Vin, 67160 Cleebourg. ☎03 88 94 50 33. www.cave-cleebourg.com. Open daily 8am–noon & 1.30–6pm (Sun and public holidays from 10am). Closed Dec 25, New Jan 1, Easter Sunday.* The estate, recreated in 1946 as a cooperative in the first land consolidation programme, grows the seven traditional Alsace grape varieties. Its two blue-chip values are Pinot Gris and Pinot Blanc. Each year one of the vintages of the Confrèrerie is selected from the wines of Cleebourg The cellar also offers a wide variety of local wines, and 4 Crémants d'Alsace. Alsace, Crémant d'Alsace.

La Sommelière – *2 r. des Tourneurs, 68000 Colmar. ☎03 89 41 20 38. Open Tue–Fri 9.30am–noon and 2–6.30pm, Sat 9.30am–6pm.* Mr and Mrs Tempé have personally tasted 90% of the wines on offer and visited every single estate, enabling them to offer knowledgeable advice to customers who appreciate the excellent range of Alsace wines, including Marc Tempé's own production.

Cave cooperative Wolfberger – *6 Grand'Rue, 68420 Eguisheim. ☎03 89 22 20 20. Open Mon-Fri 8am-noon & 2-6pm, Sat-Sun 10am-noon & 2-6pm.* Under the Wolfberger brand, the cooperative sells a selection of wines from all over Alsace, including a dozen or so Grands Crus.

Cave vinicole de Kientzheim-Kayserberg – *10 r. des Vieux-Moulins, 68240 Kientzheim. ☎03 89 47 13 19. www.vinsalsace-kaysersberg.com. Open Mon-Fri 9am-noon & 2-6pm, weekends and public holidays from 10am (closed weekends Dec to Mar).* Thanks to high wine-making standards and strict quality controls, the distinctive character of the wines of this cooperative is regularly singled out by wine specialists. The Grands Crus Schlossberg, Furstentum, and Altenberg are among Alsace's most prized.

ESTATES

Domaine Sibler – *8 r. du Château, 68770 Ammerschwihr. ☎03 89 47 13 15. jm.sibler@wanadoo.fr. Open daily by appt.* The Sibler family has been in the wine-making business for three generations. Their estate grows all the authorised Alsatian varieties except for Sylvaner. One of the house's best-sellers is its Kaefferkopf wine. The cellar has been furnished with benches and a vat has been turned into a tasting table. Alsace, Crémant d'Alsace, Alsace Grands Cru.

Domaine Thierry Martin – *Rue Westhoffen, 67520 Wangen, ☎03 88 04 11 22; www.thierry-martin.com* A female winemaker at this estate, Cécile Lorentz, can trace her viticultural roots in the area back to 1650. Well located by the old walls of this attractive village, among the many good wines is a Gewurztraminer Vieilles Vignes. Alsace, Crémant d'Alsace.

Domaine Marc Kreydenweiss – *12 r. Deharbe, 67140 Andlau. ✆03 88 08 95 83. www.kreydenweiss.com. Open by appt. Mon–Sat 10am–noon & 2–5pm.* Born into a family that has been making wine in Alsace for over three centuries, Marc Kreydenweiss has been at the head of this estate since 1971. In the company of his wife and son, he runs his 12-hectare vineyard, implementing biodynamic growing methods for the last 15 years. A happy blend of modern wine-making techniques and traditional wine-lore, such as temperature control by a water circulation regulation system; the estate produces several Grands Crus and is renowned for its distinctive wines with character. Alsace, Alsace Grands Crus Kastelberg, Moenchberg & Wiebelsberg.

Alsace Willm, *67140 Barr. ✆03 89 41 24 31. www.alsace-willm.com, Open Tues-Sun 10-7.* Founded in 1896 by the same family who continue to run the estate today, with a strong reputation particularly in the United States. Try their excellent Grand Cru - including Clos Gaensbroennel - and Vendange Tardive winesk. Alsace, Crémant d'Alsace, Alsace Grands Cru Kirchberg de Barr.

Domaine Bott-Geyl – *1 r. du Petit-Château, 68980 Beblenheim. ✆03 89 47 90 04; www.bottgeyl.com. Open by appt. Mon–Tue 9.30–11.30am & 2–6pm.* Heir to a family tradition which dates back to 1795, Jean-Christophe Bott has been running the Bott-Geyl estate since 1993. The 13-hectare estate is home to 70 vineyards spread over seven towns. Biodynamic farming methods entail low yields, severe and systematic pruning even during the growing stage. After the entirely manual harvest, the grapes are pressed by gravity and not in pneumatic presses. The wine is then left on the lees until bottling.

Domaine Roland Schmitt – *35 r. des Vosges, 67310 Bergbieten. ✆03 88 38 20 72; Open Mon–Sat by appt, www.roland-schmitt.fr.* Anne-Marie Schmitt, born in Naples, has thrown herself body and soul into maintaining the high standards set by her late husband, helped by her sons Julien and Bruno. The estate's 10.5 hectares of vineyards (south-southwest exposure, on clay and marl) is planted with seven traditional Alsatian varieties. Manual harvesting is followed by fermentation in temperature-controlled tanks. Alsace, Alsace Grands Cru Altenberg de Bergbieten.

Gustave Lorentz – *68750 Bergheim, ✆03 89 73 22 22. www.gustavelorentz.com; Open Mon lunchtime to Sat 10am–noon & 2–6pm.* A family business begun in 1750; the Lorentz family now owns some thirty hectares and also buys grapes from other growers. The vines, planted on clayey limestone soil, enjoy a south-southeast facing aspect with maximum sunshine. Temperature-controlled fermentation is followed by barrel-aging prior to bottling. Alsace, Crémant d'Alsace, Alsace Grands Crus Altenberg de Bergheim & Kanzlerberg.

Caveau Robert-Karcher – *11 r. de l'Ours, 68000 Colmar. ✆03 89 41 14 42. www.vins-karcher.com. Open daily 8am–noon & 1.30–7pm. Closed Sun afternoons, Good Friday, Easter Sunday, Dec 25–26, Jan 1.* The Karcher's wine-growing estate stands on the site of an old farm (1602) in the heart of old Colmar. The wines sold come exclusively from the vineyard known as the Harth de Colmar (6km from the centre). Wines created from seven varieties of grapes garner regular prizes and awards. Tastings and tours of the property.

Albert Hertz, *68420 Eguisheim ✆03 89 41 30 32; www.alberthertz.com; Open Mon-Sat 8am-noon and 1-7pm.* This award-winning winemaker is worth a visit. Try La Marianne pinot noir, and the excellent grand crus from south-facing hillside slopes. Biodynamic since 2007. Alsace, Crémant d'Alsace, Alsace Grands Crus Elchberg, Zinnkoepfle & Pfersigberg.

Maison Léon Beyer – *8 pl. du Château, 68420 Eguisheim. ✆03 89 23 16 16. www.leonbeyer.fr; Open Thu-Tue 10am–noon & 2–6pm. Closed Jan–Feb.* This establishment, one of the oldest in Alsace, (it is said to date back to 1580), enjoys a particularly fine reputation among many top restaurants in Europe and America for its dry white wines. The house's pride and joy are its Réserve maison and above all the Grandes Cuvées Comtes d'Eguisheim wines. Alsace, Crémant d'Alsace.

Domaine Schlumberger – *100 r. Théodore-Deck. 68501 Guebwiller Cedex. ℘03 89 74 27 00. www.domaines-schlumberger.com. Mon-Fri by appt.* A single domain of 140 hectares of vineyards, 70 hectares of which are Grands Crus, make up the Schlumberger estate, one of the largest in Alsace. The estate instigated a local quality charter for the Grands Crus Kitterlé and Kessler which has been applied since the harvest of 2001. In 2000, a modernisation process began with the inauguration of new vats and a new tasting room, plus trials are being carried out in biodynamic winemaking. Alsace, Alsace Grand Crus Kessler, Kitterlé, Saering & Spiegel.

Jean et Hubert Heywang – *7 r. Principale, 67140 Heiligenstein. ℘03 88 08 91 41. http://heywang.vins.free.fr; Open Mond-Sat by appt. 9am-noon & 1.30-6.30pm.*Jean and Hubert Heywang, at the head of this family-owned 7-hectare estate, practice organic methods such as reinforcing the vines' defences, protecting the soil and respecting local flora and fauna. They produce a full range of traditional Alsace wines including the village's speciality since 1742, the Klevener of Heiligenstein. Alsace, Alsace Grands Crus Kirchberg de Barr & Klevener de Heiligenstein.

Domaine Mittnacht Frères – *27 rte. de Ribeauvillé, 68150 Hunawihr. ℘03 89 73 62 01. mittnacht.freres@wanadoo.fr. Open Mon-Fri 9am-noon & 2-6pm; Sat 10-noon & 2-6pm.* Marc and Christophe Mittnacht, cousins, run the family estate of 23 hectares according to biodynamic principles. In 2002, the estate was certified as a result of its commitment to organic farming methods. The wine is stored in stainless steel vats, tuns and barrels for one year. Alsace, Alsace Grands Cru Ostererg, Crémant d'Alsace.

Domaine Weinbach – *25 rte. des Vins, 68240 Kaysersberg. ℘03 89 47 13 21. www.domaineweinbach.com. Open by appt. Mon–Sat 9–11.30am & 2–5pm.* Tireless ambassadors of Alsace, Mrs Faller and her daughters, Catherine and Laurence, maintain the highest quality standards in their 27-hectare vineyard spread over the Clos des Capucins, around the house and the Grands Crus Schlossberg, Furstentum and Mambourg. Biodynamic methods are employed in the cultivation of the entire vineyard. Alsace, Alsace Grands Crus Furstentum, Mambourg, Marckrain & Schlossberg.

Domaine Paul Blanck – *29 Grand' Rue, 68240 Kientzheim. ℘03 89 78 23 56. www.blanck.com. Open Mon–Sat 9am–noon & 1.30–6pm. Closed public holidays.* The Blanck family, wine-growers from father to son since 1610, has lost track of the number of medals it has won over the ages. Philippe and Frédéric continue to contribute to the fine reputation of Alsace wines with their Grands Crus Schlossberg and Furstentum and their Crus Patergarten and Altenburg. Seven varieties of grape are grown on the estate. Alsace, Crémant d'Alsace, Alsace Grands Crus Furstentum, Ambourg, Schlossberg, Sommerberg & Wineck-Schlossberg.

Gérard Neumeyer – *29 r. Ettore-Bugatti, 67120 Molsheim. ℘03 88 38 12 45. domaine.neumeyer@wanadoo.fr. Open by appt. Mon–Sat 9am–noon & 2–7pm.* Gérard Neumeyer is the guardian of three generations of know-how and passion. The southeast facing vineyard enjoys maximum sunshine and is sheltered from the cold winds by the Vosges foothills. The marl-limestone conglomerate, rich in gravel, is ideally suited to the vines which are grown according to ecologically responsible principles. Alsace, Alsace Grand Cru Bruderthal, Crémant d'Alsace.

Albert Boxler – *78 r. des Trois-Epis, 68230 Niedermorschwihr. ℘03 89 27 11 32. Open Mon–Sat 9am–noon & 2–6pm.* Mr Boxler, at the helm of this 12-hectare estate, grows and makes Riesling and Tokay-Pinot Gris wines with the help of his son Jean. Their wine-growing family is justly proud of its Grands Crus Sommerberg and Brand and its full-bodied vendanges tardives vintages. Riesling, Pinot–Gris, Alsace Grands Crus Sommerberg & Brand.

Domaine Pierre Frick – *5 rte. de Baer, 68250 Pfaffenheim. ℘03 89 49 62 99. www.pierrefrick.com. Open by appt. Mon–Sat 9am–noon, 2–6pm.* The Frick family, led today by Jean-Pierre Frick, has specialised in cultivation of the Pfaffenheim grape for 12 generations. The 12-hectare estate encompasses 12 terroirs where chalky soils dominate. Biodynamic winemaking, with no pesticides nor fertilisers, and the wines are never chaptalised. Alsace, Crémant d'Alsace, Alsace Grands Crus Eichberg, Steinert & Vorbourg.

Domaine Trimbach – *15 rte. de Bergheim, 68150 Ribeauvillé. 03 89 73 60 30. www.maison-trimbach.fr. Open by appt. Mon–Fri lunchtime 9am–noon & 2–5pm.* In the same family for 12 generations, the 35-hectare estate deals only in the very highest quality wines where residual sugar is as low as possible, and high levels of natural acidity produce beautiful wines with a long ageing potential. Each stage of the operation, from planting the vines to bottling, is executed with the utmost attention and care. Alsace, Rosacker Grand Cru.

Dopff and Irion – *1 cour du Château, 68340 Riquewihr. 03 89 47 92 51. www.dopff-irion.com. Open by appt. daily 10am–6pm.* This leading wine merchant is also at the head of an extremely well-located estate of 27 hectares, two-thirds of whose vineyards are Grands Crus. Traditional wine-growing methods including the planting of grass, severe pruning, manual harvesting and voluntarily restricted yields are applied. In 1998 the house acquired 5 hectares of the Château d'Isenbourg in the town of Rouffach. Alsace, Crémant d'Alsace, Alsace Grands Crus Schoenenbourg & Sporen.

Domaine Fernand Engel – *1 route du Vin, 68590 Rorschwihr; t03 89 73 77 27;* Open Mon-Sat 8-11.30am & 1.30-6pm, Sunday by appt; www.fernand-engel.fr. This 45 hectare domaine isAlsace's most important organically farmed vineyards, producing consistently lauded wines. The estate has an excellent tasting room and is well set up to receive visitors. Among its range of wines, try the Selection Grains Nobles for wonderfully dense, rich fruit, or Clos des Anges for its crisp delicacy. Alsace, Grand Cru Schoenenbourg, Grand Cru Sporen.

Domaine Hugel et Fils

© www.hugel.com

Domaine Hugel et Fils – *3 r. de la 1ère-Armée, 68340 Riquewihr. 03 89 47 92 15. www.hugel.com. Open by appt. Mon–Fri lunchtime 8am–noon & 2–5.30pm.* For nearly four centuries, the Hugel family has been tending this vineyard which now covers 26 hectares. The family estate is run by Jean-Philippe, Marc and Etienne, continuing the traditions set by the legendary Jean Hugel. Meticulous harvesting and wine-making methods include the absence of fertilisers, hand-picked grapes, ruthless selection of stock and voluntarily restricted yields. Alsace, Riquewihr Grand Cru.

René Muré – *Rte. des Vins, 68250 Rouffach. 03 89 78 58 00. www.mure.com. Open by appt. Mon–Fri 8am–6.30pm, Sat 10am-1pm & 2-6pm; 7P for groups.* Born into a wine-growing family whose traditions can be traced back to 1648, René Muré is at the head of a 22-hectare estate. Sylvaner, Riesling, Pinot gris, Muscat, Gewürztraminer and Pinot noir take root in a clay-limestone soil where they are grown organically. The red wines mature in barrels for one year, while the white wines are left on the lees for between 12 to 18 months. Alsace, Alsace Grand Cru Vorbourg, Crémant d'Alsace.

Le Domaine de l'Ecole, lycée viticole – *8 aux-Remparts, 68250 Rouffach, N83 exit Rouffach centre. ☎03 89 78 73 16. www.rouffach.educagri.fr. Open Mon–Fri 8am–noon & 1.30–5.30pm. Closed Dec 25, Jan 1.* The wine-making school of Rouffach works 13 hectares of vineyard, 5.5 of which are Grand Cru Vorbourg, the estate's pride and joy. High quality is consistent thanks to voluntarily restricted yields. The estate's Côte-de-Rouffach, Crémant brut, and Gewürztraminer are also worth a close look. Alsace, Alsace Grand Cru Vorbourg, Crémant d'Alsace

Domaine Schille Pierre et Fils – *14, rue du stade, 68240 Sigolsheim. ☎03 89 47 10 67, www.vinsalsaceschille.fr. Open Mon–Sat 9am–noon & 2–7pm.* Family property run by Christophe Schillé that makes wine over three Grand Crus around the Mambourg mountain, as well as an excellent sparkling wine. Just over nine hectares in total. Alsace, Crémant d'Alsace, Alsace Grands Crus Mambourg.

Paul Kubler – *32 rue de la Valle, 68570 Soultzmatt. ☎03 89 47 00 75. Open Mon-Sat 9-noon & 2-7, Sun by appt.* An excellent young winemaker, working nine hectares of vines. The family has been producing wine since 1620, but it was his grandfather who was the first to bottle the wine after WW2. Paul worked in Burgudny, Bordeaux and New Zealand before returning to the family estate in 2002. Alsace, Alsace Grand Cru Zinnkoepflé, Crémant d'Alsace.

Domaine Zind-Humbrecht – *4 rte. de Colmar, 68230 Turckheim. ☎03 89 27 02 05. Open Mon–Fri 8am–noon & 1.30–4.30pm (call two weeks in advance); www.zind-humbrecht.com.* This estate covers 41 hectares of land, and nearly every inch is covered in vines, spread over the five communes of Thann, Hunawihr, Gueberschwihr, Wintzenheim and Turckheim. A deep respect for the local terroir, the use of biodynamic winemaking and traditional vinification with as little filtration as possible characterises the approach of this reputable estate. Alsace, Alsace Grands Crus Brand, Goldert, Hengst & Rangen.

Domaine Eric Rominger – *16 r. Saint-Blaise, 68250 Westhalten. ☎03 89 47 68 60; Open afternoons only by appt; vins-rominger.eric@wanadoo.fr.* The 11.5-hectare family estate lies south of Colmar, at the Grand Cru Zinnkoepflé. Seven grape varieties thrive in the sandy, chalky soil. Biodynamic winemaking, hand harvesting, then fermentation in stainless steel casks or vats. The wine is then left on the lees for 8–10 months. Alsace, Crémant d'Alsace, Alsace Grands Crus Saering & Zinnkoepflé.

Domaine Barmès-Buecher – *30 r. Sainte-Gertrude, 68920 Wettolsheim. ☎03 89 80 62 92; www.barmes-buecher.com. Open by appt. Mon–Sat 9am–noon & 2–7pm.* Since 1985, Geneviève and François Barmès have been running this 15 hectare family estate, born out of the marriage between two well-established wine-growing families, Barmès and Buecher. Biodynamic cultivation was begun in 1998. The vines are an average of 30 years old and grow on the slopes of Wettolsheim and the surrounding villages of Leinerthal, Herrenweg and Kruel, and around 25 different wines per year, vinified according to terroir. Alsace, Crémant d'Alsace, Alsace Grands Crus Hengst & Pfersigberg.

Josmeyer (Jean Meyer) – *76 r. Clemenceau, 68920 Wintzenheim. ☎03 89 27 91 90; www.josmeyer.com. Open Mon–Fri 8am–noon & 2–6pm, Sat 9am–noon.* Founded in 1854 by Aloyse Meyer and managed today by his great-grandson Jean, the 27ha vineyard (of which 5ha are devoted to Grands Crus) is farmed according to biodynamic methods. Sand, pebbles and lime soils compose the plain, but the slopes are chalky marl. Grapes are harvested manually, pressed whole, and fermented naturally in temperature-controlled tanks. The wine is then left on the lees to age in oak. Alsace, Alsace Grands Crus Brand & Hengst.

ADDRESSES

STAY

AROUND BARR

Le Bugatti – *R. de la Commanderie, 67120 Molsheim. 03 88 49 89 00. www.bugatti.fr. Closed Dec 24–Jan 2. 48 rooms. 6.50€.* Contemporary architecture reflects the famed auto factory nearby. The rooms are sober and functional, nicely appointed with laminated wood furnishings.

Château d'Andlau – *113 vallée St-Ulrich, 67140 Barr, 2km from Barr on the rte. du Mont-Ste-Odile. 03 88 08 96 78. www.hotelduchateau-andlau.fr. Closed Jan 2–25, Nov 12–26. 22 rooms. 9€. Restaurant.* This low-lying half-timbered inn surrounded by high trees stands on the banks of the Kirneck on the road to Mont Ste-Odile. Enjoy a peaceful night's sleep and awaken to the lovely flowered garden in the morning. New restaurant with a wine list of over 1 000 bottles, including many Champagnes, the house speciality.

AROUND COLMAR

A la Vigne – *5 Grande-Rue, 68280 Logelheim, 6km SE of Colmar on the D 13 and the D45. 03 89 20 99 60. restaurant. alavigne@calixo.net. Closed June 22–Jan 9 and Dec 23–Jan 7. 9 rooms. 6€. Restaurant.* A welcoming establishment with a red-painted façade and fully renovated interior. This quiet hotel offers tasteful, spotlessly clean rooms providing an excellent stopover point just 10min from Colmar. Classical recipes served in the family dining room and tartes flambées at the bar.

Chambre d'hôte les Framboises - *128 r. des Trois-Epis, 68230 Katzenthal, 5km NW of Colmar towards Kaysersberg then the D 10. 03 89 27 48 85 or 06 82 21 76 31. www.gites-amrein.com. 4 rooms.* . Leave the bustle of Colmar and relax in the peace and quiet of this village set in the heart of vineyards.
The owner distils marc, a sort of brandy, from Gewürztraminer, and offers guests comfortable panelled rooms under the eaves. Don't miss the puppet show in the morning.

Amiral – *11A bd. Champ-de-Mars, 6800 Colmar. 03 89 23 26 25. hotelamiralcolmar@wanadoo.fr. 46 rooms. 9.50€.* A charming former malthouse offers modern, fairly spacious rooms (the quietest are in the main building) with a welcoming salon decorated in rattan.

Château de la Prairie – *Allée des Maronniers, 68500 Guebwiller, 03 89 74 28 57. 18 rooms. 8.50€.* This modest manor-house, built in 1858 for a local industrialist, features spacious bedrooms whose original moulding and wooden parquet floors have been retained and enhanced by rustic furniture. Some have a terrace. A number of wood-lined sitting rooms with fireplaces. Two hectares of fenced parkland.

Hostellerie du Château – *2 r. du Château, 68420 Eguisheim. 03 89 23 72 00. www.hostellerieduchateau.com. Closed Jan 2–Feb 10. 11 rooms. 11€.* On the main square of this picture postcard town, this old house has been entirely renovated by the owner himself, an architect by training. The contemporary, personalised rooms blend well with the old structure and the bathrooms are a joy.

Hôtel au Moulin – *Rte. d'Herrlisheim, 68127 Ste-Croix-en-Plaine, 10km S of Colmar on the A 35 then the D 1. 03 89 49 31 20. www.aumoulin.net. Closed Nov 5–Mar 31. 17 rooms. 8€. Restaurant.* This old flour-mill, dating from 1880, offers a real sanctuary for tired travellers within its flowered courtyard and surrounding half-timbered buildings. Some of the rooms, which are spacious and tastefully decorated, overlook the Vosges, while the others have a view of the plain. All are gloriously quiet. Quick snacks and mini Alsace museum.

Hôtel Turenne – *10 rte. de Bâle, 68000 Colmar. 03 89 21 58 58. www.turenne.com. 85 rooms. 7.50€.* Ideally located two minutes from Little Venice, it is impossible to miss the bright pink and yellow façade of this large establishment. The spacious rooms have been treated to a makeover and are well soundproofed. Several clean, inexpensive «singles». Breakfasts are served in a traditional Alsatian room.

AROUND RIQUEWIHR

Chambre d'hôte Maison Thomas – *41 Grand'Rue, 68770 Ammerschwihr. 03 89 78 23 90. www.maisonthomas.fr. 4 rooms and 4 gîtes.* . This former wine-grower's house stands in the most picturesque part of the village, near a fortified gate. Its large functional rooms are all equipped with a small kitchen and some have a mezzanine. Several apartments also available. Pleasant garden.

Chambre d'hôte Schmitt Gérard – *3 r. des Vignes, 68340 Riquewihr. 03 89 47 89 72. Closed Jan–Mar. 2 rooms.* . Mr Schmitt's home and garden stand in the upper part of the village on the edge of the vineyards. The wood-panelled rooms are under the eaves. Impeccable cleanliness and reasonable prices also appeal.

Cheval Blanc – *122 Grand Rue, 68150 Ribeauvillé. 03 89 73 61 38. cheval-blanc-ribeauvlle@wanadoo.fr. Closed Jan 9–Feb 8 & Nov 14–23. 24 rooms. 7€.* Glorious blooms cover the facade of this Alsatian-style structure. Rustic interior with modest rooms; the quieter ones are at the back. Modern restaurant (there's a fireplace in the salon) where you can enjoy a selection of traditional dishes.

Fief du Château – *67600 Orschwiller, 7km N of Ribeauvillé on the D 1. 03 88 82 56 25. www.fief-chateau.com. Closed Jun 30–Jul 5, Nov 3–18, Feb 17–Mar 3 and Wed. 8 rooms. 8€. Restaurant.* The resplendently Alsatian façade of this late 19C house is adorned with brightly coloured geraniums in summer. Indoors a welcoming interior reveals a beamed dining room where the local dishes do full justice to the region's wines.

Hôtel Kléber – *69 r. Kléber, 68800 Thann. 03 89 37 13 66. 26 rooms. 8.50€. Restaurant.* Near St-Thiébaut, two buildings are situated about an interior courtyard. Calm and spacious rooms are located toward the back. The two restaurants, one pleasantly rustic, serve forth traditional dishes with regional accents.

Chambre d'hôte Domaine Bouxhof – *R. du Bouxhof, 68630 Mittelwihr, 2km S of Riquewihr on the D 3. 03 89 47 93 67. Closed Jan. 3 rooms.* . A delightful 17C house set in the midst of wine-growing estate. The owners are only too pleased to take you on a tour of their magnificent listed cellar and introduce you to the estate's production. Spacious, well-equipped gîtes and modern guestrooms – minimum 2 nights' booking. Breakfast is served in the 15C chapel.

Hostellerie de l'Abbaye d'Alspach – *2 r. du Maréchal-Foch, 68240 Kientzheim. 03 89 47 16 00. www.abbayealspach.com. Closed Jan 5–March 15. 28 rooms. 10€.* This charming hostelry occupies a wing of a 13C former convent in the heart of Kientzheim. Calm, good-sized rooms are appointed with massive, rustic furnishings. Five modern suites offering every luxury. Pleasant welcome.

Hôtel l'Oriel – *3 r. des Ecuries-Seignuriales, 68340 Riquewihr. 03 89 49 03 13. www.hotel-oriel.com. 19 rooms. 9.50€.* A double oriel window and an amusing wrought-iron sign adorn the frontage of this 16C house. Indoors, a maze of corridors and staircases take guests up to rustic rooms furnished in Alsatian style. Several have a mezzanine. A recent wing also offers accommodation.

AROUND WISSEMBOURG

Chambre d'hôte Klein – *59 r. Principale, 67160 Cleebourg, 7km SW of Wissembourg on the D 7. 03 88 94 50 95. www.chez.com/cleebourg. 4 rooms.* . This 18C-19C Alsatian abode in the heart of the village of Cleebourg, renowned for its wine, will appeal to all those in search of authenticity and calm. All the ground-floor rooms are furnished with lovely antique pieces. Pleasant rear garden. Regional cooking.

Moulin de la Walk – *2 r. Walk, 67160 Wissembourg. 03 88 94 06 44. info@moulin-walk.com. Closed Jan 2–23. 25 rooms. 8€. Restaurant.* A riverside setting for these three buildings grafted onto the remains of the old water mill, the wheel of which still turns. Most of the rooms feature practical modern fixtures and fittings. Welcoming dining room lined in wood and flowered terrace. Classical dishes.

EAT

AROUND BARR

Au Bœuf Rouge – *6 r. du Dr-Stoltz, 67140 Andlau. ℘03 88 08 96 26. aubœufrouge@wanadoo.fr. Closed Feb 15–24, Jun 20–Jul 12, Wed evenings and Thu except Jul–Sept.* Set in a 17C post office, this typical Alsatian restaurant serves tasty traditional dishes in an elegant wainscoted dining room or summer terrace, while the winstub offers regional specialities including its famed *flammekeuches*.

Am Lindeplatzel – *71 r. Principale, 67140 Mittelbergheim. ℘03 88 08 10 69. Closed Feb holidays, last 10 days of Nov, Mon lunchtime, Wed evenings and Thu.* An excellent address whose à la carte menu offers delights such as sautéed artichokes in peanut oil and fried goose liver, vanilla flavoured sea bass and French toast with cardamom ice cream.

AROUND COLMAR

Au Vieux Porche – *16 r. des Trois-Châteaux, 68420 Eguisheim. ℘03 89 24 01 90. vieux.porche.@wanadoo.fr. Closed Jun 27–Jul 6, Nov 8–16, Feb 15–Mar 15, Tue and Wed.* This welcoming house built in 1707 stands under the protection of Bacchus. The owner's family still owns vineyards, the produce of which can be found on the fine wine list. Guests tuck into an interesting blend of regional dishes and personal recipes.

Aux Trois Poissons – *15 quai de la Poissonnerie, 68000 Colmar. ℘03 89 41 25 21. Closed Jul 15–Aug 1, Dec 23–27, Jan 5–18, Sun evenings, Tue evenings and Wed.* Naturally enough this establishment on the banks of the Lauch Canal specialises in fish dishes – oysters from Marennes-Oléron, mussels, sole, sea bream, pike quenelles and fried carp are just some of the delights awaiting you in this half-timbered house in Little Venice.

Bartholdi – *2 r. des Boulangers, 68000 Colmar. ℘03 89 41 07 74. restaurant.bartholdi@wanadoo.fr. Closed Jun 4–18, Nov 12–20, Sun evenings and Mon.* Everything in this excellent establishment reminds you that you are in Alsace, from the painted sign, traditional winstub decor and furnishings, friendly atmosphere and the regional cuisine (fresh foie gras, choucroute, onion tart, trout in Riesling). Terrace in a paved courtyard alongside the famous Maison des Têtes.

Chez Hansi – *23 r. des Marchands, 8000 Colmar. ℘ 03 89 41 37 84. Closed Jan 5–Feb 5, Wed and Thu.* The lively atmosphere of old Colmar can be felt in this inn next door to the former Custom's and Pilgrim's houses. Within its half-timbered façade lies a traditional, very popular, Alsatian dining room.

Winstub Flory – *1 r. Mangold, 68000 Colmar. ℘03 89 41 78 80. Closed Tue, Wed except Jul-Aug and Dec.* This is your chance to discover the convivial atmosphere of the Alsacian ***Stammtisch***: a communal table, usually for regulars. Ringing the little bell in the centre means another round of good white wine for everyone! The faultless regional fare and wall fresco are both worth the visit.

La Grangelière – *59 r. du Rempart-Sud, 68420 Eguisheim. ℘03 89 23 00 30. www.lagrangeliere.com. Closed mid-Feb–mid-Mar, Sun evenings Nov– Apr, and Thu.* Before taking charge of his own establishment, Alain Finkbeiner learnt his trade in a number of prestigious restaurants. Customers can choose between an unfussy brasserie-style decor serving regional dishes or the more elaborate restaurant with personalised service.

La Maison des Têtes – *19 r. des Têtes, 68000 Colmar. ℘03 89 24 43 43. les-tetes@calixo.net. Closed Feb, Sun evenings and Mon.* Take the time before you cross the threshold to look up and admire the superb façade of this restaurant, one of Colmar's architectural gems adorned with at least a hundred sculpted masks. Indoors an enthusiastic staff prepares and serves excellent traditional French and a few regional dishes.

AROUND MOLSHEIM

Auberge du Cerf – *120 r. du Général-de-Gaulle, 67560 Rosheim. ℘03 88 50 40 14. Closed Jan 7–18, Jun 21–Jul 7, Sun evenings and Mon.* A familial ambience pervades this simple, family-style auberge located on the main road through Rosheim. Delicious, regional classics at reasonable prices.

⊖⊖ **La Petite Auberge** – *41 r. du Général-de-Gaulle, 67560 Rosheim. ℘03 88 50 40 60. restaurant.petite.auberge@wanadoo.fr. Closed Jun 30–Jul 12, Nov 19–26 and Feb 16–28.* Whether in the comfortable wood-panelled dining room or on the summer terrace, the Petite Auberge treats its guests to a delicious selection of regional dishes. Famed for its ***baeckeofe***, the house is also known for its meat cooked in Riesling or Sylvaner, homemade foie gras and fresh fruit soup flavoured with Crémant-d'Alsace.

⊖⊖ **Winstub O'Baerenheim** – *46 r. du Général-Gouraud – 67210 Obernai – ℘03 88 95 53 77. gerard-eckert@free.fr. Closed Jan 2–30 and Nov 14–30.* As you enter, notice the barrels above the main door. Once inside, seated near a warm open hearth, you can choose from a selection of very reasonably-priced regional dishes including a wide range of meat, fish, seafood and shellfish courses and an appealing set menu.

AROUND RIQUEWIHR

⊖ **A l'Arbre Vert** – *7 r. des Cigognes, 68770 Ammerschwihr, 4km SE of Kayserberg on the N 415. ℘03 89 47 12 23. Closed Mar 1–12, Nov 15–26, Feb 1–26.* In the dining room decorated with wooden carvings inspired by wine and vineyards, the Gebel-Tournier family is rightly proud of its carefully prepared, tasty local cuisine: choucroute, coq au Riesling, and roasted pikeperch garnished with a traditional horseradish sauce and ***spätzle***, a kind of noodle.

⊖ **Caveau du Vigneron** - *5 Grand-Rue, 68150 Hunawihr. 2km S of Ribeauvillé on the D 1. ℘03 89 73 70 15. chrisbruault@aol.com. Closed Dec 20–Feb 7 and Wed.* Proprietor Christophe Bruault worked here as a chef for five years before taking ownership. The interior decoration – that of the cellar of a 17C house – is unchanged and regional Alsatian dishes continue to take pride of place.

⊖⊖ **Au Relais des Ménétriers** – *10 ave. du Général-de-Gaulle, 68150 Ribeauvillé. ℘03 89 73 64 52. Closed Jun 29–17 Jul, Dec 23–Jan 2, Thu evenings, Sun evenings and Mon.* The fiddle-playing tradition is far from dead in Ribeauvillé and the sound of the violin may well guide your footsteps to this restaurant in which the terroir is all important. Spacious dining rooms decorated in full-blown Alsatian style. Regional tasty cooking made with fresh local produce.

⊖⊖ **Aux Trois Merles** – *68770 Ammerschwihr, 4km SE of Kayserberg on the N 415. ℘03 89 78 24 35. Closed Feb holidays, Wed, Sun evenings and Mon.* A menu slanted towards fish and seafood is served in a cosy dining room and comfortable terrace – roasted pikeperch and bacon, mixed fish in a beurre blanc or tuna steak ***à la plancha***. The menu features a number of Alsatian favourites such as choucroute and *baeckeofe*.

⊖⊖ **Caveau Morakopf** – *7 r. des Trois-Épis, 68230 Niedermorschwihr. 7km SE of Kaysersberg on N 415 then on D 107. ℘03 89 27 05 10. Closed Jan 7–20, Jun 23–Jul 7, Mon lunchtime and Sun.* A warm atmosphere greets the visitor to this establishment located in the cellar of an 18C building with a terrace garden. Alsatian specialities such as ***Schwina Zingala*** (boiled pork tongue) or ***fleischschnaka*** are just a few of the delights on the menu prepared by Mrs Guidat.

⊖⊖ **La Vieille Forge** – *1 r. des Écoles, 68240 Kayserberg. ℘03 89 47 17 51. Closed Feb holidays, Jul 1–21, Mon, Tue and Thu except evenings in Sept–Oct, and Wed.* A charming dining room welcomes tourists and regulars, drawn by the establishment's flavourful country cooking. How about a preview of the menu to set your taste buds tingling? Pikeperch in Riesling, choucroute, tournedos of beef in Pinot Noir, Munster cheese, iced ***kouglof*** with cherries or warm plums.

⊖⊖ **Le Sarment d'Or** – *4 r. du Cerf, 68340 Riquewhir. ℘03 89 86 02 86. closed, Sun evenings, Tue lunchtime and Mon.* The enchanting village of Riquewihr is home to many lovely houses including this 17C building, now a restaurant. Wood panelling, beams, open fireplace and tasteful furnishings set the scene for the pleasant dining rooms where traditional dishes are spiced up by a few sprigs of modernity.

⊖⊖ **Winstub du Sommelier** – *68750 Bergheim, 3km N of Ribeauvillé on the D 1. ℘03 89 73 69 99. Closed Jul 15–29, Jan 20–29, Tue evenings and Wed.* This house built in 1746 reveals an elegant ***winstub*** atmosphere, perfectly matched by its refined regional cuisine. Diners can choose between a daily set menu or a more elaborate choice which evolves with the seasons. Handsome wine list and selection of wines by the glass.

Winstub du Château – *38 r. du Général-de-Gaulle, 68240 Kayserberg. ☎03 89 78 24 33. Closed Jan 17–Feb 4, Jun 20–29, Nov 7–16, Wed evenings and Thu.* Popular all year round, the Kohler family's restaurant is even more so around Christmas time because Kayserberg's Christmas market is one of the best known in Alsace. On the faultless regional menu are local specialities such as snails à l'alsacienne, choucroute royale, smoked fillet of trout with horseradish sauce.

AROUND THANN

Le Moschenross – *42 r. du Général-de-Gaulle, 68800 Thann. ☎03 89 37 00 86. Closed Jul 1–16. 23 rooms. 6.50€. Rooms.* Within view of the famous sloping vineyard of Rangen, this 19C hotel, is fully renovated. The rooms are small, but modern and well sound-proofed. Sample traditional specialties in the bright and pleasant dining room.

L'Aigle d'Or – *5 r. Principale, 68500 Rimbach-près–Guebwiller. ☎03 89 76 89 90. Closed mid-Feb–mid-Mar. 19 rooms. 6.50€. Rooms.* Retreat to the countryside at this simple, delightfully peaceful family auberge. Regionally-accented dishes are served about the fireplace, and you can stroll in the lovely garden.

Caveau de Thaler – *47 r. de la 1re Armée -Francaise, 68190 Ensisheim. ☎03 89 26 43 26. la-couronne@wwanadoo.fr. Closed Sat lunchtime, Mon evenings and Sun.* Enter this charming old wine cellar in the lower level of the highly-regarded La Couronne hotel, where artisan's tools form an charming decor. Simple yet well-prepared regional dishes round out the menu.

AROUND WISSEMBOURG

Auberge du Pfaffenschlick – *Col de Pfaffenschlick, 67510 Climbach, 12km SW of Wissembourg on the D 3 towards Lembach, and the pass road on D 51. ☎03 88 54 28 84. www.restaurant-du-pfaffenschlick.com. Closed Jan 15–Feb 15, Mon and Tue.* Deep in the forest, opposite a cabin which served as a canteen during the construction of the Maginot Line, stands an inn: at one time, only walkers came here, but now its wholesome and plentiful cooking is deservedly better known. Pleasant terrace.

Hostellerie du Cygne – *3 r. du Sel, 67160 Wissembourg. ☎03 88 94 00 16. www.hostellerie-cygne.com.* Two terraced houses, one dating from the 14C, the other already an inn in the 16C, have been put together. The more modern dining rooms feature woodwork and inlaid ceiling. Local produce comes into its own in dishes like boar stew, ***presskopf*** of pork, and stuffed young rabbit with oxtail.

FUN AND GAMES

Jeux de pistes dans le vignoble (A vineyard treasure hunt) – *Aglaé – 36 r. de la Forêt – 67280 Urmatt – ☎03 88 47 36 71 – www.rallyes-aglae.com Open Jul-Aug, Wed-Fri and Apr-Jun and Sep-Dec on Sun.* Join a group in the towns of Obernai, Dambach-la-Ville and Turckheim and take part in an amusing question and answer treasure hunt (in French) through the vineyards. Programme on the web site and in tourist offices.

GOURMET SHOPPING

Ferme l'Hirondelle – *100 rte. de Guémar, 68150 Ribeauvillé. ☎03 89 73 62 32. fermehirondelle@wanadoo.fr. Open Tue–Fri 2–6pm, Sat 9am–noon and 2–6.30pm, Sun and public holidays noon–7pm; daily Jul–Aug 10am–7pm.* In the Hirondelle boutique, over 100 cheeses, cooked meats, jams and dairy products are attractively displayed. The star of the show is Ribeaupierre, a local cheese which this farm has begun producing again.

Windholtz – *31 ave. du Général-de-Gaulle, 68150 Ribeauvillé. ☎03 89 73 66 61. mwhindholtz@terre.net.fr. Open Mon–Sat 9am–midday & 2–6pm.* Mr Windholtz makes eaux de vie for true connoisseurs. His brandies are distilled according to old traditions to ensure that they retain all their character and taste. His special plum, pear and cherry Réserve brandies are particularly worthy of note.

2 - BEAUJOLAIS

Beaujolais, which owes its name to its historical capital, Beaujeu, conjures up an image of good meals, good wine and good friends. It holds a special place in the hearts of many Frenchmen and women because its wines, red for the most part, are so synonymous with the friendly atmosphere of the region. Beaujolais is a relatively diverse geological region and although vines have been planted here since Roman times, it was only in the 20C that wine-making became the dominant agricultural activity.

The fortunes of its producers and merchants have varied from flourishing in the Middle Ages, to almost ignored in the 17C, followed in the 18C and 19C by a genuine revival when Lyon, known as the "siphon of Beaujolais", ceased to be France's sole market and the wines began to be shipped to Paris, and further afield as the road and rail networks evolved.

However, the region's great discovery was Beaujolais nouveau—bottled within a few months of harvest with no ageing. Every November since the 1950s, first Paris, then France and then the whole world, have been inundated by this uncomplicated, easy-to-drink wine.

Highlights

1. George Dubouef's fascinating **Hameau du Vin** (p123)
2. A November tasting of **Beaujolais Nouveau**.
3. The chapel at the summit of **Mount Brouilly** (p121)
4. The beautiful village of **Bagnols** (p125)
5. Exploring the ten village crus of **northern Beaujolais** (p117)

This style of wine has not, however, always promoted the best image of Beaujolais abroad, and after a period of relative commercial madness, there is a signifcant move today towards promoting the village appellations of Beaujolais, which have more depth and subtlety and more fully express the subtlety of the terroir. And there is plenty to be proud of in this region - not only does it have the highest planting density in the world (9-10,000 vines per hectare, which means low yields of good quality grapes), but is also the steepest vineyard in France. Particularly concentrated in northern Beaujolais, 50% of the vines are planted on slopes of over 20% gradient, meaning good drainage and excellent sun exposure for the vines. On such steep slopes, all viticultural work, and harvesting, has to be carried out by hand. Whole-cluster vinification is also routinely carried out here, unlike in most other parts of France. To discover this, you are best to find one of the many welcoming cellars of tiny villages nestling in a landscape of hills.

Theizé village

OVERVIEW

The Terroir

Michelin Local Map no 327 – Saône-et-Loire (71) and Rhône (69)
Surface area: 20,500 hectares stretching from Mâcon in the north to the Azergues valley in the south.
Production: 1 million hectolitres per year.
The region's vineyards are composed of two main types of soil: "gore", a sort of clay created by decomposing granite to the north, and sedimentary limestone or clayey-limestone soils in the centre and south. Granite rock can also be found in the upper Azergues valley. The wines made from grapes grown at over 250m are more delicate than their low altitude counterparts.

The Wines

The region has three appellations, **Beaujolais, Beaujolais-Villages** and ten AOC village wines: **Morgon, Saint-Amour, Chénas, Brouilly, Côte-de-Brouilly, Juliénas, Moulin-à-Vent, Régnié, Chiroubles** and **Fleurie.** Practically only one grape variety is grown, Gamay noir, which thrives on the sunny hills producing light, fruity wines. Chardonnay is also grown in less than 2% of the vineyard, producing a little under 10,000 hectolitres/year of white Beaujolais.

"River Beaujolais"

"Lyon is fed by three rivers: the Rhône, the Saône and... Beaujolais." This quotation is variously ascribed to René Falet or Antoine Blondin; both instrumental figures in developing the prosperity of wine-growing in Beaujolais. It was during the Second World War, when Paris' journalists had fled the capital for Lyon, that the media and therefore the wider world became acquainted with Beaujolais, over a glass of red wine at a café counter in the early morning. The tradition has remained and the "pot Beaujolais", a thick-bottomed glass bottle, remains the ideal companion to hearty regional dishes such as *gras-double*.

Beaujolais Wine Road

The road meanders through the vineyards in the northeast of the region; the A6 and the N 6 offer quick access to the main towns and points north and south. A more complete Route des Vins covering 140km is opening by the end of 2009.

- **Michelin Map:** p119.
- **Population:** 185,000, mainly concentrated around the Val de Saône.
- **Info:** www.beaujolais-wines.com
- **Location:** South of Lyon, in the Rhone Alps. Itinerary 2 covers sights away from the vineyards west from St-Amour-Bellevue through les Écharmeaux, and back toward Villefranche. itinerary 3 covers vineyards in the southern part of Beaujolais, but not along the wine route.
- **Timing:** Allow two to three days to explore the wine route.
- **Kids:** The Touroparc in Romanèche-Thorins.

DRIVING TOURS

1 VILLEFRANCHE-SUR-SAÔNE TO BELLEVILLE

35km. Villefrance-sur-Saône lies 30km N of Lyon by the A 6 or the N 6.
Michelin Local Map 327, G-H 1-3.
A sea of green vineyards spreads out like ripples over the slopes of the Beaujolais hills down to the Saône valley. The vines are as much a part of the regional

landscape as they are of the local way of life. The region lives to the rhythm of the wine-growing calendar and the precious nectar flows through the economic backbone of the entire area.

Villefranche-sur-Saône

The town owes a great deal to Guichard IV of Beaujeu who made it the capital of Beaujolais in 13C, endowing it with a charter and countless privileges. It is above all famed for its seemingly never-ending Rue Nationale, a perfect snapshot of the town's urban architecture.

Rue Nationale is lined on either side with old houses, built and transformed between the 15C and 18C. They have relatively narrow façades, because of a tax imposed on the width of the house façades in 1260 to make up for the exemption from taxes and other privileges granted the town in its charter.

At n°523, the spiral staircase, mullion windows and shell-shaped niche with elegant statue of **Hôtel Mignot de Bussy** form a delightful Renaissance picture. **Auberge de la Coupe d'Or**, at n°528, was the oldest inn in Villlefranche (14C), but was transformed in the 17C.

Eglise Notre-Dame-des-Marais owes its existence to a legend according to which a statue of the Virgin Mary, found in the marshes by peasants and transported to Eglise Ste-Madeleine, was mysteriously found again in the marshes. The inhabitants of Villefranche eagerly set about building a chapel to mark the spot. All that remains of the original 13C structure is a small Romanesque belfry (13C) above the chancel. The church has been substantially reworked over the ages: the central tower is 15C, the magnificent Late Gothic façade was a gift from Pierre II de Bourbon and Anne de Beaujeu in the 16C and the spire was rebuilt in 1862. Notice the gargoyles on the north façade one of which depicts lust.

Leave Villefranche on D 504; right on D 19 and then left onto the D 44.

Montmelas-Saint-Sorlin

The feudal **castle** (*not open to the public*), restored by Dupasquier, a pupil of Viollet-le-Duc, lies to the north. Perched in solitary splendour on a rocky outcrop, its high crenellated battlements and towers make for an imposing sight.

Continue to the pass of St-Bonnet. From the pass, a walking trail leads to the Signal de St-Bonnet (30min return).

Signal de Saint-Bonnet

The panorama from the east end of the chapel unfolds to reveal Montmelas in the foreground, set against the hills and vineyards of Beaujolais, and in the distance the Saône valley; to the southwest lie the mountains of the Lyonnais and Tarare regions.

Young (*4 years and older*) and old may enjoy romping through the acrobatic adventure course created in the trees of the **Au fil des arbres park** (*open Jul–Aug daily 10am–7pm; May–Jun Wed 2–7pm, weekends 10am–7pm; Mar, Apr, Sep & Oct weekends and school holidays 1–7pm; Nov school holidays 1–6pm; 19€, children 5€–16€; 04 74 60 03 95; www.aufildesarbres.fr).*

From the pass, take D 20 (right).

Saint-Julien

This delightful wine-growing village is the birthplace of **Dr Claude Bernard** (1813-78). A house bought by the French scientist amid vineyards bears the following inscription: "I live on the hillside overlooking the Dombes…". It now houses a museum created under the aegis of the Fondation Mérieux of Lyon, devoted to the life and works of Claude Bernard. Walk through the garden past the vineyards and you will reach the place where he was born at the rear of the property (*open Wed–Sat 2-6pm,Sun 10am–noon & 2–6pm closed public holidays; 5€; 04 74 67 51 44; www.fond-merieux.org).*

Take the D 19 to Salles.

Salles-Arbuissonnas-en-Beaujolais

Salles-Arbuissonnas-en-Beaujolais is still home to a few buildings of a **pri-**

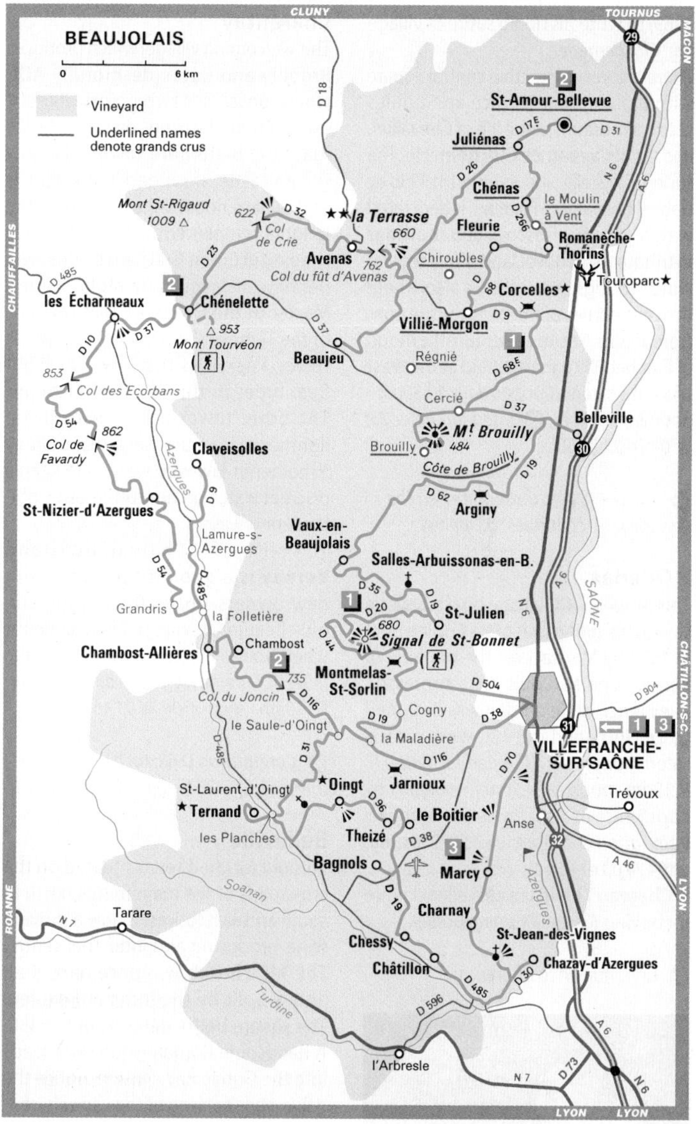

ory founded in the 10C by the monks of Cluny. A collection of souvenirs and objets d'art are exhibited in the 15C **chapter house**, reached through the garden and the cloisters to the right of the church (*45min guided tours by prior arrangement with Miss Alliès; 3€; 04 74 67 51 50).*

To the right of the church, a small Late Gothic door leads into the Romanesque **cloisters**; all of which remains is an elegant arcaded gallery. The wine produced here is Beaujolais-Villages.

From Salles, take the D 35, then the D 49E to the right.

Vaux-en-Beaujolais

This wine-growing village clinging to the slopes of the Beaujolais mountains inspired Gabriel Chevallier (1895-

1969) to write his ribald satire of village life, *Clochemerle*.

There is a very attractive central square with a panoramic terrace and boules court, a museum of the life of Chevallier, and the **Caveau de Clochemerle**. The superb 17C cellar, inaugurated in 1956 by Gabriel Chevallier in person, is decorated with humorous frescoes and drawings in tribute to his novel, and offers regular wine-tastings. The cellar is also where the ceremonies of the picturesque Confrèrerie des Gosiers Secs (Brotherhood of Parched Throats) are held at the feast of Saint Vincent (*open daily 10.30am–noon & 3–7.30pm; closed Jan 1, Dec 25; 04 74 03 26 58*).

The D 49E cuts through Le Perréon and the D 62 continues to Odenas.

Odenas

This Brouilly AOC village boasts several castles including that of **La Chaize** built in 1674 by Mansart for the nephew of Père La Chaize, Louis XIV's confessor. The French-style garden was designed by Le Nôtre and the 18C wine vat is a listed monument. (*open Jul Mon–Fri, 8.30am–noon & 2–5pm, weekends by appt.; rest of year by appt. Mon–Fri 9am–noon & 2–5pm; 2.50€ tasting; 04 74 03 41 05*).

Château Thivin is an excellent choice for buying (*see Shopping Guide*).

Continue on to Charentay.

Art of wine-making...

S. Sauvignier/MICHELIN

Charentay

This welcoming village, which produces Brouilly and Côtes-de-Brouilly AOC wines, possesses two points of interest: **Château d'Arginy**, on the Belleville road, and **Bellemère tower**. The now ruined castle, shrouded in mystery, is said to have housed the treasure of the Knights Templar entrusted to the safe keeping of Count Guichard de Beaujeu, nephew of Jacques de Molay, Grand Master of the Order. All that remains of the Templars' era is a large redbrick tower, known as the Tower of Eight Beatitudes or the Tower of Alchemy. The other tower, which rises like a lighthouse over the vines, was built by a mother-in-law who wanted to keep a discreet watch on her son-in-law's philandering ways.

The cellar of **Château du Grand Vernay** is a good local estate with new owners since 2008, producing only Beaujolais Village Charantay but where you will receive a warm welcome (*69220 Charentay; open by appt. Mon-Fri 10am–7pm; 04 74 03 46 20*).

Continue on D 68; take the D 19 on the left and D 37 to the right to Belleville.

Belleville

This old fortified town situated on the crossroads of the main routes north to south and east to west is now a thriving wine-producing and industrial centre. The 12C **church** was once part of an abbey built by the lords of Beaujeu. The square belfry dates from the 13C. A handsome Romanesque door leads into the Gothic nave. Inside, notice the naïve-style carving of the capitals, representing the Seven Deadly Sins. The **Hôtel-Dieu**, built in the 18C to replace an older hospital, was in use for the care of the sick until 1991. The three large rooms are divided into characteristic white-curtained alcoves, and are connected to the chapel through finely wrought iron gates. The dispensary houses a collection of 17C and 18C porcelain (*open May–Oct, 1hr guided tour Wed-Fri, 10am & 4pm; Sat 5pm, Sun (Jul-Sept) 5pm; 5€; 04 74 69 65 85*).

2 THE AOC VILLAGES: FROM BELLEVILLE TO ST-AMOUR-BELLEVUE

57km. Belleville lies 15km N of Villefranche-sur-Saône and 44km from Lyon by the A 6. Michelin Local Map 327, G-H 1-3. Drive W from Belleville on the D 37

You'll pass **Château de Bel-Air**, now a wine-producing school. On the same site is the **Capvignes** tourist centre, offering wine discovery courses including learning how to recognise aromas and an illustration of the different wine-growing professions. There is also a ten hectare park for picnics (*Château de Bel-Air, Rte. de Beaujeu, open Sept-Jun Mon-Fri 8am-5pm, weekends by appt; 04 74 66 62 78; www.capvignes.com).*

Saint-Lager

The territory of this wine-growing locality dominated by Mont Brouilly is dotted with opulent properties tucked in among the rows of vines. The 19C **Château des Ravatys** belongs to the Pasteur Institute and the benefits of its produce are used to fund medical research. The park and cellars are open to visits. Sales of Brouilly and Côtes-de-Brouilly (*open Mon–Sat 8.30am–noon & 2–6pm; closed Aug 1–15 and public holidays; 04 74 66 80 35; www.chateaudesravatys.com).*

An 8.5km **walk** starts out from Saint-Lager cellar and loops round Mont Brouilly to return to the starting point.

The neighbouring village of **Cercié** leads to the **Voie verte du Beaujolais** (Beaujolais Green Belt), an 11km trail tracing an old railway line, for walkers and cyclists.

Alternatively, continue on the D 37 to Beaujeu, the capital of Beaujolais.

Beaujeu

Surrounded by hillsides carpeted in vines, the historic former capital of Beaujolais is full of low-lying houses and narrow streets.

Les Sources de Beaujolais is a wine centre-cum-museum whose original, modern displays provide a historic excursion into the wine-growing world of Beaujolais. There are often tastings of regional products alongside wine, and in summer months there are bikes for hire to get out into the vineyards. However the museum's most unusual exhibit is without doubt a full-scale replica of a **barge** whose bridge visitors walk over. Regional produce on sale. *Enter through the Maison du pays, opposite the church (open Jul-Aug, Mon-Sat 10am-12.30pm & 2-7pm, Sun 10am-12.30 & 3-7pm; Mar–Jun & Sept–Dec, Wed-Mon 10am-12.30pm & 2-6pm; last admission 1hr before closing; 5€; 04 74 69 20 56; www.beaujeu.com).*

The **Musée des Traditions Populaires Marius-Audin** is also well worth a visit; a section is devoted to the cultivation of vines. (*open May–Sept 9.30am–12.30pm & 2.30–6.30pm, Jul 9pm; Mar–Apr & Oct–Nov Wed–Sun 10am–noon & 2.30–6pm; 2€; 04 74 69 22 88; www.beaujeu.com).*

The **Beaujolais-villages Caveau** is located in the cellar of the museum, and has many good bottles of wine. An individual producer to visit in the area is Jean Marc Lafont at Domaine Bel Air (*see Shopping Guide).*

Back on the road to Cercié, turn right on D 43; left on D 43E for 100m; then left again onto the Rte. Côte de Brouilly.

Mont Brouilly

These hilly slopes are where the fruity fragrant wine of Côtes-de-Brouilly is produced. Côtes-de-Brouilly and Brouilly are both produced in the towns of St-Lager, **Quincié** (*see Cave Beaujolaise and Domaine des Grandes Vignes in Shopping Guide*), Charentay, Odenas, Cercié and St-Etienne-la-Varenne. Brouilly with 1,300 hectares, is one of the largest AOCs of Beaujolais, while Côtes-de-Brouilly only covers some 300 hectares. Walk or cycle to the top of the hill, and admire the **view**★ over the vineyards, the Beaujolais hills, the Saône plain and the Dombes region. The **chapel** at the summit (altitude 484m) is a place of pilgrimage for wine-growers. Devoted to the Vierge-aux-Raisins (Virgin Mary of Grapes), it was built in the 19C to protect the vines from mildew.

Villié-Morgon vineyards

J. Damase/MICHELIN

Return to Cercié and on the way out of the village, bear left onto the D 68E towards the historic town of Corcelles. From there, turn left onto the D 9.

Château de Corcelles★

Open Mar–Nov Mon–Sat 10am–noon & 2.30–6.30pm; Dec–Feb Mon–Sat 10am–noon & 2.30-5.30pm. Closed public holidays; 2€, or MP3 audio-tour at 4€; 04 74 66 00 24.

This stronghold was originally built in the 15C to defend the border between Burgundy and Beaujolais, but transformation work carried out in the 16C has left it looking more like a manor house. The inner courtyard features Renaissance arcades and a well adorned with 15C wrought-iron work, and the chapel boasts some remarkable Gothic woodwork. The Château de Corcelles ranks among Beaujolais' most famous wine-growing estates. Its huge 17C **wine vat** is one of the most beautiful you will see in the region.

Return onto the D 9 to the right.

The road passes through some of the most prestigious vineyards of Beaujolais commanding fine views of the Saône valley. Each village has a wine cooperative or cellar where you can taste these excellent wines.

Villié-Morgon

The Morgon AOC owes its name to the small hamlet of the same name, but it is perhaps by visiting one of the 250 wine-growers of Villié-Morgon that you will discover the real meaning of the wine-word "morgonner". Morgon wines are said to "morgonne" when they throw off earthy, animal scents unlike those of any other wine. The Côte du Puy is the most well-known of the AOC. The **Domaines Piron estate** and **Jean-Marc Burgaud estate** are both to be recommended *(see Shopping Guide)*. The **Morgon** firm, located in the 18C château de Fontcrenne situated in a lovely park, can be relied on to make visitors feel at home. *(Château de Fontcrenne, 69910 Villié-Morgon; open daily 10am–noon & 2.30–7pm; 04 74 04 20 99).*

Several well-signposted **walking trails** leave from the centre of the village and up through the hilly vineyards.

From Villié-Morgon, head north on D 68 skirting the village of Chiroubles.

Chiroubles

Chiroubles is without doubt the most floral of Beaujolais wines, renowned for its subtle fragrance of violets and peonies. The altitude (400m) of the vineyards are most probably the reason for this delicate bouquet. The local hero, whose statue adorns the village square, is Victor Puillat who saved the vines from phylloxera by grafting American rootstock onto French stock.

The landscape can be savoured from a panoramic path *(signposted)*.

The friendly staff of the **Maison des Vignerons**, a local cooperative, are happy to advise visitors about its fine selection of wines; if you prefer buying from estates, try **Domaine Emile Cheysson** and **Domaine Desmures** *(see Shopping Guide).*

Fleurie

A Virgin Mary, erected in 1875 to protect the vine from phylloxera, dominates the village. Fleurie wines are reputed for their flavour of fresh grapes and fruity bouquet, to which the equally well-known Fleurie andouillette sausage is an ideal accompaniment. In addition to the get-ahead cooperative cellar of the **Producteurs des Grands Vins de Fleurie**, one of the most substantial in the region, **Chateau des Labourons estate** and **La Madonne** also produce good quality wines *(see Shopping Guide).*

From Fleurie, take the D 32 eastbound, then the D 186 to the left.

Romanèche-Thorins

This thriving market town in the heart of Beaujolais-Villages is the annual meeting-point for Beaujolais nouveau lovers who come here to see the tanks leave Georges Duboeuf's storehouse, where the vast majority of early wines from most of the region's cooperative cellars are grouped together and sold.

Romanèche-Thorins shares with Chénas the Moulin-à-Vent AOC, Beaujolais' oldest appellation, whose reputation for distinctive robust wines produced from manganese-rich soils dates back to the 18C - and the name Moulin-à-Vent comes from on old windmill standing to the northwest of Romanèche-Thorins, now preserved as the last remaining specimen in the region.

Around 1830, Beaujolais' vines were decimated by the pyralis worm, leaving the wine-growers helpless. **Benoit Raclet**, who owned vineyards in Romanèche, noticed that a vine growing along the side of his house, near to where the household's waste water was emptied, was totally unaffected by the scourge. He decided to water all his stock with hot water at 90°C in February to kill the worm's eggs, thereby saving his vines, despite his neighbours' scepticism. In the end, however, they also finally decided to adopt the technique. A festival is held each year in his honour in the last weekend of October. His **house** is also open to the public with a variety of souvenirs and tools on display. *(guided tours by appt. 2 weeks in advance; closed Nov–Apr; 03 85 35 51 37).*

The **Hameau du Vin★★**, developed by Georges Duboeuf in a former railway station, deserves its reputation as one of the most impressive pieces of wine tourism in France. It offers visitors the chance to take a child-friendly, fun and educational tour of the history of Beaujolais' vineyards and the different elements of winemaking, as well as offering a larrge tasting room and cafe. After visiting the inside exhibits, head for the **Jardin en Beaujolais** *(minitrain)* to investigate the winemaking centre *(open daily Apr–Oct 9am–7pm; Nov–Mar 10am–6pm; closed Dec 25; garden closed Dec–late Mar; 16€, under 16 no charge. 03 85 35 22 22; www.hameauduvin.com).*

The Moulin-à-Vent wines are recongised to be among the finest of Beaujlais, and we recommend **Domaine Yvon Metras** and **Chateau des Jacques** *(see Shopping Guide).*

Touroparc Zoo and Amusement Park★

At the crossroads of Maison-Blanche on the N 6, take the D 466E St-Romain-des-Iles road. Open Jun-Aug daily 9.30am–7pm (rides 1.30–6pm). Mar-May & Sept-Nov 9.30–6pm, Feb 10.30am-5.30pm (rides 1.30-5.30). 15€. 03 85 35 51 53. www.touroparc.com.

Trees and parkland dotted with ochre-coloured buildings form the setting of this breeding and acclimatisation centre whose 10 hectares are home to 120 species of birds and animals from five continents, most of whom roam free, with the exception of the big cats. Rides, play area, slides, water amusements, small aerial monorail train.

Take the D 266 through the hamlet of Moulin-à-Vent back onto the D 68.

Chénas

The Moulin-à-Vent windmill marks the border of border of Romanèche and Chénas. At only 280 hectares of land, this is one of Beaujolais' smallest AOCs. It produces an elegant relatively light wine for the most part, with the exception of the produce from the granite slopes below Pic Rémont.

The cellar of **Château de Chénas**, housed in a lovely 19C edifice, produces 45% of this village AOC and welcomes visitors. The **Domaine La Rochelle** is also an excellent choice for wine purchases *(see Shopping Guide)*.

There is a pleasant walk up to the **Cabane des Chasseurs** (hunting lodge) affording a fine view over the vineyards *(orientation table)*.

Juliénas

This village, whose name is said to be linked with that of Julius Cesar, is home to the 600 hectares of Juliénas AOC which produce excellent wines, many of which age very well. They can be tasted in the **Cellier de la Vieille Eglise**, where Bacchanalian revels have somewhat astoundingly replaced the customary pious images. *(open Jun–Sept 9.45am–noon & 2.30–6.30pm; Oct–May Wed–Mon 9.45am–noon & 2.30–6.30pm; 04 74 04 42 98)*.

Both the **Jean-Marc Monnet** and the **Domaine des Vieilles Caves estates** can be recommended for purchases *(see Shopping Guide)*.

Stretch your legs along a 2km-**signposted walk** through the vines, past the old church and cooperative cellar.

Treasure of Beaujolais

S. Sauvignier / MICHELIN

On the way out of the village, on the D 137, notice the lovely arcaded façade of the 16-17C **Maison de la Dîme** (tithe house).

Head towards St-Amour-Bellevue.

Saint-Amour-Bellevue

A number of terroirs with picturesque names such as Heaven or Madness can be found in the AOC. Seek out selections at the **Denis et Hélène Barbelet estate** *(see Shopping Guide)*. The area also produces white Saint-Véran and Mâcon wines, as it lies on the border with the Maconnais *(see BURGUNDY)*.

3 THE LAND OF GOLDEN STONE

59km. Villefrance-sur-Saône lies 30km N of Lyon by the A 6 or the N 6. Michelin Local Map n°327, G-H, 3-4.

See itinerary 3 on map p119.

The "land of golden stone" in the south of Beaujolais owes its name to the limestone houses, which turn a beautiful ochre hue as they catch the rays of the setting sun. It is an endearing region which offers visitors a picture of aristocratic graceful landscapes strewn with medieval villages guarded by rows of well-tended vines. The omnipresent vineyards produce Beaujolais and Beaujolais-Villages AOC wines which sometimes lack the finesse of their counterparts from northern Beaujolais, and are used to produce the majority of Beaujolais Nouveau. What they do offer is charm, and a round and fruity expression of the mild climate and generous soil of this land.

Leave Villefranche on the D 70 and turn left onto the D 39.

This attractive **ridge-top road**★ commands views over the Saône valley.

Anse

The town, at the confluence of the Azergues and the Saône, was a major halt in Gallo-Roman times. **Château de Tours** boasts a splendid late-2C mosaic depicting river traffic at the time.

(open Sat 3.30pm by appt.; 2€; 04 74 60 26 16, Pierres Dorées tourist office). Anse has a pleasant water-sports centre at Colombier, and a number of walking trails around the area.

Return onto the D 70 to the left.

Marcy

On the outskirts of this town *(access by a minor road signposted "Tour Chappe")* stands a telegraph **tower** built by Claude Chappe in 1799, whose semaphore mechanism with moveable arms (restored) was used to transmit visual messages up until 1850 *(open Sun Mar–Nov 2.30–5/6pm; 04 74 67 02 21)*.

Charnay

The remains of the fortifications of a 12C feudal castle can still be seen in this small country town at the summit of a hill. In the square, lined with limestone 15C and 16C houses, stands a **church**, which contains a Gothic statue of Saint Christopher (12C) in polychrome stone. Climb up to the top of the church tower to enjoy the panoramic view. Higher up, an impressive 17C castle, called La Mansarde, is now the town hall.

For wine tasting, try **Domaine des Terres Dorées** *(see Shopping Guide)*.

To the south of Charnay, take the narrow road to St-Jean-des-Vignes.

Saint-Jean-des-Vignes

The tiny high-perched church amid a riot of flowers in summer commands a fine view of the Lyon region.

The **Pierres Folles Museum** was founded to highlight important geological sites in the region. Displays, paintings and films illustrate the slow evolution of life on earth; outside there is a botanical garden that covers 8,400sq m and has over 500 species of plants. The remainder of the museum is devoted to displays on the local countryside and its industrial and tourist activities. *(open Mar–Nov, Tue–Sun; 5€; 04 78 43 69 20; www.espace-pierres-folles.com)*.

Return to D 30.

Chazay-d'Azergues

A belfry and a few 15C and 16C houses continue to add character to this fortified town overlooking the Azergues. The 15C castle *(closed to public)* was formerly the abode of the abbeys of Ainay.

Take the D 30 to Lozanne and the D 485 to Châtillon.

Châtillon

A 12C-13C fortress looms over this village, protecting the mouth of the Azergues valley. **Chapelle St-Barthélemy** *(steep walk up the hill signposted to the left of the parish church)*, extended in the 15C, originally stood within the walls of the fortress. Inside the chapel are paintings by Lavergen and H. Flandrin *(open mid-Apr–Oct Sun and public holidays 2.30–6pm; 04 78 43 92 66)*.

The Esplanade du Vingtain, further down, commands a fine view of the town.

Take D 485 lined with red slag heaps.

Chessy

The Late Gothic church contains a handsome 16C font and a statue of Saint Martha slaying a dragon. In earlier times, the locality was the site of a major copper seam belonging to Jacques Coeur. The ore obtained was known as "Chessylite", a variety of azurite with a beautiful blue colour, greatly prized by collectors. Just outside Chessy, in the village of Le Breuil, Chateau des Pertonnieres makes a good visit, where the Dupeuble family make quality Beaujolais from 40 hectares of Gamay and Chardonnay vines. Try their sparkling demi-sec rosé, launched in 2008 *(69620 Le Breuil; 04 74 71 68 40; Open 9am-noon & 2-6pm; www.beaujolaisdupeuble.com)*.

Take the D 19 to Bagnols.

Bagnols

A Watercolour Festival is held every year during the last weekend of July in this village whose 15C château has been turned into a hotel. Built at the same time, the **church** possesses a beautiful pendant keystone. Pretty 15C-16C houses with porches adorn the village square.

Head back onto the D 19 to the left. Stop at the hamlet of Le Boîtier.

Le Boitier

On the road leading out of the hamlet, on the right, is the Clos de la Platière once the home of Madame Roland, a famous French revolutionary.

Theizé

The pleasant village of Theizé is home to two castles: Rapetour in the lower part of the village and Rochebonne in the upper part. The **Chapelle Sainte Hippolyte**, with a Late Gothic chancel, is used for concerts and temporary art exhibitions. (*open Jul–Aug Wed–Mon 2-6pm; May–Jun & Sept–mid-Oct weekends and public holidays 2–6pm; 3.50€; 04 74 71 16 10).*

The **Château de Rochebonne** features a Classical façade. Exhibitions are held indoors where a handsome spiral staircase can still be seen. On the ground-floor is a wine centre poetically called "**Les Fiancés de l'automne**" (Autumnal Engagement).

The 13C stronghold of **Château de Rapetour** still boasts its original Gothic arched doorway, watchtowers, corbelled artillery holes and towers.

Oingt★

All that remains of the fortress of Oingt is Nizy gate which leads into this beautiful village that is perched high on a promontory, with charming pedestrian lanes, a 16C communal house and countless artisan workshops.

The view from the top of the **tower** over the Monts du Lyonnais and Beaujolais hills and of the Azergues Valley is quite stunning (*open Jul–Aug Mon–Fri 3–7pm; Apr–Jun & Sept weekends and public holidays 3–7pm; 45min guided tours available by appt.; 1.50€; 04 74 71 21 24).*

Saint-Laurent-d'Oingt

In addition to its unusual church with porch, this peaceful village also possesses a **cooperative**. *(69620 St-Laurent-d'Oingt; cellar: Mon-Fri 9am-noon & 2-6pm, Sat 9am-noon, Sun 3-7pm; 04 74 71 20 51; www.cavesaintlaurent.com).*

Coming in on the D 485, turn right.

Ternand★

Former bastion of the archbishops of Lyon, Ternand retains some of its fortifications: the keep and rampart walk afford fine views of the Monts de Tarare and Azergues Valley.

The Carolingian capitals of the chancel and mural paintings of the same period in the crypt make the **church** worth a visit (*guided tours by appointment; enquire at the town hall; 04 74 71 33 43).*

Another site of interest is the substantial collection of wine-growing tools accumulated by **Jean-Jacques Paire**, a Beaujolais producer from Ronzié (*open Jul–mid-Sept Tue–Sat 10am–7pm; mid-Sept–Jun Sat 10am–7pm or by appt.; 3€; 04 74 71 35 72).*

Make a U-turn, go through the town of Les Planches and continue on D 31

This **route**★★ over the Saule-d'Oingt Pass, is extremely picturesque with lovely old farmhouses overlooking fields and meadows dotted all over the hillside.

Right at La Maladière.

Jarnioux

The six-towered **castle** built in the 15C and 17C includes a particularly lovely Renaissance portion. Traces of the former drawbridge are visible in the majestic entrance providing access to two successive courtyards. (*open early Jul–mid-Jul & mid-Aug–late Sept by appt. 4€; 04 74 03 80 85).*

Take the D 116 towards Villefranche.

Liergues

Wine-making village whose fine Gothic chancel has medieval paintings.

Return to Villefranche on the D 38.

Oingt Village, Beaujolais

WINE BUYING GUIDE

INFORMATION

Union interprofessionnelle du Beaujolais – *210 bd. Vermorel, 69661 Villefranche-sur-Saône. ℘04 74 02 22 10. www.beaujolais.com.*

USEFUL TIPS

Almost half of Beaujolais wine-growers continue to practice the "métayage" (tenant farmer) system. Although it has disappeared from almost all the other wine-growing areas, this practice persists in Beaujolais because many of the vineyards belong to owners who live in Lyon or further afield. A métayer is responsible for the upkeep of the vines, their cultivation and wine-making, in exchange for which, depending on the contract, he receives roughly half of the benefits of each crop.

Beaujolais nouveau – Once a year on the third Thursday of November the entire wine-growing fraternity of Beaujolais frantically prepares dispatches of Beaujolais nouveau wine to the four corners of the earth. This uncomplicated wine, bottled less than three months after the harvest, has always represented a good deal for wine-growers who are able to quickly sell part of their stock. Recently, however, Beaujolais nouveau wines have suffered from a certain degree of disinterest on the part of consumers who are on the lookout for more distinctive wines.

The exceptional weather conditions of the summer of 2005 gave rise to the production of very good quality Beaujolais, this vintage is definitely worth looking out for. A warm July and sunny harvest period brought good results for 2006 as well, and the 2008 vintage was also of good quality.

WINE CHARACTERISTICS

The majority of Beaujolais wines are red, characterised by a deep ruby-red robe and the scent of soft red fruit and liquorice. Despite a healthy wine tang, the tannins are essentially silky.

STORAGE

Beaujolais wines can be kept for three to five years, sometimes longer in the case of good vintages. As they mature, they take on game and woody notes and "pinotent" similar to Burgundies.

PRICES

Beaujolais – 3 to 5€
Beaujolais-villages and other AOC – 5 to 15€

WINE MERCHANTS AND COOPERATIVES

Caveau des Beaujolais-Villages – *Pl. de l'Hôtel-de-Ville, 69430 Beaujeu. ℘04 74 04 81 18. Open May–Nov 10.30am–1pm & 2–7.30pm. Closed 3 weeks in Jan.*

This "bacchanalian temple" devoted to Beaujolais-Villages is located in the vaulted cellars of the town hall. A statue of Saint Vincent, patron saint of wine-growers and a wax effigy of Anne de Beaujeu watch over wine tastings of Beaujolais-Villages, white Beaujolais-Villages and Hospices de Beaujeu Beaujolais-Villages. New vintage: Pierre and Anne de Beaujeu.

Cave du Château de Chénas – *La Bruyère, 3.5km NE of Fleurie by the D 68, 69840 Chénas. ✆04 74 04 48 19. cave.chenas@wanadoo.fr. Open Mon-Sat 8am-noon and 2-6pm (Sat 7pm), Sun and public holidays 2.30-7pm; www.cavedechenas.com* The sumptuous Château de Chénas headquarters this association of wine-growers created in 1934, with a current membership of 110, and part of the Alliance des Vignerons de Beaujolais, created in 2003. The 250-hectare estate produces several AOC wines, including Moulin-à-Vent and Chénas, in its superb 17C vaulted cellars that date back to the time of Louis XIV.

La Maison des Vignerons – *Le Bourg, 3.5km SW of Fleurie by the D68, 69115 Chiroubles. ✆04 74 69 14 94. lamaisondesvignerons@wanadoo.fr. Open 10am–12.30pm & 2–6.30pm. Closed Jan 1, Dec 25.* Tucked away in the tiny village of Chiroubles, this makes wines from 100 hectares of Chiroubles, Fleurie, Morgon, Régnié and Beaujolais-Villages. Now merged with Cave de Belair in St Jean d'Ardieres (✆04 74 06 16 05, www.cave-belair.com), the boutique and cellars still warmly receive visitors.

Cave des Producteurs des Grands Vins de Fleurie – *Le Bourg, 69820 Fleurie. ✆04 74 04 11 70. www.cavefleurie.com. mid Apr-mid Oct 9.30am-1pm & 2.30-7pm, mid Oct-mid Apr Mon-Fri 9.30am-noon & 2.-6pm.* Created in 1927, this cooperative is the oldest in Beaujolais. It bottles one-third of the production of Fleurie, produces a range of "Cuvées Terroirs" (Chapelle des Bois, Garants, etc) and receives particular recognition for its Cardinal Bienfaiteur and Présidente Marguerite wines.

Cave Beaujolais de Quincié – *Le Bourg, 69430 Quincié-en-Beaujolais, 5.5km S of Beaujeu by the D 37E, then the D37. ✆04 74 04 34 17. www.cavedequincie.com. Open Mon–Fri 8.30am–noon & 2–6pm, Sat 9am–noon & 3–6pm, Sun 10am-noon & 3–6pm. Closed Jan 1, May 1, Nov 1, Dec 25.* The different AOC Beaujolais-Villages, Régnié and Brouilly wines of this cooperative established in 1928, with their exceptional fruity floral bouquets, regularly wins prizes and medals. A state-of-the-art sales and tasting room makes this an interesting visit.

La Maison des Beaujolais – *441 ave. de l'Europe, 69220 St-Jean-d'Ardières. ✆04 74 66 16 46. www.lamaisondesbeaujolais.com. Open daily, Thur-Sun noon–10pm, Tues-Wed noon-3pm. Closed Christmas holidays.* The sign outside leaves one in no doubt that the establishment is devoted body and soul to Beaujolais wine. Equipped with a tasting room, shop and restaurant, it provides an ideal introduction to the manifold delights of this wine-growing region.

ESTATES

Bruno Debize – *30 chemin des Prenelles, Apinost, 69210 Bully. ✆04 74 01 03 62. Open Mon–Sat 8am–7pm.* This 5-hectare estate employs biodynamic and organic methods in the cultivation of its Gamay, Chardonnay and Pinot Gris vines. Manual harvesting is followed by traditional winemaking methods using natural yeasts; the wines are never chaptalised. Aging takes place in oak. Beaujolais, Beaujolais Blanc.

Domaine des Terres Dorées – *69380 Charnay, ✆04 78 47 93 45. Open Mon–Fri 8.30am–noon & 2–5.30pm by appt.* Jean-Paul Brun has been in charge of the 22-hectare vineyard since 1979, cultivating Pinot Noir, Gamay and Chardonnay in a clayey-limestone soil. This wine-grower, reputed for his commitment to ancient techniques, uses only natural yeast in the wine-making process and chaptalisation is banished from a proportion of his production. The wines are fermented in concrete tanks and aged in oak barrels for six to ten months. Beaujolais, Côtes-de-Brouilly, Morgon, Moulin-à-Vent.

Domaine Bel Air – *69430 Lantignie. ✆04 74 04 82 08. www.dombelair.com Open Mon-Sat by appt.* Annick and Jean Marc Lafont have been making wine here for over 25 years, and produce excellent bottles from the grantic soils of Bel Air hil at Beaujeu. The vines have an average age of 40 years and vinification takes place in small temperature-controlled vats, followed by ageing in their impressive vaulted cellars.

Domaine Émile Cheysson – *Clos Les Farges, 69115 Chiroubles. 04 74 04 22 02. dcheysson@terre-net.fr. Open daily 8am–noon & 2–6pm.* Founded by the sociologst Émile Cheysson in 1870, and today run by Jean-Pierre Large, this 26 hectare vineyard is planted exclusively in Gamay. Granite and porphyry make up the soil in the high-altitude vineyard, and everything is harvested by hand.
The wines age in vats for 3 to 6 months for the Tradition vintage, while the Prestige is left in oak for a year. Mâcon is also produced here. Chiroubles.

Domaine A & A Desmures – *Le Bourg, 69115 Chiroubles. – 04 74 69 10 61. Open Mon-Sat by appt.* In the same family for four generations, the estate is run by Armand and Anne-Marie Desmures, and totals 6 hectares divided into 22 fields graced with a south, southwest exposure. The Gamay vines thrive in soils of granite and flint and gravel. Traditional methods entail minimal interference with the vines and manual harvesting. Chiroubles.

Domaine de la Madone – *69820 Fleurie. 04 74 69 81 51. www.domaine-de-la-madone.com. Open daily 10am–noon & 1.30-7pm.*Red-granite hillsides form this 13-hectare estate, farmed by the family of Jean-Marc Desprès for five generations. The vineyard, planted entirely in Gamay, faces south-southeast. Vine growth is carefully controlled, and traditional-style winemaking uses gravity. Beaujolais-Villages, Fleurie, Julénas.

Chateau des Labourons, Les Labourons, 69820 Fleurie. 04 74 04 13 04. Open Mon-Fri 8am-noon & 2-7pm, weekends by appt. Priska de Barry and Fabien de Lescure took over the running of their family wine estate two years ago, with 18 hectares of old vines making excellent quality organic Fleurie.

Domaine Jean-Marc Monnet – *69840 Juliénas. 04 74 04 45 46. Open 8am-*

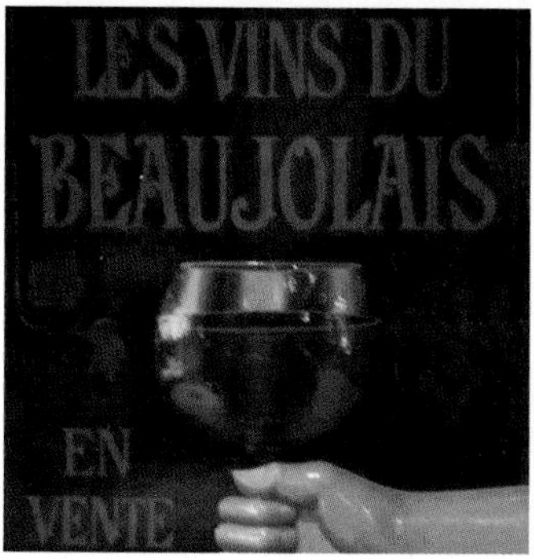

S. Sauvignier / MICHELIN

7pm. Jean-Marc Monnet is the third generation of his family to tend the vines on his 10-hectares estate. Farming methods are ecologically responsible; the grapes are hand-picked, the winemaking process is traditional. The estate also produces a Saint-Véran. Chiroubles, Juliénas.

Domaine des Vieilles Caves – *69840 Chénas. 04 74 04 48 24. Open by appt.* Fernand Charvet makes silky and seductive Chénas wines, as well as some of the most renowned Moulin-à-Vent. He is also the mayor of Chénas, and so a good source of information on the area and its wines. Beaujolais-Villages, Chénas, Moulin-à-Vent.

Château Thivin – *69460 Odenas, 04 74 03 47 53. www.chateau-thivin.com. Open Mon-Sat 9am-noon and 2-7pm.* Claude and Evelyne Geoffray, also the owners of the Manoir du Pavé at Saint-Lager, took over here in 1987 and are today helped by their son. Claude-Edouard At present, 15 hectares are devoted to AOC Côte-de-Brouilly, 6 hectares to Brouilly, 5 hectare to Beaujolais and Beaujolais-Villages. The estate also makes a white Burgundy. Hand harvesting precedes fermentation in stainless-steel tanks; the wine is then aged in oak casks down in the vaulted blue-stone cellar. Beaujolais, Beaujolais-Villages, Côtes-de-Brouilly.

Domaine des Grandes Vignes– *Chavanne, 69430 Quincié-en-Beaujolais. 04 74 04 31 02. www.ddgv.com. Open daily 9am–7pm.* Jacky and Jean-Claude make the third generation of winegrowers at this family estate. Gamay Noir and Chardonnay thrive in the 19-hectare vineyard. Hand harvesting is followed by fermentation in concrete vats for 6 to 10 days. Beaujolais-Villages, Brouilly, Côtes-de-Brouilly, Morgon, Moulin-à-Vent.

Château des Jacques – *71570 Romanèche-Thorins 03 80 22 10 57. www.louisjadot.com. Open by appt.* Bought by Louis Jadot in 1998, serious investments in the quality of the wine are really paying off. This attractive property has 35 hectares in Moulin-à-Vent. The best parts are spread over five clos - Clos de Rochegrès, covering 7 hectares; Clos du Grand Carquelin, 4 hectares; Clos de Champ de Cour, with 5 acres; Clos de la Roche, with 1.5 hectares; and Clos des Thorins, 3 hectares. Moulin-à-Vent, Morgon, Beaujolais-Villages.

Domaine Yvon Métras – La Pierre, 71570 *Romanèche-Thorins. 03 85 35 59 82. Open by appt.* The 6 hectares of this estate are planted entirely in Gamay Noir, and consist of heavily tilled granite on some of the steepest slopes of the region. Organic and traditional methods are employed in the winemaking process; around half the wine is aged in cement vats, the rest in oak barrels. Beaujolais-Villages, Fleurie.

Domaine Denis Barbelet – *Les Billards, 71570 St-Amour-Bellevue. 03 85 36 51 36. dhbarbelet@yahoo.fr. Open by appt.* Denis and Helene Barbelet employ ecologically responsible principles in the management of their 3-hectare vineyard, which is entirely planted in old vine Gamay Noir. Manual harvesting is followed by fermentation in concrete tanks. Afterward the wines are aged in oak barrels for 10 months; or in tank for 6 to 12 months. Saint-Amour.

Domaines Piron – *69910 Villie-Morgon 04 74 69 10 20. www.domaines-piron.fr. Open Mon-Sat 9am-noon & 2-6pm.* Dominique Piron works 60 hectares of vines, primarily in Morgon, at this highly regarded estate, alongside his American oenologist wife Kristine Mary. and their two daughters. Morgon, Beaujolais, Beaujolais-Villages, Brouilly, Régnié, Moulin à Vent, Chénas.

Domaine Jean-Marc Burgaud – *Morgon-le-Haut, 69910 Villié-Morgon. 04 74 69 16 10. www.jean-marc-burgaud.com. Open by appt.* Since 1989, the dynamic Jean-Marc Burgaud has run this 14-hectare vineyard to exacting standards, and is becoming increasingly well known. Planted in Gamay Noir, the estate practices ecologically responsible farming, with hand-harvesting and traditional wine-making including whole-grape maceration in concrete vats for 6 to 15 days. After that, they are left to mature in wood for 6 to 12 months. Particularly recommended is his Morgon Côte du Py. Beaujolais-Villages, Morgon, Régnié.

FESTIVALS

The arrival of Beaujolais nouveau is celebrated practically everywhere.
Belleville – Beaujolais nouveau kegs are tapped in the town hall cellar on 3rd Wednesday of November at midnight.
Juliénas – Wine Festival, 2nd or 3rd weekend of November.
Pommiers – Beaujolais nouveau pressing, 3rd Thursday of November.
Tarare – Beaujolais nouveau Festival, 3rd Thursday of November.

ADDRESSES

STAY

AROUND BEAUJEU

Chambre d'hôte Domaine des Quarante Ecus – *Les Vergers, 69430 Lantignié, 3.5km E of Beaujeu on the D 78. 04 74 04 85 80. 5 rooms.* This wine-growing estate offers a few rooms furnished in a mixture of old and new pieces and decorated with reproductions of works by Van Gogh. All command views over the vineyards or the garden and orchards. Breakfast is served in a lovely countrified room. Visit to the cellar and tasting of wines produced on the estate.

Chambre d'hôte Gérard Lagneau – *Huire – 69430 Quincié-en-Beaujolais – 5.5km SE of Beaujeu on the D 37– 04 74 69 20 70 – www.domainelagneau.com.*

4 rooms. This delightful stone-built house, nestled in the hamlet of Huire, is the property of a friendly wine-growing family who make it a point of honour to make sure you feel at home with them. Simple but faultlessly kept rooms. Breakfast is served in rustic, timbered room. Tasting of local wines in the 16C cellar.

Chambre d'hôte Mr and Mrs Bonnot – *Le Bourg, 69430 Les Ardillats, 5km NW of Beaujeu on the D 37. 04 74 04 80 20. Closed Jan. 5 rooms. Restaurant*. On the edge of the village, the stone façade and wooden shutters of this restored farmhouse immediately catch the eye. Colourfully decorated rooms with bare beams, each of which is named after a fruit: raspberry, pineapple, plum and mandarin. Tasty home cooking and as much Beaujolais as you can drink.

Domaine de Romarand – *69430 Quincié-en-Beaujolais, 5.5km SE of Beaujeu on the D 37. 04 74 04 34 49. Closed Jan 1, Dec 25. 3 rooms.* This lovely stone-built property overlooking a rockery garden and acres of vineyards belongs to a couple of wine-growers. The modern, comfortable rooms all command pleasant views. Homemade jams and pastries take pride of place on the plentiful breakfast table.

AROUND FLEURIE

Chambre d'hôte Domaine de la Grosse Pierre – *La Grosse Pierre, 69115 Chiroubles, on the D 119 towards Chiroubles. 04 74 69 12 17. www.chiroubles-passot.com. Closed Dec–Jan. 5 rooms.* An ideal choice for a prolonged stay in the heart of Beaujolais, this handsome manor surrounded by vineyards offers a handful of tasteful, if simply decorated rooms. Wine tasting in a vaulted cellar.

Chambre d'hôte les Pasquiers – *Les Pasquiers, 71570 Romanèche-Thorins, 2.5km SE of Fleurie on the D 119E. 04 74 69 86 33. www.lespasquiers.com. 4 rooms. Reservations required. Restaurant*. An immense walled garden surrounds this handsome Second Empire property many of whose original fittings and fixtures are still visible: carpets, library, grand piano in the sitting room, etc. The rooms in the main wing are furnished with lovely 19C antiques, while those in the outhouse are more "contemporary" in flavour.

Les Maritonnes – *71570 Romanèche-Thorins – 3.5km E of Fleurie – 03 85 35 51 70. www.maritonnes.com. Closed Dec 22 to Jan 20. 20 rooms. 13€. Restaurant*. This splendid property covered in Virginia creeper stands in the heart of well-tended parkland, offering spacious bright rooms. The restaurant serves traditional dishes served with the famous local wine: Moulin-à-Vent. A bistro area offers a simpler choice of menu.

AROUND ST-AMOUR

Hôtel Les Vignes – *Rte. de St-Amour, 69840 Juliénas, 3km SW of St-Amour-Bellevue on the D 17E. 04 74 04 43 70. www.hoteldesvignes.com. Closed Feb 7–22, Dec 21–28, Sun from Dec–Mar. 22 rooms. 11€.* On the road out of Juliénas, this hotel built on a hillside and surrounded by vineyards, offers colourful, renovated practical rooms. The Beaujolais-inspired breakfast, offers a choice of local cooked meats, is served in a sunny room and is more than worth a special mention. Friendly staff.

AROUND VILLEFRANCHE-SUR-SAÔNE

Hotel Émile Job – *12 r. du Pont, 01190 Montmerle-sur-Saône, 13km NW of Villefranche by the N6 to St-Georges-de-Reneins, then the D 20. 04 74 69 33 92. www.hotelemilejob.com. Closed Mar 1–15, Oct 22–Nov 14, Sun evenings Oct–May, Wed lunchtime Jun–Sept and Mon. 22 rooms. 7.50€. Restaurant*. A lovely, lime-shaded terrace along the banks of the Saône, a simple dining room, traditional cuisine and a family atmosphere all make for a pleasant experience. Rooms are bit dated, but still comfortable.

Saint-Romain – *Rte. de Graves, 69480 Anse, 7.5km NE of Charnay on the D 70. 04 74 60 24 46. Closed Nov 28–Dec 9, Sun evening from Nov–Apr. 24 rooms. 7€. Restaurant*. You could not do better than spend a night or two in this old stone farmhouse in the heart of Beaujolais where the only sounds that disturb the peace and quiet are those of birdsong and the wind in the leaves. The somewhat old-fashioned interior decoration of the rooms is fully compensated by their immaculate cleanliness and care. Tasty meals prepared with fresh produce in the restaurant.

⊜⊜ **Hotel Plaisance** – *96 ave. de la Libération, 69400 Villefranche-sur-Saône. ☎04 74 65 33 52. www.hotel-plaisance.com. Closed Dec 24–Jan 1. 68 rooms. 9€. Restaurant⊜⊜⊜.* This impeccably-kept family hotel fronts the Esplanade de la Libération. Rooms are decorating in various styles, well-maintained and clean.

⊜⊜⊜ **Le Clos de la Barre** – *14 r. de la Barre, 69400 Villefrance-sur-Saône. ☎04 74 65 97 85. www.leclosdelabarre.com. Open Apr1–Sept 30. 6 rooms.* Pretty ponds, masses of irises and century-old trees ornament the exterior of this 1830 house. Beautifully decorated rooms.

EAT

AROUND BEAUJEU

⊜⊜ **Auberge Vigneronne** – *Au Bourg, 69430 Régnié-Durette, 5km S of Beaujeu on the D 78 – ☎ 04 74 04 35 95. www.beaujeu.com. Closed Tue evenings Oct–Apr, and Mon.* Near the church, the lovely stone façade of this traditional restaurant also hides a tasting cellar. Two welcoming Beaujolais-style dining rooms, one of which has an open fireplace, and summer terrace.

⊜⊜ **Mont-Brouilly** – *Au Pont des Samsons, 69430 Quincié-en-Beaujolais, 5.5km SE of Beaujeu on the D 37. ☎04 74 04 33 73.* The owners of this pleasant restaurant at the foot of Mount Brouilly invite guests to discover the delights of traditional dishes cooked with local produce and accompanied by a fine wine list. The spacious dining room commands a peaceful view of the flowered garden.

AROUND BELLEVILLE

⊜⊜ **Beaujolais** – *40 r. du Maréchal-Foch, 69220 Belleville. ☎04 74 66 05 31. Closed Apr 13–16, Aug 4–26, Dec 22–29, Sun evenings, Tue evenings and Wed.* The culinary and decorative choices of this restaurant combine into a vibrant ode to Beaujolais: recipes and wine list, deeply anchored in local traditions, enhanced by a dining room whose local flavour and roots are equally present in the bare stone and timbers, rustic furniture and country objects.

⊜⊜ **L'Ange Couronné** – *18 r. de la République, 69220 Belleville. Closed Jan 3–25, Oct 3–11, Sun evenings, Tue lunchtime and Mon. ☎04 74 66 42 00.* On the main street of a former stronghold that is now a thriving wine-growing centre, a light contemporary dining room where you can tuck into reliable traditional dishes. The bedrooms, set around a winter garden, are sober and tasteful.

⊜⊜⊜ **Christian Mabeau** – *69460 Odenas, 15km NW of Villefrance by the D 43. ☎04 74 03 41 79. christian.mabeau@france-beaujolais.com. Closed Jan 2–12, Aug 30–Sept 12, Sun evenings and Mon except public holidays.* This small family restaurant in the heart of the village of Odenas lays a few tables on the terrace overlooking the vineyards as soon as the weather permits. A pleasant dining room where traditional recipes enhanced by local flavours are served in addition to a choice of regional wines.

AROUND ST-AMOUR

⊜⊜ **Chez Jean Pierre** – *71570 Saint-Amour-Bellevue – ☎ 03 85 37 41 26. Closed Dec 22–Jan 10, Sun evenings, Wed evenings and Thu.* The terrace and dining room of this attractive stone-built house provide a warm setting in which to savour the creative cooking of chef Alain Develay, such as wild mallard served with wild mushrooms.

⊜⊜ **L'Auberge des Vignerons-La Tassée** – *69840 Emeringes, 6.5km NW of Fleurie on the D 32. ☎04 74 04 45 72.* The bay windows of the wainscoted dining room offer a lovely view over the Beaujolais vineyards as you tuck into delicious traditional fare.

⊜⊜ **Le Coq à Juliénas** – *Place du Marché, 69840 Juliénas, 3km SW of St-Amour-Bellevue on the D 17E. ☎04 74 04 41 98. www.leondelyon.com. Closed Jan, Dec and Wed.* The boisterous strutting and cock-a-doodle-dos of the cockerel echo throughout the tasteful decor of this handsome country bistro. Here in the heart of the Beaujolais region, the cockerel however has a serious rival in the local wines and the excellent choice of regional vintages.

Le Villion – *Blvd. du Parc, 69910 Villié-Morgon. 04 74 69 16 16.* Fine old building overlooking the village, with a terrace facing the vineyard-covered hillsides. Traditional cooking.

Les Platanes de Chénas – *Aux Deschamps, 69840 Chénas, 2km N of Chénas by the D 68. 03 85 36 79 80. Closed Feb, Dec 23–28 Dec, Tue and Wed except in Jul–Aug.* In summer, meals are served mainly on the terrace overlooking row upon row of carefully tended vines. Beautifully prepared dishes ranging from regional recipes to more contemporary-inspired concoctions.

Restaurant Le Morgon – *Haut-Morgon, 69910 Villié-Morgon, 4.5km S of Fleurie on the D 68. 04 74 69 16 03. Closed Dec 15–Jan 20, public holidays, Tue evenings from Jan 20–Apr 1, Sun evenings and Wed.* The village of Villié-Morgon, in a landscape of vineyards, is an essential halting-point for all lovers of good wine. The Morgon Restaurant in the heart of this tiny town is the ideal choice for all those who are eager to combine fine vintages with tasty Beaujolais recipes.

Chez la Rose – *Place du Marché, 69840 Juliénas, 3km SW of St-Amour-Bellevue on the D 17E. 04 74 04 41 20. Closed Feb 8–28, Dec 13–17, Tue, Thu, Fri, Mon lunchtime, and Mon evenings out of season.* Your taste buds will begin to tingle as you approach the pleasant restaurant Chez la Rose in the heart of Beaujolais' vineyards whose rich soil and climate produce full-bodied robust wines which age particularly well. Carefully prepared regional dishes served in a country-style dining room or on a flower-decked terrace.

Restaurant Le Cep – *Place de l'Eglise, 69820 Fleurie. 04 74 04 10 77. Closed Dec, Jan, Sun and Mon except public holidays.* The owner of this proud embassy of the Beaujolais region, gave up luxury to devote herself wholeheartedly to her passion – regional cooking of undisputed authenticity.

Table de Chaintré – *71570 Chaintré, 4km northeast of St-Amour-Bellevue on the D 186. 03 85 32 90 95. Closed Aug 6-21, Dec 24–Jan 8, Sun evening, Mon and Tue.* In the heart of the Pouilly vineyards, this welcoming house is where Lucie Aubrac, famous resistance fighter, was born and lived. Comfortable contemporary-style dining room with a set daily menu and an excellent wine list.

AROUND VILLEFRANCHE-SUR-SAÔNE

Donjon – *64 Petite-Rue-du-Marché, 69620 Oingt. 04 74 71 20 24. Closed Mon and Tue.* Choose either the country-style dining room or the more contemporary one, but seek out a spot near the windows to drink in the view over the peaks of Lyon and Beaujolais.

Juliénas – *236 r. Anse, 69400 Villefranche-sur-Saône. 04 74 09 16 55. Closed Sun except public holidays.* This delightful bistro-style country restaurant will not empty your wallet as you tuck into a plate loaded high with inventive recipes which masterfully combine modern and traditional flavours. The wine list does full justice to the region's many delights.

GOURMET SHOPPING

Moulin à Huile – *29 r. des Echarmeaux, 69430 Beaujeu. 04 74 69 28 06. Open Mon–Sat 9am–noon & 2.30-7pm. Closed first week of Jan, Sun and public holidays.* In his parent's former ironmonger's shop, Jean-Marc Montegottero has set up an oil press to press oil traditionally. The old stone mill forgotten in a corner has come back into use and is once again working at full capacity. Argan, hazelnut and pine nut oil tastings after a visit of the workshop.

Yves Maringue – *269 rue Nationale, 69400 Villefranche-sur-Saône. 04 74 68 33 98. Open Mon–Sat 7.30am–1pm & 2-7.30pm.* The tiny shop of this master of charcuterie, rewarded countless times for his home-cured ham and saucisson, seems to overflow with mouth-watering terrines, pork pies, magnificent hams and hosts of other delicacies. The pastry-delicatessen shop a few yards away also belongs to Mr Maringue.

MARKETS

Anse – Friday morning
Beaujeu – Wednesday morning
Belleville – Tuesday morning
Juliénas – Monday morning
Villefranche – Monday morning and Sunday morning.

3 - BORDEAUX

The Romans introduced the vine to Aquitaine, although the wine produced at the time was of poor quality: laced with honey and enhanced with spices, it bore no resemblance to the quality bottles that mature in Bordeaux's cellars today. The vine still reigns supreme in the countryside around the city, and the region is a sea of green, dotted with a splash of colour from the occasional rosebush. Its vineyards extend right up to the edge of forests and towns., and the chateaux are opening up to visitors like never before. The itineraries listed below will provide a wonderful insight into this delightful region, from the most famous properties to tiny villages dedicated to the production of some of the world's finest wines.

Highlights

1. Climb the bell tower in Place du Marche for views over the vineyards of **Saint-Émilion** (p147)
2. Pair oysters with a glass of white wine in **Cap-Ferret** (p159)
3. Soak in a red-wine filled barrel at **Sources de Caudalie** (p145)
4. Take a wine class at Bordeaux's **Ecole du Vin** (p160)
5. Ride through the **Entre deux Mers** vineyards from the Creon Station Velo (p136)

Background

Although in evidence since the Roman conquest, the region's vineyards only really developed from the 4C onwards. And it wasn't until the 300 years of English domination, from the 12C to the 15C, that the reputation of Bordeaux's wines spread overseas. The wines enjoyed then were a pale, thin version of what the Bordelais produce today (known as clairet, the origin of the word claret meaning red wine, but in fact a light red more similar to today's rosé and a style still made in the region today), but they ensured the prosperity of a region which, from the Renaissance onwards, was of great commercial interest to merchants from Ireland, the Netherlands and Germany. In fact, it could be said that Bordeaux owes its success as much to these durable links as it does to its soil and climate, for it was these same traders who established a system based on merchants (négociants), estate owners and brokers (courtiers) which is still in place today – the first sold the wine, the second produced it, and the third acted as an intermediary.

Harvesting by hand in Saint-Émilion vineyard

S. Sauvignier/MICHELIN

The 18C was Bordeaux's Golden Age, with the creation of large handsome chateaux which were built from the profits of a burgeoning industry. A "cork aristocracy" subsequently developed, thanks to the famous classification of 1855, which established a ranking system for the properties of the Médoc and Sauternes.

A victim, like other areas, of phylloxera and other vine diseases, Bordeaux experienced difficulties in the mid 20th century, and again in recent years. But it has adapted and survived, and its best wines continue to reach enormously high prices at auction. Even if reforms are underway to face up to competition from the wines of the New World, the name Bordeaux remains synonymous with excellence.

OVERVIEW

The Terroir

Michelin Local Map 335 – Gironde (Département 33).

Area: 120 000ha in the Gironde *département* alone.

Production: 4.79 million hectolitres in 2008, representing 13% of total French *Appellation d'Origine Contrôlée* (AOC) production. with 54 appellations.

The climate is temperate-oceanic, characterised by relatively mild winters, wet springs, hot summers and sunny autumns.

Between the Garonne and the Dordogne (Entre-Deux-Mers), the soil is a mix of clay and limestone or clay and gravel. Gravel predominates on the left banks of the Garonne and Gironde, offering natural drainage for the vineyards. On the right bank of the Dordogne, the soil is clay or limestone (Blayais) or sand and gravel (Libournais).

Wines

The region can be divided into six main production areas:

Right bank of the Garonne – AOC Cadillac Cotes de Bordeaux, Saint-Macaire, Loupiac and Sainte-Croix-du-Mont.

Entre-Deux-Mers – AOC Entre-Deux-Mers, Haut-Benauge and Graves-de-Vayres.

Left bank of the Garonne – AOC Graves, Pessac-Léognan, Graves-Supérieures, Sauternes, Barsac and Cérons.

Libournais – AOC Fronsac, Canon-Fronsac, Pomerol, Lalande-de-Pomerol, Saint-Émilion, Saint-Émilion Grand Cru, Montagne-Saint-Émilion,Puisseguin-Saint-Émilion, Saint-Georges-Saint-Émilion, Lussac-Saint-Émilion, Saint Foy Bordeaux, Castillon Cotes de Bordeaux, Francs Cotes de Bordeaux

Blayais and Bourgeais – AOC Côtes-de-Bourg, Blaye Cotes de Bordeaux:

Médoc – AOC Médoc, Haut-Médoc, Moulis, Listrac, Saint-Estèphe, Pauillac, Saint-Julien, Margaux.

Bordeaux wines are blended using the following main grape varieties:

Reds and rosés: Cabernet Franc, Cabernet Sauvignon, Merlot, Malbec, Petit Verdot, Carmanere.

Whites: Sauvignon, Semillon, Muscadelle, Colombard, Ugni Blanc.

Useful Tips

While many larger estates welcome visitors, don't expect to taste the very best Grands Crus, whose prices have reached stratospheric levels.

As a rule, you're likely to receive a warmer welcome in the region's smaller estates, although in recent years many of the big names have opened boutiques.

Classifying Bordeaux

It was at the Paris Fair-Exhibition of 1855 that Bordeaux wines received their first classification, which was based primarily on cost. Only Médoc and Sauternes wines, as well as Château Haut-Brion in the Graves region, were included; Médoc wines were divided into five levels, and the wines of Sauternes three. In 1973, the classification was revised to include Château Mouton Rothschild in the list of Premiers Crus, but it has basically remained unchanged for over 150 years. In the 1930s, the Médoc also established the Crus Bourgeois category, which since 2009 is once again mark of quality on wine labels. In 1955, the wines of Saint-Émilion were also classified; this list is subject to a 10-yearly revision. The wines of the Graves region also have their own classification - and this is the only area that has both its red and white wines classified.

While they remain generally valid, wine classifications are subject to debate, and are contested on a regular basis… especially by those wine producers who do not appear in them. However, the only true classification is that of the consumer, who is able to compare the value for money that the wines are able to offer.

Right Bank of the Garonne

The right bank of the Garonne is bordered by hills which, for a distance of some 60km, form the appellation known as Castillon-Côtes-de-Bordeaux (formerly Premières **Côtes).This region is particularly attractive with fine landscapes dotted with small châteaux once occupied by the artists Henri de Toulouse-Lautrec and Rosa Bonheur, and the writers François Mauriac and Anatole France. The Cadillac-Côtes-de-Bordeaux appellation covers 6 400ha of clayey-limestone and clayey-gravelly soil. The area encompasses the Cadillac AOC** appellation, known for its liquoreux whites. First and foremost, the region produces well-constituted, robust reds, dominated by Merlot which gives the wines their characteristic overall roundness and suppleness. The rosés and *clairets* (pale reds) are a particular speciality of this area, where the whites range from mellow to liquoreux.

- **Michelin Map:** 335, H-J 5-7. Local map p140; on this map, the loop along the D 14 and D 20 is a suggested route for those wishing to visit the church in St-Genès-de-Lombaud, which is not described here.
- **Location:** Stretching southwards from the city of Bordeaux, on the right side of the Garonne river, this area ecompasses the beautiful steep slopes of the Cotes, and the gentle hills and valleys of Entre deux Mers.
- **Don't Miss:** The bastide towns such as Sauveterre de Guyenne and Creon.

DRIVING TOURS

1 CÔTES-DE-BORDEAUX

105km Bordeaux – Ste-Croix-du-Mont.

Bordeaux★★★

The capital of the wine industry is graced by long avenues and attractive town-houses with their limestone facades. For centuries a centre of trade, Bordeaux is vibrant, diverse city which continues to evolve: recent projects include a new tramway system, the renovation of the quays along with river, and the appearance of new parks and paved squares filled with pavement cafés.

More than 5 000 buildings dating from the 18C can be seen in the **old town**★★, situated between the Chartrons and St-Michel districts. The immense **esplanade des Quinconces** (126 000m^2) takes its name from the formal arrangement of the trees along one side. On the esplanade, note the striking **monument aux Girondins** with its two magnificent bronze **fountains**★.

At the end of place de la Comédie, the recently restored **Grand Théâtre**★★, built by the architect Victor Louis between 1773 and 1780, is considered to be one of the most beautiful theatres in France.

The attractive **place de la Bourse**★★, overlooking the banks of the river was laid out between 1730 and 1755. The square is bordered by the Palais de la Bourse to the north and the old Hôtel des Fermes, which houses the Musée National des Douanes, to the south. Directly in front of the Bourse, the Miroir d'Eau is one of the city's most striking attractions - a shallow reflective lake of 3450m2 designed by architect Michel Corajaud.

On **place du Parlement**★ the façades are adorned with mascarons carved into grotesque heads or representing vine branches and wine barrels.

The 11C-15C **Cathédrale St-André**★ is the most impressive church in Bordeaux. Its main features of architectural interest are the attractive 13C **Porte Royale**★, with its impressive sculptures, and a fine Gothic nave and **chancel**★ *(open daily*

9–11.30am & 2.30–5.30pm; first Sun of month 2.30–5.30pm, t 05 56 52 68 10).
The **Tour Pey-Berland**★, built in the 15C by the archbishop of the same name, has always stood separately from the rest of the cathedral. There is a wonderful panoramic **view**★★ from the top of the tower *(231 steps; open year-round; 5€; 05 56 81 26 25).*

Follow cours Pasteur.

Housed in the old university, the **Musée d'Aquitaine**★★ retraces the life of the people of Aquitaine from prehistoric times to the present day, with scenes illustrating traditional settlements and farming. It also contains France's first permanent exhibition to the country's role in the slave trade *(20 cours Pasteur; open Tue–Sun 11am–6pm; closed public holidays; 05 56 01 51 0; www. mairie-bordeaux.fr).*

Turn left into cours Victor-Hugo.

Note on your left the Porte de la **Grosse Cloche**★, all that remains of a 15C bell tower that once stood here.

Continue along cours Victor-Hugo and turn right into rue des Faures.

Construction of the **Basilique St-Michel**★ began in 1350 and lasted two centuries. This imposing building is dominated by the late-15C **Tour St-Michel** (114m), the highest bell tower in southern France *(open Jun–Sep, 2–7pm; 3€; 05 56 00 66 00; www. bordeaux-tourisme.com).*

Take the tram back along the river to esplanade des Quinconces.

In the Allées de Tourny you'll find the **Maison du vin de Bordeaux** *(See Shopping Guide) which has an excellent Wine School for getting an overview before heading out to vineyards.*
The Chartrons district, once the centre of the wine trade, lies to the north of place des Quinconces. The **Musée d'Art Contemporain**★ *(7 r. Ferrère)* is

A. Thuillier/MICHELIN

Place de la Bourse and Fontaine des Trois Grâces, Bordeaux

housed in the old **Laîné warehouse**★★, which was once used to store sugar. Its permanent collection illustrates artistic trends from the 1960s to the present day *(open Tue–Sun 11am–6pm; Wed 11am–8pm; closed public holidays; 5€, no charge first Sun of month; 05 56 00 81 50).*
Continue your visit on **cours Xavier-Arnozan**, where prestigious Bordeaux wine merchants have their offices, then walk up through the antiques of rue Notre Dame. The merchant's house at 41 rue Borie, built in 1720, is the only one in the area to boast an upper-floor storehouse and today hosts a small museum looking at the history of the area's wine traders.

Leave southeast on D 113, then follow the D 10 along the River Garonne.

Quinsac

This wine-producing village, situated on the edge of the city limits, has a **cave coopérative** which specialises in pale reds or clairets *(see Shopping Guide).*

Continue along the D 10 to Langoiran.

It is worth stopping at **Cambes** to admire the Romanesque church of St-Martin.
On the **Tabanac** hills overlooking the River Garonne stands the Château de Plassan (www.chateauplassan.fr), a unique example of Palladian architecture in the Bordeaux region.

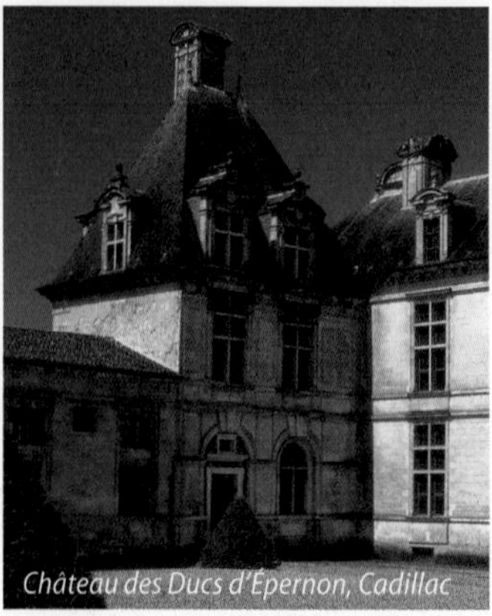
Château des Ducs d'Épernon, Cadillac

A. Thuillier / MICHELIN

Langoiran
A private association looks after the upkeep of the charming 13C **castle** in Langoiran. Surrounded by ramparts, the estates hosts various medieval festivals over the summer months. There is a splendid **view**★ of the Garonne valley from the esplanade *(open Jul–Aug 10am–12.30pm & 2–7pm; Sep–Jun 2–6pm; Closed Jan 1, Dec 25; 3€; 05 56 67 12 00).*

East of Langoiran in the **Capian** area, the attractive Château de Ramondon with its four delightful towers, is home to a vineyard that was the property of the kings of England until 1453. The area boasts some of the most beautiful châteaux in the *côtes*. Surrounded by four-hundred-year-old sequoias, the **Château du Sainte-Marie** in **Targon** produces excellent wines in the Entre deux Mers appellation *(see Shopping Guide).*

Rions
Enter this small fortified village through the Porte du Lhyan, a 14C gateway which has retained its original defensive appearance. Rions is a pleasant place for a stroll, with attractive old houses and a market hall dating from the 18C. In the village, stop at the *cercle* – this is the name for village bistros in this part of the Gironde – to taste the sweet white wine produced by the owner.

Before arriving in Cadillac, the road passes through the village of **Béguey**, home to the beautiful **Château Reynon**. This château produces a number of very good red, dry white and Cadillac liquoreux white wines under the aegis of Denis Dubourdieu, a renowned oenologist and the owner of the estate *(see Shopping Guide).*

Cadillac
This bastide, founded in 1280, gave its name to **Cadillac**, a small appellation of liquoreux white wine that ages extremely well.

Antoine de **Lamothe-Cadillac**, lord of the town (or more probably someone who simply borrowed the town's name), founded Detroit, which became the capital of the motor industry; the famous saloon car was created in his honour.

The **Château des Ducs d'Épernon** was built between 1598 and 1620. Of particular interest here are the eight richly decorated monumental fireplaces. *(open Jun–Sept 10am–1.15pm & 2–6pm; Oct–May Tue–Sun 10am–12.30pm & 2–5.30pm; closed Jan 1, May 1, Dec 25; 4.60€; no charge first Sun of month Oct–May; 05 56 62 69 58).*

At the southern exit to the town, the **Maison des Vins des Côtes-de-Bordeaux et de Cadillac** sells wine from most of the region's wine producers.

Loupiac
The **Loupiac** AOC lies just below Cadillac, directly opposite from Barsac and Sauternes on the left bank of the river, and like them makes fine liquoreux white wines; the **Château Dauphiné-Rondillon** is particularly reputed for its excellent wines *(see Shopping Guide).* The town already existed in Roman times, as vestiges of a **Gallo-Roman villa** in the Château le Portail Rouge testify; note the beautiful mosaics in the baths *(guided tours by appt,; 3€; contact the Château le Portail Rouge, 05 56 62 93 82 or 06 07 01 64 88).*

Continue to Verdelais on D 117.

Verdelais
Notre-Dame de Verdelais **basilica**, which is said to protect the afflicted, is dedicated to the Virgin Mary. Rebuilt

in the 17C, its walls are almost entirely covered with **ex-votos**.
In the peaceful cemetery to the right of the basilica lies the grave of the painter **Henri de Toulouse-Lautrec-Monfa** (1864-1901). His simple tombstone can be seen at the end of the central pathway, on the left-hand side. Among the several worthy estates here, we recommend **Château Les Guyonnets** *(see Shopping Guide).*

Continue 3km NEon D 19.

Château de Malromé

Open for tastings by appt.
05 56 76 44 92. www.malrome.com.
Built in the 14C and enlarged in the 16C and 19C, this château was home to Toulouse-Lautrec, who spent the last few years of his life here with his mother, Countess Adèle de Toulouse-Lautrec. The famous painter died at the age of 37. The château comprises four buildings arranged around a courtyard: the seigniorial dwelling, the staff quarters, the wine storehouse and the stables. Toulouse-Lautrec is portrayed on the château's wine labels and there is a small museum about his life.

Rejoin D 19; south to St-Macaire.

Domaine de Malagar

Open Jun–Sept guided tours (30min) 10am–12.30pm & 2–6pm. Oct–May Tue–Sun 2–5pm, weekends and public holidays 10am–12.30pm & 2–6pm. Closed May 1, Dec 22–Jan 1. 5.50€. 05 57 98 17 17. http://malagar.aquitaine.fr/.
Overlooking the St-Maixant valley, this estate was once the holiday home of the writer **François Mauriac** (1883-1970). A museum in one of the storehouses is dedicated to his life and work. A walk through the beautiful gardens leads to the stone terrace where Mauriac used to enjoy the view of his vineyards and the Landes in the distance.

Saint-Macaire★

This medieval town overlooks the River Garonne. The **Côtes-de-Bordeaux-St-Macaire** appellation, which covers the area to the southeast, is little used. The **Maison du Tourisme en Coteaux Macariens** sells local wines and organises wine-tastings, as well as providing information on walks through the vineyards (*open Jun–Sept 10am–1pm & 3–7pm; Oct–May Tue–Sun 10am–noon & 2–6pm).*
The **walls** of the town, which have retained three old gates, date back to the 12C. Also of interest is **Église St-Sauveur** (13C-14C) which overlooks the valley; note the 14C **wall paintings**★ in the transept crossing and on the vault of the eastern apse. There is a view of the River Garonne from the terrace.
The Place du Mercadiou or Marché-Dieu, is surrounded by Gothic and Renaissance structures, and handsome 15C–16C residences.

Cross the Garonne on the N 113 and continue along this road to Sainte-Croix-du-Mont.

Sainte-Croix-du-Mont★

This hilltop village has given its name to liquoreux and moelleux AOC white wines, which are very fruity and less heady than Sauternes.
From the terrace of the Château de Tastes *(now the town hall)*, there is a fine **view**★ south to the Pyrenees from the viewing table. Admire the Romanesque door of the **church** at the end of the hill. **Caves**★ can be seen below, dug out from a bed of fossilised oysters. Of the many interesting estates in this appellation, Chateau de Vertheuil makes excellent wines and is open for visits (8.30am-12.30pm, 2pm-6pm. 05 56 62 02 70).

Chateau de Roquetaillade★★

10km SW of St-Macaire by the D 222.
Visit by guided tour only (1hr, last departure 1hr before closing) Jul–Aug 10.30am–6.30pm. Rest of the year Sunday, public holidays and school holidays visits at 3pm and 4pm. Closed Dec 25. 7€. 05 56 76 14 16. http://chateau roquetaillade.free.fr.
This imposing chateau was built in 1306 by Cardinal Gaillard de la Mothe, nephew

of the French Pope Clement V. An striking example of feudal architecture, the structure is part of a compound of two fortresses (12C and 14C) built within the same outer wall.
The interior is equally dramatic but dates from a 19C renovation, with an elaborate staircase in the entrance hall; early Art Nouveau in the dining room; and incongruously ornate **pink and green** bedrooms. There is a small farm outside for children.

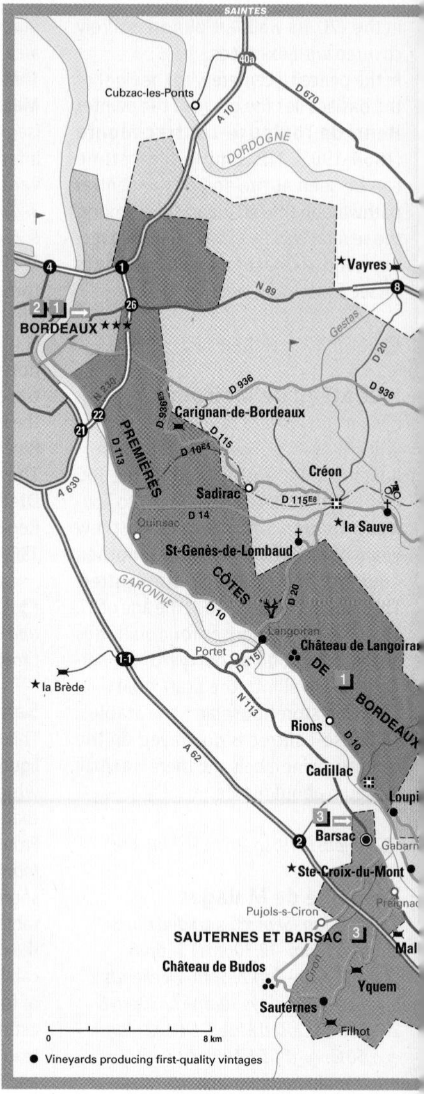

2 ENTRE-DEUX-MERS

115km starting from Bordeaux.
The rolling green hills of the Entre-Deux-Mers region between the River Garonne and River Dordogne are covered with vineyards, small copses and meadows. The **Entre-Deux-Mers** AOC label is granted to dry white wines from the region made predominantly from Sauvignon grapes. These fruity wines are an excellent accompaniment for oysters from the Arcachon basin.

Leave Bordeaux to the E along the D 936 and turn right onto the D 936E5.

Carignan-de-Bordeaux

The **Ginestet wine company**, founded in 1897, is open to the public, providing visitors with information on not only wine production but also the commercial side of Bordeaux.
(1h30min guided tour by appt; 9am–12pm, 2–5pm, closed weekends & public holidays; 05 56 68 81 82; www.ginestet.fr.)

Head SE along the D 10E4, then turn onto the D 115.

Sadirac

Housed in an old workshop, the **Maison de la Poterie-Musée de la Céramique Sadiracaise** displays ceramics dating from the 14C-18C (*open Tue–Sun 2–5pm; Wed 2-4pm closed public holidays; 2€. 05 56 30 60 03).*
Also of interest is the fascinating **"Oh! Légumes oubliés"**, a farm growing and selling rare plant and vegetable varieties (*open Apr–Nov Mon-Sat 2–6pm; 7.90€; 05 56 30 62 00; www.ohlegumesoublies.com).*

Follow the D 115^{E8} and the D 671 to Créon.

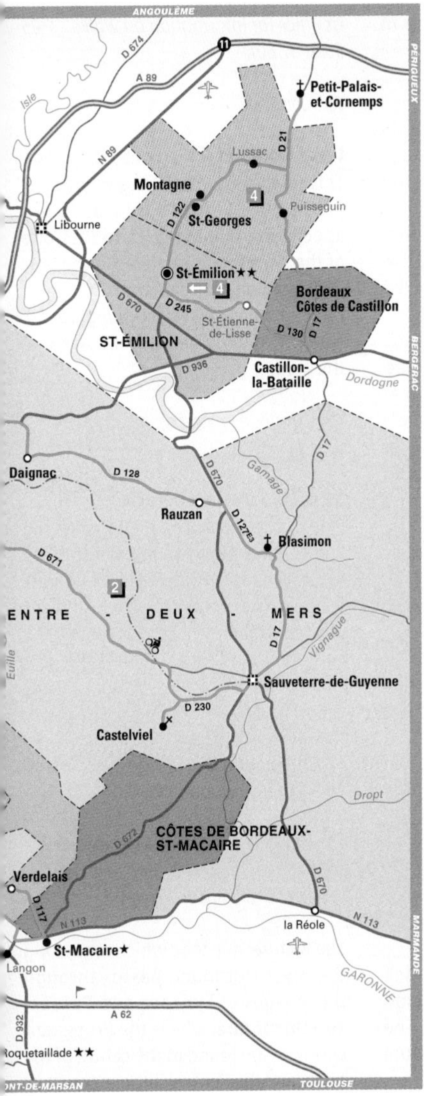

Créon

Centred on an attractive 14C arcaded square, this old English bastide village holds a lively market every Wednesday morning. Créon was the first village in the Gironde to be awarded the **Station Vélo** (Cycling Resort) label; a large number of bicycles are available for hire in the old railway station.

An attractive 16km cycle route, "Les Vignes du Seigneur", can be followed through the vineyards *("La gare", blvd. Victor-Hugo, 33670 Créon; 05 57 34 30 95; http://creonstation-velos.free.fr; open May 16-Nov 15 8.30-12.30, 1.45-6.45pm, Feb-May 15 8.30-12.30pm, 1.45-5.30pm, closed Nov 16-Feb 1.*

A number of good vineyards for white wine are found in Creon, including Chateau Bauduc and Chateau Thieuley (see Shopping Guide).

La Sauve★

The **old Abbaye de la Sauve-Majeure**★, founded by the Benedictines in 1079, was once a powerful landowning estate.

It became a prison in 1793, and was subsequently used as a quarry before being completely abandoned. The abbey is a good example of the transition from the Romanesque to Gothic architectural styles.

Note the magnificent **capitals**★ on top of the columns in the right bay of the chancel. Remains of the 13C cloister, chapter house and refectory can be seen to the right of the abbey building *(open Jun–Sept 10am–6pm; Oct–May Tue–Sun 10.30am–1pm & 2.00–5.30pm; closed Jan 1, May 1, Dec 25; 7€; 05 56 23 01 55).*

The **Maison de l'Entre-Deux-Mers**, housed in the abbey's old tithing barn, provides information on local wines, which can be tasted and purchased here at estate prices *(see Shopping Guide).*

Continue along the D 671. At St-Brice, turn right and follow the D 123 and D 230.

Église de Castelviel

The main feature of interest in this church is the superb Saintonge-style **Romanesque doorway**★. Note the rich carving on the capitals and arches, which makes this one of the most beautiful architectural monuments in the Gironde.

Sauveterre-de-Guyenne

This typical bastide, built by Edward I in 1281, finally became French in 1451 after changing hands between the French and English no fewer than 10 times. The village has retained its four fortified gates and a large, attractive arcaded square, which comes to life every Tuesday on market day. Around fifty regional wines can be tasted and purchased in the **Maison du Sauveterrois**, which also provides information on walks in the area. Increasingly renowned wines are also available for tasting at **Château des Léotins** (*see Shopping Guide*).

Head E along the D 230. This circuit is not shown on the map on p140.

Castelmoron-d'Albret

The smallest *commune* in France (3.5ha) stands on a rocky outcrop surrounded by fortifications. About 60 people live in this charming village.

Continue along the D 230, then turn immediately left onto the D 139.

Abbaye de Saint-Ferme

Open Jun–Sept Tue–Sat 2.30–6pm. Oct–May Tue–Fri 2.30–5pm. 3.50€. 05 56 61 69 92.

This Benedictine abbey was founded in the 11C, on the route to Santiago de Compostela in northern Spain. The courtroom, scriptorium and a museum of old tools are open to the public.

Continue north on D 16 & D 672.

Pellegrue

Two attractive Romanesque churches can be seen in this old bastide town which also has a traditional market sqaure.

Several wine estates, such as the medieval Château de Lugagnac (*www.chateaudelugagnac.com*), are dotted around the vineyards amid rolling scenery that is perfect for walkers (*contact the tourist office for information on walks; 05 56 61 37 80*).

Continue along the D 672.

Les Lèves-et-Thoumeyragues

This small wine-producing town, situated in the **Sainte-Foy-Bordeaux** appellation, is home to **Univitis**, one of the largest cooperatives in the Bordeaux region, vinifying over 2,000 hectares of vines (*see Shopping Guide*). Note the gabled bell tower, typical of the area.

Continue to Ste-Foy-la-Grande along the D 672.

Sainte-Foy-la-Grande

One of the most colourful markets in France is held in this 13C bastide every Saturday. Once a Protestant stronghold, Sainte-Foy is proud to be the birthplace of several famous citizens, including the surgeon Paul Broca, the art critic Elie Faure, and the geographers and anarchy theorists, Élie and Élysée Reclus. Note the splendid medieval house in rue de la République, whose façade is decorated with strange wooden carvings.

Leave Sainte-Foy-la-Grande to the south along the D 672, then turn right onto the D 130 toward Eynesse.

The picturesque road which runs along the River Dordogne passes through the villages of **Eynesse** and **Pessac-sur-Dordogne**, where the Protestant churches are found in the centre of the town, and the Roman Catholic churches on the outskirts. Search out the gravestones, mostly Protestant, among the vines. Wine estates to visit include Chateau de Carbonneau which is run by a New Zealand-French couple, has very attractive gardens and a popular chambres d'hotes (*www.chateau-carbonneau.com, 05 57 47 46 46*)

Gensac

This hilltop village, with its splendid viewpoint from "Calvin's throne" on the old ramparts, overlooks the Durèze valley. The efficient **tourist office** is able to provide information on a wide range of walks in the area and also sells local wine at estate prices. *(05 57 47 46 67).*

Continue W to Pujols along the D 18.

Pujols

A lovely view of the countryside can be admired from the remains of the old feudal castle, now the town hall. The area produces good dry Bordeaux whites. Just outside of Pujols, in St Pey de Castets, Chateau Cablanc winery offers an excellent nature trail arund its own private valley, where children can learn about winemaking through games and explanatory boards along the walk, and then enjoy a picnic at the end on tables that overlooks the vines (*05 57 40 52 20, www.chateaucablanc.com. Open Jun-Sept daily 11am-7pm, Apr-May 11am-6pm. 5€*).

Head SW to Blasimon on D 17.

Before entering the village, note the **Moulin de Labarthe**, an interesting example of a fortified medieval mill.

Blasimon

Hidden at the bottom of a valley is an old Benedictine **abbey**, now in ruins. Admire the Romanesque and Gothic features in its 12C-13C church *(open Mon–Fri by request; weekends no restrictions; enquire at the tourist office; 05 56 71 59 62).*

Rauzan

The **Château de Rauzan**, built in the late 13C, has retained its magnificent keep (30m). Also worthy of note is the late-15C tower decorated with striking rib vaulting *(open Jul–Aug 10am–noon & 2–6pm; rest of the year Tue–Sun 10am–noon & 2–5pm; guided tours by reservation; 3€; 05 57 84 03 88).*

Pujols

© Jimjag/Fotolia.com

The **Grotte Célestine** is worth visiting for its varied stalactites and stalagmites, and stunning rock formations. Visitors can walk the 250m through 5–15cm of water to admire these fascinating natural features *(45min guided tours daily Jul–Aug 10am–noon & 2–6pm; rest of the year Tue–Sun 10am–noon & 2–5pm; 6.50€; 1.20m minimum height requirement; 05 57 84 08 69; www.rauzon.fr; reservations required; 14°C in the cave so bring a sweater, all other equipment is provided).*

The **Union des Producteurs de Rauzan** is one of the largest wine cooperatives in France *(see Shopping Guide).*

Return to Bordeaux along the D 128 towards Daignac, then take the D 936.

Montesquieu

In 1689, **Charles de Segondat**, the future Baron de Labrède et de Montesquieu, was born at the château. Montesquieu later became President of the Parliament of Bordeaux (despite considering himself a mediocre magistrate), but preferred the peace of the countryside to the town and was often found at his La Brède property: "It is the most beautiful rural scenery that I know."

At the château, he would take care of his business correspondence (he sold much of his wine to England), walk in his vineyards and visit his storehouses. Of an even and easy-going temperament, Montesquieu, like Montaigne, found his intellectual work relaxing: "Study has been for me the main antidote to life's problems – I have never had a worry that could not be cured by an hour's reading."

Left Bank of the Garonne

On the left bank of the Garonne and the outskirts of Bordeaux, the name for the Graves region comes directly from its soils, which is made up of small stones. Cultivated for grape production since the Middle Ages, these well-drained gravelly hills were created by the erosion of the Pyrenées. The biggest concentration of big name chateaux is found in the northern section of Graves, which was granted the Pessac-Léognan AOC in 1987 in recognition of its strong concentration of good quality properties. The southern Graves comprises the Barsac and Sauternes appellations where the best sweet wines of the region are made (*see tour 3***). The smaller Graves-Supérieures AOC area also produces sweet white wines. The Maison des Vins de Graves in Podensac is avery attractive building that houses are large wine shop where you can try many of the wines.**

- **Michelin Map:** Sauternes driving tour (3) is marked on the map on p140. For the Graves Vineyards, see Michelin Map 335, H-I 6-7.
- **Info:** www.sauternais-graves-langon.com
- **Location:** The Left Bank is not just the Médoc (p154), but also the land stretching south of Bordeaux from the Jalle de Blanquefort to the handsome market town of Langon, containing some of the oldest vineyards of the region.
- **Don't Miss:** The historical monuments of Chateau de la Brede and Chateau de Malle. The white wines of the region should also be sought out.

DRIVING TOURS

THE GRAVES VINEYARDS

57km.Head SW out of Bordeaux on N 250; follow signs to "Pessac Centre".

Pessac

Less than 4km from the centre of Bordeaux, **Château Haut-Brion** is nowadays completely surrounded by suburbs. This Premier Cru wine was first listed in 1855. With its vineyards covering an area of 43ha, the château - and its sister property of La Mission Haut Brion across the street - produce some of the most celebrated wines of the region, and organise efficient visits. They also have a barrel maker on site (*see Shopping Guide*). Another renowned estate in the area is **Château Pape-Clément** which belonged to Bishop Bertrand de Got during the Middle Ages, later to become Pope Clement V, and today to Bernard Magrez, who owns a number of chateaux both in Bordeaux and further afield. The 19C neo-Gothic château is particularly imposing and has been restored to a very high standard. There is a slick tourist circuit, plus an excellent wine boutique that is open seven days a week, holding regular tasting evenings (*see Shopping Guide*).

Rejoin the bypass heading towards Toulouse. Leave the ring-road at exit 18 and take the D 651 to Léognan.

Léognan

It is well worth visiting the **Domaine de Chevalier** with its ultra-modern wine cellars and excellent wines;. At **Château Carbonnieux** an interesting historical anecdote relates how "Carbonnieux water" sent to the Sultan of Constantinople in the 18C was in fact an excellent white wine produced by local monks. Today, the white wines are equally well recognised, and often reach higher prices than the estate red (*see Shopping Guide*).

Château La Louvière is a beautiful late-18C château designed by the archi-

tect François Lhote, which became a listed building in 1991.
New cellars opened in 2009 and there is a large boutique that sells wines from a number of Bordeaux properties, all belonging to André Lurton *(149 ave. de Cadaujac, 33850 Léognan; open by appt. Mon-Fri, 9am-noon & 2-5pm; Sat 9am-noon by appointment. 05 56 64 75 87; 5€ www.andrelurton.com).*

Head southeast along the D 109 to Martillac.

Martillac

Known both for wine and its lily of the valley perfume, this village has an attractive **Romanesque church** with a highly ornate interior. Close by, the aptly-named **Domaine de la Solitude** was a 16C-18C convent which is now a good quality wine estate *(33650 Martillac; open by appt. Mon–Fri 8.30am–12.30pm; 05 56 72 74 74; www.domainedelasolitude.com).*
Château Smith-Haut-Lafitte is home to a wine estate and a vinotherapy centre, **Les Sources de Caudalie**, as well as a good quality hotel. The spa offers an interesting range of treatments, combining a mineral-rich water taken from their own underground spring with the antioxidant benefits of grape extracts and grape seed oil, all of which help to moisturise and tone the skin. Treatments on offer vary from a Chardonnay facial scrub to sitting in a wine-barrel jacuzzi in grape-extract juice. It's rather pricey (the "half day discovery" costs 195€) but it is undoubtedly a good way to splurge *(Chemin de Smith-Haut-Lafitte, 33650 Martillac, 05 57 83 82 82; www.sources-caudalie.com)*
Good places to stock up on wine include **Château Latour-Martillac** and **Château Haut Bailly** which has a small outport of the Mollat bookshop in Bordeaux (*see Shopping Guide*).

Follow the D 109 south to La Brède.

The road now enters the Graves du Sud region, a vast wine-producing area once home to Montesquieu, where the vineyards stretch between the River Garonne and the Landes forests of the Gironde.

Château de La Brède★

Visit by guided tour (30min) only, Jul–Sept Wed–Mon 2-6.45pm. Early-Oct–mid-Nov weekends and public holidays 2–5.30pm. Apr–Jun weekends and public holidays 2–6.30pm. 7€. 05 56 20 20 49.
The austere silhouette of this Gothic-style château is reflected in its moat, making your walk up to the main building rather dramatic. The building dates from the 12C-15C, and it has hardly changed since it was inhabited by the writer Montesquieu. The tour starts at the moat, which is crossed by small bridges linking two old fortified structures. On the first floor is the 5,000-book library and Montesquieu's simple **room**, furnished exactly as it would have been during the writer's residence.

Head east along the D 108, then turn right onto the N 113.

Portets

The lofty silhouette of the 18C **Château de Portets** dominates this village on the banks of the Garonne. The **Musée de la Vigne et du Vin** at the **Château Lagueloup** displays an interesting collection of equipment found in the wine storehouses. *(open Jul-Aug 10am–6pm; Sept-Jun Sat-Sun 2-6pm; 6P 05 56 67 13 90).*

Head southeast to Podensac along the N 113.

Podensac

This large village is the home of **Lillet**, a wine-based aperitif flavoured with herbs and quinine that is available in both red and white versions, and is the typical early-evening drink of the Bordeaux region. The distillery, which has a collection of Art Deco vats and labels, is open to the public *(open mid-Jun–mid-Sept 9am–6pm; mid-Sept–mid-Jun Mon–Fri 9.30am–5pm by appt; 05 56 27 41 41; www.lillet.com).*

Follow the N 113 to Cérons.

Cérons
This tiny appellation of liquoreux wines covers an area of less than 100ha.

Head S along the N 113 to Barsac.

3 SAUTERNES AND BARSAC
30km. Barsac lies 40km SE of Bordeaux by the N 113. *See map p140.*

The Sauternes and Barsac vineyards are located near the confluence of the Ciron with the Garonne. The AOC **Barsac** wines are also entitled to use the **Sauternes** appellation. The grapes for both wines are allowed to undergo the process of "noble rot" or *botrytis cinerea*, which is caused by the mist rising from the River Ciron - Sauternes gets around 100 misty or foggy days in a year on average. It is the enzymes in this mould that concentrate the sugars in the grape.

Barsac
Altogether Barsac is home to a dozen châteaux whose architectural styles are as elegant as their wines; **Château Climens** and **Château Coutet** are of particular interest (*see Shopping Guide).*

Château Nairac (17C-18C) is an attractive example of the Classical style, both in terms of its architecture and its wine. Today owned by the Heeter-Tari family, the rose gardens are open to the public, and make for a charming visit in summer *(33720 Barsac; open by appt.; 05 56 27 16 16, www.chateau-nairac.com).*

Pujols-sur-Ciron
Clos Floridène, headed by Denis Dubourdieu, a renowned professor of oenology who specialises in white wine and consults at a number of leading properties in the region, produces elegant dry white wines here at his own family estate (*see Shopping Guide).*

Sauternes
Visitors are assured of a warm welcome at the **Maison du Sauternes.** The mysteries of noble rot and the Sauternes production process are explained here and some 70 wines are available at estate prices (*see Shopping Guide).*

Northwest of Sauternes, the village of Bommes is home to the prestigious **Château La Tour Blanche**, which was given to the state in 1909 by the philanthropic financier Daniel Iffla and now houses a wine school as well as a working chateaux that offers good tours and tastings. *(open Mon–Fri 9am–noon & 2–5pm by appt.; 05 57 98 02 73; www.tour-blanche.com).*

Château d'Yquem
www.yquem.fr.

L:ocated at the highest point of the Sauternes appellation, the wines produced by this prestigious château enjoyed a fine reputation as early as the 16C; they were much appreciated by Thomas Jefferson. The château (*not open to the public*), dates from the 15C and 17C, and even from the road you can see its attractive lines, and the large trees in the grounds. The chateau was a military hospital during WW1, and the cedar tree in the gardens was planted by recovering patients at the end of the war.

Château de Malle
Open Apr–Oct 2–6pm; guided tours (30min) mornings by appt. 7€. 05 56 62 36 86. www.chateau-de-malle.fr.

This attractive estate has Italian-style summer gardens and the interior houses a 17C collection of trompe l'oeil silhouettes, unique in France. There are also over 50 hectares of vines, in the Sauternes, red Graves and white Graves appellations. These are Château de Malle, Sauternes, "Grand Cru Classé" in 1855, Château de Cardaillan, a red Graves, and the M. de Malle a dry white Graves., so a good range of styles to try during your visit. Although unihabited for two centuries, the same family has owned this property since it was built in circa 1620. In the 1950s, the family undertook extensive renovations, not only of the château itself but also completely replaning the vineyards.

Take the D 8E4 to Preignac; return to Barsac along the N 113.

Libournais

The River Dordogne widens to the west of Libourne, joining the Garonne at Bec d'Ambès. On the right bank of the river lie the gentle rolling hills of the Fronsadais vineyards. East of Libourne, the renowned wine-producing areas of Pomerol and St-Émilion stand in the heart of a region with a rich historical past.

- **Michelin Map:** 335
- **Location:** Attractive vineyards on slopes and limestone plateaux around 40km east from Bordeaux, along the Dordogne river.
- **Don't Miss:** The medieval village of Saint-Émilion, with its underground monuments.

DRIVING TOURS

4 SAINT-ÉMILION AREA

52km. St-Émilion lies 40km E of Bordeaux by the D243. *See map on p140.*

St-Émilion, the most beautiful wine-producing village in the Bordeaux region, is listed as a UNESCO World Heritage Site. This attractive village of limestone houses and red-tiled roofs is set amid rolling hills carpeted with vines, and is entirely dedicated to wine. It is partly as a result of the limestone sub-soil that the vines here produce such high-quality wines, and partly as a result of the slow ageing process which takes place in old quarries now used as wine cellars.

The St-Émilion vineyards cover an area of 5,400ha, extending across nine *communes*. Other "satellite" appellations, such as Montagne, Puisseguin, Lussac and St-Georges, cover an area of just under 4 ,000ha.

Both AOC Saint-Émilion and AOC Saint Emilion Grand Cru can be produced in the geographic region of Saint-Émilion, but only the latter appellation can further classify its wines, with a ranking system dating from 1955, and revised every ten years.

Saint-Émilion★★

Excellent views of the village and surrounding area can be enjoyed from the top of the church bell tower or from the Tour du Roi. Local specialities here include St-Émilion **macaroons**, a delicious biscuit made from almonds, sugar and egg whites.

Start your tour of the village with the monuments in the **Place du Marché** (*guided tours only: tickets from the tourist office)*. Of particular interest is the underground **monolithic church**★ built

St-Émilion and its famous vineyards

S. Sauvignier/MICHELIN

from "a single stone" between the late 8C and 12C, the largest of its kind in Europe. The interior is striking for its wide aisles carved into the rock and for the imposing quadrangular pillars. The **collegiate church** above the place du Marché is a huge building with a Romanesque nave and Gothic chancel. Entrance to the church is through a magnificent doorway dating from the 14C. Of particular interest in the chancel are the imaginatively carved characters adorning the 15C **choir stalls**. The 14C **cloisters**, refectory and monks' dormitory, all of which have been restored, form the "Doyenné", which now houses the local tourist office.

The four sights that follow are open by guided tour (45min). Hours for English tour Jul–mid Sept 11.30am, 2.30pm, 4.30pm; Jun 11.30am, 2pm, 4pm; Apr–May 11.15, 4pm; no English visits in winter; 6.50€; 05 57 55 28 28; www.saint-emilion-tourisme.com.

The cave of the **St-Émilion hermitage** was built in the form of a cross by the hermit Émilion. Legend says that women hoping to have a child should sit on Émilion's chair, which is carved into the rock.

The **Chapelle de La Trinité** was built in the 13C by Benedictine monks. The building has retained some attractive **Gothic frescoes**, hidden for many years under a layer of soot.

A series of **catacombs** – underground galleries originally used as a necropolis – can be seen in the next section of the rock. The hole visible in the central cupola was originally used to lower the bodies into the catacombs.

In the place du Marché, climbing the 187 steps of the **monolithic church bell tower** mean you will be rewarded with a lovely **view** of the village and the surrounding Dordogne valley.

East of this square, above the main rue Guadet, stands the **Cloître des Cordeliers**★. Built in the 14C, these romantic cloisters comprise a series of Romanesque arches supported by columns. Underneath the cloisters and park are **cellars** dug from the rock at a depth of 20m, which are home to the sparkling Crémant-de-Bordeaux wine *(05 57 24 42 13; www.lescordeliers.com. Visits Mon-Fri 2.30pm, 3.30pm and 4.30pm).*

To the south, the rectangular keep of the **castle** (32m), known as the **Tour du Roi**, stands alone on a rocky base, providing splendid **views**★ of the town and surrounding area from its summit. It is from this tower that the jurade proclaim their judgement of the new wine in spring and the vintage banns in autumn *(open Jun–Sept 10.30am–8.30pm; off-season enquire at the tourist office; access to the top of the tower 1€).*

The **Maison du Vin de St-Émilion** offers an introduction to the local wine industry with a short video and an exhibition highlighting typical aromas found in the wines. The centre organises wine tastings in summer and provides a guide to the estates. Wines from 225 châteaux available at estate prices *(see Shopping Guide)*. Also worth a visit is the **Union des Producteurs de St-Émilion** cooperative, where visitors are guar-

Jurade and Jurats

The famous wines of St-Émilion were known in the Middle Ages as "honorary" wines because they were often presented in homage to sovereigns and other important personalities. During this period, the municipal council, was responsible for checking the quality of the wine. The *Jurade*, re-formed in 1948, upholds the tradition.

Every Jun *(3rd Sun)*, the *jurats*, dressed in their silk hoods and scarlet robes, attend mass before proceeding to the collegiate church cloisters, where they carry out the induction of new members. At the end of the afternoon, they proclaim their judgement of the new wine from the top of the Tour du Roi. In Sep *(3rd Sun)*, the jurats announce the *bans des vendanges* (new vintage) from the same tower. Today this is purely ceremonial and is accompanied by a lively wine festival.

anteed a warm welcome in its impressive modern winery (*see Shopping*).

There is no fixed route for touring the **St-Émilion wine estates**, unless you decide to join the **Train des Grands Vignobles** tour which visits the Grands Crus châteaux and includes a commentary and wine-tasting (*every 45 mins from 10.30am–5pm; closed Oct 15–Easter except school holidays; 6€; Tasting at Château Rochebelle 05 57 51 30 71; www.visite-saint-emilion.com).*

Château Franc-Mayne is a delightful château typical of the Gironde style. With magnificent underground cellars, a well-stocked boutique and a new tourist centre since summer 2009, the château also offers bed and breakfast accommodation (*33330 St-Émilion; 05 57 24 62 61; www.chateau-francmayne.com*).

Château La Gaffelière is situated on the site of an old Gallo-Roman villa.

A mosaic from the villa representing a vine bearing fruit testifies to the presence of a vineyard here since the 4C (*BP 65, 33330 St-Émilion; open by appt. daily Jun–Aug 8am–noon & 2–6pm, 5pm Fri; rest of the year Mon–Fri 8am–noon & 2–6pm, 5pm Fri; 05 57 24 72 15; www.chateau-la-gaffeliere.com*).

Another attractive estate to visit, located at one of the highest points of the appellation and unusually laid out with terraces cut into the slopes around the property, is Chateau de Pressac. This elevated estate was the location chosen on July 20, 1453, when the English surrendered after the Battle of Castillon, thereby returning Bordeaux to France. (*St Etienne de Lisse, t05 57 40 18 02, www.chateau-de-pressac.com; Open 9am-12pm, 2-6pm*).

Visitors can purchase wine (*see Shopping Guide*) at **Château Angélus** and **Château Figeac**.

Leave St-Émilion via the Porte Bourgeoise and head north along the D 122.

Saint-Georges

The **Saint-Georges-Saint-Émilion** AOC is a small appellation, covering an area of 170ha. Just before you come into the village of St-Georges on the road from St-Émilion, note the **Château St-Georges** on the right. This beautiful Louis XVI-style building was designed by Victor Louis, the architect of the Grand Théâtre in Bordeaux. The 11C Romanesque church's bell tower stands 23m high.

Montagne

The **Montagne-St-Émilion** appellation is the largest of the St-Émilion "satellite" vineyards, covering an area of 1,560ha. The **Maison des Vins** provides a good introduction to the four "satellite" appellations and has approximately 250 different wines for sale. Also worth a visit is the **Groupe des Producteurs de Montagne**, which gives a good general introduction to the appellation (*see Shopping Guide*).

Château Montaiguillon enjoys an excellent hilltop location offering stunning views of the surrounding countryside (*33570 Montagne, open Mon–Fri; tours by appt.; 05 57 74 62 34; www.montaiguillon.com*).

The nearby **Écomusée du Libournais** provides a full introduction to the Libournais wine-producing area, plus offers walks through the vines (*open Apr–Nov 11 10am–noon & 2–6pm; 5.50€; 05 57 74 56 89; www.ecomusee-libournais.com*).

Continue along the D 122 to Lussac.

Lussac

Lussac has given its name to an appellation covering an area of 1,430ha. Respected producers in the area include **Châteaux Bonnin** and the **Union des Producteurs**, an umbrella organisation for 140 wine producers offering quality wines (*See Shopping Guide*).

Follow the D 122 for 2km, then turn left onto the D 21 for 4.5km.

Petit-Palais-et-Cornemps

Surrounded by a cemetery, the **Église St-Pierre** dates from the late 12C. It has a delightful Romanesque **façade**★ whose delicately carved style is typical of the Saintonge and is heavily influenced by Moorish architecture.

Return to the D 21 to Puisseguin.

Puisseguin

The Puisseguin-Saint-Émilion appellation covers an area of 746ha to the northeast of Saint Emilion. Among the stars of this area is **Château Teyssier**, a 15th century property that today covers 50 hectares. Michel Rolland is the consultant, and makes a fruit-forward, succulent wine thta is increasingly well-recognised *(1 Teyssier, 05 57 74 63 11).*

Take the D 17 to Castillon-la-Bataille.

The road now enters the **Côtes-de-Castillon** appellation (2,945ha), which produces well-structured and generally fruity red wines that often offer very good value for money.

The vineyards lie mainly on the hills to the north of Castillon-la-Bataille, and the winding roads and steep slopes make this particularly attractive driving country. Shortly after Puisseguin, a scenic road (D 123E7) leads to **Saint-Philippe-d'Aiguilhe.** There is a pleasant spot at Candeleyre for a picnic.

Continue along the D 17.

Castillon-la-Bataille

Castillon overlooks the right bank of the Dordogne. In 1453, the English troops commanded by General Talbot suffered a heavy defeat here, marking the end of English domination in Aquitaine. Every summer, the re-enactment of the battle with a cast of 600 provides a dramatic spectacle, with horse-backed soldiers riding through the valley *(Château Castegens, 33350 Castillon-la-Bataille; shows every weekend mid-Jul–mid-Aug;10.30pm; 05 57 40 14 53; www.batailledecastillon.com).*

The **Maison des Vins des Castillon Côtes de Bordeaux** has a choice of 54 wines on sale at estate prices *(see Shopping Guide)*. It also offers wine tastings and every summer organises tours of the châteaux which take place before the re-enactment of the battle. *(reservation required; meet at the Maison des Vins at 5pm).*

POMEROL AND FRONSAC

30km. Libourne is located 33km E of Bordeaux by the N 89.

Libourne

The prosperity of this smart town has long been linked to wine. Interest in the wine trade was revived here, at the confluence of the River Dordogne and River Isle, in the early 20C by families from the Corrèze, many of whom are still active in the industry.

Place Abel-Surchamp is lined with houses from the 16C and 19C. The **Tour du Grand-Port**, on quai des Salinières, was once part of the town's fortifications. Quai du Priourat, to the left of the bridge on the town side, is home to several wine merchants, including Maison Moueix, owner of the world-famous Petrus. Although this is not open to the public, a stroll along the quays at this point is a pleasant way to get a feel for the area, and there are a number of guingette restaurants where you can get an open-air lunch.

Drive NE from Libourne along the N 89.

Pomerol

Covering an area of only 780ha, **Pomerol** enjoys an excellently consistent reputation. This region has few grand châteaux buildings, but many famous wines. The Petrus estate, which produces one of the best – and most expensive – wines in the world, is an understated stone property with barely a sign outside, and the equally renowned Le Pin has barely even a house. Neither is open to the public.

Pomerol wines owe their delicacy and bouquet to the complex soil of pebbles, gravel, sand and clay.

The dominant grape variety used is Merlot, which gives the wines a fruity intensity, but the clay and iron-oxide soil here gives a more intense expression of the grape than elsewhere on the Right Bank. These wines are pleasant to drink when young, but also age well.

To discover this appellation which borders that of St-Émilion, contact the **Château La Fleur de Plince**, the smallest Pomerol estate, with an area of just 28ha. The friendly owner, Pierre Choukroun, will be happy to introduce you to his estate and provide information on the local area *(Le Grand Moulinet, 33500 Pomerol; 05 57 74 15 26, www.pomerol.com).*

The **church** at Pomerol dates mainly from the 19C, although it once was part of a commandery of the Knights Hospitaller of St John of Jerusalem.

To the northeast, the 17C **Château de Salles** is the only real château in the area. Built on one level, with two wings, the château served as a model for the 18C country houses of the Bordeaux region. One of the few Pomerol chateaux to have a visitor centre is Chateau Petit Village (33500 Pomerol, |*t05 57 51 21 08; www.petit-village.com*). There is a tasting room overlooking the vines, a modern architect-designed winery and a small boutique.

Head N on the D 245 for 2.5km.

Lalande-de-Pomerol

Surrounding the village of Lalande-de-Pomerol, whose 12C **church** was built by the Knights Hospitaller of St John, the vineyards of Lalande-de-Pomerol cover a larger area than those of Pomerol. The Lalande wines are fleshy, robust and well-structured, and are a good place to look for the signature style of Pomerol without the same price tag. **Chateau Siurac** is one of the top producers in the appellation, with a beautiful building and extensive park. *(see Shopping Guide).*

Return towards Libourne along the D 910, then turn right onto the D 670.

Fronsac

The Fronsac vineyards, west of Libourne, extend for 816ha across six *communes*. The textured red wines produced here will lay down well. Wines from Fronsac and St-Michel-de-Fronsac are permitted to use the **Canon-Fronsac** name.

The Romanesque and Gothic **Église St-Martin** is thought to have been founded by Charlemagne.

The **Maison des Vins** here has a selection of 70 wines for sale at estate prices, including several old vintages. **Château Lamarch-Canon**, **Château La Dauphine** and **Château Richelieu** are particularly noted for their quality *(see Shopping Guide).*

Château de La Rivière (16C-19C) was restored by Viollet-le-Duc and is the largest wine estate in the appellation, with 3ha of underground cellars and large grounds with plenty of hidden corners *(33126 La Rivière; open Jun–Sept 9am–noon & 2–5pm; closed Sun mornings; 05 57 55 56 56; www.chateau-de-la-riviere.com).*

As you continue along D 670, stop at **Saint-Michel-de-Fronsac** to admire its attractive Romanesque church (12C-13C). The imposing Chateau de Carles sits at one of the highest points of the appellation in the village of Saillans, with views over the Dordogne valley. Its Haut Carles wine is one of the best of Fronsac. *(33141 Saillans, 05 57 84 32 03, www.haut-carles.com).*

Continue to St-André-de-Cubzac.

Saint-André-de-Cubzac

A dolphin dancing in the centre of a roundabout in Saint-André-de-Cubzac carries a small red cap in its mouth as a reminder that Jacques Cousteau was born here. The fortified 13C-14C Romanesque church has arrow-slits in the towers.

Château du Bouilh, surrounded by its vineyards and attractive park, was designed by Victor Louis with its buildings laid out in a crescent shape *(open mid-Jul–Aug daily 2.30–6pm; mid-Apr–mid-Jul & Sept–Oct weekends & public holidays 2.30–6pm; 5€; 05 57 43 01 45).*

Bourgeais and Blayais regions

The limestone hills on the right bank of the Gironde offer a combination of undulating landscapes and rustic charm, characterised by small family-owned wine estates rather than grand châteaux and Crus Classés. Covering an area of 3,800ha, the Côtes-de-Bourg appellation produces well-structured reds which lay down well, as well as a few dry whites, renowned for their fruity and rounded characteristics.

Michelin Map: 335, H-I 4

Location: 32km drive. Bourg is located 35km N of Bordeaux by the N 10, on the right bank of the Dordogne, on a series of hills and valleys as it converges with the Garonne river. From many parts of Bourg and Blaye, you can see the Médoc vineyards on the other side of the Garonne.

Don't Miss: The attractive market town of Bourg, and the imposing Blaye Citadel.

DRIVING TOUR

Bourg

The steep narrow streets of this small hilltop town situated on the banks of the Dordogne are perfect for a leisurely stroll. Shaded by old elm and lime trees, the **Terrasse du District** has lovely views of the siena-coloured rooftops of the lower town; in the distance, the Dordogne and Garonne meet at Bec d'Ambès to form the Gironde *(viewing table)*. The 18C **Château de la Citadelle** is surrounded by formal French-style gardens. The château now houses the **Musée Hippomobile "Au temps des calèches"**, with a collection of 40 carriages dating from the 19C *(open Jun–Aug 10am–1pm & 2–7pm; Mar–May & Sep–Oct weekends & public holidays 10am–1pm & 2–7pm, weekdays by appt; closed May 1; 4.50€; 05 57 68 23 57)*.

The **Maison des Côtes-de-Bourg**, housed in an attractive vaulted cellar, has a large choice of wines on sale *(see Shopping Guide)*.

The **Château de la Grave**, restored in Louis-XIII style, is worth a visit for its fine setting, as well as for its good quality wines *(bed and breakfast available; 33710 Bourg; open by appt.; 05 57 68 41 49; www.chateaudelagrave.com)*.

Before continuing to Blaye, stop in Pain de Sucre, at the foot of the cliff, where the **Maison Brouette** produces Crémant-de-Bordeaux sparkling wine *(Pain de Sucre, 33710 Bourg; open 8.30am–noon & 2–5/6pm; closed Jan 1 & Dec 25; 05 57 68 42 09)*.

Head east along the D 669.

Grottes de Pair-non-Pair

Visit by guided tour only (45min, last tour 1hr before closing) mid-Jun to mid-Sept tours at 10am, 11.15am, 12.30pm, then every hour until 5.30pm, 5.30pm; mid-Sept–mid-Jun, 10am, 11.15am, 2.30pm, 4pm. Closed Jan 1, May 1 & Dec 25. 7€ (no charge first Sun of month Oct-May). Reservation recommended. 05 57 68 33 40.

The name Pair-non-Pair is said to come from a village lost by a nobleman in a gambling game. These caves cut into the limestone rock house Aurignacian engravings of horses, mammoth, ibex and bison from the Palaeolithic Era (20 000-25 000 BC) but rediscovered in the late-19C. It was acquired by the French State in 1900 and was the first cave in France to be listed as a historic monument.

Head north along the D 133.

Tauriac

Tauriac, situated in the heart of the appellation, is home to several renowned wine producers. The vibrant **Cave Viticole de Bourg-Tauriac** always has a friendly welcome for visitors, offering a large selection of quality wines and a good explanation of the typical qualities of the local wines (*Shopping Guide*).

Return to Bourg; go west on D 669.

The scenic road follows the estuary, offering views of the Gironde and Bec d'Ambès. The Château de Tayac and Château d'Eyquem produce respected wines and enjoy panoramic views.

Bayon-sur-Gironde

Château Falfas is an attractive 17C manor house that produces excellent wines (*33710 Bayon; open by appt. Mon–Fri 9am–noon & 2.30–6pm; 05 57 64 80 41; www.chateaufalfas.fr*).

Return to Gironde; continue to Blaye.

The road now passes through a series of small hamlets, many of which have dwellings built into the cliff face. Square fishing nets known as carrelets hang on winches above the river, by huts built on piles over the water. There are very good views at several points over the Estuary and the Médoc.

Right at Roque de Thau onto D 250

At **Villeneuve**, stop to admire **Château de Mendoce**, a fine 15C manor house with four corner towers. The château is open for tastings of its excellent Côtes-de-Bourg, which take place in a large, imposing tasting room (*33710 Villeneuve; open daily by appt. 9am–noon & 2–6pm; 05 57 68 34 95; www.mendoce.com*).

Return to the D 669.

Plassac

The remains of three **Gallo-Roman villas** dating from the 1C-5C AD have been found behind the church in this village. A museum provides information on the history of the villas and exhibits artefacts excavated here (*open May–Sept 9am–noon & 2–7pm; Apr & Oct Mon-Sat 9am–noon & 2–6pm, Sun 2-6pm; unaccompanied visit of the museum; 30min

Old washhouse and a view of the upper town, Bourg

S. Sauvignier / MICHELIN

guided tours; 3€; 05 57 42 84 80*).

Château Mondésir-Gazin produces an excellent red (*see Shopping Guide*).

Blaye

The Blaye region produces reds and dry whites in an area of approximately 6,000ha, which includes the **Côtes-de-Blaye**, **Blaye**, and Blaye Côtes de Bordeaux appellations. The red wines are robust and fruity; the whites fresh and rounded. The **Maison du Vin** has a selection of 270 wines from the appellation, including a number of different vintages (*see Shopping Guide*).

The **citadel**★, originally built to protect Bordeaux from the English fleet, was completed by Vauban in 1689. This is now almost a small village in its own right. Excellent **views** can be enjoyed from the **Tour des Rondes** and the esplanade on place d'Armes (*free visit year round. Tours from Jun-Sept 2pm, 3.30pm and 5pm; 5€; 05 57 42 12 09*).

The **Manutention** was built in 1677 to house the prison; it now houses interesting **exhibitions** on the ecosystem of the estuary (*open Apr–Oct 1.30–7pm; 2.80€; 05 57 42 80 96; www.estuaire-gironde.net*). A **cycle path** from Blaye to Étauliers runs for 13km through the vineyards. A ferry also leaves from Blaye to Lamarque in the Médoc.

Leaving head east along the D 937.

St Paul de Blaye

The **Château La Rivalerie** produces a range of good quality wines and is also open for visitors (*see Shopping Guide*).

Médoc

The Médoc peninsula is wedged between the Gironde estuary and the Atlantic Ocean. Its name is synonymous with good wine, although almost 80% of the region is covered with forest. Water is an ever-present influence in the region, which has a mild climate and is well watered by rain coming in from the Atlantic. The soils, however, are well drained because of the gravelly terroir, and the high density of plantation (10,000 vines per hectare instead of the 4 ,000 that is typical of other areas) means wines are intense and powerful. The other secret of the Médoc - as elsewhere in Bordeaux - is the highly skilled blending of different grape varieties and the maturing wine in oak barrels.

Michelin Map: Local Michelin Map 335, F-H 3-5. See tour on the map p155.

Info: www.medoc-bordeaux.com

Location: 130km drive, starting from Bordeaux. A long peninsula stretching northwest of Bordeaux from Blanquefort Jalle to the Pointe de Grave at the tip of the Gironde Estuary. On one side lies the Garonne river, on the other a bank of pine trees before the Atlantic Ocean.

Don't Miss: The Routes des Chateaux, tightly packed with famous classed growth properties.

DRIVING TOUR

The terroir comprises mainly gravelly hills, which slope towards the Gironde. Although the entire 16,000ha area is entitled to use the **Médoc** appellation, only the vineyards to the north do so. The closest part of the region to Bordeaux is the Haut-Médoc, a vast appellation of 4,200ha, which includes the six village Crus of Margaux, Moulis, Listrac, Saint-Julien, Pauillac and St-Estèphe.

Leave Bordeaux to the NW along the N 215, then turn right onto the D 2 at Eysines. Visitors leaving from the Parc des Expositions should follow the D 209.

The first village you come to in the **Haut-Médoc** AOC upon leaving Bordeaux along the D 2 is **Blanquefort**, home to the supposedly haunted ruins of an 11C-15C castle which once belonged to the mysterious Black Prince.

At Blanquefort, leave D 2, join D 210; road runs parallel to and east of the D 2.

More and more vineyards appear after **Parempuyre**. Here the splendid **Château Clément-Pichon**, typical in style of the "neo" architecture of the 19C, produces an excellent Cru Bourgeois *(30 ave. du Château-Pichon, 33290 Parempuyre; open by appt; 05 56 35 23 79, www.vignobles.fayat.com).*

Ludon-Médoc

Just before Ludon-Médoc, note the elegant **Château d'Agassac**, an old 12C fort transformed into a Renaissance château. The château produces offers iPod tours and picnics *(15 r. du Château-d'Agassac, 33290 Ludon-Médoc; open Jul-Aug, daily 10.30-6.30pm; Jun, Sept Tue–Sat 10.30am–6.30pm; Oct–May by appt. Mon–Fri 9.30–12.30pm & 1.30–4.30pm; 05 57 88 15 47; www.agassac.com).* The main property of note in the town is the prestigious 18C **Château La Lagune**, producers of a Troisiéme Cru Classé *(see Shopping Guide).*

Macau

The port has a few open-air cafés where people come from Bordeaux to sample shad, lamprey or eels, depending on the season. The delicious small prawns fished in the estuary and served with aniseed are available all year round. Macau is renowned for artichokes.

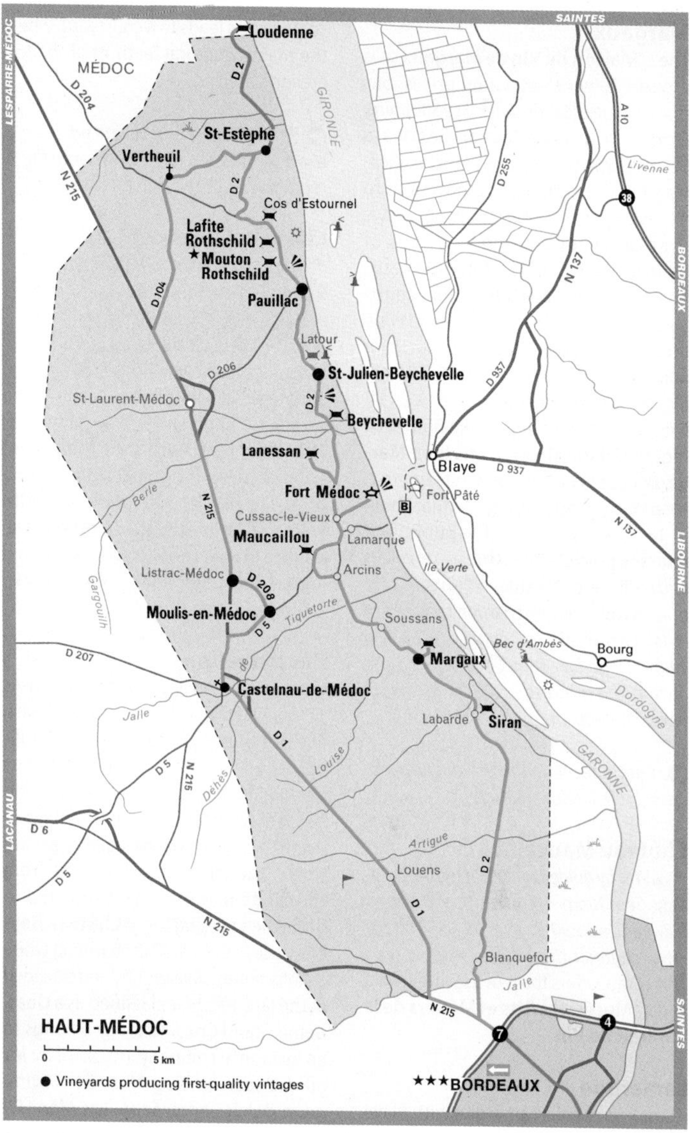

Return to the D 2.

Labarde

The **Margaux** appellation, covering an area of 1,410ha and producing some of the finest wines in the Médoc, begins at Labarde. These wines contain a blend of Cabernet Sauvignon and Merlot, resulting in strong tannins and a mellow flavour. The appellation is home to 19 Crus Classés. The beautiful 18C **Château Dauzac** produces an excellent wine (*see Shopping Guide*). Another jewel of the region is **Château Giscours**, an attractive Second Empire building which is open for visits, has a small boutique and also offers two guest rooms *(10 rte. de Giscours, 33460 Labarde; open by appt; 5€; 05 57 97 09 09, www.chateau-giscours.fr).*

Margaux

The **Maison du Vin de Margaux** sells around 50 wines at estate prices, but does not offer tastings (*See Shopping Guide*). **Chateau Rauzan Gassies**, a Second Growth from the 1855 classification, has just completed renovations to its tasting room, which now has views over the neighbouring vineyards of Château Palmer and Château Margaux. There is also an attractive inner courtyard, and a possibility of food and wine matching (*visits by appointment 9am-noon & 1.30-5.30pm; 5€; 05 57 88 71 88; www.domaines-quie*).

One of the top names in the Bordeaux region, **First Growth Château Margaux** covers an area of 82ha. The harmoniously proportioned château, built in 1812, is not open to the public, but tours are possible round the barrel cellars and vinification facilities (*visit by 1hr guided tour only, reservation required at least two weeks in advance, Mon–Fri 10am–noon & 2–4pm; closed Aug and during the harvest; 05 57 88 83 83; www.chateau-margaux.com*).

Continue along the D 2 and turn left onto the D 5 before Lamarque.

Château Maucaillou

Visit by guided tours (1hr30min) only, May–Sept 10am–5pm. Oct–Apr 10–11am & 2–4pm. 6.90€. 05 56 58 02 58; www.chateau-maucaillou.com.

This estate offers tours of its wine cellars and its **Musée des Arts et Métiers de la Vigne et du Vin**.

Lamarque

A small ferry links Lamarque with Blaye on the opposite bank of the Gironde.

Turn right at Cussac-le-Vieux.

Fort Médoc

Opening times vary year-round. 2.20€. 05 56 58 91 30.

This fort was built by Vauban in 1689, along with the citadel at Blaye on the other side of the estuary, to protect the approach to Bordeaux from the English fleet. A gate adorned with Louis XIV's coat of arms leads to a courtyard, where the main structural features of the fort are indicated.

Pass through Cussac and on towards Pauillac, turning left onto the road that leads to Château Lanessan.

Château Lanessan

Visit by guided tour (1hr) only 9.30am–noon & 2–6pm. Vinification or horse visit, 8€ each, or both for 15€. 6€. 05 56 58 94 80. www.lanessan.com.

Situated on a hill surrounded by a 400ha estate, Château Lanessan was built in 1878 in a mix of Dutch and Spanish Renaissance styles. The property offers a tour of its wine storehouses, which concludes with a tasting. The **Musée du Cheval**, housed in the outbuildings, exhibits an interesting collection of horse-drawn carriages dating from 1900.

Beychevelle

The Saint-Julien appellation comprises 11 Crus Classés produced from just 909ha. The fine wines produced here are full-bodied and are sometimes described as combining the qualities of Margaux and Pauillac wines. The name Beychevelle (from the French baisse-voile, meaning "lower the sails") is said to come from the salute that ships were required to give when passing the **Château Beychevelle** in the 17C. This charming white country house, rebuilt in 1757 and extended in the late 19C, was classified as a Quatrième Grand Cru, and today belongs to an insurance company. (*visit by 1hr guided tour Jul–Aug Mon–Sat 10am–noon & 1.30–5pm; Sept–Jun Mon–Fri 10am–noon & 1.30–5pm; reservations preferable; 8P for visit with tasting at 2.30pm, other visits free closed public holidays; 05 56 73 20 70; www.beychevelle.com*). Beyond Beychevelle there are lovely views of the Gironde estuary.

Saint-Julien-Beychevelle

Château Ducru-Beaucaillou, a fine country house, produces a Second Cru Classé. This wine compares favourably with the higher-rated Premiers Crus, highlighting the full expression of the Cabernet Sauvignon grape *(see Shopping Guide)*.

Pauillac

Pauillac is situated halfway between Bordeaux and the Pointe de Grave. The town and its surrounding area are above all renowned for their Grands Crus with 17 Classified growths, including three Premiers Crus: Mouton-Rothschild, Lafite-Rothschild and Latour. The 1,200ha of the **Pauillac** appellation cover an area of well-drained gravelly hills, which provide the ideal conditions for the Cabernet Sauvignon grape. Pauillac wines are powerful and full-bodied. As they age, they develop an extraordinary bouquet.

The **Maison des Vins et du Tourisme** provides a wealth of information on the local vineyards and surrounding area, as well as on sporting activities available in the region, including fishing from the traditional huts along the river. Pauillac is the starting point for **6 circuits** *(5-21km)* which can be followed on foot or by bicycle *(for further information, contact the Maison du Tourisme, La Verrerie, 33250 Pauillac; 05 56 59 03 08; www.pauillac-medoc.com)*.

Château Pichon-Longueville-Comtesse-de-Lalande is home to a small museum of glass and wine-related exhibits. The château produces an excellent Second Cru Classé and enjoys a fine view of the Gironde estuary from its terrace *(33250 Pauillac; open by appt; 05 56 59 19 40; www.pichon-lalande.com)*.

Château Mouton Rothschild★

Visit by guided tour (1hr) only, reservations required 15 days in advance; Mon–Thu 9.15–11am & 2–4pm; Fri 9.15–11am 2–3pm. Closed weekends & public holidays. 5€. 05 56 73 21 29. www.bpdr.com.

One of the Médoc's most famous châteaux stands in the heart of the vineyards surrounding Pauillac. The wine produced here was classified as a Premier Cru in 1973 as a result of the relentless efforts of Baron Philippe de Rothschild, who has made his wine a work of art, symbolised by the labels designed every year by a renowned artist. In addition to the **wine storehouses**★, the château houses the **Musée du Vin dans l'Art**★★ displaying a collection of wine-related art from different periods, with a large section dedicated to contemporary trends.

Château Lafite Rothschild

Rte. des Châteaux, D 2, 33250 Pauillac. Visit by guided tour (45min) only, reservations required 7 days in advance off-season, 15 days in advance in high season; Mon–Fri 2–3.30pm. Closed Aug–Oct & public holidays. Reservations by fax 05 56 59 26 83 or visites@lafite.com. 05 56 73 18 18. www.lafite.com.

The circular storehouse at the home of the finest and most discreet of the Grands Crus was designed by the Catalan architect Ricardo Bofill. The château stands on a terrace planted with beautiful cedar trees and enclosed by a Louis XIV balustrade; since the time of the Second Empire (1868) it has belonged to the English branch of the Rothschild family.

Bages

This small village, next to Pauillac, has been re-invented in recent years as a centre of wine and gastronomy. Renovated by Jean Michel Cazes of Chateau Lynch Bages (www.lynchbages.com), it contains a bakery, a wine shop, a bistro and a children's play area around a central fountain in an attractive cobbled square. A tour around the Chateau Lynch Bages, where art exhibitions are held over the summer months, will end in Bages village (*05 56 73 24 00; daily guided visits (1hr) 9am-noon, 2-5.30pm, by appt; 8€*).

Saint-Estèphe

The small town of St-Estèphe, dominated by its unusual **church** of Romanesque origin with a Baroque interior, is situated on a hillock in the centre of a sea of vineyards.

St-Estèphe, the northernmost of the Médoc appellations, covers an area of 1,300ha and produces wines which acquire a fine quality as they age. The area includes five Crus Classés.

At the entrance to the appellation, stands the Eastern silhouette of the Indian pagodas belonging to **Château Cos-d'Estournel** - built in memory of the founder's overseas expeditions.
In 2009, a visitor centre and impressively modern new winery of glass and stainless steel opened its doors, in addition to the existing wine museum *(33180 St-Estèphe; open by appt only Mon–Fri 9am–12.30pm & 2–5.30pm; 05 56 73 15 50).*
Not far from here, in the hamlet of **Marbuzet**, **Château Haut-Marbuzet** produces a Cru Bourgeois worthy of a Cru Classé; a good place to purchase this wine is at the **Marquis de St-Estèphe** wine cellar in Leyssac *(see Shopping Guide).*

Saint-Seurin-de-Cadourne

Several quality Crus Bourgeois are produced around the village of Saint-Seurin-de-Cadourne. Estates worthy of particular note here include **Château Sociando-Mallet** and the **Cave Coopérative La Paroisse** *(see Shopping Guide).*
The **Château de Verdus** has a splendid dovecote (14C-17C) and a small museum dedicated to the history of the Médoc; wine tasting *(Domaine Dailledouze Père et Fils, Bardis, 33180 St-Seurin-de-Cadourne; open Jun–Sept Mon–Sat 9.30–noon & 2–6pm; Sun 3–6pm; Oct–My afternoons only; 05 56 73 17 31; www.chateau-verdus.com).*

Return to St-Seurin, turn right towards Pez, then follow the D 104E3 to Vertheuil. Continue along the D 104, then rejoin the N 115. Continue as far as Listrac.

Listrac-Médoc

Moulis and **Listrac**, two neighbouring village appellations, are characterised by a complex mix of soils that includes clay, limestone and gravel.
Listrac produces wines that are more robust, and sometimes rustic; however, the tendency to replace Cabernet Sauvignon with Merlot is resulting in wines that are more rounded.
Standing at an altitude of 46m, the village is the highest point in the Médoc. Its most impressive architectural feature is its 12C church. The **Maison du Vin de Listrac** sells all the appellation's wines at estate prices. The **Château Fourcas-Dupré** is one of the appellation's most renowned estates *(see Shopping Guide).*

Moulis-en-Médoc

Moulis, the smallest appellation in the Médoc, produces some very fine wines.
In Grand-Poujeaux, the **Maison du Vin de Moulis** sells the appellation's wines as well as offering visitors the opportunity to enjoy a 12km walk through the surrounding vineyards. In the same area, the romantically named Cru Bourgeois, **Château Chasse-Spleen**, means 'chasing away melancholy' in English, with some believing that it owes its name to Baudelaire, others to Lord Byron, www.chasse-spleen.com.
Just part Moulis, on the way back to Bordeaux, ensure a stop at **La Winery de Philippe Raoux**, a new wine and arts centre that has a large boutique, a gourmet restaurant and regular farmer's markets held through the summer months (*Rond-Point des Vendangeurs 33460 Arscac-en-Médoc, 05 56 39 04 90 www.lawinery.fr); open Tues-Sun 10am-7pm*).

Follow the D 1 to return to Bordeaux.

ALONG THE COAST

Lacanau-Océan

55km NW of Bordeaux along the D 6.
The resort of Lacanau-Océan stands at the foot of sand dunes carpeted in maritime pines, making it the ideal base from which to explore the surrounding *lèdes* (sandy valleys swathed in forest) and the 20km of glorious beaches. More active visitors can take advantage of the 120km of coastal cycle routes which dissect the pine forest.
The area is also renowned for its surfing, with a choice of popular areas such as the plage Centrale, Nord, Sud and Super Sud, all of which are subject to the fre-

quent displacement of sand dunes. Golfers are also well catered for with three local clubs, including one 18-hole course. Another activity centre popular with the whole family is the **Monkey Beach**, an adventure park with elevated trails built through the forest, along with rope bridges and "Himalayan" walkways (*Rte. du Baganais, 33680 Lacanau-Océan;* ○*closed 1 week in the spring, 1 week in the autumn outside of school holidays and Nov 15–Apr 1;* ℘ *06 64 74 50 51).*

The 8km-long **Lac de Lacanau**★, covering 2,000ha, is popular with fishing enthusiasts with abundant stocks of pike, eel and perch, as well as offering sailing, windsurfing (particularly at the gently sloping Le Moutchic), water skiing, canoeing and kayaking, and the opportunity to rent boats, dinghies and pedalos.

Soulac-sur-Mer⌂
40km NW of Vertheuil along the N 215.
On the Médoc coast, Soulac is relatively well protected from the Atlantic swell by a deep offshore bank, although the four beaches here are still supervised by lifeguards. In common with every resort along this coastline, Soulac is the ideal base for all water sports enthusiasts, as well as those who enjoy land-based activities such as hiking, cycling and fitness trails. There is also a traditional steam train that runs between Soulac and Bordeaux for the yearly festival in June. The main beach is accessible via a dedicated cycle route from the town's Amélie district.
The resort's pine trees provide welcome shade on a hot summer's day.

Cordouan Lighthouse★★
100km NW of Bordeaux by the N 215, then by ferry. ⌒*Departures from Pointe de Grave (Verdon-sur-Mer) late Mar–late Oct Sat–Thu weather permitting. Reservations suggested.* ○*28€ (ferry and lighthouse admission). La Bohême II.* ℘*05 56 09 62 93. www.vedettelaboheme.com.*
In the 14C, the Black Prince erected an octagonal light tower here, dispatching a hermit to maintain its continuous

bonfire. In the 16C this early tower eventually fell into ruin, replaced by another designed by the architect and engineer Lous de Foix in the 17C. The domed and lanterned belevedere with its Renaissance levels and balustrade projected an image of invincibility. A staircase of 311 steps climbs to the top.

AROUND THE BASSIN D'ARCACHON
Cap-Ferret⌂
71km SW of Bordeaux along the D 106.
This thin strip of land between the Atlantic and the Bassin d'Archachon runs for approximately 20km. Cap-Ferret is a chic holiday destination with plentiful options including cycling through the pine forests, swimming in the calm waters of the *bassin* or the surf of the Atlantic, sampling the delicious local oysters in open-air restaurants, or visiting oyster farms.

Arcachon⌂
70km SW of Bordeaux along the A 63.
The town of Arcachon is the main coastal resort from the city of Bordeaux, and has a lively centre with large numbers of shops and restaurants, and a large waterfront with a marina and popular beach. The writer Alexandre Dumas once lived in Arcachon's Ville d'Hiver. A number of boat trips can be organised from the main port in the town, and a regular taxi-boat shuttles back and forth between Arcachon and Cap Ferret in summer (enquire at the Tourist Office).

Beach of Arcachon

E. Larribère / MICHELIN

Parc Ornithologique du Teich★

50km SW of Bordeaux by the A 63, the A660, then the D 650. Open Jul–Aug 10am–8pm; Sept–Jun 10am–7pm. 7€. 05 56 22 80 93. www.parc-ornithologique-du-teich.com.

This 120ha nature reserve is located in the Eyre delta, which flows into the Bassin d'Arcachon. It is a popular stop on the migration route of several species of birds, which can be viewed in the four theme parks within the reserve. Walking shoes or boots and binoculars are recommended. In total there are 260 different species of birds who can be seen here, and over 60 of these make their nests and raise their young on the site.

Dune du Pilat★★

65km SW of Bordeaux by the A 63, the A 660 and the D 218. Access via the D 218 to the S of Pilat-Plage. Leave your car in the car park (pay parking).

To reach the top, climb up the side of the sand dune (the ascent is relatively difficult) or climb the steps (only in use during the summer season). Climbing or hiking footwear advisable; the sand can also be very hot, so care is recommended.

This bulbous mass of sand is the highest dune in Europe. Currently measuring 2.7km in length, 500m in width and 107m high, it swells in size every year in line with the effects of the wind and ocean currents.

A set of steps have been built into the side of the dune for making the steep climb up to the top, but getting back down again is more about running as fast as you can. A visit here is an invigorating experience and should not to be missed - but remember that the sun can get very hot, and is reflected further off the white sand and surrounding sea, so ensure that you apply plenty of suncream.

WINE BUYING GUIDE

INFORMATION

Conseil Interprofessionnel du Vin de Bordeaux – *1 cours du 30-Juillet, 33000 Bordeaux. 05 56 00 22 66. www.vinsbordeaux.fr. Open Mon–Fri 9am–5pm. Closed weekends and public holidays.*

Syndicat Viticole Côtes-de-Bordeaux et Cadillac – *05 57 98 19 20. www.premierescotesdebordeaux.com.*

Syndicat Viticole de Loupiac – *05 56 62 92 22. www.vins-loupiac.com.*

Syndicat Viticole de l'Entre-Deux-Mers – *05 57 34 32 12. www.vins-entre-deux-mers-com.*

Syndicat de l'Appellation Sainte-Foy-Bordeaux – *saintefoy-bordeaux.com.*

Syndicat Viticole des Graves – *05 56 27 09 25. www.vins-graves.com.*

Syndicat Viticole de Pomerol – *05 57 25 06 88. www.vinspomerol.fr.*

Syndicat Viticole de Saint-Émilion – *05 57 55 50 50. www.vins-saint-emilion.com.*

Syndicat Viticole des Blaye Côtes de Bordeaux – *05 57 42 91 19. info@aoc-blaye.com*

Syndicat Viticole des Côtes de Bourg – *05 57 94 80 20. www.cotes-de-bourg.com.*

CHARACTERISTICS

Red wines – The colour of Bordeaux's reds ranges from crimson to ruby to deep purple. On the nose, they express hints of dark fruits (blackcurrants and blackberries) for Cabernet Sauvignon, and red fruits (strawberry and cherry) for Merlot, with those wines which have matured in barrels developing aromas of roasted coffee and vanilla. Upon ageing, further complexity develops with the appearance of hints of undergrowth, truffles, leather and smoke. On the palate, Bordeaux's reds are tannic when young, but soften with age, at the same time retaining their fleshy character.

Dry white wines – Clear with green tints when young, and straw-coloured to light gold upon ageing. Aromas of citrus and exotic fruit, boxwood and mint in their infancy, and crystallised fruits and the peel of citrus fruit upon ageing.

Sweet white wines – Pale yellow when young, to caramel when very mature. Exotic fruits, pear and pineapple on the nose, evolving towards underlying aromas of grilled almonds, crystallised citrus fruit and wild strawberries. Silky in the mouth with a touch of acidity.
Rosés and clairets – From bright pink rose petals to bright crimson. Fruity on the nose, with hints of red fruits and fruit drops. Pleasantly acidic.

STORAGE

Red wines – A good Bordeaux should age well in the bottle for at least five years. The best wines can continue ageing for fifty years and more.
Dry white wines – Most dry whites should be drunk within five years, although Graves whites can age for up to twenty years.
Sweet white wines – 10 to 100 years.
Rosés and clairets – Best consumed when young.

PRICES

Entre-Deux-Mers, Fronsac – 5 to 18€.
Bordeaux Supérieurs, Premières-Côtes-de-Blaye, Côtes-de-Castillon – 5 to 15€.
Bordeaux, Premières-Côtes-de-Bordeaux, satellites of St-Émilion, Graves, Côtes-de-Bourg – 5 to 20€
Médoc, Lalande-de-Pomerol – 8 to 15€.
Pessac-Léognan, Haut-Médoc – 8 to 40€.
St-Émilion, Ste-Foy-Bordeaux, Canon-Fronsac, Listrac-Médoc, Cotes-de-Blaye – 10 to 15€.
St-Émilion Grand Cru, Moulis, Pauillac – 10 to 40€.
Margaux, St-Julien, St-Estèphe – 15 to 50€.
Pomerol – 20 to 76€.
Loupiac, Cadillac – 8 to 43€.
Sauternes – 8 to 43€
Barsac – 8 to 43€
Classified growths (Crus) from all appellations – 20 upwards€.

MAISONS DES VINS

Maisons des Vins have the advantage of being able to offer a good choice of wines from their appellation at the same price as those purchased directly from the estate. They are also a valuable source of information on their particular wine area.

Vineyards of Château Margaux
S. Sauvignier/MICHELIN

Maison du Vin de Barsac – *Pl. de l'Église, 33720 Barsac. ℘05 56 27 15 44. www.maisondebarsac.fr. Open Jan–Apr Tues-Sun 10am–12.30pm & 2–6pm; May–Dec daily 10am–1pm & 2–7pm.*

Maison du Vin de Blaye Côtes de Bordeaux – *12 cours Vauban, 33390 Blaye. ℘05 57 42 91 19. www.premierescotes-blaye.com. Open daily 8.30am–12.30pm & 2–6.30pm. Free introduction to wine tasting Tue–Thu 4.45–5.45pm. Closed public holidays.*

Maison du Vin de Bordeaux – *3 cours du 30-Juillet, 33075 Bordeaux Cedex. ℘05 56 00 22 88. www.bordeaux.com. Open Mon-Thu 8.30am-12.30pm & 1.30-5.15pm, Fri 8.30am-12.30pm. Wine bar open Mon-Sat 11am-10pm.*

Maison du Vin des Côtes de Bourg – *1 pl. de l'Éperon, 33710 Bourg. ℘05 57 68 22 28. Open mid-Jun–mid-Sept 10am–1pm & 2–7pm. Sept 15–Jun 15 Mon–Sat 9.30am–12.30pm & 2–6pm.*

Maison des Vins des Côtes de Bordeaux et Cadillac – *D 10, rte. de Langon, 33410 Cadillac. ℘05 57 98 19 20. www.premierescotesdebordeaux.com.*

Maison des Vins de Castillon Côtes de Bordeaux – *6 allée de la République, 33350 Castillon-la-Bataille. ℘05 57 40 00 88. Open Jul–Aug Mon–Sat 9am–1pm & 2–6pm; Sept–Jun Mon–Fri 8.30am–12.30pm & 3.30–5.30pm.*

Maison des Vins de Fronsac – *Le Bourg, 33126 Fronsac, 15km SE of St-André-de-Cubzac by the D 670. ℘05 57 51 80 51. Open mid-Jun–mid-Sept Mon–Sat 10.30am–7pm. Mid-Sept–mid-Jun Mon–Sat 10.30am–12.30pm & 2–6pm. Closed public holidays.*

S. Sauvignier / MICHELIN

Maison du Vin de Listrac – *36 ave. de Soulac, 33480 Listrac-Médoc. ℘05 56 58 09 56. Open June–mid-Sept Tues-Sat 9.30am-1pm & 2-6.30pm. mid-Sept-May 10am-12.30pm & 2.30-6pm.*

Maison du Vin de Moulis – *Pl. du Grand-Poujeaux, 33480 Moulis-en-Médoc. ℘05 56 58 32 74. www.moulis.com. Open Jun 15–Sept 15 Tue, Thu, Fri 9am–12.30pm & 2–6pm; Sat 10am–6.45pm. Sept 16–Jun 14 Mon, Tue, Thu Fri 9am–noon & 2–6pm. Closed 1 week in Jan, 1 week in Feb, 1 week in May, 1 week in Jun, 1 week in Oct and public holidays.*

Maison du Vin de Margaux – *Pl. de la Trémoille, 33460 Margaux. ℘05 57 88 70 82. Open Jun–Sept 10am–1pm & 2–7pm. Apr–Oct Mon–Sat 10am–12.30pm & 2–6pm. Jan–Mar Tue–Fri 10am–noon & 2–6.30pm. Nov–Dec Mon–Sat 10am–noon & 2–6pm. Closed public holidays in winter.*

Maison des Vins de l'Union des Satellites de Saint-Émilion – *Le Bourg, 33570 Montagne. ℘05 57 74 60 13. www.montagnesaintemilion.com. Open May–Oct Mon–Fri 9am–12.00pm & 2–7pm. Nov–Apr Mon–Fri 9am–12.30pm & 2–5.30pm.*

Maison des Vins de Ste-Foy-Bordeaux – *6 rue de Notre Dame, Port St Foy. 33220 Pineuilh. ℘05 53 58 37 34. www.sainte-foy-bordeaux.com. Open Tues-Fri 2-5pm.*

La Maison des Vins de Graves – *61 cours du Mar.-Foch, 33720 Podensac. ℘ 05 56 27 09 25. www.vins-graves.com. Open Mon–Fri 9.30am–6.30pm weekends and public holidays 10.30am–6.30pm. Nov–Apr Mon–Fri 9.30am–6.30pm.*

Maison du Vin de St-Émilion – *Pl. Pierre-Meyrat, 33330 St-Émilion. ℘05 57 55 50 55. www.vins.saint-emilion.com. Open Sept–Jul daily 9.30am–12.30pm & 2–6.30pm. Aug daily 9.30am–7pm. Closed Dec 25 & Jan 1.*

Maison du Sauternes – *14 pl. de la Mairie, 33210 Sauternes. ℘05 56 76 69 83. Open Mon–Fri 9am–7pm, weekends 10am–7pm. Closed Dec 25 & Jan 1.*

Maison de l'Entre-Deux-Mers – *4 r. de l'Abbaye, 33670 La Sauve. ℘05 57 34 32 12. www.vins-entre-deux-mers.com. Jun–Sept Mon–Sat 10am–1pm & 2–5.30pm. Oct–May Mon–Fri 10am–12.30pm & 2–5.30pm.*

Maison du Sauveterrois – *2 r. St-Romain, 33540 Sauveterre-de-Guyenne. ℘05 56 71 53 45. Open mid-Sept–early Jun Mon–Sat 9am–noon & 2–6pm; early Jun–mid-Sept 9am–noon & 2–7pm.*

COOPERATIVES

Cave Coopérative du Blayais – *9 Le Piquet, 33390 Cars. ℘05 57 42 13 15. www.la-cave-des-chateaux.com. Open Mon–Sat 9am–noon & 2–6pm.* This cooperative sells a number of interesting estate wines.

Univitis – *1 r. du Gén.-de-Gaulle, 33220 Les Lèves-et-Thoumeyran. ℘05 57 56 02 02. www.univitis.fr. Open Jul–Aug 9am–12.30pm & 2.30–7pm. Sept-Jun 9am –12.30pm & 2.30–6pm. Closed public holidays.* The Bordeaux region's largest cooperative offers its customers a fine range of wines from various estates.

Union des Producteurs – *33570 Lussac. ℘05 57 55 50 40. Open Mon–Sat 9am–12.30pm & 2–6.30pm;* A grouping of 140 wine-makers producing a range of quality wines.

Groupe des Producteurs de Montagne – *La Tour Mont d'Or, 33570 Montagne. ℘05 57 74 62 15. Open Mon–Fri 9am–noon & 2–6pm; Sat 9am–noon.* This group of producers offers a good overview of the Montagne-St-Émilion appellation.

Cave Coopérative Larose – *44 ave du Mar.- Joffre, 33250 Pauillac. larosepauillac@wanadoo.fr. ℘05 56 59 26 00. Open Tue–Fri 8am–noon & 2–6pm. Mon & Sat 9am–noon & 2–6pm*

(Jul–Aug 7pm). More than 75 years since its founding, the winery continues to produce, noteworthy wines according to natural methods. Generally aged 3 years before its release La Rose Pauillac is a popular choice, as is la Fleur Pauillac, sold a bit younger.

Cave Coopérative *de Quinsac, 33360 Quinsac, ☎05 56 20 86 09. www.cave-de-quinsac.com. Open Mon–Sat 9am–noon & 2–6pm; Sun and public holidays 8am–noon & 3–6pm.* Production here includes clairet, an intense rosé obtained following a brief maceration.

Union des Producteurs de Rauzan – *Aiguilley, 33420 Rauzan. ☎05 57 84 13 22. Open Mon–Sat 9am–12.30pm & 2–6pm; open Sun in Jul–Aug.* One of the largest cooperative wineries in France with an annual production of 135,000hl. Around thirty reasonably priced wines on sale.

Union des Producteurs de St-Émilion – *In the lower section of St-Émilion, near the railway line on the D 670. ☎05 57 24 70 71. www.udpse.com. Open Mon–Sat 8am–noon (8.30am Sat) & 2–6pm (6.30pm Jul–Aug). Closed public holidays.* This cooperative produces some sixty estate wines here. Warm, friendly welcome and service from the wine producers themselves.

Cave Marquis de St-Estèphe – *Leyssac, 33180 St-Estèphe. ☎05 56 73 35 30. Open Mon–Fri 8.30am–12.15pm & 2–6pm, Sat 10am-noon & 2-5pm.* The Cave Marquis brings together a number of local wine-makers producing a selection of good quality wines.

Cave Coopérative La Paroisse – *2 r. Clément-Lemaignan, 33180 St-Seurin-de-Cadourne. ☎05 56 59 31 28. cavecooperativevinification@wanadoo.fr. Open Sept–May Mon–Fri 8.30am–12.30pm & 2–6pm (Fri 5pm). Jun–Jul Mon–Sat 8.30am–12.30pm & 2–6pm. Aug 8.30am–12.30pm & 2–7pm.* This cooperative is renowned for its excellent-value Haut-Médocs.

Cave Viticole de Bourg-Tauriac – *3 ave. des Côtes-de-Bourg, 33710 Tauriac. ☎05 57 94 07 07. Open 9am–12.30pm & 1.30–6pm.* An extensive choice of quality wines.

ESTATES

Remember that, to buy wine directly from a Bordeaux château, it is usually necessary to book a visit. Take advantage of appellation open days, known as Portes Ouvertes. (*see **Sales, Fairs and Markets***)

Château Coutet – *33720 Barsac. ☎05 56 27 15 46. www.chateaucoutet.com. Open by appt. Mon–Fri 9am–noon & 2–5pm.* This estate extends across 38.5ha of uninterrupted vineyards planted with Semillon, Sauvignon and Muscadelle vines with an average age of 35 years. In addition to the Coutet estate in Barsac, classified as a Grand Cru, which they have run since 1977, Philippe and Dominique Baly also own several hectares of Graves, where they produce the Château Marc Haut-Laville. Barsac, Graves, Sauternes.

Château Climens – *33720 Barsac, ☎05 56 27 15 33. www.chateau-climens.fr. Open by appt. Mon–Fri 9am–noon & 2–5pm.* Owned by Lucien Lurton since 1971, the château has been managed by his daughter, Bérénice, since 1992. Located in the commune of Barsac, the vineyard covers 30ha of red sand and pebbles on a limestone base. A single grape variety, Semillon, is grown here. Traditional wine production methods, with limited yields, and fermentation and ageing in barrels. Barsac.

Château Reynon – *21 rte de Cardan. 33410 Béguey. ☎05 56 62 96 51. reynon@wanadoo.fr. Open by appt.* The vineyard, located in the community of Pujols-sur-Ciron, near Barsac, encompasses 30.76ha of clayey-limestone soil. Thriving here are Sémillon (45%), Sauvignon (50%), and Muscadelle (5%) for the white wines; and Merlot (30%) and Cabernet-Sauvignon (70%) for the reds. The winemaking process employs a long maceration period; the wines are then matured in wooden barrels, of which a third are new. Graves.

Château Carignan – *33360 Carignan-de-Bordeaux. ☎05 56 21 21 30. www.chateau-carignan.com. Open by appt. Mon–Fri 8am–noon & 2-6pm.* Purchased in 1981 by Philippe Pieraerts, the vineyard covers 150ha, 65 of which are under production. Merlot, Cabernet

Sauvignon and Cabernet Franc grape varieties on clayey-limestone and gravelly soil. Manual harvesting, followed by de-stemming, vinification in thermo-regulated vats and maturing in the barrel. Blaye-Côtes-de-Bordeaux.

Château La Rivalerie. *route de Saint Christoly de Blaye, 33390 Saint Paul de Blaye. 05 57 42 18 84. www.larivalerie.com. Open by appt.* The Bonaccorsi family bought this 35 hectare estate in 2005, and it is today run by son Jerome. The grapes pass through a low temperature cooling system after picking, followed by a cold soak before fermentation, to maximise fresh fruit flavours. The top 1858 cuvée is aged for 24 months in new oak. Blaye-Côtes-de-Bordeaux.

Château Lamarche-Canon – *33126 Fronsac. 05 57 51 28 13. bordeaux@vgas.com. Open by appt.* Situated at the foot of the Canon hills, this estate encompasses 22ha of Bordeaux Supérieur and 5ha of Canon-Fronsac. The vineyards, planted in Merlot (80%), and Cabernet-Sauvignon (20%), is farmed along ecological principles, with manual harvesting. The wines mature in oak barrels, of which 40% are new wood, for 6 to 12 months. Bordeaux-Supérieur, Canon-Fronsac.

Château de La Dauphine – *33126 Fronsac. 05 57 74 06 61. www.chateau-dauphine.com. Open by appt.* This dynamic 31-hectare estate is owned by Jean and Guillaume Halley and has been subject to serious investment since their purchase in 2001 from the Moueix family. The Cabernet Franc and Merlot vines are an average of 35 years old, and the wine itself is vinified in new cellars in a style that maximises intense but supple fruit. Fronsac.

Château Richelieu – *Chemin du Tertre, 33126 Fronsac. 05 57 51 13 94. www.chateau-richelieu.com. Open daily 9am–12.30pm & 2–5pm.* Merlot, Cabernet-Franc and Malbec flourish in this 12.5ha vineyard, farmed traditionally with no fertilisers or chemicals. Harvesting is by hand. Natural yeasts are used in the vinification process, and the wine is then matured on the lees for 12 months in French oak barrels. Fronsac.

Château Dauzac – *33460 Labarde. 05 57 88 32 10. Open by appt. Mon–Fri 9am–noon & 2-5.30pm.* Since 1988, Château Dauzac has been owned by the MAIF insurance company.
In 1992, the job of running the estate was handed to renowned wine expert André Lurton, whose daughter Christine succeeded him in 2005. 45ha of vineyards on deep gravelly soil, 58% of which is planted with Cabernet Sauvignon, 37% with Merlot and 5% with Cabernet Franc. With an average age of 30 years and planted with a density of 10 000 plants per hectare, the vines are double-guyot pruned with de-budding and manual harvesting. Vinification is in thermoregulated stainless steel vats, followed by twelve months' ageing in barrels, 50-80% of which are new. Haut-Médoc, Margaux.

Domaine de Chevalier – *Chemin de Mignoy, 33850 Léognan. 05 56 64 16 16. www.domainedechevalier.com. Open by appt. Mon–Fri 9am–noon & 2–6pm.* The Bernard family, fine Bordeaux wine and brandy merchants, acquired Domaine de Chevalier in 1983. Over the past two decades, Olivier Bernard has perpetuated the spirit of balanced production on this estate covering 34ha with a mix of Cabernet Sauvignon, Semillon, Merlot and Cabernet Franc vines. Planted on black sandy soil and fine white gravel, they have an average age of twenty-five years. Traditional vinification, followed by maturing in the barrel for twenty-one months. Pessac–Léognan.

Château Carbonnieux – *33850 Léognan. 05 57 96 56 20. chateau.carbonnieux@wanadoo.fr. Open by appt. Mon–Fri, 8.30am–11am and 2–5pm.* Bought by Marc Perrin in 1956, the property is now run by his son, Antony. The vineyard, extending across 45ha, produces both reds and whites, and is planted with Cabernet Sauvignon, Merlot, Cabernet Franc, Cot, Malbec, Petit Verdot, Semillon and Muscadelle. Traditional growing methods, with manual harvesting. Three-week vinification in stainless steel vats, followed by a ten-month maturing process in the barrel for the estate whites, and eighteen months for its reds. Pessac–Léognan.

Château Fourcas Dupré – *Le Fourcas, 33480 Listrac-Médoc. ✆05 56 58 01 07. chateau-fourcas-dupre@wanadoo.fr. Open by appt. Mon–Fri 8am–noon & 2–5pm.* Since 1985, Patrice Pagès has overseen this family business. The estate's vineyards are planted on Pyrenean gravel and extend across an unbroken area covering 46ha, with 44% dedicated to Cabernet Sauvignon, the same area to Merlot, 10% to Cabernet Franc, 2% to Petit Verdot, and a planting density of 8 500 vines per hectare. Over the past few years, the vinification area has been completely renovated. The wines are matured in barrels, a third of which are replaced every year. Listrac-Médoc.

Château Dauphiné-Rondillon – *33140 Loupiac. ✆05 56 62 61 75. vignobles-darriet@wanadoo.fr. Open Mon–Fri 8.30am–12.30pm & 2–6pm; weekends by appt.* This family estate, created in 1784, has been handed down through the generations. Jean-Christophe Darriet heads the enterprise today, following his father Guy, an oenologue with more than fifty years' experience. The 60ha vineyard, of which 20ha are in the Loupiac appellation, 36ha in the Premières-Côtes-de-Bordeaux appellation, and 4ha in the Graves appellation, extends along both banks of the Garonne. Grape varieties include Semillon, Sauvignon Blanc, Muscadelle, Merlot, Cabernet-Sauvignon and Cabernet Franc. The majority of the vines are at least 40 years old, with some 80-year-old vines near the chateau. Bordeaux, Graves, Loupiac, Premières-Côtes-de-Bordeaux.

Château La Lagune – *81 ave. de l'Europe, 33290 Ludon-Médoc. ✆05 57 88 82 77. lalagune@club-internet.fr. Open by appt. Mon–Thu 9am–11am & 2–5pm.* The château changed hands several times prior to its acquisition in 2000 by Jean-Jacques Frey. Today Frey's daughter Caroline manages the estate along with Denis Dubourdieu. The 80 hectares are planted with Cabernet Sauvignon, Cabernet Franc, Merlot and Petit Verdot on sandy gravel soil. The new vinification area was put into operation for the 2004 harvest. Wines are matured in oak barrels (55% are new), for 15 to 18 months. Haut-Médoc.

S. Sauvignier / MICHELIN

Château Bonnin – *Blanchon, 33570 Lussac. ✆05 57 74 53 12. Open daily by appt. 8am–noon & 2–6pm.* Acquired by Patricia and Phillippe in 1997, the property consists of clayey-limestone soil. Traditional methods hold sway in the 6.5ha vineyard (85% Merlot, 10% Cabernet-Sauvignon, 5% Cabernet Franc), including de-budding and low-yield harvesting. The grapes are macerated before fermenting in cement tanks; ageing follows in barrels for 12 months. Lussac-Saint-Émilion.

Château Latour-Martillac – *Chemin de La Tour, 33650 Martillac. ✆05 57 97 71 11. www.domaines-kressmann.com. Open by appt.* Alfred Kressmann, a Bordeaux wine merchant, bought this estate in 1929. In 1940, his son Jean took over the running of the estate, developing it to its current size. Following the complete renovation of the wine storehouses in 1989, his two youngest sons, Tristan and Loïc, are perpetuating the family tradition. Traditional vinification and hand-picking. Reds account for the majority of production. Pessac–Léognan.

Château Haut Bailly – *33850 Leognan. Tel: 05 56 64 75 11. www.chateau-haut-bailly.com. Open by appt. Mon–Fri, 9am–12.30pm & 2–6pm.* Owned by American Robert G Wilmers and run by Veronique Sanders, this 30 hectare estate sits on one of the highest ridges in the appellation. It planted with 64% Cabernet Sauvignon, 30% Merlot, and 6% Cabernet Franc, at 10,000 vines per hectare, with its oldest vines dating back over 100 years. The wines produced here are elegant and restrained, and increasingly celebrated. An excellent second wine also, La Parde de Haut Bailly. Pessac-Léognan.

Château Chasse-Spleen – *2558 Grand-Poujeaux-Sud, 33480 Moulis-en-Médoc. ℘05 56 58 02 37. infos@chasse-spleen.com. Open Mon–Thu 8am–noon & 2–5pm; Fri 8am–noon, by appt. (except Jul–Aug).* Madame Castaing gave the château its name in the 19C. A century later, another exceptional woman, Bernadette Villars, reinforced the prestige of this Grand Cru, and now it is the turn of her daughter, Céline, who is running this 83ha estate with great enthusiasm. Harvesting by hand, traditional growing methods, maturing in barrels for eighteen months, and bottling on the estate ensure the quality and traditions of this renowned château. Moulis.

Château Haut-Brion – *33600 Pessac. ℘05 56 00 29 30. www.haut-brion.com.* The estate was purchased in 1935 by Clarence Dillon, an American citizen; today his great-grandson, Prince Robert of Luxembourg, heads the Dillon Company, which operates Haut Brion, La Mission Haut-Brion, La Tour Haut-Brion and Laville Haut-Brion estates. The vines, including Merlot, Cabernet Franc and Cabernet Sauvignon, are harvested by hand, followed by traditional vinification and barrel ageing for 9 to 22 months. Pessac–Léognan.

Château Pape-Clément – *216 ave. du Dr-Nancel-Penard, 33600 Pessac. ℘05 57 26 38 38. www.pape-clement.com. Open daily, by appt. Guided tours at 10.30, 11.30, 14.30, 16.30. Sunday at 10.30.* Owner Bernard Magrez has made this 32.5 hectare estate one of the most sought after of the appellation. The majority of the vineyard is devoted to Cabernet Sauvignon and Merlot, with smaller areas set aside for Sauvignon (2.5ha), Semillon and Muscadelle. The wines are matured in new barrels made from French oak. Good boutique where you can taste across Magrez's 35 estatres. Pessac–Léognan.

Château Mondésir-Gazin – *10 Le Sablon, 33390 Plassac. ℘05 57 42 29 80. www.mondesirgazin.com.* Marc Pasquet, a winemaker of Breton origin, moved to Plassac in 1990. Mondésir-Gazin's 14ha of vineyards are planted with Merlot, Malbec and Cabernet Sauvignon vines with an average age of 30 years. Hand-picking is followed by a rigorous sorting process. Vinification in stainless steel vats, with maturing in the barrel. Côtes-de-Blaye, Côtes-de-Bourg, Premières-Côtes-de-Blaye.

Château de Chantegrive – *Rte. de St-Michel-de-Rieuffret. 33720 Podensac. ℘05 56 27 17 38 www.chateauchantegrive.com. Open Mon–Sat 8.30am–5.30pm.* Following the redistribution of land by Henri and Françoise Levêque, the vineyard now covers around 100ha. In thirty years, the estate has seen the introduction of the best traditional equipment to enhance growing methods and the winemaking process, as well as the latest techniques to improve vinification, including the installation of fifteen vats, a temperature regulation system and automatic cap punching equipment. The estate also has an impressive bottling facility, with a capacity of 500 000 bottles. Cérons, Graves.

Château Bastor-Lamontagne – *33210 Preignac. ℘05 56 63 27 66. www.bastor-lamontagne.com. Open by appt. Mon–Fri 8.30am–12.30pm & 2–6pm.* The château's vineyards extend across 58ha of silico-gravelly soil on a limestone base. Harvesting is by hand, with low yield. The estate's wines are aged in stave-wood oak barrels for a period of between fifteen and eighteen months. Graves, Sauternes.

Clos Floridène – *33210 Pujols-sur-Ciron. ℘05 56 62 96 51. reynon@wanadoo.fr. Tasting and sales at the Chateau Reynon, 21 rte. de Cardon. 33410 Béguey. Open by appt.* The vineyard, located in the community of Pujols-sur-Ciron, near Barsac, encompasses 30.76ha of clayey-limestone soil. Thriving here are Sémillon (45%), Sauvignon (50%), and Muscadelle (5%) for the white wines; and Merlot (30%) and Cabernet-Sauvignon (70%) for the reds. The winemaking process employs a long maceration period; the wines are then matured in wooden barrels, of which a third are new. Graves.

Château Siaurac – *33500 Néac. ✆05 57 51 64 58. www.baronneguichard.com. Open daily by appt.* Very attractive estate covering 37 hectares of vines and the same again of parkland. At the back of the property, you have views over the churches of St.Emilion, Pomerol and Néac. The wines are 80% Merlot, 20% Cabernt France, with vines at around 40 years old. The same family owns Vray Croix de Gay in AOC Pomerol. Lalande-de-Pomerol.

Château Angélus – *33330 St-Émilion. ✆05 57 24 71 39. www.chateau-angelus.com. Open by appt. Mon–Fri 9am–noon & 2–5pm.* This estate has remained in the hands of the same family for seven generations. Through the unstinting efforts of Hubert de Boüard de Laforest and his cousin, Jean-Bernard Grenié, the estate was awarded Premier Grand Cru status in 1996. Today, the vineyard covers 23.4ha of uninterrupted land on soil that varies from clayey-limestone to sandy-limestone, planted with Merlot, Cabernet Franc and Cabernet Sauvignon, all of which are harvested by hand. The winery was renovated in 2001. Saint-Émiliion-Grand-Cru.

Château Figeac – *33330 St-Émilion. ✆05 57 24 72 26. www.chateau-figeac.com. Open by appt. Mon–Fri 9am–noon. Closed Aug and public holidays.* Thierry and Marie-France Manoncourt are ably supported in the running of this 40ha property by their daughter Laure d'Aramon and their son-in-law Éric. The vineyard, planted with Cabernet Franc (35%), Cabernet-Sauvignon (35%) and Merlot (30%), is cultivated traditionally, with manual harvesting. Tanks and vats of stainless steel, wood and oak are used in the winemaking and ageing processes. The estate also produces Chateau Petit Figeac, Chateau La Fleur Pourret and Chateau de Millery. Saint--Émilion-Grand-Cru.

Château Haut-Marbuzet – *33180 St-Estèphe. ✆05 56 59 30 54. info@haut-marbuzet.net.* When Hervé Duboscq bought this 7ha Cru property on a life annuity in 1952 he had no experience of the wine industry. Ten years later he was joined by his son Henry, who is now in charge of operations at this 58ha estate, now one of the appellation's most respected names. Every vine is harvested by hand, with a preference for overmaturing and complete de-stemming. The wines are then aged in barrels. St-Estèphe.

Château Ducru-Beaucaillou – *33250 St-Julien-Beychevelle. ✆05 56 73 16 73. Open by appt. Mon–Fri.* This estate, spread across 55ha of low-lying pebbly hills, has belonged to the Borie family since 1929. Three grape varieties are grown here: Cabernet Sauvignon, Merlot and Cabernet Franc. The maturing process takes place in oak barrels, from 12 to 18 months depending on the vintage. Saint-Julien.

Château Sociando-Mallet – *33180 St-Seurin-de-Cadourne. ✆05 56 73 38 80. scea-jean-gautreau@wanadoo.fr. Open by appt. Mon–Thu 9am–noon & 2–5pm; Fri 9am–noon.* Jean Gautreau fell in love with this château superbly situated alongside the Gironde, and created a wine whose quality has earned it international acclaim. 72ha of vines on land that is pebbly in nature, with a clayey-limestone subsoil, and planted with Cabernet Sauvignon, Cabernet Franc and Merlot with an average age of 25 years. Vinification occurs over 15–40 days in stainless-steel and cement vats, followed by ageing in oak barrels, for a period of between twelve and fifteen months. Haut–Médoc.

Château des Léotins – *33540 Sauveterre-de-Guyenne. ✆05 56 71 50 25. Open Mon–Fri 8am–noon & 2–9pm; weekends by appt.* In 1980 Claude Lumeau took the reins of the family estate. 85% of the 100ha estate are planted in red-wine grapes; 8ha in whites. Clayey-limestone soils support the Merlot, Cabernet-Sauvignon, Cabernet Franc, Sémillon and Sauvignon Blanc vines that thrive here. Bordeaux, Bordeaux Clairet, Entre-Deux-Mers.

Château Sainte-Marie – *51 rte. de Bordeaux, 33670 Targon. ✆05 56 23 64 30. Open by appt. Mon–Sat 8am–6pm.* This 45ha vineyard lies over to sunny hilltops atop clay-limestone soil. The vines, with an average age of 25 years, include Merlot, Cabernet-Sauvignon, Cabernet Franc, Sauvignon, Semillon and Muscadelle, and are planted 6,000-10,000 vines to the hectare; unusually high for the appellation. The white grapes are harvested by hand, then left on the lees for 6 month, the reds, are aged n oak vats. Bordeaux, Bordeaux Clairet, Bordeaux Supérieur, CastillonCôtes-de-Bordeaux, Entre-Deux-Mers.

Chateau Bauduc - *33670 Creon. 05 56 23 06 05. www.bauduc.com. Open Mon-Fri by appt.* English couple Gavin and Angela Quinney produce award-winning white and red wine here that is served at many leading restaurants in the UK. 30 hectares of Cabernet Sauvignon, Merlot, Sémillon and Sauvignon Blanc vines that have been extensively replanted in recent years at 6,500 vines per hectare, as part of an ongoing and successful quality drive. Cotes de Bordeaux, Bordeaux Blanc, Bordeaux.

Chateau Thieuley – *33670 Creon. 05 56 23 00 01. www.thieuley.com.* Consistently impressive wine from sisters Sylvie and Marie Courselle.

Low temperature vinification, early picking dates for the rosé wine and cold soaking for the reds, make this a quality range of fruit-forward, highly appealing wines.

Château Les Guyonnets – *33490 Verdelais. 05 56 62 09 89. didiertordeur@aol.com. Open Mon–Sat 9am–noon & 2–6pm.* Managed by Sophie and Didier Tordeur since 2000, this estate covers 25ha planted in Merlot and Cabernet-Sauvignon for the reds; and Sémillon and Sauvignon for the whites. The vineyard extends over clayey-limestone hillsides, is cultivated with the environment in mind, using no fertlisers or mowing. Temperature-controlled fermentation in stainless-steel tanks follows manual harvesting; the wines are then aged for the most part in wooden barrels (a third of them new) for 12 to 18 months. Bordeaux, Bordeaux Clairet, Bordeaux Sec, Bordeaux Supérieur, Cadillac, Premières-Côtes-de-Bordeaux, Sainte-Croix-du-Mont.

ADDRESSES

STAY

Gîtes Bacchus – *21 cours de l'Intendance, 33000 Bordeaux. 05 56 81 54 23. gites-de-france-gironde@wanadoo.fr.* The Gîte Bacchus label, created in 1996 by the Gîtes de France de Gironde, is awarded to accommodation run by wine producers on their own properties. Guests are given a personalised introduction to the region's wine industry, with a presentation of the main grape varieties, access to wine cellar, tastings etc.

AROUND BLAYE

Chambre d'hôte Château Pontet d'Eyrans–*25 le Pontet Nord-Est, 33390 Eyrans, 9km NE of Blaye along the D 937. 05 57 64 71 07. www.chateaupontet.fr. Reservation required. 5 rooms.* This château is quite simply a delight. Housed in the former stables, the modern bedrooms are all equipped with brand-new bathrooms and all overlook the swimming pool.

Closerie des Vignes – *Village Arnaud, 33710 St-Ciers-de-Canesse, 10km SE of Blaye along the D 669, then the D 250. 05 57 64 81 90. www.la-closerie-des-vignes.com. Open Apr–Oct. 9 rooms. 9€. Restaurant*. This modern house is surrounded by the vineyards of Blaye. Spacious bedrooms with stylishly modern furniture, and a panelled dining room looking onto the vineyards and garden. The culinary emphasis here is on simple, traditional cuisine.

Chambre d'hôte Villa Prémayac – *13 r. Prémayac, 33390 Blaye. 05 57 42 27 39. www.villa-premayac.com. 5 rooms.* This charming 18C villa at the foot of the citadel has a handful of pleasant rooms individually furnished with antiques, pleasant colours and elegant fabrics. The owner, a former golf coach, organises breaks which combine the region's fairways and vineyards.

AROUND BORDEAUX

Château Lantic – *10 rte. de Lartigue, 33650 Martillac. 05 56 72 58 68. www.chateau-de-lantic.com. 8 rooms. 8€.* This adorable château houses rooms furnished in the style of yesteryear (some with kitchenettes). An outbuilding hosts temporary exhibitions.

Châlet Lyrique – *169 cours Générale-de-Gaulle, 33170 Gradignan, 3.5km S of Pessac. 05 56 89 11 59. info@chaletlyrique.fr. 44 rooms. 9.50€.* Two buildings with contrasting styles add a certain cachet to this hotel. Rooms of varying size with differing levels of comfort – the renovated bedrooms are perhaps preferable. The restaurant, housed in the former village café, has lost none of its local atmosphere.

Hôtel de la Tour Intendance – *16 r. de la Vieille-Tour, 33000 Bordeaux. 05 56 44 56 56. www.hotel-tour-intendance.com. 24 rooms. 8€.* A nicely renovated hostelry in the heart of downtown, with a Bordeaux-style facade and charming interior accented with stone. Comfortable, modern, individual rooms add to the charm of this spot, as does the friendly welcome.

Une Chambre en Ville – *35 r. Bouffard, 33000 Bordeaux. 05 56 81 34 53. www.bandb-bx.com. 5 rooms. 8€.* This entirely renovated building in the old town features impeccably-kept rooms, each with its own individual décor. Try the "Bordelaise" suite, done in warm colors with modern appointments; or the "Nautique" displaying a seagoing theme. The "Oriental" sports vivid colors and furniture from Mahgreb.

AROUND LANGON

Chambre d'hôte Chassagnol – *33410 Ste-Croix-du-Mont, 12km S of Cadillac along the D 10. 05 56 62 00 58. 4 rooms.* This large 19C house at the heart of the Ste-Croix-du-Mont vineyards is a popular choice with wine aficionados. Spacious bedrooms furnished with antique furniture, plus a garden and terrace with the added attraction of a barbecue.

Chambre d'hôte Château du Broustaret – *33410 Rions, 4km NW of Cadillac by the D 10. 05 56 62 96 97. www.broustaret.net. Closed Nov–Easter holidays. 5 rooms.* The tradition of hospitality has been maintained for a quarter of a century at this wine property at the heart of the Premières-Côtes-de-Bordeaux appellation. Woods and meadows surround the house, in which the guest rooms are simply furnished yet comfortable. A peaceful retreat from which to explore the region's vineyards.

Chambre d'hôte Les Logis de Lestiac – *71 rte. de Bordeaux, 33550 Lestiac-sur-Garonne. 05 56 72 17 90. 5 rooms. Restaurant.* The owner, an impassioned decorator, has superbly restored this 18C house. The guestrooms on the upper floor each represent a different season, and there is a duplex on the ground level. Tasty meals available.

Relais du Château d'Arche – *Rte de Bommes, 33210 Sauternes. 05 56 76 67 67. chateau-arche@terre-net.fr. 9 rooms. 10€.* This fine 17C country house dominating the village stands at the heart of the vineyards of the Château d'Arche, an estate famous for its Sauternes Grand Cru. The luxurious bedrooms enjoy the benefits of peace and tranquillity, plus views across the vineyards.

AROUND LIBOURNE

Henri IV – *Pl. du 8-Mai-1945, 33230 Coutras, 15km N of Lussac along the D 17. 05 57 49 34 34. www.hotelcoutras.com. 16 rooms. 8€.* This 19C mansion opposite the railway station is fronted by a garden-courtyard. Solid pine furniture in the somewhat basic yet well-maintained bedrooms – those on the top floor are air-conditioned and attic in style. Efficient double-glazing and double windows to combat noise from passing trains.

Hôtel des Vignobles – *35 r. André-Nhévoit, 33500 Libourne. 05 57 51 23 29. 8 rooms. 6.50€.* This tiny hotel located between the stadium and the train station surrounds a delightfully verdant courtyard, setting for breakfast in fine weather. Functional rooms are

Chambres d'hôte at the Château Le Foulon

S. Sauvignier/MICHELIN

well-equipped and maintained. There is a fully-equipped kitchenette at clients' disposal.

La Tour du Vieux Port – *23 quai Souchet, 33500 Libourne. 05 57 25 75 56. http://latourduvieuxport.com. 14 rooms. 6€. Restaurant*. This hotel-restaurant next to the Tour du Port overlooking the Dordogne River offers spacious rooms with personal touches, all tastefully renovated by the owner. Three dining rooms, all offering traditional, seasonal fare.

Chambres d'hôte Château de La Rivière – *In la Rivière, 33500 Libourne, 6km W of Libourne. 05 57 55 56 51. www.chateau-de-la-riviere.com. Closed Dec 15–Jan 15. 5 rooms.* In the Renaissance wing of the Chateau de la Rivière, standing amid the vines, five spacious guestrooms are a happy blend of old and new. As a bonus, the property features a large park and tours of the cellars.

IN MARGAUX

Chambre d'hôte Château Cap Léon Veyrin – *33480 Listrac-Médoc – 4km from Listrac along the D 5E2 – 05 56 58 07 28 – capleonveyrin@aol.com – Closed Dec 25–Jan 1. 5 rooms.* The same family has run this attractive property at the heart of a 20ha estate since 1810. All the Louis XV-style bedrooms are equipped with impressive bathrooms. Delightful breakfast room opening onto the wine storehouse.

Chambre d'hôte Domaine de Carrat – *Rte. de Ste-Hélène, 33480 Castelnau-de-Médoc, 5km S of Listrac-Médoc by the N 215 – 05 56 58 24 80. Closed Dec 25. 4 rooms.* This red-shuttered house surrounded by a pine forest and leafy woodland once served as the stables for the neighbouring château. Friendly and attentive owners and bedrooms offering good levels of comfort. On arrival, you will pass under the splendid stone entrance used in former times by horse-drawn vehicles.

France et Angleterre – *3 quai Albert-Pichon, 33250 Pauillac. 05 56 59 01 20. contact@hoteldefrance-angleterre.com. Closed Dec 19–Jan 15. 29 rooms. 9€. Restaurant*. A 19C building along the waterfront with functional yet tastefully renovated bedrooms, with those on the main façade enjoying pleasant views of the Gironde estuary. Traditional and local cuisine, including Pauillac lamb, served in the modern dining room and veranda.

Chambre d'hôte Château Le Foulon – *Rte de St-Raphaël, 33480 Castelnau-de-Médoc, 5km S of Listrac-Médoc along the N 215. 05 56 58 20 18. www.au-chateau.com. Closed Dec 15–Jan 2. 4 rooms.* This château dating from 1840 is the perfect base from which to discover the Grands Crus of the Médoc. The four bedrooms, all furnished with antiques, have retained their original spaciousness, with views of the park, lake and resident swans. An apartment with a fully-equipped kitchen is also available.

Le Pavillon de Margaux – *3 r. Georges-Mandel – 33460 Margaux – 05 57 88 77 54. 14 rooms. 12€. Restaurant*. It's hard to imagine that this delightful 19C building on the edge of Margaux's vineyards was once the local school. Inside, each bedroom is named after and decorated in the style of a Médoc château. Those in the most recent wing are on the smaller side. Outstanding wine cellar.

AROUND ST-ÉMILION

Auberge de la Commanderie – *R. des Cordeliers, 33330 St-Émilion. 05 57 24 70 19. 18 rooms. 9.50€.* Within the walls of a former 17C command-post, the hotel's rooms are small, but pleasant updated; those in the annex are larger, and better suited to families.

⊜⊜ **Chambre d'hôte Château Monlot** – *St-Hippolyte, 33330 St-Émilion, 3km SE of St-Émilion by the D 245. ☏ 05 57 74 49 47. www.chateaumonlot.com. 6 rooms.* ☕. This "château" is the archetype of the many bourgeois residences in the region. Bedrooms with period furniture, paintings and old photos, each named after a particular grape variety: Merlot, Cabernet, Sauvignon etc. Attractive breakfast room with viticultural decor. Tree-shaded garden for the summer months.

⊜⊜ **Logis des Remparts** – *18 r. Guadet, 33330 St-Émilion. ☏05 57 24 70 43. www.saint-emilion.org. Closed Dec 15–Jan 31. 16 rooms. ☕12€.* This building, dating from the 17C, has a pleasant, meticulously maintained private terrace, as well as a garden facing onto the local vineyards. Comfortably furnished bedrooms, plus a breakfast veranda.

AROUND SAUVETERRE-DE-GUYENNE

⊜ **Hôtel les Remparts** – *16 r. du Château, 33890 Gensac. ☏05 57 47 43 46. 7 rooms. ☕7.50€. Restaurant⊜⊜⊜.* Located near the church, this hostelry features charming rooms outfitted in a former medieval presbytery. The restaurant boasts a panoramic view from its beautifully appointed tables. Lovely garden.

⊜⊜ **Chambre d'hôte La Lézardière** – *Boimier-Gabouriaud, 33540 St-Martin-de-Lerm, 8km SE of Sauveterre-de-Guyenne by the D 670, D 230, then the D 129. ☏05 56 71 30 12. www.lalezardiere@free.fr. Closed Jan–Feb. 4 rooms and 1 gîte.* 🚭 ☕. *Restaurant⊜⊜.* The half a dozen rooms on the first floor of this 17C farm overlooking the Dropt valley have been attractively converted with a focus on colour. Evening meals in the upper barn. A lounge containing documentation on wine and the region is located behind the old livestock feeding troughs. Swimming pool, plus a large gîte.

⊜⊜ **Chambre d'hôte Domaine de la Charmaie** – *33190 St-Sève, 12km S of Sauveterre-de-Guyenne by the D 670, then the D 129. ☏05 56 61 10 72. http://monsite.orange.fr/domainedelacharmaie. 4 rooms.* 🚭 ☕. *Restaurant⊜⊜.* This 17C mansion is tucked away in a verdant setting. Bedrooms with a harmonious decor of pastel shades, elegant fabrics and furniture showing the patina of age, and attractive bathrooms.

⊜⊜⊜⊜ **Le Château de Sanse** – *33350 Ste-Radegonde. ☏05 57 56 41 10. www.chateaudesanse.com. Open Mar 1–Nov 30. 16 rooms. ☕15€. Restaurant⊜⊜⊜.* Its light-stone facade dominating countryside and vineyard, this noble 18C residence features a large park and a fine swimming pool. Spacious, calm rooms.

EAT

AROUND BLAYE

⊜ **Le Troque-Sel** – *1 pl. Jeantet, 33710 Bourg. ☏05 57 68 30 67. Closed Sun evenings, Tue evenings and Mon.* The key to the success of this restaurant is the old adage that simplicity is best. The wine list here features a wide choice of Côtes-de-Bourg and Crus from the Bordeaux region to accompany dishes such as lamprey *à la Bordelaise* and duck magret with *cèpe* mushrooms.

⊜⊜ **La Citadelle** – *5 pl. d'Armes, 33390 Blaye. ☏05 57 42 17 10. www.hotel-la-citadelle.com. 21 rooms ⊜⊜.* A wonderful location in the heart of the Citadelle de Blaye is the major selling point of this hotel-restaurant. Modern, bright dining room with large bay windows, and splendid views of the Gironde estuary from the terrace. The emphasis here is on traditional cuisine. Functional bedrooms. Swimming pool.

⊜⊜ **La Filadière** – *Rte. de la Corniche, Furt, 33710 Gauriac, 8km SE of Blaye by the D 669. ☏05 57 64 94 05. lafiladiere@tiscali.fr. Closed Dec 2–14, Tue evenings from Sept 15–Jun 30 and Wed.* The airy dining room is decorated in bright colours with exquisite rattan furniture. In summer, guests can enjoy the panoramic view from the Filadière's terrace. Appetising local recipes.

AROUND BORDEAUX

⊜⊜ **Auberge du Marais** – *22 rte. de Latresne, 33270 Bouliac. ☏05 56 20 52 17. Closed Feb 15–Mar 1, Aug 15–Sept 6, Sun evenings and Wed.* Regional southwestern fare tempts the palate at this lovely country home, graced with modern paintings. Weather permitting, take a seat on the pretty shaded terrace.

⊖⊖ **Auberge la Forêt** – *Rte. de la Forêt, 33370 Salleboeuf, 10km N of Créon along the D 671. ℘05 56 21 25 49. www.aubergelaforet.com.Closed Sun evenings and Wed.* Spacious, rustic-style dining room occupying a house in a residential suburb. Pleasant veranda opening onto an attractive garden for alfresco dining in the summer months. Appetising traditional cuisine at reasonable prices.

⊖⊖ **Gravelier** – *114 cours de Verdun, 33000 Bordeaux. ℘05 56 48 17 15. amgravelier@yahoo.fr. Closed Jul 31–30 Aug, Sat and Sun.* Run by Yves Gravelier and his wife in the Les Chartrons district, this restaurant has garnered a reputation for its inventive, contemporary cuisine based on high-quality, rigorously sourced products. New, trendy decor enhanced by refined furnishings and contrasting colours.

⊖⊖ **La Cape** – *Allée Morlette, 33150 Cenon, 6km W of Bordeaux along the A 630 ring road. ℘05 57 80 24 25. Closed Sat, Sun and public holidays.* This discreet house is home to two contemporary, brightly coloured dining rooms, in addition to a pleasant garden-terrace. Attractive, inventive cuisine, plus an interesting local wine list.

⊖⊖ **Le Bistro du Musée** – *3 pl. Pey-Berland, 33000 Bordeaux. ℘05 56 52 99 69. bistrodumusee@wanadoo.fr. Closed for a fortnight at Christmas, 3 weeks in Aug and Sun.* You'll take an instant liking to this bistro with its attractive dark green wood frontage and elegant interior with exposed brick walls, oak flooring, moleskin benches and a decor embellished with tools from the wine trade. Cuisine from the southwest accompanied by a comprehensive Bordeaux wine list.

⊖⊖ **Le Cohé** – *8 ave. Roger-Cohé, 33600 Pessac. ℘05 56 45 73 72. lecohe@free.fr. Closed Aug 4–29, Sun evenings and Mon.* An old house with a pleasant white stone façade, hushed, contemporary interior and clean, elegant layout. Cuisine with a modern edge, with an emphasis on fish and seafood.

⊖⊖ **Tupina** – *6 r. Porte-de-la-Monnaie, 33000 Bordeaux. ℘05 56 91 56 37. www.latupina.com.* A country-style atmosphere and thoughtful decor are the hallmarks of this restaurant which has been visited by former President Jacques Chirac. Dishes from the southwest roasted over an open fire or prepared on the stove according to time-honoured traditions. Impressive wine list, plus a superb collection of Armagnacs and Cognacs.

⊖⊖⊖ **L'Olivier du Clavel** – *44 r. Charles-Domercq, 33000 Bordeaux. ℘05 57 95 09 50. fgclavel@wanadoo.fr. Closed Aug, Jan 2–10, Sat lunchtime, Sun and Mon.* The chef here uses different appellations of oil from far and wide to produce cuisine inspired by seasonal produce and the Mediterranean. Neo-bistro decor in Provençal tones.

AROUND LANGON

⊖ **Braises et Gourmandises** – *RN 113, 33210 Preignac, 8km W of Verdelais. ℘05 56 62 30 58. braises-gourmandises@ot-sauternes.com. Closed Tue evenings and Sun evenings.* Pay no attention to the unremarkable facade; just push through the front door into this charming interior done in wood, accented by copper pots. Grilled meats and fish selections, to sample indoors or on the shaded terrace. Efficient, unobtrusive service.

⊖⊖ **Cyril** – *62 cours Fossés, 33210 Langon. ℘05 56 76 25 66. cyril.baland@wanadoo.fr.* This restaurant takes its name from the chef, who divides his time between the kitchen and local markets, where he sources the very best products to create unpretentious yet high-quality traditional dishes. A warm welcome from Karine in the freshly revamped dining room. Excellent value for money.

⊖⊖ **L'Abricotier** – *2 r. François-Bergoeing, 33490 St-Macaire, 3km N of Langon by the N 113. ℘05 56 76 83 63. Closed Nov 12–Dec 12, Tue evenings and Mon.* Set back slightly from the N 113, "The Apricot Tree" offers guests the choice of its smart, modern dining rooms or, on sunny days, a terrace in the shade of mulberry trees. In the kitchen, the culinary focus is on simple yet good quality local dishes, washed down perhaps with a bottle from the judicious wine list.

Le Cap – *12 r. Gemin, 33210 Preignac, 8km NE of Sauternes by the D 125, then the D 8. 05 56 63 27 38. lecaphorn@wanadoo.fr. Closed Feb 3-10 Feb, Mar 24–Apr 9, Sept 15–Oct 8, Mon from Jun–mid-Sept and Sun evenings.* The charming dining room (with seating for just 20) and the fine terrace of this venerable building on the banks of the Garonne are popular with both professional and amateur sailors who come here to enjoy contemporary cuisine, including dishes that include river fish.

Le Saprien – *R. Principale, 33210 Sauternes. 05 56 76 60 87. saprien@tiscali.fr. Closed Dec 1–26, Feb school holidays, Sun evenings and Mon.* Choose between the elegant dining room, veranda or terrace with pleasant views of the vineyards. The excellent sweet wine produced locally takes centre-stage here with dishes such as Terrine in Sauternes jelly, Parfait Glacé au Sauternes, plus the obligatory fine cellar!

L'Entrée Jardin – *27 ave. du Pont, 33410 Cadillac. 05 56 76 96 96. Closed 1 week in Feb, Aug 15–31, Thu evenings, Sun evenings, and Mon off-season.* Local innkeepers without exception recommend this restaurant, which handily blends a friendly welcome, efficient service and pleasant atmosphere. Regional cuisine (practically everything is made in-house) handily satisfies even the biggest appetites.

Claude Darroze – *95 cours Général Leclerc, 33210 Langon. 05 56 63 00 48. www.darroze.com. Closed Oct 21–Nov 10, Jan 6–28, Sun evenings and Mon lunchtime Nov–Jun.* An old-style dining room and plane tree-shaded terrace provide the backdrop for delicious classic cuisine (Gironde lamprey in Bordeaux wine, warm duck foie gras with caramelised apples etc) and a comprehensive Bordeaux-dominated wine list. A traditional address for serious gourmets.

AROUND LIBOURNE

Chez Carles – *1 barrail-de-Tourenne, 33240 St-Germain-de-la-Rivière, 8km NW of Libourne by the D 670. 05 57 84 44 50. jocelyne@lunerouge.net. Closed Sun evenings and Mon.* Housed in the same building as the Maison du Pays Fronsadais, this restaurant borders the mirror-like waters of a small inlet. The chef offers his own take on traditional recipes, all accompanied by good regional wines. Try something grilled over vine cuttings!

Chez Servais – *14 pl. Decazes, 33500 Libourne. 05 57 51 83 97. Closed Aug 12–25, Sun evenings and Mon.* Behind the engaging façade of this small stone house is a charming dining room attractively laid-out with flower-decked tables, cane chairs and tasteful furniture. Popular with locals who flock here to enjoy a choice of enticing traditional menus.

Le Vieux Presbytère – *Pl. de l'Église, 33570 Montagne, 4km SW of Lussac along the D 122. 05 57 74 65 33.* This restaurant occupies a former presbytery next to a Romanesque chapel. Meals are served in the rustic-style dining room or on the attractive terrace in season. Traditional cuisine complemented by a selection of Crus.

Le Villagosia – *12 r. de la République, 33141 Villegouge, 12km N of Libourne along the D 128. 05 57 84 40 50. Closed Fri lunchtime and Sun evenings.* Opened a couple of years ago in a small village surrounded by vineyards in the hills to the north of Libourne, this restaurant has already built up a loyal following. Fresh decor, bright tones and good-quality cuisine.

AROUND MARGAUX

Le Lion d'Or – *Pl. de la République, 33460 Arcins, 6km NW of Margaux along the D 2. 05 56 58 96 79. Closed Jul, Dec 24–Jan 1, Sun, Mon and public holidays. Reservations required.* This old coaching inn has been converted into a modern gastronomic staging post with an unpretentious atmosphere which, like its owner-chef, is full of character! The slate board on the side of the road highlights the daily menu for avid regulars who flock here for copious, well-prepared local cuisine.

Café Lavinal – *in Bages, pl. Desquet, 33250 Pauillac. 05 57 75 00 09. Closed Dec 26–Feb 5, Sun evenings.* Attractive "neo-retro" bistro opened in 2006 in the downtown Pauillac. Open kitchen, and updated decor with slate accents. Local wines.

Auberge des Vignerons – *28 ave. Soulac, 33480 Listrac-Médoc. 05 56 58 08 68. Closed Feb school holidays, Sat lunchtime, Sun evenings and Mon from Oct–May.* The dining room in this auberge, standing next to the Maison des Vins de Listrac-Médoc, occupies a former wine cellar. Enjoy pleasant views of the vineyards of this famous appellation from the terrace. Traditional cuisine, plus a cellar resolutely based on the quality wines of Listrac!

Ferme-Auberge Château Guittot-Fellonneau – *33460 Macau, 6km SE of Margaux by the D 2 and then the D 209. 05 57 88 47 81. Closed Feb school holidays and Aug 16–Sept 5.* Fine wining and dining is guaranteed on this wine-producing estate in the Médoc. Indulge in the typical fare of the southwest on a shady terrace overlooking the vines, with dishes such as rillettes, confits, foie gras etc, all prepared on the property by the owner.

La Table d'Olivier – *La Mare aux Grenouilles, 53 rte. de Lesparre, 33340 Gaillan-en-Médoc. 05 56 41 13 32. Closed Sat lunchtime, Sun evenings and Mon.* A charming address overlooking a frog pond. Contemporary cuisine, served in a pleasant, modern décor of wooden tables, iron chairs and paintings.

Auberge de Savoie – *1 pl. Trémoille, 33460 Margaux. 05 57 88 31 76. Closed Feb and Christmas school holidays and Sun evenings.* A friendly welcome is assured in this attractive 19C stone inn next to the tourist office. Meals are served in two pleasant and colourfully decorated dining rooms and, in fine weather, on the attractive terrace. Enticing cuisine prepared on a coal-fired stove. Impressive Bordeaux wine list.

AROUND ST-ANDRÉ-DE-CUBZAC

Coq Sauvage – *in Cavernes, 33450 St-Loubès, 15km S of St-André-de-Cubzac by the D 911, then the D 242. 05 56 20 41 04. Closed Aug 2–29, Dec 24 –Jan 9, Sat and Sun.* The Dordogne flows past this house in a small village in the Entre-Deux-Mers area. In winter, the regional fare on offer here is served in the attractively rustic dining room, and in summer on a flower-decked patio. Quiet bedrooms.

AROUND ST-ÉMILION

Le Bouchon – *1 pl. du Marché, 33330 St-Émilion. 05 57 24 62 81. franckherman@tiscali.fr. Closed Nov–Feb.* One of the most pleasant of several restaurants on the place du Marché, the hub of St-Émilion life. The dining room, repainted in yellow and blue tones, is adorned with black and white photos. Refined traditional cuisine accompanied by a lively choice of wines.

L'Envers du Décor – *11 r. du Clocher, 33330 St-Émilion. 05 57 74 48 31, enversdudecor@nerim.fr. Closed Dec 22–Jan 9.* This wine bar adjoining the collegiate church serves seasonal dishes in a dining room where the style is a fusion of wood, old stone and aluminium. Quiet, relaxing terrace adorned with flowers and fig trees. A choice of high-quality wines is also on sale for consumption off the premises.

De France – *7 p. du Marché, 33420 Branne. 05 57 84 50 06.* Sample intriguing local recipes, some grilled over vine cuttings either in the rustic dining room or on the lovely shaded terrace. At lunchtime, a daily fixed menu is on offer at the bar.

Le Tertre – *R. du Tertre-de-la-Tente, 33330 St-Émilion. 05 57 74 46 33. Closed Jan 5–Feb 11, Nov 12–Dec 18, Thu from Oct–Apr and Wed.* The elegant dining room, with its seafood tank and cellar dug into the rock containing a number of prestigious vintages, is sure to whet your appetite. Enticing contemporary cuisine with a definite Gascon influence.

AROUND SAUVETERRE-DE-GUYENNE

⊜⊜ **Les Fontaines** – *8 r. Verdun, 33190 La Réole, 14km S of Sauveterre-de-Guyenne by the D 670. ✆05 56 61 15 25. Closed Feb 23–Mar 1, Nov 17–Dec 1, Wed eve nings off-season, Sun evenings and Mon.* This large bourgeois building adjoins a delightful wooded garden. Two dining rooms which have retained their original elegant feel, plus a terrace for summer dining. Delicious traditional cuisine at prices that remain digestible!

⊜⊜ **Le Flore** – *1 Petit-Champ-du-Bourg, 33540 Coirac, 7.5km W of Sauveterre-de-Guyenne by the D 671, then the D 228 beyond St-Brice. ✆05 56 71 57 47. Closed 2 weeks in Feb, 2 weeks in Nov, Wed evenings, Sun evenings and Mon.* Creative, high-quality cuisine prepared by an up-and-coming chef is served in the flower-decked dining room of this small house. Easy-going yet professional service from the chef's wife, who will guide you effortlessly through the enticing menu.

⊜⊜⊜ **Auberge Saint-Jean** – *8 ave. du Pont, 33420 St-Jean-de-Blaignac, 17km N of Sauveterre-de-Guyenne by the D 670. ✆05 57 74 95 50. Closed Jan 5–9, Nov 15–Dec 12, Tue evenings and Wed.* Generous regional cuisine mixed with a dash of inventiveness, with dishes such as foie gras with tobacco, turbot and langoustine pot au feu, lamb with lavender sauce etc. Enjoy an unbeatable view of the Dordogne from the veranda of this former coaching inn.

GOURMET SHOPPING

Baillardran – *55 cours de l'Intendance, 33000 Bordeaux. ✆05 56 52 92 64. Open Mon–Sat 10.30am–8pm, Sun 10.30am–1pm& 2–7.30pm. www.baillardran.com.* This attractive boutique decked out in marble, mirrors and gilding sells just three products: macaroons, nougatine and the famous canelé. Originally created in the 16C but popular as ever, this Bordeaux speciality is a caramelised cake flavoured with vanilla and rum which takes the shape of the mould it is baked in.

Bordeaux speciality – Cannelés

S. Sauvignier/MICHELIN

Pierre Oteiza – *77 r. Condillac. 33000 Bordeaux. ✆05 56 52 38 76. www.pierreoteiza.com. Open Tue–Sat 10am–1pm & 2.30–7.30pm.* This temple of Basque gastronomy is overflowing with hams, sausages, and jars and tins of preserves. Its owner offers his customers the very best of the region's products from the renowned piperade to the famous Les Alludes leg of pork, which is rubbed in pepper and is prepared on the premises.

Recette des Anciennes Religieuses – Mme Blanchez – *R. Guadet, 33330 St-Émilion. ✆05 57 24 72 33. Open Mon–Sat 8am–12.30pm & 3-7pm; Sun 9am–12.30pm & 3–7pm. Closed 2 wks in Feb, 3 wks in Nov.* Archives confirm the existence of macaroons in Saint-Émilion as early as 1620. Following an eventful history, the recipe finally came into the hands of the Passama family in 1930. Made from eggs, sugar and almonds, these delicious cakes are still made in this shop according to traditional methods.

MARKETS

Bordeaux – Marché des Capucins, every morning except Tue; Marché du Chartrons, along the Garonne, Sun morning; Marché St-Michel, Sat morning; organic market every Thu morning along the river opposite the Esplanade des Quinconces.

Libourne – Sun, Tue and Fri mornings.

Pauillac – Sat morning; Fri evening market in summer.

Sauveterre-de-Guyenne – Wed morning.

4 – BURGUNDY

Nowhere is the idea of "terroir" more prized than in Burgundy. Here centuries of observation and experience have made it possible to adapt grape varieties to soils and climatic conditions, so that each village, estate or plot can produce a unique, inimitable wine. Indeed, the word "climate" (climat) has a special sense in Burgundy, where it is used to refer to a wine-growing area producing a specific wine. However, this geographical diversity would be useless without the human factor: the monks of Cîteaux and Cluny abbeys were the true pioneers of Burgundy wine. The modern-day wine region, between the Auxerrois and Mâconnais areas, represents only a tiny part of historic Burgundy, once as mighty a dukedom as any in France. Burgundy's diversity lies in its vineyards within their walled-in plots, in the neatly cultivated slopes of the hillside estates, but also in charming villages, their bell towers capped with colourful glazed tiles; in castles combining military austerity with rich ornamentation, and in cellars where the fruit of human labour is left to mature beneath the earth.

Highlights

1. A tour around the **Hospices des Beaune** (p189)
2. A **kir** (creme de cassis and white wine) to start a meal (p211)
3. A visit to Nuit St George's **Imaginarium** (p188)
4. A leisurely trip down the **Burgundy canals** (p199)
5. A stroll around the pictureque **Montagny-les-Buxy** (p194)

Background

In its methods and standards, Burgundy has always been something of a world apart, even reckoning its parcels of ground not in hectares but by the *ouvrée* (about 0.04ha). Historically, this was defined as the area a man with a pick could work in a day. A small unit of measurement also makes it easier to determine the geological diversity of the soils which depends in part on the gradient of the slope, and the amount of sunshine, wind and frost it receives. There are, for instance, 59 soil types in the Côte de Nuits area alone.

This extremely precise information about each plot of ground has enabled Burgundian wine growers to give a name to each **climat** or **vineyard**. These names are often picturesque and their origin varies. It can be based on botany: Blanches Fleurs (white flowers), Clos des Chênes from the oak trees growing in a particular plot, La Truffière from truffles; from zoology: Grenouilles (the frogs), Clos des Mouches (flies), Dent de Chien (dog's tooth), Les Corbeaux (the crows); or from the local climate: Les Brouillards (fog), Bel Air (clean air), Côte Rôtie (sun-roasted slopes), Vigne du Soleil (sunny vines); or geology: Les Terres Blanches (white soil), Les Gravières (gravel). Other names are drawn from an anecdote or a fanciful idea: La Pucelle (the virgin), Les Amoureuses (the lovers), Paradis (paradise), Clos l'Évêque (bishop's enclosure), Les Joyeuses (the happy ones), Chevalier (the knight), Les Procès (the legal cases), L'Homme Mort (the dead man), Tonton Marcel (uncle Marcel). All of them give you an idea of how personally attached Burgundian winemakers get to their land, and are key to understanding that the whole aim of wine-making in the region is about ways to maximise the personality of the land in each bottle of wine.

The patchwork of small-sized plots can make the area seem difficult to approach for wine tourists, but it makes up the richness of Burgundy, and the winemakers that you meet when exploring the villages and towns are usually only to happy to invite you in to taste their wines in the cellars beneath their estates, and explain to you the origin and characteristics of their wines.

You will often find them uncorking any number of old vintages just to enjoy sharing them with an interested party.

Clos de Vougeot – a Burgundian jewel set in the heart of its vineyard

B. Kaufmann / MICHELIN

OVERVIEW

The Terroir

Michelin Local Maps 319 and 320 – Yonne (89), Côte-d'Or (21) and Saône-et-Loire (71).

Area: 27,670ha (5% of the total wine-growing land in France), extending from north to south over 160km.

Production: about 1.53 million hl (203 million bottles) in five wine-growing regions, the Chablis, Auxerre, Tonnerre and Vézelay areas in the Yonne *départment*; the Côte de Nuits and Hautes-Côtes de Nuits between Dijon and Corgoloin in the Côte-d'Or *départment;* the Côte de Beaune and Hautes-Côtes de Beaune between Beaune and Les Maranges astride the Côte-d'Or and Saône-et-Loire *départments*; the Côte Chalonnaise and Mâconnais in Saône-et-Loire.

The vineyards, backing on to the eastern foothills of the Massif Central, extend over the slopes of the Jurassic escarpments, at an altitude varying from 80m to 350m. The semi-continental climate features oceanic influences. Winters are cold, summers temperate and sunny. Rainfall is most abundant in springtime.

Grape varieties

Burgundy features a remarkable ampelographic unity, with the almost exclusive dominance of two grape varieties: Pinot Noir for red wines (36% of grapes planted) and Chardonnay for white wines (46% of grapes planted). Also present are Gamay, Sauvignon and minor grape varieties such as Sacy, Aligoté and Melon for white wines, César for the reds and Pinot-Beurot for some rosé wines. Mention of the grape variety linked with a regional appellation is allowed, but on AOC Villages and Premier Cru labels the name of the appellation alone is allowed.

Appellations

In Burgundy, there are four grades of appellation:

23 regional appellations: eg Bourgogne, Bourgogne-Passetoutgrain, Mâcon-Villages, Bourgogne-Vézelay.

44 village appellations: eg Beaune, Chablis, Nuits-Saint-Georges, St-Romain.

635 villages + Premier Cru climats (vineyards): eg Nuit St Georges 1er Cru Les Cailles, Chablis 1er Cru Fourchaume

33 Grands Crus: eg Corton, Musigny, Montrachet, Romanée-Conti, Clos-de-Vougeot, Clos-de-Tart. (32 in Cotes d'Or, 1 in Chablis with 7 climats).

Yonne Valley Wine Road

The northern parts of the Burgundy vineyard begin just 90 minutes south of Paris, and run alongside the Aube region of Champagne, then down through Chablis and Vezelay. This is an attractive landscape, with gently undulating slopes, less steep than the Cotes regions of Burgundy.

- **Population:** 323,000 in the Yonne Valley.
- **Michelin Map:** 319, D4, E5, G4, H4.
- **Info:** www.vins-bourgogne.fr.
- **Location:** The Yonne Wine Route is 260km long
- **Don't Miss:** The Yonne Wine Route festival, held in the third weekend of May.
- **Timing:** Two days for a leisurely explore.
- **Kids:** A picnic in the vines around Saint Bris le Vineux

DRIVING TOURS

AUXERROIS, CHABLIS & TONNERROIS VINEYARDS

Joigny

Joigny is a picturesque little town clinging to the slopes of the Côte Saint-Jacques, on the edge of the forest of Othe; its steep streets, lined with half-timbered old houses and Renaissance monuments, plunge down towards the River Yonne. Joigny was long an important wine-growing centre and its inhabitants were referred to as "maillotins", after the mallets they used to make their wine barrels. Today, the Côte-Saint-Jacques vineyards are being slowly revived thanks to the care of a handful of enthusiastic wine growers and to the attention drawn by the renowned chef **Jean-Michel Lorain**.

On top of the Côte Saint-Jacques★

1.5km north along D 20. The road, climbing in hairpin bends, reaches Croix de Guémard where a path on the right runs across the vineyards. Fine **view** over Joigny and the Yonne Valley.

Leave Joigny southwest along D 67.

Pressoir de Champvallon

Closed while work is in progress.

Located inside a monumental cellar, in the heart of the village, this winepress boasting a 12C pendulum mechanism is still in working order.

Drive south on D 367, then D 955; first road left after the motorway bridge.

Musée rural des Arts populaires de Laduz★

Open daily Jul–Aug 2.30–6.pm. Jun & Sept: weekends and public holidays 2.30–5.30pm. Rest of year by appt. 6€ 03 86 73 70 08; www.art-populaire-laduz.com.

This folk museum, situated at the south-east entrance to the village and with beautiful parkland around it, recalls rural working life before 1914.

Drive 20km along D 31 to Auxerre.

Auxerre★★

The cathedral and old houses of the capital of Lower Burgundy proudly rise in terraces above the River Yonne. The town used to be renowned for its wine, but the vineyards have disappeared with the exception of Clos de la Chaînette, a 5.4ha estate belonging to a psychiatric hospital. Its production is shared between the employees of the establishment, who are only entitled to 12 bottles a year.

The fine Gothic **Cathédrale St-Étienne**★★ was built over a period of nearly four hundred years, from 1215 to 1525. It is therefore a blend of Gothic and Renaissance features. The interior boasts a splendid array of 13C **stained-glass windows**★★. The **Romanesque crypt**★ is adorned with medieval frescoes. Take a look at the **Treasury**★ before leaving (*open Easter Sunday–Nov 1* *daily 9am–6pm (closed Sunday morning except for religious service); rest of the year 10am–5pm; ☎03 86 52 23 29).*

To reach the abbey follow the north side of the cathedral and rue Cochois.

The famous **Abbaye St-Germain**★★, founded in the 6C by Queen Clotilda, the wife of Clovis, was a centre of learning which attracted many saints including St Patrick. Inside the **abbey church**, the most interesting part is the **crypt**★★. This underground church contains **frescoes**★ dating from 850. The **Musée d'Art et d'Histoire**, located in the conventual buildings, houses an archaeological museum *(open Jun–Sept Wed–Mon 10am–6.30pm; Oct–May Wed–Mon 10am–noon, 2–6pm; last admission 1hr before closing; 45min guided tours of the crypt; closed May 1 & 8, Nov 1 & 11, Dec 25, Jan 1; 4.30€; no charge 1st Sun of the month; ☎03 86 18 05 50).*
For a scenic drive through the Auxerre vineyards, follow the D 362 to Augy rather than N 6, then cross the River Yonne towards Vaux. The Vaux vineyard, stretching along the Yonne, was revived in the 1980s.

Drive Son river to Escolives.

Escolives-Sainte-Camille

The charming Romanesque **church** has an 11C crypt where the relics of St Camille were once kept. The 17th century, fortified **Domaine Borgnat**, opposite the church *(1 rue de l'église - Escolives Sainte Camille - ☎03 86 53 35 28)*, offers a warm welcome to visitors and tastings of its AOC Bourgogne in the vaulted cellars. At the northern end of the village, excavations are in progress to explore the **remains** of a Gallo-Roman village and public baths (1C to 3C) and a Merovingian cemetery.
A 2C fresco discovered on the site testifies to the long-standing presence of vineyards in the region *(visit by guided tour Apr–Oct 10 & 11am, then hourly 2–5pm; Nov–Mar by appt.; closed Jan 1, May 1, Nov 1 & 11, Dec 25; ☎03 86 53/53 39 09).*

Coulanges-la-Vineuse

The very name of this hilltop village suggests an ancient wine-growing tradition. The vineyard, extending over 135ha, produces Bourgogne-Coulanges-la-Vineuse wines: soft, light reds, fruity whites and good rosés.
In addition to its display of old wine-growing implements, the **Musée du Vieux Pressoir et de la Vigne** houses a winepress of the kind used in medieval times *(55 bis, rue André Vildieu; open Jun–Sept Wed, Thur, Fri 8am-noon & 2–6pm, rest of week by appt.; Oct-May Mon-Thur 8am-noon & 2-5.30pm, rest of week by appt. 2.30€; ☎03 86 42 54 48).*

Follow D 85 to Vincelottes, then D 362 towards Auxerre until you reach Bailly (3.5km).

Vincelles and **Vincelottes** are ancient moorings for river boats loading wine bound for Paris. They make attractive stopping points, with many walking and cycling routes.
On the way to Auxerre, one comes across the hillside **Caves de Bailly**. These underground quarries, which used to supply Paris with building stones, were turned in 1972 into cellars covering 3ha where members of the wine growers' cooperative stock bottles of Crémant-de-Bourgogne. Take the guided tour of the rooms decorated with sculptures, followed by an introduction to the making of Crémant and wine tasting to finish *(Boutique open Jul-Aug Mon-Fri 8am-6.30pm, Sat-Sun 10am-6.30pm; rest of year Mon-Fri 8am-noon & 2-6.30pm, Sat-Sun 10am-noon & 2-6.30pm; Guided tours Mar-Nov 2.30–5.30pm; Nov–Mar weekends and public holidays 4pm and 5pm; 4€ ☎03 86 53 77 77; www.bailly-lapierre.fr).*

Return to Vincelottes then drive 2.5km along D 38 to Irancy.

Irancy

This village, lying in a dale planted with cherry trees, produces **Irancy** AOC wines that are the most renowned red wines yielded by the Auxerre vineyards.

They are made partly from an original grape type, César, believed to have been imported by Roman legions. Palotte and Côte du Moustier are the best Irancy vineyards.
Local wine growers are very friendly. Among others, pay a visit to **Domaine Cantin** (*see Shopping Guide*): one of the rising stars of the appellation.

Continue along D 38 towards St-Cyr-les-Colons and turn left onto a minor road climbing towards St-Bris.

Saint-Bris-le-Vineux

One of the most charming villages of the Yonne region gave its name to the **Saint-Bris** AOC which only produces white wines from Sauvignon and Sauvignon Gris grapes - very unusual in this Chardonnay-dominated region. Built over an amazing network of vaulted cellars covering 3.5ha at 60m underground, Saint-Bris boasts fine old stone houses and a 13C Gothic church. The main sight is the **Baphomet**, a strange sculpture representing the horned head of a man surrounded by angels, which is believed to have been a symbol of the Knights-Templars.
The **Maison du Vignoble Auxerrois** offers an excellent selection of wines (*see Shopping Guide*). Also, **Ghislaine and Jean-Hugues Goisot** make excellent organic wines, and are open for wine-tasting and tours of their medieval cellars (*30 r. Bienvenu-Martin, 89530 St-Bris-le-Vineux; open by appt. Mon–Fri 8am–noon & 1.30–6pm, Sat 9am-noon & 1.30-5pm; 03 86 53 35 15; www.goisot.com*).

Village of St-Bris-le-Vineux and its vineyards
S. Sauvignier/MICHELIN

Follow D 62 towards Chablis.

Chitry

This pleasant village boasts an imposing 14C fortified church. The terroir is famous for its white Burgundy wines.

Drive 4km on D 62 towards Chablis.

Shortly before reaching Courgis, there is a picnic area with a viewpoint offering a fine panorama of the vineyards.

Courgis

Although situated within the Chablis Appellation, this village, with its network of narrow streets, also produces red Burgundy wines. Every Sunday before Assumption Day, a pilgrimage is staged here to celebrate the "holy thorn" from Christ's crown, kept in the church.

A minor road runs south to Préhy.

Préhy

The **Domaine Jean-Marc Brocard** organises one and two-day tours of the vineyards, along with picking days during harvest and detailed tasting classes. The wine-tasting room is located at the foot of Ste-Claire Church, in the middle of the vineyards (*3 rte. de Chablis, 89800 Préhy; Open by appt. Mon–Sat 9.30am–7pm; From 7€ depending on visit; 03 86 41 49 00; www.brocard.fr*). Also in Prehy is **Domaine Tixier** (see Shopping Guide).

Drive to Chablis along D 2.

Chablis

This opulent village, entirely devoted to the reputation of its white wines, has retained a few old houses, monuments and shops which testify to the wealth derived from the "golden liquid". Although less famous than its wines, the chitterling sausages of Chablis are considered to be among the best anywhere, and make a good accompaniment to the wines, particularly when served alongside some oysters. The **William Fèvre** and **Vincent Dauvissat** estates together with the **Château Long-Depaquit** are among the most famous estates. You can also visit **La Chablisienne** cooperative, founded in 1923, which produces a quarter of the Chablis Appellation and has a monopoly on Château Grenouille *(see Shopping Guide).*

The excellent **Domaine Laroche** has a recently renovated visitor centre with a wine bar and bistro, two boutiques (both in the centre of the village), hotel and cellar visits. The main focus of the visit is the Obédiencerie, a former monastery dating from the 9C; the cellars house a 13C winepress and a small crypt which, between 877 and 887, contained the relics of St Martin *(10 r. Auxerroise and 18 r. des Moulins, 89800 Chablis; open daily 10am–noon & 2–6pm; daily guided tours at 2pm from r. Auxerroise;10€; 03 86 42 89 28; www.larochewines.com).*

Villages of the Chablis region

Twenty villages are entitled to the **Chablis** Appellation. We suggest visiting some of the most charming of them before going on to Tonnerre.

Beine

6km W of Chablis along D 965.

The high spire of the Église Notre-Dame (12C-16C) towers above the village. A 15ha artificial lake was created on municipal land to supply water to the sprinklers used in the vineyards against spring frost. At the **Domaine Alain Geoffroy**, you can browse the charming **Musée de la Vigne et du Tire-Bouchon**, with its collection of 1,500 corkscrews and winemaking implements, before sampling the estate's products *(open Mon–Fri 8am–noon & 2–5pm; 03 86 42 43 76; www.chablis-geoffroy.com).*

Maligny

7km N of Chablis along D 91.

This small hillside village boasts one of the finest terroirs of the Chablis Appellation. Here, you will find many pleasant local estates, such as the **Chateau de Maligny**, run by Jean Durup Père et Fils *(see Shopping Guide).*

Béru

11km E of Chablis along D 45 and D 98.

The old fortified village is overlooked by a vast **castle** with 12C, 15C and 17C features.

Noyers-sur-Serein★

26 km SE of Chablis along D 961 and D 956.

Tucked inside a meander of the Serein and enclosed by ramparts, Noyers (pronounced noyère) is a small, delightful **medieval town**★★; its old timber-framed or stone houses all have cellars opening directly on to the street, a reminder that this was wine country before the phylloxera crisis.

Place de l'Hôtel-de-Ville is surrounded by lovely half-timbered houses, dating from the 14C and 15C and by arcaded houses. The triangular **place du Marché-au-Blé** is lined with old houses. From there, walk through an archway and along the picturesque **rue du Poids-du-Roy**. The street leads, via a covered passage, to the tiny **place de la Petite-Étape-aux-Vins**, framed by half-timbered houses, some of them adorned with sculptures. Turn left onto the main street, **rue de la Petite-Étape-aux-Vins**, also lined with old houses, which leads to place du Grenier-à-Sel. Not far from the **Église Notre-Dame**, a vast late-15C church featuring gargoyles, a Renaissance west front and a square tower, you can take in the **collection of naive art**★ in the **Musée d'Art Naïf** *(Rue de l'Eglise 89310 Noyers sur Serein; open Jun–Sept Wed–Mon 11am–6.30pm; Oct–May weekends and holidays 2.30–6.30; closed Jan and Dec 25; 3.05€; 03 86 82 89 09).*

Return to Chablis then drive on to Tonnerre, 18km E via D 965.

Tonnerre

This small city backing on to a hill and surrounded by vineyards lies on the banks of the Canal de Bourgogne and the Armançon. The once flourishing vineyards covered over 1,000ha at the end of the 19C. Having practically disappeared during the 1970s, they have now found a new lease of life and in 2006 received its own appellation – Bourgogne Tonnerre. Today is covers about 150ha in the localities of Tonnerre, Épineuil, Danemoine, Molosmes and Vaulichère. Roughly equal quantities of white, red and rosé wines are produced from traditional grape types. To try some of the wines, try Domaine Clement *(Route de Tissey, 89700 Tonnerre, t03 86 55 16 30; Open 9am-noon & 2-7pm; www.domaineclement.fr)*.

When in Tonnerre, go and see the **Fosse Dionne**★. This circular basin, filled with blue-green water, was used as a wash-house. It is fed by a spring emerging out of the rocks at the centre of the pool, its flow varying according to rainfall.

The **Hôtel Dieu** (also known as the Vieil Hôpital or old hospital)★, erected between 1293 and 1295 by Marguerite de Bourgogne, the widow of Charles d'Anjou, has survived intact, with its impressive roof covering an area of 4,500m². Every Easter weekend, the great hall (90m long, 18m wide) is the venue of the local wine fair, Les Vinées tonnerroises. *(open Apr–Oct 9am–noon & 2–6pm; Sun & public holidays 10am–noon & 2–5pm; Nov–Mar Mon–Sat 9–11.30am & 2–5.30pm; last entrance 45min before closing; closed Dec 25–Jan 1, May 1; 4.50€; 03 86 55 14 48; www.hotel-dieu-tonnerre.com)*.

From Tonnerre, follow D 188.

Vézelay

S. Sauvignier/MICHELIN

Épineuil

The village gave its name to the **Épineuil** Appellation which includes 80ha of hillside grapevines planted on steep slopes combining marl and clay soils. Pinot Noir, the dominant variety, produces light reds and full-bodied rosés. Among the producers, try the **Domaine de l'Abbaye du Petit Quincy** located on the site of a former abbey *(see Shopping Guide)*.

Drive on to Molosmes, 5km NE via a steep minor road to Vaulichères, then along D 202. The tiny village of ***Molosmes****, nestling among hills, is surrounded by Chardonnay terroirs. Return to Tonnerre along D 202.*

VÉZELAY AND THE SURROUNDING VINEYARDS

Vézelay is located 52km S of Auxerre by the N 6 and the D 951.

The hillsides surrounding Vézelay have always been planted with grape vines and the wines they produced were once much appreciated by pilgrims. However, successive crises had almost wiped out the vineyards when a handful of indomitable wine growers decided to revive them. Marc Meneau, the famous restaurant owner, and a small local cooperative, were the main driving force behind this revival. Red and white Burgundy is produced today, but the **Bourgogne-Vézelay** appellation is reserved for white wine made from the Melon grape, also used for Muscadet.

Vézelay★★

Situated on the borders of Morvan, Vézelay extends over the slopes and top of a hill towering above the Cure Valley. Such was the spiritual influence of Vézelay, a main stop on the way to Santiago de Compostela, that many writers settled in the town. From place du Champ-de-Foire, at the lower end of the town, walk along the promenade des Fossés, following the line of the old ramparts, to the château terrace, behind the basilica. Return by Grande-Rue lined with shops established in old houses with carved doors and mullioned windows.

The monastery founded in the 9C was dedicated in 1050 to Mary Magdalene whose relics it retained. The old abbey became a parish church in 1791 and was elevated to a **basilica**★★★ in 1920. Visitors should take time to examine the sculptures on the doorways dating from the early 12C. Those of the tympanum of the **central doorway**★★★ show Christ surrounded by the Apostles. You will get a good idea of the local production when you visit the small **Henry de Vézelay** cooperative (*see Shopping Guide*). In the town itself, the **Caves du Pèlerin** stock wines produced by all the cooperatives of the Yonne region and offer guided tours of medieval cellars laid out on 3 levels. *(332 r. St-Étienne, 89450 Vézelay; open Thu–Tue 9.30am–noon & 2–6pm; closed Jan–mid-Mar; 03 86 33 30 84; cavesdupelerin@wanadoo.fr).*

Côtes Road

The Côte de Nuits and Côte de Beaune stretch from Dijon to Santenay, over a distance of 85km. Every signpost announces legendary names: Nuits-Saint-Georges, Vosne-Romanée, Vougeot, Aloxe-Corton, Puligny-Montrachet... These hillside villages are at the heart of a region that produces some of the rarest and most precious wines in the world.

- **Population:** 800,000.
- **Michelin Map:** 320, J-K 5-7. Local map p187.
- **Info:** www.route-grands-crus-borgogne.com
- **Location:** Following the wine growing slopes of both the Cote de Nuits and Cote de Beaune.
- **Timing:** Two days.
- **Don't Miss:** World-famous villages such as Pommard and Gevrey Chambertin.
- **Kids:** Cycling along the canals.

DRIVING TOURS

1 TERROIRS OF THE CÔTE DE NUITS

About 60km.

The **Côte de Nuits** extends from Fixin to Corgoloin, almost exclusively producing reds. The most famous Crus are, from north to south: Chambertin, Musigny, Clos-Vougeot and Romanée-Conti. Rich and full-bodied, these wines take eight to ten years to acquire superlative qualities of body and bouquet. The road, known as the "Champs-Élysées of Burgundy", runs at the foot of vine-covered hills and through opulent towns and villages with evocative names. To the south, on the western slopes of the Côte, the **Hautes-Côtes-de-Nuits** vineyards produce less complex wines.

Dijon★★★

The former capital of the dukes of Burgundy is a museum town with a prestigious past and well-preserved architectural heritage. A major university, intensive cultural activity and numerous shops bring a continuous flow to the city and enliven the streets running through the conservation area. Lovers of Burgundy wine will find Dijon the ideal starting point of the Grands Crus road.

The old district around the Palais des Ducs et des États de Bourgogne is full of character. As you stroll along the streets, often pedestrianised, you will come across handsome stone mansions and numerous half-timbered houses dating from the 15C and 16C. **Rue des Forges**★ is one of the busiest streets in town. Lined with several 13C-15C mansions, it starts from **place François-Rude** in the centre of the pedestrian zone, overlooked by the statue of the

"Bareuzai", a wine grower clad only in verdigris and looked upon as the local guiding spirit. He is busy grape-treading, but the product of his work only flows during the wine festivals.

Musée des Beaux-Arts★★ *(open Apr-Nov daily 2-6pm, Dec-Mar Wed–Mon 2-6pm; closed major public holidays; 5,50€ 03 80 24 98 70)* – Even if you don't have a lot of time to visit Dijon, try not to miss this huge fine arts museum housed in the **Palais des Ducs et des États de Bourgogne★★**. Created in 1799, the museum is famous above all for its **Salle des Gardes★★★**, which contains art treasures from the Chartreuse de Champmol (*see below*), the necropolis of the dukes of Valois. The prize exhibit is the **tomb of Philip the Bold★★★**. Several Flemish artists worked successively on this masterpiece from 1385 to 1410. The recumbent figure is watched over by 41 extremely realistic statuettes. You will also be able to admire the **tomb of John the Fearless and Margaret of Bavaria★★★**, carved between 1443 and 1470, and marvel at the richly carved decoration of two wooden altarpieces: the **Crucifixion altarpiece★★★** and the **altarpiece of the Saints and Martyrs★★★**. In the centre, note an **altarpiece of the Passion★★**, carved in an Antwerp workshop at the beginning of the 16C.

In the basement of the **Musée archéologique★** two 11C Romanesque rooms contain a collection of Gallo-Roman sculptures. In the former chapter house, the **goddess Sequan★** sits enthroned in her boat; this bronze statuette was found during the excavation of the sanctuary of the source of the River Seine. In the former monks' cells there is a rich display of prehistoric remains including, in particular, a **solid-gold bracelet** found in **La Rochepot** (9C BC) and the **Blanot Treasure★**, a group of objects from the late Bronze Age *(5 rue Docteur Maret; open May–Sept daily 9am–12.30pm & 1.30-6pm; Oct-Mar Tues–Sun 9am–12.30pm & 1.30–6pm; closed major public holidays; 03 80 48 83 70)*.

Housed in the cloisters of the Bernardines' monastery built around 1680, the **Musée de la Vie Bourguignonne★** illustrates local history through regional costumes and collections of typical trades and houses until the end of WWII, brought to life by imaginative displays. The same museum houses the **Musée d'Art Sacré** displaying Catholic liturgical objects from the 12C to the 20C *(R. Ste-Anne; open May–Sept Wed–Mon 9am–12.30pm & 1.30–6pm; Oct–Apr Wed-Mon 9am-noon & 2-6pm guided tours (1hr) available on request; closed major public holidays; 03 80 48 80 90)*.

Wanting a burial place of royal standing, Philip the Bold founded **Chartreuse de Champmol★**, a Carthusian monastery, in 1383. All that remains today are the **chapel doorway★** and the **Puits de Moïsea★★★**: six large statues of Moses and the prophets (14C-15C) leaning back against a hexagonal pillar *(1 bd.*

The Knights of the Tastevin

The Brotherhood of the Knights of the Tastevin has owned the Château du Clos de Vougeot since 1944. In 1934, a small group of Burgundians met in a cellar of Nuits-St-Georges and, in order to fight against the wine slump, they decided to form a society whose aim was to promote "the wines of France in general, and in particular, those of Burgundy". The brotherhood was founded and its renown grew so fast that it soon spread throughout Europe and America. Every year, several chapter meetings of the order, famous the world over, are held in the Great Cellar of the Château du Clos de Vougeot. Five hundred guests take part in these "disnées" (banquets), at the end of which the Grand Master and the Grand Chancellor, surrounded by high dignitaries of the brotherhood, initiate new knights according to a rite strictly established in pseudo-Latin and inspired by Molière's Malade Imaginaire.

Chanoine-Kir; follow signposts marked "Puits de Moïse"; open by reservation at the tourist office; 03 80 44 11 40).

It would be a shame to leave Dijon without visiting the **Musée de la Moutarde Amora**, created by the world's leading mustard manufacturer. This museum recounts the history of this staple product and its origins, and has an interesting collection of old advertising posters *(48 quai Nicolas-Rolin; visit by guided tour only May–Sept Mon–Sat 3pm; Oct–Apr Tues & Sat 2-6pm; reserve at the tourist office 03 80 44 11 44).*

Leave Dijon via the D 122, appropriately named "route des Grands Crus".

Chenôve

Located in the old village, the **Cuverie des ducs de Bourgogne** (winery of the dukes of Burgundy) contains two magnificent 13C winepresses. *(guided tours available Jul–Sept, 2-7pm; rest of the year, by request 10 days in advance at the town hall; 03 80 51 55 00.*

Marsannay-la-Côte

The terroir of the **Marsannay** AOC is famous for its rosé wines obtained after a short maceration of Pinot Noir grapes. The **Domaine Regis Bouvier** and the **Château de Marsannay** both offer wine tasting in a pleasant setting *(see Shopping Guide).*

A tourist office and small museum of local heritage houses the **Maison du Patrimoine et du Tourisme**, exploring the life of winegrowers and their economic impact on the region *(41, rue de Mazy; open Jun–Sept Mon–Sat 9am–12.30pm & 2–6.30pm; Sun 9am–1pm; rest of the year hours vary slightly; 03 80 52 27 73).* This is the starting point of several **hiking trails** leading to the municipal forest and across the vineyards.

Fixin

The vineyards of the **Fixin** AOC only spread over some 100ha which produce very fine wines with a deep bouquet. The most famous of these are Clos-du-Chapitre, Clos-de-la-Perrière and Les Arvelets. The **Philippe Naddef** estate, which produces fine wines, also offers three guest-house rooms *(see Shopping Guide).* The village commemorates Napoleon through a monument erected by the sculptor Rude at the request of a former soldier of the Imperial Guard and through a museum located in Parc Noisot.

Brochon

Situated on the edge of the Côte de Nuits, Brochon produces excellent wines. The **château** was built in 1900 by the poet Stephen Liégard. The title of one of his works, honoured by the French Academy in 1887, was destined to a brilliant future: its author had just coined the phrase "Côte d'Azur".

Gevrey-Chambertin

Situated at the opening of a gorge, Combe de Lavaux, the town is framed by hillside vineyards. **Chambertin**, which comes from the two vineyards of Chambertin-Clos-de-Bèze and Chambertin, is the most famous of the Côte-de-Nuits great wines. The area producing it only covers 28ha whereas the **Gevrey-Chambertin** AOC covers almost 450ha and can be produced in Gevrey-Chambertin and the neighbouring commune of Brochon. It is possible to compare the two wines at the **Domaine Trapet Père et Fils** *(see the shopping guide).*

In the upper part of the village stands the square-towered **Château du Gevrey-Chambertin** erected in the 10C by the lords of Vergy and given to

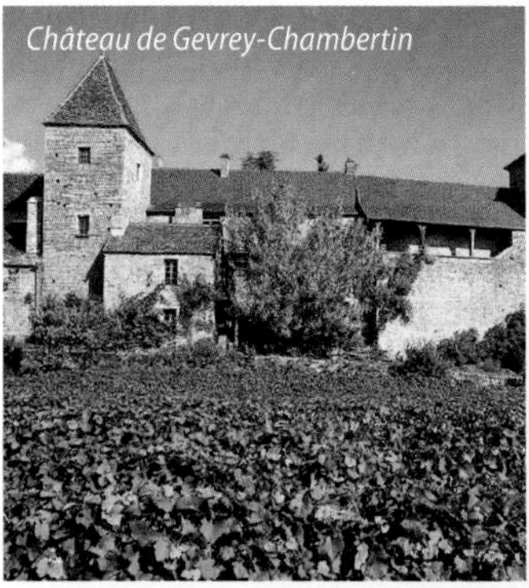
Château de Gevrey-Chambertin

B. Kaufmann/MICHELIN

the monks of Cluny in the 11C. The great tower has retained its watchroom and bowmen's room.
Vintage wines are stored in the vaulted cellars. The vineyards of the château produce, among others, the Charmes-Chambertin Grand Cru and Lavaux-St-Jacques Premier Cru and Clos du Chateau (*1hr guided tours available by request one day in advance May—Sept 10am–noon & 2–6pm; rest of the year by appt; 5€; 03 80 34 36 77; www.chateau-de-gevrey-chambertin.com).*
A clear star of the appellation is **Alain Burguet** (*18 rue de l'Eglise, 21200 Gevrey-Chambertin, 03 80 34 36 35*) who doesn't offer individual tastings, but makes wines well worth hunting out.

Morey-Saint-Denis

Situated in the heart of the Côte de Nuits, the east-facing vineyards include five prestigious Grands Crus: Clos-des-Lambrays, Clos-de-Tart, part of Bonnes Mares, Clos-St-Denis and Clos-de-la-Roche. **Morey-Saint-Denis** AOC wines combine richness and subtlety and the Grands Crus can be aged for fifteen to twenty years. The **Domaine Arlaud** is worth a visit (*see Shopping Guide*).

Follow N 74 south.

Vougeot

The terroir which produces the highly valued Clos de Vougeot wines was owned by the abbey of Cîteaux from the 12C to the Revolution. The vineyard of **Clos de Vougeot** covers 50ha divided between 70 wine growers. Its fame outshines the small **Vougeot** appellation (just 15 hectares in total), but there are other excellent wines to discover - try the **Christian Clerget estate** (*see Shopping Guide*).
Surrounded by vineyards, the **Château du Clos de Vougeot★** is visible from afar. Completed during the Renaissance, it was restored in the 19C. The visit includes the 12C Grand Cellier where the ceremonies of the Order of the Tastevin are held, the 12C cuverie containing four huge winepresses, the 16C kitchen and the monks' dormitory with its spectacular 14C roof structure. There is a slide show (15min) about the Brotherhood of the Knights of the Tastevin (*visit by either 45min guided tour or self-guided Apr–Sept Sun–Fri 9am–6.30pm, Sat 9am–5pm; Oct–Mar 9-11.30am & 2–5.30pm, Sat 9–11.30am & 2–5pm; closed Jan 1, Dec 24–25 and 31. 3.90€; 03 80 62 86 09; www.tastevin-borgogne.com).*

Drive W along D 122H.

Chambolle-Musigny

Yet another highly prestigious name, where the AOC dates back to 1936, making it one of the first in France to be designated. Here, the terroirs have evocative titles such as Les Amoureuses, Les Groseilles or Les Charmes and produce extremely subtle wines bearing the **Chambolle-Musigny** and **Musigny** AOC. The Les Musigny Grand Cru is located above the Clos de Vougeot, and synonymous with excellence, as is the other Grand Cru of this village, Bonnes Mares. The **Amiot-Servelle estate** is worth a visit (*see Shopping Guide*).

W along D 122H, then turn left onto D 116. Pass the village of Reulle-Vergy, then drive SE through Curtil-Vergy to Vosne-Romanée on a peaceful road running along the edge of Mantua Forest.

Vosne-Romanée

The **Vosne-Romanée** AOC is only represented by rich, subtle and delicate red wines. Among the vineyards which make up the appellation, those of **La Romanée-Conti**, La Tâche and Richebourg produce some of the best, and most expensive, wines in the world. To seal Vosne-Romanée's reputation as a connoisseur's paradise, the surrounding woods are known to supply good Burgundy truffles (*Tuber incinatum*).
In addition to its wines, the estate of **Armelle and Bernard Rion** sells tinned truffles all year round (*8 r. Nationale, 21700 Vosne-Romanée; open by appt. Mon–Sat 9am–6pm; 03 80 61 05 31; www.domaineriion.fr).*

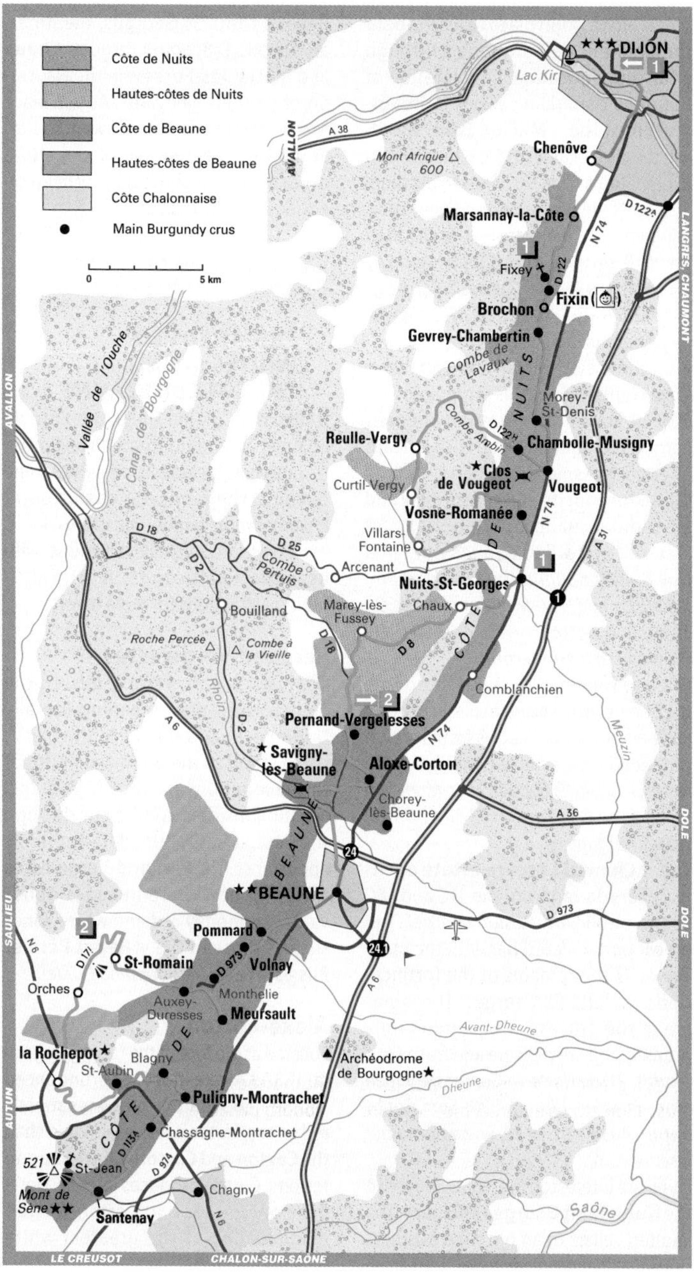

Nuits-Saint-Georges

The attractive "capital" of the Côte is known for its **Nuits-Saint-Georges** AOC and its Cru Saint-Georges established as early as AD 1000. Its wines owe much of their reputation to the dynamic wine merchants settled in the town. There are no Grand Crus here, but 41 Premier Crus (or Climats).

This is also a good place to learn about the Crement de Borgogne - through a fun and educational exploration of Bugundy's sparkling wines at **Imaginarium** at the **Maison Louis Bouillot**; the visit includes videos, models and explanations from the vines to bottling, and ends with a tasting of three sparkling wines. An expansiaon is planned for 2010. *(Ave. du Jura; open Apr–Oct 10am–1pm &2–7pm; closed Mon Nov–Mar; 6.90€; 03 80 62 61 40; www.imaginarium-bourgogne.com).*

Blackcurrant is the town's other treasure - five companies in this region provide 80% of France's production of Cassis cordial and liqueur. If you wish to learn all about the small black berry, visit the **Cassisium**, for its museum display and an audio-visual presentation *(R. des Frères-Montgolfier; open Apr– mid Nov daily1hr 30min tour, 10-11.30am, 2-5.30pm; mid Nov–Mar Mon–Sat 10.30–11.30am & 2–4pm; 7€; 03 80 62 49 70; www.cassissium.com).*

Offering a more family-style atmosphere, the **Ferme Fruitrouge** makes red-berry jams and other delicacies from its own production *(Hameau de Concoeur, 21700 Nuits-St-Georges; open Thur-Mon–Sun 9am–noon & 2–7pm 03 80 62 36 25; www.fruirouge.fr).*

The **Chantal Lescure estate** opens its cellars dating from the 11C and 18C to the public *(admission charge)*. The oldest part, located beneath the Black Tower, is the remains of the fortifications of Nuits-St-Georges. The wines are in the process of becoming fully organic, and are delicate and fresh *(34 r. Thurot, 21700 Nuits-St-Georges; open Mon–Fri 9am–12pm & 1.30–5pm, Sat by appt; 03 80 61 16 79; www.domaine-lescure.com).*

If you are interested in archaeology, visit the **Nuits Saint Georges Museum**. The vaulted cellars of an old wine business house archaeological collections from the Gallo-Roman site at Les Bolards, as well as Merovingian funerary objects and jewellery *(12 rue Camille Rodier; open May–Oct Wed–Mon 10am–noon & 2–6pm; rest of year by appt. 2.25€; 03 80 62 01 37).*

Beyond Nuits-St-Georges, the itinerary follows D 8, going through **Chaux** and **Marey-lès-Fussey**, in the Hautes-Côtes de Nuits vineyards. As you leave Marey-lès-Fussey, you may want to stop at the very pleasant picnic area. Note the blackcurrant and raspberry fields on either side of the road.

Drive to Pernand-Vergelesses situated 5km S via D 18.

2 FROM REDS TO WHITES ALONG THE CÔTE DE BEAUNE

Unlike the Côte de Nuits, the Côte de Beaune, extending from Aloxe-Corton to Santenay, includes great white-wine terroirs. The landcape at this point becomes more gentle, with sharp slopes morphing into soft valleys. Beaune, with its architectural treasures, is full of fascinating attractions for wine lovers.

Pernand-Vergelesses

"Pernand je bois, verre je laisse": the French word-play, meaning literally "I drink Pernand but leave the glass", could stand as the unofficial motto of this charming wine-growing village. Nestling inside a combe cut through the Côte, it has retained its authentic appearance. The **Pernand-Vergelesses** AOC produced here includes good-value-for-money red and white wines such as those of the **Rapet Père et Fils estate** *(see Shopping Guide).*

Aloxe-Corton

Located at the foot of the "Corton mountain", the **Aloxe-Corton** (pronounced 'alosse') appellation produces mostly red wines, but it is less renowned than the **Corton** and **Corton-Charlemagne** terroirs. Corton produces intense, slow-developing reds and Corton-Charlemagne some of the greatest white Burgundy wines.

The **Château de Corton-André**, roofed with polychrome Burgundian tiles, is one of the most photographed buildings in Burgundy. The estate produces top-quality wines which can be bought on the premises and tasted in a fine

14C vaulted cellar (*21420 Aloxe-Corton; open by appt. 10am–1pm & 2.30-6pm; 03 80 26 44 25; www.pierre-andre.com*). **Domaine Comte Senard** is another estate well worth visiting and offers a wine-tasting lunch *(see Shopping Guide.)*

Aloxe-Corton is situated near the villages of **Chorey** and **Ladoix-Serrigny** which include part of the Corton and Corton-Charlemagne terroirs. Their red wines are supple and their whites are light. The **Edmond Cornu et Fils** estate, in Ladoix-Serrigny *(see Shopping Guide)* offer good advice.

Savigny-lès-Beaune

Tucked away in its valley, Savigny comprises the largest wine-growing area of the Côte-d'Or, covering around 300ha. The light and fruity red wines of the **Savigny** Appellation are best drunk rather young. White wines are lively, becoming rounder after two or three years in the bottle. They are available at the **Simon Bize et Fils** estate *(see Shopping Guide)*.

Pay a visit to **Château Savigny-lès-Beaune**★ and its amazing collections. At the entrance stands the 17C "small château" adapted to include an area for tasting and buying wines as well as an exhibition of **Abarth racing cars**. The second floor is devoted to **motorbikes**,★ with a display of more than 500 items from the most prestigious to the short-lived, and another to **fire engines** with over 100 examples *(open Apr–Oct daily 9am–6.30pm; Nov–Mar daily 9am–noon & 2–5.30pm, last entrance 1hr 30min before closing time; closed part of Jan; 7€; 03 80 21 55 03; www.chateau-savigny.com)*.

Beaune★★

A prestigious wine town, Beaune is also an incomparable artistic city. Its Hôtel-Dieu, its museums, its Église Notre-Dame, its ring of ramparts with bastions housing the most important cellars, its gardens, all combine to make it the jewel of Burgundy, but it is also a lively town, whose highlights include the Festival du Film Policier (thriller movies), held in April (*www.beaunefestivalpolicier.com*). The **Beaune** AOC produces very subtle red and white wines. The most famous Crus are Les Grèves and Les Bressandes and Le Clos-du-Roy.

Place de la Halle marks the town centre. The beautiful roof of the Hôtel-Dieu dominates the area. The square and neighbouring streets are lined with shops selling regional specialities, wines and spirits, plus plenty of welcoming cafes and restaurants.

Hôtel-Dieu★★★

Open late Mar–mid-Nov 9am–6.30pm; rest of the year 9–11.30am & 2–5.30pm. Guided tours (1hr) available. 6.50€. 03 80 24 45 00. www.hospices-de-beaune.com.

The Hôtel-Dieu, a marvel of Burgundian-Flemish art, was founded in 1443 by Nicolas Rolin, Philip the Good's chancellor. It was used as a general hospital until 1971. You have to enter the **main courtyard** to appreciate the extent of the buildings: with their roofs of multi-coloured glazed tiles, they form a group which looks more like "a dwelling fit for a prince than a hospital for the poor". The **Grand'salle** or **Chambre des Pauvres**★★★ has retained a magnificent polychrome timber roof in the shape of an upturned keel. At the end of

Ceremonial

Every year the Hôtel-Dieu is the venue of the famous sale of wines from the Hospices de Beaune vineyards, now run by Christie's auction house. Bids are called out by the auctioneer (since 2008 these can be received either in person, by phone or by the internet), and the bids last only as long as it takes for two small candles to burn, hence the name of "sale by candlelight". The proceeds of what has been called "the greatest charity auction in the world" are used for charitable works, and for maintenance of the Hôtel-Dieu.

Hôtel-Dieu, Beaune

© Senai Aksoy/Dreamstime.com

the room stands a larger than life-size, polychrome wooden statue (1.76m seated) of **Christ bound**★ (15C). The **Salle du Polyptyque** contains Roger Van der Weyden's famous rendering of the **Last Judgement**★★★, a masterpiece of Flemish art made between 1445 and 1448. The kitchen *(commentary and "son et lumière" show every 15min)* and the **pharmacy** can also be visited.

Musée du Vin
Rue d'Enfer; ○*Open Apr–Nov 9.30am–6pm. Dec–Mar, Wed–Mon 9.30am–5pm.* ○*Closed Jan 1 & Dec 25.* ⊚*5.40€;* ℘*03 80 22 08 19.*
The 14C cellar of this wine museum contains an impressive collection of presses and vats. On the first floor is the headquarters of the "Ambassade des Vins de France" (Embassy of French wines). The history of Burgundian vineyards and of wine growing is related on the ground floor. The **Collégiale Notre-Dame**★, begun around 1120, is a fine example of Burgundian Romanesque art. Numerous sculptures in 15C and 16C Burgundian style adorn the chapels. Behind the high altar, there is a magnificent set of **tapestries**★★ depicting the Life of the Virgin Mary, which mark the transition from medieval to Renaissance art. Since May 2009, the restoration work at **l'Hotel Boussard de la Chapelle** has been completed, with a new public park and attractive walkway between rue Paradis and la Collégiale.

▷ *Leave Beaune S along D 973.*

Pommard
Pommard takes its name from an ancient temple dedicated to Pomona, the goddess of fruits and gardens. Red wines of the **Pommard** AOC, which are firm, deeply coloured, and age well, were much enjoyed by Renaissance poet Pierre de Ronsard, kings Henri IV and Louis XV, and Victor Hugo. Premiers Crus such as Les Épenots, Les Vaumuriens and Les Rugiens are very much sought after. The **Château de Pommard** is a fine 18C building surrounded by a park, once the home of the mathematician Gaspard Monge (1746-1818); the **Domaine des Éperneaux** estate is also one of the reliable producers of this appellation *(see Shopping Guide).*

Volnay
Its wines, exclusively red, have a delicate bouquet and silky taste and are often described as "feminine". It is said that Louis XI was very partial to them. The **Volnay** Appellation includes no fewer than 34 Premiers Crus, among them Les Caillerets, Les Santenots and les Champans.
There is a fine view of the vineyards from the esplanade below the small 14C church. The village is very attractive with its picturesquely named streets, such as rue d'Amour, rue de l'Abreuvoir or rue de la Piture. The **Domaine Henri Delagrange** is one of the many cellars waiting to welcome you *(see Shopping Guide).*

Meursault
This prosperous little town, dominated by a beautiful 53m-high Gothic spire, owes its name to a gap separating the Côte de Meursault and the Côte de Beaune, known as the "Rat's Leap", in Latin *Muris Saltus.*
Although red **Meursault** wines are made, the appellation is devoted to top-quality white wines with characteristic hazelnut aromas, which can age for as long as fifteen years. The most renowned vineyards are Les Perrières, Les Genevrières and Les Charmes.

The **Château de Meursault** is the largest estate of the appellation. It boasts a fine 17C building, later remodelled, with extensive, much older cellars (*see Shopping Guide).*

Drive 6.5km NW to St-Romain via Monthélie and Auxey-Duresses.

Monthélie and **Auxey-Duresses** are not among the best known appellations despite their undeniable quality. They mainly produce red wines, which are robust and improve with age. White wines are similar to Meursaults.
In **Auxey-Duresses**, the **Château de Melin** and **Vincent Prunier** estates are worth a visit (*see Shopping Guide).*

Saint-Romain

This locality is made up of two distinct villages. St-Romain-le-Haut is perched on a limestone spur surrounded by a semicircle of cliffs, with the ruins of its 12C-13C castle on the southern edge (*archaeological site; 200m visitor trail).* Right at the top stands the beautifully restored 15C church. The town hall, located lower down,
Red and white wines of the **St-Romain Appellation** have no Premier or Grand Crus, but are generally good value for money. **Alain Gras** is one of the most reliable estates of the appellation and has been making good wine here for over 20 years (*see Shopping Guide).*

Drive towards La Rochepot along D 171.

Just before **Orches**, a village set in a rocky site, the road offers a fine **view**★ of St-Romain, Auxey, Meursault and the Saône Valley.

Beyond Orches, drive 4km further S.

Château de la Rochepot★

Visit by guided tour (1hr) only Jul–Aug 10am–6pm. May–Jun & Sept 10am-5.30pm, Apr & Oct 10–11.45am & 2–4.30pm. 7.50€. 03 80 21 71 37. www.larochepot.com.

The 13C castle rises above the woods, on top of Nolay peak, like a fairy-tale apparition. Tours include the guardroom and its weaponry, the kitchen with its monumental stove, the richly furnished dining room and the former chapel.

Drive to Nolay along D 973, then follow D 33 towards St-Aubin.

Saint-Aubin

The vineyards surrounding this pretty village, dominated by a belfry shaped like a sugar loaf, produce excellent slow-developing white wines under the **Saint-Aubin** AOC, on fine terroirs such as the picturesque Murgers des Dents de Chien *climat*. St-Aubin also makes delicate, fruity red wines.
The **Henri Prudhon et Fils**, **Hubert Lamy** and **Patrick Miolane** estates are excellent examples of the appellation (*see Shopping Guide).*

Leave St-Aubin towards Puligny-Montrachet, then take the minor road running through Blagny.

In the hamlet of **Gamay**, which boasts a "castle" immortalised by the artist Utrillo, a steep minor roads leads to the hamlet of **Blagny**, a small red-wine enclave in an area given over to great white wines.

Puligny-Montrachet

This is the world capital of great dry white wines. They seem to draw their richness from the pebbly limestone soils which are better at releasing the heat of the sun than any other in Burgundy. Their intense bouquet is very rich and their colour almost green. The Puligny terroir is shared between prestigious Grands Crus **Montrachet**, Bâtard-Montrachet and Chevalier-Montrachet. If you wish to buy, visit the **Louis Carillon et Fils** estate (*see Shopping Guide).*
Situated 3km south, the village of **Chassagne-Montrachet** has given its name to the **Chassagne-Montrachet** appellation which also produces great white wines such as the Criots-Bâtard-Montrachet Cru.

Santenay

Surrounded by cliffs, Santenay wines are mainly red and characterised by their great diversity due to the variety of geological elements making up the soils of the appellation. Of all the Santenay wines, those from the estates of **Françoise et Denis Clair** and **Anne-Marie et Jean-Marc Vincent** offer some the best value for money (*see Shopping Guide*).

In spite of its numerous alterations, the **Château de Santenay** (also known as the castle of Philip the Bold, the first duke of Burgundy) looks handsome with its roof of multicoloured tiles. *(1 r. du Château, 21590 Santenay; open Apr–Oct 10am–6pm; Nov–Mar 9am–noon & 2–5pm; 03 80 20 61 87; www.chateau-de-santenay.com).*

Côte Chalonnaise

Situated to the south of Burgundy region, the Côte chalonnaise stretches east of D 981 over 100km, across land where the vineyards alternate with the pastures of Charolais cattle.
The Côte Chalonnaise appellation applies to red and white wines produced within an area which also includes the village appellations of Bouzeron, Rully, Mercurey and Givry, picturesque little towns in the heart of a region marked by strong rural traditions.

- **Michelin Map:** 320, I 8-9; local map p187.
- **Info:** wwwww.laroutedesgrandsvins.com.
- **Location:** South of Beaune, from Changy down to Montagny.
- **Timing:** A leisurely two days on foot or by bike is most enjoyable.
- **Don't Miss:** The 80km green route along the canal du Centre
- **Kids:** Rully castle

DRIVING TOURS

CÔTE CHALONNAISE TOUR

Chagny

This peaceful city lying along the Canal de Bourgogne is a famous gourmet stop-over, boasting the renowned Lameloise restaurant.

Follow D 974 W.

The road runs through **Remigny**, where you can enjoy a flight over the vineyards in a **hot-air balloon** *(71150 Remigny; open Apr-Oct; 03 85 87 12 30; www.air-escargot.com).*

Les Maranges

This small wine-growing "republic" comprises 3 picturesque hamlets, **Dezize-lès-Maranges, Sampigny-lès-Maranges and Cheilly-lès-Maranges**, rising like islands above a sea of vines. The **Maranges** AOC mostly includes red wines, which are both fruity and robust, and a few very subtle white wines.

Return to Chagny then follow D 219 S towards Bouzeron.

Bouzeron

The 12C church of this quiet village, entirely given over to wine growing, has a nave paved with funerary steles. The grape variety grown here is Aligoté, a white grape which flourishes on local ferruginous clay soils and produces floral white wines, at their best when drunk young. The **Chanzy** estate is worth a visit (*see Shopping Guide*).

Continue S until you reach Rully.

Rully

The **Rully** AOC produces twice as much white wine as red wine. The whites are, best drunk within three to four years. The reds are light and fruity. Rully is a large prosperous village dominated by its **Chateau de Rully**, a fortress erected round a 12C keep with features of military architecture. Stroll through the beautiful English-style park and try the wines of the estate *(71150 Rully; open by appt Mon–Fri morning 9am–noon & 1.30–6pm; 03 85 98 12 12; www.chateau-rully-bourgogne.com).*

Leave Rully S and follow the small road running just beneath the castle.

Mercurey

Mercurey is the largest and best known of the village appellations of the Côte Chalonnaise. The red and white wines produced here are at their best within a few years and reasonably priced. The **Michel Juillot estate** and **Domaine Brintet** are both rewarding visit (*see Shopping Guide*). The **Château de Chamirey**, a fine 17C edifice, has a cellar classified as a historic monument and produces wines matured in oak barrels *(71640 Mercurey; open by appt. Mon–Fri morning 9.30–noon & 1.30–6pm; 03 85 98 12 12; www.chamirey.com).*

Drive east along D 978 to Chalon-sur-Saône.

Chalon-sur-Saône

Situated in the heart of the Côte Chalonnaise vineyards, Chalon is the economic capital of a region sharing its activities between industry, arable farming and stockbreeding. Its festivals are very popular, especially the Paulée de la Cote Chalonnaise which celebrates the end of the grape harvest. For wine purchases, stop at the **Maison des vins de la côte chalonnaise** (*see Shopping Guide*).

Some of the houses in the old town, particularly in the St-Vincent district, boast fine half-timbered façades. The **Cathérale St-Vincent** has features dating from the 11C to the 19C. The chapel is lit through a beautiful stained-glass window depicting "the woman with the twelve stars" of the Apocalypse.

The flowerbeds of the prestigious **Roseraie St-Nicolas**★(including some 25 000 rose bushes) are scattered over huge expanses of lawn *(4km S from the banks of the Saône, via the bridges across the Saône islands then left along rue Julien-Leneveu; 5km rambling trail starting from the St-Nicolas leisure park: 1hr 30min though the rose garden).*

Housed in an 18C annexe of the former Ursulines convent, the **Musée Denon**★ is named after Vivant Denon, a local engraver who drew up a list of Egypt's antique monuments during Napoleon's campaign there. The museum displays works by Bassano and Caravaggio as well as fine 17C Dutch paintings. The *Portrait of a Black Man* by Géricault is one of the museum's prize pieces *(open Wed–Mon 9.30am–noon & 2–5.30pm; closed public holidays; 3.10€; no charge Wed and 1st Sun in the month; 03 85 94 74 41).*

The **Musée Niépce**★★ is dedicated to the pioneer of photography, Nicéphore Niépce (1765-1833), a native of Chalon. Housed in the Hôtel des Messageries, the museum exhibits a rich collection of vintage equipment illustrating the evolution of photography, together with some excellent contemporary exhibitions *(open Jul–Aug Wed–Mon 10am–6pm; Sept–Jun Wed–Mon 9.30–11.45am & 2–5.45pm; closed public holidays; 3.10€, no charge Wed and 1st Sun in the month; 03 85 48 41 98; www.museeniepce.com).*

Leave Chalon-sur-Saône along D 69 towards Givry, 9km E.

Givry

The **Givry** AOC produces red and white wines which Henri IV drank every day. They are similar to Mercurey wines. Good examples of the wines are made on the estate of **Guillemette and Xavier Besson** (*see Shopping Guide*).

Givry looks like a small 18C city with its town hall housed inside a monumental gatehouse dating from 1771, its fountains and its **church** surmounted by cupolas. The **Halle ronde**, a former corn exchange was built in the early 19C.

Leave Givry W along D 170.

The road runs through several wine-growing villages, **Jambles**, **Moroges** and **Bissey-sous-Cruchaud**, where there are many pleasant cellars. If you feel like enjoying an overall view of the vineyards, stop in Moroges and treat yourself to a hot-air balloon flight; 3-hour flights at the start and close of the day are available from **Bourgogne-montgolfières**, *(1390 Moroges; 180€/person; 03 85 47 99 85; www.eole71.com).*

D 125 leads S from Bissey to Buxy.

Buxy

This large village on the border of the Mâconnais has an important cooperative, the **Cave des Vignerons de Buxy** *(see Shopping Guide).*

The small **Musée du Vigneron** illustrates work in the vineyard and in the cellar over a period of a year. Display of old implements *(in the village centre; open Jul–Aug Tue–Sat 2–6.30pm; 03 85 92 00 16).*

Drive 2km W along D 977.

Montagny-lès-Buxy

The small **Montagny** appellation, exclusively devoted to white wines, surrounds a picturesque village clinging to a hillside above Buxy. Not far from the village, there is a fine viewpoint with a statue of the Virgin Mary and a picnic area.

1 WHITE WINES OF THE MÂCONNAIS

93km from Tournus to Mâcon (Itinerary 2 indicates a route for discovering aspects of the Mâconnais apart from its vineyards).

Although its wines are, in theory, entitled to the **Bourgogne** appellation, the Mâconnais differs from the Côtes area in several aspects: a geological homogeneity featuring a high proportion of limestone and red clay, a higher production-to-area ratio, the use of Gamay grapes for red wines and the predominance of white wines. It is a fine hilly region, heading down to Beaujolais, dominated by the high rocky spurs of Vergisson and Solutré.

Tournus

This transition town between "oc" and "oïl" country (southern and northern France) is worth a visit for its provincial character, its fine restaurants and its splendid Romanesque abbey.

The **Église abbatiale St-Philibert**★★ boasts a remarkably high nave and lovely 12C mosaics discovered in 2000, which illustrate work in the fields. The **crypt**★ dates from the late 10C. The 12C fresco decorating the south chapel is the best preserved of all.

You can buy local wines at the **Cave des Vignerons de Mancey** *(see Shopping Guide).*

Leave Tournus SW along D 14

Driving through a dale, you will come to the village of **Ozenay**, with its small 13C castle and rustic 12C church. *Beyond Ozenay, the road runs over the Brancion pass on its way to Brancion.*

Brancion★

Cars are not allowed in town; use the parking area provided outside the walls.

This feudal market town is perched on a spur overlooking two deep ravines, forming one of the strikingly picturesque settings of the region.

Once through the portcullised gateway set in the 14C ramparts, visitors discover the imposing ruins of the fortress, narrow streets lined with medieval houses, the 15C covered market and the church standing proudly at the end of the spur. The feudal **castle** dates back to the early 10C. From the top platform (87 steps, viewing table), there is a fine **view**★ of the village and its surroundings *(open Apr–15–end Sept 10am–1pm & 2–6.30pm;*

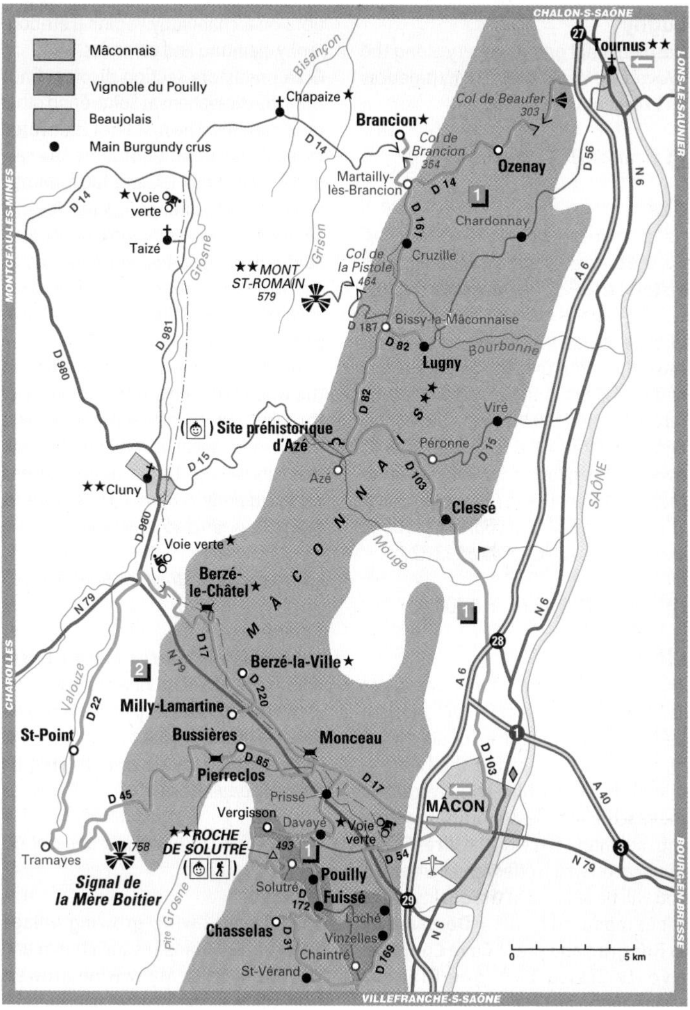

Oct–early Nov 2–5.30pm; 5€; 03 85 32 19 70; www.brancion.fr).

The **Église St-Pierre** is a squat 12C church built in the Cistercian Romanesque style, surmounted by a square bell tower. Inside there are 14C frescoes and many tombstones. The church terrace affords a panoramic view of the valley.

Leave Brancion towards Tournus then turn right on D 161.

Cruzille

This wine-growing village, which produces red and white Mâcon-Cruzille wines (**Mâcon-Villages** AOC), boasts an unusual wash house looking like an antique temple. The **Musée de l'Outillage artisanal rural et bourguignon** contains an amazing collection of several thousand old implements used by 32 different trades. It is housed in an estate pioneering organic wine growing *(Domaine des Vignes du Maynes; open daily 9.30–11.30am & 2.30–5.30pm; closed during harvest; 03 85 33 20 15, www.vignes-du-maynes.com).*

Continue on D 161 to Bissy-la-Mâconnaise and turn left on D 82.

Lugny

Nestling amid green scenery along the "Mâconnais Wine Road", Lugny produces an excellent white wine.

Return to Bissy then head south.

Azé

Azé produces mostly light white wines. But the town is known mainly for its **prehistoric site**. The **museum** displays numerous items found during the course of the excavations. An arboretum precedes the entrance to the **caves**. The first of these, 208m long, served as a refuge for cave bears (300,000-year-old bones) and prehistoric men. An underground river can be followed for 800m; it flows through another cave (*open Apr–Oct 10am–noon & 2–5.30/6pm; 1hr 30min guided tours; 6€; 03 85 33 32 23).*

East on D 15; right on D 103.

Clessé

This wine-growing village has a late 11C **church** with a small yet elegant bell tower and a spire covered with glazed tiles. Situated in the heart of one of the best white-wine terroirs in the Mâconnais, Clessé forms, together with neighbouring Viré, the **Viré-Clessé** Appellation which offers excellent value. You will be amazed at the quality of the wines produced by the **Domaine de la Bongran** and the **Cave Coopérative de Clessé-La Vigne Blanche** (*see Shopping Guide).*

Continue S along D 103 to Mâcon.

Mâcon

Spread between the Saône and the Mâconnais hillsides planted with vines, the town plays host every May to one of the most important French wine competitions (Concours des vins de France). The **Maison Mâconnaise des vins** is a good place to buy wine and a reliable source of information about local wines, in particular the **Mâcon** AOC (*see Shopping Guide).*

Housed in a former 17C convent, the **Musée des Ursulines**★ contains sections on archaeology, regional ethnography, painting and ceramics.

A prehistory section displays finds from the excavations at Solutré and other regional sites. The first floor is devoted to local crafts and traditions. The second floor exhibits 17C and 18C furniture, ceramics and paintings (*open Tue–Sat 10am–noon & 2–6pm, Sun & public holidays 2–6pm; closed Jan 1, May 1, Jul 14, Nov 1, Dec 25; 2.50€; 03 85 39 90 38).*

Inside the **Hôtel-Dieu**, the Louis XV **dispensary**★ has retained a fine collection of glazed earthenware. In addition to the wood panelling, the woodwork of the windows, blending perfectly with the general decor, is remarkable. Note the frescoes in the chapel (*open Jun–Sept daily 2–6pm; closed Jul 14; 2.50€; 03 85 39 90 38).*

West on D 17; then left for Prissé.

Prissé

This village produces Mâcon-Prissé white wine (Mâcon-Villages AOC). The **Groupement des producteurs de Prissé-Soligny-Verzé** is one of the most important cooperatives in the region (*see Shopping Guide).*

South on D 209, passing under N 79.

Davayé

This pleasant wine-growing village boasts a 12C Romanesque church and two 17C castles. Many wine growers from all over the region attended its wine-growing school.

D 177 runs W to Vergisson.

Vergisson

Tucked between the rocks of Solutré and Vergisson, this village, with its typical ochre-coloured stone houses, is included in the Pouilly-Fuissé Appellation. The **Barraud estate** is worth a visit (*see Shopping Guide).* Just like Solutré, it is a prehistoric site where remains of Neanderthal men have been excavated. A 3m-high menhir towers above the vines. **A footpath**, to the right along the road to Pierreclos, leads

Roche de Solutré, looking like the "Sphinx with its claws clutching the vines"

H. Champollion/MICHELIN

to the summit of the rock of Vergisson. Donkey rides along the paths running through the vineyards, at the foot of the rock of Vergisson, are organised by **Ânes et Sentiers** *(Martelet, 71960 Vergisson; open May–Sept; from 26€; 03 85 35 84 28; www.anes-sentiers.com).*

Drive W to Solutré.

Roche de Solutré★★

This true emblem of southern Mâconnais, on the borders of Beaujolais and in the heart of the Pouilly-Fuissé vineyards, can be seen from miles away between Bourg-en-Bresse and Mâcon. The superb limestone escarpment, with its slender outline and sphinx's profile, is one of the major prehistoric sites in France.

Before the Solutré cemetery, take the second left to the parking. Follow yellow markings, 45min on foot return.

A path leads to Crot-du-Charnier where the **Musée départemental de Préhistoire**, buried at the foot of the rock, is devoted to the prehistoric archaeology of southern Mâconnais. Exhibits include depictions of horses and hunting in the Solutré area during the Upper Palaeolithic Age and Solutrean man *(closed Nov, Dec; 3.50€; 03 85 35 85 24).*

Pouilly

This hamlet gives its name to various white Crus of the Mâconnais region: Pouilly-Fuissé, Pouilly-Loché, Pouilly-Vinzelles. Beyond the village, the vineyards spread over the gentle curves of the hillsides. **Fuissé** *(1.5km S of Pouilly)* shares with Pouilly the renown of **Pouilly-Fuissé**, the greatest white wine produced in the Mâconnais, although its quality varies a lot from one estate to the next. Try the **Château de Fuissé** *(see Shopping Guide).*

From Fuissé, drive W along D 172.

Chasselas

This village, dominated by an outcrop of grey rock showing through the heath, is situated on the borders of Beaujolais. The local vineyards produce well-known dessert grapes.

Leave Chasselas SE along D 31.

Saint-Vérand

Nobody really knows why St-Vérand lost its "d" on becoming the **St-Véran** AOC, producing lively, dry white wines such as can be bought at the **Domaine de l'Ermite de St-Véran** *(see Shopping Guide).* The hilltop village looks picturesque with its Romanesque church and its large wine growers' houses.

East via Chânes on D 169.

Vinzelles

The main point of interest in this village on the outskirts of Mâcon is its **Cave des Grands Crus Blancs** bringing together wine growers from Vinzelles and Loché; the **Domaine de la Soufrandière** is also worth a visit *(see Shopping Guide).*

Legendary Abbeys

Ancienne abbaye de Cluny★★

26km NW of Mâcon along D 17, then N 79 and D 980. Open 9.30am–5/6.30pm. 5€ during renovations, 7€ once completed in 2010; ticket combined with the Musée d'Art et d'Archéologie. 03 85 59 15 93; cluny.monuments-nationaux.fr.

The name of Cluny evokes the monastic order which exercised an immense influence on Western Christendom during the Middle Ages. For 200 years, the Benedictine abbey, founded in 910 by Guillaume of Aquitaine, was tremendously prosperous, as testified by the huge abbey church completed in the 12C.

The foundation of the austere Cistercian order and the Hundred Years War followed by the Wars of Religion progressively reduced the influence of the abbey, which was finally closed in 1790 and the abbey's stones were used for various buildings throughout the region. Extensive renovations are currently ongoing to the chapel, the transept and the cloisters, due to completed by 2010. Housed in the former abbey palace, an elegant 15C residence, the **Musée d'Art et d'Archéologie**★ contains the remains of the abbey found during excavations. There are models in the entrance hall and, upstairs, an audio-visual **Maior Ecclesia**★ *(9min)* reconstructs Cluny III by means of computer-generated images giving a realistic idea of the size of the abbey church.

17km NE of Auxerre via N 77.

Abbaye de Cîteaux

23km S of Dijon along D 996. Guided tour (1hr 15min) May–Sept; call for times. 7€. 03 80 61 32 58. www.citeaux-abbaye.com.

Under the great driving force of St Bernard, who joined the community in 1112 three years before becoming abbot of Clairvaux, this off-shoot of Cluny spread its influence throughout the world.

There is very little left of this important centre of Western culture: all that remains are the ruins of the former library dating from the 15C. There is also a handsome 18C building, at present inhabited by the monks who make the excellent Cîteaux cheese, a perfect companion for the regional wines. The **boutique** offers cheese, honey candies, caramels and other monastery products for sale.

Garden Paradise

Grand-Courtoiseau★★

38km W of Joigny between Triguères and Château-Renard by the D 943. Visit by guided tour (1hr 15min) in late spring – summer; call for times. 7€. 06 80 24 10 83.

Designed by landscape architect Alain Richert, this 6ha garden is a charming marriage of greenswards, flowerbeds and kitchen gardens laid out around an 18C manor house. Enjoy a stroll about its various sections, and don't miss the striking avenue of lime-trees planted in the 18C, nor the antique roses.

Gourmet Delights

Burgundy truffle and wine trail

Agence de développement touristique de l'Yonne, 1-2 quai de la République, 89000 Auxerre. Open Mon–Fri (Sat in high season). 03 86 72 92 10. www.tourisme-yonne.com.

The Loisirs-Accueil service of the Yonne *département* offers a wide choice of themed courses, without having to organise anything. From mid-Sept–mid-Dec, Saturday mornings are devoted to Burgundy truffles (lecture, demonstration, tasting).

ABC of haute cuisine (Yonne)

Hôtel La Côte St-Jacques, 14 faubourg de Paris, 89300 Joigny. Closed Jan 2–Feb 1. 3 86 62 09 70. www.cotesaintjacques.com.

Jean-Michel Lorain, from La Côte Saint-Jacques, shares his gastronomic experience and introduces his guests to contemporary cuisine.

Down the Cure

Club Canoë-kayak

3km N of Vézelay. R. de la Guinguette, 89460 Cravant. Gérard Valdiviesso. ℘03 86 42 20 31.

This club organises equipment and transport for a day trip (or longer) down the magnificent Cure Valley, from the Malassis dam to the Sermizelles dam and down the Yonne.

Ab Loisirs

3km E of Vézelay by the D 957. Rte. du Camping, 89450 St-Père. ℘03 86 33 38 38. www.abloisirs.com.

This leisure park offers a trip down the Cure from Malassis to Sermizelles *(4hr, 18km)*, an adventure trail with swinging footbridges, rope ladders, high-wire slides and Nepal bridges in Pierre-Perthuis, and rafting in the Morvan region *(starting 20km S of St-Père)*.

Along the Canals

Over 1,200km of canals, now almost free of commercial transport, are waiting for leisure-cruising enthusiasts. Mostly built from the 17C onwards, these canals, together with navigable rivers (the Yonne, the Saône and the Seille), provide an exceptional network for those who wish to discover Burgundy's soul. Hiring a house-boat with a capacity for four to 12 people for a day, a weekend or a week, enables visitors to get a different perspective of the sites encountered along the canals. Rates vary according to the period, the size and degree of comfort of the boat. No licence is required (the control lever only moves to two positions), but the helmsman gets a quick lesson before the start of the cruise. The main starting points are Auxerre, Digoin, Joigny, St-Jean-de-Losne, Tournus.

Aquafluvial – *Port des Pougeats, 58110 Baye-Bazolles; ℘03 86 38 90 70; www.aquafluvial.com.*

France Fluviale – *89270 Vermenton; ℘03 86 81 54 55; www.bourgogne-fluviale.com.*

Saône fishing

The **Mâcon Pêche au gros** association can introduce you to catfish fishing in the Saône. Michel, a fishing guide, explains all you need to know to track down this river giant which can be over 2.5m long. All the necessary tackle and a specially equipped boat are at your disposal. Meals are taken on location. Three-hour introduction or trips lasting one day or more, suitable for everyone *(4 r. de la Liberté, 71000 Mâcon; ℘03 85 39 07 50; www.peche-au-silure.com)*.

Keeping Fit

The "Green Trail"

This 44km trail between Givry and Cluny follows the route of a former railway line linking the Mâconnais and Chalonnais regions. Mostly tarmacked, it is reserved for pedestrians, in-line skaters and cyclists; there is a special track for horses between Massily and Cluny. The *Guide de la Voie verte* is available free from the Comité départmental de tourisme. It lists all the stops, the accommodation on offer, the restaurants and the cycle-hire companies. *Kits Voie verte* are also available for bikers: they enable them to follow the green trail one way only and to return to their starting point between Dijon and Mâcon by loading their bike on to a bus or a train *(available in SNCF stations, valid for 1–6 persons; N°7 bus line between Chalon and Mâcon, 6 buses daily; TER from Dijon, Nuits-Saint-Georges, Beaune, Chagny, Chalon, Tournus, Mâcon. 7.50€ to 21€.*

Cycling Auxerre and Chablis

This round trip of about 80km across hilly countryside will take someone with trained muscles one weekend to complete, starting from Auxerre. The route runs through Coulanges-la-Vineuse, Irancy, St-Bris-le-Bineux, Chablis, Ligny-le-Châtel, Pontigny and Appoigny *(information from the Comité départemental du tourisme de l'Yonne, 1-2 quai de la République, 89000 Auxerre; ℘03 86 72 92 10; www.trouisme-yonne.com)*.

WINE BUYING GUIDE

INFORMATION

Bureau interprofessionnel des vins de Bourgogne (BIVB) – *12 bd. Bretonnière, BP 150, 21024 Beaune Cedex. ✆03 80 25 04 80. www.bivb.com* The BIVB provides extensive information and publishes several brochures about wines, including an *Annuaire des caves de Bourgogne* listing the names and locations of the various estates, cooperatives and merchant-producers.

USEFUL TIP

"From vineyards to cellars" – Over 250 wine-growing estates, producers, merchants and cooperatives signed the Charter entitled "De vignes en caves", guaranteeing a quality welcome in the vineyards of Burgundy. A sign at the entrance to their property identifies them and a free guide available from various tourist organisations and wine centres gives their location.

CHARACTERISTICS

Burgundy wines are referred to by the name of their appellation. This can include the name of the village appellation, of the Cru, the locality, the vineyard and, the name of the wine grower. Crémants-de-Bourgogne wines have no Cru or village name.

Auxerrois and Tonnerrois – White wines are light and tangy with aromas of flower and honey. Red wines are not very tannic, relatively clear, with fine red-berry flavours. Irancy wines are more structured and age well.

Chablis – These white wines are crisp and minerally when young; the best of them acquire aromas of honey, roasts and dry fruit when very old.

Côte-de-nuits – These red wines are famous for being both robust and subtle. Their quality and characteristics vary considerably according to the village appellations, the Crus and the vineyards. White wines are fat with a lingering flavour.

Côte-de-beaune – Great white wines, round and generous, becoming very rich with age. Red wines are generally full-bodied and always very aromatic.

Côte chalonnaise – Fairly light red and white wines, best drunk within three to four years.

Mâconnais – White wines made from Chardonnay, fairly unpretentious (except for the more complex Pouilly-Fuissé), for drinking young. The same thing applies to the reds made from Gamay. Those made from Pinot Noir are entitled to the Burgundy Appellation.

STORAGE

White wines – They age well owing to their good levels of acidity. Most can easily be kept for 3 to 5 years and the richest even much longer. **Red wines** – The best bottles can be kept for 20 years and more. Maturing red and white wines in casks is common practice in Burgundy. Most of the time casks are made of French oak: this gives young wines vanilla or roast aromas, which fade with ageing.

Sparkling wines – These are normally drunk as soon as they are released, but some may be held for a few years.

PRICE

The price range of Burgundies here is very wide.

Regional Bourgognes, Aligotés de Bouzeron – 3 to 11€.

Bourgognes Hautes-Côtes-de-Nuits, Hautes-Côtes-de-Beaune, Petits Chablis, Côte chalonnaise, Mâcon, Rully, Mercurey and Givry – rarely more than 8€.

Chablis – 5 to 10€; Chablis Premier Cru: 8 to 12€, sometimes over 20€; Chablis Grand Cru: 20 to 30€.

Auxey-Duresses, Ladoix, Maranges, Pernand-Vergelesses, Saint-Aubin, Saint-Romain, Santenay – less than 15€.

Beaune, Chassagne-Montrachet, Côte-de-Beaune, Meursault, Pommard, Volnay and Puligny-Montrachet – 11 to 30€.

Grands Crus from Montrachet and subsidiary appellations – over 70€.

Bourgognes Grand Ordinaire and Bourgogne-Passetoutgrain – 3 to 11€.

Côte-de-nuits – 20 to 50€.

Crémants – rarely more than 8€.

WINE MERCHANTS

Les Agapes – *13 r. Preuilly, 89000 Auxerre. ✆03 86 52 15 22. marcragaine@wanadoo.fr; open 9am-12.30pm & 2-7pm.* Excellent selection of fine wines, in bulk and bottled, as well as spirits and objects for your cellar…

La Cave des Cordeliers – *6 r. de l'Hôtel-Dieu, 21200 Beaune. ✆03 80 25 08 85. Open daily 9.30am–noon & 2–6pm. Closed Jan 1–22, Dec 24, 25 & 31.* The former Couvent des Cordeliers in Beaune (1243) houses this cellar which you can visit before tasting a few Grands Crus from Burgundy. The firm stocks 80 different wines, among them some Côte-de-Beaune, Côte-de-Nuits and wines from the Hospices de Beaune vineyards. There is also a choice of regional products.

La Carte des Vins – *20 r. d'Alsace – 21200 Beaune. ✆03 80 22 44 20 – www.lacartedesvins.fr. Open daily 10am-8pm. Closed Dec 25–26.* Well laid out shop with interesting choice of well known and up-and-coming producers. Knowledgeable staff help you select from over 2,000 references, and there are regular tastings held in store. A store in Macon, Beaune, Dijon and Lyon.

Le Cellier de l'Abbaye – *13 r. Municipale and r. du 11-Août-1944, 71250 Cluny. ✆03 85 59 04 00. www.cellier-abbaye.com. Open Tue–Sat 9.30am–12.30pm & 3.30–7pm; Sun 10am–12.30pm; Mon 14 Jul– 15 Aug; public holidays 10am–noon. Closed Sun Jan–Mar.* It is better to go into this historic and prestigious cellar through the entrance on rue du 11-Août-1944. A superb stone-vaulted corridor leads to the shop furnished with wooden racks, shelves loaded with bottles and a few casks. Over 300 local wines are sold here at prices set by the estates, but you will also find whiskies, brandies and liqueurs.

Nicot Yves – *48 r. Jean-Jacques-Rousseau, 21000 Dijon. ✆03 80 73 29 88. nicotvins@infonie.fr. Open Mon–Fri 8am–12.30pm & 3–8pm; Sat 8am–8pm; Sun 8am–12.30pm.* Mr Nicot has a real passion for wine. That is the reason why he founded this business in 1985. Four years later, he opened a wine school where he gives courses in wine tasting and oenology. Fine selection of Burgundies.

Caves de Saint-Valérien – *58 r. du Dr-Privey, 71700 Tournus. ✆03 85 51 78 74. Open Tue–Sat 9am–12.30pm & 2.30–7.30pm; Sun 9am–12.30pm.* In his cellar, where he stocks over 1 000 different wines, Mr Bayet, who loves his terroir and specialises in Grands Crus from Burgundy, gives pride of place to wines from the Mâconnais such as Pouilly-Fuissé, Saint-Véran or Mâcon-Solutré, yet he also favours Côte chalonnaise and Côte de Beaune wines.

COOPERATIVES AND WINE CENTRES

Cave des Vignerons de Buxy – *Les Vignes-de-la-Croix, 71390 Buxy. ✆03 85 92 03 03. Open Mon-Sat 9am–12pm & 2–6.30pm.* This cooperative makes Bourgogne-Côte-Chalonnaise, Montagny and Mercurey wines.

La Chablisienne – *8 bd. Pasteur, 89800 Chablis. ✆03 86 42 89 89. www.chablisienne.com. Open 9am–12pm, 1.30-6pm. Closed Jan 1, Dec 25.* This cooperative has around 300 wine growers as members; they represent a quarter of the Chablis vineyards and produce the 6 Grands Crus of the appellation: Bougros, Blanchot, Les Clos, Les Preuses, Valmur, Vaudésir and Grenouille. The wine-tasting room is the ideal place to discover the range of Premiers Crus and Petits Chablis. Bourgogne, Bourgogne Aligoté, Chablis, Chablis Grand Cru, Chablis Premier Cru, Crémant-de-Bourgogne, Irancy, Petit Chablis, Saint-Bris.

Maison des vins de la côte chalonnaise – *2 prom. Ste-Marie, 71100 Chalon-sur-Saône. ✆03 85 41 64 00. Open Mon–Sat 9am–7pm.* This renowned centre, run by an association of wine growers of the Côte chalonnaise, only sells regional wines at prices set by the estates. Givry, Montagny, Rully or Mercurey, have all been selected through blind tasting.

Cave Coopérative de Clessé-La Vigne Blanche – *Rte. de la Vigne-Blance, 71260 Clessé. ✆03 85 36 93 88. Open Mon–Sat 9am-noon & 2-6.30pm; www.vire-clesse.com.* Founded in 1927, this cooperative covers 130ha planted in Chardonnay, Pinot Noir and Gamay. Traditional cultivation, with mechanical harvesting followed by traditional winemaking in temperature-controlled stainless-steel tanks. Since 2006, wines have been aged in oak barrels. Bourgogne, Crémant-de-Bourgogne, Macon, Macon-Villages, Viré-Clessé.

Maison Mâconnaise des Vins – *484 ave. de Lattre-de-Tassigny. 71000 Mâcon. 03 85 22 91 11. www.maison-des-vins.com. Open daily 9am–10pm (restaurant 11.30am-10pm). Closed Jan 1–20.* Showroom, bookshop, boutique, wine tastings conducted by professionals… The Maison des vins de Mâcon is really worth a visit. In addition, its restaurant offers some regional specialities (fish in white wine, chicken in cream sauce, coq au vin) served with selected Crus from the Mâconnais.

Groupement de producteurs de Prissé-Sologny-Verzé – *Les Grandes Vignes, 71960 Prissé. 03 85 37 88 06; open Mon-Sat 9am-12.30pm & 1.30-7.30pm; Sun 2-7pm; www.cavedeprisse.com.* This association of wine growers from Prissé-Sologny-Verzé is the result of the merger of three cooperatives. It includes 500 members and covers 1,000ha of vineyards. It is today the second most important cooperative in Burgundy and holds an ISO 9002 certificate. Bourgogne, Bourgogne-Aligoté, Bourgogne-Passetout-Grain, Crémant-de-Bourgogne, Mâcon, Mâcon-Villages, Pouilly-Fuissé, Saint-Véran.

Maison du vignoble auxerrois – *14 rte. de Champs, 89530 St-Bris-le-Vineux. 03 86 53 66 76. maison.du.vignoble.auxerrois@wanadoo.fr. Open Mon–Tue & Thu–Fri 9am–12pm & 3–7pm; Sat 9am–12.30pm& 2.30–7pm; Sun 2.30–6.30pm. Closed Jan–Feb.* Centre run by an association of wine-growing unions of the Grand Auxerrois region. Wine tastings (sometimes thematic) and sale of 25 Crus selected by the wine growers themselves in an attempt to show the best of their know-how. There are also guided tours of the vineyards.

Cave Henry de Vézelay – *4 rte. Nanchévres, 89450 St-Père. 03 86 33 29 62. www.henrydevezelay.com. Open Mon–Fri 9am–noon & 2–6pm, weekends 10am–12.30pm & 2.30–7pm. Closed Dec 25 & Jan 1.* BIVD Welcome Charter. The cooperative has brought together 12 wine growers and 31ha of vineyards producing a good Bourgogne-Vézelay (white, red, rosé), a Ratafia-de-Bourgogne and a Melon-de-Bourgogne (now rare in Burgundy, but experiencing a resurgence in Vézelay).

Cave des Vignerons de Mancey – *N 6, 71700 Tournus. 03 85 51 00 83. Open daily 8am–noon & 2-6pm.* This cooperative is the showroom of an association of 80 wine growers tending 140ha of vineyards. Their wines are varied but never fail in quality. Among the better ones are Les Essentielles, a fine range including a Mâcon-Villages, a Mâcon-Mancey and a Bourgogne-Pinot Noir (all three remarkable), Crémants and Aligotés.

Cave des Grands Crus Blancs – *Rte des Allemands, 71680 Vinzelles. 03 85 27 05 70.* This popular cooperative offers the whole range of white wines produced in the Mâconnais at very reasonable prices.

ESTATES

Domaine du Château de Melin – *21190 Auxey-Duresses. 03 80 21 21 19. www.chateaudemelin.com. Open by appt.* This 23ha family estate cultivates Pinot Noir and Chardonnay vines on clayey-limestone soils. Grapes are harvested mechanically, and vinified by traditional methods. Maturation takes place in oak barrels, a quarter of them new, for 15 months. Bourgogne-Hautes-Côtes-de-Beaune, Chambolle-Musigny, Chassagne-Montrachet, Gevrey-Chambertin, Maranges, Meursault, Pommard, Puligny-Montrachet, Saint-Romain, Santenay.

Domaine Michel Prunier et Fille – *Rte. de Beaune, 21190 Auxey-Duresses. 03 80 21 21 05. Open by appt. Mon–Sat 9am–noon, 2–7pm.* The estate, founded in 1968, today covers 12ha planted in Pinot Noir and Chardonnay. Premier Crus include Clos du Val, Les Sizies and Les Caillerets. Vineyards are cultivated along ecologically responsible principles. In 2004, Estelle joined her father in the enterprise. Auxey-Duresses, Beaune, Bourgogne, Bourgogne-Aligoté, Bourgogne-Hautes-Côtes-de-Beaune, Bourgogne-Passetoutgrain, Chorey-lès-Beaune,

Côte-de-Beaune-Villages, Crémant-de-Bourgogne, Meursault, Pommard, Volnay.

Domaine Chanzy – *1 r. de la Fontaine, 71150 Bouzeron. 03 85 87 23 69. www.chanzy.com. Open Mon–Fri 8am–noon & 2–5.30pm, weekends by appt.* This estate was taken over by Catherine and Daniel Bouzeron in 1974 today joined by their children Anne-Sophie and Olivier. Now covering 38ha, it is planted with Aligoté, Chardonnay and Pinot Noir varieties. It includes seven appellations in the three Côtes areas: Côte de Beaune, Côte de Nuits and Côte Chalonnaise. Wines are matured in oak casks, a third of them new. Bourgogne, Bouzeron, Crémant-de-Bourgogne, Mercurey, Puligny-Montrachet, Rully, Santenay, Vosne-Romanée.

Domaine William Fèvre – *10 R. Jules-Rathier, 89800 Chablis. 03 86 42 12 06. www.williamfevre.com. Open daily 9.30am-12.30pm & 1.30-6pm.* The Henriot family has owned the estate since 1998. With its 15ha of Grand Cru land, and 12ha of Premier Cru, the vineyard boasts one of the most prestigious ranges of Chablis Grands Crus. Practices include harvesting by hand, careful sorting of the grapes, maturing in casks and stainless-steel tanks for ten to fifteen months depending on the vintage. Chablis, Chablis Grand Cru, Chablis Premier Cru, Saint-Bris.

Château Long-Depaquit – *45 r. Auxerroise, 89800 Chablis. 03 86 42 11 13 – chateau-longdepaquit@albert-bichot.com. Open Mon–Sat 9am–12.30pm & 2–6pm. Closed Dec 25–Jan 1, and on Saturdays from Nov to Feb.*

This vast wine-growing estate which, until the Revolution, was owned by the Cistercian abbey of Pontigny, produces Chablis AOC Premier and Grand Cru wines, matured in oak casks. The wine made from grapes grown on the plot of La Moutonne is considered to be the "eighth Chablis Grand Cru". Wine-tasting cellar, boutique and very attractive park arround the chateau. Chablis, Chablis Grand Cru, Chablis Premier Cru.

Domaine Tixier *37, Grande Rue de Chablis, Préhy 89800, tel: 03 86 41 42 72. Open by appt.* Owned by the dynamic

S. Sauvignier/MICHELIN

Martine Tixier, the vineyard covers a surface of more than 7 hectares and extends over the villages of Courgis and Chablis. Try the excellent Chablis Premier Cru Montmains. Martine is more than happy to welcome visitors, while her husband Momo is usually out in the vines. In 2007 their son Thomas joined the team. Chablis, Chablis Premier Cru.

Domaines Jean Durup Père et Fils – *4 Grande-Rue, Maligny, 89800 Chablis. 03 86 47 44 49. www.durup-chablis.com. Open Mon–Fri 9am–noon & 1.30-5.30pm.* Jean Durup, a Paris lawyer, who comes from a long line of wine growers from Chablis, heads one of the two wine growers' unions; his son Jean-Paul ensures continuity in running the estate covering 180ha. Vinification and maturing methods are still traditional. The wines are left in stainless-steel tanks for a minimum of five to six months depending on the appellation. Chablis, Chablis Grand Cru, Petit Chablis.

Domaine Amiot-Servelle – *21220 Chambolle-Musigny. 03 80 62 80 39. www.amiot-servelle.com. Open by appt. Mon–Sat.* Having practiced ecologically responsible cultivation methods for a decade, in 2003 Christian Amiot converted entirely to organic winegrowing. The yields are low and harvesting is done by hand, with rigorous sorting of the grapes. The wines then mature in oak barrels. The estate produces several Premier Crus: Les Charmes, Derrière-la-Grange, les Amoureuses, les Feusselottes and les Plantes. Bourgogne, Bourgogne-

Aligoté, Chambolle-Musigny, Clos-de-Vougeot.

Domaine Comte Senard – *Les Meix, 21420 Aloxe-Corton. ℘03 80 26 41 65; domainesenard.com. Open by appt. Mon–Sat 9am–12pm & 2–6pm. Lunches also by reservation Tues-Sat 10am-6pm.* Winemaker Count Philippe Senard and his daughter Lorraine offer a wonderful wine-tasting lunch where you match typical dishes of the region with the estates own wines. Tours of the cellars are also available. Aloxe Corton, Corton Charlemagne, Savigny-lès-Beaune Premier Cru, Savigny-lès-Beaune, Beaune and Chorey-lès-Beaune.

Domaine de la Bongran – *71260 Clessé. ℘03 85 36 94 03. www.bongran.com. Open by appt.* Jean Thévenet believes in methods that respect nature: weeding by machine instead of chemicals, harvesting by hand, slow fermentation without adding yeasts etc. Wines are aged 18 to 24 months. Mâcon-villages, Viré-Clessé.

Domaine de l'Abbaye du Petit Quincy – *R. du Clos-de-Quincy – 89700 Épineuil. ℘03 86 55 32 51. Open Mon–Sat 10am–12.30pm & 2.30–6pm. Closed public holidays.* In this 13C building owned by the monks of the Cistercian abbey of Quincy, Dominique Gruhier produces quality wines over 24ha: Bourgogne Épineuil made with grapes from a recently recreated vineyard, Chablis and Crémant-de-Bourgogne. Ask someone to show you the interesting wine press. Bourgogne, Chablis, Crémant-de-Bourgogne, Petit Chablis.

Château de Fuissé – *71960 Fuissé, ℘03 85 35 61 44. www.chateau-fuisse.com. Open Mon–Thu 8.30–noon & 1.30–5.30pm (Fri 4.30pm).* Elegant building flanked by a 15C tower standing opposite two bottle-shaped yew trees, in the middle of a 30ha estate. Visit of the cellar and opportunity to taste the Pouilly-Fuissé originating from renowned terroirs, some of which are the exclusive property of the estate (Le Clos, Les Combettes, Les Brûlés). Mâcon, Mâcon-Villages, Pouilly-Fuissé, Saint-Véran.

Vineyard of Aloxe-Corton

B. Kaufmann/MICHELIN

Domaine Philippe Naddef – *30 rte. des Grands-Crus, 21220 Fixin. ℘03 80 51 45 99. Open by appt. Mon–Sat.* In 1983, Philippe Naddef took over 2.5ha of Gevrey-Chambertin, forming part of the family estate originally created by his grandfather. Since then, the estate has spread to the Fixin and Marsannay terroirs to cover 5ha, 4ha of Pinot Noir and the rest of Chardonnay.
He produces two Gevrey-Chambertin Premiers Crus, Les Cazetiers and Les Champeaux. Bourgogne, Fixin, Gevrey–Chambertin, Marsannay, Mazis-Chambertin.

Domaine Trapet Père et Fils – *53 rte. de Beaune, 21220 Gevrey-Chambertin. ℘03 80 34 30 40. www.domaine-trapet.com. Open by appt. Mon–Fri 9–11am & 2–5pm.* The vineyard extends over 14.5ha: Chambertin, Chapelle-Chambertin and Latricières-Chambertin Grands Crus, and two Gevrey Premiers Crus, Clos-Prieur and Petite-Chapelle. On this estate having used bio-dynamic methods since 1998, harvesting is done by hand. For these wine growers, who value traditional wine growing, it is very important to respect the terroir. Red wines are matured for up to twenty months in oak casks. Bourgogne, Chambertin, Gevrey-Chambertin, Latricières-Chambertin, Marsannay.

Domaine Guillemette et Xavier Besson – *9 r. des Bois-Chevaux – 71640 Givry. ℘03 85 44 42 44.* The vineyards cover some 7ha planted with Pinot Noir and Chardonnay, including several plots of Givry Premier Cru and of Beaune Premier Cru. Harvesting is done by hand and vinification is traditional with full de-stalking, temperature control, etc. The wines are then left to mature in oak casks. Beaune, Givry.

Domaine Cantin – *35, chemin des Fossés, 89290 Irancy; ✆03 86 42 21 96. Open by appt.* Benoît Cantin runs this 13.5 hectare estate along organic principles, with no weedkillers and as little intervention as possible. His increasingly lauded wines are fruity but elegant, and are all aged in barrel (in recently updated cellars and winery). Try the Irancy Cuvee Emeline (named after Benoit's daughter). Bourgogne, Bourgogne-Passetoutgrain, Irancy.

Domaine Edmond Cornu et Fils – *Le Meix Gobillon, r. du Bief, 21550 Ladoix-Serrigny. ✆03 80 26 40 79. Open Mon–Sat 9am–12pm & 3–6pm.* Extending over 14ha spread within a 3km radius, this family-owned estate with its various buildings stands inside a walled perimeter. Harvesting is done by hand. The grapes are then fermented in tanks and matured in casks. The estate produces Aloxe-Corton and Ladoix Premiers Crus, and a Corton Grand Cru. Aloxe-Corton, Bourgogne Aligoté, Chorey-lès-Beaune, Corton, Côte-de-Nuits-Villages, Ladoix, Savigny-lès-Beaune.

Domaine Regis Bouvier – *52 route de Mazy, 21160 Marsannay la Cote. ✆03 80 51 33 93. Open by appt. Mon–Fri 9am–noon & 2–7pm.* This 15 hectare estate has been subject to extensive work in the vineyard over the past five years. All chemicals have been banned, and the soils have been worked to encourage the roots to go down as far as possible. In the cellars, the emphasis is on fruit, meaning gentle extraction and use of gravity rather than pumps. It's also family run – Regis and his wife alongside their children Christophe and Julie. Bourgogne Aligoté, Chambolle-Musigny, Fixin, Marasannay, Santenay.

Château de Marsannay – *Rte. des Grands-Crus. 21160 Marsannay-la-Côte. ✆03 80 51 71 11. www.chateau-marsannay.com. Open Mon–Sat Nov–Mar 10am–6pm0pm. Closed Dec 23–Jan 14.* The Château de Marsannay estate owns a 38ha vineyard. A tour of the old cellar and of the storehouses stocked with casks and bottles (around 300 000) ends with a wine tasting in the shop. A showroom illustrates the history of the Marsannay tournament (1443). Bourgogne, Chambertin, Clos-de-Vougeot, Fixin, Gevrey-Chambertin, Marsannay, Ruchottes-Chambertin, Vosne-Romanée.

Domaine Michel Juillot – *59 Grande-Rue, BP 10, 71640 Mercurey. ✆03 85 98 99 89. www.domaine-michel-juillot.fr. Open daily 9am–6pm.* Laurent Juillot took over from his father Michel in 2002, after having worked with him for nearly fifteen years. With his wife Carine, he now works 30ha. The vineyard is cultivated by ecologically responsible methods, and the wines are matured in casks. Aloxe-Corton, Bourgogne, Corton, Corton-Charlemagne, Mercurey, Santenay.

Domaine Brintet - *Grande Rue, 71640 Mercurey, ✆03 85 45 14 50; www.domaine-brintet.com* - Véronique and Luc Brintet own this 13 hectares estate, and vinify each plot of vines seperately to ensure the greatest authenticity. Try the Mercurey Rouge Les Vieilles Vignes, and their three Premier Crus: Les Vasées, Les Crêts et La Lévrière. Cote Maconnais, Mercurey., Mercurey Premier Cru.

Château de Meursault – *R. du Moulin-Foulot, 21190 Meursault. ✆03 80 26 22 75. Open daily by appt. 9.30am–noon & 2.30–6pm.* Bought by André Boisseaux in 1973 from the count of Moucheron, the 60ha estate is now run by his son Jacques with the help of Jean-Claude Mitanchey. The vineyard is planted with Pinot Noir and Chardonnay. Following a careful sorting, the black variety is slightly crushed, fermented and transferred into casks. White wines are either fermented in tanks or in casks. Aloxe-Corton, Beaune, Bourgogne, Meursault, Pommard, Puligny-montrachet, Savigny-lès-Beaune, Volnay.

Domaine Arlaud – *41 rue d'Epernay, 21220 Morey Saint Denis. ✆03 80 34 32 65; www.domainearlaud.com.* Newly-modernised cellars have just added to the sense of dynamism around this family-run estate, producing consistency high quality wines. Cyprien Arlaud, sister Bertille and brother Roman have taken over here from their father Herve. Organic winemaking, with horses in the vines. Bourgogne, Chambolee Musigny, Morey-Saint-Denis.

Domaine Rapet Père et Fils – *21420 Pernand-Vergelesses. 03 80 21 59 94. Open by appt. Mon–Sat; www.domaine-rapet.com.* This 18ha estate spreads across the municipalities of Pernand-Vergelesses, Aloxe-Corton, Savigny and Beaune. It is run by Vincent Rapet. The vineyard, planted with Pinot Noir and Chardonnay, is cultivated by ecologically responsible methods. The Rapets have always made a point of respecting the terroir and the specificity of the appellations. Aloxe-Corton, Beaune, Bourgogne, Bourgogne Aligoté, Corton, Corton-Charlemagne, Pernand-Vergelesses, Savigny-lès-Beaune.

Domaine du Clos des Épeneaux – *Pl. de l'Église – 21630 Pommard. 03 80 24 70 50. www.domaine-des-epeneaux.com. Open by appt.* Limited to 5ha for its exclusive Pommard Premier Cru, Clos des Éperneaux, the estate was extended by the purchase of the Volnay Premier Cru Frémiets, of a plot of red Auxey-Duresses Premier Cru, and of a few acres of Bourgogne-Villages. It has remained a family-owned vineyard, with Benjamin Leroux in charge of winemaking, and covers 7.5ha of biodynamic vineyards. Auxey-Duresses, Bourgogne, Pommard, Volnay.

SCEA Louis Carillon et Fils – *1 impasse Drouhin, 21190 Puligny-Montrachet. 03 80 21 30 34. Open by appt.* The Carillon family works a 12ha vineyard planted with Chardonnay for white wines and Pinot Noir for red wines. Matured in oak casks for a year, the wines spend an additional six months in stainless-steel tanks before being bottled. Bienvenues-Bâtard-Montrachet, Puligny-Montrachet, Saint-Aubin.

Domaine Hubert Lamy – *Le Paradis, 21190 St-Aubin. 03 80 21 32 55. Open by appt.* Successive generations of the Lamy family have been wine growers in Saint-Aubin since 1640. The 17ha estate, planted with Pinot Noir for red wines and Chardonnay for white wines, is now run by Olivier Lamy, Hubert's son. He cultivates the vineyard by ecologically responsible methods. The wines are matured in oak casks and small barrels in modern cellars extended in 2003. Chassagne-Montrachet, Criots-Bâtard-Montrachet, Puligny-Montrachet, Saint-Aubin, Santenay.

Henri Prudhon et Fils – *32 r. des Perrières, 21190 St-Aubin. 03 80 21 36 70. Open by appt. Mon–Sat.* The estate owns around 14ha within the "sacred triangle" formed by Saint-Aubin, Chassagne and Puligny-Montrachet. The steep hillsides, consisting of ancient geological strata of limestone and clay, enjoy a splendid aspect with plenty of sunshine; they are planted with Chardonnay and Pinot Noir. Chassagne-Montrachet, Puligny-Montrachet, Saint-Aubin.

Domaine Patrick Miolane – *21190 St-Aubin. 03 80 21 31 94. Open by appt. Mon–Sat 9am–noon & 2–6pm.* The estate covers 9ha spread across the villages of Saint-Aubin, Puligny-Montrachet and Chassagne-Montrachet. Chardonnay and Pinot Noir grape varieties, planted in clayey limestone soil, face south-east. The Chardonnay vines are 15 years old and the Pinot Noir vines are 25 years old. The wines are matured in oak casks. Chassagne-Montrachet, Puligny-Montrachet, Saint-Aubin.

Domaine Alain Gras – *21190 St-Romain-le-Haut. 03 80 21 27 83. Open by appt. www.domaine-alain-gras.com.* Since the 1997 vintage, Alain Gras has been working nearly 12ha of vines. He uses traditional methods and creates delicate, aromatic wines. Auxey-Duresses, Meursault, Saint-Romain.

Domaine de l'Ermite de St-Véran – *Les Truges, rte. de Pruzilly. 71570 St-Vérand. 03 85 36 51 09. Open by appt.* This wine-growing estate, created in 1978, spreads over 12ha. White grape varieties are planted in clayey limestone soil and red varieties in sandy soil mixed with silica and granite. Traditional growing methods are used and harvesting is done by hand. The estate also produces three Beaulolais wines, a Beaujolais-Villages, a Juliénas and a Saint-Amour. Saint-Véran.

Domaine Françoise et Denis Clair – *14 r. de la Chapelle, 21590 Santenay.* ***℘03 80 20 61 96. Open by appt. daily 8am–noon & 2-6pm.*** Having run a family estate for ten years, Françoise and Denis Clair decided in 1987 to create their own estate over an area of 5ha. Today, the vineyard covers 14ha. The estate produces several Premier Crus. Bourgogne Aligoté, Bourgogne-Hautes-Côtes-de-Beaune, Puligny-Montrachet, Saint-Aubin, Santenay.

Domaine Anne-Marie et Jean-Marc Vincent – *3 r. Ste-Agathe. 21590 Santenay.* ***℘03 80 20 67 37. Open by appt.*** This family-owned estate covers 5ha mostly devoted to the Santenay Premier Cru and Auxey-Duresses appellations. Wine-growing methods are environment-friendly: ploughing, grassing. The vines are pruned back short and strict disbudding is applied. The wines are matured in oak casks and bottled almost unfiltered. Auxey-Duresses, Santenay.

Simon Bize et Fils – *12 r. Chanoine-Donin, 21420 Savigny-lès-Beaune.* ***℘03 80 21 50 57. www.domainebize.com. Open by appt. Mon–Fri 9am–12pm & 3-6pm.*** The vineyards of this domaine cover 22ha, spread across the villages of Savigny-lès-Beaune, Aloxe-Corton and Pernand-Vergelesses. The estate also owns a plot of Latricières-Chambertin Grand Cru. Anxious to respect Burgundian traditions, Patrick Bize leaves his wines to mature in oak casks for a minimum of one year. Aloxe-Corton, Chambertin, Charlemagne, Latricières-Chambertin, Savigny-lès-Beaune.

Domaine Barraud – *Le Bourg – 71960 Vergisson.* ***℘03 85 35 84 25. www.domainebarraud.com. Open by appt. Mon–Fri 9am–noon & 2–6pm.*** This family estate, extending over 7ha of clayey limestone soil, offers a wide range of Crus, the finest of them being the Pouilly-Fuissé Les Crays. Mâcon-Villages, Pouilly-Fuissé, Saint-Véran.

Domaine de la Soufrandière – Bret Brothers – *La Soufrandière, 71680 Vinzelles.* ***℘03 85 35 67 72. Open by appt. www.bretbrothers.com.*** In 1947, Jules

A. Cassaigne / MICHELIN

Bret, a professor of medicine, bought 1ha of Pouilly-Vinzelles Les Quarts AOC vines. In 1998, La Soufrandière welcomed Jean-Guillaume and Jean-Philippe, two of Jules's three grand-children. Today, the vineyard covers 4.5ha planted with Chardonnay. Wine growing is done both by modern and traditional methods: the land is worked by machines, yields are limited, bio-dynamic methods are tested, harvesting is done by hand. Mâcon-Villages, Pouilly-Fuissé, Pouilly-Loché, Pouilly-Vinzelles, Saint-Véran, Viré-Clessé.

Domaine Hentri Lagrange – *7 cours Francois Blondeau, 21190 Volnay.* ***℘03 80 21 64 12. Open by appt; www.domaine-henri-delagrange.com.*** The vineyard of the estate extends over 15 hectares - owner Didier Delegrange has just added one hectare of the Volnay Premier Cru Les Santenots. Beaune, Pommard, Aloxe Corton, Mersault, Borgogne Haut Cotes de Beaune.

Domaine Christian Clerget – *21640 Vougeot.* ***℘03 80 62 87 37. Open Mon-Fri 9am-noon & 2-7pm, Sat-Sun 9am-noon.*** This 6ha estate produces two Premiers Crus. Harvesting, pruning and disbudding are done by hand. Vinification takes place in enamelled tanks and in concrete tanks, inside the cellar built in 1999. The wines are then matured in oak casks for eighteen months. Bottling is done on-site, without filtration or fining. Chambolle-Musigny, Échezeaux, Morey-Saint-Denis, Vosne-Romanée, Vougeot.

ADDRESSES

STAY

AROUND AUXERRE

Chambre d'hôte M. et Mme Piedallu – *5 ave. de la Gare, 89160 Lézinnes, 11km SE of Tonnerre along D 905. 03 86 75 68 23. 3 rooms.* This new house built in traditional style is full of charm. The garret rooms are nevertheless spacious and decorated with antique furniture. The veranda of the dining room offers a pleasant breakfast setting. There is a small drawing room for those who wish to read or rest.

Chambre d'hôte Domaine Borgnat Le Colombier – *1 r. de l'Église, 89290 Escolives-Ste-Camille, 9.5km S of Auxerre along D 239. 03 86 53 35 28. www.domaineborgnat.com. 5 rooms. Restaurant.* This magnificent 17C fortified farmhouse is the head-quarters of a fine wine-growing estate. You will have a choice between guest-house rooms and the self-catering cottage housed in the dovecot. Meals introduce guests to the wines produced by the estate; these can also be tasted when visiting the superb cellars. There is also a heated pool, and wine-themed courses available.

Chambre d'hôte Le Calounier – *r. de la Fontaine, hameau de Arton, 89310 Môlay, 8km N of Noyers along D 86 and a minor road. 03 86 82 67 81. www.lecalounier.fr. Closed Jan–Feb. 4 rooms. Restaurant.* Everything is aimed at seducing you in this splendidly restored Burgundian farmhouse; its name in local dialect is also that of the walnut trees planted around the estate. The half-British, half-regional decoration of the rooms located in the two wings is very attractive. The cuisine is based on products of the terroir.

Chambre d'hôte Château de Ribourdin – *89240 Chevannes, 7km SW of Auxerre along N 151, D 1 and a minor road. 03 86 41 23 16. www.chateauribourdin.com. 5 rooms.* This splendid, small 16C castle and its dovecot, standing beneath the village, in the middle of a wheat field, look very elegant. The former 18C barn houses the bedrooms, each one named after a local castle, and the breakfast room adorned with a fireplace.

Hôtel Maxime – *2 qui Marine, 89000 Auxerre. 03 86 52 14 19. contact@lemaxime.com. 26 rooms. 10€.* In the old mariners' quarter (wood panelled houses), this family hotel dates from the 19C. Choose a room with a view over the Yonne, or one of the quieter ones overlooking the courtyard.

Rive Gauche – *R. Port-au-Bois, 89300 Joigny. 03 86 91 46 66. www.hotel-le-rive-gauche.fr. 42 rooms. 9.50€ Restaurant.* Contemporary building erected on the west bank of the River Yonne. Fairly spacious, refurbished rooms with a sensible layout. Pleasant park with ornamental pond and helipad. The contemporary dining room-veranda and the terrace both look out towards the river.

Hôtel La Côte St-Jacques – *14 faubourg de Paris, 89300 Joigny. 03 86 62 09 70. www.cotesaintjacques.com. 27 rooms. 27€. Restaurant.* A luxury hotel overlooking the River Yonne, so far from everything… and so close to perfection. There's also a private boat for river cruising and a shop. The splendid inventive cuisine and a profusion of Grands Crus are the strong points of this leading gastronomic establishment.

AROUND BEAUNE

Hôtel du Parc – *13 r. du Golf, 21200 Levernois, 5km SE of Beaune via rte. de Verdun-sur-le-Doubs, then D 970 and D 111L. 03 80 24 63 00. www.hotelleparc.fr. Closed Nov 28–Jan 27. 25 rooms. 7.50€.* An attractive courtyard bedecked with flowers separates the two buildings which make up the hotel. The façades are decorated with Virginia creeper; the rooms contain antique furniture, retro lights and colourful draperies which create a warm atmosphere. The park situated at the back ensures peace and quiet. Attentive family-style service.

Hôtel Grillon – *21 r. Seurre, 21200 Beaune. 03 80 22 44 25. www.hotel-grillon.fr. Closed Feb. 17 rooms. 7.50€.* This elegant pink house with almond-green shutters, nestling inside an enclosed garden, contains fresh-looking rooms partly furnished with items found in antique shops. Lounge-bar in the vaulted cellar and flower-decked terrace where breakfast is served in fine weather.

Domaine du Moulin aux Moines – *Auxey-Duresses, 21190 Meursault. ✆03 80 21 60 79. www.laterrasse.fr. 7 rooms and 1 apt. ☕7€.* This fine residence set in the middle of a vineyard once belonged to Cluny Abbey. The spacious, tastefully decorated rooms are full of charm. Those located in the mill are particularly attractive. Wine-tasting cellar for sampling the wines produced by the estate and small wine-growing museum (handsome winepress).

Hôtel La Villa Fleurie – *19 pl. Colbert, 21200 Beaune. ✆03 80 22 66 00. www.lavillafleurie.fr. Closed Jan. 10 rooms. ☕8.50€.* The branches of a fragrant wisteria intertwine on the railings of this small 1900-style villa which has three kinds of rooms: contemporary, bourgeois-style or family-style, the latter – two maisonettes – located on the top floor. Attractive, slightly British-looking breakfast room and garden-terrace.

AROUND CHALON

Adélie – *21200 Montagny-les-Beaune. ✆03 80 22 37 74. www.hotel-adélie-beaune.fr. 19 rooms. ☕7€.* Family hotel located in the heart of a peaceful village. Renovated rooms are painted in pastels, accented with pine furnishings.

Chambre d'hôte Au Temps d'Autrefois – *Pl. Monge, 21340 Nolay. ✆03 80 21 76 37. www.terroirs-b.com/gite. 3 rooms, 1 suite and 1 self-catering cottage.* A charming old-world atmosphere pervades this lovely 14C timber-framed house standing in a small square adorned by a fountain. The interior is very welcoming, with its share of exposed beams, antique furniture and red-brick floor tiles, and the rooms are attractive and quiet. Breakfast is served on the terrace in summer.

Fontaine de Baranges – *R. Fontaine-de-Baranges, 71390 Buxy. ✆03 85 94 10 70. www.hotelfb.com. 18 rooms. ☕9€.* A master winegrower long resided here, preserving the building's 19C charm. Spacious, individually decorated rooms, a third of which boast private terraces overlooking a romatic garden. Breakfast is served in a pretty vaulted cellar.

Hôtel St-Jean – *24 quai Gambetta, 71100 Chalon-sur-Saône. ✆03 85 48 45 65. 25 rooms. ☕6€.* Perfectly situated on the banks of the Saône, this family hotel will welcome you with open arms. The rooms are beautifully kept, with floral accents. Breakfast is served in a glassed room that feels like a winter garden.

Hostellerie du Château de Bellecroix – *Rte. de Chalon, 71150 Chagny, 18km W of Beaune by the N 74 then the N 6. ✆03 85 87 13 86. www.chateau-bellecroix.com. Closed Dec 19–Feb 13 and Wed in low season. 19 rooms. ☕17€. Restaurant.* The two towers of this 18C château rise above a tree-filled park. Behind them, you'll see the former command-poste of the Chevaliers de Malte (12C). Old-fashioned furnishings in the guestrooms, and good reproductions of medieval woodwork in the dining room.

AROUND DIJON

Chambre d'hôte Les Brugères – *7 r. Jean-Jaurès, 21160 Couchey, 10km S of Dijon via N 74 and D 122D. ✆03 80 52 13 05. www.francoisbrugere.com. Closed Dec–Mar. 4 rooms. ☕.* If you wish to talk about wine and taste it, this charming 17C wine grower's home is the perfect place for you. Attractively decorated bedrooms featuring exposed beams and pieces of antique furniture. Pleasant breakfast room. The cellar is open to visitors who are invited to taste the wine.

Hôtel La Musarde – *7 r. des Riottes, 21121 Hauteville-lès-Dijon. ✆03 80 56 22 82. www.lamusarde.fr.*

Place François Rude, Dijon

B. Kaufmann/MICHELIN

Closed Dec 23–Jan 15; restaurant closed Sun evening and Mon. 12 rooms 9€. Restaurant. The terrace of this hotel is very pleasantly shaded in fine weather by cypress, hazelnut and oak trees mingling their foliage, and the peaceful village all around adds to the appeal of the place. The rooms, plainly furnished in rustic style, look out on the quiet garden.

Hôtel Les Grands Crus – *R. de Lavaux, 21220 Gevrey-Chambertin. 03 80 34 34 15. www.hoteldesgrandscrus.com. Closed Dec–Feb. 24 rooms. 12€.* Treat yourself to a break here, in the heart of wine country: the old village, celebrated by so many writers – one of them, Gaston Roupnel, even tried his hand at wine growing – is understandably popular with wine lovers. The hotel rooms, in either bourgeois or rustic style, offer fine views of the vineyards.

La Bonbonnière – *24 r. des Orfèvres, 21240 Talant, 5km NW of Dijon along D 107A. 03 80 57 31 95. labonbonniere@wanadoo.fr. Closed Jan 1–7, Jul 29–Aug 15 and Dec 23–31. 20 rooms. 9€.* Private house turned into a hotel in a lovely village overlooking Lake Kir. The interior decor lives up to the name of the establishment: period furniture and pastel colours add a slight "bijou" touch to the place. Spacious, quiet bedrooms, bourgeois-style sitting rooms and convivial breakfast room.

AROUND MÂCON

Auberge du St-Véran – *71570 St-Véran. 03 85 23 90 90. www.auberge-saint-verain.com. Closed Jan 9–29, Mon and Tue midday in low season. 11 rooms. 10€. Restaurant*. In the heart of the St-Véran terroir, a charming refurbished watermill with a country feel. Comfortable rooms.

Chambre d'hôte Château de Salornay – *71870 Hurigny, 6km W of Mâcon along D 82 and a minor road. 03 85 34 25 73. 4 rooms and 2 self-catering cottages.* This castle, dating from the 11C and 15C, looks very elegant with its handsome towers and thick walls crowned by a watch path. The spacious rooms, one of them in the keep, contain antique furniture and look out on the surroundings fields. Two distinctive, self-catering cottages are also available.

Chambre d'hôte Le Château d'Escolles – *71960 Verzé, 2km N of La Roche-Vineuse along D 85. 03 85 33 44 52. www.gite-escolles.com. 4 rooms.* You will be given a friendly welcome in this outbuilding of a 17C castle, located on the edge of a 5ha park. The garret rooms are cosy: thick wall-to-wall carpet, exposed beams, antique furniture... Breakfast features a selection of homemade jams and fresh fruit juice. Charming terrace.

Chambre d'hôte Le Tinailler du Manoir de Champvent – *Lieu-dit Champvent, 71700 Chardonnay, 11km SW of Tournus via D 56 and D 463. 03 85 40 50 23. Closed Nov–Feb. 5 rooms.* The outbuildings of this handsome yellow-stone manor contain several rooms decorated with antique furniture, still-lifes and abstract paintings. There is a large meadow where children can let off steam and a lovely courtyard bedecked with flowers. Shows (plays, concerts, humour etc) and exhibitions are regularly staged in the theatre.

Chambre d'hôte Côté Vigne – *Domange, 71960 Igé. 03 85 33 46 64. www.cotevigne.fr. 5 rooms. Table d'hôte (by reservation Wed–Sun).* A handsome early 19C residence overlooking the vineyards. The welcome is warm, the rooms are comfortable, and the meals in the best taste. Swim in the heated pool! Wine tasting in the vaulted cellar.

AROUND VÉZELAY

Chambre d'hôte Au Porc-Épic – *80 R. St-Pierre, 89450 Vézelay. 03 86 33 32 16. www.le-porc-epic.com. Closed Jan. 3 rooms.* This artist's home dates from the 12C, but has been magnificently restored. Enter through the studio-cum-art gallery. Despite their slightly monastic appearance, the rooms are very comfortable and well-kept. A nice, if somewhat atypical spot.

Hôtel Crispol – *Rte d'Avallon, à Fontette, 89450 Vézelay, 5km E of Vézelay along D 957. 03 86 33 26 25. www.crispol.com. Closed Jan 10–end Feb, Tue lunchtime and Mon. 12 rooms. 9€. Restaurant*. This stone building, located in a hamlet of the Vézelay area, features rooms decorated in contemporary style and brightened up by the artist-owner's works. You will appreciate the peace and quiet of the garden, in spite of the hairpin bend in the road at that very spot. Elegant restaurant looking out towards Vézelay hill.

EAT

AROUND AUXERRE

Le Bistrot des Grands Crus – *8 r. Jules-Rathier, 89800 Chablis. 03 86 42 19 41. www.bistrotdesgrandscrus.com. Closed Dec 20–Jan 20.* There is a choice of appetising regional dishes on the menu of this restaurant where one eats in cramped conditions in the dining room or outside in summer. Try a small dish of Burgundy snails, eggs cooked in Pinot Noir sauce or chitterling sausage flavoured with Chablis!

Relais St-Vincent – *89144 Ligny-le-Châtel, 9km N of Chablis. 03 86 47 53 38. relais.saint.vincent@libertysurf.fr. Closed Dec 21–Jan 6.* The town bailiff lived in this 17C building, today transformed as a hostelry. Local recipes are served about the fireplace, accompanied by the delightful wines of the Chablis region. Guestrooms preserve the charm of yesteryear.

La P'tite Beursaude – *55 r. Joubert, 89000 Auxerre. 03 86 51 10 21. auberge.beursaudiere@wanadoo.fr.* The regional-sounding name, the plain, convivial country-style dining room, the staff dressed in local costume and copious dishes based on regional cuisine: it's Burgundy in miniature!

Le Bourgogne – *15 r. Preuilly, 89000 Auxerre – 03 86 51 57 50 – closed Jul 31–Aug 29, Dec 23–Jan 2, Thu evenings, Sun and Mon, and public holidays.* The signboard out front announces the daily menu, created from the freshest market ingredients. There's a lovely paved terrace bedecked with flowers which welcomes gourmets in summer.

Le Moulin de la Coudre – *2 r. Gravottes, 89290 Venoy. 03 86 40 23 79. www.moulindelacoudre.com. Closed Jan 6–29, Sun evenings and Mon.* This 19C mill nestling in pastoral surroundings is a real haven of peace only a few minutes' drive from Auxerre. Sitting outside under the trees or in the comfortable dining room, you will be able to enjoy to the full the tasty cuisine which combines tradition with regional trends.

Le Saint Père – *2 ave. Georges-Pompidou, 89700 Tonnerre. 03 86 55 12 84. Closed Dec 29–Jan 20, Sun evenings and Wed.* The menu of this small Tonnerre restaurant does credit to local products. Joint of beef gratinéed with Époisses cheese, Chablis-style ham or pork cheek braised in red wine delight gourmets sitting comfortably in the pleasant dining room decorated with a fine collection of coffee grinders.

Hostellerie des Clos – *18 r. Jules-Rathier, 89800 Chablis. 03 86 42 10 63. www.hostellerie-des-clos.fr. Closed 22 Dec to 16 Jan.* This hostelry in the heart of the village occupies the former hospital. Pleasant restaurant looking out on a patio, copious dishes and extensive wine list. Well-furnished rooms.

AROUND BEAUNE

Auberge des Vignes – *N 74, 21190 Volnay. 03 80 22 24 48. elisabeth.leneuf@free.fr. Closed Feb 3–Mar 3, Nov 29–Dec 9, Sun and Wed evenings and Mon.* Appreciated by kings, red Volnay wine has had a long, illustrious history. If you wish to be introduced to its subtle bouquet while enjoying eggs in red-wine sauce, braised knuckle of beef or a thick steak of Charolais beef, go to this restaurant with its veranda overlooking the vineyards.

Aux Vignes Rouges – *45 r. Maufoux, 21200 Beaune. 03 80 24 71 28. Closed Aug 15–31 and Tue.* Unusual setting: the kitchen forms an integral part of the dining room and the chef works in full view of the guests.

La Bouzerotte – *21200 Bouze-lès-Beaune. 03 80 26 01 37. www.labouzerotte.com. Closed Jan 2–20, Sept 1–9, Dec 22–Jan 1, Mon and Tue.* The menus of this restaurant, featuring an unassuming rustic setting, combine regional specialities with trendy dishes: it is possible to enjoy a traditional coq au vin as well as fillet of ling in lime sauce, or pancetta served with confit of pork cheek seasoned with lemon and clove.

La Ciboulette – *69 r. de Lorraine, 21200 Beaune. 03 80 24 70 72. Closed Feb 2–25, Aug 2–18, Mon and Tue.* This small, convivial establishment offers its guests a typical Burgundian cuisine. The concise menu concentrates on sure-fire regional favourites such as Burgundy-style pork cheek fillet, ham seasoned with parsley or thick steak of Charolais beef with Époisses cheese. This limited choice enables the chef to take even more care over each dish.

La Cuverie – *5 r. Chanoine-Donin. 21420 Savigny-lès-Beaune. 03 80 21 50 03. Closed Dec 20–Jan 20, Tue and Wed.* Here in the heart of the Savigny vineyards, everything points to the terroir: the name refers to the place where wine is fermented. The spacious dining room is furnished in Burgundy style and the cuisine is based on regional produce: try snails in their shell or stewed, ham seasoned with parsley or Charolais beef.

Le Fleury – *16 pl. Fleury, 21200 Beaune. 03 80 22 35 50. www.lefleury.com. Closed Jan 5–9, Tue and Thu Oct–May.* Paintings hanging on soft-toned walls, dishes of slow-cooked bœuf bourguignon by a chef trained at Guy Savoy's in Paris: this restaurant, overlooking a lively square in Old Beaune, delights both the eyes and the taste buds of its guests. Appetising menus inspired by the terroir.

AROUND CHALON-SUR-SAÔNE

Auberge du Camp Romain – *71150 Chassey-le-Camp. 03 85 87 09 91. www.auberge-du-camp-romain.com.* Between the woods and the vines, a comfortable spot near a Neolithic camp. Simple rooms in the main building, with larger, more modern spaces in the annex. Copious portions of traditional cuisine in the rustic dining room. Veranda reserved for non-smokers.

Aux Années Vins – *71390 Buxy. 03 85 92 15 76. www.aux.annees.vins.com.* Very pleasant spot located in the ramparts of the town. Enter through a rear courtyard to the warmly-coloured dining room with stone walls and fireplace. Terrace overlooking the village. Attentively prepared dishes at reasonable prices.

L'Air du Temps – *7 r. de Strasbourg, île St-Laurent, 71100 Chalon-sur-Saône. 03 85 93 39 01.* The name of this charming spot is reflected in the decor of the small dining rooms as well as the savoury dishes made from fresh local ingredients, all offered at reasonable prices.

Le Bourgogne – *28 r. de Strasbourg, 71100 Chalon-sur-Saône. 03 85 48 89 18. Closed Jul 4–19, Dec 25–30, Sun evenings and Mon.* In a charming setting of the sort you only ever find in fine old buildings – you are sure to enjoy regional dishes (snails, eggs in red-wine sauce or tournedos of Charolais beef) as well as a few trendier ones such as red mullet bavarois, brochette of spicy scallops or duck breast with caramelized peaches.

Le Magny – *71530 Sassenay. 03 85 91 61 58.* This restaurant cultivates a pleasantly provincial atmosphere, what with the armoires, the fireplace, the poultry-themed artwork… Vintages of the terroir figure prominently on both the wine list and the menu.

Le Terroir – *Pl. du Jet-d'Eau, 21590 Santenay, 5km W of Chagny along D 62 and D 113. 03 80 20 63 47. www.restaurantleterroir.com. Closed Dec 10–Jan 10, Wed evening Nov–Mar, Sun evenings and Thu except Jul 20–Aug 20.* This stone house nestling in a peaceful village, situated at the end of the prestigious "Grands Crus road", has two comfortable dining rooms where guests enjoy a tasty cuisine combining tradition and regional flavours. The essential finishing touch to this feast of the palate comes from the cellar well stocked with local Crus.

Le Vendangerot – *6 pl. Ste-Marie, 71150 Rully. 03 85 87 20 09. www.vendangerot.com. Closed Jan 2–15, Feb 15–Mar 10, Wed except evening Jul-Sept, and Tue.* This house, bedecked with geraniums, awaits you in the heart of a real wine-growing village. In the dining room, decorated with a collection of old photographs on the theme of wine growing, you will discover the chef's tasty Burgundian dishes, successfully blending local produce with Rully wines.

Le Chassagne – *2 imp. Des Chenevottes, 21190 Chassagne-Montrachet. 03 80 21 94 94. www.restaulechassagne.com. Closed Jul 25–Aug 10, Dec 19–Jan 12, Sun and Wed evenings, and Mon.* Wild turbot glazed with orange peel candied with ginger, truffle salad served with artichoke chips, veal cooked with citrus fruit… All these delicacies, enhanced by a very fine selection of Chassagne-Montrachet wines, offer you a glimpse of gourment paradise!

AROUND DIJON

La Toute Petite Auberge – *N 74, 21700 Vosne-Romanée. 03 80 61 02 03. Closed Feb, Tue evening and Wed.* The regional and traditional dishes served in both dining rooms or on the terrace overlooking the small park and the vineyards are truly delicious. Burgundy-style crispy beef cheek, for instance, reveals subtle flavours enhanced by a rich red-wine sauce.

Le Bistrot des Halles – *10 r. Bannelier, 21000 Dijon. 03 80 49 94 15. Closed Sun and Mon.* The 1900-style bistro faces the covered market. Among the must-try specialities, choose the pie, the snails or the unusual Dijon-style cod in mustard cream. On the other hand, the description of some specialities might arouse your curiosity: their roast duck with pineapple and gingerbread springs to mind…

Ma Bourgogne – *1 av. Paul-Doumer, 21000 Dijon. 03 80 65 48 06. Closed Aug 10–25, Sun evening and Sat.* The chef of this restaurant deliberately limits the number of his guests in order to be able to control everything from A to Z himself and to prepare regional dishes which justify the good name of the house. His wife and his daughter welcome and serve their guests with a smile in the simple, well-kept dining room.

Chez Guy – *3 pl. de la Mairie, 21220 Gevrey-Chambertin. 03 80 58 51 51. Closed Wed.* Ham seasoned with parsley, pastilla of snails, Burgundy-style beef cheek, blackcurrant cake or gingerbread ice cream are on the menu and the wine list includes the best Crus: you are in one of the most famous wine-growing villages of the Côte, and in the perfect place to make the most of it.

Le Chambolle Musigny – *28 r. Basse, 21220 Chambolle-Musigny. 03 80 62 86 26. Closed Jul 1–6, Dec 19–Jan 20, Sun evenings Dec–Apr, Wed and Thu.* A friendly greeting welcomes you to this small dining room where you can enjoy dishes inspired by the terroir. Eggs in red-wine sauce, Burgundy snails, coq au vin and boeuf bourguignon are cooked slowly, with the greatest care by the chef who will advise you to wash it down with a Chambolle-Musigny as tradition requires.

Les Deux Fontaines – *16 pl. de la République, 21000 Dijon. 03 80 60 86 45. Closed Jan 1–11, 3 wks in Aug, Sat and Mon.* The menu of this attractive bistro begins with a tribute to the owner's grandmother, a true cordon bleu. The decor of the dining room, housed in a former warehouse, brings about a nostalgic feeling. As for the dishes, drawn from recipes of the past, they are brought up to date through the use of spices and flavours from around the world.

AROUND MÂCON

Au P'tit Pierre – *10 r. Gambetta, 71000 Mâcon. 03 85 39 48 84. Closed Jul 25–Aug 15, Tue evenings, Wed Sept-Jun, Mon lunchtime and Sun Jul-Aug.* A favorite spot with local residents, this recently opened bistro features enticing decor, pretty tables, a well-executed menu, and very good value for money.

Le Fin Bec – *Pl de la Mairie, 71570 Leynes. 03 85 35 11 77. Closed Jul 25–Aug 10, Nov 13–22, Jan 1–11, Thu evenings except in Jul–Aug.* Warm welcomes issue forth from this rustic dining room accented with Beaujolais-themed art. Generous helpings of regional cuisine.

Le Restique– *56 r. St-Antoine, 71000 Mâcon. 03 85 38 38 76. Closed 3 wks in Aug, late Dec–early Jan, Mon and Tue evenings, and Sun.* Three menus on offer at this rustic restaurant: terroir, matelot or lyonnais, all at very reasonable prices. Simple wooden furnishings and decor, all befitting the warm welcome.

Pouilly Fuissé – *Le Bourg, 71960 Fuissé, 9.5km from Mâcon along D 17, D 54 and D 172. ☎03 85 35 60 68. Closed Jan 2–26, Jul 28–Aug 6, Sun, Mon and Tue evenings, and Wed.* This establishment named after the famous local Cru favours regional wines, of course. Served by the glass or the bottle, they go perfectly well with the good-value, tasty cuisine which combines traditional and typically Burgundian dishes: chitterling sausage with Époisses cheese and vacherin flavoured with Burgundy marc.

Aux Terrasses – *18 av. du 23-Janvier, 71700 Tournus. ☎03 85 51 01 74. www.aux-terrasses.com. Closed Jan 2–Feb 2, Jun 6–14, Nov 16–22, Sun evenings, Tue lunchtime and Mon.* It is unthinkable to go through Tournus without tasting Michel Carette's delicious, classical cuisine: hot mallard pie, Bresse chicken braised in Chardonnay wine or pikeperch with ham from Morvan, which you wash down with a Cru selected from the inspiring wine list. Attractive dining rooms. Friendly welcome.

Le Terminus – *21 ave. Gambetta, 71700 Tournus. ☎03 85 51 05 54. www.leterminustournus.com. Closed Wed.* Spacious dining room and shaded terrace where you will feel perfectly at ease to enjoy the tasty traditional dishes prepared by the chef. Worth noting: the "100% Charolais menu." All dining rooms non-smoking.

IN VÉZELAY

Les Aquarelles – *6 ruelle des Grands-Prés, in Fontette, 89450 Fontette. ☎03 86 33 34 35. Closed Nov12–Dec 5, Dec 26–Mar 12, Mon and Tue in Nov–Dec.* Former farmhouse located in a peaceful hamlet, where you will be welcomed as among friends. The rooms are small yet fresh and well kept. Table d'hôte offering simple meals prepared with regional produce and served on two large farm tables. Tasting of the wines produced on the estate.

Le St-Étienne – *39 r. St-Étienne, 89450 Vézelay. ☎03 86 33 27 34. www.le-saint-etienne.fr. Closed mid-Jan–late Feb, Wed and Thu.* This 18C building rises next to the main street leading to the basilica. Within, a welcoming rustic dining room with exposed beams, and invitations to sample the selections of the day.

GOURMET SHOPPING

Au Fin Palais – *3 pl. St-Nicolas, off quai de la Marine, 89000 Auxerre. ☎03 86 51 14 03. aufinpalais@club-internet.fr. Open Apr–Oct daily, 9am–7.30pm. Nov–Mars Tue–Sun 9am–12.30pm & 2–7.30pm.* This shop sells renowned specialities of Burgundian gastronomy, bought from the best local producers: terrine from Morvan, streaky salted pork with lentils, boeuf bourguignon, gingerbread, nonnettes (small iced gingerbread), croquets (dry crispy biscuit with almonds),

Burgundian speciality – escargots

R. Marcialis/MICHELIN

various kinds of jam, mustard and vinegar… and the famous snails. A small space is set aside for wines and spirits.

Amuse-Bouche – *7 pl. Carnot, 21200 Beaune. ✆03 80 25 06 62. Open Tue-Sat 10am–1pm & 2–7pm; Sun 10am–1pm; Closed Feb school holidays.* This shop specialises in rare delicacies: morels, truffles, caviar and prestigious wines are prominently displayed on the shelves, among Espelette Pimentos, smoked hams, various kinds of olive oil and homemade dishes like boeuf bourguignon and coq au vin.

Au Cep Gourmand – *15 r. Auxerroise, 89800 Chablis. ✆03 86 18 97 83. Open Mon–Sat 9am–5pm, Sun, 9am-1pm.* This shop stocks many products manufactured by local cottage industries intended for the palate and the table. You will find, among others, terrines, foie gras, chitterling sausages, biscuits, a selection of local wines and some fresh produce as well as a selection of tableware and gifts.

Légendes Gourmandes – *4 pl. St-Vincent, 71100 Chalon-sur-Saône. ✆03 85 48 05 64. www.legendes-gourmandes.com. Open Tue-Sat 9.30am–noon & 2.30–7pm; Sun 9.30am–noon.* Mesdames Lotz and Sotty offer their clients a real gastronomic tour of France: from Provence to Brittany via Lorraine or Burgundy of course, they have selected all kinds of products for the quality of their taste: vinegars, terrines, fruit drinks, caramels, sardines, spirits etc.

Bourgogne Street – *61 r. de la Liberté, 21000 Dijon. ✆03 80 30 26 28. Open Mon –Sat 9am–7pm; Sun 10am–1.30pm & 2.30–7pm.* Orange-flavoured gingerbread brought fame to this establishment taken over in 1974 by the renowned Dijon company, Mulot et Petitjean. The recently enlarged shop offers a great variety of local products (try the chocolat du foux!) including nonnettes, gingerbreads, gimblettes, blackcurrant liqueur, Fallot mustard, wines, confectionary, jams and biscuits.

Ph. Gajic / MICHELIN

L'Escargotière de Marsannay-le-Bois – *9 rte d'Épagny – 21380 Marsannay-le-Bois ✆03 80 35 76 15 – sylvainmansuy@wanadoo.fr – daily, 10am-8pm.* Tours of the snail farm, from the breeding stage to the final product, are regularly organised. In the shop, you will find snails prepared according to the traditional Burgundian recipe, others cooked in white wine with fresh vegetables, empty shells ready to be filled and ready-cooked specialities.

MARKETS

Joigny – *Wed and Sat mornings, pl. du Marché.*
Auxerre – *Tue and Fri mornings, l'Arquebuse market. Sun morning, Ste-Geneviève market.*
Chablis – *Sun morning, in the town centre.*
Tonnerre – *Sat morning, pl. de la Gare.*
Dijon – *Tue, Fri and Sat mornings, in the town centre.*
Nuits-St-Georges – *Fri morning, covered market.*
Beaune – *Wed and Sat mornings.*
Buxy – *Thu morning, in the town centre.*
Tournus – *Sat morning, in the town centre.*
Châlon-sur-Saône – *Wed morning, pl. de l'Hôtel-de-Ville.*
Mercurey – *Sat morning, in the town centre.*
Mâcon – *Sat morning, esplanade Lamartine.*

5 - CHAMPAGNE

Champagne, a wine that has fascinated and intrigued ever since its creation, has been called the "nectar of gods" and the "wine of kings". Often imitated but never equalled, this legendary wine, born out of the meeting between the terroir, the know-how of wine-growers and the marketing genius of wine merchants, has become the epitome of French sophistication throughout the world. Given its international reputation, it's easy to forget that the only true Champagne is grown and made in the Champagne region of France, from Chardonnay, Pinot Noir and Pinot Meunier grapes grown on a mixture of Champagne terroirs. The vineyards of Champagne are spread over five French départements, although the vast majority can be found on the hillsides of the Marne and the Aube. These sunny slopes bring strength and aroma to the wine which in turn brings prosperity to the entire region.
Despite periods of hardship, France's Champagne vineyards thrive today, thanks to a burgeoning demand for the sparkling nectar. A trip to Reims, Épernay and the Aisne and the Marne valleys offers pleasant insights into the intricacies of this complex world, quite unlike that of any other wine-growing region. Like the subtle nuances of the wine itself, the region's way of life and the skills of its wine-makers are best discovered at leisure.

Highlights

1 The Gothic architecture of **Reims Cathedral** (p218)
2 A crumbly pink **Fossier biscuit** with a glass of Champagne (p252)
3 A stroll along Avenue de Champagne in **Épernay** (p226)
4 A hike through the national park of **Montagne de Reims** (p218)
5 A boat trip along the Marne river from **Cumières** (p229)

Mysteries behind the making

The first stage consists in hand picking and carefully selecting the bunches of grapes. These are then pressed according to very strict regulations. With red grapes, the juice is immediately separated from the skins so no trace of colour is imparted to the wine. No more than 4,000kg of grapes may be pressed at one time and the juice collected must not exceed 2,050 litres.
The must (juice) is then left to ferment in vats to around 11% alcohol by volume, before being blended in the spring. If the wine is to become a vintage Champagne it can only be made from wine from a single year. The wine is then drawn into thick glass bottles and selected yeasts and sugar are added. As a result a second fermentation takes place in bottle and as the extra sugar is transformed into alcohol, the carbon dioxide produced as a by-product of any fermentation can not escape, thereby dissolving into the wine and forming bubbles.
The bubbles take about two months to develop, after which time the bottles are stored in dark cellars for at least fifteen months for non-vintages and three years for vintage wines. The bottles are kept upside down on racks where they are rotated either manually or automatically, in order to progressively move the deposit that has formed down to the neck of the bottle: the *dégorgement* process then takes place. The bottles are placed in a refrigerated solution, which freezes the deposit and makes it easy to remove when opened. The now fined and sparkling wine is topped up with a "liqueur d'expédition", a blend of wine and sugar, depending on the taste wanted (demi-sec, sec, brut, extra brut or brut zero). It is then corked, wired, labelled and ready for shipping.

Different types of Champagne

The blend of vines, terroirs and often years enables each brand to develop its own distinctive character and style.
A **blanc de blancs** is a Champagne made only from white Chardonnay grapes.
A **blanc de Noirs** contains only black Pinot Noir and Pinot Meunier grapes.

OVERVIEW

The Terroir

Michelin Local Map 306 and 313 – Marne (51), Aisne (02) and Aube (10).

Surface area: a little over 32,902 hectares with 23,780 in the Marne, 6,772 in the Aube and Haut Marne, and 2,350 in the Aisne and Seine-et-Marne.

Production: Around 350-400 million bottles annually.

Grapes: 38% Pinot Noir, 33% Pinot Meunier, 29% Chardonnay.

In the Marne, the vineyards are located mainly on the hillsides around the Montagne de Reims, in the Marne Valley and around Épernay on the Côte des Blancs. The latter comprises an area in its own right in the south of the *département* around Sézanne. **In the Aisne**, the vineyards dominate the valley of the Marne from Charly to Dormans. **In the Aube**, the wine-growing area stretches from the densely-planted Côte des Bars around Bar-sur-Seine, to the more dispersed area around Bar-sur-Aube, predominantly on a base of chalky marl. It also includes the sector around Les Riceys to the south. **In the Marne**, the soil is mainly chalky and clayey-limestone. The climate is partly oceanic, partly semi-continental. Harsh winters and springs are softened by dense forests which raise the temperature. Summers and autumns are warm and sunny. In March 2008, the Institut National des Appellations d'Origine (INAO) approved the idea of expanding the area of production for champagne to around 35,000ha across 357 communes from the current 319. These proposals are now being debated, and may become law in 2015.

The Wines

Champagne has three appellations d'origine contrôlée:

Champagne AOC – Champagne is defined as a sparkling wine made from grapes only from the region of Champagne which are pressed and made into wine using the Champagne method, described later in this chapter. The different varieties of vines used are Chardonnay, which adds floral, refreshing notes, Pinot Noir, pressed without skin contact to keep the juice white and brings body and substance, and Pinot Meunier, a cousin of the Pinot Noir, used for its full-bodied yet supple notes. Within this area, 44 villages Premier Cru and 17 villages are classified Grand Cru.

Coteaux-Champenois AOC – These are non-sparkling red and white wines. The white wines are made from Chardonnay and the red and rosé wines from Pinot Noir and Pinot Meunier.

Rosé-des-Riceys AOC – The only Champagne AOC village which makes rosé wines from Pinot Noir grapes.

A Sparkle in the Eye

"Champagne", wrote Louis XV's mistress, Madame de Pompadour, "is the only wine that leaves a woman beautiful after drinking it. It gives brilliance to the eyes without flushing the cheek." Wines from other countries have attempted for many years to use the name, but the Champagne board (CIVC) finally won a legal battle that forced other producers of sparkling wines to stop calling their products "Champagne".

A **Rosé Champagne** is made by adding a measure of red Coteaux-Champenois before the bottle fermentation stage. A vintage Champagne is a blend of wines from different plots of land and/or different varieties of grapes, all of which are harvested in the same year. Wines of several years which are blended together are sometimes referred to as "brut sans année". The terms "cuvée prestige" or "cuvée spéciale" refer to Champagnes which are often vintage and made from the best wines of the year.

Champagne Wine Routes

The roads around Reims, Epernay, Troyes or Château-Thierry lead the traveller from huge cellars to tiny museums and from opulent Champagne firms to lush hillsides covered in vineyards of Chardonnay, Pinot Noir and Pinot Meunier.

- **Population:** 1.3 million people, one of France's least populated regions.
- **Michelin Map:** p220. Michelin Local Map 306.
- **Info:** www.champagne.fr
- **Location:** Reims is about an hour east of Paris by the A 4 motorway.
- **Kids:** Zig Zag park in Verzy.
- **Timing:** Allow two days to visit both Reims and Epérnay.

DRIVING TOURS

REIMS AND MONTAGNE DE REIMS

100km. Map p220.

The Montagne de Reims refers to a promontory south of Reims which rises to an altitude of 287m. The picturesque massif is covered with forests and its north and southeast slopes are planted with vineyards. The entire sector now makes up the Regional Nature Park of the Montagne de Reims.

Reims★★★

If you can't decide between Champagne tasting or Gothic art, Reims is just the place for you, offering the unforgettable prospect of a visit to the cathedral and the Palais du Tau combined with ventures into the underground cellars of prestigious Champagne firms.

Cathédrale Notre-Dame★★★

Reims Cathedral, a gem of Gothic art, has witnessed great moments in French history: it was on this site that Clovis, king of the Franks, was anointed and where Charles VII was crowned in the presence of Joan of Arc. But the succession of cathedrals which have stood here have endured a troubled past, culminating in the heavy German bombardment of 1914. The first cathedral to be built here was erected by Saint Nicaise in 401, very probably on the site of a Gallo-Roman temple of worship. This was replaced in the 9C by a larger edifice, destroyed by a fire in 1210. At this point, Archbishop Aubry de Humbert decided to rebuild in Gothic style, taking the great cathedrals of Paris, Soissons and Chartres as his models. The first stone was laid in 1211, but the towers were not completed until the late 15C due to a fire which delayed building. A long restoration programme carried out during the 19C had just been completed when the First World War broke out. On 19 September 1914, heavy shelling set fire to the timber framework, causing the bells and the lead of the stained glass to melt and the stone to split. The walls held up, however, and at the end of the war a new restoration programme was launched, partly financed by the Rockefeller Foundation.

The **exterior** of the cathedral was originally decorated by some 2 300 statues, but most of these are now copies. The **façade**, composed of three doorways, is reminiscent of Notre-Dame in Paris. The central doorway is devoted to the Virgin and depicts several periods of her life.

Inside the **nave** is three storeys high. The oldest capitals are decorated with carvings of acanthus leaves, monsters and two wine-growers carrying a basket of grapes *(6th pillar in the nave on the right)*. The 13C **stained-glass windows**★★ suffered considerable damage; those of the apse are still intact. The great 13C rose-window, dedicated to the Virgin, is a masterpiece of Gothic art.

Palais du Tau★★

2 pl. du Cardinal-Luçon. Open Tue–Sun. Closed Jan 1, May 1, Nov 1 & 11, Dec 25. 7€. 03 26 47 81 79; http://palais-tau.monuments-nationaux.fr.

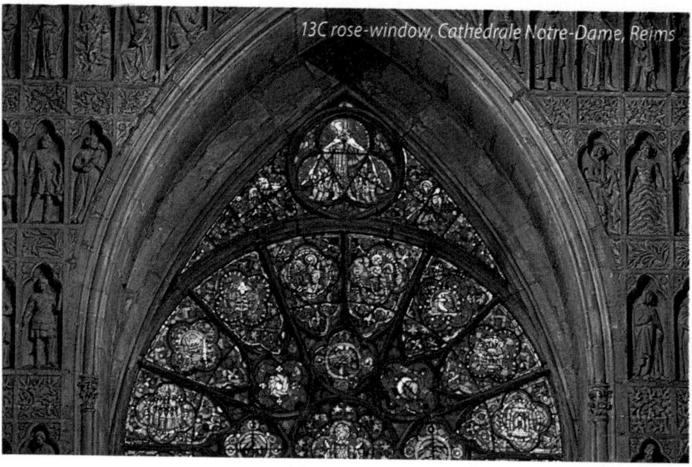

13C rose-window, Cathédrale Notre-Dame, Reims

Ph. Gajic/MICHELIN

The former palace of the archbishops of Reims, first built in 1138, was reworked in the 15C in a Late Gothic style and towards 1670 in a Classical style. Listed on the Unesco World Heritage List, it is now home to the cathedral treasure and to many of the original statues from the cathedral's façade.

Basilique St-Remi★★

Pl. Saint-Remi. The oldest church in Reims. In 533, Saint Remi was buried in a small chapel dedicated to Saint Christopher. Shortly after a basilica was erected on the site and in the second half of the 8C a group of Benedictine monks moved in and founded the Abbaye de Saint-Remi.

Work on the present building began c 1007 and the church was formally consecrated by Pope Leo IX in October 1049. The building was remodelled in the 12C, 15C, 16C and 17C. Many archbishops of Reims and the first kings of France are buried here; the Holy Phial used during the Royal coronations was also kept here. Behind the altar, Saint Remi's grave, rebuilt in 1847, has retained its 17C statues representing St Remi, Clovis and 12 peers who took part in the coronation.

Chapelle Foujita★

33 r. du Champ-de-Mars. Open May–Oct Thur-Tue 2–6pm; Rest of year by appt. Closed Jan 1, May 1, Jul 14, Nov 1 & 11, Dec 25. 3€ (no charge 1st weekend of the month). 03 26 40 06 96. www.ville-reims.fr

Donations by the Champagne firm Mumm led to the construction of this chapel, designed and decorated in a primitive Christian style by Léonard Foujita (1886-1968): Foujita, a Japanese painter who belonged to the early-20C school of art known as the Ecole de Paris, was aged 80 at the time. Inaugurated in 1966, the chapel commemorates the mystical inspiration felt by the Japanese painter in the Basilique St-Remi, leading him to convert to Christianity and be baptised in Reims Cathedral.

Champagne cellars of Reims★★

See the Shopping Guide.

The world-famous Champagne cellars of Reims are located in the Champ de Mars district and along the limestone slopes of St-Nicaise hill, which are riddled with 250km of underground chalky cellars, known as crayères, dating from the Gallo-Roman period. The depth and extent of these make them ideal Champagne cellars.

Pommery

5 pl. du Général-Gouraud. Visit by guided tour (1h) only, Mar–Nov Mon-Fri 9.30am–7pm, Sat-Sun 9.30am-6pm. Dec–Feb 10am–6pm. Closed 2 wks at Christmas. 10-17€. 03 26 61 62 56. www.pommery.com

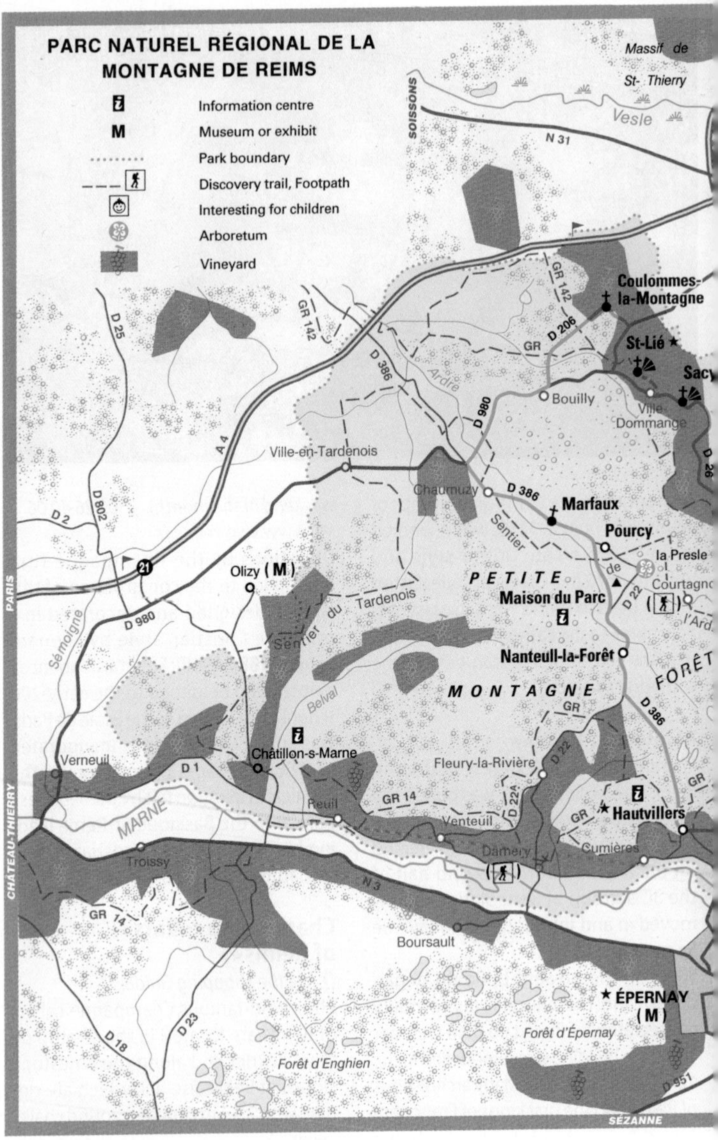

Founded in 1836 by Narcisse Gréno and Louis-Alexandre Pommery, the firm was expanded by the latter's widow who inaugurated Brut Champagne and had the present buildings erected in 1878. She also linked the 120 Gallo-Roman crayères by 18km of tunnels (galleries). Pommery now belongs to the Vranken group. The tour explains the different stages of Champagne-making through galleries decorated with 19C sculptures and displays a 75,000-litre tun by glass sculptor Emile Gallé.

Taittinger

9 pl. St-Nicaise. Guided tours (1hr) mid-Mar–mid-Nov 9.30am-1pm & 2-5.30pm. Rest of the year Mon–Fri 9.30am–1pm & 2–5.30pm; Closed Jan 1, Dec 25. 10€. 03 26 85 84 33.

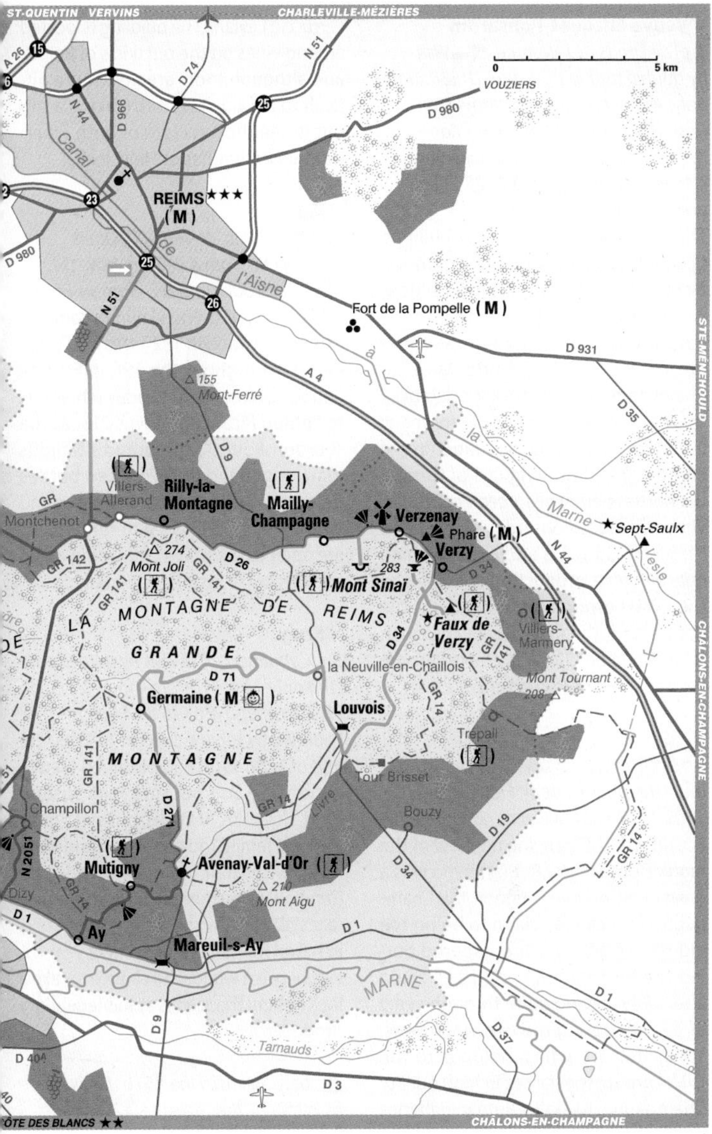

In 1734 the Fourneaux family of wine merchants from Reims began producing sparkling wines. In 1932, Pierre Taittinger took over the management of the firm which was renamed after him, and it is today - after some wrangling - the largest family-owned Champagne company still carrying the family name. Today the Taittinger vineyards extend over 250ha and the firm owns six grape-harvesting centres on the Montagne de Reims, the Château de la Marquetterie in Pierry and the Hôtel des Comtes de Champagne in Reims in addition to superb cellars. Visitors are taken on a fascinating tour of the cellars where 15 million bottles are stored in the cool Gallo-Roman galleries and in the crypts of the former 13C Abbaye St-Nicaise, destroyed during the Revolution.

Veuve Clicquot-Ponsardin
1, pl de Droits de l'Homme. Visit by guided tour with tasting (1hr30min) only, Apr–Oct Mon–Sat 10am–6pm (last departure 4.15pm). Nov–Mar Mon–Sat 10am–6pm (last departure 4.15pm). 13€. 03 26 89 53 90. www.veuve-clicquot.com
The firm founded in 1772 by Philippe Clicquot was considerably expanded by his son and later by his son's widow, Barbe Nicole, whose maiden name was Ponsardin, thus explaining the firm's present name. The "Grande Dame" of Champagne, after whom a special cuvée was named, was responsible for many initiatives including remuage (art of blending) and riddling (art of turning the bottles before *dégorgement*). Today, Veuve Clicquot-Ponsardin, which owns 515ha of vineyards and exports three quarters of its production, is owned by the LVMH group and is run by Cécile Bonnefond, the first female chairman since Madame Clicquot. The cellars are located in Gallo-Roman *crayères*.

Ruinart
4 r. des Crayères. Visit by guided tour (1hr) only, by appt. From 26€. 03 26 77 51 51. www.ruinart.com.
Founded in 1729 by the nephew of the monk Dom Thierry Ruinart, who was a great friend of Dom Pérignon, this Champagne firm can lay claim to being the oldest in existence. It prospered during the Restoration period and again after 1949, having gone through years of decline during the two world wars. Today Ruinart, which belongs to the LVMH group, specialises in high quality Champagne. Its Gallo-Roman galleries on three levels, starting 18m underground, are particularly interesting.

Piper-Heidsieck
12, allee du Vignoble. Appt only. 03 26 8443 00. www.piper-hiedsieck.com.
The firm, founded in 1785 by Florens-Louis Heidsieck, now belongs to the Rémy Cointreau group. The company moved in 2008 to impressive new head offices in gleaming steel and glass, designed by Jacques Ferrier with interior design by Ferruccio Laviani. The buidling is located among vines on the outskirts of Reims, and although tours are now more difficult to obtain, it is worth taking a trip out to see the new face of both Piper-Heidsieck and Charles Heidsieck.

Mumm
29 r. du Champ-de-Mars. Open Mar–Oct 9–11am & 2–5pm. Nov–Dec Mon–Sat 9.30–11am & 2–5pm. 8€. 03 26 49 59 70. www.mumm.com.
After its creation in 1827, this firm prospered throughout the 19C in Europe and the United States. Today it belongs to Pernod Ricard and owns 218ha. The "Cordon Rouge", the brand's famous logo, originated in 1875 when bottles delivered to the best clients were bound with a red ribbon. Its 25km-long cellars are open to the public; including a film and display of historic winemaking.

Krug
5, r. Coquebert. Visit by guided tour (1hr) only, Mon-Fri10am–noon & 3-5pm. No tastings. 03 26 84 44 20
Founded by Johann Josef in 1843, by the end of 1846 Josef had obtained French nationality and became Jean Joseph Krug. Now part of LVMH, but still run by the Krug family, today by Henri and Remi Krug, with their children Olivier and Caroline. All fermentation at this house takes place in barrel, and the wine stays in barrel for a minimum of five years. A visit here is a wonderful chance to take a look behind the scenes at this legendary producer.

Leave Reims by the N 51 as far as Montchenot, then take the D 26 towards Villers-Allerand.

The D 26 skirts the northern flank of the Montagne de Reims, winding its way past the vineyards and villages of Champagne.

Rilly-la-Montagne
Countless wine-growers and merchants have brought prosperity to this well-off village. One excellent address among many is **Domaine Daniel Dumont** (*see Shopping Guide*).

From the D 26, at the top of the hill to the right, you can see a contemporary sculpture by Bernard Pages in celebration of the Earth and in tribute to works by the philosopher Gaston Bachelard.

Mailly-Champagne

The name of Mailly is inextricably linked with that of its cooperative cellar located in elegant modern buildings which produce excellent Champagnes under the brand of **Mailly Grand Cru** (*see Shopping Guide).*

You c an take a trip back to prehistory at the **Carrière pédagogique de Mailly-Champagne**, a geological quarry showing a complete cross-section of the Tertiary formations of the eastern Paris Basin *(1km beyond Mailly-Champagne; geological specimens discovery path open all year; departure from the village hall of Mailly-Champagne; visitors who wish to go on their own are advised to purchase the "Guide de Mailly-Champagne" guide for 7€ from the reserve's offices in Pourcy; guided tours are organised by the Montage de Reims regional nature reserve for 5.50€; contact the reserve's offices for the programme; 03 26 59 44 44; www.parc-montagnedereims.fr).*

Verzenay

This renowned wine-growing village is dominated by a windmill to the west and by the unusual sight of a lighthouse in the middle of the vines. This unexpected monument is the work of Joseph Goulet who had it built in 1909 in order to promote his Champagne firm. Originally an outdoor café with swings and a croquet lawn, it was used by the English in 1940 as an anti-aircraft machine gun post. After being superbly restored, it is now home to the **Musée de la Vigne**★, which is reached by a hanging bridge. Inside visitors are invited to get better acquainted with Champagne through videos, art exhibitions, historical recreations and clear photography and explanations. There is also a picnic area and a good boutique that sells local gourmet products, including the lighthouse's own shortbread biscuits. *(open May-Dec Tue–Sun10am–6pm closed Dec 25; 6€; 03 26 07 87 87; www.lepharedeverzenay.com).*

Verzy

This ancient wine-growing village prospered under the protection of the Benedictine abbey of St-Basle founded in the 7C by the archbishop of Reims, Saint Nivard, and destroyed in 1792. It is still home to a number of reputable wine estates such as that of **Etienne Lefevre**. Under the buildings of this 19C property are amazing pointed vaulted cellars at a depth of 15m. A collection of old wine-growing tools and presses is on display including a press which dates from the 18C. Tasting and sales after the visit. *(30 r. de Villiers, 51380 Verzy; open Mon–Sat 9am–noon & 2–5pm; closed Dec 25, Easter Sun and a fortnight in Aug; 03 26 97 96 99; www.champagne-etienne-lefevre.com).*

However the main claim to fame of this area are the **Faux de Verzy**★. Verzy Forest is home to a thousand specimens of a very rare species, Faux (from the Latin *fagus*, meaning birch). These twisted, stunted birches are the result of a genetic phenomenon, of which there are only two other examples in Europe *(in Verzy, take the D 34 towards Louvois; from the plateau, take the second left towards the Parking des Pins and follow the path over a distance of about 500m; guided tours organised by the Montagne de Reims nature reserve park depending on the time of year; 5.50€; enquiries and brochure available at the reserve offices; 03 26 59 44 44).*

For children, Verzy is home to **Zig Zag Park** which is built around 10ha of labyrinths and mazes. *(06 87 27 84 44; Wed-Sun 2-7pm; 7€; www.zigzagparc.fr).*

Return onto the D 34 towards Louvois.

Château de Louvois

Not open to the public.

Erected by Mansart for Louis XIV's minister, the château became the property of Louis XV's daughters. This splendid residence, surrounded by a park designed by Le Nôtre, was for the most part demolished between 1805 and 1812.

The present castle consists of a pavilion partly rebuilt in the 19C and is owned by Champagne house Laurent Perrier.
From Louvois, the road continues towards **Bouzy** *(5km SE on the D 34)*, reputed for its subtle Coteaux-champenois red wines; tasting at **Georges Vesselle** *(see Shopping Guide)*.
Leave the village by the Chemin des Vaches, which has excellent views over the Chalons plain.

Ambonnay

Although it also produces red wines, this area is far better known for its Champagnes, particularly those produced by the **Egly-Ouriet**, **Serge Pierlot** and **Paul Dethune** firms *(see Shopping Guide)*.

Back in Louvois, return to the D 9 and head N as far as Neuville-en-Chaillois, then turn left onto the D 71 through the forest via Germaine (see "Back to Grass Roots" at the end of this chapter).

Avenay-Val-d'Or

Eglise St-Trésain, 13C and 16C, has a fine Late Gothic west front.
A **discovery trail** starting from the station *(brochure available from the Maison du Parc in Pourcy)* enables visitors to discover a rural community.
Avenay produces vintages made from Chardonnay and Pinot Noir varieties.

Opposite Avenay station, take D 201, and immediately after the railway line, take the small road uphill to Mutigny.

Mutigny

Surrounded by vineyards and forest, this village stands on an outcrop at an altitude of 240m. There is a fine view from the simple country church of Ay and the Côte des Blancs to the right and over Châlons and the plain to the left.
A 2.2km **wine-growers' trail** starts from the village; it is dotted with signposts which inform the walker about the vineyards and how the vines are cultivated from season to season, and finishes with a tasting *(by appt. mid-Apr–Nov 1; 7.50€; 03 26 52 31 37; www.mutigny-en-champagne.com)*.
The road down to Ay offers good views of Epernay and the Côte des Blancs.

Ay

This ancient city, well known in Gallo-Roman times, was well liked by several French kings including Henri IV who was known as "Sire 'Ay". It lies in a secluded spot at the foot of a hill among famous vineyards. **Eglise St-Brice** has a flamboyantly Gothic doorway paired with a Renaissance belfry. On Rue St-Vincent, the visitor will see a lovely timber-framed house called the **Pressoir Henri IV**.
The **Institut International des vins de Champagne** (Villa Bissinger) is situated in a former 19C manor house. Equipped with a documentation centre, it is devoted to research into Champagne and offers visitors a range of tasting classes, from short introductions to food and wine matching to vineyard visits *(15 r. Jeanson, 51160 Ay; open Apr–Oct 1st Sat of the month at 2.30pm; 38€ (English class); 03 26 55 78 78; www.villabissinger.com)*.
At n°69 Rue Jules-Blondeau stands the **Gosset firm** whose founder was listed as a wine-grower in the city's records of 1584, making it the oldest firm in the Champagne region *(www.champagne-gosset.com; not open to public)*.
The **Bollinger firm** *(www.champagne-bollinger.fr; not open to public)*, despite an international reputation and its frequent appearances in James Bond films, remains a family affair committed to upholding ancestral traditions. It possesses one of the last remaining cooperages in Champagne, as well as a portion of "Vieilles Vignes Françaises", which is ungrafted stock that survived the phylloxera epidemic. In 2005, the Jacques Bollinger Group bought neighbouring Ay Champagne brand, Ayala.

In Ay, left on D 1.

Mareuil-sur-Ay

The château was erected in the 18C for J.-B. de Dommangeville whose daughter fell in love with the poet André Chénier.

The estate was bought in 1830 by the duke of Montebello who created his own brand of Champagne.

Founded in 1818, the **Billecart-Salmon** family firm, known for its pink Champagne, is the proud possessor of vats which combine state-of-the-art technology with traditional methods. Take a stroll round the ornamental walled garden, designed by Charles Roland-Billecart in 1926 *(40 r. Carnot, 51160 Mareuil-sur-Ay; open by appt. Mon–Fri by appt; 7€ 03 26 52 60 22; billecart@champagne-billecart.fr).*

The Clos des Goisses vintage is the pride and joy of the **Philipponat estate** *(see Shopping Guide).*

Return to Ay and continue towards Dizy, then turn onto the N 2051 towards Champillon.

Between Dizy and Champillon, the road rises to command a good **view**★ of the vineyards, the Marne Valley and Epernay.

Hautvilliers★

In this attractive village in the heart of Champagne, the famous 17C monk Dom Pérignon is said to have invented the art of blending wines to produce sparkling champagne. He was in charge of the cellars of the Benedictine abbey of Saint-Pierre in Hautvilliers for 47 years. Although he may not have "discovered" Champagne, his contribution to the transformation from non-sparkling into sparkling wines was essential. Dom Pérignon's knowledge of wine-making was extensive and his discoveries include the benefits of blending grapes from different terroirs into "vintages", the quick, successive pressing of black grapes to produce a perfectly clear white juice, the use of the first thick glass bottles to withstand the pressure of the second fermentation, and corks to contain the bubbles instead of pieces of chestnut wood as was common at the time, and even the digging of chalk cellars to enable the wine to age at a constant temperature. In 1715 he was laid to rest in the abbey church of St-Sindulphe, where his black

Hautvilliers Abbey

S. Sauvignier/MICHELIN

marble tombstone can be seen at the foot of the high altar to the left. A vast chandelier (1950) made up of four wheels from winepresses hangs over the high altar. Founded in 650 by Saint Nivard, nephew of King Dagobert, the **abbey of Saint-Pierre** now belongs to the Moët et Chandon firm. Visits to the abbey are open to the public, but try to book in advance to visit the Dom Pérignon Musuem, also on site, that contains his old workroom and some 16C bottles *(03 26 51 22 00).*

Leave Hautvilliers on D 386, then right on the D 1 as far as Reuil (14km).

Reuil

In Reuil, park your car and go for a ride round town in a horse-drawn carriage. **Calèche Evasion** offers a variety of themed excursions from a short ride to a full-day trip around the surrounding hillsides and vineyards. "Calèche et terroir", a combination of ride and tasting, "Calèche et danse" for music lovers or "Calèche et Champagne" to discover the cellars *(Open mid-Apr– mid-Oct; options include ride with riverside Champagne tasting 12€; ride with cellar visit 15€; reservation required; 03 26 55 68 19; www.caleche-evasion.net).*

Make a U-turn and return on the D 1, then turn left on the D 22 (14km). Head for Venteuil, then Nanteuil-la-Forêt.

Nanteuil-la-Forêt
This village, tucked away in a narrow pastoral vale surrounded by forest, once possessed a Templar's priory. Today's visitors come here to admire the plants in the **Centre botanique de la Presle** (botanic gardens). A couple of nursery-owners organise exhibitions in the garden which has a fine collection of spirea, willow and a dozen or so species of rose, including the Marne rose (*Carrefour de la Presle; open Mon–Fr 2-6pm; Sat 9am–noon & 2–6pm; closed public holidays; 5€; 03 26 59 43 39; www.jardin-brochetlanvin.com).*

North on D 386, via Pourcy and the Montagne de Reims' Maison du Parc.

Marfaux
The **church** boasts fine capitals carved with acanthus foliage.

Beyond Chaumuzy, turn right on D 980; as you reach Bouilly, left on D 206 towards Coulomnes-la-Montagne.

Coulomnes-la-Montagne
In this flower-decked village, there is a lovely Romanesque **church**.

Turn right to rejoin the D 980 via Pargny-les-Reims, 1.5km further on, turn left towards Saint-Lié.

Chapelle St-Lié★
This chapel, dating from the 12C, 13C and 16C, stands in a secluded spot near Ville-Dommange, at the centre of a copse which was probably a holy grove in Roman-Gallo times. Dedicated to a 5C hermit, the chapel is surrounded by its cemetery. There is an extended **view**★ of Ville-Dommange, the Côte d'Ile-de-France, Reims and its cathedral, the plain as far as the St-Thierry massif and the Tardenois region.

Sacy
Eglise St-Remi has a late 11C east end and a 12C tower. Admire the view over Reims from the adjoining cemetery.

Return to Reims via Bézannes (9km).

2 CÔTE DES BLANCS
28km from Épernay to Mont Aimé. Map p232.

From Épernay to Vertus, the north-south facing Côte des Blancs lies on the edge of the Plateau de Brie. It owes its name to its white-grape vineyards consisting almost exclusively of Chardonnay vines. This elegant variety is used to produce prestigious vintages and blanc de blancs, as Champagnes made exclusively from white grapes are known. The majority of the great Champagne firms own vineyards and wine-making facilities in this area.

This itinerary, which runs half-way up the slopes, offers splendid views of the vineyards and the immense Châlons plain below.

Épernay★
Although both claim the title of capital of Champagne, Épernay, which is home to prestigious firms such as Moët et Chandon and Mercier to name but a few, may have a slight edge over Reims. Avenue de Champagne in the east of town is lined with Champagne firms of international repute, many of which date back for centuries. The avenue runs above a limestone cliff riddled with miles of galleries whose temperature remains constant (9-11°C) all year round. Some of the cellars are open to the public.

Moët et Chandon
18 Ave. de Champagne. Visit by guided tour (1hr) mid-Feb–mid-Nov daily 9.30am–4.30pm. Rest of the year by appt.; closed public holidays. 13€. 03 26 51 20 20, www.moet.com.

The leading Champagne house in terms of number of bottles produced, the firm owes its name to Claude Moët, who founded the house in 1743 and to his grandson's son-in-law, Pierre Gabriel Chandon, whose name was added later. The brand now belongs to LVMH (Louis Vuitton Moët-Hennessy) which has done much to promote the image of French luxury goods in general and Champagne in particular, teaming up with icons such as Karl Lagerfield for its advertising campaigns. Moët et Chadon's Brut Imperial is the world's best selling Champagne, with 18 million bottles per year.

Mercier

75 Ave. de Champagne. Car park and reception opposite the firm. Visit by guided tour, including small train (45min) early Mar–mid-Nov daily 9.30–11.30am & 2–4.30pm. Rest of the year Thu–Mon 9.30–11.30am & 2–4.30pm. Closed Christmas holidays and Jan 1. 6.50€. 03 26 51 22 00.

Eugène Mercier created his firm in 1858 and had 18km of galleries dug. To celebrate the World Exhibition of 1889 he asked a sculptor, Navlet, from Châlons, to decorate a huge tun with a capacity of 215,000 bottles which was placed on a cart drawn by 24 oxen with 18 horses to help the uphill sections and taken to Paris. This exceptional convoy took twenty days to travel from Épernay to Paris: some bridges had to be reinforced and walls demolished along the way. The 34-ton barrel is now displayed in the main reception hall. The visit here is particularly enjoyable (or touristy, depending on your point of view), with a short film, a glass lift down to the chalk cellars then an electric train through the galleries explaining the process of production, followed by a tasting.

Champagne Boizel *46, av de Champagne. Open by appt. Closed Aug. 8€. 03 26 55 21 51; www.champagne-boizel.fr*

Still on the illustrious avenue de Champagne, this smaller house makes an excellent visit. Founded in 1834 by August Boizel, this is run by the charming Evelyne and Christophe Roques-Boizel, and is today part of the Boizel-Chanoine-Champagne Group. Working with growers in around 50 villages, the Champagnes here are delicate and elegant. Try the cuvée Joyau de France.

Musée municipal

13 av. de Champagne. 03 26 51 90 31. Closed for renovations but park open for visits, and access for research by appt.

The city museum is housed in the former Château Perrier, a copy of a castle in the Louis XIII style built in the mid-19C by a wine merchant. Two rooms are devoted to the life and work of a wine-grower. Collection of Champagne labels.

Leave Épernay on D 951 to the SW.

Pierry

The town of Pierry is justly proud of its handsome 18C **Château de Pierry**, whose reception rooms, small apartment, wine-press museum and cellars are open to the public. Visitors to the property are offered a flute of Champagne at the end of the visit. *(open Mon-Wed, Thu-Fri 9.30-11.30am & 2-4.30pm; Sat 9.30-11.30am & 2-4pm; guided tours with tasting (1hr 30min) by appt; 8-10€; 03 26 54 02 87; www.chateau-de-pierry.fr).*

The **Domaine Henri Mandois** cellars, dating from the 18C, are located beneath the church of Pierry *(66 r. du Général-de-Gaulle, BP 9, 51530 Pierry; >open by appt. Mon–Sat 10am–noon & 2–5pm; 03 26 54 03 18; www.champagne-mandois.fr.*

The **Vollereaux firm** can also be recommended *(see Shopping Guide).*

Those with a sweet tooth shouldn't miss **Chocolaterie Thibualt**, where you can watch artisanal chocolates being made. Free tour and tasting *(ZA de Pierry, Pôle d'activités St-Julien, 51530 Pierry; open Mon–Sat 9am–noon & 2–7pm; tours 9–11am & 2–6pm. No visits during the fortnight before Christmas and the fortnight before Easter; closed last week of Jan and public holidays; 03 26 51 58 04; www.chocolaterie-thibaut.com).*

Take the D 40 to Cuis, overlooked by a Romanesque church, and continue on the D 10 to Cramant.

Cramant★

Cramant lies in a pleasant setting and is the capital of Chardonnay vines. At the entrance to the village stands an enormous bottle (a rheoboam, equivalent to 6 bottles) over 8.6m high and 7.9m round at its base.

Lilbert Fils and **Bonnaire** both have a fine selection of local wines *(see Shopping Guide).*

Vineyards of the Côte des Blancs in the early morning mist

S. Sauvignier/MICHELIN

Avize

After a stroll round the town, walk out to the west for extended views of the whole area, or stop at the house of **Marie-Hélène Waris-Larmandier**, wine-grower, painter and potter, specialised in the decoration of Champagne bottles *(608 Rempart du Nord, 51100 Avize; open by appt.; 03 26 57 79 05; www.champagne-waris-larmandier.com).*

Known for its wine, Avize also runs a school for future Champagne wine-growers. The Champagnes of **Franck Bonville** and **Agrapart et Fils** are among the best-known of this prestigious locality (*see Shopping Guide*).

The **Corbon** firm offers visitors the chance to get better acquainted with the subtleties of Champagne through a choice of two tasting courses: the first focuses on food matches, while the second teaches the rudiments of tasting. The theory is accompanied by a series of practical tests and trials. Children can also join in the fun and learn to distinguish the aromas and flavours of a variety of different fruits. *(541 Ave. Jean-Jaurès, 51100 Avize; open by appt.; closed late Dec–late Jan; 03 26 57 55 43; www.champagne-corbon.com).*

Oger

Despite its wealth of picturesque fountains, wash-houses and weather-vanes, Oger is far more than just a pretty flower-decked village, even if it is ranked among the "Most Beautiful Villages of France". It is also the regional capital of marriage thanks to its highly unusual **Museum** devoted to "Love and Champagne". Wedding traditions between 1820 and 1920 are illustrated through a series of objects including an interesting collection of bride's mementoes under glass covers. The museum also houses a collection of 19C Champagne labels, bottles and tools which retrace the history of Champagne making. Tasting at the end of the visit. There is also a restaurant, by advance reservation (*open Tues-Sun 10am-12.30 & 2-6pm; guided tour available (1hr30min); 6€; 03 26 57 50 89; www.mariage-et-champagne.com).*

The **Milan** firm, founded in 1864 and renowned for its blancs de blancs, organises guided tours of its presses, storehouses and cellars, followed by a tasting session. There are also rooms to stay here. *(6 r. d'Avize, 51190 Oger; open daily by appt.; closed Jan; 03 26 57 50 09; www.champagne-milan.com).*

Le Mesnil-sur-Oger

This vine-growing village is known for producing excellent quality wines, and two of the regions's most prestigious cuvees - Salon's Le Mesnil and Krug's Clos du Mesnil - come from here.

The wine-growing and producing **Launois** family has created an interesting **Musée de la Vigne et du Vin★**. In addition to an impressive collection of 17C, 18C and 19C presses, the museum also boasts countless pumps, corking and other wine-making machinery. The high point of the visit is the entrance to the secret tasting cellar, followed by a ride round the vineyards on board a small train *(visit by guided tour (1hr30min) by appt.; closed Jan 1, Easter Sun, Dec 25; 7€; 03 26 57 50 15. www.champagne-launois.fr.*

The **Domaine Pierre Moncuit** has a fine selection of vintage Champagnes. **Jean Louis Vergnon**can also be recommended *(see Shopping Guide).*

A small road winds its way across the vineyards to Vertus.

Vertus

Vertus, at the foot of the Côte des Blancs with 450 hectares of vineyards is a tiny town whose twisting lanes are dotted with pretty squares and countless fountains. **Eglise St-Martin** (11C and 12C), built over four crypts and restored after the Second World War, has preserved its pointed vaulting and a 16C Pietà.

Treat yourself to a visit to the **Veuve Fourny et Fils** and the **Duval Leroy** firms *(see Shopping Guide).*

South of Bergères-lès-Vertus, turn right onto the road leading to Mont Aimé.

Mont Aimé★

Once part of the Ile-de-France cliff, this isolated hill reaches 237m.

VALLÉE DE LA MARNE

You can choose between two possible round trips, one out of Épernay and one out of Château-Thierry.

The villages in this valley lined with vineyards and dotted with forests are spread out on either bank of the Marne river. The Pinot Meunier variety reigns supreme over the area producing fruity, characterful Champagne.

3 ROUND TRIP FROM ÉPERNAY

63km. Map p232.

Mardeuil

Bound to the north by the Marne, and to the south by vineyards, this ancient commune is home to the **Maison Beaumont des Crayères** and its winegrowers' museum *(see Shopping Guide).*

Cross over the Marne and continue alongside the river to Cumières.

Cumières

Located beneath a cirque of vineyards, this riverside town is reputed for its red Coteaux-champenois wines and those produced by **René Geoffroy** are to be recommended *(see Shopping Guide).*

Cumières is the starting point for **boat trips** on board the *Champagne Vallée* which take you past vineyards and through locks *(1hr 30min cruises on the Marne; Croisi-Champagne, BP 22, 51480 Cumières; 03 26 54 49 51; www.champagne-et-croisiere.com).*

Damery

Damery offers walks along the banks of the River Marne at the foot of vineyards. In former times, horse-drawn barges used to stop alongside its embankments. The 12C-13C **church** possesses a *Virgin and Child by Watteau* (18C). The main wing of the **A.R. Lenoble wine estate** with its vaulted 18C cellars and wooden presses is a fine example of regional architectural styles *(35 r. Paul-Douce, 51480 Damery; open by appt. Mon–Fri 8.30am–12.30pm & 1–5pm; 03 26 58 42 60, contact@champagne-lenoble.com).*

Another worthwhile address is that of the **Domaine Louis Casters** *(see Shopping Guide).*

Turn right towards Fleury-la-Rivière.

Fleury-la-Rivière

The **wine cooperative** is decorated with a huge 500m² **fresco** by artist from Greg Gawra. The fresco depicts the history of Champagne from phylloxera up until the

Frescoes of the wine cooperative of Fleury-la-Rivière

Ph. Gajic/MICHELIN

present day. Little by little this work of art is being transferred indoors where it will be better protected from the weather (*45min guided tours on request Mon afternoon, Tue, Thu, Fri 8.30am–12.30pm & 2–5.15pm; Sat 9am–12.30pm& 2–6pm, Sun and public holidays by appt; 4€; 03 26 58 42 53).*

At Cuchery, bear left towards Châtillon-sur-Marne.

Châtillon-sur-Marne

Camped on a vine-covered hill overlooking the Marne, this ancient fortified town stands at an altitude of 148m at the mouth of the vale of Cuchery.

Leave your car in the car park; take Rue de l'Eglise then turn right into Rue Berthe-Symonet. The 33m-high **statue** of Pope Urban II was erected in 1887 on a mound formerly crowned by the castle keep, in homage to this local boy who instigated the first crusades. It is made from eighty blocks of granite which were brought all the way from Brittany by ox-cart. Inside, a staircase leads up the arm of the statue (*open May–Sept daily 10am–12.30pm & 2–6pm; Mar–Apr Mon–Fri 11am–5pm, weekends 10am–12.30pm & 2.30–6pm; 1.50€; 03 26 58 32 86; www.otchatillon51.com).*

Enjoy the view from the nearby viewing table over the 22 villages in the valley and the vineyards.

Head west on the D 1 towards Vandières.

Vandières

Whether the town's name comes from vinum dare ("give wine") or from vendemiare ("to harvest the grapes"), its close relationship with wine is clear. An 18C château stands in the middle of a park at the top of the village, and the 11C church has a beautiful porch.

Continue on the D 1.

Verneuil

The small 12C-13C **church**, carefully restored, stands on the banks of the Sémoinge, a tributary of the Marne.

Continue towards Vincelles then Dormans.

Dormans

A park, lined with trees, including a beautiful sequoia near the Chinese bridge, is the setting for the **Chateau de Dormans** which houses temporary exhibitions, receptions and the tourist office. The **Mémorial des Deux Batailles de la Marne**, a memorial chapel dedicated to the battles of the Marne from 1914-1918, stands to the rear of the park on a spot chosen by Maréchal Foch (*open Apr–mid-Nov Mon–Sat 2.30–6.30pm, Sun 10am–noon & 2.30–6.30pm; guided* *tours on request; ℘03 26 57 77 87; www.tourisme-dormans.fr.*

The **Moulin d'en Haut**, a former communal mill, houses an old mill wheel, in addition to a collection of rural tools related to wine-growing and making over the ages *(open Jun–Aug 2-6pm, Sun & public holidays 3–6pm; rest of year by appt.; 4€; ℘03 26 58 85 16).*

Also worth a visit locally is the **Snail Museum** *(8, rue des plumons, 51700 Try; t03 26 58 10 77)* to explore a renowned regional delicacy.

Continue on the N 3 as far as Port-à-Binson, from where you will be able to see Châtillon, dominated by the statue of Pope Urban II. Take the N 3 to Œuilly.

Œuilly

This ancient fortified hillside town is home to several museums grouped under the Eco-Musee d'Oeuilly. The **Maison Champenoise** (1642) features a typical wine-grower's house of the late 19C. The **Musée de la Goutte**, devoted to the brandy of the same name, possesses the village's old alambic (1850) and an exhibition about the 1911 riots which took place in Champagne, and another about cooperage techniques. The **1900 village school** still has its original desks, stove, blackboard and even a dunce's hat *(visit by guided tour (1hr 15min) Apr–Oct Wed–Mon 2–6pm; Nov–Mar Wed–Mon 2–5pm; closed Christmas holidays, May 1; 5.50€; ℘03 26 57 10 30; www.ecomusee-oeuilly.fr.st).*

Take D 222 towards Boursault.

Château de Boursault

Built in 1848 by architect Arveuf for the legendary widow Veuve Clicquot, this sprawling Renaissance-inspired edifice. It was the venue of magnificent receptions organised by Madame Clicquot, and was later given to her daughter and great-grand daughter. The estate produces wonderfully subtle blanc de blancs Champagnes *(Chateau not open to public, but boutique open, Fri 1.45-5pm, Sat 10am-12.30pm & 1.45-5pm, Sun 10am-12.30pm, www.champagne-chateau.com).*

Continue on towards Vauciennes and the D 22 to the Marne, then the N 3 back to Epernay.

3 ROUND TRIP FROM CHÂTEAU-THIERRY

60km. *See map p232.*

The Aisne vineyards which follow the River Marne from Crouttes to Trélou, near Dormans, belong to the Champagne wine-growing region.

Château-Thierry

Although it is located in the Aisne, Château-Thierry is genuine Champagne territory both by its origins and by its vineyards. It is built on the slopes of an isolated hill crowned by an old 14C **castle**, which has become a favourite walking spot with fine views of the Marne valley. Walking down from the Tour Bouillon on the hilltop, you will go past the **birthplace** of the world-famous fable writer and poet, **Jean de la Fontaine**. The reception rooms display magnificent editions of the author's *Fables* and *Tales*, including volumes illustrated by Oudry (1755) and Gustave Doré (1868). There is also a collection of unusual objects decorated with scenes from the *Fables*, plus an attractive courtyard and gardens *(open Tues-Sun 9.30am–noon & 2–5.30pm; 3.60€; ℘03 23 69 05 60; www.musee-jean-de-la-fontaine.fr).*

A visit to the **cellars of the Pannier Champagne house** located in 13C stone quarries makes a good finish to your tour of the town; audiovisual display and guided tours of the one thousand year old cellars *(23 r. Roger-Catillon, west of the town; visit by 1hr guided tour by appt. Mon–Sat 9am–12.30pm & 2.30–6.30pm; closed public holidays; 5€; ℘03 23 69 51 30; www.champagnepannier.com).*

Leave Château-Thierry westbound on Avenue J. Lefebvre, then take the D 969.

Essômes-sur-Marne★

The **interior**★ of **Eglise St-Ferréol**★, founded in 1090, is characteristic of Decorated Gothic architecture. The 38 stalls of the chancel are Renaissance in style *(guided tours available by appt; enquire at the town hall Sept–Jun; ℘03 23 83 08 31).*

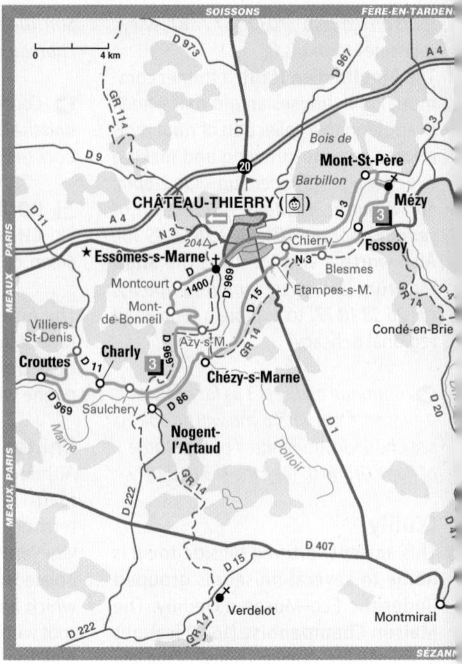

From Essômes, make for Montcourt then bear left onto the D 1400.

The road runs through vineyards, offering an interesting **panorama** of a meander of the Marne between Mont-de-Bonneil and Azy, with the wooded Brie region in the distance.

At Azy, rejoin the D 969 and continue past the built-up suburbs of Saulchery, to Charly.

Charly-sur-Marne

This is the most important wine-growing centre of the Aisne département. It is impossible to miss the statue of Emile Morlot, mayor and member of parliament, to whom the Aisne owes its current status of AOC Champagne.

Take the D 11 towards Villiers-Saint-Denis, then the D 842 to Crouttes. On the way, admire the sweeping views to the south of the meanders of the Marne.

Crouttes

This wine-growing village owes its name to its cellars dug out of the rock (from the Latin *cryptae*). Park your car in the Place de la Mairie and walk up the hill to the picturesque church. A visit to **Francoise Bedel** gives an interesting insight into a biodynamic Champagne house *(see Shopping Guide)*.

From Crouttes, return to Charly on the D 969 and cross the river. Once on the other side, take the D 86 to Nogent-l'Artaud.

Nogent-l'Artaud

All that remains today of the former abbey of the Poor Clares Order, founded in the 13C by Blanche d'Artois, Queen of Navarre, can be seen in the Convent district near the school.

The picturesque road which looks down over the Marne takes you past hillsides covered in vines. It passes through **Chézy-sur-Marne**, a delightful village popular with painters and tourists, offering fine walks along the banks of the Dolloir.

Take the D 15. The road runs under the D 1 to Etampes-sur-Marne and joins the N 3 in Chierry. Between Chierry and Blesmes, the road commands a fine panorama of the valley. 1.5km beyond Blesmes, turn left onto a minor road.

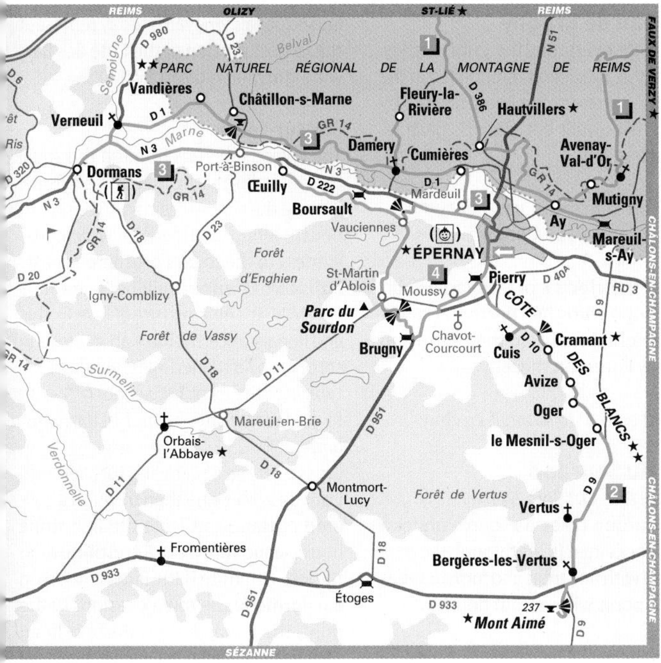

Fossoy

The Déhu firm, run by the seventh generation of a wine-growing family, welcomes tourists along the Champagne wine road. They have created a small **Musée de la Vigne et du Vin** (Le Varocien) in former stables. In addition to explanations of the three grape varieties, there is a collection of old wine-making equipment (note the refractometer dating from 1863 used to measure alcohol content) and wine tasting classes are possible.
(3 r. Saint-Georges, 02650 Fossoy; visit by 20min guided tour by appt. Mon–Fri; contact Mr Déhu; closed public holidays; 4€ ; 03 23 71 90 47; www.champagne-dehu.com).

Continue along the minor road as far as Mézy (Gothic church), then cross the Marne to take a left on the D 3 and along the north bank.

Mont-Saint-Père

The 1,000 or so paintings by Léon Lhermitte (1844-1925), born in Mont-Saint-Père, were inspired by rural life and landscapes. He painted *The Harvesters' Wages*, which Van Gogh so admired (and which now hangs in the Musée d'Orsay in Paris) in the fortified farmhouse, Rue Chailly in Fossoy, on the south bank of the Marne.

The D 3 skirts the wood of Barbillon, before rejoining Château-Thierry.

4 ROUND TRIP SOUTH OF EPERNAY

28km. Map above.
Leave Epernay on the D 51.
The road follows the Cubry Valley with vineyards on both sides of the river. As you come to Moussy, look left towards the church of Chavot (13C) perched on a peak. At Moussy, the place known as la Loge-Pinard commands a fine view of the Cubry Valley and Epernay framed by hills.

1km beyond Vaudancourt, turn right onto the D 951.

Château de Brugny

The castle overlooks the Cubry Valley. Built in the 16C, it was remodelled in the 18C. The square stone keep, flanked by round brick-built bartizans, is particularly attractive.

At the crossroads, turn right onto the D 36 towards St-Martin-d'Ablois.

Admire the **views**★ of the glacial Sourdon cirque with the church of Chavot to the right, Moussy in the centre and Epernay Forest on the left.

Left on D 11 to Mareuil-en-Brie.

Parc du Sourdon

Open Apr–Oct 9am–7pm.

The Sourdon takes its source under a pile of rocks then flows through the park planted with fine trees and forms a series of rock pools where trout flourish.

Return to D 22; turn left. The road runs through Epernay Forest (private property) and village of Vauciennes, then reaches the N 3 (right for Epernay).

CÔTE DES BARS

Although traditionally looked down on by the growers from the Marne region, the Champagne vineyards of the Aube *département* have forged a name and a reputation for themselves; they now produce one-quarter of the output of Champagne. On the borders of Burgundy, the Aube is the kingdom of Pinot Noir, and the warmer climate here makes fruitier, rounder wines than elsewhere in Champagne. The tiny parcels of vineyards are dotted around a landscape of forest, and on the high slopes of Bar-sur-Seine and Bar-sur-Aube. Vines also grow on the mound of Montgeux near Troyes, the surroundings of Villenauxe-la-Grande in the south and the regions of Les Riceys closer to Burgundy.

Le Barséquanais

56km from Bar-sur-Seine.

Michelin Local Map 313, G-H 5-6.

Since the Roman Empire, vines have been grown on the hillsides of the Aube. The Barséquanais vineyards today represent the largest portion of the Côte des Bars wine-growing region of 7,000ha.

Bar-sur-Seine

The River Seine runs through this small town, nestling at the foot of the hillside. Admire the timber-framed 16C and 17C houses along Grande-Rue, which bear witness to the town's prosperous past. **Église St-Etienne**, built between 1505 and 1616, is a fine mixture of Late Gothic and Renaissance. **Inside**★ an interesting set of grisaille stained-glass windows are typical of the local 16C school *(visit by guided tour only, by appt. at the tourist office; 03 25 29 94 43).*

Cross over the square and turn left into Cour de la Mironne then through a covered passageway. Note the fine stone house along **Rue de la République**, on the left. Opposite is the largest house in Bar, formerly the town's casino. To the right, the Passage de la Poste is lined with half-timbered houses with carved beams. At n°17, you can identify Saint Roch and his dog in a small alcove of the Renaissance house on the corner.

Turn right into Avenue Paul-Portier. On the corner you will see the oldest house of Bar-sur-Seine, the 15C **Maison de l'Apothicaire**. On the way at the end of Rue Lagesse is **Maison du Charron**, so called because of its wheel-shaped timber frame.

Turn into Rue des Fossés, built on the site of old graveyards, then turn right into **Rue de la Résistance**. At **n°118**, admire the Corinthian-inspired pilasters of the Chapelle de la Passion, founded in the 12C. At **n°135** of **Grande-Rue**, behind the porch, a stone staircase *(173 steps)* up the hill leads to the former castle of the counts of Bar, all of which that now remains is the **Clock** or Lion Tower, rebuilt in 1948.

A fine selection of Champagnes and Rosé-des-Riceys wines can be found at **Devaux Champagne** *(see Shopping Guide)*, a brand of Champagne belonging to the dynamic cooperative **Union Auboise**.

Leave Bar-sur-Seine south on N 71; head for Celles-sur-Ource by D 67.

Celles-sur-Ource

This welcoming village is home to forty or so wine-growers.

A **wine trail** *(11km, 3hr 30min)* winds its way through the vineyards commanding fine views of the valleys of the Ource and the Seine *(Map available at the town hall; 03 23 38 52 68).*

During the grape harvest, the **Marcel Vezien et Fils** firm organises afternoon beginners' courses in grape picking and pressing by appointment. After a hot afternoon's work, your efforts will be rewarded by a bottle of Champagne *(68 Grande-Rue, 10110 Celles-sur-Ource; open Mon–Fri 9am-noon & 2–5pm; weekends by appt.; 03 25 38 50 22, www.champagne-vezien.com).*

Head for Landreville by the D 67.

Landreville

In the winding lanes of this delightful market town are a remarkable set of 12C to 16C edifices including a castle, road-side cross, chapel and church; inside the latter is an altarpiece by Bouchardon.

René Jolly makes a splendid rosé Champagne; after a tour of the 18C cellars, don't miss the firm's museum which unveils the secrets of Champagne-making *(10 r. de la Gare, 10110 Landreville; open Mon–Sat 10am–4pm; closed public holidays; 03 25 38 50 91; www.jollychamp.com).* We also recommend a stop at **Richardot** cellars in **Loches-sur-Ource** *(see Shopping Guide).*

Continue on the D 67 as far as Essoyes.

Essoyes

Auguste Renoir (1841-1919) bought a house in Essoyes, his wife's birthplace, in 1865, and for 25 years the family spent all their summers here. Many of his paintings depict the surrounding countryside and his **studio** is open to the public. A collection of photos, documents and personal belongings is on display *(7 r. Extra; open May–Sept Mon afternoon–Sun 10.30am–12.30pm & 2–6.30pm; Apr & Oct 2–6.30pm; 2€; 03 25 38 56 28).*

All around the village, the Chemins de Rnoir, are marked out, and you continue your pilgrimage to the **cemetery**. The busts by Guino remind visitors that Auguste Renoir is buried here in the company of his wife and their three sons, Pierre, actor, Jean, film director and Claude, ceramicist.

Take the D 79 southbound then take a sharp right onto the D 117 through the forest and then bear right onto the D 17.

Mussy-sur-Seine

Former residence of the bishops of Langres, this town has retained its 15C and 16C houses, including an old salt storehouse.

It is difficult not to be impressed by the dimensions of the huge late 13C **Eglise St-Pierre-ès-Liens**. In the baptismal chapel, a 2m-high sculpture of Saint John the Baptist dates from the 14C; it was the work of craftsmen whose reputation was known throughout the Aube and Burgundy. For visits to the church, and the excellent **Musée de la Resistance** that details the town's exploits during WW2, enquire at the tourist office *(03 25 38 42 08).*

Continue heading SW on the D 17.

After passing through the forest, the road reaches the vine-covered hillsides of Les Riceys countryside. On the way down, it is possible to make out three hamlets, each of which is dominated by a Renaissance church.

Les Riceys

On the border with Burgundy, this unusual village is made up of three hamlets dotted along the banks of the River Laignes (Ricey Haut, Ricey Haute Rive, Ricey Bas). Together, they boast three listed churches, six chapels and seven wash houses. However its main claim to fame is its delicious Pinot Noir rosé wine, considered to be one of the best in France.

Church of Ricey-Bas and the vineyards

S. Sauvignier/MICHELIN

Rosé-des-Riceys

Rosé-des-Riceys is among the most rare and prized rosé wines of France. The geographic location of the vineyards and strict regulations mean that wine-growers are not able to make it every year. Exclusively from Pinot Noir grapes grown on the steepest and sunniest slopes, the harvest takes place only in dry weather and only the highest quality grapes are picked.
A slow maceration is followed by a carefully monitored fermentation, checking hour by hour when the wine takes on the distinctive Rosé-des-Riceys taste: a delicate bouquet of wild flowers, violets and hazelnuts. Only skill and experience tells the winemaker the right time to take the wine from the casks.
The wine was a favourite with Louix XIV, who was introduced to it by the workmen from Riceys who were employed to build the Palais de Versailles.

The lovely 16C **Eglise St-Pierre-ès-Liens** (in Riceys-Bas) possesses a richly carved porch. The oldest section dates back to the 13C and inside, two carved wooden altarpieces adorn the Chapelles de la Passion on the north and south sides (*open by appt. at the tourist office; 03 25 29 15 38)*.
Eglise St-Vincent (in Riceys-Haut) is unusually made up of two churches, joined together by extending the transept of the second church. On the square, note the imposing timber frame (18C) of the **Halle au Vin**, where the annual Grand Jeudi fair is held.
The **Morel**, **Jacques Defrance** and **Morize** firms are among the best known producers (*see Shopping Guide)*.
From Les Riceys, head north on the D 452 to Polisy, then take the D 207 via **Polisot**, a village surrounded by vineyards and woods.

Rejoin Bar-sur-Seine by the N 71.

Baralbin Region

70km from Bar-sur-Aube, located 53km E of Troyes by the N 19. Michelin Local Map n°313, I4.

More spread out than those of the Barséquanais, the vineyards around Bar-sur-Aube stretch over the best-facing hillsides of the region as far as the *département* of Haute-Marne.

Bar-sur-Aube

During the era of the counts of Champagne, Bar-sur-Aube was been a thriving wine centre; its medieval fairs were major events, and among the six annual Champagne events which drew visitors from all over Europe. The Foire aux Bulles in early September perpetuates the tradition and it is the ideal moment to taste the Champagne of Bar-sur-Aube, whose vineyards cover the area.
The town is surrounded by boulevards, laid out on the site of the former ramparts, with 16C to 18C houses.
Eglise St-Pierre★ (12C) was built on the site of a sanctuary, the floor of which remains; visitors may notice that the entrance to the nave is, unusually, down eight steps. The high altar was originally in Clairvaux Abbey and the organ in Remiremont Abbey. Some fifty tombstones mark the graves of local lords and wealthy merchants.
At n°16 and 18 of **Rue d'Aube** is the post office, an 18C edifice with beautiful wrought-iron balconies. **Eglise St-Maclou** (*not open to the public)* was the former chapel of the counts of Bar's castle, destroyed in the late 16C. The 12C belfry was the castle keep.

Eglise St-Pierre, Bar-sur-Aube

Ph. Gajic / MICHELIN

Rue Nationale is the town's main street. At n°14 note the deconsecrated **Chapelle St-Jean** (11C-12C).
The former town house of the monks of Clairvaux, the **Cellier des Moines** has retained a fine cellar covered with 12C ribbed vaulting, now a restaurant. It was used as the wine-growers' headquarters during their rebellion in 1912 which cemented the Bar region's right to the name Champagne.

Leave Bar-sur-Aube southbound on the D 4. 3km further on, turn left, in a bend, onto a steep lane and park your car.

Chapelle Sainte-Germaine
The footpath leads up to a pilgrimage chapel dedicated to Saint Germaine, a virgin martyred by the Vandals in 407. Walk beyond the chapel and around the house to reach the viewing table which offers **views** of Bar-sur-Aube, the valley, Colombey-les-Deux-Eglises and its cross of Lorraine, as well as the Dhuits and Clairvaux forests.
Those more energetic might prefer to walk along the "Côte d'Aube" path *(10km, 2hr 30min)* up the hill from Bar-sur-Aube and through the vineyards *(enquire at the tourist office)*.

Rejoin the D 4 and continue for 6km to Meurville.

Meurville
This village is home to several Champagne producers. A fine view of the village can be had from the picnic area known as Quatre-Napoléon.

Continue northbound on the D 44 as far as Spoy.

Spoy is a delightful flower-decked village which possesses a recently restored Roman bridge.

Return to Meurville and take the D 4 to Bligny.

Château de Bligny
Open Jun–Aug Mon–Sat 10.30am–6.30pm. 3€. 03 25 27 40 11; www.champagnechateaudebligny.com.
One of the rare châteaux to have given its name to a Champagne. The 18C edifice built by the marquis of Dampierre and restoration work in 1999 has restored the painted ceilings and lovely neo-Gothic glass roofs. The visit includes a tour of the château, the cellar and a tasting session.

Rejoin the D 4 via Meurville, then turn right onto the D 44 towards Urville.

Urville
The wine-growing village of Urville is home to a number of traditional old houses and to the family-run **Drappier** firm, who were official suppliers of

KIDS

Nigloland★

At Dolancourt, 9km NW of Bar-sur-Aube on the N 19. Open mid-Jul–end Aug Mon–Sat 10am–7pm. Early Apr–early May & mid-Jun–mid-Jul daily 10am–6pm, Sun 10am–7pm. Early May–mid-Jun Mon–Tue & Thu–Fri 10am–6pm, Sun 10am–7pm. Sept weekends 10am–6pm. Oct & Nov holidays Sun 10.30am–5.30pm. 17€ 03 25 27 94 52. www.nigloland.fr.

This amusement park in a green setting traversed by River Landion, the fourth largest in France, offers attractions for young and old alike. Discover the park aboard a small train or along the meandering enchanted river. Those who prefer more thrills should head for the Gold Mine Train, the Canadian River Ride and the Space Shuttle, while the Bat Roller Coaster hurtles up and down steep slopes at almost 100kph. Don't miss the Niglo Show (electronic automata) staged in the theatre of the Canadian village. A balloon ride provides a splendid bird's eye view of the park.

Grass Roots

Parc naturel Régional de la Montagne de Reims★★

Created in 1976, the Regional Nature Park of the Montagne de Reims covers an area of 50,000ha between the towns of Reims, Epernay and Châlons-en-Champagne. The forest, consisting mainly of deciduous trees such as oaks, beech and chestnut trees, covers 20,000 hectares, more than a third of the park. Numerous footpaths and hiking trails thread their way through the park, including the GR 14 and its offshoots such as the 141 and 142. Discovery trails have been created on the banks of the canal which runs alongside the Marne: 41 information panels on the stretch between Condé-sur-Marne and Damery, provide walkers with insights into the local flora, fauna, know-how and traditions. Picnic areas abound, as do viewpoints.

Maison du Parc, Pourcy

21km SW of Reims on the D 980 and the D 386 to the left. Chemin de Nanteuil, 51480 Pourcy. Open Easter Sun–Nov 11 2.30–6pm. 03 26 59 44 44. www.parc-montagnedereims.fr.

Anyone even the slightest bit interested in the nature park of the Montagne de Reims really should stop at the Maison du Parc. Offering documentation about the wildlife and the region, calendar of events and excursions, exhibitions, guides and maps, the Maison du parc is a treasure-trove of information. Make sure you pick up a copy of the *Journal du parc*, with a list of everything going on in the region.

In Champagne, some species of fruit tree are threatened by more dominant varieties. The **Verger conservatoire** *(access via the Maison du parc)* protects rare species such as the Montmorency de Sauvigny cherry, the Rousselet pear or the Imperial plum of Boursault.

Maison du bûcheron

In Germaine. 24km S of Reims on the N 51, then take a left onto the D 71. Rte. du Pré-Michaux. Open Easter Sun to Nov 11 Sun and public holidays 2.30-6.30pm. 2€ (children no charge). 03 26 59 44 44. www.parc-montagnedereims.fr.

This appealing small museum is devoted to different aspects of forestry (marking, clearing, cutting, felling, carrying) and its corresponding trades and professions. Documents, tools and photographs illustrate each aspect. Nearby is a nature trail through the forest.

Lac de l'Orient

14km E of Troyes on the N 19.

Created in 1966, the artificial Lac de l'Orient covers 2,500ha set in a superb landscape of forests, the peace and quiet of which are disturbed only by the flight of thousands of migratory birds (bird sanctuary to the northeast) and the multicoloured sails of yachts, catamarans, windsurfers and little sailing dinghies.

Champagne to General de Gaulle and who continue to supply the Elysées palace today. The12C vaulted cellars built by the monks of Clairvaux are open to the public.
This Champagne-producing firm is the only one in the world to use a single bottle throughout the entire process *(rue des Vignes, 10200 Urville; open Mon–Sat by appt. 8am-noon & 2-6pm; closed public holidays; 03 25 27 40 15, www.champagne-drappier.com).*

Continue on the D 44, then turn right onto the D 70 to Champignol-lez-Mondeville.

Champignol-lez-Mondeville
This peaceful village has a 12C chapel with an unusual wooden door and an 18C church which possesses a Baroque altarpiece and staffs from brotherhoods of wine-growers. The **Dumont** establishment has a fine selection of local wines.

Rejoin Baroville NE on the D 70.

Baroville
Champagne is the main attraction of Baroville, but the town's wine-growers also make excellent red Coteaux-Champenois wines.

Head eastbound on the D 170 then take the D 396 left.

Bayel
Founded by a Venetian master glass-worker, Jean-Baptiste Mazzolay who was granted a letter of patent by Louis XIV, the **Royal crystal-works of Champagne** is famous the world over. Since its foundation in 1666, its kilns have never been extinguished and glass-blowers and cutters continue to uphold ancient traditions.
A mixture of sand, lime, soda and lead heated for 12 hours to a temperature of 1,450°C produces a kind of paste which is ready to be shaped by blowing or casting; all the items are handmade *(2 r. Belle Verriere, 10310 Bayel, visit by guided tours (1hr 30min) Mon–Fri 9am-1pm & 2-6pm (Jul-Aug til 7pm); 5.30€; 03 25 92 42 68; www.bayel-cristal.com).*
The **Ecomusée du Cristal** is housed in three small workers' cottages (entrance through the tourist office).
A series of models offers an insight into the origins of crystal, its various components, the manufacturing process and the different methods used to decorate glass such as guilloche and engraving *(open Apr–Sept Mon–Sat 9.15am–1pm & 2.15–6pm; Sun & public holidays 2.15–6pm; closed Sun Oct–Mar, May 1, Nov 1, Dec 25, Jan 1; 3.80€; combined ticket for the crystal-works and ecomusée 7.60€; 03 25 92 42 68).*

Leave Bayel NE on the D 47 and head for Rouvres-les-Vignes via Lignol-le-Château. At Rouvres, take a left onto the D 74.

After driving through the forest, the attractive sight of hillsides carpeted in vineyards once again comes into view from Rouvres-les-Vignes. This area is the oldest section of the Baralbin vineyards, originally planted by monks in the High Middle Ages.

Colombé-le-Sec
Despite its name (Colombé the Dry), this picturesque flower-decked village was the site of an immense storehouse where the monks of Clairvaux used to keep their wine in the 12C. The **Charles-Clément** brand, made up of several producers, continues to uphold the monks' traditions *(see Shopping Guide).*
Bernard Breuzon offers a tour with commentary explaining the various stages of Champagne making, finishing with a tasting of the firm's Colombine vintage Champagne *(R. St-Antoine, 10200 Colombé-le-Sec; 03 25 27 02 06; www.champagnebreuzon.com).*
The village has retained an interesting octagonal wash-house thought to date back to the 12C.

Rejoin Bar-sur-Aube on the D 13.

WINE BUYING GUIDE

INFORMATION

Comité interprofessionnelle des vins de Champagne – *5 r. Henri-Martin, 51204 Epernay. ℘03 26 51 19 30. www.champagne.fr.*

Syndicat général des vignerons de la Champagne – *44 Avenue Jean-Jaurès – 51205 Epernay. ℘03 26 55 19 79 – www.champagnesdevignerons.com.*

USEFUL TIPS

Les carnets des Champagnes
Published by the Comité Interprofessionnelle des vins de Champagne, these guides of around twenty pages each (in French) initiate the reader into the world of Champagne. Wine hints, tips and characteristics, food and wine, and the ins and outs of Champagne etiquette are all covered.

CHARACTERISTICS

Champagne is generally light gold or rosé in colour. The streams of bubbles in the glass should be persistant and the wine should be sparkling with a slight head of froth but without being aggressive. The range of aromas varies greatly from fresh brioche bread and white flowers to ripe grapes and soft red fruit. In terms of taste, Champagnes can be brut, sec or demi-sec depending on the quantity of sugar added. The Coteaux-Champenois are still red wines with a deep, rich robe and a distinctive bouquet of raspberry and cherry notes. The deep pink Rosé-des-Riceys are still, rosé wines, which are fruity and intense with a hint of bitterness.

STORAGE

Champagne, once it has been bottled, and whether it be a vintage wine or not, is rarely kept for more than five years. Coteaux-Champenois and Rosé-des-Riceys can be kept for between five to eight years.

PRICES

The 2004, 2005 and 2006 harvests were excellent, in terms of both quality and quantity. The appellation is nearly entirely planted with vines and sales continue to climb, leading to talk of shortages and the extension of boundaries discussed in the Overview (p217). Even with drops in sales from the 2009 financial crisis, Champagne, the wine of celebrations and special events, remains expensive.

Wine-growers Champagne – Between 11€ and 15€.
Vintage Champagne – Between 15€ and 30€.
Grande cuvée prestige Champagne – Between 50€ and 100€.
Coteaux-Champenoise – 15€ to 20€.
Rosé-des-Riceys – 15€ to 20€.

WINE MERCHANTS

Confrérie la St-Vincent de Rizaucourt et Argentolles – *Cellier St-Vincent, Musée de la Vigne et du Vin, 52330 Argentolles. ℘03 25 02 58 05. Open appt only, call 48hrs in advance.* It is not very surprising to find that an oenological brotherhood has chosen to name itself after Saint Vincent, who is the patron saint of wine-growers; his saint's day is in late January, at a time when the vines require the least care. The establishment, which is also home to a small wine museum sells locally produced Champagnes.

Les Delices Champenoises – *2 r. Rockefeller, 51100 Reims. Open daily 9.30am-7pm; ℘03 26 47 35 25.* Not a single Grand Cru Champagne is missing from the roll call in this cellar, which is barely two minutes from the cathedral. Row upon row of Veuve Clicquot, Pommery, Perrier-Jouët, Taittinger, Jacquart, Bollinger and Mumm, to name but a few, stand smartly to attention, alongside wine from Bouzy, pink Champagne biscuits, Reims mustard and chocolates stuffed with marc de Champagne.

GROUPS OF CHAMPAGNE-PRODUCERS

Mailly Grand Cru – *28 r. de la Libération, 51500 Mailly-Champagne. ℘03 26 49 41 10; Open Mon-Fri 8.30am-noon & 2.30-6pm, Sat 9am-5pm; Sun 11am-5pm; www.champagne-mailly.com.* In 1923 six wine-growers joined forces to press their grapes, make wine and sell their produce together. Six years later, their ranks had risen to 20 and they founded the Société des producteurs de Mailly-Champagne. The firm, which now has

77 members who cultivate some 70 hectares of vineyards, is a particularly get-ahead enterprise which combines traditions, state-of-the-art technology and a permanent quest for excellence. Champagne, Coteaux Champenois.

WINE ESTATES

Serge Pierlot – *10 r. St-Vincent, 51150 Ambonnay. 6.5km SE of Louvois on the D 34 and D 19. 03 26 57 01 11. champagne-serge-pierlot@wanadoo.fr. Open daily by appt. Closed Jan, late Aug–early Sept.* The south- and southeast facing Côte d'Ambonnay-Bouzy is renowned for its AOC Champagnes and red Coteaux-Champenois. Stop at Agnès and Serge Pierlot's wine-growing estate and taste their wines after visiting their small museum complete with an 18C press and old vine and wine-making tools. Champagne, Coteaux Champenois.

Paul Dethune – *2 rue du Moulin, 51150 Ambonnay; 03 26 57 01 88. Open by appt; www.champagne-dethune.com.* Pierre and Sophie Dethune make an excellent Champagne at this understatedly glamorous ivy-clad building, with impeccably maintained underground cellars. The family has been making Champagne since 1610. Seven hectares of Pinot Noir and Chardonnay vines, and seven Grand Cru Cuvees. Champagne, Coteaux Champenois.

Egly-Ouriet – *15 r. de Trépail, 51150 Ambonnay. 03 26 57 00 70. Open Mon-Fri 9am–noon & 2–6pm.* Charles Egly founded his Champagne firm in 1936; today it is run by his son Michel and his grandson is in charge of the 11.7ha, 9ha of which are Grand Cru class. The Egly family also produces red Ambonnay wines. The estate continues to employ traditional agricultural methods and the vines are tended and pruned extremely carefully, optimising the quality of the grapes. The vineyards are cultivated using ecologically responsible methods and the soil is regularly ploughed and aired. All the estate's wines are stored for three years before their release to the market. Champagne, Coteaux Champenois.

Agrapart et Fils – *57 ave. Jean-Jaurès, 51190 Avize. 03 26 57 51 38. champagne.agrapart@wanadoo.fr. Open by appt.* It was in 1894 that Arthur Agrapart created this estate in Avize, now run by his heirs Fabrice and Pascal Agrapart. Together the two men work 9.5ha of vineyard spread over Avize (Côte des Blancs Grands Crus), Oger, Cramant and Oiry. The chalky soil is ideally suited to Chardonnay. The vineyards are still regularly ploughed (mechanical weeding) to ensure constant microbic life and enable the roots to draw rich mineral elements from deep down in the ground. The grapes are harvested manually and selectively depending on the health and maturity of each plot of land. Champagne, Coteaux Champenois.

Franck Bonville – *9 r. Pasteur, 51190 Avize, t03 26 57 52 30; open Mon-Sat by appt; www.champagne-franck-bonville.com.* Attractive cobble-stoned courtyard and large underground cellars. Olivier Bonville is today in charge, but still works with his parents, and his grandparents still live on the estate. The family has 20 hectares of Grand Cru Vines in Avize, Cramant and Oger. Champagne.

Georges Vesselle – 16 r. des Postes, *51150 Bouzy. 03 26 57 00 15 ; www. champagne-vesselle.net. Open Mon-Fri 8am-noon & 2-5pm, weekends by appt.* This Champagne producer also makes an excellent Bouzy red wine. Georges is pretty much retired now, and his sons Bruno and Eric are in charge of the18ha of vines in Montagne de Reims; south-facing with a sunny exposure. The red is made from oldest vines, and only during vintage years for the champagne – ie only in the best years, when the grapes are most ripe. Pinot noir 90% planted in the vines. Champagne, AOC Buuzy.

Champagne Dumont – *Rte. de Champagne, 10200 Champignol-les-Mondeville. 03 25 27 45 95. rdumontetfils@wanadoo.fr. Open Mon–Fri 9am–6pm; weekends by appt.* This family of wine-growers has owned and worked the vineyard for over two centuries. Staunch champions of the merits of traditional methods, it has recently managed to introduce new technology to maintain its rank in the profession. Tours are organised of the wine-making premises (presses, vats, etc) with Champagne tasting. Champagne, Coteaux Champenois.

Champagne Charles-Clément – *R. St-Antoine, 10200 Colombé-le-Sec. 03 25 92 50 70. www.champagne-charles-clement.fr. Open mid-Jun–Aug 8am–noon & 1.30–5.30pm; Sun 10am–noon & 2–6.30pm; rest of the year 8am–noon & 1.30–5.30pm (Fri 4.30pm). Cellar visits 10am; last entry 3:30pm; Closed Jul 14.* This wine cooperative is a happy mix of old and new with pneumatic and traditional presses. Excellent selection of rosé Champagnes and still Coteaux-Champenois wines. Many of the wines and Champagnes on sale have won medals. Champagne, Coteaux Champenois.

Lilbert Fils – *223 r. du Moutier, BP 14, 51530 Cramant. 03 26 57 50 16. www.champagne-lilbert.com. Open Mon–Sat 10am–noon & 2–6pm.* Specialised in the production of white Champagne for which he has received countless medals and awards, Georges Lilbert has even gone so far as to forego rosé Champagne completely. Born into a family of wine-growers from father to son since 1746, Georges upholds ancient traditions and the bottles are still turned by hand on traditional racks and the dégorgement process is also carried out according to ancestral customs. Champagne.

Mr Bonnaire checking his wine at Bonnaire

© Bonnaire

Bonnaire – *120 r. d'Epernay, 51530 Cramant. 03 26 57 50 85. www.champagne-bonnaire.com. Open by appt. Mon-Sat 8.30–11.30am & 2–7pm.* The same family of wine-growers and producers has been at the helm of this house created in 1932 for three generations. Today, the firm of Champagne Bonnaire works 22 hectares of vineyards, the majority of which is classed in the Grand Cru or Premier Cru categories. Champagne.

Champagne René Geoffroy – *150 r. du Bois-des-Jots, 51480 Cumières. 03 26 55 32 31. www.champagne-geoffroy.com. Open Mon–Sat 9am–noon & 2–6pm, Sun by appt.* This Champagne firm has been handed down from generation to generation since the 17C. René Geoffroy and his son Jean-Baptiste, both dedicated and enthusiastic wine-growers, supervise every step of the wine-making process of each of their wines, leaving nothing to chance. This attention to detail can be felt in every aspect of the production process from the vine stock to the thick heavy glass bottles. Their 13ha estate is planted with Pinot Noir, Pinot Meunier and Chardonnay, all according to ecologically responsible methods. The grapes are harvested by hand and subjected to a stringent selection process. The wine is fermented mainly in small oak tuns. Champagne, Coteaux Champenois.

Louis Casters – *26 r. Pasteur – 51480 Damery. 03 26 58 43 02. champagne.louis.casters@wanadoo.fr. Open by appt. Mon–Sat 10am–noon & 2–5pm.* The10ha vineyards of this estate are spread over the communes of Damery, Vauciennes, Reuil, Binson-Orquigny and Villers-sous-Châtillon. In 1985, this traditional family-run affair took on the status of néogociant-manipulant (buyer and blender). Since then, it has been buying grapes from a further 25 hectares of carefully selected vineyards. Champagne.

Champagne René Geoffroy

Francoise Bedel – *71 Grande Rue, 02310 Crouettes sur Marne, ℘03 23 82 15 80; www.champagne-francoise-bedel.fr – Open daily by appt.* Francoise Bedel makes her own biodynamic Champagne from this 7ha estate, and has used no chemical fertilisers or treatments since 1997. Half the estate was converted to biodynamics in 1998, the other half in 1999. The majority of the vineyard is planted to Pinot Meunier (at 78%) giving a fleshy but delicate wine.

Champagne Richardot – *38 r. René-Quinton, 10110 Loches-sur-Ource. ℘03 25 29 71 20. champagne.richardot@wanadoo.fr. Open Mon–Fri 9–11.30am & 2–6pm; weekends by appt. Closed Jan 1, Dec 25.* The superb vaulted cellars of the Richardot firm are adorned with a collection of old wine-grower's tools and utensils. The view over the vineyards as you sip a glass of Champagne in the pleasant tasting room is well worth the visit. Champagne.

Beaumont des Crayères – *64 r. de la Liberté, 51530 Mardeuil. ℘03 26 55 29 40. www.champagne-beaumont.com. Open Mon–Fri 9am–noon & 1.30-5pm. Closed 2 weeks in Aug, Jan 1, Dec 25.* The Beaumont firm, whose reputation for outstanding wines is a secret to no one, was awarded the Grand Prix d'Excellence by the French Union of Oenologists in 2004. Among other exhibits, its museum devoted to Champagne boasts the largest bottle of Champagne in the world. Tasting, sales and guided tours of the cellars. Champagne.

Philipponnat – *Domaine Clos des Goisses, 13 r. du Pont, 51160 Mareuil-sur-Ay. ℘03 26 56 93 01. www.champagne philipponnat.com. Open Mon-Fri by appt 9am-noon & 1.30-5pm.* Established in Champagne since the early 16C, the Philipponnat family has earned its living from the making and selling of fine wines for centuries. Today the firm run by Charles Philipponnat is located in Mareuil-sur-Ay in the heart of the Champagne region; it offers a selection of wines, made primarily from Pinot Noir grapes. Grapes grown on the estate are augmented by others from the Montagne de Reims, the Côte des Blancs and the Vallée de la Marne. Vinification occurs in wood, with no malolactic fermentation. Champagne.

Pierre Moncuit – *11 r. Persaut-Maheu, 51190 Le Mesnil-sur-Oger. ℘03 26 57 52 65. Open Mon–Sat 10.30am–noon & 2–3.30pm.* Yves and Nicole Moncuit, who have taken over from their parents, are now at the head of a vineyard which rose to fame at the inauguration of the Universal Exhibition of 1889. Yves is in charge of the sales side of the business and customer relations, while his sister Nicole devotes herself to running the 19ha of vineyards planted exclusively with Chardonnay. The estate has retained a vine over 80 years old which is at the origin of the "Pierre Moncuit –

Musée de la Vigne et du Vin, Launois Père et Fils

© Launois Père et Fils

Deos" prestigious Champagne. Champagne.

Jean-Louis Vergnon– *1 Grande Rue, 51190 Le Mesnil sur Oger* *03 26 57 53 86. www.champagne-jl-vergnon.com. Open Mon-Fri by appt 9am-noon & 2.30-5.30pm.* Christophe Constant is a name to watch in this high quality winemaking village, and a visit to the estate of Jean Louis Vergnon is the place to catch him. The son of a local restaurateur, Constant has worked at prestigious houses including Veuve Cliquot before managing this small 5ha estate. Try the Cuvée Confidence 2003, a zero dosage wine. Champagne.

Launois Père et Fils – *2 ave. Eugène-Guillaume, 11km S of Epernay by the D 40 and D 10, 51190 Le Mesnil-sur-Oger.* *03 26 57 50 15. Open Mon-Fri 9am-noon & 2-5pm, Sat-Sun 10am-1pm; 7€; www.champagne-launois.fr.* This négociant-manipulant (buyer and blender) firm founded in 1872 has its own museum devoted to vines and wine. The two-hour tour ends with a tasting session of three of the firm's own brand. Champagne.

Champagne Vollereaux – *48 r. Léon-Bourgois, BP 4, 51530 Pierry.* *03 26 54 03 05. Champagne.vollereauxsa@wanadoo.fr. Open Mon–Sat 10.30am–noon & 3–6pm; Sun by appt.* The Vollereaux wine-growing family, established in Pierry and Moussy since 1805, owns 40 hectares of vineyards spread throughout the Champagne AOC, although most of it is on the hills around Epernay. The three traditional varieties of vines are cultivated according to ecologically responsible methods; the harvests are by hand. Fermented in modern vats, the Champagne is then stored for four years in the estate's own cellars. Champagne.

Piper-Heidsieck – *51 blvd. Henry-Vasnier, 51100 Reims.* *03 26 84 43 44. www.piper-heidsieck.com. Open strictly by appt, apply one month in advance.* Florens-Louis Heidsieck, son of a Lutheran pastor, founded his Champagne firm in 1785. His success was swift and he was granted the privilege of presenting Queen Marie-Antoinette with a wine made specially in her honour. On his death, his nephew Christian Heidsieck took over the company with a partner Henri-Guillaume Piper. The outstanding salesmanship of the latter propelled Heidsieck Champagne into the international arena and the brand acquired its current name of Piper-Heidsieck. In 1989 the house was purchased by the Rémy-Martin group, now the Rémy-Cointreau group. Its Champagnes are blended from a variety of different wines. Champagne.

Champagne Pommery –*5 pl. du Général-Gouraud, BP 1049, 51689 Reims Cedex 2.* *03 26 61 62 63. www.pommery.fr.* Every year, the head of the Pommery wine cellars endeavours to ensure that the year's vintage will be representative of the distinctive, elegant Pommery style initiated by Madame Pommery over a century ago. In April 2002, the Vranken group, founded by Paul-François Vranken, and owner of Heidsieck & Co Monopole, acquired the Pommery firm of Champagne.

Champagne Taittinger – *9 pl. St Nicaise, 51100 Reims. ℘03 26 85 45 35.* Founded in the early 1930s by Pierre Taittinger, since 1960 the firm has been run by his son, Claude. With property in all the major Champagne-producing regions (Epernay, Montagne de Reims and Essoyes), the vineyards are located on hillsides and worked according to ecologically responsible methods. Its 270 hectares are planted with Chardonnay (40%), Pinot Noir (45%) and Pinot Meunier (15%). The Taittinger firm also purchases high-quality produce from a selection of the best Champagne vineyards. The firm's cellars store some 19 500 000 bottles. In addition to vineyards in France, Taittinger also owns 70 hectares of vines in the Carneros region of California.

Daniel Dumont – *11 r. Gambetta, 51100 Rilly-la-Montagne. ℘03 26 03 40 67. Open daily by appt. 8am–noon & 1.30–5.30pm; www.champagne-danieldumont.com.* Daniel Dumont planted his vineyard in 1962 and in 1970 he began to sell a few hundred bottles under his own brand. Today his three children, Alain, Jean-Michel and Marie-Claire all work on the estate with him. Their vineyards cover some 10 hectares of Premiers Crus, planted with Chardonnay (40%), Pinot Noir (40%) and Pinot Meunier (20%). The presses and the storehouse have both been modernised in keeping with Champagne traditions dear to the hearts of wine-growers. The wine is bottled and aged (between four and seven years) in the estate's cellars. Annual production ranges between 75 000 and 90 000 bottles. Champagne

Champagne Devaux – Domaine de Villeneuve, 10110 Bar-sur-Seine, t03 25 38 30 65. *Open 10am-noon & 2-5pm, www.champagne-devaux.fr.* One of the largest and most dynamic cooperative houses in Champagne, who own 1,400ha of vines and produce Champagne under the brand Devaux and are located in the beautiful Domaine de Villeneuve. The Union Auboise was founded in 1967 by a merger of eleven co-operative houses, and today has 800 vine growers. This gives them excellent control over the growing conditions of their vines, and its Champagnes are increasingly lauded. Maison Devaux also makes a well regarded Rosé-des-Riceys. Champagne, Rosé-des-Riceys.

Champagne Morel Père et Fils – *93 r. du Général-de-Gaulle, 10340 Les Riceys. ℘03 25 29 10 88. www.champagnemorelpereetfils.com. Open daily by appt. Closed harvest period, and Sun.* Five generations of family winegrowers have managed this property, headquartered in a magnificent regional-style building. Tastings occur in the vaulted cellars of their excellent Rosé des Riceys, plus a Rosé Champagne. Champagne, Rosé-des-Riceys.

Jacques Defrance – *28 rue de la Plante 10340 Les Riceys℘03 25 29 32 20. Open Mon–Fri by appt. 9am–noon & 2–5pm; www.champagnejacquesdefrance.fr.* An excellent Champagne is made here, as well as a delicate and perfumed Rosé-des-Riceys. The family is now in its fourth generation of winemakers, and the estate is a blend of Pinot Noir and Chardonnay, made with a mix of traditional viticulture, modern winery and aged in classic underground cellars. Champagne, Coteaux Champenois, Rosé-des-Riceys.

Champagne Morize Père et Fils – *122 r. du Général-de-Gaulle, 10340 Les Riceys. ℘03 25 29 30 02. www.champagnemorize.com. Open Mon–Sat 9–11am & 2.30–5pm. Closed public holidays.* The cellars which date from the 12C are as welcoming as they are attractive. After the ritual tour of the property in the company of the owner, you can choose between sipping a glass of Champagne at the stone bar or taking a seat for a gourmet meal. Whatever you decide, you will be spoilt for choice by the estate's 100 000 bottles of sparkling nectar. Champagne, Coteaux Champenois, Rosé-des-Riceys.

Veuve Olivier et Fils – *10 rte. de Dormans, 2.5km west of Dormans on the D 6. 02850 Trélou-sur-Marne. ℘03 23 70 24 01. www.champagne-veuve-olivier.com. Open Mon–Fri 9am–noon & 2–5pm; Sat 9am–noon & afternoons by appt.* This admirably situated estate commands a splendid panoramic view of the Marne valley. A video and guided tour of the premises includes a look at the traditional press and an explanation of how Champagne is made. Tasting of several wines is possible, and there is a boutique for sales on the estate. Champagne.

Duval-Leroy – *69 ave. de Bammental, BP 37, 51330 Vertus. ℘03 26 52 10 75. www.duval-leroy.com. Open by appt. Mon–Fri 9–11.30am & 2–4.30pm.* Located right in the heart of the prestigious Côte des Bars since 1859, this establishment now owns and cultivates over 170 hectares of vineyards which provide it with one-quarter of its needs in grapes. Since 1991, Carol Duval-Leroy has made a name for herself in the exclusive circle of women Champagne blenders. Her dynamic, get-ahead outlook and that of her team are fundamental in turning this family affair into a highly successful enterprise. Champagne.

Veuve Fourny et Fils – *Domaine du Clos du Faubourg-Notre-Dame, 5 r. du Mesnil, 51130 Vertus. ℘03 26 52 16 30. www.champagne-veuve-fourny.com. Open Mon–Fri 9am–noon & 2–6pm., Sat 10am-noon & 3-5.30pm* Four generations of the Fourny family have been running this Premier Cru class vineyard in Vertus. Monique Fourny directs operations today along with sons Emmanuel (an oenologist) and Charles-Henry. The Premier Cru vineyard is planted with Chardonnay, with an average vine age of 40 years. All cultivation is ecologically responsible. Wines are aged a minimum of 3 years; vintage Champagnes age from 10 to 25 years. Champagne, Coteaux Champenois.

FESTIVALS

Ay – Fête Henri IV, first weekend of July in even years. The festival lasts two days, the first is devoted to visits to the cellars and tasting. The second day is given over to a parade of some 2,000 people, 40 horses and 15 carriages and carts, all in honour of King Henry IV.

Epernay – Grand Cochelet des Vendanges – a popular festival held on the last day of the grape harvest, includes music, dancing and a huge wine-growers' meal.

One of the Marne towns – Festival of Saint Vincent de Champagne, Sunday after 22 January.

Les Riceys – Walking festival, 1 May. Sign up with the tourist office.

One of the towns of the Massif of St-Thierry – Traditional-style grape harvesting, 3rd Sat-Sun of Oct, odd years.

ADDRESSES

STAY

AROUND BAR-SUR- AUBE

Le St-Nicolas – *2 r. du Général-de-Gaulle, 10200 Bar-sur-Aube. ℘03 25 27 08 65. www.lesaintnicolas.com. 27rms. 8€.* Three appealing houses whose main wing dates from the 18C and two other wings overlooking the swimming pool, make up this town centre establishment. The rooms, all renovated, have practical painted wooden furnishings. Delightful breakfast area. Sauna available.

Moulin du Landion – *R. St-Léger, 10200 Dolancourt. 9km NW of Bar-sur-Aube by the N 19 toward Troyes. ℘03 25 27 92 17. www.moulindulandion.com. Closed Nov 15–Feb 15. 16 rooms. . Restaurant .* Calm and quiet reign at this historic timber-mill, where guestrooms open onto a pastoral park. The dining room windows overlook the water-wheel. Swimming pool available in summer.

AROUND BAR-SUR-SEINE

Le Val Moret – *10110 Magnant, 9km NE of Bar-sur-Seine near the motorway interchange. ℘03 25 29 85 12. www.le-val-moret.com. 42 rooms. 7€. Restaurant .* This large modern flower-decked building has a definite motel style. The simple practical rooms are all on the ground floor and are well soundproofed. Good value-for-money. Traditional unpretentious cuisine.

⊜⊜ **Les Voyageurs** – *6 r. de la Nation, 10250 Gué-sur-Seine. ℘03 25 38 20 09. hotel-voyageurs-gye@wanadoo.fr. Closed Aug 16–24 and Feb holidays. 7 rooms. ☕8€. Restaurant* ⊜⊜. Fresh, bright rooms await you in this old 19C lodge fronted by a stone facade.

AROUND CHÂTEAU-THIERRY

⊜ **Chambre d'hôte La Grange du Moulin** – *15 r. du Moulin, 02810 Bussiares. 13km W of Château-Thierry by the N 3 and D 9. ℘03 23 70 92 60. lagrangedumoulin@hotmail.fr. Closed Dec 15–Jan 15. 4 rooms. ☕. Restaurant* ⊜. This distinctive ivy-covered house offers comfortable, beautifully renovated rooms and an appealing dining room complete with exposed beams and antique furniture. The small garden is delightful in summer.

⊜ **Chambre d'hôte M et Mme Leclère** – *1 r. de Launay, 02330 Connigis. 12km E of Château-Thierry by the N 3 and D 4. ℘03 23 71 90 51. Closed 24 Dec to 1 Jan. Reservations required. 5 rooms. ☕. Restaurant* ⊜. The 16C castle of Connigis is located in an immense park surrounded by vineyards. The estate makes its own Champagne which guests are invited to taste before dinner. A country style prevails indoors. The table is laden high with home-made produce and as much wine as you can drink.

AROUND EPERNAY

⊜ **Chambre d'hôte La Boursaultière** – *44 r. de la Duchesse-d'Uzès, 51480 Boursault. 9km W of Epernay by the N 3 and the D 222. ℘03 26 58 47 76. Closed Feb. 2 rooms.* ☕. This appealing house built out of local stone extends a faultless welcome to guests who are treated to delightful rooms hung with medieval- or Renaissance-style printed fabrics. The luxurious bathrooms boast beautiful Italian glazed tiles and the paved courtyard is a riot of lush green plants.

⊜ **Chambre d'hôte "Terroirs de Champagne"** – *R. de la Coopérative, 51480 OEuilly. 13km W of Epernay by the N 3 (Dormans road). ℘03 26 58 30 60. Closed Oct–Mar. 4 rooms.* ☕. Take advantage of your stay with a real wine-grower to find out more about how Champagne is made, and taste your host's own wine. The ground-floor rooms of this unpretentious house are wonderfully spacious and all afford a relaxing view of the surrounding vineyards. Courteous welcome and family ambience.

⊜⊜ **Hôtel Les Berceaux** – *13 r. des Berceaux, 51200 Epernay. ℘03 26 55 28 84. www.lesberceaux.com. 18 rooms. ☕11€. Restaurant* ⊜⊜. Guests to this hundred-year-old flower-decked house are assured of a warm welcome. Ask for one of the tastefully renovated rooms. The elegant restaurant offers tasty classic dishes served with AOC Champagne and Coteaux-champenois wines. Wine by the glass and simpler fare in the Wine Bar.

⊜⊜ **La Famille Guy Charbaut** – *12 r. du Pont, 51160 Mareuil-sur-Ay. 8km E of Epernay on the D 1. ℘03 26 52 60 59. www.champagne-guy-charbaut.com. Closed Jan 1, Dec 25. 6 rooms. ☕ Restaurant* ⊜⊜⊜. Wine-growers from father to son since 1930, the Charbaut family bends over backwards to make guests feel welcome in their attractive 19C home, taking them on tours of the cellars and organising tasting sessions of their best Champagnes. Antique furniture in the bedrooms. Meals are served in a magnificent old storeroom.

⊜⊜⊜ **Chambre d'hôte Manoir de Montflambert** – *51160 Mutigny, 7km NE of Epernay on the D 201. ℘03 26 52 33 21. manoir-de-montflambert@wanadoo.fr. 6 rooms.* ☕. This former 17C hunting lodge on the edge of a wood commands a splendid view of the Marne and the vineyards. The price is more than compensated for by the manor's lovely woodwork, impressive staircase up to the rooms, quiet ambience and rich past – its walls are said to have witnessed the romance between Henry IV and the Countess of Montflambert.

⊜⊜⊜ **Touraine Champenoise** – *R. du Magasin, 51150 Tours-sur-Marne. ℘03 26 58 91 93. touraine-champenoise@wanadoo.fr. Closed 1–15 Jan and Thu. 8 rooms.* ☕. Country home alongside the canal, maintained by the same family since 1907! The rooms are simple, comfortable, country-style. Locally-inspired dishes served in the rustic dining-room.

⊜⊜⊜⊜ **Clos Raymi** – *3 r. Joseph-de-Venage, 51200 Épernay. ℘03 26 51 00 58. Closraymi@wanadoo.fr. Closed Sun* *from Dec 15–Feb 15. 7 rooms. ☕14€.* This lovely brick home belonged to the Chandon family. Guestrooms are refined, and individually decorated. Start your day in the pleasant breakfast-room overlooking the garden.

AROUND REIMS

Ardenn' Hôtel – *6 r. Caqué, 51100 Reims. ℘03 26 47 42 38. ardennhotel@wanadoo.fr. 14 rooms. ☕5.50€.* Behind a pretty brick façade, this establishment offers a quiet location not far from the town centre, impeccably well-kept premises, tastefully decorated rooms and ever-smiling staff. In short, a sound, affordable choice.

Chambre d'hôte Delong – *24 r. des Tilleuls, 51390 St-Euphraise-et-Clarizet. 16km SW of Reims by the D 980 and D 206. ℘03 26 49 74 90. jdscom@wanadoo.fr. 4 rooms.* ☕. In the heart of a wine-growing estate, this former cowshed has been beautifully converted: lovely old stone walls and exposed timbers in the rooms which also have attractive bathrooms. The estate organises visits to the cellars, the wine press and Champagne tasting.

Chambre d'hôte Lapie – *1 r. Jeanne-d'Arc, 51360 Val-de-Vesle. 21km SE of Reims by the N 44 and D 326 on the left. ℘03 26 03 92 88. joyhello@free.fr. Closed Dec 15–Jan 15. 5 rooms.* ☕. Five bedrooms stylishly decorated in pastel colours have been fitted out in the main wing of this farmstead in the heart of the village: a happy blend of old and new. The pleasant ground-floor dining room is ideal for breakfasts.

Hôtel Crystal – *86 pl. Drouet-d'Erlon, 51100 Reims. ℘03 26 88 44 44. www.hotel-crystal.fr. 31 rooms. ☕9€.* An amazing haven of greenery and tranquillity right in the heart of town and yet protected from the busy town bustle is what this 1920s house offers tired travellers. All the rooms have been treated to a fresh coat of paint and excellent bedding. In summer, breakfast is served in a charming flower-decked garden-courtyard lined with trees.

Hôtel La Cathédrale – *20 r. Libergier, 51100 Reims. ℘03 26 47 28 46. hoteldelacathedrale@wanadoo.fr. 17 rooms. ☕7€.* Notre-Dame Cathedral rises majestically at the far end of the street where this smart establishment is located. The pretty rooms with cosy inviting beds are bright and comfortable. Tasteful old engravings adorn the walls of the breakfast room. Warm welcome, faultless upkeep.

Hôtel du Cheval Blanc – *51400 Sept-Saulx. 18km SE of Reims by the N 44 and the D 37. ℘03 26 03 90 27. www.chevalblanc-sept-saulx.com. Closed Feb, Mar, Wed from Oct–Mar. ☕11€. Restaurant.* Peace and quiet guaranteed in this former coaching inn off the main roads. Attractive rooms overlooking a well-tended garden on the banks of a branch of the Vesle. Plush comfortable dining room and flower-decked courtyard which doubles as a dining terrace in summer. Tennis and mini-golf.

Hôtel Porte Mars – *2 pl. de la République, 51100 Reims. ℘03 26 40 28 35. www.hotelportemars.com. 24 rooms. ☕10€.* A charming place to have a cup of tea by the fireplace of the cosy sitting room, or a drink before dinner in the sophisticated bar. The comfortable personalised rooms are all excellently soundproofed. Copious breakfasts served in an attractive conservatory decorated with old photos and mirrors.

Les Barbotines – *1 pl. A,-Tritant, 51150 Bouzy. ℘03 26 57 07 31. www.lesbarbotines.com. Closed Aug 1–14, Dec 15–Jan 15. 5 rooms.* ☕. Handsome 19C winegrower's home near the famed Route du Champagne. Charming rooms outfitted with antiques.

Hôtel Continental – *93 pl. Drouet-d'Erlon, 51100 Reims. ℘03 26 40 39 35. www.grandhotelcontinental.com. Closed Dec 21–Jan 7. 50 rooms. ☕11.50€.* The smart late-19C façade of this hotel overlooks a pedestrian square which is the liveliest spot in town. Renovated rooms in a variety of styles reached by a magnificent staircase; avoid the rooms overlooking Boulevard du Général-Leclerc for maximum peace and quiet. Elegant Belle Epoque reception rooms.

Assiette Champenoise – *40 ave. Paul-Vaillant-Couturier, Tinqueux, 51100 Reims. ℘03 26 84 64 64. www.assiettechampenoise.com. 55 rooms. ☕14€. Restaurant.* An immaculate park provides the setting for this elegant mansion to which an extra wing has been recently added with attractive renovated rooms; some have a private sitting room.

EAT

AROUND BAR-SUR-AUBE

Auberge de la Plaine – *10500 La Rothière. ℘03 25 92 21 79. www.auberge-plaine.com.* Welcoming little roadside spot at the edge of the Forêt d'Orient regional park. The dining room is simply and comfortably appointed in a country style, with regional dishes on the menu.

La Toque Baralbine – *18 r. Nationale, 10200 Bar-sur-Aube. ℘03 25 27 20 34. toquebaralbine@wanadoo.fr. Closed Jan 5–25, Sun evening and Mon.* An attractive setting along the main commercial thoroughfare, where you can sample up-to-date dishes with a delicious local flavour. Lovely flowered terrace.

Natali et Hostellerie de la Montagne – *17 r. Argentolles, 52330 Colombey-les-Deux-Eglises. ℘03 25 01 51 69. www.hostellerielamontagne.com. Closed Jan 17–Feb 2, Mar 8–16, Sept 13–21, Dec 20–29, Mon and Tue. – 26/52P.* A peaceful inn, just outside the village which rose to fame as the home of Charles de Gaulle. Traditional creative cooking made from fresh market produce, against a décor of bare stone walls and exposed beams. The rooms overlooking the Champagne countryside are perfect for a weekend getaway.

AROUND BAR-SUR-SEINE

Le Commerce – *30 pl. de la République, 10110 Bar-sur-Seine. ℘03 25 29 86 36. hotelducommerce.bar-sur-seine@wanadoo.fr. Closed Feb holidays, Aug 21–28, Dec 25–31, Fri evenings during Jul–Aug and Sun.* The tiny Aube capital of Champagne houses this deliciously simple inn run by a determined and enthusiastic owner-couple. Seated in the dining room with bare beams and a fireplace, guests are treated to traditional recipes full of regional flavour.

Le Magny – *38 r. du Général-Leclerc, 10340 Les Riceys. ℘03 25 29 38 39. www.le-magny.com. Closed Sept–Mar, Sun evenings, Tue evening out of season and Wed.* The restoration of this country inn surrounded by a garden is faultless. A comfortable dining room is the backdrop for tasty traditional dishes and excellent local AOC wines: Rosé-des-Riceys, Coteaux-champenois and Champagne. Quiet rooms. Swimming pool.

S. Sauvignier/MICHELIN

Auberge de la Seine – *1 faubourg de Bourgogne, 10260 Fouchères. ℘03 25 40 71 11. contact@aubergedelaseine.com. Closed Aug 21–28, Feb 19–Mar 11, Sun evenings and Wed.* Welcoming 18C route-house, with the charming addition of a terrace overlooking the Seine. Traditional dishes are served beneath the beams of the cosy, updated dining room.

Parentèle – *32 r. Marcellin-Léveque, 10260 Villemoyenne. ℘03 25 43 68 68. Closed Jul 24–Aug 12, Jan 2–10, Feb 26–Mar 15, Sun evening, Mon and Tue except holidays.* You'll feel welcome as can be in this restored family home. Choose a table in the attractive dining room or on the garden terrace and peruse the selection of carefully prepared dishes on the menu. Good wine list and advice.

IN CHÂTEAU-THIERRY

L'Estoril – *1 pl. des Granges, 02400 Château-Thierry. ℘03 23 83 64 16. norberto.fran@wanadoo.fr.* Brightly coloured sponge-painted walls and azulejos tiles set the scene for this small restaurant in a little square whose Portuguese inspiration is equally noticeable in the culinary menu. Fish and seafood dishes rub shoulders with Portuguese specialities and traditional fare, to the delight of discerning palates.

Auberge Jean de la Fontaine – *10 r. des Filoirs, 02400 Château-Thierry. ☎03 23 83 63 89. infos@auberge-jean-de-la-fontaine.com. Closed 2 weeks in Dec.* All the paintings on wood in the small dining room illustrate the fables of La Fontaine. The chef's impeccable traditional recipes are as appreciated by a steadfast core of regular customers as by passing travellers lucky enough to stop here. To do full justice to the meal, make sure you leave room for some cheese.

Auberge Le Relais – *2 r. de Paris, 02850 Reuilly-Sauvigny. ☎03 23 70 35 36. auberge.relais.de.reuilly@wanadoo.fr. Closed Aug 20–Sept 7, Jan 28–Mar 2, Tue & Wed.* You'll enjoy every moment in this charming auberge, where tradition coexits with modernity in both menu and décor. Lovely veranda.

AROUND EPERNAY

Auberge de la Chaussée – *La Chaussée de Damery, 51480 Vauciennes. 6km W of Epernay on the N 3. ☎03 26 58 40 66. Closed 1 week in Feb, Sun evenings and Fri. 9 rooms. 7€.* Lovers of traditional French cuisine will be enchanted by this well-located inn by the side of the main road. An unaffected setting with black and white floor tiles. Clean simple accommodation.

Au Bateau Lavoir – *3 r. Port-au-Bois, 51480 Damery. 8km W of Epernay on the N 3 and the D 22. ☎03 26 58 40 88. www.au-bateau-lavoir.com. Closed 1 week in Feb, 2 weeks in Aug and Mon.* This pretty flower-decked house is admirably situated on the banks of the Marne in the birthplace of a famous French actress, Adrienne Lecouvreur. Tasty traditional fare served in an attractive modern dining room with huge bay windows.

La Cave à Champagne – *16 r. Gambetta, 51200 Epernay. ☎03 26 55 50 70. www.la-cave-a-champagne.com. Closed Tue evenings in Jul–Aug and Mon.* In a neighbourhood rich in restaurants, the Cave à Champagne stands out from the competition thanks to a trump card: its very reasonably priced wine list. This is the perfect opportunity to treat yourself to Champagne throughout the entire meal, served in a dining room decorated with a collection of bottles of this precious nectar.

La Table de Kobus – *3 r. du Dr-Rousseau – 51200 Epernay. ☎03 26 51 53 53 – closed 1–9 Jan, 19–26 Apr, 1–19 Aug, 24–31 Dec, Sun evening, Thu evening and Mon – 24/33€.* Decorated in a turn-of-the-19C style, this bistro provides the ideal setting to break open a bottle of Champagne, even one from your own cellar, at no extra cost! So do as the locals do, and enjoy the appetising bistro cuisine rustled up by a chef whose culinary talents leave nothing to be desired.

La Table Sourdet – *6 r. du Dr Moret, 51700 Dormans. ☎03 26 58 20 27. Closed Jul 1–15 and Fri.* La Table Sourdet has been run by the same family for six generations. A plush bourgeois interior decoration provides the backdrop to appetising classical recipes. At lunchtime La Petite Table veranda serves simple meals at low prices.

Le Caveau – *R. de la Coopérative, 51480 Curnières. 5km NW of Epernay on the D 301. ☎03 26 54 83 23. www.lecaveau-cumieres.com. Closed Sun evenings, Mon evenings, Tue evenings and Wed.* As you venture into this establishment you will first pass through a small room decorated on a vine theme, before a long corridor takes you into a magnificent vaulted dining room carved out of the local chalk. Immaculate table layouts. Regional specialities.

Le Mesnil – *2 r. Pasteur, 51190 Le Mesnil-sur-Oger. ☎03 26 57 95 57. mesnil@chez.com. Closed Aug 16–Sept 7, Jan 22–Feb 8, Mon evenings, Tue evenings and Wed.* It would be a crime to pass through this delightful wine-growing town without tasting the hospitality of the Jaillant husband and wife team. Claude supervises the kitchen while Yvette is in charge of the dining room. The result is sophisticated classical dishes served with a smile, all to the accompaniment of a fine wine list.

Le Théâtre – *8 pl. Mendès-France, 51200 Epernay. ☎03 26 58 88 19. www.epernay-rest-letheatre.com.* This handsome early 20C building is home to an attractive dining room where efficient staff masterfully maintain a pleasant muted atmosphere. A refreshing up-to-date interpretation of a classical French repertoire.

Auberge St-Vincent – *1 r. St-Vincent, 51150 Ambonnay, 20km E of Épernay on the D 201, D 1 and D 37. ℘03 26 57 01 98. www.auberge-st-vincent.com. Closed Feb holidays, Aug 18–Sept 1, Sun evenings and Mon.* This smart regional-style inn is located in the heart of the village surrounded by acres of vineyards and forest. A pleasing flower-decked façade leads into a light dining room complete with fireplace and ancient cooking utensils. Tasty traditional fare prepared by a chef who favours local produce. Renovated rooms.

Vieux Puits – *18 R. Roger-Sondag, 51160 Ay. ℘03 26 56 96 53. Closed Aug 16–31, Dec 23–Jan 7, Feb 26–Mar 11, Wed & Thu.* Take a seat in one of three rustic dining rooms or, in summer, in the interior courtyard, featuring a charming old well.

AROUND REIMS

Brasserie Le Boulingrin – *48 r. Mars, 51100 Reims. ℘03 26 40 96 22. www.boulingrin.fr. Closed Sun.* Home to Le Boulingrin since 1925, this brasserie is a favourite with the town locals who appreciate its Art Deco style and Bacchanalian-inspired frescoes of grape harvests. Tuck into appetising bistro-style dishes or treat yourself to a platter from the well-stocked oyster bar.

Au Chant des Galipes – *2 r. Chanzy, 51380 Verzy. ℘03 26 97 91 40. chantdesgalipes@wanadoo.fr.* This wine-grower's house has been converted into an inn with two contemporary-style dining rooms and an appealing courtyard-terrace. The up-to-date menu with a distinctly regional preference is full of delightful surprises, thanks in particular to the subtle use of Champagne, both on the plate and in the glass.

Au Petit Comptoir – *17 r. de Mars, 51100 Reims. ℘03 26 40 58 58. aupetitcomptoir@wanadoo.fr. Closed Dec 24–Jan 2, Sat lunchtime, Mon lunchtime and Sun.* This trendy bistro is greatly in vogue with the locals who adore its unabashed contemporary spirit and the creative culinary talents of Patrice Maillot. The kitchen is in full view of the dining room. The well-stocked wine list boasts 170 names.

La Table Anna – *6 r. Gambetta, 51100 Reims. ℘03 26 89 12 12. www.latableanna.com.* Champagne takes pride of place in the window of this establishment next to the Music School. Some of the paintings on the walls inside are the work of the owner, an artist in his spare time. His creative talent can also be appreciated in the delicious traditional dishes made with fresh market produce.

Le Jamin – *18 blvd. Jamin, 51100 Reims. ℘03 26 07 37 30. Closed Jan 15–29, Aug 14–31, Sun evenings and Mon.* Mr Milon, a trained chef, is the enthusiastic owner of this small neighbourhood restaurant. Guests are served faultless traditional dishes in an attractive country-style dining room. The daily suggestions, chalked up on the traditional slate, offer excellent value-for-money.

Café du Palais – *14 pl. Myron-Herrick, 51100 Reims. ℘03 26 47 52 54. www.cafedupalais.fr. Closed Aug 1–21, Sun, public holidays.* Founded in 1930, this cheerful café stands next to the law courts. The inhabitants of Reims appreciate its simple unfussy cuisine and dining room decorated with red hangings under the original glass roof. Copious salads, assorted cold meats, menu of the day and homemade pastries. Reasonably priced Champagne by the glass.

Grand Hôtel Continental – *93 Place Drouet-d'Erlon, 51100 Reims. ℘03 26 47 01 47. www.le-continental.fr.* The inhabitants of Reims have long

S. Sauvignier/MICHELIN

S. Sauvignier/MICHELIN

favoured this attractive bourgeois establishment along a pedestrian square in the heart of the city. Faultless, personalised service and equally impeccable contemporary cuisine.

La Vigneraie – *14 r. de Thillois, 51100 Reims. ℘03 26 88 67 27. www.vigneraie.com.* Drouet-d'Erlon Square, complete with night-clubs, theatres and cinemas, is the city's liveliest neighbourhood. La Vigneraie, the proud owner of a splendid collection of carafes, lies just off the square. Classic, tasty cuisine. Good wine list. Excellent value for money.

Le Cheval Blanc – *51400 Sept-Saulx. ℘03 26 03 90 27. www.chevalblanc-dspt-saulx.com.* Three buildings, one of them a former postal station, rise amid the Champagne vineyards. The rooms open onto a large garden bordered by a river.

Le Millénaire – *4 r. Bertin, 51100 Reims. ℘03 26 08 26 62. www.lemillenaire.com.* Two minutes from Place Royale, this spacious modern dining room is decorated with exhibitions of local art work; private lounges up in the mezzanine. Up-to-date menu oozing with creative inspiration to tantalise the taste buds of gourmets from far and near.

GOURMET SHOPPING

Deléans – *20 r. Cérès, 51100 Reims. ℘03 26 47 56 35. www.deleans.fr.* Everything is home-made and of superb quality in this delicious chocolate shop. Hundred-year-old carvings and mouldings frame the window displays, piled high with mouth-watering delicacies such as the ginger and orange flavoured Péché au diable, cognac cherry Nelusko and the Perle de Champagne, made with vintage liqueur.

Fossier – *25 Cours Jean-Baptiste-Langlet, 51100 Reims. ℘03 26 47 59 84. www.biscuits-fossier.com.* Founded in 1756, the Fossier biscuit shop and factory has long been an institution in Reims. It is the last place still to produce the legendary half-crumbly, half-crunchy pink biscuits. If you're not comfortable with the idea of dipping a biscuit into your glass of Champagne without making an awful mess, make a beeline for this shop to learn the proper etiquette of eating these sophisticated biscuits.

La Petite Friande – *15 Cours Jean-Baptiste-Langlet, 51100 Reims. ℘03 26 47 50 44.* It was in this institution of Reims founded in 1832 that the mythical dark chocolate Bouchon au marc de Champagne was first invented in 1951. It was also here that the Bulle made with vintage Champagne was created in 1987. Nowadays such inventions rank high in "France's national heritage list of delicacies".

MARKETS

AISNE

Charly-sur-Marne – *Thursday morning.*

Château-Thierry – *Friday morning, Place de la Mairie.*

Nogent-l'Artaud – *Sunday morning.*

MARNE

Avize – *Thursday morning.*

Ay – *Friday morning, Place Henri-Martin.*

Epernay – *Thursday and Saturday morning, Halle Saint-Thibault, Sunday, Place Auban-Möet.*

Reims – *Monday morning, Avenue de Laon; Tuesday morning, Place and r. St-Maurice; Wednesday, Esplanade Paul Cézanne; Thursday, Boulevard Carteret; Friday morning, Boulevard Wilson; Saturday morning, Place du Boulingrin; Sunday morning, Avenue Jean-Jaurès.*

AUBE

Bar-sur-Aube – *Saturday morning.*

Bar-sur-Seine – *Friday morning.*

Essoyes – *Tuesday morning.*

Les Riceys – *Thursday morning.*

Little Red Riding Hood

But Little Red Riding Hood had her regional map with her, and so she did not fall into the trap. She did not take the path through the wood and she did not meet the big bad wolf. Instead, she chose the picturesque touring route straight to Grandmother's house, and arrived safely with her cake and her little pot of butter.

The End

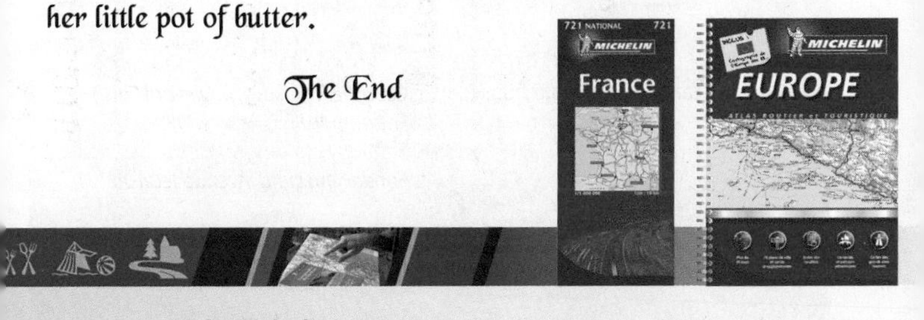

With Michelin maps, go your own way.

MICHELIN
A better way forward

6 - COGNAC

Cognac owes its very existence to the River Charente, a peaceful little waterway that allowed for shipping of the precious spirit from France to the rest of the world. Over the years, cognac has become such a widely (and sometimes inaccurately) used term that its producers have had a difficult time bringing it back into the fold of protected appellations. Its fascinating history is written on the green banks of the river, along the 80km stretch between Saintes and Angoulême. The massive storehouses rising alongside the river have been blackened over time by mould that thrives on what is known as the "Angels' Share", caused by the natural evaporation of the spirit while it is maturing in the cask. You'll also see splendid Romanesque churches and quiet little towns with red tile roofs. Throughout Charentes, with its characteristic "art de vivre", the gentle pace of life will enable you to savour the region's subtle blends of nature and culture.

Highlights

1. The Festival de la Bande Desinee in **Angoulême** (p260)
2. A picnic on the banks of the **Charente** (p255)
3. Soul and funk music at the **Fête du Cognac**.
4. Blending your own cognac at **Camus** (p258)
5. A **boat trip** (p259)

Cognac is a spirit or *eau-de-vie* that is made by distilling white wine from grapes grown in the Charentes region. The distilling process takes place until the end of March and is completed in two stages, both of which involve heating the wine through a copper alembic still. The first stage yields a liquid known as *brouillis,* a light spirit of around 30% alcohol. The second further distils the *brouillis* to obtain a colourless spirit with a maximum strength of 72%.

This is then stocked in oak casks where it takes on its characteristic colour and matures slowly, gradually losing some of its alcoholic strength. To be ready for sale, cognac has to mature for at least thirty months and have a minimum strength of 40%.

As it takes a long time to reach this point, producers are allowed to add distilled water. The same goes for the colour, which can be modified by adding an infusion of oak shavings or caramel. The secret of a good cognac lies in the blending of different growths and vintages.

Fins Bois vineyards

M. Thierry/MICHELIN

OVERVIEW

The Terroir

Michelin Local Map 327 – Charente (16) and Charente-Maritime (17).

Surface area: the Cognac vineyards cover 75,013ha divided into six districts, each with its own distinctive quality: Grande Champagne (3,428ha), Petite Champagne (15,570ha), Borderies (4,127ha), Fins Bois (31,693ha), Bons Bois (9,164ha) and Bois Ordinaires (1,031ha).

Production: 610,901hl (2007/2008).

The climate is oceanic and temperate, with relatively mild winters, warm to hot summers, rain in the spring and quite a lot of sunshine in the autumn. The soil is chalky, or part clay, part lime, with the best growing areas located on the chalkiest soil.

Wines and Spirits

The Cognac vineyards are almost exclusively made up of white grape varieties. Ugni Blanc is the most widespread, followed by Folle Blanche and Colombard. These varieties produce light acidic wine suitable for distilling.

Over the past few years, new grape varieties have been introduced to make the **vins de pays Charentais** (the Charentes region's local wines) – Chardonnay and Sauvignon for the whites, and Merlot and Cabernet for the reds and rosés.

The fortified wine **Pineau des Charentes** is made exclusively with a red or white grape juice base that derives its alcohol content from the addition of cognac that has been aged for at least a year.

Since the 2008 vintage, the system of "double fin" has ended, and producers must declare which type of product the grapes are destined for before harvest begins.

Useful Tip

If you are driving through the Cognac area in summer, make the most of the picnic sites laid out on the banks of the Charente. It's an absolute delight to stop and enjoy the shade in peaceful surroundings; and you won't have any trouble stocking up on delicious products in the local markets.

Along the Charente

Located just to the north of the vineyards of Bordeaux, there are miles of Atlantic coastline to be explored - and the Marenne-Oleron oysters to be enjoyed. Away from the sea, this region is dominated by its rivers, perfect for canoeing and boating.

- **Population:** Charente is home to around 350,000 people.
- **Michelin Map**: See the map of Cognac vineyards on p256.
- **Info:** www.cognac.fr
- **Location:** Saintes is located about 70km SE of La Rochelle by the N 137. Michelin Local Map 324, G-H-I 5, J-K 6.
- **Kids:** Atlantys water park in Saint-Jean-d'Angély
- **Timing:** Two days.

DRIVING TOUR

The River Charente, dotted with locks, bridges and ferries, winds its way between Saintes and Angoulême, telling the story of the flat-bottomed *gabares*. These were barges that travelled up-river carrying salt and spices and returned, laden with "liquid gold."

Saintes★★

With its plane trees and white houses with tiled roofs, Saintes has a southern look about it. To broach its historic and

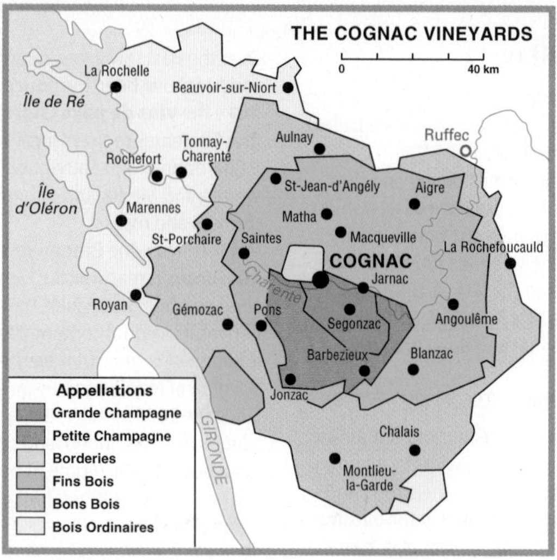

artisitic heritage, take a stroll through the **old town**★, which abounds in remarkable sights. **Cathédrale St-Pierre** was built on the site of a Romanesque church, of which only a dome remains. The cathedral dates mostly from the 15C. The original spire has been replaced by a lead dome. The Flamboyant doorway within the porch at the foot of the tower is adorned with fine carvings.

The **Présidial** *(r. Victor-Hugo, set back at the far end of the garden)*, a mansion built in 1605, now houses the **Musée des Beaux-Arts**★, mainly devoted to painting from the 15C to the 18C. One of the rooms contains 14C-19C ceramics from Saintonge province *(open Jun–Sept Tue–Sun 10am-12.30pm & 1.30–6pm; Oct–May Tue–Sun 2–5pm; closed May 1; 1.70€; no charge Wed & Sun; 05 46 93 03 94. www.saintes.fr)*.

To reach the 11C **Église St-Eutrope**, head west through the old town. The church was an important stop on the pilgrim route to Santiago de Compostela. The only remaining parts of the original building are the transept and the Romanesque chancel, with magnificent historiated **capitals**. The plan of the **crypt**★ is identical to that of the church above it. Follow the signs from the church to the amphitheatre, or **Arènes**★ *(access via r. St-Eutrope and r. Lacurie)*, built in the early 1C AD. One of the oldest amphitheatres in the Roman world, it held 20 000 spectators *(open Jun–Sept daily 10am–8pm; Oct–Mar Mon–Sat 10am–12.3-pm & 1-5pm, Sun 1.30–5pm; Apr-May Mon-Sat 10am-6.30pm, Sun 1.30-6pm; closed Jan 1, May 1, Nov 1, Dec 25; 2€; 05 46 97 73 85)*.

Standing on the opposite bank of the Charente is the **Arc de Germanicus**★, with twin arcades, erected in the year AD 19. It was a votive – not a triumphal – arch. Behind it, the **Musée Archéologique**★ houses an interesting Roman lapidiary collection and the metal remains of a **ceremonial chariot**★ (late 1C AD) *(open Jun–Sept Mon–Sat 10am–6pm, Sun 2–6pm; Oct–May Mon–Sat 10am–5pm, Sun 2–5pm; closed Jan 1, May 1, Dec 25; 1.80€, no charge Sun & Wed; 05 46 74 20 97; www.ville-saintes.fr)*.

A few hundred yards east, you come to the large **Abbaye aux Dames**, which was consecrated in 1047. It was placed in the hands of Benedictine nuns who were entrusted with the education of young daughters of the nobility. The Abbey Church, **Église Abbatiale**★ is in the local Saintonge Romanesque style and is surrounded by convent buildings. The main **doorway** is adorned with fine sculptures Inside, thirteen tapestries illustrate the book of Genesis *(open*

Apr–Sept daily 10am–12.30pm & 2–7pm; Oct–Mar daily 2–6pm; 1hr 30min guided tours available late Jun–3rd Fri in Sept; closed Dec 25–Jan 1; 2€; 05 46 97 48 48; 05 46 97 48 48).

Head SW out of Saintes along D 128.

You leave Saintes by driving alongside the quays on the left bank of the Charente, passing a row of fine mansions belonging to wine merchants. The buildings gradually give way to pastureland and then you reach the vineyards around **Courcoury**, where tall houses flanked by storehouses indicate that this is wine-making country. From April to late October you can take the ferry across to **Chaniers** to see the pretty Romanesque church.

Alternatively, continue on D 128, then turn left towards Beillan. After crossing the Charente, bear right on D 24 heading towards Cognac.

Dompierre-sur-Charente

The stores lining the Charente testify to a long-standing wine-making tradition. The chain ferry to the opposite bank is the last of its kind operating in France. At **Domaine de Flaville**, which you reach along a narrow road, there is an excellent choice of Pineau des Charentes, cognac and vins de pays, including a worthwhile Chardonnay Moelleux. Mireille et Jacky Bureau make welcoming hosts and are the fifth generation at the estate *(302 rte. du Pineau, 17610 Dompierre-sur-Charente; open mid-Jun–mid-Sept 8.30am–7.30pm; rest of the year Mon–Sat 8.30am–7pm, Sun 8.30am–12.30pm; 05 46 91 00 45).*

The picturesque road between Dompierre and Cognac runs alongside the shady banks of the Charente.

Cognac★

The handsome town of Cognac is very atmospheric, partly because of the contrast of the smart buildings and the blackened wine cellars that you frequently pass. This black soot is in fact *torula compniacensis*, a mould that

Cognac cellar

© Alain Couillaud/iStockphoto

thrives on the alcohol fumes released through the natural evaporation known as the "Angels' Share". The cellars, where the precious nectar matures away from the light, have similarly blackened inside walls. The steep streets of old Cognac run up between the quays and the Church of St-Léger. Access to the town was once through the 15C gateway, **Porte St-Jacques**, which leads on to **rue Grande** and the old quarter. Rue Grande, originally the main street in Cognac is lined with 15C houses with timber fronts. Rue Saulnier, on the other hand, is Renaissance in style. Its name recalls one of the traditional activities of Cognac – the salt trade. It has retained its irregular cobblestone surface and its handsome 16C and 17C houses. Also of interest are **rue du Palais**, **rue Henri-Germain**, and **rue Magdeleine** with its Maison de la Salamandre.

For a good introduction to the surrounding area, visit the **Espace Découverte en Pays du Cognac**, charmingly arranged in an old wine merchant's premises. There's a model of the countryside, as well as interactive exhibits and an excellent audio-visual show cocnetrating not on cognac the prodcut, but the river, the history and the surrounding landscape *(Pl. de la Salle-Verte; open Jul–Aug daily 10am–6.30pm; June and Sept Tue–Sun 10am–6.30pm; Apr-May and Oct Tue–Sun 10.30am–6pm; Mar and Nov Tue–Sun 2–6pm; no charge; 05 45 36 03 65; www.espace-decouverte.fr).*

The **Musée des Arts du Cognac**★★, the only one of its kind in France, has recently been set up near the quays along the Charente. It is dedicated to cognac, focusing on the economic role of the brandy through a description of the trades and techniques associated with it: wine-growing, distilling, glass-making, cooperage, corks and labelling. You can also see clips of famous films in which cognac is featured *(Pl. de la Salle-Verte; open Jul–Aug daily 10am–6.30pm; Apr–Sun and Sept–Oct Tue–Sun 11am–6pm; Nov–Mar Tue–Sun 2–5.30pm; closed Jan 1, Nov 1, Dec 25; 4.50€; 05 45 32 07 25. www.musees-cognac.fr).*

The cognac trading companies or **Maisons de Cognac**★ stretch out along the riverside quays, near the port.

Camus

Visit by guided tour (45min) June–Sept Mon 2-6pm, Tue–Sat 10.30am–12.30pm & 2-6pm. Oct–Apr by appt. Closed public holidays. 7€ with tasting of one cognac, 20€ with tasting of three, 160€ for masterclass where you blend your own cognac. Enquire for price of other tours. 05 45 32 28 28. www.camus.fr.

The tour offered by this cognac trading company, founded in 1863, has recently been refurbished, and is very slick, looking at the history of cognac, its distillation, ageing and blending through beautifully-presented exhibits, and with a lovely stop at the end in the library of old cognacs. Visitors can select from a number of tours, including matching foods to cognac, or even travel with Camus up to the cognac producing island of the Ile de Ré.

Otard

In the castle. Visit by guided tour (1hr, last departure 1hr before closing) Apr–Oct 11m–noon & 2–6pm. Nov–Dec Mon–Fri 11am–noon & 2–5pm. Closed May 1, Nov 1, Nov 11, Dec 25. 8€. 05 45 36 88 88. www.otard.com.

This 15C and 16C château recalls the memory of the Valois family and François I, who was born here. It was sequestrated by the Republicans during the Revolution before being bought in 1795 by Baron Otard, who was from Charentes and of Norwegian and Scottish extraction. During the tour you can see some of the old castle rooms, such as the Helmet Room or Salle au Casque, where Richard the Lionheart married his son Philip to Amélie de Cognac. The room contains a magnificent chimney-piece. There is also a small museum with a collection of 1920s advertising posters, and the tour ends with a visit to the wine store and a tasting.

Hennessy

Visit by guided tour (1hr 15min) May 2–Sept 10am–6pm. Mar–April and Oct–Dec 10am–5pm. Closed May 1, Dec 25. 10€. 05 45 35 72 68. www.hennessy-cognac.com.

Richard Hennessy, a former captain of Louis XV's Irish Brigade, settled in Cognac in 1760. In 1765 he founded a trading company that was to prove very prosperous, and is today owned by LVMH. The warehouses of the company are located on both banks of the River Charente, which you can cross by boat. One of the buildings displays the three symbols of cognac: copper (for the still), oak (for the casks) and glass (for the bottles). In the wine stores the various stages of brandy making are explained with the help of special effects involving sounds and smells.

Martell

Visit by guided tour (1hr; reservations advised) Apr–Oct Mon–Fri 10am–5pm; weekends and public holidays noon–5pm. 8€. 05 45 36 33 33. www.visitez-martell.com.

Jean Martell, a native of Jersey, settled in 1715. The tour includes the semi-automated bottling process, and the stores and cellars where the brandy is left to age. In the blending room cognacs of different origins are mixed. Some of the blends, such as the Cordon Bleu, are famous worldwide. Rooms in the house of the founder recreate the life and work of an entrepreneur in the early 18C, but most interesting of all is the recreation of the *gabare* boat, taking the cognac to market in the 18C.

Rémy Martin
4km south-west on D 732. Head towards Pons, then turn left onto D 47 towards Merpins. Visit by guided tour (1hr 30min; reservations required) May–Sept. Mon-Sat 9am-12,30 & 1.30-6pm. Rest of year by appt. 8€ 05 45 35 76 66. www.remy.com.
This firm, founded in 1724, makes its cognac exclusively from the elite Grande Champagne and Petite Champagne wines. A small train takes visitors on a tour of the plant, going through the cooper's shop, part of the vineyard and various cellars and stores used for ageing.

Head E for Jarnac via St-Brice (D 157)

The narrow road follows the winding course of the Charente. Near the magnificent 16C **Logis de Garde-Épée**, a dolmen comes into view. Not far from there in the middle of a field stands a very fine church, **Église de Châtre**★. It was the abbey church of a convent destroyed during the Wars of Religion. Note the festoons on the main doorway and the beautifully carved motifs.

Bourg-Charente

Bourg-Charente stands on the left bank of the Charente, looking over the spot where the river branches out into several arms, forming low islands covered in meadows. The façade of the **church** in the Saintonge Romanesque style consists of three levels, with a triangular pediment at the top. Note the Latin Cross plan of the church, and the three domes on pendentives. Inside, on the left wall of the nave, there is a 13C fresco of the Adoration of the Magi. The **château** standing on a rise on the other side of the Charente dates from the time of Henri IV. Visitors are warmly welcomed to **Domaine de la Grange du Bois**, which produces a good Pineau des Charentes aged in casks for ten years *(SCEA Cartais-Lamaure, 16200 Bourg-Charente; open daily by appt. 10am–7pm; 05 45 81 10 17)*.
Also worth visiting in the area, in the attractive town of **Segonzac**, is Chateau Fontpinot, the home base of **Frapin Cognac**, one of the smaller, more exclusive houses that produce excellent quality *(05 45 83 40 03 ; www.cognac-frapin.com)*.

Jarnac

The native town of the former President of France, François Mitterrand, whose family ran a vinegar factory, has changed so little over the years that it could easily provide a backdrop to a 1930s-style film. Visitors can go on a **boat trip** aboard the *Chabot*, between Jarnac and Bourg-Charente, for a commentary on the history of the Salt and Cognac Route *(Jarnac bridge; departures Jul–Aug 10.30am, 2.15pm, 4.15pm; May weekends and bank holidays 3.30pm; Jun, Sept Tue, Sat, Sun 3.30pm; reservations advised; 7.50 € 05 45 82 09 35)*.
You can also find out about the origin of the cooperage industry and the all-important interaction between wood and alcohol by going on the **Circuit du chêne** *(2hr 30min)* which includes explanatory visits with a woodcutter and a barrel-maker. The tour finishes up with a traditional tasting at a distillery *(tourist office 05 45 81 09 30; www.jarnac-tourisme.com)*.
The former **Abbey Church** dates from the 11C and has a square tower. The sober-looking **Protestant Church** was built in 1820 and is open in summer.
The **Musée François-Mitterrand**, known as the Orangerie Cultural Centre is housed in a former brandy store on the banks of the Charente. The exhibition contains some of the works of art presented to François Mitterrand by people from all over the world during his 14-year presidency. On the way out, peruse the *Livre d'Or*, where visitors leave their comments. The President is buried in Grands-Maisons cemetery to the west of Jarnac *(open Jul–Aug 10.30am–12.30 & 2.30–6.30pm; Sept–Oct and Jan–Jun Wed–Sun 2–6pm; closed May 1; 5€; 05 45 81 38 88)*.
Maison Courvoisier is set up in a former warehouse that has been attractively refurbished. The museum proposes an interesting tour through the blending workshop, which resem-

bles a perfumery. Stills and barrels are on display to explain how cognac is produced. You are then greeted by the heady fumes of the evaporating "Angels' Share" as you enter the reconstructed *chai (Pl. du Château; guided tour (1h) April 25–Sept 10am-1pm & 2–6pm; 8€; ☏05 45 35 56 16; www.courvoisier.com).*

The *Espace Voyage* in **Maison Louis Royer** presents the production of cognac and its global exportation. *(Quai de la Charmille; open Jul–Aug Wed–Fri 10am–noon & 2–5pm; Sat 10m–noon & 2–6pm; Sun 2–6pm; no charge; ☏05 45 81 02 72; www.louis-royer.com).*

Leave Jarnac E on D 22 to Bassac. Visit abbey; continue on D22.

Châteauneuf-sur-Charente

The church, **Église St-Pierre** has a doorway with intricate carvings of foliage, animals and figures on its mouldings. The upper level of the façade, separated from the lower by a cornice supported by carved modillions (amusing figures of people), is pierced by a bay with a statue of an Apostle on either side. On the left, there is an equestrian statue of Emperor Constantine (with the head missing).

Drive to Angoulême along D 699.

Angoulême★★ and Comic Strips

The 'other' capital of the Charente, Angouleme is an attractive town with wide tree-lined avenues mixed with Art Nouveau housing, and upsacle graffiti of comic book heros. Definitely an interesting place to spend a few hours exploring.

- **Population:** The town itself has around 43,000 inhabitants.
- **Info:** www.angouleme-tourisme.com
- **Location:** In the Charente.
- **Kids:** The whole city will appeal to children.
- **Timing:** It has to be the cartoon festival in January.

Angoulême★★

Angoulême is pleasant to explore on foot, with its maze of narrow streets, its beautiful old buildings and wonderful views from the ramparts of the **upper town**★★. It is also fun in late January when the place goes wild during the Comic Strip *(Bande Dessinée)* Festival. The whole town bears the mark of the festival, from the **painted walls** to the plaques of street names shaped like comic strip speech bubbles.

Electronic Games and Interactive Media School (ENJMIN)★

121 r. de Bordeaux. Open Jul–Aug Mon–Fri 10am–7pm, weekends 2–7pm. Sept–Jun Tue–Fri 10am–6pm. Closed Jan 1, May 1, Dec 25. 5€. ☏05 45 38 65 68. www.enjmin.fr.

The centre (connected to the Centre National de la Bande Dessinee et de l'Image) pays homage to great comic strip authors including Töpffer, Christophe (*La Famille Fenouillard*), Pinchon (*Bécassine*), Forton (*Les Pieds Nickelés*), and Alain St-Ogan (*Zig et Puce*), as well as the Belgians Hergé (*Tintin*) and Franquin (*Gaston Lagaffe*), the Americans Raymond (*Flash Gordon*) and Schulz (*Peanuts*), and the French Goscinny and Uderzo (*Astérix*).

Musée du Papier "Le Nil"

134 r. de Bordeaux (opp. the CNBDI). Open Jul–Sept Tue–Sat noon-6.30pm. Oct–Jun Tue–Sun 2–6pm. ☏05 45 92 73 43. www.alienor.org.

The former Bardou-Le Nil paper mill, which specialised in the manufacture of cigarette papers, operated here until 1970. It has since been converted into a museum on the papermaking industry, where you can learn about a tradition that grew up in Angoulême thanks to the purity of its river water. In the 17C, the town counted almost 100 mills that supplied Holland with watermarked paper. An exhibition called *Imaginaires d'usines* describes the different stages in the industrial manufacture of paper and cardboard.

Cathédrale St-Pierre★

This dates from the 12C. It was partially destroyed by the Calvinists in 1562, and restored in 1634, followed by a more complete restoration started by the architect Abadie in 1866.

The sculptures on the **façade**★★ form an impressively lively tableau carved in the Poitiers style. More than 70 characters, statues and bas-reliefs illustrate the Last Judgement. The ensemble is presided over by a Christ in Majesty, surrounded by the symbols of the Evangelists, and angels and saints set in medallions. Note also the archivolts and friezes above and around the side doors with their finely carved foliage, animals and figures. On the lintel of the first blind doorway, on the right, are strange scenes of combat based on episodes from the medieval epic *La Chanson de Roland* (Song of Roland).

Atlantys Water Park, *Avenue de Marennes, 17400 Saint Jean d'Angely t05 46 59 21 50; Open Wed-Mon 10am-8pm (Tue til 9.30pm); 4.50€; www.casilis.fr* A very popular water park close to Angouleme.

WINE BUYING GUIDE

INFORMATION

Bureau National Interprofessionnel du Cognac (BNIC) – *23 allées du Champs-de-Mars, BP 18, 16101 Cognac Cedex. ✆05 45 35 60 00. www.cognac.fr.*

Comité National du Pineau-des-Charentes – *112 ave. Victor-Hugo, 16100 Cognac. ✆05 45 32 09 27. www.pineau.fr.*

OVERVIEW CHARACTERISTICS

Cognac – Before a cognac can be sold it has to be at least two and a half years old, counting from 1 October of the year the grapes were harvested. It is the age of the youngest *eau-de-vie* in the blend that determines the age of the cognac.

What cognac labels mean: **VS (Very Special:** The youngest *eau-de-vie* is at least two years old. **VSOP (Very Special Old Pale) or ★★★**: The youngest *eau-de-vie* is at least four years old.

Napoléon, **XO**, **Hors d'âge**: The youngest *eau-de-vie* is at least six ears old. The term "*fine*" is allowed for *eaux-de-vie* made with a wine that has AOC *(Appellation d'origine contrôlée)*

Architecture graffitti, Angoulême

© Marc/Fotolia.com

status, such as Grande Champagne.

Pineau des Charentes – The fortified wines bearing this label are liqueurs, or *mistelles*, obtained by mixing fresh (unfermented) grape juice with cognac. They may be white or rosé, young or old.

Vins de pays – The Charentes region's *vins de pays* are white, red or rosé. They should be drunk young. The whites go well with seafood.

PRICES

Cognac – from 15€ upwards.

Pineau des Charentes – 8€ to 15€.

Vins de pays – from 3€.

ADDRESSES

STAY

Chambre d'hôte Anne et Dominique Trouvé – *5 r. de l'Église, 17810 St-Georges-des-Coteaux, 9km northwest of Saintes heading for Rochefort on N 137 then D 127. 05 46 92 96 66. adtrouve@yahoo.fr. Closed Nov 15–Mar 28. 4 rooms.* . A stay in this 18C Charentes farmhouse set in a large garden is a must. The stables and hayloft have been converted into a huge space combining sitting room, library and billiards room. The bedrooms with regional furnishings are all named after famous authors.

Hôtel Résidence – *25 ave. Victor-Hugo, 16100 Cognac. 05 45 36 62 40. www.hotellaresidence-cognac.com. – Closed Dec 20–Jan 3. 18 rooms. 6.50€.* The hotel's sober façade with its exposed stones provides a contrast with the colour scheme inside. Sitting room in shades of green and garnet, modern breakfast room in pink and fuchsia, and functional rooms in brightly coloured prints.

Messageries – *R. des Messageries, 17100 Saintes. 05 46 93 64 99. www.hotel-des-messageries.com. Closed Dec 19 –Jan 7. 33 rooms. 7€.* Ideally located in the heart of the old town, this former stagecoach inn built around a courtyard dates from 1792. It is bathed in a quiet atmosphere and gives onto a peaceful alleyway. Country-style rooms. Convenient garage.

Logis de l'Astrée – *17770 St-Bris-des-Bois. 05 46 93 44 07. www.logisdelastree.com. 4 rooms. 7€.* Elegance and good taste abound in this fine residence tucked away in a sheltered garden. Spacious rooms are decorated with good antiques, and you'll enjoy breakfast with a vineyard view.

Valois – *35 r. du 14-Juillet, 16100 Cognac. 05 45 36 83 00. hotel.levalois@wanadoo.fr. Closed Dec 24–Jan 2. 45 rooms. 7.80€.* This recently built hotel has a wonderful location a stone's throw from the storehouses, right in the centre of town. Spacious rooms with functional furniture, a pleasantly redecorated bar-lounge in the lobby, and a sauna and gym for guests.

EAT

L'Amaryllis de Courcoury – *Pl. de l'Église, 17100 Courcoury. 05 46 74 09 91. amaryllisdecourcoury@wanadoo.fr.* Ths pleasant country restaurant near the Romanesque church in a small village on the Charente serves up tasty traditional dishes. Rustic-style décor with southern flair.

Taverne du Coq d'Or – *Pl. François-Ier, 16100 Cognac. 05 45 82 02 56.* The mosaic cockerel on the sign proudly welcomes clients who come to the restaurant (founded in 1908) for the calf's head in gribiche sauce (vinaigrette, chopped boiled eggs, gherkins, capers and herbs) or the veal chops with ceps and Pineau des Charentes gravy. Strictly Limousin beef and beautifully fresh ingredients contribute to the place's popularity. Recently renovated.

Le Bistrot Galant – *28 r. St-Michel, 17100 Saintes. 05 46 93 08 51. Closed Sun except lunch on public holidays, and Mon.* The chef Patrick Aumon creates temptingly inventive dishes with market-fresh produce that you can eat in one of the bright dining rooms.

Le Saintonge – *Rte. de Royan, at Complexe Stes-Végas, 17100 Saintes. 05 46 97 00 00. Closed evenings on Sun and Mon.* The 1970s-style decor and neat layout set the scene for Guy Gireau's classical fare. You can try crayfish tempura, choice meat ***à la plancha***, salmon and mussel blanquette, or boned quail with truffle sauce. Bon appétit!

Les Pigeons Blancs – *110 r. J.-Brisson, 16100 Cognac. 05 45 82 16 36. Closed Jan 1–15, Sun evenings and Mon lunchtime.* Pleasant lodge located in a quiet residential neighbourhood. Nicely appointed dining room, shaded terrace fronting on the garden, and individually-decorated guestrooms.

Château – *15 pl. du Château, 16200 Jarna. 05 45 81 07 17. Closed Jan 17–31, Aug 9–31, Sun evenings, Tue evenings, Wed evenings and Mon.* This town house covered in attractive Virginia creeper gives onto the square where the castle once was. Inside, the dining room is bright and stylish and serves personalised traditional cuisine with flavours from Charentes.

7 - CORSICA

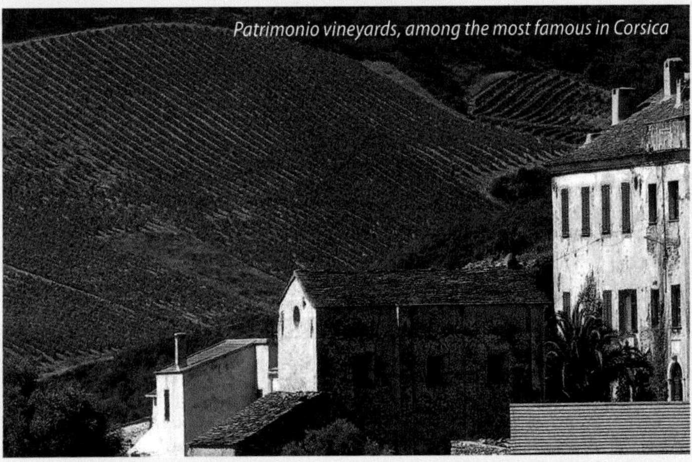

Patrimonio vineyards, among the most famous in Corsica

G. Magnin / MICHELIN

The "Island of Beauty", as the French call it, is half way between the Cote d'Azur and Italy; a tranquil island rising steeply out of the deep blue Mediterranean sea. Wild vines have been part of the scenery since the Phoenicians settled here thousands of years ago, but commercial wine production only developed relatively recently. Vineyards were established on gravelly slopes, along sun-drenched ravines and on arid soils, where vines roots have to struggle deep into the ground in search of nourishment; the struggle develops complexity in the resulting wine. There are vineyards right around the coast, so that a wine tour is a perfect opportunity for a complete tour of Corsica - although remember that winding cliff roads make driving slow going at times, and if you venture inland, things get mountainous very quickly.

Corsica is a popular destination for French and Italian holidaymakers, so try to plan your visit for spring or autumn, when the summer crowds are gone and weather conditions are ideal. The island is sunnier than anywhere else on mainland France, with an average of 2,750 hours of sunshine per year), so you don't need to worry about going off-season. Corsica has been subject to numerous territory disputes over the years, and there are ruined castles and crumbling fortifications to explore, while for children there are watersports at every point along the coast, and inland hiking, mountain biking and even skiing in winter.

With all of this, tourism is the key economic activity on the island, but wine is the most important export in volume and value, and you will be warmly welcomed. The drive from north to south is around 180km, and you will encounter enthusiastic wine growers, proud of producing quality wines which are only one of the fascinating charms of this jewel of the Mediterranean.

Highlights

1 The Italian paintings in the Fesch Musuem in **Ajaccio** (p268)

2 The coast-to-coast walk **across Cap Corse** (p270)

3 An aperitif overlooking the busy harbour of **Saint-Florent** (p267)

4 Scuba diving in **Figari Bay** (p271)

5 The traditional Corsican village of **Pigna** (p265)

OVERVIEW

The Terroir
Michelin Local Map 345 – Corse-du-Sud (2B) and Haute-Corse (2A).
Area: about 7,000ha spread all round the island.
Production: about 350,000hl (114,000 in AOC), including 45% rosés, 40% reds, 10% whites and 5% Muscat-du-Cap-Corse. In this Mediterranean climate, expect hot, dry summers, temperate springs and autumns and cold winters in the mountains.
The effects of the sun are tempered by altitude and the influence of the sea. The soil varies, featuring a predominance of schist in the north, granite in the south and west, limestone in the Patrimonio area and clayey sand along the east coast.

The Wines
Corsican wines bear the effects of the sun, characterised by a rather high alcohol content. They are made from traditional grape varieties: Vermentino for the whites, Nieluccio and Sciaccarello for the reds and rosés. Continental grape varieties are used to make the *Vins de Pays de l'Île-de-Beauté:* Chardonnay, Pinot Noir, Cinsault, Grenache.
AOC – Corse AOC over most of the island except in the Patrimonio and Ajaccio terroirs: Corse, Corse-Coteaux-du-Cap-Corse, Muscat-du-Cap-Corse, Corse-Calvi, Corse-Sartène, Corse-Figari, Corse-Porto-Vecchio, Ajaccio, Patrimonio.
Vins de Pays – Vins de Pays de l'Île-de-Beauté, produced all over the island.

Corsican Wine Routes

Follow our routes through the coasts and mountains of Corsica for an insight into its wines and history.

- **Michelin Map:** 345, or local map p266.
- **Info:** www.vinsdecorse.com
- **Location:** Most vineyards lieon the coast, concentrated around Cap Corse.
- **Timing:** Due to inaccessibility, allow four to five days.
- **Don't Miss:** The fishing villages of Centuri-Port, Erbalunga.

DRIVING TOURS

1 BALAGNE VINEYARDS

63km starting from Calvi.

A tour of the Balagne vineyards offers a good opportunity of discovering splendid mountainous landscapes between Lumio and Belgodère, with vines clinging to the screes. Attractive stone villages, with red-tiled houses and increasing numbers of restaurants and artisan workshops, make this a rewarding area to explore. This is where **Corse-Calvi AOC** and Vins de Pays are produced.

Calvi★

Proudly established round a luminous bay, against a background of often snow-covered mountains, Calvi is one of the most beautiful Corsican sites. The ochre-coloured walls of the **Citadel**★★ tower above the lower town. A walk along the watch path offers fine **views**★. The **fortifications**★ were erected by the Genoese at the end of the 15C. The 13C **Église St-Jean-Baptiste**, overlooking the place d'Armes, was rebuilt in 1570 after being severely damaged by the explosion of a powder magazine.
The **seafront**★, with its cafés and restaurants along the quayside lined with palm trees, offers an ever lively spec-

tacle. There is also a long sandy beach stretching 5km from the town itself. Wine producers in Calvi include the excellent **Clos Landry** (*see Shopping Guide*).

N 197 towards Île-Rousse.

AOC Calvi winemakers have also established a Route des Vins to encourage you to visit the vineyards (for the full route, contract Domaine de la Figarella in Calenzana *t04 95 65 07 24, Open Mon-Sat 11am-1pm & 4-8pm*). Also in Calenzana, **Domaine Orsini** offers a good visit (*see Shopping Guide*).

Lumio★

Rising like an amphitheatre above its large Baroque church flanked by a lofty openwork campanile, this opulent market town of the Balagne region stands amid olive trees and orchards, offering panoramic views of the gulf of Calvi. The long winding street offers a pleasant stroll. As far as wine is concerned, the **Clos Culombu** is worth a visit (*see Shopping Guide*).

Sant'Ambroggio Marina

The Sant'Ambroggio marina offers good facilities for yachtsmen, and has a sand beach set inside the curve of the bay.

Turn right onto the narrow D 313, then right again onto D 151 towards Pigna.

Corbara's convent

After 2km, take the minor road on the left (statue of St Dominic).
The entrance to the convent is in the centre of the main façade. Cloister and church: visit by guided tour only Jul–Aug Tue-Sun 3pm. Rest of the year guided tours by request at 3pm. No tour required to visit the church in summer. 04 95 60 06 73.

This former orphanage, founded in 1430 at the foot of Monte Sant'Angelo and turned into a convent in 1456, was ruined during the Revolution then rebuilt and extended by the Dominicans from 1857 onwards. The **conventual church**, dating from 1735, overlooks

View of Calvi
S. Sauvignier/MICHELIN

the bay of Algajola, the lower Balagne region and the village of Pigna.

Pigna★

Lined with carefully restored houses bedecked with flowers, the cobbled or stepped winding streets and the paved village square are very attractive.
Since the end of the 1960s, Pigna has become a symbol of the revival of traditional crafts and music. Various Corsican crafts, and locally produced musical instruments, are promoted in the **Casa di l'artigiani** (*open Jul–Aug 10am–1.30pm & 2.30–8pm; Apr–Jun and Sept–Oct Mon 2.30-6.30pm, Tue–Sat 10.30am–12.30pm & 2.30–6.30pm; 04 95 61 75 55; www.casa-artigiani.com*).

Turn left onto the mountain road separating the Regino and Algajola basins and leading to the mountain village of Sant'Antonino.

Sant'Antonino★★

Like an eyrie towering some 500m above the last slopes of the Balagne, the village offers a harmonious maze of narrow cobbled streets and vaulted passages. Following its successful restoration, it has become a popular tourist sight and a centre for the revival of Corsican crafts. As you walk clockwise round the village, you will see the remarkable **panorama**★★ encompassing the Regino

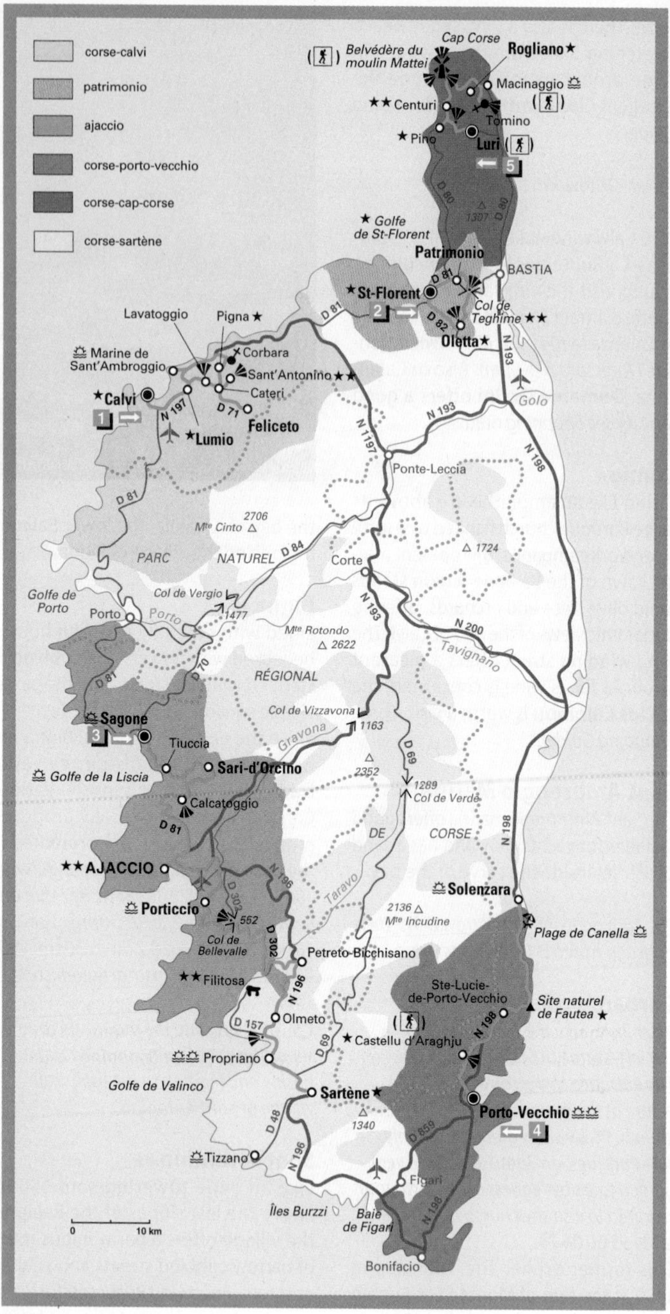

Valley, the undulating Balagne region between Belgodère and Lumio, the snow-covered mountains, Algajola bay and the sea.

Return to D 151 then turn left onto D 71.

Feliceto
This village, surrounded with orchards, overlooks the Regino Valley where excellent wines, such as those of the **Clos Reginu e Prove** (*see Shopping Guide*), are produced. Below stands the Baroque church with its dome and tiered tower.

Turn back and, at the crossroads, continue along D 71 towards Lumio.

Cateri
Nestling among olive trees, Cateri rises above the Algajola basin. Walk to the end of the village through narrow cobbled streets linked by vaulted passages and lined by lofty granite houses occupied by various craftsmen.

Lavatoggio
From the platform in front of the church or from the terrace of Le Belvédère restaurant (100m further), the **view**★ extends over the fine beach of Algajola, the coast and the foothills of the Balagne, west of the crest-line separating them from the Regino basin. The village was once famous for the quality of its springs.

Drive to Lumio, then to Calvi along N 197.

2 PATRIMONIO VINEYARDS
60km.

The **Patrimonio AOC** vineyards surrounding the gulf of St-Florent owe their reputation to their red wines grown on an enclave of limestone soil barely covering an area of 400ha.
Wine growers here were the first to go in for quality. A tour of the area will enable you to discover not only fine wines but also splendid landscapes and mountain villages which seem to defy time.

Saint-Florent★
Set inside a beautiful **gulf**★, St-Florent is a seaside resort and a marina lined with colourful houses, dominated by the fortifications of its citadel. Nearby vineyards include **Clos Teddi** that has joined forces with two other local vineyards to open a boutique in the town (*see Shopping Guide*).
The **old town**★ surrounds the church and its belfry overlooking the harbour protected by a long pier. **Place des Portes**, surrounded by outdoor cafés, is the real centre of the city. Built on a promontory by the Genoese, the **citadel** founded in 1439 towers above the town and the harbour. The **former Cathédrale du Nebbio**★★ **(Église Santa-Maria-Assunta)** is one of the most significant examples of religious architecture in Corsica. Built in the Pisan Romanesque style, it was probably completed around 1140 *(1km along the narrow street starting opposite the war memorial and heading towards Poggio-d'Oletta; to visit, enquire at the tourist office 04 95 37 06 04)*.

Leave St-Florent S along D 82.

The **Nebbio** is an area of vineyards, olive groves, orchards and pastures, criss-crossed by drystone walls, very appropriately named the "golden conch".

Oletta★
The tall white, ochre and pink houses of Oletta rise in terraces up the green slopes of a hill. The pleasant **view**★ encompasses the gulf of St-Florent and the Nebbio. The surrounding area is famous for its ewe's-milk cheese, which goes very well with the rich wines produced in the neighbouring village of **Poggio-d'Oletta**. **Domaine Leccia** is among the leading producers of Patrimonio wine (*see Shopping Guide*).

Rejoin D 38 and turn right.

The road offers extended **views**★ over the next 9km. The **Teghime pass**★★, situated at an altitude of 536m, is often swept by the violent *libecciu* wind blowing from the west, but offers **views**★★ over the gulf of St-Florent.

At the pass, turn left onto D 81 towards Patrimonio.

Patrimonio
The houses and large church of Patrimonio are scattered over fertile hillsides covered with orchards and vineyards. The Domaine **Antoine Arena** (*see Shopping Guide*) is one of many prominent estates in the area. Most wine growers also produce Muscat-du-Cap-Corse.
The **Église St-Martin**★ (16C and 19C) has a 2.29m limestone statue of the **Nativu**★, standing next to the war memorial, protected by wire fencing. This statue features prominent shoulders and ears, a protruding chin and a mysterious engraving on the torso.

Return to St-Florent along D 81.

3 THE AJACCIO AND SARTÈNE VINEYARDS
150km starting from Sagone.

Alongside Napoleon, Ajaccio takes pride in its small vineyard, hardly more than 20ha of **Ajaccio AOC**, covering the hillsides overlooking the gulfs of Ajaccio.

Sagone
Sagone has a large beach, a marina and facilities for water sports (sailing and diving schools). The **Genoese tower**, to the west of the town, stands guard over the cove of Sagone and the harbour.

Tiuccia
This small seaside resort lies inside the **gulf of La Liscia**; it is overlooked by the ruins of Capraja castle.

Beach in Golfe d'Ajaccio

A. de Valroger / MICHELIN

Turn left onto D 601.

Sari-d'Orcino
This is an area of terraced olive groves and orchards of orange and lemon trees, as well as vineyards which wine-growers have worked hard to keep going.

Head S along D 101.

Calcatoggio
This large hamlet and its fruit gardens overhang the gulf of Sagone and the inland area. Fine **view**★.

Turn left onto D 81.

Ajaccio★★
In the **old town**★, which corresponds to the ancient Genoese city, the 200m long pier of the citadel offers an excellent **view**★ of the seafront. The 2-year-old Napoleon was christened in the Renaissance **cathedral** in July 1771. Rue Bonaparte leads to place du Maréchal-Foch, the very hub of daily life in Ajaccio.
The Quatre-Lions fountain is surmounted by the statue of **Bonaparte Premier Consul**. The town hall houses the **Salon napoléonien**★, an exhibition room displaying mementoes of the Emperor and his family. (*open Mon–Fri 9–11.45am & 2–5.45/6.45pm; closed public holidays; 2.30€; 04 95 51 52 62).*
Rue du Cardinal-Fesch (U Borgu), a long, bustling shopping street, runs through the former "Borgo". The **Musée Fesch**★★ houses the most important collection of **Italian painting**★★★ in France apart from the Louvre collection (*closed for renovations; 04 95 21 48 17. www.musee-fesch.com.)*

Leave Ajaccio along N 193 and follow N 196 towards Sartène.

At the N 196 / D 302 intersection, at a place called Pisciatello, you will find the **Clos Capitoro** (*see Shopping Guide*).

Turn back and turn left onto D 55 towards Porticcio.

Porticcio

The tourist trade of this seaside resort, located within easy striking distance of Ajaccio, is developing fast. Sand beaches, numerous hotels and restaurants, a thalassotherapy centre and residential complexes attract many holidaymakers. From the extremity of the headland, the view extends over the Ajaccio roadstead and Sanguinaires islands, recalling Alphonse Daudet's atmospheric tale of the Sanguinaires lighthouse.
On leaving Porticcio, the road skirts the long stretch of **Agosta beach**. *Turn left onto D 255A*. At the end of the road, the **Bellevalle pass** offers a fine view of the gulf and the alluvial plain of La Gravona.

Turn right onto D 302

On the way, stop in **Pila-Canale** where the **Domaine de Pratavone** is worth a visit *(see Shopping Guide)*.

7km further on, turn left onto D 757.

Petreto-Bicchisano

Situated at an important intersection, this village actually consists of two villages: Bicchisano, the lower one, along N 196 and Petreto, the upper one, along D 420. Bicchisano spreads its massive granite houses on both sides of the road.

Drive S along N 196.

Olmeto

The fine granite houses of this large village rise in tiers up the steep south-facing slope of the Punta di Buturettu (alt 870m). The ruins of the **Castello della Rocca** crown the isolated hill which stands opposite the village, to the east.
N 196 runs down towards Propriano, offering fine **glimpses**★ of the gulf of Valinco and the plain of Baracci planted with olive trees.

Propriano

Sheltering deep inside the gulf of Valinco with its calm, clear waters, this small harbour is today a busy tourist centre and a seaside resort sought after for its water sports facilities and numerous beaches of fine sand.

Sartène★

The **Corse-Sartène Appellation** covers a relatively wide area extending from the shores of the gulf of Propriano to the back country around Sartène. These are the sunniest vineyards on the island. Some ten producers get good results. This is the case, in particular, of the **Domaine Saparale** *(see Shopping Guide)*.
Sartène has lots of character, with old austere houses. Place de la Libération, with its cafés and its market, is the liveliest part of the **old town**★★.

4 PORTO-VECCHIO VINEYARDS

46km from Porto-Vecchio to Solenzara.

The **Corse-Porto-Vecchio AOC** is scattered around the town of the same name; it is the smallest Corsican appellation. Made from grape varieties grown on steep granite screes, sometimes overhanging the sea, these wines are generally extremely subtle.

Porto-Vecchio

Built deep inside a vast gulf with an indented coastline, Porto-Vecchio is a thriving seaside resort and the third largest town in Corsica. Some of the finest Corsican beaches nestle nearby.
The cours Napoléon cuts across the old town and, on either side of it, there is a maze of narrow streets, vaulted passages and flights of steps.
Outdoor cafés liven up the shaded place de la République in the city centre. The former Genoese fortifications have retained their bastions and bartizans towering above the seafront.

Leave Porto-Vecchio N along D 368 towards L'Ospédale; 4km further on, turn right onto D 759 towards Araggio.

Castellu d'Araghju★

Leave the car in the parking area on the right. Walking shoes recommended. The path leading to the site starts in the hamlet (follow signs). 1hr return.

Built on a rocky spur and looking like a crow's nest above the gulf of Porto-Vecchio, the Castellu (fortress) d'Araghju is a typical large Torrean building. The **view★★** extends over the coastal plain and the gulf.

At the end of D 759, turn left onto N 198.

In order to break the journey, you could stop in **Lecci** and try the wines produced by the **Domaine de Torraccia** (*see Shopping Guide*).

Site naturel de Fautea★

The **Genoese tower** *(lit at night by solar panels)* marks the northern limit of the two coves which are one of the sites protected by the Conservatoire du littoral, the coastline authority. The site is close to the Cerbicale nature reserve and it is possible to see black **shags** (*marangone* in Corsican) flying low over the sea then diving in to catch their food.

Solenzara

This seaside resort separates the **rocky Côte des Nacres** in the south from the flat northern coast. It offers the facilities of its marina and combines pleasures derived from the sea and from the nearby mountains. It is also appreciated for its local wine, such as that produced by the **Domaine de Solenzara** (*see Shopping Guide*).

Poster of the Luri wine fair, attended by many Corsican wine growers

G. Magnin/MICHELIN

5 CAP CORSE VINEYARDS

53km starting from Luri, about 30km N of Bastia by the D 80.

One of the island's oldest vineyards, renowned for its Muscat fortified wines, is located at the northern extremity of Cap Corse. Traditional **Corse-Coteaux-du-Cap-Corse Appellation** wines are also produced here. It is a magnificent wind-swept region, affording some of the most beautiful landscapes in Corsica, and the wines tend to be good quality.

Luri

This locality is split into several hamlets spread across a green valley, sheltered from the wind. The **Domaine Pieretti** produces a good-quality Muscat and has one of the few female winemakers on the island (*see Shopping Guide*). There is also a **wine museum** in Luri, with opportunities to taste local wines *(Marie de Luri, 20028 Luri t04 95 35 06 44; Open Jul-Aug 10am-noon & 3-6pm; rest of the year, times vary; www.acunfraternita.com; 4€).*

Follow D 180 W towards Pino.

A half-ruined watchtower, dating from the Middle Ages and known as the **Tour de Sénèque**, stands in a remote **site★**, on one of the peaks of Monte Rottu (alt 564m).

On reaching the Ste-Lucie pass, take the road starting near the chapel. It leads to a parking area. A trail *(1hr 15min on foot there and back)* leads along a steep path departing from the southwestern extremity of the platform. In clear weather, the **view★** extends as far as the islands of Elba and Capraia.

Pino★

The houses, Genoese towers and numerous chapels of this charming village rise in tiers up the mountain slopes.

Continue N along D 80.

Morsiglia slopes down in terraces to the sea. The main hamlet, surrounded by tall cliffs, is guarded by large square towers.

S. Sauvignier/MICHELIN

The road narrows and offers a spectacular bird's-eye view of the coastline.

Centuri★★

This is one of the most charming villages of the Cap Corse area; D 35 leads down to the **seaside area**★★ which forms a pleasant resort.

Beyond Centuri on the left, a minor road leads to the lovely village of **Cannelle**★, with its traffic-free, flower-decked alleyways. A little further on, it is possible to take a short walk starting from the **Mattei mill** viewpoint *(30min on foot there and back; parking area).* From the pass, follow the path on the right which climbs to the old mill rising above the maquis at an altitude of 404m. Restored by Mattei, who produce the famous Cap Corse Mattei aperitif, this old windmill became the symbol of the modern trade name. It offers a vast **panorama**★★ extending from the island of La Giraglia in the north to the Centuri cove and the rocky coast in the west.

Rogliano★

The locality of Rogliano, inhabited since Roman times, comprises seven hamlets perched on rocky spurs. Rogliano spreads its towers, churches and tall old houses in tiers inside a green hollow sheltered by Monte Poggio. The **Clos Nicrosi** produces Muscat and Coteaux-du-Cap-Corse wines *(see Shopping Guide).*

Leave D 80 before Macinaggio and turn left onto D 353.

Tomino

From the square in front of the church, the **view**★★ plunges down to the bay and the port of Macinaggio, extending far towards the islands of Finocchiarola and Capraia. The inhabitants of Tomino share the running of the vineyards with their neighbours in Rogliano.

Macinaggio

This seaside resort has mooring facilities for 600 boats in its modern marina. Genoese towers are dotted along the splendid **Sentier des Douaniers**★ (customs officers' path) which starts from the beach and skirts the protected coastline *(about 3hr from Macinaggio to Barcaggio; 45min as far as Santa Maria Chapel; easy hike; wear walking shoes and take water with you; enquire beforehand about weather conditions 08 36 68 02 20).*

UNDERWATER ADVENTURES

Corsican shores have abundant underwater flora and fauna. Wearing only a mask and snorkel it is possible to get a clear view to a depth of 15m. The best spots are the gulf of Valinco, the Tizzano area, the bay of Figari, the islands of Burzzi and the Centuri area in Cap Corse. For scuba-diving, contact the **Comité corse de la Fédération française de sports sous-marin**, It has the list of diving clubs and provides information about local regulations *(BP 12, 20145 Solenzara; 04 95 57 48 31; www.plongee-corse.org).*

A SHORT WALK IN THE NEOLITHIC
Site archéologique de Filitosa★★

17km NW of Propriano along N 196, D 157 and D 57. Open early Apr–mid-Oct 8am–dusk. Information in four languages. 6€. 04 95 74 00 91.

The remains on this site offer a summary of early Corsican history from the Neolithic period (6000-2000 BC) to Roman times. Among the 70 menhir-statues which have been excavated, Filitosa V is the largest. On one side, it appears with a long sword and a slanted dagger in its sheath.

WINE BUYING GUIDE

INFORMATION

Comité intersyndical des vins de Corse – *7 bd. du Gén.-de-Gaulle, 20200 Bastia. 04 95 32 91 32. www.vinsdecorse.com.*

CHARACTERISTICS

Red wines – Wines with a fairly high alcohol content, full-bodied and rich. Their colour varies from deep garnet red to dark purple. Typical aromas include stewed fruit, prune, developing into hints of spices and game. **Rosé wines** – Fairly rich colour with orange highlights at times. Their aromas point to red berries, citrus fruit and spices. **White wines** – Generally bright, well-structured, with aromas of citrus fruit, white fruit, almonds and honey. **Muscat-du-cap-corse** – These wines are generous, silky, with fine aromas of candied citron, honey and spices.

STORAGE

Reds – 10 years and more for best quality. Other wines: 5 years at least. **Rosés** – Best drunk young. **Whites** – Good-quality wines: within 5 years. Other wines: within 2 years.

PRICE

Between 3 and 20€. The Patrimonio AOC wines are generally sold between 8 and 15€. The Muscats generally cost between 10 and 20€.

BUYING

Clos Reginu e Prove – *leaving Feliceto on the way to Muro, follow D 215 towards Santa-Reparata; Domaine Maestracci, 20225 Feliceto. 04 95 61 72 11. www.clos-reginu-eprove.com. Open May-Oct Mon–Sat 9am–noon & 2–7.30pm; Nov-Apr call first.* Planted on a glacial moraine, the vineyard of this estate, situated in the Reginu Valley, produces two excellent vintages (matured for three years in wooden vats and casks). You will be able to taste them on the premises after a tour of Michel Raoust's cellars. Corse-Calvi.

Domaine Leccia – *20232 Poggio-d'Oletta, 04 95 37 11 35. Open daily by appt. 9am–noon & 3–6pm.* The 22ha vineyard is planted with Nielluccio, Vermentino and Muscat à Petits Grains, all espaliered and trained horizontally. Following the restructuring of the vineyard and the building of the new storehouse, the estate now produces red Petra Bianca. Muscat-du-Cap-Corse, Patrimonio.

Clos Culombu – *Chemin San-Petru, 1.5km from Lumio on the way to Calvi; follow the road on the left leading to the cemetery, 20260 Lumio. 04 95 60 70 68. www.closculombu.com. Open Mon–Sat 9am–noon & 3–7pm.* The 55ha estate extends into the communes of Lumio and Montegrosso. The growing success of his wines is encouraging for Étienne Suzzoni who makes it a point of honour to grow his vines as ecologically responsibly as possible. Corse-Calvi.

Clos Landry - *Rte de l'Aeroport, 20260 Calvi, t04 95 65 04 25. Open by appt; closlandry.com* Founded in 1990 by Timothy Landry, and is now owned by Fabien Paolini and his daughter Cathy, who look after 25ha of vines. The estate is known for its rosé gris. Corse-Calvi.

Domaine Orsini – *Rochebelle, 20214 Calenzana, t04 95 62 81 01, Open daily 9.30am-12.30pm & 2-8pm (last tasting 1hr30 before closing); www.vins-corse.com.* Excellent quality wines at this family-run property headed up by Tony Orsini. The estate now stretches to over 100ha, making it one of the biggest on the island, planted with traditional grape varieties. There is a very good wine tasting room and boutique, where you can buy local jams, patés and liqueurs aswell as the wines. Corse-Calvi.

Domaine Pieretti – *Santa-Severa, intersection of D 80 and D 180, 20228 Luri. 04 95 35 01 03. Open Jun–Sept daily 10am–1pm & 4.30–8.30pm. Offseason by appt.* The fifth generation of Pierettis today manages the 9ha vineyard (Nielluccio, Vermentino) of the family estate, situated by the sea. You will be given the opportunity to taste some delicious crus. Coteaux-du-Cap-Corse.

Domaine Arena – *Morta-Majo, at the southern entrance to the village, 20253 Patrimonio. 04 95 37 08 27. Open daily 8-11.30am & 3.30-7.30pm.* In his small 11ha estate, Mr Arena produces high-quality, entirely natural wines such as the Muscat-du-Cap-Corse, the Patrimonio (100% Vermentino and 100% Nielluccio) or the "Bianco Gentile" (a grape variety which he has revived). Muscat-du-Cap-Corse, Patrimonio, Vin de Pays de l'Île de Beauté, Vin de Pays des Portes de la Méditerranée.

Domaine de Pratavone – *20123 Pila-Canale. 04 95 24 34 11. Open daily 8.30am–noon & 3.30–7.30pm; public holidays by appt.* Isabelle Courrege is an oenologist and produces excellent wines at this 32ha estate, where she lives with her young family. A family estate since the early 1960s, they produce red, white and rosé wines in both stainless steel and oak. Corse-Sartène.

Clos Capitoro – *Rte de Sartène, Pisciatella, intersection N 196/D 302, 20166 Porticcio. 04 95 25 19 61. www.clos-capitoro.com. Open Mon–Sat 8am–noon & 2–6pm. Cllosed public holidays.* Owned by the Bianchetti family since 1856, the Clos Capitoro produces Ajaccio AOC wines and fortified wines used as aperitifs (made from Grenache grapes) and dessert wines (Les Malvoisies: sweet wines also served with foie gras and white meat). Tour of the cellar, wine tasting and sale. Ajaccio.

Domaine de Torraccia – *N 198, Lecci, 20137 Porto-Vecchio. 04 95 71 43 50. Open Jun-Sept Mon-Sat 8am-8pm, Sun 9am-1pm; Oct-May Mon–Sat 8am–12.30pm & 2–6pm.* Mr Imbert manages his attractive 43ha vineyard by traditional methods. He produces red, rosé and white Corse-Porto-Vecchio AOC wines which are increasingly renowned The domaine also produces home-made olive oil. Corse-Porto-Vecchio.

Clos Nicrosi – *20247 Rogliano. 04 95 35 41 17. Open May-Sept Mon-Sat 10am-noon & 4-7pm. Oct-Apr by appt; clos.* In 1959, the 10ha Clos Nicrosi vineyard was entirely recreated at the foot of the village of Rogliano by Toussaint and Paul Luigi. Today, it is managed by Paul's son Jean-Noël. Renowned for its white wine and its Muscat, the estate uses the ***passerillage*** method: packed in wooden trays, the grapes are left out in the sun to concentrate the natural sugar content and the aromas. Coteaux-du-Cap-Corse, Muscat-du-Cap-Corse.

Clos Teddi– *Boutique 20217 St-Florent. Vineyard: Casta 20217 St Florent. 06 10 84 11 73. Boutique open Apri-Sept daily 10am–1pm & 4–8pm.* This 35 hectare estate (11ha white, the rest in red) is run by Marie Brigitte Poli, who wisely decided a few years ago to team up with two other fairly inaccessible vineyards (Clos Santamaria and Clos Alivu) and open a wine-tasting space and boutique in the centre of the small village of Saint Florent. Muscat-du-Cap-Corse, Patrimonio.

Domaine Saparale – *5 cours Bonaparte, 20100 Sartène. 04 95 77 15 52. Open by appt;* The 20ha Domaine Saparale spreads over granitic sand. Grape varieties planted on its south-eastern hillsides include Sciacarello, Vermentino and Nielluccio. White and rosé wines are vinified by direct pressing with thermo-regulated fermentation in stainless-steel tanks. The wines are matured on fine lees and bottled early. For red wines, harvesting is done by hand. The Cuvée Casteddu, a special vintage, comprises red, rosé and white. Corse-Sartène.

Domaine de Solenzara – *20145 Solenzar. 04 95 57 44 10. Open daily by appt. 2.30–7pm.* This 16ha vineyard is the only one in Solenzara to be classified as Corse-Porto-Vecchio AOC. It produces white, rosé and red from traditional grape varieties. Corse-Porto-Vecchio.

ADDRESSES

STAY

Santa Maria – *Pl. de l'Église, 20210 Olmeto. 04 95 74 65 59. www.hotel-restaurant-santa-maria.com. Closed Nov–Dec. 12 rooms. 6€. Restaurant.* Family atmosphere in this former oil mill near the church. A flight of stairs leading up to the guestrooms lends it quite an air.

Hôtel Les Voyageurs – *9 ave. du Mar.-Sébastiani, 20200 Bastia. 04 95 34 90 80. www.hotel-lesvoyageurs.com. Closed Dec 20–Jan 10. 24 rooms. 8€.* A modern hotel with a good location along one of the main avenues of town. Guests will be absolutely comfortable in contemporary rooms decorated in blue and yellow. A nice place to stay.

Hôtel Mare E Monti – *20225 Feliceto. 04 95 63 02 00. Closed Oct 16–Mar. 16 rooms. 7€.* Fine 19C family home; ask the manager to let you see the little chapel and the salon-museum. Guest rooms are individually decorated.

Hôtel Marengo – *2 r. Marengo, 20000 Ajaccio. 04 95 21 43 66. www.hotel-marengo.com. Closed Nov 6–Mar 24. 17 rooms. 7€.* A good, inexpensive hotel a bit off the beaten track and therefore calm and quiet. Bright, well-maintained rooms, simply furnished. Warm welcome.

Hôtel San Giovanni – *20137 Porto-Vecchio. 3km SW of Porto-Vecchio by the D659 rte. d'Arca. 04 95 70 22 25. www.hotel-san-giovanni.com. Closed Nov 3–Feb 26. 30 rooms. 9€.* Those seeking peace and tranquility will love this beautiful spot. The owner is a passionate gardener who pours his heart into the vast grounds festooned with Mediterranean plants, a swimming pool and a pretty basin. Soberly decorated rooms; traditional dishes on the menu.

Hôtel Thalassa – *Rte. de Propriano, 20217 St-Florent. 04 95 37 17 17. 41 rooms. 7€.* Settle right down by the flower-decked swimming pool, surrounded on three sides by hotel buildings. Spacious, comfortable rooms with modern fittings, all just steps away from the beach.

Hôtel Villa Piana – *Rte. de Propriano, 20100 Sartène. 04 95 77 07 04.* You could hardly ask for more at this spot just a few minutes from the beach: charming rooms, some with private terraces, a lovely view, swimming pool, all within the lovely village of Sartène.

Chambre d'hôte Château Cagninacci – *20200 San-Martino-di-Lota, 8km NW of Bastia along D 80 (towards Cap-Corse) then onto D 131 in Pietranera. 06 78 29 03 94. www.chateau cagninacci.com. Closed Oct–May 14. 4 rooms.* Clinging to the mountain slopes, this 17C Capucines monastery, remodelled in the 19C in the style of a Tuscan residence, has been tastefully restored and offers spacious, traditionally furnished rooms and modern, spotlessly kept bathrooms. It is extremely quiet and the panorama is superb.

Kallisté – *Rte. du Vieux-Molini, Agosta-Plage, 20166 Porticcio. 04 95 25 54 19. www.hotels-kalliste.com. Closed Nov 12–14 Mar. 9 rooms. 10€.* A pretty walled garden creates a tranquil haven for this villa tucked away in a residential neighbourhood of Porticcio, a popular seaside resort. Sober rooms overlooking sea or garden.

Hôtel Balanea – *6 r. Georges-Clemenceau, 20260 Calvi. 04 95 65 94 94. www.hotel-balnea.com. 38 rooms. 12€.* Follow the pedestrian street up from the yacht harbour to this little hotel, with its rose-and-ochre facade. Spacious rooms, some with balcony or terrace, open their windows onto the bay and the boats. Eclectic furnishings in an imaginative decor.

EAT

A Mandria – *Rte. de Ghisonaccia, pont de Solenzara, 20145 Solenzara. 04 95 57 41 95. Closed Jan, Sun evening and Mon off-season.* This converted sheep barn offers a choice of mouth-watering Corsican dishes. Other strong points are the reasonable prices and a shaded terrace.

Auberge Santa Barbara – *Rte. de Propriano, 20100 Sartène. 04 95 77 09 06. Closed Oct 16–Mar 14, Mon except evenings in-season.* An unimpressive facade belies the lovely terrace and verdant garden, with a view of the village. Good food with local flavour.

Aux Bons Amis – *R. Georges-Clemenceau, 20260 Calvi. ℘04 95 65 05 01. Closed Oct 16–Mar 31, Thu off-season and Sun in-season.* Fish is the theme here, both on the menu and in the decor. Try the bouillabaisse, paella or other seafood specialities.

La Corniche – *Castagneto, 20200 San-Martino-di-Lota. ℘04 95 31 40 98. www.hotel-lacorniche.com. Closed Jan 1–Feb 15, Tue lunchtime and Mon.* "Climb up" to this establishment and sit at a table under the old plane trees shading the terrace. You will enjoy tasty traditional dishes while admiring an unforgettable panorama.

La Table du Marché St. Jean – *Pl. du Marché, 20200 Bastia. ℘04 95 31 64 25. Closed Sun.* This convivial restaurant offers impeccable cuisine prepared from fresh produce. Fish with garlic mayonnaise and traditional Corsican charcuterie are among the dishes served on the terrace in fine weather.

L'Antigu – *51 r. Borgo, 20137 Porto-Vecchio. ℘04 95 70 39 33. Closed Jan–mid-Feb, Sun lunchtime early Apr–early Nov, and Mon.* The rooftop terrace affords a magnificent panorama of the gulf of Porto-Vecchio and the copious, well-prepared regional dishes, served with care, are a delight to the palate!

Le Guaïtella – *10 hameau de Guaïtella, 20200 Ville-di-Pietrabugno. ℘04 95 34 20 51. www.leguaitella.com. Closed lunchtime.* . Perched on the heights overlooking Bastia, the Guaïtela with a spectacular view of the town and the harbour. Dishes are well prepared but never over-elaborate: try fillet of beef and slice of foie gras with chestnut flavouring, or a swordfish steak with capers.

Le Grand Café Napoléon – *10 cours Napoléon, 20000 Ajaccio. ℘04 95 21 42 54. Closed Dec 24–Jan 1, Sat evenings, Sun and public holidays.* One of the oldest houses in Ajaccio, this prestigious mansion offers a fine "grand café" terrace, a Second Empire-style dining room and an energetic young chef at the helm.

Osteria di San Marinu – *20253 Patrimonia. ℘04 95 37 11 93. Closed Oct–Mar, Wed lunchtime in Apr, May & Sept.* This little "osteria" is a summer hotspot, with chefs plying the barbecue on the pergola-shaded terrace. Sample traditional Corsican dishes, washed down with the Patrimonia wines made by the owner's brother.

Chez Charles – *20260 Lumio. ℘04 95 60 61 71. www.hotel-chezcharles.com. Open mid-Mar–mid-Nov.* Refined cuisine served in a pleasant dining room or on the shaded terrace. Guestrooms and swimming pool.

U Licettu – *Plaine-de-Cuttoli, 20167 Mezzavia, 15km NE of Ajaccio along the Bastia road, then the Cuttoli road (D 1) and the Bastelicaccia road. ℘04 95 25 61 57. Closed Jan, Sun evening and Mon except Jul–Aug – reservations required.* Have a seat at this lovely villa isolated in the maquis and enjoy generous Corsican dishes. Enjoy the terrace and a garden full of flowers. One gourmet menu only, drinks included.

GOURMET SHOPPING

U San Petrone – *Pl. de l'Ancienne-Poste, 20217 St-Florent. ℘04 95 37 10 95. Tue–Sun 9am–noon & 3–7pm, Mon in Jul–Aug. Closed mid-Sep–Easter.* Mr Rinaldi, who is both a farmer and a pork butcher, can tell you all about the lonzu, coppa and hams he has dealt with. As for other products (cheeses, liqueurs, wines), he calls on craftsmen who, like him, use good local produce.

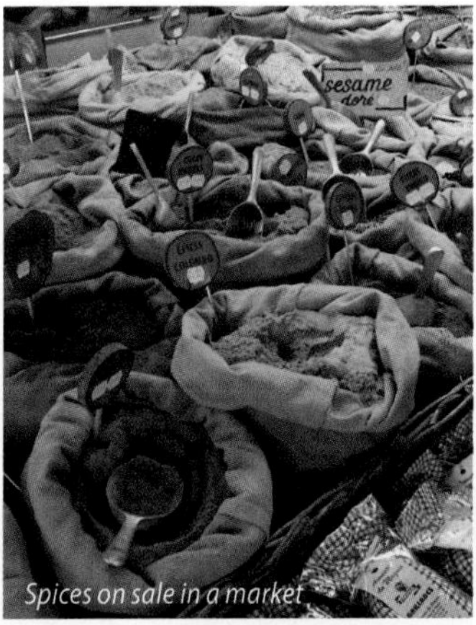

Spices on sale in a market

© Valerio Lo Bello/stock.xchng

8 - JURA

Secluded, even secretive, the Jura wine-growing area has a resilient identity, characterised by wines with mysterious-sounding names – *vin de paille, vin jaune, vin d'Arbois* **– produced from grape varieties that are found nowhere else. The area stretches north–south for some 100km, backing onto the Revermont, a limestone plateau formed by the foothills of the Jura as they descend towards the eastern edge of the Bresse plain. Everywhere you will come across enthusiastic wine-growers, proud of their identity and ready to extend a warm welcome. The region's Comté cheeses, freshwater fish and smoked pork make it a gastronome's paradise. But if you want to stretch your legs, the Jura also offers countless opportunities for walking, in both vineyard and forest. With the saltworks of Arc-et-Senans, Arbois, Poligny and Lons-le-Saunier, the region is also home to an historical and architectural heritage that is second to none.**

Highlights

1 A tasting of Comté cheese, at the museum in **Poligny** (p281)

2 The breathtaking views from the **Roche de Baume** (p287)

3 Enjoying some spa therapy at **Salin-les-Bains** (p278)

4 Celebrating the distinctive wine at the **Percée du Vin Jaune** (p14)

5 A drive along the **Revermont Corniche** (p282)

As well as being known by their appellation, Jura wines are described in terms of the way they are made.

The **vin jaune**, a white wine made exclusively from the Savagnin grape, is left to age for around six years in 228l containers, without topping-up. In other words, the wine is left to slowly evaporate. In contact with the air, a film of yeast – the "veil" – forms on the surface of the wine. This protects it from oxidisation and fosters development of the wine's characteristic flavours, which range from fresh walnut to curry. *Vin jaune* is a very dry wine and newcomers may be surprised by its strong personality. It is sold in a *clavelin* bottle, which contains just 62cl.

Vin de paille derives its name from the practice of spreading the best grapes on beds of straw and leaving them to dry slowly to concentrate the sugar. Nowadays, this practice has been replaced by a ventilation process but still produces a very sweet wine with walnut flavours.

Fruitières – The Jura was one of the first French regions to establish cooperative wineries. Here they are referred to as "fruitières", a name borrowed from cheese-making. The five Jura *fruitières* are those of Arbois, Pupillin, Poligny, Voiteur, and the Caveau des Byards.

Vineyards on the slopes below Château-Chalon

S. Sauvignier/MICHELIN

OVERVIEW

The Terroir

Michelin Local Map 321 – Jura (39).
Area: approximately 1 850ha – equivalent to a mere two per cent of the Bordeaux wine-growing area – located at altitudes of between 250 and 400m, spread over 81 *communes* (local authority areas).
Production: approximately 90 000 hl. The soils consist mainly of clays and marls, with extensive limestone areas in the southern sector. The region has a continental climate with cold winters, relatively little rainfall, plenty of sunshine and temperate-to-hot summers.

The Wines

Côtes-du-Jura – The area found north of Arbois to the south of Lons-le-Saunier. White wines here are made from Chardonnay and Savagnin grapes, the latter is virtually unique to the Jura region and reds (Pinot Noir, Poulsard and Trousseau).
Arbois – Whites (Chardonnay and Savagnin) and reds (Pinot Noir, Poulsard and Trousseau). **Arbois-pupillin** is a local name for certain reds and rosés.
Château-Chalon – North of Lons-le-Saunier, an area which produces exclusively *vin jaune*, made from the Savagnin grape.
L'Étoile – Southwest of Château-Chalon, where they make only traditional whites, *vins jaunes* and *crémants* (sparkling wines, less effervescent than champagne) from Chardonnay (90%), Poulsard and Savagnin.

Jura Wine Route

The Route Touristique des Vins de Jura was recently designated a "Pays d'Eden" by the European Union, reflecting the natural beauty of its landscape and its emphasis on celebrating local traditions.

- **Population:** 64,000.
- **Michelin Map:** See map on p284.
- **Info:** www.laroutedesvinsdujura.com
- **Location:** Approximately 100km. Michelin Local Map 321, E-F 4-7
- **Kids:** The underground caverns at Osselle.
- **Timing:** Allow one to two days, including stops to visit places of interest

DRIVING TOURS

1 ARC-ET-SENANS TO POLIGNY

Leaving the Arc-et-Senans saltworks, you will not see any vineyards for several kilometres, until you come to a bend in the River Loue, near Port-Lesney. There is less evidence of wine-growing around Salins-les-Bains, but there are vineyards all the way from Montigny-les-Arsures to Poligny.

Saline Royale d'Arc-et-Senans★★

Open Jul–Aug 9am–7pm. Apr–Jun & Sept–Oct 9am–noon & 2–6pm. Feb–Mar & Nov–Dec 10am–noon & 2–5pm. Closed Dec 25. 7.50€. Guided tour by request for groups. 03 81 54 45 45. www.salineroyale.com.

The former Royal Saltworks stands between the River Loue and the Forest of Chaux. A prime example of 18C industrial architecture, it is a UNESCO World Heritage Site. Here salt was produced by evaporation, boiling the brine drawn from below ground at Salins-les-Bains in immense cauldrons. The brine was conveyed to the works by gravity in wooden "saumoducs", which formed a sort of underground pipeline.

The building is striking for the beauty of its geometrical arched vaults and futuristic architecture. The architect, Claude-Nicolas Ledoux, in fact designed an entire community complex, with dwellings for 250 workers and the management, workshops, and even a prison for those who stole salt, a very valuable commodity at the time. In spite of its value, the saltworks were never very profitable, and the vast amount of wood it consumed for fuel led to the virtual destruction of the Forest of Chaux. Having gone to wrack and ruin, the saltworks closed in the late 19C, and the building was later used by the Vichy regime as an internment camp for gypsies. After intensive restorations, it reopened as a museum in 1996.

Chemin des Gabelous (salt-tax collectors' path) d'Arc-et-Senans

On leaving the saltworks, turn left, then right at the roundabout into the Rue des Graduations. The waymarked path begins at the camp site. 5hr 30min on foot, 2hr 30min by bicycle.

This 24km path roughly follows the route of the "saumoduc" which carried brine from the salt mine at Salins to the works at Arc-et-Senans.

Take the D 17E then the D 121 and finally the D 48E.

Port-Lesney★

The road to this pretty riverside village cuts through vineyards contained by a bend in the Loue. One of Port-Lesney's former mayors was President Edgar Faure, who played an important political role during the Fourth and Fifth Republics. On Sundays, anglers, boating enthusiasts and lovers of trout and fried fish converge on this spot. The harbour district, on the left bank of the Loue, has some fine wine merchants' houses.

From the Chapelle de Lorette, a pathway *(1hr there and back)* leads through undergrowth to the **Edgar-Faure viewing point**, which overlooks the village and the whole of the valley.

From Port-Lesney, take the D 48 to the hamlet of Pagnoz, then the D 472 to Salins-les-Bains.

Salins-les-Bains

As its name suggests, the town owed its former prosperity to salt, an inexhaustible source of taxation under the Ancien Régime, levied in the form of the gabelle or salt tax. Dominated by **Fort Belin** and **Fort Saint-André**, Salins is strung out along the valley bottom of the Furieuse. The town still has fragments of its ramparts and towers. Nowadays, it is a pleasant spa town, whose waters are used for treating rheumatic and gynaecological conditions *(see "Water Sports and Spas")*.

The impressive buildings and tall chimneys of the **saltworks** still stand on the banks of the Furieuse. Here the brine was extracted before being conveyed by "saumoduc" (a primitive pipeline) to the Royal Saltworks at Arc-et-Senans. Salt is no longer extracted from the mines, but the salt spring is still used by the local spas. The underground tunnels (13C),

Claude-Nicolas-Ledoux (1736-1806)

Inspector General of the Saltworks of Lorraine and Franche-Comté, Ledoux was a visionary architect who was influenced by Enlightenment ideas. His greatest achievement was the Arc-et-Senans Saltworks, but he was also the creative mind behind some other bold projects, as the museum devoted to him at the saltworks explains: he had a hand in the design of the pavilions of the Fermiers Généraux complex in Paris – and the rotundas of La Villette and the Parc Monceau – the Château de Bénouville in Normandy, and the theatre in Besançon. In 1804, he published a treatise on architecture and its relation to the arts, the law and customs, which enlarged on his plans for an ideal settlement at Chaux.

200m long and supported by impressive medieval vaulting, are well worth a visit. (*visit by 1hr guided tour Jul–Aug daily 10am–5pm (English visits at 11.15am, 12.15pm, 2.15pm); mid-Apr–Jun, Sept-Oct daily 10am, 11.30am, 2.30pm–5.30pm; Nov–Feb weekends and school holidays 10.30am & 3pm; Mar–mid-Apr daily 10.30am & 3pm; bring something warm to wear; closed Dec 25; 5€; 03 84 73 01 34; www.salins-les-bains.com).*

Travel S from Salins on the D 472, turn right onto the D 94, then right again onto the D 271. In Marnoz, take the D 105 towards Arbois then the D 249 in the Montigny-lès-Arsures direction.

Montigny-lès-Arsures

This traditional wine-growing village, where every house has its own cellar, backs onto the Revermont. It has a fine Romanesque church. In the hamlet of Les Rosières (below the village, near the N 83), is a sign indicating the **"Vigne historique Pasteur"**, a property belonging to the Académie des Sciences. It was here that Louis Pasteur performed his first experiments on yeasts.

He demonstrated that the juice from bunches of grapes wrapped in cotton, and therefore not in contact with the atmosphere and the yeasts it contains, did not ferment, unlike the juice from grapes that had been exposed to the air. The village is situated in the Arbois appellation area and there are at least ten vignerons selling local wines.

The terroir is known for red wines made from the Trousseau grape, the full character of which is expressed in the wines produced by **André and Mireille Tissot** (*see Shopping Guide*).

The **Frédéric Lornet** winery is housed in a former 16C abbey and you can taste its wares in the old chapel *(Abbaye de la Boutière, 39600 Montigny-lès-Arsures; open daily by appt. 9am–noon & 2–6pm; no charge; 03 84 37 44 95).*

If weather permits, you can take advantage of a picnic area laid out on the outskirts of the village, heading towards Arbois, with views of the vineyards.

Drive to Arbois on the N 83.

Arbois★

Arbois derives its name from two Celtic words, Ar and Bos, meaning "fertile soil". The capital of wine-growing in the Jura, Arbois lent its name to the region's first *appellation d'origine contrôlée* (AOC) in 1936. In the past, its wine was praised by Rabelais, Voltaire and Henry IV, who knew how to appreciate good things. However, this did not prevent Henry from besieging the town in 1595 and looting it when it fell. Arbois has a number of wine cellars and wine merchants in the Place de la Liberté area.

It has a well-deserved reputation for gastronomy. But Arbois also owes much to the great **Louis Pasteur**, who through his scientific research and advice made an important contribution to the revival of the wine-making industry after it had been devastated by phylloxera.

Take time to stroll around Arbois and absorb its rural elegance. A tour of the old walls *(map/brochure from the tourist office)* brings you to the picturesque **Gloriette Tower** and the **Pont des Capucins** over the Cuisance, a small river whose banks were formerly crowded with paper mills and tanneries. Also take a walk in the **Faubourg Faramand**, the old wine-merchants' district, where you will see, on the pavement in front of each house, the "trappon" (trap-door) giving access to the cellar below. Nowadays, Arbois is home to just a few dozen wine growers, but in the 18C there were more than a thousand of them. You will receive a warm welcome at the celebrated **Maison Henri Maire**, or the estate of **Domaine Ligier Père et Fils** (*see Shopping Guide*).

Fruitière Vin. Château Béthanie

2 r. des Fossés, 39600 Arbois. Cellar tours Jul–Aug Tue–Sat 11am, 2.30pm, 4.30pm. Closed May 1, Dec 25. 03 84 66 11 67. www.chateau-bethanie.com.

Founded in 1906 by 26 wine-growers overwhelmed by competition from the South of France, this *fruitière* was France's second cooperative winery. Nowadays, it is an extremely well-equipped

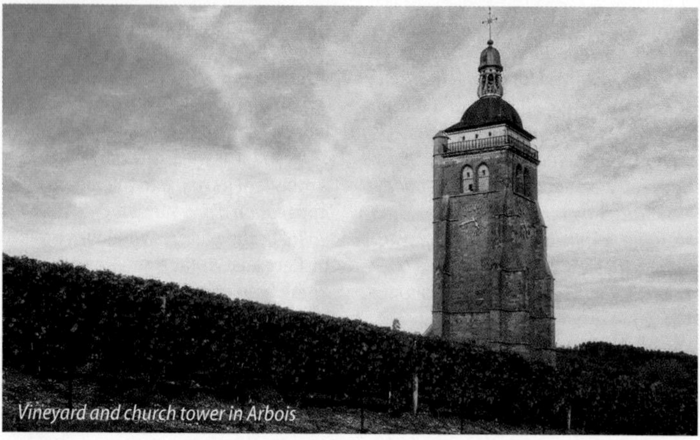

Vineyard and church tower in Arbois

enterprise which produces wines from approximately 200ha of vineyards and has made a name for itself with its Béthanie vintage, a pleasant white made from Savagnin and Chardonnay grapes, with a pronounced *vin jaune* character. A tour of the cellars will give you a thorough knowledge of how *vin jaune* is made, and you can taste the winery's products in a former chapel building.

Musée du Vin et de la Vigne

Open Jul–Aug 10am–noon & 2pm–6pm. Mar–Jun & Sep–Oct Wed–Mon 10am–noon & 2pm–6pm. Nov–Feb Wed–Mon 2pm–6pm. Guided tours available(1hr). Closed Jan, May 1, Dec 25. 3.50€. 03 84 66 40 45, www.juramusees.fr.

A vestige of the town's ancient fortifications, the **Château Pécauld** houses the region's wine museum and institute. Outside, the work of the vigneron is introduced by a tour of small plots of different grape varieties. Inside, the history of the vineyards and the wine-growing community, past and present, is illustrated by photographs and artefacts, with new exhibitions being introduced to enliven children's visits. The visit includes an opportunity to taste some selected wines.

Maison de Louis Pasteur★

Visit by guided tour (30min) Jun–Sept 9.45am, 10.45am, 11.45am and 2pm–6pm. Apr–May and early Oct 2.15pm, 3.15pm, 4.15pm, 5.15pm. 6€. 03 84 66 11 72. www.academie-sciences.fr. Call ahead to book in summer.

A visit to the family house where Louis Pasteur spent part of his life is a surprisingly moving experience. Standing on the bank of the Cuisance, his father's tannery was gradually extended and modernised by the famous scientist. The house has lost nothing of its opulent decor and the family atmosphere is faithfully preserved. Pasteur's bedroom appears to be untouched: his penholder, inkwell and blotter await him on the bureau; his trade-mark fur hat is still there. In the laboratory, you can see the instruments and apparatus he used for his experiments on wines, and where he discovered pasteurisation.

Église St-Just★

Beside the building is an esplanade, giving a good view of the Cuisance. The outstanding feature of this priory church (12-13C) is its bell tower, 60m high, which lords it over the town. Built in the 16C of golden-ochre coloured stone, it culminates in an onion-shaped dome housing a chime of bells.

On the first Sunday in September each year, the wine-growers pay homage to the parish's patron saint, processing to the church of St Just with a giant bunch of grapes, the Biou, plaited from grapes from all over the commune.

This time-honoured tradition is celebrated by the whole town, whose prosperity is closely bound up with the life of its vignerons.

Leave Arbois and travel S on the D 246.

Pupillin

After climbing up onto the plateau, with a fine view of the red roofs of Arbois in your rear mirror, you will reach Pupillin, a village totally devoted to wine-growing. It likes to think of itself as the "world capital" of Poulsard (or Ploussard), a grape variety which does well on the blue and red marls of the area. It produces light wines, pale in colour, whose flavours are reminiscent of cherry, and are slightly smokey. Of the Arbois-Pupillin estates, those of **Pierre Overnoy** and the **La Borde** can be relied on for quality *(see Shopping Guide)*. Another good address is that of the **Fruitière Vinicole de Pupillin** *(R. Poulssard, 39600 Pupillin; open 8.30am-noon & 2-6pm; 03 84 66 12 88)*.

Pupillin is also a centre of hazelnut growing. You will see plantations on either side of the road as you travel towards Poligny. A viewing point has been laid out on the outskirts of the village, from which you can survey some of the vineyards while making use of the picnic tables.

Continue on the D 246 as far as Buvilly, then turn left onto the N 83 towards Poligny.

Poligny

To the great joy of connoisseurs, Poligny successfully combines the production of excellent wines with the manufacture of Comté cheese, of which the town is the acknowledged centre. For centuries, its rich soils, at the heart of the AOC Côtes-du-Jura wine-growing area, have ensured its prosperity, and this is borne out by the town's cultural heritage, and it is today classed as a "Petit Cité Comtoise de Caractere".

Poligny's main place of interest is the unusual **Caveau des Jacobins**. A former 13C church, deconsecrated at the time of the Revolution, it passed into public ownership and was purchased by the local vignerons for use as a winery. This marriage between Christ and Bacchus seems to have worked well, as the winery now sells some excellent *vins jaunes*, together with a whole range of high-quality Côtes-du-Jura wines *(1 r. Hyacinthe Friant, 39800 Poligny; open Jul–Aug daily 9.30am–noon & 2–7pm; rest of the year Mon–Sat morning 9.30am–noon & 2–6.30pm, Sun 10am–noon; 03 84 37 14 58, www.caveaudesjacobins.com)*.

In the town itself, you will find several well-regarded wine merchants', such as the **Xavier Reverchon** and **Benoît Badoz** establishments *(see Shopping Guide)*.

After wine, cheese: be sure to visit the **Maison du comté**, which also houses the Comté trade association, for an explanation of the various operations involved in cheese-making, from collecting the milk to maturing of the finished cheese. It will certainly stimulate your appetite and talks about not only Comté but other local cheeses Morbier and Mont d'Or *(visit by 1hr 30min guided tour Jul–Aug Tue–Sun 10–11.30am & 2–5.30pm; Apr–Jun, Sept–Oct and school holidays Tue–Sun 2–5pm; closed Jan 1, May 1, Dec 25; 4€; 03 84 37 23 51; www.maison-du-comte.com)*.

You should still have time to see the **Collegiate Church of St-Hippolyte**. Under the porch, the dividing pillar of the doorway supports a 15C polychrome sculpture of the Virgin Mary. Above the doorway is a bas-relief depicting the quartering of St Hippolytus. In the right-hand doorway, a 15C Pietà stands on a console. Inside, there is a remarkable wooden **calvary cross**, on the rood beam dominating the entrance to the choir, and a fine collection of statues of the 15C Burgundian school.

The **ramparts walk** *(roughly 2hr; map from the tourist office)* through the old parts of Poligny follows the line of the ancient ramparts, with the keep of Saint-Laurent and the tower of the Sergenterie still in good shape. You can climb up to the site of the former Château de Grimont for a good view over the town.

2 FROM POLIGNY TO LONS-LE-SAUNIER

After Poligny, the itinerary follows minor roads along the Revermont corniche, where in many places the vineyards cling to very steep slopes.

From Poligny, take the D 259 S, then the D 194 for about 8km.

Saint-Lothain

Huddled at the foot of its hill, this village, named after a local saint, is dominated by vineyards interspersed with meadows and pinewoods. The village boasts some imposing vignerons' houses and an interesting little church in the late-Romanesque style peculiar to the Franche-Comté region. On the outskirts of the village, on the right-hand side of the Passenans road, is a well-equipped picnic site.

Continue for 3km on the D 57, until you come to Passenans.

Passenans

This pretty village has some solid stone houses with steep-pitched roofs and crow-step gables. In a relaxed atmosphere, you can investigate the excellent crémants and Côtes-du-Jura wines of the **Grand Frères estate**, on the outskirts of the village *(see Shopping Guide)*.
Then climb the narrow road to the site of **Frontenay**, where an avenue of ancient lime trees leads to a 15C church surrounded by a cemetery. The **château**, further up, was a stronghold of the counts of Frontenay, standing guard over the salt route. Its 14C keep survives. At the entrance to the château, about 1km up the road from the church, you will find a display panel showing the routes of several country walks.
From Passenans, you can make a detour via **Toulouse-le-Château**★, and return on the N 83. Drive up to the **viewing point**★, at the summit of which stands a church in the local 15C style, near the ruins of the former castle, and enjoy a magnificent view over the Revermont and the Bresse plain.

Take the D 57 to Menétru-le-Vignoble then the D5, climbing all the way to Château-Chalon.

Château-Chalon★

A former stronghold, solidly anchored on its rocky escarpment, this splendid village reigns over a small but prestigious terroir. The Château-Chalon appellation, which covers a mere 50ha spread over the communes of Menétru-le-Vignoble, Nevy-sur-Seille, Voiteur and Domblans, in fact only applies to vin jaune. It is an untypical terroir of marly soils, whose sun-drenched slopes are clothed in vines. Another contributing factor is the wide temperature range of its dry, well-ventilated cellars, where this "solid gold" wine matures slowly, apparently benefiting from the vagaries of wind and weather.
The **Berthet-Bondet winery**, housed in a fine 16C mansion in the upper part of the village, has very attractive tasting rooms that are open to the public. The **Jean-Claude Crédoz estate** also has a good reputation *(see Shopping Guide)*.
Everywhere about the village are reminders of the historical importance of a site that was fortified as early as Gallo-Roman times, even before the building of its castle and Benedictine abbey (7C). The flower-bedecked **streets** have plenty of character, featuring multi-storey vignerons' houses, some of which have flights of steps up to them and outside access to the cellars below. Since 2008, a **Pole Decouvèrte du Froid Pignon** museum has opened in an old stone building on a rocky promotory overlooking the village, explaining the history of Chateau Chalon and Vin Jaune. There is also a **Circuit Pedèstre du Vin Jaune** that goes for 5km from the village *(information from Haut Seille Tourist Office t03 84 44 62 47; www.hauteseille.com)*.
To find out how well vin jaune complements Comté cheese, pay a visit to the **fromagerie Vagne**. Housed in the cellars of the former abbey building, this *fructerie* sells cheeses which have been matured for up to two years. A guided

tour reveals all the mysteries of this famous cheese *(R. St-Jean, 39210 Château-Chalon; guided tour with cheese tasting mid-Jun–mid-Sept 2.30–6.30pm; rest of the year Wed, Fri, Sat, Sun and public holidays 2.30pm & 3.30pm; 4€ Shop: Daily 11am–12.30pm & 2–5.30pm; 03 84 44 92 25; www.comte-vagne.com).*

Leave Château-Chalon on the D 5.

Voiteur

The **Fruitière Vinicole** is the chief place of interest in this little market town located in the plain below Château-Chalon, where several roads meet. The cooperative has some fifty members, who own 75ha of vineyards, 13ha of which qualify for the Château-Chalon appellation. The blue marls of the surrounding terroirs are well suited to Savagnin, while the Chardonnay grape does better on limestone scree *(Rte. de Nevy, 39210 Voiteur; open Jul–Aug Mon–Fri 8.30am–noon & 1.30–7pm, Sat 8.30am-noon; Sept-June Mon-Fri 10am–noon & 2–6pm; 03 84 85 21 29; www.fruitiere-vinicole-voiteur.fr).*

Take the D 70 S towards Vernois.

Le Vernois

This tiny village is something of a Mecca for lovers of Jura wines, as it has so many estates producing high-quality wines. Like many others, **Baud Père et Fils** *(see Shopping Guide)*, are the descendants of a long line of growers who have made the best of their Chardonnay and Savagnin vines, cépages which are completely at home here on the clayey-limestone and blue-marl soils.

For a better idea of local wine production, make a stop at the **Caveau des Byards**; France's smallest wine cooperative with just 15 members, almost half of whom belong to the same family. They produce mainly Côtes-du-Jura whites from Chardonnay grapes, wines which keep well *(see Shopping Guide).*

On leaving Vernois, turn right in the direction of Plainoiseau, then travel back N on the N 83 towards Arlay.

Château d'Arlay★

Open mid-Jun–mid-Sept 2–6pm; guided tour (30min) of the château. 8€ (6€ for garden only). Boutique for wine tasting 9am-noon & 2-6pm for wine tasting. 03 84 85 04 22. www.arlay.com.

On the banks of the Seille, in the heart of a highly regarded wine-growing area, this village is still associated with the knightly deeds of the powerful Arlay family from Chalon. The medieval fortress was abandoned in the 17C and replaced in the 18C with an impressive country mansion. It has a fine collection of **furniture** in the Restoration style. Note particularly the library and doll's house.

In the **park**, a pleasant path climbs the hill to the ruins of the medieval fortress. Along the route you will encounter driveways lined with lime trees and decorative features – a grotto, an open-air theatre and extensive lawns – and enjoy fine views over the Bresse plain, the Revermont and the château's own vineyards. The ruins of the fortress provide a romantic setting for the **Jurafaune** collection of birds of prey. The staff give demonstrations, which are always impressive, especially for children.

The Laguiche family, who own the estate, were originally from Burgundy, which explains why 45% of the 30ha of **vineyards** are planted with Pinot Noir, something quite exceptional in the Jura. As well as his black-cherry flavoured reds, Alain de Laguiche, who manages the estate, produces a very pleasant *"rosé corail"* and a particularly fine red macvin *(see Shopping Guide).*

From Arlay, drive W on the D 120 towards Bletterans, then turn immediately left and continue for 7km as far as L'Étoile, passing through Quintigny.

L'Étoile

Unusually, this village owes its name to a marine invertebrate, the five-tentacled crinoid or feather star, fossils of which are abundant in the local soil.

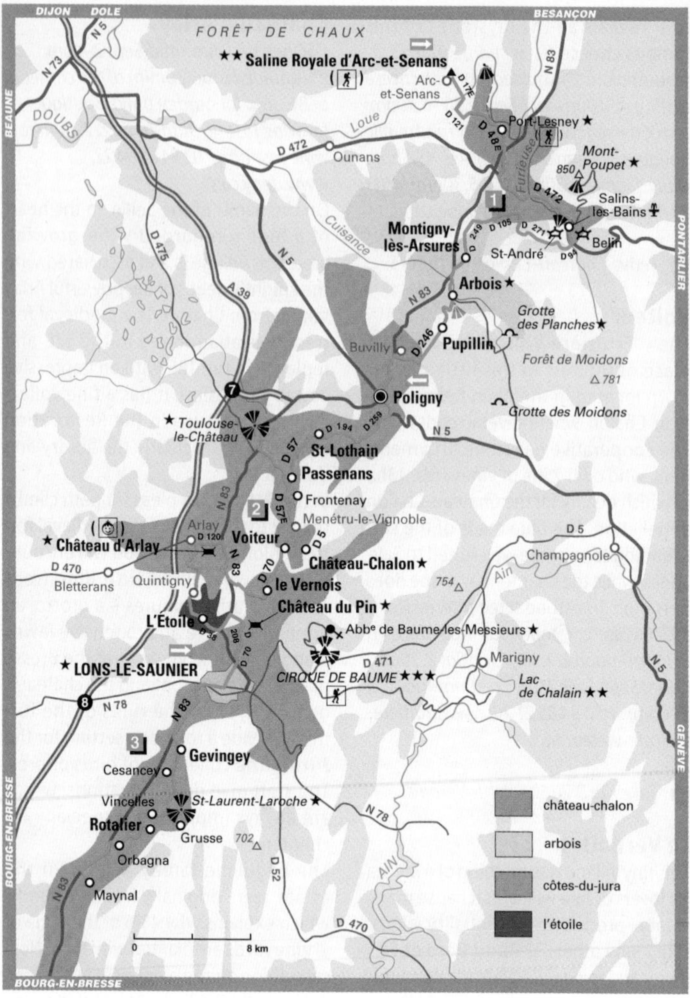

This is an excellent terroir for Chardonnay and Savagnin and the Étoile appellation (AOC) applies exclusively to white wines, more or less distinctively of the *vin jaune* type. One of the more picturesque wineries is that run by the Vandelle family at the **Château de L'Étoile**. The **Montbourgeau** estate also produces reliable wines (*see Shopping Guide*).

Leave L'Étoile south and join D 38. Travel N on the N 83 for about 1km, then turn right towards the Château du Pin.

Château du Pin★

Open Jul–Sept 1–7pm. 5€. 03 84 25 32 95.

The château stands in a setting of meadows and vineyards. Built in the 13C by Jean de Chalon, count of Burgundy and lord of Arlay, then destroyed by Louis XI, it was reconstructed in the 15C and has been restored in recent times. From the 15C keep there are magnificent views of the surrounding countryside.

Drive to Lons-le-Saunier via the D 208, then the D 70.

Lons-le-Saunier★

The hills around the town were formerly covered in vines. Now, only the fine vignerons' houses in the Place de la Comédie bear witness to the importance of this activity, as urbanisation has gradually separated Lons-le-Saunier from its wine-growing roots.

The real heart of Lons-le-Saunier is the **Place de la Liberté**, where much of the town's activity takes place. At one end is the imposing rococo façade of the **theatre**★, whose clock grinds out two bars of the *Marseillaise* before striking the hours. Why this patriotic tune? Simply because Rouget de Lisle, the author of France's national anthem, was born in Lons: there is a statue of him on the Promenade de la Chevalerie.

The arcaded **Rue du Commerce**★, with its 146 arches dating from the second half of the 17C, is a picturesque sight. No 24, the house where Rouget was born, is now the **Musée Rouget-de-Lisle**. Little of the original furniture remains, but memorabilia and documents bear witness to the extraordinary destiny of the artist and of the Marseillaise itself. There is also a video presentation *(open mid-Jun–mid-Sept Mon–Fri 10am–noon & 2–6pm; weekends & public holidays 2–5pm; no charge; 03 84 47 29 16).*

Begun in 1735, the 18C **Hôtel-Dieu** has a very handsome wrought-iron gateway. Though no longer in use as a hospital, it still houses a superb **pharmacy**★, the wooden panelling of which sets off a collection of ceramic, pewter and copper pots *(visit by 1hr guided tour mid-Jul–mid-Sept Tue 10am and Sat 3pm; meet in front of the iron gateway; 5€; 03 84 24 65 01).*

The **Place de la Comédie**, to the right on the way to the Rue du Puits-Salé, is lined with former wine-growers' houses. The lintels of nos 20 and 22 are decorated with pruning knives, symbols of their occupation. At the bottom of the Rue du **Puits-Salé**, in a small park, flows the mineral-water spring known as the Puits-Salé, once used by the Romans and around which the town grew up. Finally, a visit to Lons would not be complete

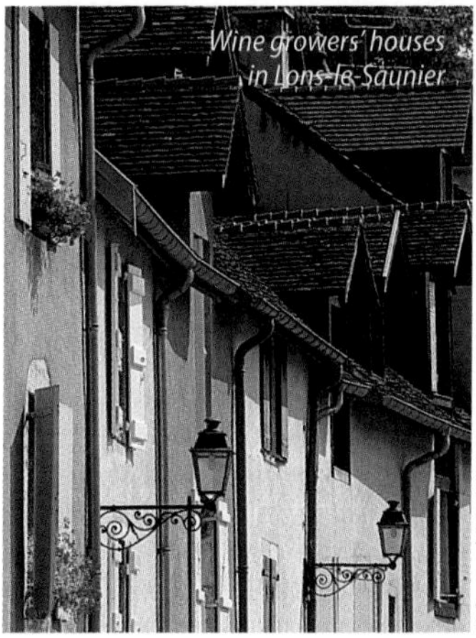

Wine growers' houses in Lons-le-Saunier

M. Paygnard / MICHELIN

without seeing the **Archaeological Museum**, where you are greeted by the famous plateosaurus, the fossil remains of which were found in the region. The museum is awaiting an extension to its premises so that it can properly display its fine collections, which include an exceptional outrigger canoe dating from the Bronze Age, found in the Lac de Chalain. In the meantime, it draws on its reserves to stage some fascinating temporary exhibitions *(25 r. Richebourg; open Wed–Sun 10am–noon & 2–6pm; weekends & public holidays 2–7pm; closed Jan 1, May 1, Dec 25; 2€, no charge Wed and 1st Sun in month; 03 84 47 88 45).*

A good selection of wines from the region is available at the **Maison du vigneron** *(see Shopping Guide).*

3 WINE VILLAGES OF THE SOUTHERN REVERMONT

Côtes-du-Jura vineyards abound a few kilometres south of Lons-le-Saunier, in countryside criss-crossed by winding roads. Most of the wines produced here are white, but you'll also see Pinot Noir thriving in the region.

Along the 20km stretch of the Sud-Revermont, the route passes pretty wine-growing villages in verdant little valleys.

Drive S from Lons on N 83.

Gevingey

This picturesque village was the scene of a terrible tragedy during the Second World War, recorded on a plaque on the front of the Mairie. The mixed limestone-scree and blue-marl soils favour good Savagnin whites.

Continue towards Cesancey.

Country lanes link the charming wine-growing villages of **Cesancey**, **Grusse**, **Vincelles**, **Rotalier** and **Orbagna**. They all have fountains and wash-houses.

At Grusse, drive up to the **viewing point**★ at **Saint-Laurent-Laroche**★ *(2.5km)* for a magnificent overview of the Sud-Revermont villages and the Bresse plain.

You can then continue southwards to **Maynal**, which also has a fine viewing point and an interesting church with a fortified bell tower, visible from miles around. While you're here, stop in at the **Domaine Claude Buchot** *(see Shopping Guide)*. The wine-growing estates of this region are small in area, but produce a wide variety of wines. Good examples are the **Domaine Labet** at **Rotalier**, for its Pinots and Chardonnays, and the **Domaine Ganevat** *(see Shopping Guide)*.

A PLACE FOR REFLECTION

Abbey of Baume-les-Messieurs★

7km SE of Voiteur on the D 70. Open mid-Jun–end Sept 10am–noon & 2–5pm. 3.50€. 03 84 44 95 45.

The abbey was founded in 890. It was self-governing from 1157 to 1186, thanks to Frederick Barabarossa, the Holy Roman Emperor, who married the heiress of the county of Burgundy, and from this time the foundation enjoyed "imperial" status. In the 16C, the humble monks were replaced by aristocratic canons, who changed the name of their establishment from Baume-les-Moines to Baume-les-Messieurs.

In 1793, at the time of the Revolution, their pride was dashed when the abbey was closed down and its property auctioned off.

In the front doorway (15C) of the **church** is a sculpture of God the Father in the act of blessing and, in the niches on either side, angels blowing wind instruments. In the **Chalon Chapel** *(on the left)* and on either side of the choir, you will see a fine collection of 15C **Burgundian statues**. However, the abbey's chief treasure is its magnificent early 16C **Antwerp altarpiece**★★ *(on display during the guided tour)*, the central subject of which is Christ's Passion.

On the right, a door gives access to the former **cloister**. The monks' refectory and dormitory opened onto this courtyard, which still has its fountain. If you pass through an archway on the left, you will come to another courtyard, surrounded by buildings which housed the aristocratic canons. Then return to the former cloister and first courtyard via a vaulted passageway through the former cellars (13C).

Baume-les-Messieurs village and the Cirque de Baume

R. Mattès/MICHELIN

MAGNIFICENT VIEWS

Cirque de Baume★★★

12km NE of Lons-le-Saunier via the D 471. Shortly before Crançot, turn left onto the D 471, then right to reach the Roche de Baume viewing point.

To get to the magnificent **Roches de Baume viewpoint**★★★, walk along the edge of the cliff which forms the celebrated Roches de Baume "belvedere", commonly known as the "belvédère de Crançot". The natural amphitheatre before you is impressive and, when you come upon it suddenly, takes your breath away.

Near the viewing platform furthest to the right, you will see steps cut in the rock to form the **Échelles de Crançot**, a steep pathway leading down to the bottom of the cirque *(the descent is difficult: proceed cautiously).*

Mont-Poupet★

10km N of Salins-les-Bains via the D 492. After 5.5km, turn left onto the D 273, then 1km farther on, again on the left, is a road leading to the Mont Poupet cross (car park).

From the viewing point (alt 803m; *15 min on foot there and back*), there is a magnificent **view**★ over the Salins basin and the fort of St-André; in the distance, you can see as far as Mont Blanc, the Alps and the Jura; in the opposite direction, the Bresse plain and, beyond, the mountains of Burgundy and Beaujolais.

For an easy initiation into flying in this magnificent area, contact the **Poupet gliding school (École de vol libre du Poupet)** *(9 r. du Poupet, 39110 Saint-Thiébaud; 03 84 73 04 56. www.poupetvollibre.com)* offering first flights in two-seaters; beginners' and improvers' courses from March to September.

Fort Saint-André

4km S of Salins-les-Bains via the D 472, the D 94 right, the D 271 right and right again. Open Jul–Aug 10am–6pm. Apr–Jun and Sept–mid-Oct weekends & public holidays 10am–6pm. 2€. 03 84 73 16 61.

Built in 1674 to plans by Vauban, the fort is a fine example of 17C military architecture. At the foot of the ramparts on the right, is a viewing platform with a good **view**★ over Salins.

Kids will have a fine time at the **Salins Forts Aventure** *(39110 Salins-les-Bains; open Jul-Aug 11am–5pm; Jun, Sept weekends & public holidays 11am–4.30pm; 03 84 73 06 79 or 06 89 71 39 44; www.salins-aventure.com),* an adventure playground laid out around Fort Saint-André. Play at being Tarzan, swinging through the trees-tops and climbing rock-faces. There are various routes to suit different ages and levels of fitness and daring.

Cirque du Fer à Cheval viewing point★★

7km SE of Arbois on the D 469.

10min there and back. Leave your car at the inn below and follow the waymarked path, which starts off to the left.

As you come out of a small wood, the natural amphitheatre yawns before you (safety barrier). From the vantage point, some 200m above the valley, there is a superb view of the Reculée des Planches, a steep-sided blind valley carved into the limestone plateau.

VENTURING UNDERGROUND

Grotte des Planches★

6km SE of Arbois via the D 107. By the church in Mesnay, turn right onto the D 247, which soon enters the valley bottom. At Planches-près-Arbois, after the church, you will cross a stone bridge and, immediately on your left, find a narrow metalled road which runs along the foot of the cliffs. Leave your car 600m further on (kiosk). Visit by guided tour (1hr) mid-Jul–Aug 10am–6pm. Early Apr–mid-Jul and Sept–mid-Oct 10am–noon & 2–5pm. Closed Mon in Oct. 7.50€. 03 84 66 13 74.

There are over 2,000 grottos in the Jura, but this is one of the most spectacular, where tunnels run 250m beneath the Jura plateau, carved by water erosion out of the base of a cliff under a prodigious overhang. The lower tunnel, which serves as the bed of the Cuisance in the wet season, is occupied in the summer months by a string of pools formed by the eddying waters. Known as **marmites de géants** (giants' cooking pots), the water they contain is of a striking bluish colour. In an adjoining tunnel is a display showing how the cavern was formed, explored and is now managed, and how the *reculée* itself was formed. Under the overhang at the entrance to the cavern, excavations have brought to light evidence of Palaeolithic, Neolithic and Bronze Age settlement. When it rains, part of the itinerary is flooded, but the rush and roar of the raging Cuisance is a truly awesome spectacle.

Grottes des Moidons

10km SE of Arbois by the D 469. Visit by guided tour (45min) Jul–Aug daily 9.30am–5.30pm. Apr–May Thu–Tue 2–5pm. Jun & Sept hours vary. 6.90€; 03 84 51 74 94.

In the depths of the Moidons forest, a fascinating aspect of these caverns is their many stalactite and stalagmite formations. The visit ends with a son et lumière display featuring the cavern's underground pools.

Grottes d'Osselle★

16km N of Arc-et-Senans via the D 17, D 12 and D 13. Visit by guided tour (1hr 10min) Jun–Aug daily 9am–7pm. Apr–May & Sept daily 9am–noon & 2–6pm. Oct–early Nov Mon–Sat 2–5pm, Sun & public holidays 9am–noon & 2–5pm. 7€; 03 81 63 62 09. http://grottes.osselle.free.fr.

These caverns are carved in a cliff dominating a meander in the River Doubs. The dry tunnels were used as a place of refuge and worship by Catholic priests during the Revolution. A clay altar is still visible. The skeleton of a cave-dwelling bear has been reconstructed from bones found under fallen rock.

Of a total of 8km of tunnels, 1,300m of long, regular stretches have been opened up for visiting. The first "halls" have been dulled by the smoke from visitors' torches. Then, after negotiating a low passageway, you come upon white stalagmites of almost pure calcite, and others coloured by iron, copper or manganese oxides.

WATER SPORTS AND SPAS

Bathing and archaeology at the Lac de Chalain★★

26km E of Lons-le-Saunier via the D 471 and the D 39. Parking not allowed on the shores of the lake; car parks available near the beaches (fee).

This 232ha lake is undoubtedly the most beautiful in the Jura region. Our ancestors evidently thought so too, since they established a lake-dwellers' village here in prehistoric times.

At the leisure centre, you can enjoy wind-surfing, canoeing, or just swimming in the lake. However, the water is not warm all the year round, and anglers also have opportunity to test their skills and patience; the lake is classed in category 2 for fishing purposes and is a paradise for pike and perch.

Chalain is not only a place to relax. It is also a **site of archaeological interest**, where you can visit the former lacustrine village. **Neolithic dwellings on piles** have been reconstructed on the shores of the lake, using Stone Age techniques. For the purposes of experimentation, they are being left to deteriorate naturally. *Access via La Pergola camp site (pay parking) at Marigny.* There are just three guided tours and one conference each year. An annual exhibition is also organised to report on the progress of the excavations. Information can be obtained from the Clairvaux-les-Lacs tourist office.

Canoeing and kayaking on the River Loue

You can take a 6hr trip down the River Loue by canoe or kayak, covering the 21km stretch between Port-Lesney and Ounans through a magnificent landscape of mountains and vineyards. The **Val d'Amour Loisirs sportifs association** also organises introductory courses to different kinds of fishing *(39380 Ounans; 03 84 37 72 04).*

Valvital Spa

Parc des Bains, 39000 Lons-le-Saunier. Open Mon–Fri 10am-6.30pm, Sat 9.30am-6.30pm, Sun 9.30am-2.30pm. 03 84 24 20 34, www.valvital.eu.

This establishment uses strong (305g/l) and medium (10g/l) sodium-chloride-enriched waters in treating rheumatic conditions, child development problems and psoriasis, but as with most spas, there are treatments and fitness sessions open to the general public. The 7ha park surrounding the buildings is a pleasant place for a stroll.

Les Thermes de Salins

Pl. des Alliés, 39110 Salins-les-Bains. Open 2–5.30/6.30pm. 9€. 03 84 73 04 63; www.thermes-salins.com. This centre is officially approved for specialised treatments for rheumatic, gynaecological and children's conditions. Completely refurbished, along with residential facilities.

WINE BUYING GUIDE

INFORMATION

Comité interprofessionnel des vins du Jura (trade association) – *Château Pecauld, 39600 Arbois. 03 84 66 26 14. www.jura-vins.com.*

CHARACTERISTICS

Jura wines are distinguished by appellation, but also on a varietal basis.

Chardonnay – Gives dry whites, with a floral character when young, which acquire a fine golden hue and more honeyed flavours as they age.

Savagnin – Generally produces vin jaune style wines, distinguished by walnut and spicy notes on ageing. An extremely distinctive bouquet, similar to no other wine. Château-Chalon wines, which are served at room temperature, have a golden robe and a nutlike fragrance.

Poulsard – Gives pale-coloured reds with smokey and berry-fruit flavours.

Trousseau – Gives dark red wines, cherry-flavoured when young, gamey on ageing.

Pinot Noir – Highly coloured, with berry-fruit notes when young, acquiring a black-cherry flavour as it ages.

STORAGE

Vin jaune wines age exceptionally well, even for a century or more. *Vins de paille* also keep very well. Dry whites made from Savagnin will keep for up to ten years, while Chardonnays and reds can be aged for between three to five years.

PRICES

White Chardonnays, crémant-du-jura and red wines – 5 to 8€.
Whites made from Savagnin, Macvins – 8 to 13€.
Vin jaune and Château-Chalon – 20 to 30€ (62 cl).
Vin de paille – 11 to 20€ (50 cl).

COOPERATIVES

Maison du vigneron – *23 r. du Commerce, 39000 Lons-le-Saunier. 03 84 24 44 60. mbailly@cguj.fr. Open Mon–Sat 10am–noon & 2–6.30pm. Closed public holidays.* This winery, whose entrance is opposite the house of Rouget de Lisle, represents approximately 150 growers. The diversity of Jura wine-production is expressed in a wide range of AOC wines: Côtes-du-Jura, Arbois, vin jaune, vin de paille… They also sell liqueurs and local brandies.

ESTATES

Domaine Ligier Père et Fils – *56 Rue du Pupillin, 39600 Arbois. 03 84 66 28 06, www.vins-jura-ligier.com. Open Mon-Sat 9am–noon & 2–5pm. Sun by appt.* brandy) aged in oak barrels. A new tasting room and modern cellar make this 10ha estate an interesting place to visit - and if the weather is good, there is a lovely spot on the terrace for a glass of wine. Ably run by Hervé and Jean-Pierre Ligier, with everything harvested by hand and vinified plot-by-plot, according to grape variety and terroir. Arbois, Côtes-du-Jura, Crémant-du-Jura, Vin Jaune.

Henri Maire, Les Deux Tonneaux – *Pl. de la Liberté, 39600 Arbois. 03 84 66 15 27. www.henri-maire.fr. Open Jul-Aug 9am-7pm; May-Jun 9am-noon & 2-7pm; Sept-Apr 9am-noon & 2-5.30pm.* It is hard not to be aware of the Henri Maire establishment in Arbois; the firm's advertising and its immense and tempting display windows are the measure of its standing in the region. They show films, hold wine-tastings and organise visits to the cellars and

S. Sauvignier / MICHELIN

the winery (book ahead for cellar visits). Arbois, Château-Chalon, Côtes-du-Jura, Crémant-du-Jura, LÉtoile, Macvin-du-Jura.

Domaine Jacques Tissot, *39 r. de Courcelles, 39600 Arbois. 03 84 66 14 27. www.domaine_jacques_tissot.fr. Open Mon-Sat 9am-12.15pm &2-7pm, Sun 10am-12.15pm & 3-7pm.*This 30ha estate was established in 1962 by Jacques Tissot. Traditional methods hold sway here from manual harvesting to maturing in oak (3 years minimum; up to 7 years for vin jaune). Arbois, Arbois-Pupillin, Côtes-du-Jura, Crémant-du-Jura, Macvin-du-Jura.

Château d'Arlay – *39410 Arlay. 03 84 85 04 22; Open Mon–Sat 9am–noon (wine tasting) & 2–6pm (chateau visits); www.arlay.com.* The Château has one of the Jura's oldest vineyards, which was already going strong in the Middle Ages. Consisting of clayey-limestone soils, its 27ha are planted with Pinot Noir, Trousseau, Poulsard, Savagnin and Chardonnay. The grapes are harvested by hand and vinified in temperature-regulated vats. The wines are matured in old barrels for at least three years. Côtes-du-Jura, Macvin-du-Jura.

Domaine Berthet-Bondet, *39210 Château-Chalon. 03 84 44 60 48, www.berthet-bondet.net. Open daily by appt. 10am–noon & 2–7pm.* After training as an agricultural engineer and learning as he went along, Jean Berthet-Bondet set up his winery in 1985, and is the current mayor of Chateau Chalon. He now has 10ha of vines, facing south and west, planted on marly soil under a surface layer of limestone scree. He grows Chardonnay and Savagnin for making white wines; Poulsard, Trousseau and Pinot Noir for the reds and rosés. After pressing and fermentation, his whites and vins jaunes are aged in oak barrels. Attractive tasting room in the centre of the village. Château-Chalon, Côtes-du-Jura, Crémant-du-Jura, L'Étoile, Macvin-du-Jura.

Domaine Jean-Claude Crédoz – *R. des Chèvres, 39210 Château-Chalon. 03 84 44 64 91. domjccredoz@aol.com. Open daily 8am–noon & 1.30–7pm.* Founded by Victor Crédoz and still in the family, the estate now runs to 6ha. The property is in the throes of reorganisation and, since 2004, the vinification, cellaring and marketing operations have been performed in Château-Chalon. The wines are aged in oak barrels for several years, two as a minimum and up to seven for his vin de paille. Château-Chalon, Côtes-du-Jura, Crémant-du-Jura, L'Étoile, Macvin-du-Jura.

Château de L'Étoile – *994 r. Bouillod, 39570 L'Étoile. 03 84 47 33 07. www.chateau-etoile.com. Open daily by appt. 8am–noon & 2–7pm.* Passion and conscientiousness are the watchwords of this estate, which was acquired by Auguste Vandelle in 1883 and has been managed on the same principles generation by generation. Its 16ha are planted with Chardonnay, Savagnin, Poulsard and Trousseau vines. Both vineyard and buildings are situated on the slopes of Mont Muzard, the marly sub-soil of whose eastern, southern and western flanks are particularly well suited to wine-growing. Côtes-du-Jura, Crémant-du-Jura, L'Étoile, Macvin-du-Jura.

Domaine Claude Buchot – *4A, Grande-Rue, 39190 Maynal. 03 84 85 94 27. Open Sat 9am–7pm, rest of week by appt.* This 5.5ha estate raises Chardonnay, Savagnin, Pinot Noir and Poulsard for the reds. Biodynamic methods are practised in the vineyard, with manual harvesting. Fermentation occurs in thermo-regulated stainless-steel tanks, followed by maturation for 18 to 30 months in 228l barrels of Burgundy oak. Claude Buchot also makes a vin de paille. Côtes-du-Jura, Crémant-du-Jura, Macvin-du-Jura.

Domaine de Montbourgeau – *53 r. de Montbourgeau, 39570 L'Étoile. ℘03 84 47 32 96, www.vin-du-jura.com. Open by appt. Mon–Sat 9am–noon & 2–7pm.* A family property purchased in 1920, today run by Nicole Gros. The estate runs to 30ha, 8ha of which are planted with vines. The principal grape varieties are Chardonnay, Poulsard and Savagnin. The vineyard is managed with sustainable agriculture and the grapes are harvested by hand. Vin de paille and Vin jaune are also made here. Crémant-du-Jura, L'Étoile, Macvin-du-Jura

Domaine André et Mireille Tissot – *Quartier Bernard, 39600 Montigny-lès-Arsures. ℘03 84 66 08 27 – Boutique daily 9am-12.30pm, 2.30pm-7pm; Winery visits by appt; www.stephane-tissot.com.* From 0.25ha in 1962 to 30ha in 2000, this estate has registered spectacular growth. Wanting to manage their terroir responsibly, André and Mireille Tissot have converted the whole of the vineyard to biodynamic status. In 2000 and 2001, they produced their first vintages without using sulphur. The owners have invested in truncated wooden vats for vinifying their Pinot Noirs. Since 2004, André and Mireille have been officially retired, but their retirement is a very active one, as they continue to help their son, Stéphane, who has run the estate since 1999 with his wife Bénédicte. Arbois, Côtes-du-Jura, Crémant-du-Jura, Macvin-du-Jura.

Domaine Grand – *R. du Savagnin, 39230 Passenans. ℘03 84 85 28 88; www.domaine-grand.com. Open by appt 8am-noon & 2-6.30pm.* The Grand brothers, working in partnership, have been producing wines since 1976 on a family property whose origins date back to the 17C. The grey marls of the area are particularly well suited to the Savagnin and Trousseau varieties. The vineyards, covering 22ha, are planted with Chardonnay and Savagnin, vinified separately or in a blend, to produce white wines; and with Poulsard, Trousseau and Pinot Noir for reds and rosés. The musts are processed in temperature-regulated vats, and the resulting wines are matured in wooden barrels or tuns. In 2004 the winery was modernised with the addition of thermoregulated stainless-steel tanks. Château-Chalon, Côtes-du-Jura, Crémant-du-Jura, L'Étoile, Macvin-du-Jura.

Domaine Xavier Reverchon – EARL Chantemerle – *2 r. du Clos, 39800 Poligny. ℘03 84 37 02 58. reverchon.chantemerle@wanadoo.fr. Open daily 9am-noon & 2–6pm.* For four generations, this family firm has been tending 6.6ha of vines: Poulsard (1.4ha), Trousseau (0.25ha) and Pinot Noir (0.75ha) for making red wines; Chardonnay (2.5ha) and Savagnin (1.7ha) for whites. The estate's small size allows Xavier Reverchon to vinify each varietal separately. Arbois, Côtes-du-Jura, Crémant-du-Jura, Macvin-du-Jura.

Benoit Badoz – *15 r. du Collège, 39800 Poligny. ℘03 84 37 11 85. infos@badoz.fr. Open by appt. Mon–Sat 8am–7pm.* Wine-growers since 1659, the Badoz family manage 8ha of vines with careful attention to vines and grapes. As well as Côtes-du-Jura and macvins, the estate specialises in making vin jaune and vin de paille. Côtes-du-Jura, Crémant-du-Jura, Macvin-du-Jura.

Domaine de la Borde – *Chemin des Vignes, 39600 Pupillin. ℘03 84 66 25 61, http://domaine-de-la-borde.fr. Open Mon-Sat 8am-7pm & Sun by appt; www.domaine-de-la-borde.fr.* Established in 1983 by Julien Mareschal, the estate encompasses 4.5ha of 100% Ploussard vines, ranging in age from 22 to 50 years. The southwest-facing vineyard is farmed with respect for the environment, and is currently converting to biodynamism. Arbois, Arbois-Pupillin.

Pierre Overnoy – *R. de l'Abbé-Guichard, 39600 Pupillin. ℘03 84 66 24 27. emmanuel.houillon@wanadoo.fr. Open by appt.* The wines of this 5.5ha estate are produced as naturally as possible: hand-digging, no inputs of chemicals. The main varieties grown are Poulsard, Chardonnay and Savagnin, which draw their sustenance from the clayey-limestone soils of the area. Taken over on 1 January 2001 by Emmanuel Houillon, the estate is biodynamic. The wines are vinified in stainless-steel vats, then aged in tuns, barrels or 600-litre vessels (demi-muids). Arbois, Arbois-Pupillin.

Domaine Ganevat – *R. du Pont – La Combe, 39190 Rotalier. 03 84 25 02 69. Open daily by appt. 10am–7pm.* After ten years as winery manager at Chassagne-Montrachet, in 1998 Jean-François Ganevat took over the running of the business, which has been in the family since 1650! Organically farmed since 2001, the vineyards consist of Pinot Noir, Savagnin, Trousseau and Chardonnay. Manual harvesting. In addition to its traditional vins de paille and vins jaunes, the estate produces an original liqueur, Zarby. Côtes-du-Jura, Crémant-du-Jura, Macvin-du-Jura.

Domaine Labet – *Pl. du Village, 39190 Rotalier. 03 84 25 11 13. Open by appt Mon-Sat 9am-noon & 2-5pm.* On the Labet's property the grapes from different plots are vinified separately in consideration of the differing terroir and exposition. Alain Labet believes in organic farming: no fertilisers, hand pruning, careful staking and hand-digging. His vineyard covers 10ha; a third of vines are more than 60 years old. The grapes are harvested manually. The Pinot Noir and Trousseau vintages are aged in new barrels, Poulsard in older ones. Côtes-du-Jura.

Caveau des Byards – *D 70, 39210 Le Vernois. 03 84 25 33 52. www.caveau-des-byards.com. Open Mon-Sat 9am–noon & 2–6pm, Sun 10am-noon & 3-6pm.* Established in 1953, this 30ha vineyard lies at the heart of the Jura massif and enjoys a fine sunny position. The varieties grown are Chardonnay, Savagnin, Poulsard, Trousseau and Pinot Noir. Wines intended for storage are matured in oak barrels. New cellar facilities opened in 1998, and there is today an attractive tasting area and boutique. The estate also produces vin de paille and vin jaune. Arbois, Château-Chalon, Côtes-du-Jura, Crémant-du-Jura, L'Étoile, Macvin-du-Jura.

Domaine Baud Père et Fils – *Rte. de Voiteur, 39210 Le Vernois. 03 84 25 31 41. Mon-Sat 9am–noon & 2–6pm. Cellar visits at 10am and 3pm.* Managed by the Baud family since 1875 (when there were just 6ha of vineyards), the estate now runs to 18ha, planted with Chardonnay, Savagnin, Pinot Noir, Poulsard and Trousseau. Environmentally responsible cultivation, manual harvesting and traditional vinification in temperature-controlled tanks. Château-Chalon, Côtes-du-Jura, Crémant-du-Jura, L'Étoile, Macvin-du-Jura.

ADDRESSES

STAY

AT ARBOIS

Hôtel Les Messageries – *R. de Courcelles, 39600 Arbois. 03 84 66 15 45. www.hotellesmessageries.com. Closed Jan & Dec. 26 rooms.* . On one of the town's main streets, this old lodge has an attractive ivy-clad façade. The bedrooms are gradually being refurbished. Book one of the rooms at the rear, which are quieter and have fully equipped bathrooms.

Annexe Le Prieuré – *R. de l'Hôtel-de-Ville, 39600 Arbois. 03 84 66 05 67. Closed Dec, Jan, Wed Sept–Jun and Tue. 7 rooms 16.70€.* This rambling but comfortable old 17C building is the annex of the Jean-Paul Jeunet hotel-restaurant some 200m up the street. The bedrooms are stylishly furnished, some overlooking an attractive garden.

AROUND ARC-ET-SENANS

Chambre d'hôte Les Traversins du Val d'Amour – *29 rte. de Salins, 39380 Ounans, 13km SW of Arc-et-Senans via the D 17E then the D 32 and D 472. 03 84 37 62 28. lestraversins@wanadoo.fr. 4 rooms. . Restaurant* . You will receive a friendly welcome in this quiet private house not far out of Arc-et-Senans. In fine weather, you can take your breakfast on the terrace, overlooking fields and meadows. The rooms are simple but cosy.

AROUND LONS-LE-SAUNIER

Nouvel Hôtel – *50 r. Lecourbe, 39000 Lons-le-Saunier. 03 84 47 20 67.*

www.nouvel-hotel-lons.fr. Closed Dec 17–Jan 9. 26 rooms. 7.50€. Superb models of French warships, made by the owner, adorn the entrance hall of this town-centre hotel. The rooms are of varying sizes, furnished in rustic style. Those on the third floor are the least spacious.

Chambre d'hôte Le Jardin de Misette – *R. Honoré-Chapuis, 39140 Arlay, 12km W of Château-Chalon on the D 5 as far as Voiteur then D 120. ℘03 84 85 15 72. 4 rooms. Restaurant.* Former restaurateurs and authors of the recipe book Saveurs comtoises, Misette and her husband fell in love with this vigneron's property on the banks of the Seille. The bedrooms are calm and comfortable. The most agreeable is the curiously named "Chabotte" (anvil stand), in a separate little house at the bottom of the garden. Convivial atmosphere, family cooking.

Hôtel Le Parc – *9 ave. Jean-Moulin, 39000 Lons-le-Saunier. ℘03 84 86 10 20. 16 rooms. 6€. Restaurant.* Spend the night in one of the functional, updated rooms and awake to the sounds of the Marseillaise issuing forth from the neighbouring clocktower. Quiet dining-room serving simple dishes made from local ingredients.

Le Comtois – *39130 Doucier. ℘03 84 25 71 21. restaurant.comtois@wanadoo.fr. Closed Nov 28–Feb 11, Sun evenings, Mon evenings and Wed except from Jun 15–Sept 15. 8 rooms. 7€. Restaurant.* Appealing country decor, comfortable rooms, generous regional cooking and an enthusiastic welcome are the hallmarks of this cosy auberge. Good selection of Jura wines on the list.

Hôtel La Parenthèse, *300 chemin du Pin, 39570 Chille, 3km N of Lons-le-Saunier on the D 157. ℘03 84 47 55 44. www.hotelparenthese.com. 34 rooms. 11€. Restaurant.* On the Jura wine route, this is a modern hotel with rooms offering two different levels of comfort. Most have balconies and views over the hotel's park-like garden. The restaurant offers dishes combining local ingredients and non-local ideas.

AROUND POLIGNY

La Ferme du Château – *R. de la Poste, 39800 Bersaillin, 9km W of Poligny via N 83 then D 22. ℘03 84 25 91 31. Closed Jan. 9 rooms. 9.50€.* This magnificently restored 18C farmhouse has retained many of its original features, including a room with fine vaulting and pillars, which in summer is used for concerts and art exhibitions. The sober but elegant bedrooms overlook open countryside.

EAT

AROUND ARBOIS

SARL Le Grapiot – *R. Bagier, 39600 Pupillin, 3km S of Arbois on the D 246. ℘03 84 37 49 44. Closed Thu evenings, Sun evenings and Mon. Reservations recommended.* In the heart of a wine-growing village, this friendly little inn is characteristic of the local style of architecture. Seated by the large fireplace in the dining room, you can enjoy typical regional dishes.

Chalet Bel'Air –*39330 Mouchard. ℘03 84 37 80 34.* A nice place to stop, with a comfortable dining room and very attentive service. Watch meat dishes being roasted in the grand fireplace; terrace overlooking the road.

La Balance Mets et Vins – *R. de Courcelles, 39600 Arbois. ℘03 84 37 45 00. Closed Jun 30–Jul 7, Dec 12–Jan 28, Sun evenings, Tue evenings and Wed except public holidays.* The patron presides over his casseroles on an old stove in full view of his diners. His recipes are often matched with wines from the Franche-Comté region, some at very affordable prices: if you're looking for an interesting local wine list, this is a good place to try. The decor is simple and there is a pleasant terrace.

Le Caveau d'Arbois, *3 rte. de Besançon, 39600 Arbois. ℘03 84 66 10 70. www.caveau-arbois.com. Closed Sun evenings and Mon.* This restaurant's menu is a good introduction to the culinary wealth of the Franche-Comté region. Traditional French cuisine emphasises regional specialities, accompanied by local Crus. Sober, elegant dining room.

AROUND ARC-ET-SENANS

⊖ **Le Relais** – *9 pl. de l'Église, 25610 Arc-et-Senans. ℘03 81 57 40 60. Closed Dec 15 –Jan 15 and Sun evenings.* This family-run inn near the magnificent Royal Saltworks designed by Claude-Nicolas Ledoux has a pleasant terrace at the front. If the sun refuses to shine, enjoy the chef's regional specialities indoors under the exposed beams in one of three rustic dining rooms.

AROUND LONS-LE-SAUNIER

⊖ **Le Mirabilis** – *41 Grande-Rue, 39570 Mirebel, 15km E of Lons-le-Saunier via the D 471. ℘03 84 48 24 36. www.lemirabilis.com. Closed Jan 2–10, Mon, Tue and Wed lunchtimes offseason.* Well-known to local gourmets, this restaurant is tucked away in a little village in the Jura countryside. Sophie and Hugo Meyer invite you to savour their home-grown cuisine: suprême de pintade (guinea fowl) in a morel and vin jaune sauce, and baked trout flambé in vieux pontarlier, a kind of local absinthe.

⊖⊖ **Les Grottes** – *Aux Grottes, 39210 Baume-les-Messieurs, 9km NE of Lons-le-Saunier. ℘03 84 48 23 15. Closed Oct 16–Mar 19, and Mon except in Jul–Aug. Reservations required.* This fine early-20C pavilion and its well-shaded terrace is a good vantage point from which to view the natural wonders of Baume-les-Messieurs, in particular its waterfalls. Savour such local dishes as terrine comtoise, émincé de volaille au macvin – thinly sliced poultry in a macvin sauce – and entrecôte with morels.

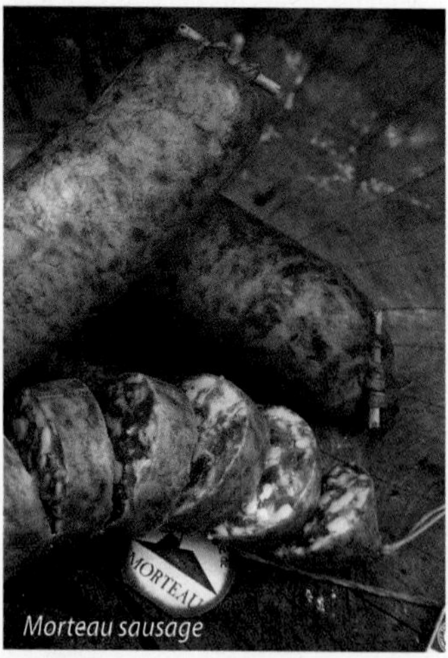

Morteau sausage

S. Sauvignier/MICHELIN

⊖⊖ **Ferme-auberge La Grange Rouge** – *39570 Geruge, 9km SW of Lons-le-Saunier on the D 117. ℘03 84 47 00 44. Closed Aug 25–Sept 17. Reservations recommended. 5 rooms ⊖.* This dairy farm, perched at an altitude of 500m, draws lovers of good food from all over the region, with such dishes as its duck in a cream and morel sauce, croûtes aux champignons and home-made cottage cheese. The spacious, comfortable bedrooms are enhanced by the bucolic peace and quiet of the location.

⊖⊖ **Les 16 Quartiers** – *Pl. de l'Église, 39210 Château-Chalon, 10km N of Lons-le-Saunier via the D 70. ℘03 84 44 68 23. seizequartiers@wanadoo.fr. Closed mid-Nov–end Mar; evenings except weekends Mar–Jun; Thu evenings Jul–Aug.* Time seems to have stood still on the shady terrace or in the semi-cave dining room of this charming 16C house, tucked away at the heart of a little town famed for its vin jaune. Enjoy its local cuisine, accompanied by Jura wines, which are available by the glass.

⊖⊖ **La Bonne Étoile** – *1 r. de la Poste, 45460 Les Bordes. ℘02 38 35 52 15. Closed Aug 22–28, Feb 1–7, Tue evenings, Sun evenings and Mon.* Attractive little country auberge near the roadway. The dining room serves up tasty traditional dishes in a rustic, colourful dining room.

AROUND POLIGNY

⊖⊖ **Le Chalet** – *7 rte. de Genève, 39800 Poligny. ℘03 84 37 13 28. Closed Wed evenings, Thu evenings and Sun.* Local specialities are the pride of this simple, friendly restaurant: escalope polinoise, Morteau sausage with Comté cheese, or salade montagnarde with Gex blue cheese and smoked ham, all served with the best Jura wines, by the bottle, carafe or glass.

AT SALINS-LES-BAINS

⊖⊖ **Les Bains** – *1 pl. des Alliés, 39110 Salins-les-Bains. ℘03 84 73 07 54. hotel.bains@wanadoo.fr. Closed Jan 1–16, Tue lunchtime, Sun evenings and Mon.* "Morillette" and "comtine" are two of the mouth-watering inventions devised by chef Maurice Marchand, who also has plenty of other tasty recipes up his sleeve. Classic cuisine is served in the country-style dining room, regional dishes in the brasserie.

⊜⊜ **Le Relais de Pont d'Héry** – *Rte. de Champagnole, 39110 Salins-les-Bains. ℘03 84 73 06 54. Closed Oct 18–Nov 4, Feb 15–Mar 3, Tue Sept–May and Mon.* Behind the somewhat bland façade of this small house are two very pleasant dining rooms where appetising traditional dishes are served: try breaded quail fillets with hazelnuts, baked turbot aux herbes, noix de saint-jacques in flaky pastry with candied lemons, foie gras soufflé or gratin d'écrevisses.

GOURMET SHOPPING

Charcuterie Guyon – *5 r. de l'Hôtel-de-Ville, 39600 Arbois. ℘03 84 66 04 25.* Everything is wholesome and home-made chez Jean-Claude Guyon, high priest of local pork butchery: wild boar ham, ham steeped in vin jaune, sausage incorporating Comté cheese or pine honey, red deer brési (dried salted meat). A glance in the window is enough to get your taste buds working.

Hirsinger, *38 pl. de la Liberté, 39600 Arbois. ℘03 84 66 06 97. www.chocolat-hirsinger.com. Open Mon–Tue & Fri–Sun 8am–7.30pm.* It would be an unforgivable oversight to pass through Arbois without paying a short visit to this chocolate-maker (winner of the Meilleur Ouvrier de France award, 1996), who produces a succulent range of chocolates – flavoured with mint, ginger or spices – as well as celebrated local specialities such as galets d'Arbois biscuits or Bouchons.

Au Prince d'Orange – *Éts Pelen, 1 r. St-Désiré, 39000 Lons-le-Saunier. ℘03 84 24 31 39. Shop open Mon–Fri 9am–12.15pm & 2.30–7pm; Sat 9am–12.30pm & 2.30–7.15pm; Sun 9am–12.30pm. Tea room open 2.30–6pm.* Since 1899, the Pelen family has been spoiling the inhabitants of Lons-le-Saunier with its galets de Chalain (nougatine and praline robed in chocolate), gâteau Écureuil (praline-hazelnut butter cream on an almond-hazelnut base, all covered in marzipan) and many other delicious sweetmeats. Stylish tea room upstairs.

Maturing Comté cheese

S. Sauvignier / MICHELIN

Juraflore – *15 pl. des Déportés, 39800 Poligny. ℘03 84 37 13 50. Open Mon–Wed 8.30–7pm; Thu–Sat 8am–12.30pm & 2.30–7pm; Sun 9am–noon.* Over three generations, the maturing of Comté cheese has been raised to an art form by the family which owns this shop. At every stage of maturity (6, 12, 18 or 23 months), mild, medium or intensely mature and salty, it is worthy of the highest praise. Also try their Mont d'Or, Morbier and Tomme de Castelviel.

Fumé du Jura – *Hameau de Moutaine, 39110 Pont-d'Héry, 8km S of Salins-les-Bains on the D 467. ℘03 84 73 02 49. Open summer daily Tue–Sun 8am–7:30pm; closed Mon in winter.* Ham on the bone, dried sausages, palette (shoulder of pork), brési, tongue, sausage marinaded in vin jaune, pâtés of various kinds: these delicious delicatessen products are made exclusively with pork meat and offal from the Franche-Comté region. Some are smoked by local craftsmen, always using juniper wood. Temptations no gourmet could resist…

MARKETS

Poligny – *Monday and Friday morning, Place des Déportés.*

Lons-le-Saunier – *Thursday, Place de la Liberté.*

Arbois – *Friday morning.*

9 - LANGUEDOC-ROUSSILLON

Cultivated by the Iberians from 7C BC, the grapevines in this region were extended by the Romans and then by the monastic orders, but remained confined within their ancient limits until the Canal du Midi was dug in the 17C, enabling a better distribution of the wines. But it was the railway in the 19C that caused the extraordinary expansion of the wine industry here. Between 1850 and 1870 production increased from 4 million to 15 million hectolitres, fuelling a cultural and economic explosion in the region. From Carcassonne to the Mediterranean, and from Banyuls to Nîmes, a sea of vines swept over Languedoc and Roussillon, and today there are many wine routes in the region, each traversing areas full of character where the architectural heritage is as remarkable as the natural landscape. Wine is part of the soul of the Languedoc-Roussilon, and passion for it runs deeply.

Highlights

1 The largest fortress in Europe at **Carcassonne** (p311)

2 A chocolate dessert and a glass of **Banyuls** (p321)

3 A stroll through the Medieval streets of **Lagrasse** (p315)

4 Cruising along the **Canal du Midi** (pp306, 309, 315, 323)

5 An afternoon siesta under the plane trees of **Perpignan** (p318)

Despite its increasing dynamism today, the Languedoc still bears the marks of a difficult past. The phylloxera crisis, which broke out in the late 19C, was a disaster and in 1907 the wine-growers, reduced to penury by competition from imported Algerian wines, finally rebelled. Led by charismatic café owner Marcelin Albert, hundreds of thousands of demonstrators clashed with the army, who mutinied out of solidarity in Narbonne. It took all of the Interior Minister Georges Clemenceau's skill as a tactician to restore order. Afterward, groups of astute wine-growers founded the first cooperatives, but high-quality production did not emerge for another two generations. Indeed, the wine-growing Midi made large quantities of basic table wine until the 1980s, when drinking trends suddenly shifted. Everyone wanted higher-quality wines, and winegrowers scrambled to modify their products accordingly. The replacement of the traditional grape varieties by quality varieties, limitation of yields, and the creation of *appellations d'origine contrôlée* formed the basis of the new regime. Today, the Languedoc-Roussillon still produces 40% of French wine, but despite the tremendous efforts made, competition from New World wines has scored a direct hit on the region.

Vineyards of the Corbières

D. Pazery/MICHELIN

Ramparts of Carcassonne

A. Thuillier/MICHELIN

OVERVIEW

The Terroir

Michelin Local Maps 339 and 344 – Gard (30), Hérault (34), Aude (11) and Pyrénées-Orientales (66).

Surface area: the vineyards of Languedoc cover 290,000ha in the Hérault, Aude and Gard *départements*; the vineyards of Roussillon cover 9,000ha in the Pyrénées-Orientales.

Production: 40% of French wines, around 16-18 million hl, 90% of which are local wines *(vins de pays)* and table wines *(vins de table)*.

The climate is Mediterranean with mild winters and hot dry summers. The soils vary: schist in Faugères, St-Chinian, the Corbières, Minervois and Roussillon; round pebbles in the Minervois, Rivesaltes and the Val d'Orbieu; limestone soils in Roussillon and the Corbières; alluvial land and granitic soils in the Coteaux du Languedoc.

The Wines

The Languedoc-Roussillon region produces red, white, fortified and sparkling wine. Since 2007, AOC Languedoc has been introduced. This is a base appellation, but there remain more specific ones also; 18 in total. The intention is to grow AOC wines to 20% of the region's output.

Gard – Appellations here include AOC Clairette-de-Bellegarde (white) and Coteaux-du-Languedoc (red, rosé, white). The AOC Costières-de-Nîmes (red, rosé, white) is connected to the Rhône Valley vineyards.

Hérault – AOC Clairette-du-Languedoc (white), Coteaux-du-Languedoc (red, rosé, white), Faugères (red, rosé), Minervois (red, rosé, white), Minervois-La-Livinière (red), Saint-Chinian (red, rosé), Muscat-de-Frontignan (fortified wine), Muscat-de-Lunel (fortified wine), Muscat-de-Mireval (fortified wine), Muscat-de-St-Jean-de-Minervois (fortified wine).

Aude – AOC Blanquette-de-Limoux (sparkling), Côtes-de-Cabardès (red, rosé), Crémant-de-Limoux (sparkling), Corbières (red, rosé, white), Côtes-de-la-Malepère (red, rosé), Coteaux-du-Languedoc (red, rosé, white), Fitou (red), Limoux (red, white), Minervois (red, rosé, white).

Pyrénées-Orientales – AOC Banyuls and Banyuls Grand Cru (fortified wine), Collioure (red, rosé, white), Côtes-du-Roussillon (red, rosé, white), Côtes-du-Roussillon-Villages (red), Maury (fortified), Muscat-de-Rivesaltes (fortified), Rivesaltes (fortified).There are also 61 *vins de pays*.

9 - LANGUEDOC-ROUSSILLON

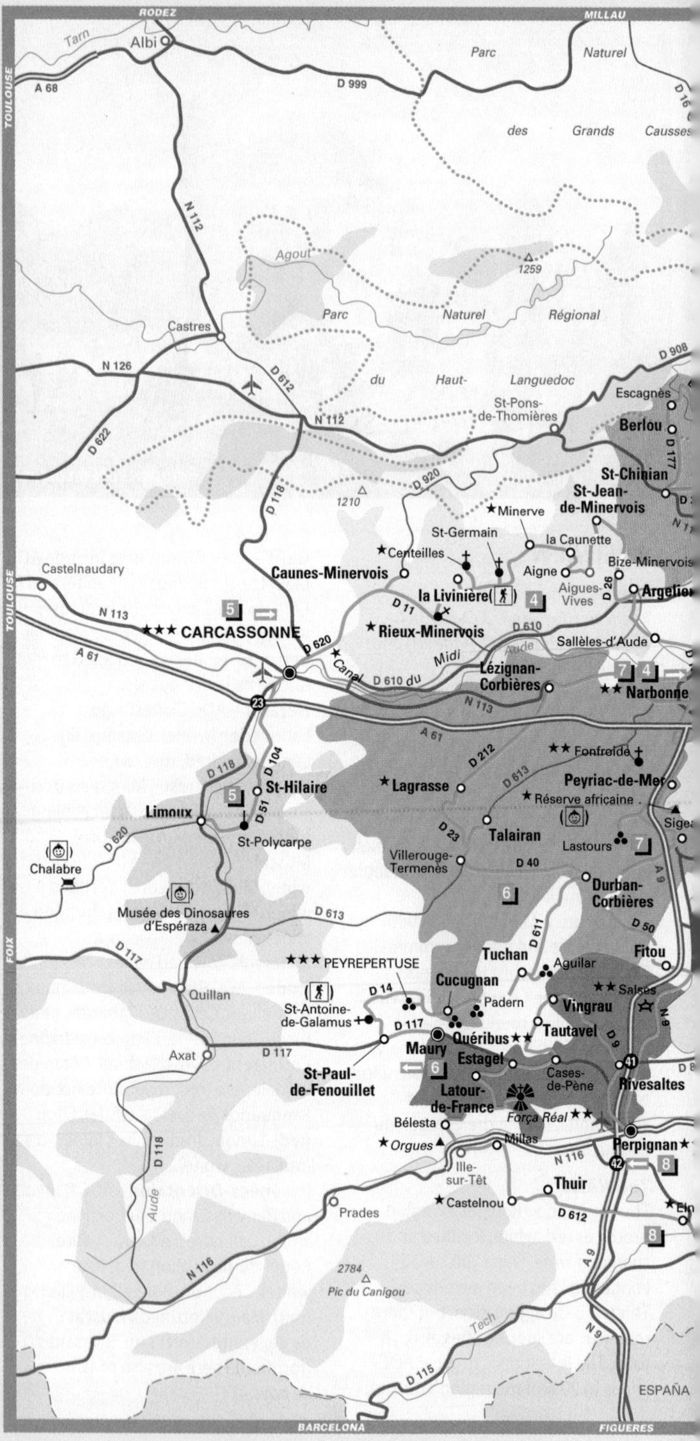

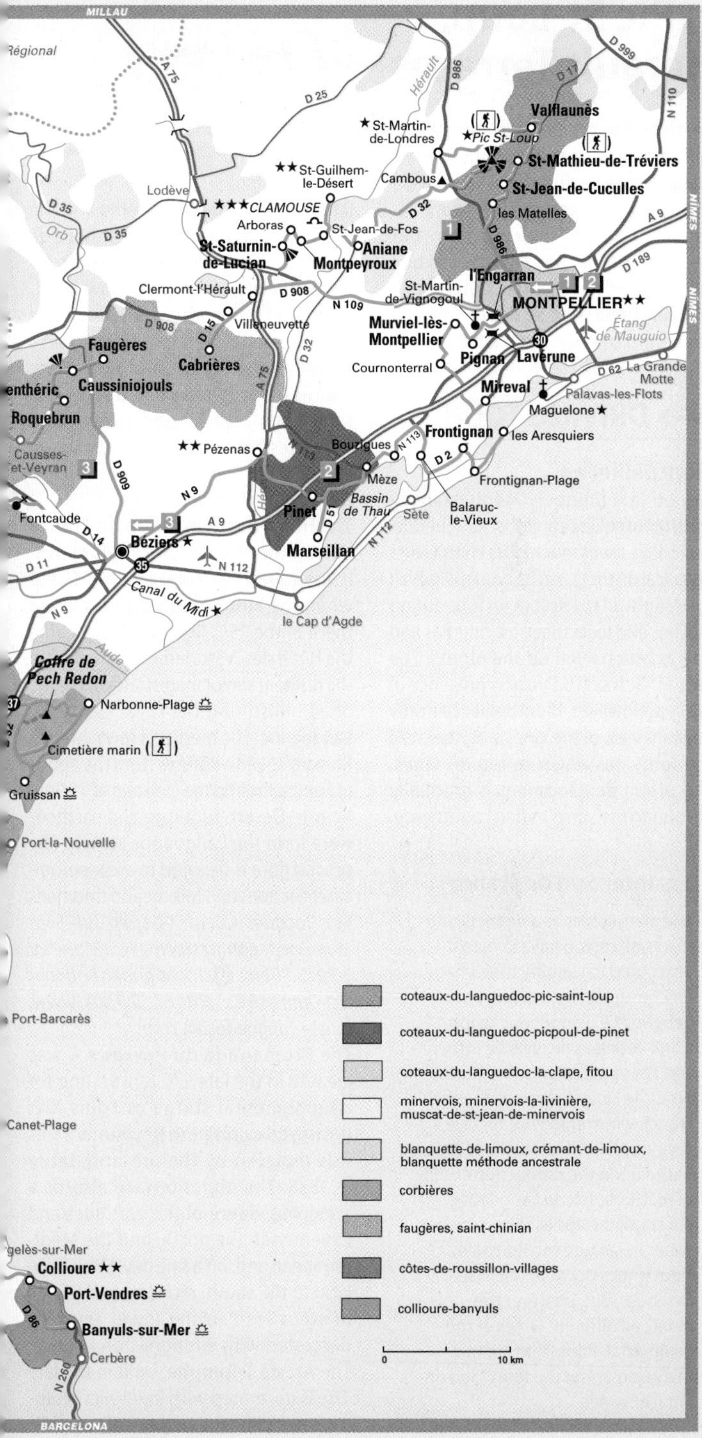
MILLAU
Régional
D 25
Hérault
D 986
D 999
D 17
N 110
★ St-Martin-de-Londres
★Pic St-Loup
Valflaunès
St-Mathieu-de-Tréviers
St-Jean-de-Cuculles
les Matelles
★★ St-Guilhem-le-Désert
Cambous
Lodève
★★★CLAMOUSE
D 32
D 35
Orb
Arboras
St-Jean-de-Fos
St-Saturnin-de-Lucian
Aniane
Montpeyroux
A 9
D 189
NÎMES
l'Engarran
St-Martin-de-Vignogoul
MONTPELLIER★★
Clermont-l'Hérault
D 908
N 109
Villeneuvette
Murviel-lès-Montpellier
Étang de Mauguio
Faugères
D 15
Cabrières
D 32
Pignan
Lavérune
Cournonterral
D 62
La Grande Motte
Caussiniojouls
A 75
Mireval
Palavas-les-Flots
Maguelone★
Roquebrun
N 113
Frontignan
les Aresquiers
Causses-et-Veyran
D 909
★★ Pézenas
Bouzigues
Mèze
D 2
Frontignan-Plage
N 9
Pinet
D 51
Bassin de Thau
Sète
Balaruc-le-Vieux
Fontcaude
A 9
Béziers★
Marseillan
N 112
D 14
D 11
N 112
Canal du Midi★
N 9
le Cap d'Agde
Aude
Coffre de Pech Redon
Narbonne-Plage
Cimetière marin
Gruissan
Port-la-Nouvelle
Port-Barcarès
Canet-Plage
coteaux-du-languedoc-pic-saint-loup
coteaux-du-languedoc-picpoul-de-pinet
coteaux-du-languedoc-la-clape, fitou
minervois, minervois-la-livinière, muscat-de-st-jean-de-minervois
blanquette-de-limoux, crémant-de-limoux, blanquette méthode ancestrale
corbières
faugères, saint-chinian
côtes-de-roussillon-villages
collioure-banyuls
0
10 km
gelès-sur-Mer
Collioure★★
Port-Vendres
D 86
Banyuls-sur-Mer
Cerbère
N 260
BARCELONA

1 Pic St-Loup, Hérault Terraces

North of Montpellier, the summit of Pic St-Loup rises 658m above the garrigue, facing the white mass of the Hortus plateau. The clayey limestone soils of their northern and western approaches are covered by the vineyards of the AOC Coteaux-du-Languedoc-Pic-St-Loup; a short drive from the city, but a world away.

- **Michelin Map:** 339, F-I 6-7. See itinerary 1 on the map on p298.
- **Distance:** 115km.

DRIVING TOUR

Montpellier★★

Bathed in a uniquely Mediterranean light, Montpellier, capital of Languedoc-Roussillon, owes much of its charm to its historical districts and its gardens, which are delightful to explore on foot during the day, and to its theatres, cinemas and opera, which liven up the nights. The salty air betrays the nearby presence of the sea. However, Montpellier has only a distant view of the vineyards; the city's economy has never relied on vines, and urban development is gradually devouring the surrounding countryside.

Inter Sud de France

The many wines and districts of this large region have in recent years tried to simplify their image for consumers by creating a generic AOC Languedoc to form a link between the vins de pays and the appellation wines (until now, the Languedoc was the only French wine region not to have a generic AOC), This new appellation, based upon the production criteria of AOC Coteaux du Languedoc, covers all the appellation growing zones in Languedoc-Roussillon, from Nîmes down to the Eastern Pyrenees. But whatever the name, all different wines of the Languedoc-Roussillon are now marketed under the term "Sud de France" wines

Between place de la Comédie and the Peyrou Arc de Triomphe, on either side of rue Foch, lie the **historic districts** ★★ of Montpellier, with their narrow, winding streets, the last vestiges of the original medieval town. Lining these streets are superb 17C and 18C private mansions, or *hôtels particuliers*, with their main façades and remarkable staircases hidden from the public eye in inner courtyards. *Itinerary available from the tourist office.*

The **Hôtel des Trésoriers de France** houses the **Musée Languedocien**★. It was called the Hôtel Jacques-Coeur when the king's treasurer was living there in the 15C. In the 17C it became the Hôtel des Trésoriers de France, after the resident senior magistrates in charge of administering the royal estates in Languedoc. The medieval room houses Romanesque sculptures from the abbey of Fontcaude and the cloisters of St-Guilhem-le-Désert, furniture and earthenware from the Languedoc region. The second floor is devoted to archaeological collections and folk art and traditions *(7 r. Jacques-Coeur; open Jul–Sept Mon–Sat 3–6pm; rest of the year Mon–Sat 2.30–5.30pm, closed public holidays Oct–Jun; 6€;. 04 67 52 93 03; www.musee-languedocien.com).*

The **Promenade du Peyrou**★★ was created in the late 17C as a setting for a monumental statue of Louis XIV; destroyed during the Revolution, this was replaced by the present statue in 1838. The upper terrace affords a sweeping **view**★ of the garrigues and Cévennes in the north, and the Mediterranean and, on a fine day, Mont Canigou to the south. Monumental flights of steps lead to the lower terraces decorated with wrought-iron railings.

The **Arc de Triomphe**, built in the late 17C, is decorated with low-relief sculptures depicting the victories of Louis XIV.

Behind the Polygone shopping centre and office complex *(starting from place de la Comédie, walk to the Antigone district via Le Polygone shopping centre)*, the **Antigone District★** is the creation of Catalan architect Ricardo Bofill. Covering the 40ha of the old polygonal army exercise ground, this vast neo-Classical project combines prefabrication techniques (the prestressed concrete has the grain and colour of stone) with rigorously harmonious design on a gigantic scale.
Lastly, take the time to visit the **Agropolis Museum★**, devoted to agriculture throughout the world.
The presentation is as attractive as it is educational; the "Dining Table of the World" display illustrates the variety and inequality inherent in this theme. In addition, there are thematic exhibitions, a Cyber Museum, and activities for children *(6km north of the Hôpitaux-Facultés district; access by car or tram to St-Éloi then shuttle to Agropolis-Lavalette; open Mon-Fri 10am-12.30pm, 2-6pm; 5€; 04 67 04 75 00; www.museum.agropolis.fr)*.

D 986 NW out of Montpellier and, after 10km, turn right to Les Matelles.

Les Matelles
This fortified village has beautiful houses with external staircases. In the Neolithic age, nomadic herdsmen settled here; this period is illustrated in the **Musée Municipal de Préhistoire** (*open summer Tues-Thu, Sat-Sun 3–6pm; rest of the year Fri–Sun 3–6pm; 04 67 84 18 68)*.

East on D 17 (3km); left on D 113.

Saint-Jean-de-Cuculles
This tiny village has a pretty Romanesque church. A very respectable Coteaux-du-Languedoc Pic St Loup is produced here at the **Domaine Haut-Lirou** (*see Shopping Guide)*.

Carry on D 113.

Saint-Mathieu-de-Tréviers
A **walk** in the garrigue *(2hr there and back)* will take you up to the ruins of the old Château de Montferrand. Lovely view of the vineyards.

Take the D 17 to Valflaunès.

Valflaunès
This is where most of the estates of the Coteaux-du-Languedoc-Pic-St-Loup *appellation* can be found. If youre buying wine try **Domaine Mas Bruguière**; **Domaine de l'Hortus** remains a benchmark (*see Shopping Guide)*.

SW on D 1, joining D 1, then take the D 122 to Saint-Martin-de Londres.

Saint-Martin-de-Londres★
Vines are scarcer on the southern side of the Causse de l'Hortus (Hortus limestone plateau), and give way to an austere landscape of garrigue. The word "Londres" comes from the Celtic word *lund* meaning "marsh". In the centre of the old village, the defences of the "old fort" date from the 12C; its bounds are marked by a gateway. The 11C Romanesque **church★** is delightful.

D 32 for Viols-le-Fort; left on D 113.

Cambous Prehistoric Village
Access road is bumpy; leave the car in the Cambous car park and walk. Open Jul–Aug Tue–Sun 2–7pm. Sept–Oct, Apr-Jun weekends & hols. 2.50€. 04 67 86 34 37; www.archeologue.org.
The substantial remains of stone dwellings, with 2.5m-thick drystone walls and openings forming corridors, date from 2800-2300 BC. A prehistoric house has been reconstructed.

D 113 to Cazevieille; park in car park.

Pic Saint-Loup★
3hr return. Follow signs to Pic St-Loup. Limestone is slippery when wet.
The wide stone path leads up to a calvary. From there, take a little winding footpath which climbs up to the chapel and observatory. From the summit, there is a magnificent **panorama★★** of the whole region.

Take the same road back to Cambous. Turn left onto the D 32.

Aniane

Aniane has lost all trace of the abbey founded here in the 8C by St Benedict. A stroll through the streets takes in the church of St-Jean-Baptiste-des-Pénitents, built in a mixture of architectural styles and now used to house temporary exhibitions. The Aniane terroir is shared by the Coteaux-du-Languedoc and *vins de pays*. The **Mas de Daumas Gassac** produces some great regional red and white wines, with a character as atypical as their prices *(see Shopping Guide)*. The 10 ha **Brugas estate**, situated between the villages of La Boissière and Argelliers, southeast of Aniane, is also a name to watch due to its relative cool micro-climate and hard-working owners Ludivine Delaeter and Olivier Zébic who have been making wine here since 2006 *(34150 La Boissière; 04 67 54 92 56, www.brugas.com; open by appt)*.

North on D 32; left on D 27

The road crosses the River Hérault by a modern bridge near the **Pont du Diable** (Devil's Bridge) which, though you might not guess so by the name, was actually built by Benedictine monks in the early 11C. View of the Hérault gorge and the bridge aqueduct that irrigates the vineyards of the St-Jean-de-Fos region.

Grotte de Clamouse★★★

Visit by guided tour (1hr) daily Jul–Aug 10am–7pm. June & Sept 10.30am–6pm. Mar–May & Oct 10.30am–5pm. 8.70€. 04 67 57 71 05. www.clamouse.com.

This cave is renowned for its wealth of crystalline formations. It takes its name from the resurgent spring that cascades noisily into the Hérault after very heavy rain, hence its Occitan dialect name of *Clamosa*, the "howler".

Drive 4km along D 4.

Saint-Guilhem-le-Désert★★

This village is built around an old abbey at the mouth of untamed river gorges, where the Verdus flows into the Hérault. It owes much of the story of its origins to legend, related in the 12C *chanson de geste* by Guillaume d'Orange. It relates that Guilhem, one of Charlemagne's officers, founded the abbey after bringing back a piece of the real Cross. This relic is on display in the 11C **abbey church**★ and is carried in a procession to the village square every year in May. From the alley lined with old houses, admire the rich decoration of the church's **chevet**★. Flanked by two apsidal chapels, it features three windows and a series of arched openings separated by slender columns.

D 4 in other direction.

Saint-Jean-de-Fos

This old fortified village was once a major centre of pottery production and has an interesting Romanesque church.

Continue on D 141 to Montpeyroux.

Montpeyroux

At the foot of an old fortress in ruins, Montpeyroux has lent its name to the **AOC Coteaux-du-Languedoc-Montpeyroux**. Here full-bodied, intense red wines are produced, such as those of the renowned **Domaine l'Aiguelière** *(see Shopping Guide)*.

D 9 N to Arboras.

Arboras

A splendid **panorama**★ can be enjoyed from the terraces of the old castle, of which only one tower remains.

D 130 SW to St-Saturnin-de-Lucian.

Saint-Saturnin-de-Lucian

The old town still has a few old houses. St-Saturnin lends its name to the **AOC Coteaux-du-Languedoc-Saint-Saturnin**. The organic **Domaine Virgile Joly**, established in 2000, is a good place to stop *(see Shopping Guide)*. From the village, a little road runs up to the **Rocher des Vierges** (Virgins' Rock), a pilgrimage place with a **panorama**★★.

D 130 and the D 141 as far as Ceyras; then turn right onto the D 908.

Clermont-l'Hérault

Like Lodève, Clermont-l'Hérault specialised for a long time in the manufacture of military cloth. It is now an important wine-growing centre and a market for dessert grapes. The narrow alleys climb up a hill crowned by the ruins of a 12C castle (beautiful view of the village and surrounding area). The fortified **Church of St-Paul**★ (13C-14C) gives an impression of solidity and strength.

Villeneuvette

Guided tour of the town (2hr) Jul–Aug daily 3.30pm and Tue–Fri 10.30am. Sept–Jun by appt. 4€. Contact the town hall, 04 67 96 06 00.

This former royal textile factory was founded by Colbert in the 17C and has retained its architectural unity. The square, main street and approaches to the workers' houses have been recobbled as in the 17C and the houses, now with pleasant, flower-filled gardens, have been converted and restored.

Left onto D 15 after Villeneuvette.

Cabrières

Decomposing shale and high slopes produce the quality of **Coteaux-du-Languedoc-Cabrières**, powerful wines that should be kept. The surrounding area also produces the **AOC Clairette-du-Languedoc**, a dry or smooth white wine which, upon ageing, takes on a "*rancio*" quality: a sweet, golden character and a nutty aroma. Make the most of your time in Cabrières to visit the hamlet of **Les Crozes**, entirely built of schist and set in magnificent scenery. You can also tour the old **Pioch-Farrus copper mine**, which dates back to prehistoric times (*visit by 45min guided tour Apr-Nov Sun-Thur 2–7pm, last departure 1hr before closing time, rest of year by appt); 7€; 06 14 91 46 02).*

D 908 to Gignac then the N 109.

2 Wine and Shellfish Route

Eaten away by urban sprawl around Montpellier, the vineyards begin to come into their own about a dozen kilometres west of the city proper. Even further away, the shores of the Thau lagoon still have some protected areas which attract pink flamingos. Sample oysters and other shellfish from Bouzigues, washed down with AOC Coteaux-du-Languedoc-Picpoul-de-Pinet.

Michelin Map: 339, F-I 7-8. See itinerary 2 on the map on p298.
Distance: 145km.

DRIVING TOUR

Leave Montpellier on the D 5 towards Lavérune then turn right onto the D 5E.

Château de l'Engarran

34880 Lavérune. Boutique open daily; chateau by appt only. 04 67 47 00 02. www.chateau-engarran.com.

Beyond the superb entrance gate stands a Louis XV style building. There is a musuem of old wine-making instruments in an attractive vaulted cellar, and a boutique selling, among the estate's other wines, a good red Coteaux-du-Languedoc-St-Georges-d'Orques.

Continue on D 5. The château is on the far west side of the village.

Château de Lavérune

Open weekends 3–6pm. 2€. 04 99 51 20 00 (town hall) or 04 99 51 20 25 (museum); www.laverune.f.

This former residence of the bishops of Montpellier (17C-18C) stands in the middle of a park and houses works by contemporary artists.

Road to St-Georges-d'Orques. Before the village; right on D 5^E5 (Pignan).

Abbey of St-Martin-de-Vignogoul

Open Mon–Fri 10am–noon & 2–5pm. Guided tours; call 04 67 42 76 68.
Not much remains of the former 11C Cistercian abbey. The 13C Gothic church stands surrounded by some of the oldest Carignan vine stock in the Languedoc.

Pignan

This once fortified wine-growers' town is at the heart of the **Coteaux-du-Languedoc-Saint-Georges-d'Orques** appellation.

D 27 NW to Murviel.

Murviel-lès-Montpellier

Some results of the excavations of the Gallo-Roman *oppidum* (fortified town) of Le Castellas are on display in the town hall *(open by appt. 04 67 47 05 14).* You will find out more by going to the **Domaine des Belles Pierres** where you can discuss archaeology over a glass of white Coteaux-du-Languedoc *(24 r. des Clauzes, 34570 Murviel-lès-Montpellier; open Wed & Sat 9am–7pm; Tue, Thu & Fri 5–7pm; 04 67 47 30 43; www.domainebellespierres.com).*

D 102 S to Cournonterral.

Cournonterral

In autumn each year, during the Paillasses festival, straw-covered monsters hunt down young people dressed all in white and plunge them into a tub of wine lees. Purple, squelching fun guaranteed.

D 114 SE to Mireval; left on N 112.

Mireval

The village is famous for the **AOC Muscat-de-Mireval** vineyards, which grow between the Étang de Vic and the slopes of the Massif de la Gardiole. The **Domaine Mas Renée** in Vic la Gardiole is a fine example *(see Shopping Guide).*

Frontignan

Frontignan lends its name to a famous, golden Muscat, whose 800ha of vineyards grow near the shores of the Étang d'Ingril. The door of the **Gothic church** (12C-14C) has a beautiful frieze of fish and boats. The **Cave Coopérative de Frontignan** *(guided tour possible)* produces 80% of the **Muscat-de-Frontignan** appellation. It offers several cuvées corresponding to different stages of maturity as well as some "forgotten wines" that have aged for many years in oak tuns *(see Shopping Guide).*
The **Musée d'Histoire locale** (local history museum) houses prehistoric collections and illustrates the production of Muscat *(4 bis r. Lucien-Salette, next to the church; open Jul–Aug daily 10am–noon & 2.30–6.30; Apr–Jun & Sept–Nov Wed–Mon 10m–noon & 2–6pm; no charge; 04 67 18 50 05).*

Frontignan-Plage and Les Aresquiers

From the beach at Frontignan *(2km S)*, you can follow the narrow offshore bar to the shingle beach of Les Aresquiers, a popular spot for nude sunbathing. The *guinguettes*, as the open-air cafés are called, serve *bouillabaisse* (fish stew) and sometimes have musical evenings.

Return to Frontignan; take D 2 west; right on D 2^E, alongside Thau lagoon.

Balaruc-le-Vieux

Perched on a hill overlooking the lagoon, the village still has its original circular layout. Some of the houses feature striking arched doorways.

D 2 to Bouzigues; left on N 113.

Bouzigues

The evolution of shellfish farming techniques is illustrated at the **Musée de l'Étang de Thau** *(on the quay of the fishing harbour; open Jul–Aug 10am–12.30pm & 2.30–7pm; Mar–Jun &*

Oyster beds in Thau lagoon

Sep–Oct 10am–noon & 2–6pm; Nov–Feb 10am–noon & 2–5pm; closed Jan 1, Dec 25. 4€. 04 67 78 33 57).
From the shores of the small bay in the far north of the lagoon you can see groups of pink flamingos and enjoy the view of Balaruc-le-Vieux.

N 113 to Mèze.

Mèze

The port of Mèze, its narrow streets, 15C church, oysters and friendly bistros attract a large number of tourists. The **Étang de Thau** is nearby. This vast lagoon (8,000ha) stretches out along the Languedoc coast, separated from the sea by the isthmus of Onglous (Sète beach). On the north shore a few fishing villages, their huts hidden by reeds, specialise in oyster and mussel farming. Admire the rigorous geometry of the shellfish parks whose delicious produce you can sample to your heart's content, washed down with a fresh white wine from the region such as a refreshing Picpoul-de-Pinet.

D 159 W, then turn left onto the D 51.

Marseillan

Probably founded in the 6C BC by sailors from Marseilles, Marseillan is the home of **Noilly-Prat**. The Noilly-Prat **storehouses** *(near the harbour)* are open to the public. One of the distinctive stages of the production of dry vermouth is the ageing of the blend in 600-litre open air casks (*visit by 1hr guided tour, plus boutique May–Sept 10–noon & 2.30–7pm; rest of year times vary; 3.50€; 04 67 77 75 19. www.noillyprat.com*).

6km to the south, **Marseillan-Plage** boasts miles of sandy beaches.

D 51 (opposite direction); left on D 18^E1.

Pinet

This small village is famous for the Picpoul (or Piquepoul) grape, formerly used to make vermouths. Since vermouth is no longer in fashion, it is now used to make a pleasant white wine that is dry and fruity and goes well with shellfish.
The welcoming **Château de Pinet** makes Coteaux-du-Languedoc-Picpoul-de-Pinet wines and produces high-quality cuvées (*see Shopping Guide*).

D 161^E2 NW; then D 161 to Castelnau-de-Guers; then D 32^E5 N.

Pézenas★★

This little artistic town is set in the "garden of the Hérault", a fertile plain covered in vineyards. In old **Pézenas**★★ you can stroll among magnificent mansions, 17C hôtels, inner courtyards and restored streets full of crafts and antiques shops *(a historic route leaflet is available from the tourist office)*. Pézenas has one big literary claim to fame: Molière stayed there from 1653 to 1657. Don't forget to try the delicious local speciality, petits pâtés, made of mutton, preserved lemon peel and curry.
The owners of **Prieuré St-Jean-de-Bébian** make a fine coteaux-du-Languedoc (*see Shopping Guide*).

Take the N 9 SW to Béziers.

3 Faugères and Saint-Chinian

The southwest edge of the Larzac plateau forms a mass covered in peaks reaching heights of between 600 and 700m. In the lowest parts, vines thrive on the schist, which alternates with limestone scree. Vineyards are this austere region's only resource, and they produce red wines renowned for their strong character on the *terroirs* of Faugères and St-Chinian. More recently the area has seen the growth of aromatic, complex white wines.

Michelin Map: 339, C-E 7-9. See itinerary 3 on the map on p298.
Distance: 125km.

DRIVING TOUR

Béziers★

The town of Béziers, with its cathedral perched on high, drops steeply down to the plain where the long silvery corridor of the **Canal du Midi**★ snakes along, and provides some wonderful photo opportunities. It is also the capital of the Languedoc vineyards, which stretch as far as Carcassonne and Narbonne. Béziers was the hometown of Pierre-Paul Riquet, the famous creator of the Canal du Midi. The town comes alive during the annual *féria* (festival) in August and every Sunday when it comes out to support its legendary rugby team, the ASB. In 1907 the **allées Paul-Riquet**, a broad avenue shaded by plane trees and lined with cafés and restaurants, provided the stage for the mutiny of the 17th infantry regiment which took place when the regiment – made up of wine-growers' sons – refused to shoot at the crowd of angry wine-growers.

The old **Cathédrale St-Nazaire**★, perched on a terrace above the River Orb, symbolised the might of the bishops of Béziers between 760 and 1789. The Romanesque building was damaged in 1209 during the Albigensian Crusade, and alterations were carried out on it from 1215 until the 15C. Go round the south side of the cathedral to the **cloisters** then take a flight of steps to the Jardin de l'Évêché, from which there is a lovely view of the church of St-Jude and the River Orb spanned by a 13C bridge, the Pont-Vieux.

Housed in the old St-Jacques barracks on Place des Casernes, the **Musée du Biterrois**★ contains substantial collections on local archaeology and natural history. A major part of the museum is given over to the region's Gallo-Roman heritage. The highlight of the exhibition is the *"Trésor de Béziers"*, consisting of three large chased silver platters discovered in 1983 in a vineyard on the outskirts of town. Various aspects of local economy are also illustrated, including fishing, wine-growing and the construction of the Canal du Midi (*open Tue–Sun 9/10am–5/6pm; closes for lunch during autumn and winter; closes Jan 1, Easter Sunday, May 1, Dec 25; 2.70€; 04 67 36 71 01*).

D 14 west ; after 15km, left on D134[E1]

This is Saint-Chinian country. The **AOC St-Chinian** covers 3,300ha scattered over a vast area of schist, limestone scree, sandstone and red clay. The wines of St-Chinian, which have been enjoyed since the Middle Ages, had a reputation for being robust. With the planting of new vines and the aid of new techniques, more supple and fruity red wines can now be produced.

Abbaye de Fontcaude

Open Jul–Aug 10am–7pm; Jun & Sept 10am–noon & 2.30–7pm, Sun & public holidays 2.30–7pm; Oct–May 10am–noon & 2.30–5.30pm, Sun & public holidays 2.30–5.30pm. Closed Jan, Dec 25. 4.50€. 04 67 38 23 85.

Set on the road to Santiago de Compostela, the abbey reached the peak of its influence during the Middle Ages before being ruined. In summer, concerts are

held here. A **museum** is housed in the large room where the monks illuminated manuscripts. A 12C bell foundry is still standing, as is the canons' oil mill.
If you wish to sample the wines of **Domaine Cazal-Vieil**, take the D 38 NE then the D 14 to Cessenon-sur-Orb *(see Shopping Guide).*

At end of D 134^{E1}, right on D 134.

Before reaching St-Chinian the road passes through the pretty red-stone villages of **Cazedarnes** and **Pierrerue**.

Left on D 20.

Saint-Chinian

The entire town – its name associated throughout France with its enjoyable wines – exudes a relaxed way of life, from its little squares edged with plane trees to its pleasant cafés, which could have been taken straight from a Marcel Pagnol story. The church contains a fine Baroque organ.
You will gain good insight into the production of the AOC at the friendly **Maison des vins**, where you can taste and buy more than 300 items at the producer's price, and different producers are on hand for tasting every day over July and August. It also offers wine-tasting courses, weekend ideas, and vineyard tours *(1 ave. de la Promenade, 34360 St-Chinian; open daily 9am–noon & 2–6.30; 04 67 38 11 69; www.vin-saintchinian.com)*. The **Domaine Canet Valette** produces good wines *(see Shopping Guide).*

D 20 E then left on D 117.

This little road passes through splendid scenery where small areas of old vine stock clinging to the red earth play hide-and-seek with the garrigue, dotted with the occasional olive tree.

Berlou

Stop at the **Cave des Coteaux du Rieu**, where a fossil exhibition will give you an insight into the character of the terroir. The cooperative has also signposted four mountain-bike circuits through the vineyards, and there are numerous "Balades des Vignerons" walks over the summer months. *(34360 Berlou; open Mon–Sat 9.30am–noon & 2.30–6pm, Sun 10am–1pm & 2.30–6pm; closed Jan 1, May 1 & Dec 25; 04 67 89 58 58; www.berloup.com).*

Continue N on D 177.

The corniche road becomes increasingly narrow and affords picture-postcard views of **Escagnès**, and of the medieval village of **Vieussan**, perched on high.

D 14 S to Roquebrun.

The sometimes lazy, sometimes raging River Orb runs through the valley, canoes gliding along its surface while swimmers, sunbathers and picnickers gather along its banks, which are equipped with facilities in some places (for example on the outskirts of **Ceps** and Roquebrun).

Roquebrun

Backed by a mountain cirque, the village is dominated by a medieval tower, and hosts a lively festival the second weekend of February. Its exceptional climate enables it to maintain a **Mediterranean garden** containing 400 Mediterranean and exotic specie *(open Jul–Aug 9am–7pm; mid-Feb–late Jun & Sept–mid-Nov Sun-Fri 9am–noon & 1.30–5.30pm, Sat 1.30–5.30pm; 5€; 04 67 89 55 29; www.jardin-mediterraneen.fr).*

D 19 to Causses-et-Veyran.

All the goodness of the excellent limestone soil of **Causses-et-Veyran** goes into **Château Maurel Fonsalade**, one of the musts of the AOC St-Chinian.

Minor road E from Causses-et-Veyran; rejoin D 136^{E2}; becomes D 136 as it cuts through the woods at Fabrègues.

You are entering the terroir of the **AOC Faugères**. This appellation covers 2,000ha extending over seven com-

with tastings of both olive oil and olives *(Hameau de Cabezac, 11120 Bize-Minervois; open in winter Mon–Fri 8am–noon & 2–6pm; summer Mon–Fri 8am–noon & 2–7pm, Sat 9am-noon & 2-7pm, Sun 10am-noon & 2-7pm; closed Jan 1, Dec 25; 04 68 41 88 88; www.loulibo.com).*

Continue on D 26; left on D 177.

Saint-Jean-de-Minervois

In an austere landscape of causse (limestone plateau) dotted with a few capitelles, the old twisted Muscat vines take all the goodness from the limestone scree to produce a fortified wine with a rich and complex bouquet. The **Coopérative du Muscat de St-Jean-de-Minervois** will give you a very warm welcome *(34360 St-Jean-de-Minervois; open Mon–Fri 8am–noon & 2–6pm; weekends 2–6pm; if closed, there are several other sales outlets in the village; 04 67 38 03 24; http://muscat.chez-alice.fr).*
The **Domaine de Barroubio**, outside the village, is an excellent establishment *(see Shopping Guide).*

D 176 south; left on D 175 to Aigues-Vives, then D 910 to Aigne.

Aigne

Vines are so much part of this attractive town that its coat of arms, on the church font, depicts a vine bearing bunches of grapes. Take a stroll around the winding streets before admiring the panorama on the road to Minerve.

D 177, then D 907 to La Caunette.

La Caunette

This old fortified village still has a 13C monumental gateway. Outside the village, the Romanesque church of Notre-Dame is set amid charming scenery.

Take the D 10 to Minerve.

Minerve★

Minerve stretches out on a rocky promontory, a veritable island detached from the causse by the combined effects of glacial and then fluvial erosion. Dominating an arid, seemingly scorched passage crisscrossed by rugged gorges, the town occupies a very picturesque **site**★★ boasting a number of rare features, such as its **natural bridges**★. Nothing remains of the proud fortress that stood atop this spur in the Middle Ages, and the echo of the Cathar tragedy caused here by Simon de Montfort is now muffled by an ocean of vineyards. In the narrow rue des Martyrs are a few crafts workshops and a number of wine-growers' shops.

D 10 west then D 182 for Cesseras.

Canyon de la Cesse

At the beginning of the Quaternary Era, the waters of the Cesse hollowed out a canyon, enlarging existing caves and making new ones.

Turn left onto the road to Cesseras, which leads down to the plain and vineyards. Go through Cesseras and turn right onto the D 168 to Siran. After 2km, turn right again.

Chapelle de Saint-Germain

This Romanesque chapel, which nestles in a grove of pine trees, is particularly interesting on account of the decoration of its apse.

Return to the D 168 and carry on towards Siran.

Chapelle de Centeilles★

North of Siran. Open Sun 2.30pm-5pm. 04 68 91 50 07.
Surrounded by cypress trees, holm oaks and vines, this 13C chapel has beautiful 14C-15C **frescoes**★ inside.

Take the D 168 to La Livinière.

La Livinière

This wine-growing village has lent its name to the AOC Minervois-La-Livinière, which produces red wines only, in five communes. Their powerful, fruity character sets them apart, and some fine examples are to be found at **L'Oustal Blanc** *(see Shopping Guide).*

Take the D 168 SW.

Starting from **Félines-Minervois**, a 12km **footpath** *(3hr 30min, average difficulty)* allows you to explore woods, *capitelles* and vineyards of the Minervois. Afterward we recommend a stop at **Domaine Borie de Maurel** *(see Shopping Guide)*.

Turn back then turn right onto the D 52, before making a left turn to Rieux-Minervois.

Rieux-Minervois

Rieux boasts a beautiful 12C **church★** with an interior decorated with remarkable carved capitals.

Carry on to Caunes-Minervois via the D 11, turning right onto the D 620.

Caunes-Minervois

The village is known for the red marble with grey and white veins quarried nearby and much sought after in the 18C. Two fine mansions stand round the town hall square: Hôtel Sicard (14C) with its corner mullioned window and **Hôtel d'Alibert** (16C), now a charming hotel and restaurant, which opens onto a delightful Renaissance courtyard. The abbey church of the former Benedictine abbey has retained its beautiful 11C Romanesque east end.
Outside the village, the welcoming cellar of the splendid **Château Villerambert-Julien** (16C) is a good place to stop to discover a wide range of local wines. The Château houses a small and tastefully arranged repository of winegrowers' tools *(11160 Caunes-Minervois, open Jun-Sept daily 9–11.30am & 1.30–6.30pm; Oct-May Mon-Fri 9-11.30am & 1.30-6.30pm, weekends by appt; 04 68 78 00 01; www.villerambert-julien.com).*

5 Blanquette Trail

Michelin Map: *344, E 3-4.* See itinerary 5 on the map on p298.
Distance: 60km.

South of Carcassonne, the Limoux region remains very attached to its festive and cultural traditions. With respect to wine growing, it is distinguished by its sparkling wines produced under three different appellations: Blanquette-de-Limoux, Crémant-de-Limoux and Blanquette Méthode Ancestrale. Blanquette is made mainly with Mauzac grapes, while Crémant contains a good proportion of Chardonnay. The region also produces well-constructed red and white still wines under the Limoux appellation.

DRIVING TOUR

Carcassonne★★★

Prepare for a breathtaking sight when you reach the outskirts of Carcassonne. The town was renovated in the 19C by the architect Viollet-le-Duc and dominates the wine-growing plain, with the garrigue-covered mountains of the Corbières in the background.
The *"Cité"* of Carcassonne is the largest fortress in Europe. It consists of a fortified nucleus, the Château Comtal, and a double curtain wall: the outer ramparts, with 14 towers, separated from the inner ramparts (24 towers) by the outer bailey, or lists *(lices)*. The main entrance, the **Porte Narbonnaise**, is flanked by two massive towers which house temporary exhibitions of modern art.
The **rue Cros-Mayrevieille** leads directly to the castle, although visitors might prefer to take a less direct route through the medieval town, with its narrow, winding streets lined with many shops (crafts, souvenirs). To the right of

place du Château is a large well, nearly 40m deep.
Built in the 12C by Bernard Aton Trencavel, with its back to the Gallo-Roman fortified wall, the **Château comtal** was originally the palace of the viscounts. It was converted into a citadel after Carcassonne was made part of the royal estate in 1226 (*visit by 45mi guided tour Apr–Sept 9.30am–6.30pm; Oct–Mar 9.30am–5pm; last entry 45min before closure closed Jan 1, May 1, Nov 1 & 11, Dec 25; 8€, no charge 1st Sun Oct-Mar; 04 68 11 70 70. www.monuments-nationaux.fr.*

Leave the castle and follow rue de la Porte-d'Aude on the left.

The **Porte d'Aude** is the main feature of the **outer bailey**, the part between the two walls. It is reached by a fortified path from the lower town and is heavily defended on all sides.
Enter the Cité through the Porte St-Nazaire. All that remains of the old **Basilique St-Nazaire**★ consecrated in 1006, is the nave. The interior is a combination of Romanesque and Gothic architecture. The **stained-glass windows**★★ (13C-14C) are considered the most interesting in the South of France. Remarkable **statues**★★ adorn the chancel walls.

South out of Carcassonne on D 104.

Carnival in Limoux
M.-H. Carcanague/MICHELIN

Saint-Hilaire
The discovery of the Blanquette's sparkle is traditionally attributed to the Benedictine monks of St-Hilaire.
From the foot of the church apse, take the ramp to the trapezium-shaped **cloisters** before entering the much altered Romanesque **church**. Inside, in the chapel on the right, is the "ossuary of St Sernin", a sarcophagus believed to be the work of the 12C Master of Cabestany.

Drive S along the D 51 to St-Polycarpe.

Saint-Polycarpe
Beneath the high altar of the **fortified church** various items from the old treasury are on display, all 14C works, and fabrics from the 8C. The two side altars feature Carolingian decoration carved with knot-work and palm leaves. On the walls and vault are the remains of 14C frescoes (restored).

Take the D 129 W.

Limoux
Limoux has gained a reputation for its carnival, which runs from January to April; every Sunday, processions of masked people (the *"fécos"*) accompanied by musicians dance through the arcades on place de la République. The town's skyline is dominated by the distinctive outline of the Gothic spire of St Martin's church, which overlooks the river. The lively narrow streets are still partly enclosed within a fortified wall built in the 14C.
The **Sieur d'Arques** wine cooperative is the main producer of Blanquette and Crémant-de-Limoux. Private tours and wine tastings with commentaries are available by appointment. The cooperative organises an auction of white AOC Limoux wines and devotes part of the funds raised to conservation of the local architectural heritage. Wine appreciation and wine-tasting courses are also available here *(Ave. de Carcassonne, 11300 Limoux; open daily 9am–noon & 2–6pm; 04 68 74 63 00, www.sieurdarques.com).*

6 Les Corbières

The Corbières, a mountainous region in the Aude *département* bordering the eastern Pyrenees, towers above the furrow of the Fenouillèdes. Here stand the vertiginous fortresses that staged famous episodes of the Cathar drama, surrounded by the spiny, sweet-smelling scrub known as garrigue. The AOC Corbières is the biggest in the Languedoc region, covering 13,500ha, and another 1,430ha in Corbières Boutenac. After years of producing table wine, the region underwent a transformation in the 1980s-1990s and now produces quality wines.

Michelin Map: 344, F-H 3-6. See itinerary 6 on map p298.
Distance: 125km.
Advice: The itinerary for Les Corbières provides an opportunity to visit several of the castles that played a part in the Cathar epic. Be prepared for very strong winds. A hat, sturdy footwear, sunscreen and drinking water are essential. Binoculars may come in handy.

DRIVING TOUR

Maury

At the foot of the arid mountain pass known as the Grau de Maury, this village has lent its name to an appellation of fortified wine, Maury, made from Grenache Noir grapes growing on 1,700ha schist. **Mas Amiel** is the appellation's star estate. You can visit its open-air store of demijohns (3,000 in all), where the wine is left to age. Guided walks through the vineyards are also possible *(66460 Maury; open 9am–noon, 2–6pm; tours by appt.; 04 68 29 01 02, www.masamiel.fr)*. You can also visit the **Vignerons de Maury** cooperative.

D 117 west.

Saint-Paul-de-Fenouillet

This peaceful place was once a border town between France and Roussillon. One of the local specialities is *biscottin*, an almond biscuit. The D 7 to Cubières follows a winding route before threading its way through vines. A bend in the road gives a view of the Canigou (left).

Ermitage Saint-Antoine-de-Galamus

Leave the car in the car park before the tunnel. 30min on foot there and back.

The path runs down from the hermitage terrace (view of Canigou). The hermitage building conceals the chapel in the dim depths of a natural cave.

The road enters the **Gorges de Galamus**★★ and follows a very narrow corniche. The gorge is so narrow and steep that you only gets rare glimpses of the mountain stream gushing below.

At Cubières, turn right onto the D 14.

Château de Peyrepertuse★★★

From the car park, follow a steep path up to the entrance (30min on foot; sturdy footwear recommended). Visitors should proceed with caution if the "cers" – a strong southwesterly wind – is blowing. Open daily Jun–Sept 9am–7pm; Apr–May and Oct 9am–7pm; Nov–Mar 10am–5pm. Closed Jan;

Wine-growers' stone huts in the Corbières
A. Thuillier/MICHELIN

no access in stormy weather. 5€. 04 68 45 40 55. www.chateau-peyrepertuse.com.
The craggy outline of the castle on its rocky spur can be seen clearly from the outskirts of Rouffiac, to the north. It is not only one of the finest examples of fortification in the Corbières, but also the biggest and probably the most evocative of the Cathar castles. Peyrepertuse comprises two adjacent but separate castles, on the east (Peyrepertuse) and west (St-Georges) ends of the ridge, and measures 300m at its longest point.

Château de Quéribus★★

Audioguides available. Open Feb–Dec; times vary. 5€ (combined ticket with Achille-Mir Theatre in Cucugnan). 04 68 45 03 69; www.queribus.fr.
This lofty castle seems to melt into the rock, looking for all the world like a thimble on a thumb. At an altitude of 729m, this sentinel watches over the plain of Roussillon, defying the winds. In 1255, it was the last Cathar fortress to be taken by the crusaders. Three successive lines of fortifications protect the two-storey polygonal keep. The high **Gothic hall**★ has vaulting resting on a central pillar.

Cucugnan

Dominated by its restored mill, this village is well known for the sermon of its parish priest, a jewel of Oc folklore which was adapted into French by Alphonse Daudet. The tiny **Achille-Mir Theatre** on place du Platane hosts a theatre performance on the theme of the "Sermon du curé de Cucugnan" (*open Jul–Aug 10am–9pm; Apr–Jun & Sept 10am–8pm; Oct & Mar 10am–7pm; Feb 10am–6.30pm; Nov–Dec 10am–6pm; closed Jan except school holidays, Dec 25; 5€ (combined ticket with Château de Quéribus); 04 68 45 03 69*).
Under the dual protection of the parish priest and the Château de Quéribus, the village of Cucugnan can quietly go about tending its vines; most of the wine is produced by the wine cooperative.

Continue on D 14.

Padern

To reach the castle, follow the yellow-marked "sentier cathare", 20min on foot there and back. The ruins are dangerous in places. The Château de Padern, now in ruins, was rebuilt in the 17C. Fine view of the village and the River Verdouble.

At end of D 14; left on D 611.

Tuchan

Tuchan is surrounded by Fitou vineyards. Some good Muscat-de-Rivesaltes and Rivesaltes are also produced at the **Producteurs du Mont Tauch** wine cooperative. Visitors are welcomed in the converted cellar that has been transformed into an impressive visitor centre and tasting room; a film recounts the vine cycle and reveals the secrets of winemaking (*11350 Tuchan; open Jul-Aug daily 9am-1pm & 2-7pm; Sept-Jun Mon–Sat 9am–noon & 2–6pm; 04 68 45 44 73; www.mont-tauch.com*).

East of Tuchan, a surfaced path through vineyards branches off the D 39 to the left and leads to Aguilar Castle.

Château d'Aguilar

10min on foot there and back from the parking area. Enter the enclosure from the SW.
Aguilar became a royal fortress in 1257. Built on top of a small rounded hill rising up from an ocean of vines, it was reinforced in the 13C on the orders of Louis IX. There is an attractive view of the vineyards in the Tuchan basin and, to the west, the ruins of Donneuve Castle.

Return to Tuchan; right on D 611.

Durban-Corbières

The castle overlooking the village consists of a rectangular two-storey building. Durban is one of the terroirs shown to advantage by the Corbières AOC appellation. The combination of black schist and clayey limestone soils results in high-flying cuvées such as those of organic wine estate **Château Haut-Gléon**. Every summer there is an exhibition of works by the young artists invited to the Château to paint on the theme of vines *(CD 611, Villesèque-des-Corbières, 11360 Durban-Corbières; open daily 9am–12.30pm & 1.30–6pm; 04 68 48 85 95, www.hautgleon.com).*

D 40 west.

Villerouge-Termenès

At the heart of the village stands the **castle** with its four towers (12C and 14C). It was owned by the archbishops of Narbonne and in 1321 was the scene of the burning at the stake of the last Cathar Parfait, Guillaume Bélibaste. The castle has been renovated and now houses an audiovisual exhibition on Bélibaste and on daily life in the Middle Ages. One wing of the castle houses a medieval restaurant (La Rôtisserie), which serves 13C and 14C dishes – with the same decorum – as well as hypocras, a wine flavoured with plants and spices *(opening times vary; closed Jan; 6€; 04 68 70 09 11).*

Continue on D 613.

Talairan

The chapel of Notre-Dame-de-l'Aire (13C-14C), which dominates the village, contains a touching St Vincent holding two bunches of grapes. If you wish to take a look, contact Jean-Pierre Mazard at the **Domaine Serres-Mazard**; he can tell you all about the vineyards and also about the wild orchids in the region, which are a passion of his *(11220 Talairan; open daily 9am–7pm; 04 68 44 02 22; www.serres-mazard.com).*

U-turn then right on D 23.

Lagrasse★

With its fragile bridges, ruined ramparts and old houses, Lagrasse is a striking sight. Set on the banks of the River Orbieu, the town serves as the setting for a famous abbey. The surrounding area constitutes one of the best terroirs of the Corbières, as illustrated in particular by **Château Pech-Latt** (*see Shopping Guide).*

A pleasant stroll through the narrow streets will take you past medieval houses where a number of craftsmen have set up their workshops.

The **Abbaye Ste-Marie-d'Orbieu** consists of a palace and a church with a 13C **bell-tower** that affords an attractive view from the top. The **abbot's chapel**★ opens onto the courtyard of the **Palais vieux** and has some rare 14C ceramic paving with geometric motifs. On the upper floor of the Palais Vieux is the monks' dormitory with its fine timber frame. A staircase leads, via the "pre-Romanesque tower", to the cellars, store rooms and bakery are located *(closed Jan; 3.50€. 04 68 43 15 99.*

D 212 north of Lagrasse.

Beyond Fabrezan, you can take a little detour by the D 161 to the right *(toward Ferrals-les-Corbières, then Boutenac)* to tast the wines at the **Château La Voulte Gasparets** in **Boutenac** (*see Shopping Guide).*

Lézignan-Corbières

In the undulating landscape of the Corbières, half way between Carcassonne and the sea, Lézignan is a small active town which relies on wine-growing and the wine trade. You can explore the tiny squares and alleyways around the church of St-Félix, and enjoy the shade of the promenades lined with plane trees.

The **Musée de la Vigne et du Vin** is a vine and wine museum that has been set up in an old vineyard. The main courtyard opens onto the saddle room, the stables and a winepress. The winemaking cellar contains a large vat for treading the grapes. On the first floor, the tools used for tending the vine are displayed by season, and include swing ploughs, pruning shears, grafting knives, back-baskets and wooden tubs. A room is devoted to wine transport along the Canal du Midi from the 18C to the present time. The museum also offers an introduction to tastes and smells. *9am-noon & 2-7pm. 5.35€ 04 68 27 07 57.*

Return to Narbonne via the N 113.

7 La Clape and Fitou

Michelin Map: 344, I-J 3-5. See itinerary 7 on map on p298.
Distance: 137km.

To the west and south of Narbonne the vineyards sweep down to the sea and cover the slopes overlooking the lagoons. The nearby Mediterranean tempers the heat of the sun a little, but the wines still have plenty of character. The small limestone island that forms La Clape mountain has become joined to the continent by the process of silting. This great "pile of stones", which rises to a height of 214m, is crowned by pine trees and garrigue, which give way to well-ordered vineyards on the slopes down to the sea. The AOC Coteaux-du-Languedoc-La-Clape, which covers 625ha, produces heady reds, fruity rosés and robust whites. The Fitou territory, split, unusually, into two parts, yields full-bodied wines.

DRIVING TOUR

Take the D 168 E out of Narbonne.

Narbonne-Plage

This resort stretching along the coast is typical of the traditional Languedoc seaside resorts.

The D 332 S leads to Gruissan.

Cité de la Vigne et du Vin

Domaine INRA de Pech Rouge. Open Jul–Aug daily 10am–8pm. Jun & Sept–Dec weekends and public holidays 2–6pm. 5€; www.cite-vigne-vin.com.

Set in the heart of the Languedoc region, on the grounds of the National Institute of Agronomic Research, this museum installation offers insights into winemaking at every level from the most basic to the most specialised. The visit is organised around the various areas of viticulture and oenology. A greenhouse lets you see vines as they pass through the seasons; a vineyard is planted with different varieties and shows irrigation and pruning techniques. You can even see and operate machinery used in the winemaking process. Video screens, interactive stations and sensory challenges make for an interesting, educational visit, especially for kids.

Gruissan

Gruissan is no longer isolated in the middle of lagoons as it once was, but the very distinctive houses of fishermen and wine-growers still coil around the ruins of the castle. The houses of the **old village**, home to fishermen and salt-pan workers, are set out in concentric circles around the ruins of the Barbarossa tower.

D 32 to Narbonne; at the crossroads beyond the tennis courts, take the road signposted to N.-D.-des-Auzils into the Massif de la Clape; keep left all the way.

Cimetière marin

4km, then 30min on foot there and back. Leave the car in the car park (in front of the Rec d'Argent nursery) and walk up to the chapel. Or, you can drive the 1.5km of forest track signposted to Les Auzils, leave the car on a piece of rough ground and continue on foot.

All along a stony path, among the broom, umbrella pines, holm oaks and cypresses, are touching memorials and plaques to sailors lost at sea. From the **Chapel of Notre-Dame-des-Auzils** in the heart of a thicket at the top of the hill, there is an extensive view over Gruissan and La Clape mountain.

Follow the little road across the lower slopes of La Clape. At the D 32, right for Narbonne. At Ricardelle, take a steep, narrow little road on the right.

Coffre de Pech Redon

This marks the summit of La Clape mountain. From it, there is a scenic view over the lagoons and Narbonne. The stony soil, which looks rather inhospitable, provides a happy home for the local vineyards.

Return to Narbonne on D 32. Stay on the city's bypass until the N 9 in the S; left on D 105 passing under it.

The road runs alongside the Bages lagoon *(Étang de Bages)*.

Peyriac-de-Mer

This village with its 14C fortified church stands on the shores of the little Étang du Doul, a welcome stopping place for migratory birds. The nearby **Domaine des Deux Ânes**, which uses organic farming methods, produces some interesting red wines *(see Shopping Guide)*.

Réserve africaine de Sigean★

Open daily Apr–Sept 9am–6.30pm. Rest of the year hours vary. 25€ (children 13€). 04 68 48 20 20. www.reserveafricainesigean.fr.

A paradise for pink flamingos, egrets and gulls, the wild landscape of the Sigean African Safari Park stretches for 300ha along the coast. Large areas of garrigue dotted with lagoons have been made to resemble the species' original native environment as closely as possible. Visitors who are quiet and patient enough, and equipped with a good pair of binoculars, will be rewarded with sightings of lions, zebras and antelopes.

D 611A to Portel-des-Corbières.

Portel-des-Corbières

A botanical path leads to the entrance of **Terra Vinea**, a former gypsum quarry converted into cellars where the wines of the cooperatives operating under the name of Caves Rocbère are left to age. Visitors can learn about the wine-growing activity in the old quarrying galleries. A Gallo-Roman villa illustrates life in ancient times. Wine-tasting at the end of the tour (*Boutique open daily 10.30am–5.45pm; restaurant Tues-Sun 11.30am-2pm. closed Jan 1, Dec 25. 8.50€; 04 68 48 64 90; www.terra-vinea.com)*.

D 3 towards Sigean. Continue for Port-la-Nouvelle before turning right on Chemin de Lapalme. At the first roundabout turn left, following the road that passes over the motorway until the little bridge. Continue on foot up the path.

Parc Éolien des Corbières Maritimes★

Spread atop the summit of Castanière Hill, this windmill park supplies electricity equivalent to the consumption of 10,000 people, not counting heating. The five wind turbines installed here in 1991 were joined in 2000 by 10 additional "desmoiselles." Signs and plaques provide the technical explanations for this silent, futuristic landscape.

Return to Sigean; left on N 9 & D 175.

Lapalme

In this village bordering the Lapalme lagoon, stop for a taste of the excellent products of the **Domaine des Mille Vignes** *(see Shopping Guide)*.

D 709 around the lagoon; left on N 9 and turn right on the D 27 toward Treilles, then the D 50 toward Fitou.

The road starts by winding through a rocky landscape where pines and holm oaks stand at the mercy of fierce winds. Then, before reaching Fraissé-des-Corbières, a dense host of vine plants invades the landscape, covering the red earth shared by the Fitou and Corbières appellations. In a heroic struggle against the wind, the vineyards, protected by cypress hedges, nestle in the most sheltered recesses of the surrounding bare mountains. Between Treilles and Fitou the landscape is sublime.

Fitou

This seaside village has given its name to an appellation which covers 2,600ha in two separate areas: Fitou Maritime and Haut Fitou. The traditional Fitou, matured in tuns, is appreciated for its *tuilé* (reddish-brown) colour and slightly oxidative character. The more fruity, new-style Fitou is very similar to Corbières.

8 Roussillon Wine Route

Michelin Map: 344, G-J 5-8. See itinerary 8 on map on p298.

Distance: 185km.

Roussillon, united with France under Louis XIV, has for a long time reaped the benefits of its dessert wines, of which Spain was particularly fond. Proud of its Catalan identity, the region is full of charm and always reserves a warm welcome for visitors. There are three major production areas here: the Côtes-du-Roussillon-Villages to the north of Perpignan, Côtes-du-Roussillon to the south, and Collioure and Banyuls on the coast, near the border with Spain. The Rivesaltes and Muscat-de-Rivesaltes fortified wines are produced throughout Roussillon.

DRIVING TOUR

Perpignan★★

Both close to the sea and to the Pyrenees, Perpignan is still part of France but also very much part of Catalonia. Walks shaded by plane trees, cafés serving tapas with aperitifs, and a pace of life between siesta and busy nightlife are all part of Perpignan's appeal. Here, the architecture speaks of the past: of the counts of Roussillon and the kings of Majorca, of the Catalans and the people of Aragon, and of the French.

Le Castillet★, an emblem of Perpignan, dominates place de la Victoire with its two towers crowned with crenellations and machicolations. It houses the Casa Pairal, which is devoted to the popular arts and traditions of the Catalans.

The **place de la Loge** and the pedestrianised rue de la Loge form the lively centre of town life. In the centre, the **Loge de Mer**★ housed a commercial tribunal for maritime matters in the 16C. In the arcaded courtyard of the **Hôtel de Ville**★ stands a bronze by Aristide Maillol, entitled *The Mediterranean*.

The **Cathédrale St-Jean**★, begun in 1324 by Sancho, second king of Majorca, was not consecrated until 1509. The façade of bricks and pebbles is flanked by a square tower with a fine 18C wrought-iron campanile. The impressive nave rests on robust interior buttresses separating the chapels, which feature sumptuous 16C and 17C altarpieces.

Away from the town centre, on the hill of Puig del Rey, stands the **Palais des Rois de Majorque**★, a palace built during the reign of the kings of Majorca (1276-1344). Today the Queen's suite (superb ceiling painted with Catalan colours) and the Flamboyant Gothic style chapel-keep are open to the public (*open 10am–5/6pm, last entry 30min before closing; tours on request; 4€; 04 68 34 48 29*).

To return to the world of wine, we suggest a trip to the **Comptoir des Crus**, where the terroirs of Roussillon are presented with the aid of geological samples; wine tasting in the company of the producers and a magnificent choice of wines from the region (*67 r. du Gén.-Leclerc, 66000 Perpignan; open Tue–Sat 9.30am–12.30pm & 2.30–7.30pm; closed public holidays; 04 68 35 54 44; www.lecomptoirdescrus.com*).

Take the D 117 N out of Perpignan.

Rivesaltes

This is one of the wine-producing capitals of Roussillon and the birthplace of Maréchal Joffre (1852-1931), a statue of whom graces the main square. The name of Rivesaltes is attached to that of Muscat, although Muscat-de-Rivesaltes is produced throughout the *département*. Several producers are to be found on the beautiful avenues in the town centre. The **Domaine Caze** is a good bet (*see Shopping Guide*). A rising star can be found in the nearby village of Calce, **Domaine de l'Horizon**, producing Vins de Pays de Cote de Catalan (*see Shopping Guide*).

Take the D 12 NW to Vingrau.

Vingrau

Tautavel Man, the oldest European human fossil, could have been called Vingrau Man since the Caune de l'Arago cave where he was discovered is closer to Vingrau than to Tautavel. A narrow hillside path leads up to the cave, but the excavation site is closed to the public. Present-day Vingrau Man is above all a wine-grower, producing good Rivesaltes like those at the **Domaine des Chênes** (*see Shopping Guide*).

Take the D 9 S to Tautavel.

Tautavel

The man who lived in this area 700,000 years BC has been named after the town of Tautavel. The **Centre européen de préhistoire**★★ (European Centre of Prehistory) enables visitors to appreciate the wealth of this important place from the past. The rooms are equipped with interactive consoles and video screens illustrating man's place in the universe and the lifestyle of Tautavel Man. The main attraction is the reproduction of the Caune de l'Arago (*open Jul–Aug 10am–7pm; Apr–Jun & Sept 10am–12.30pm & 2–6pm; Oct–Mar 10am–12.30pm, 2–5pm; 8€; 04 68 29 07 76. www.tautavel.com*).
Another museum on the same theme is the **Musée de la Préhistoire européenne – Préhistorama**. Five "virtual theatres" offer visitors 3D illustrations of the daily life of Europe's first inhabitants (*open Jul–Aug, guided tour 1hr 30min 10am–7pm; Apr–Jun & Sept 10am–12.30pm & 2–6pm; Oct–Mar 10am–12.30pm & 2–5pm; 8€; 04 68 29 07 76; www.tautavel.com*).
Les Maîtres Vignerons de Tautavel, next to the Centre of Prehistory, will give you a very warm welcome and offers a large number of interesting cuvées. Free admission to an exhibition on the work of wine-growers through the seasons (*24 ave. Jean-Badia, 66720 Tautavel; open 9am-noon & 2–6pm; 04 68 29 12 03; www.vignerons-tautavel.com*).

Take the D 59 S.

Cases-de-Pène

A picturesque road joins the Agly Valley at Cases-de-Pène, a wine-growing area of which the **Château de Jau** is the star attraction (*see Shopping Guide*). A walk up to the **Ermitage Notre-Dame-de-Pène** will reward you with a fine panorama.

Estagel

This is the birthplace of the great physicist and politician **François Arago** (1786-1853) and an important wine-growing centre that produces good Côtes-du-Roussillon-Villages.

Continue W to Latour-de-France along the D 17.

Latour-de-France

The remains of a castle stand in this one-time border village. The Macabeu grape thrives on the schist and produces remarkable Rivesaltes.

Take the D 79 and turn right onto the D 612. At the Col de la Bataille, turn right onto the D 38.

Ermitage de Força Réal

A 17C chapel stands on the summit (altitude 507m). There is a magnificent **panorama**★★ over the plain, the coast from Cap Leucate to Cap Béar, the Albères mountains and Mont Canigou.

Return to the Col de la Bataille and go straight ahead.

A pleasant stretch of road along the crest between the valleys of the Têt and the Agly leads to the Col and then to the **Château de Caladroy**, in the middle of a park planted with exotic trees (*see Shopping Guide*).

Bélesta

This remarkable village perched on a rocky outcrop rising up out of the surrounding vineyards used to be a border town between the kingdoms of Aragon and France. The town has been of interest for some time to archaeologists who have found numerous prehistoric remains, including a collective grave dating from roughly 6 000 years ago (Middle Neolithic). Visitors can see a reconstruction of the archaeological site at the **Château-Musée** (○ *open mid-Jun–mid-Sept 2–7pm; mid-Sept–mid-Jun daily except Wed & Sat 2–5.30pm;* ○ *closed Dec 24–Jan 1;* ○ *4.50€;* ℘ *04 68 84 55 55).*

▷ *Take the D 21 S.*

The road bends back into a little valley dominated by amazing geological formations consisting of *cheminées de fées* or "fairy chimneys", columns of soft rock eroded by rain and capped with hard, erosion-resistant conglomerate; they are known as the **Orgues**★ or "Organ Pipes" of **Ille-sur-Têt**. These phenomena are grouped on two sites, one of which, to the east, is accessible to the public. In the centre stands an impressive fairy chimney known as "the Sibyl" (▮*15min on foot;* ○ *open Jul–Aug 9.30am–8pm; Apr–Jun & Sept 10am-6.30pm; Feb–Mar 10am–12.30pm, school holidays 10am–5.30pm; Oct 10am–12.30pm & 2–6pm; Nov–Jan 2–5pm;* ○ *3.50€.* ℘ *04 68 84 13 13. www.ille-sur-tet.com).*

▷ *Drive to Ille-sur-Têt then turn left onto the D 916.*

You can make one last stop at **Millas**, at the ⚜**Domaine Força Réal**, from where there is an extraordinary view of the plain of Roussillon (⚜*see Shopping Guide).*

▷ *D 612 SE then right onto the D 58 and cross the D 615 to go to Castelnou.*

Castelnou★

The tiny cobbled streets of this splendid fortified village are clustered around the foot of the 10C feudal **castle**, remodelled in the 19C. Several rooms are open to the public (○ *open Jul–Sept 10am–7pm; Apr–Jun & Oct 10.30am–6pm; Nov–Mar 11am–5pm;* ○ *closed Jan;* ○ *4.50€;* ℘ *04 68 53 22 91).*

▷ *Take the D 48ᴱ.*

Thuir

Thuir is known mainly for its wine cellars, the ⚜**Caves Byrrh**. The "Cellier des Aspres" offers information on local wines and crafts in neighbouring villages *zvisit by 45min guided tour Jul–Aug 10–11.45am & 2–6.45pm; Apr–Jun and Sept–Oct 9–11.45am & 2.30–5.45pm; Nov–Mar 10.45am, 2.30& 4pm;* ○ *closed Mon from Nov–Mar, Jan 1, Dec 25;* ○ *1.70€;* ♿ ℘ *04 68 53 05 42).*

▷ *Take the D 612ᴱ.*

Elne★

This little town surrounded by ramparts is the oldest in Roussillon. The superb **cloisters**★★ of the **Cathédrale Ste-Eulalie-et-Ste-Julie**★ testify to Elne's former splendour. Building work began on the cathedral in the 11C and was completed in the 14C-15C. The superb capitals (12C-14C) on the columns are decorated with imaginary animals, biblical figures and plants. From the east gallery, a spiral staircase rises to a terrace from which there is a fine view of the surrounding area (○ *open Jun–Sept 9.30am–6.45pm; Apr–May 9.30am–5.45pm; Oct 9.30am–12.15pm & 2–5.45pm; Nov–Mar 9.30–11.45am & 2–4.46pm;* ○ *closed Jan 1, May 1, Dec 25;* ○ *4€;* ℘ *04 68 22 70 90).*

▷ *Take the N 114 to Collioure.*

After Argelès, the road reaches the first foothills of the Albères mountain range, from then on endlessly crossing the spurs that form headlands washed by the Mediterranean.

Collioure★★

With its fortified church next to the sea, its two little ports with their bobbing Catalan boats, its old castle, anchovies and wine, Collioure is a delight for both the eyes and the palate.
The AOC Collioure has just 480ha and covers the same area as the AOC Banyuls. Collioure Blanc recently joined the red and rosé wines.

The disused church of the old Dominican monastery (13C) on the road to Port-Vendres now houses **Le Dominicain** wine cooperative which has a small museum and often hosts art exhibitions *(Rte. de Port-Vendres, 66190 Collioure; open daily 8am–noon & 2–6pm; closed Sun Sept–Apr; Guided tours Apr-Sept Mon & Thurs at 4pm 04 68 82 05 63; www.dominicain.com).*

A waymarked route through Collioure, the **Chemin du Fauvisme**, leads past some of the views painted by Henri Matisse and André Derain. Each stage – there are 20 in all – is indicated by the reproduction of the relevant painting on a panel *(guided tours are also available on Thu; contact the tourist office or Espace Fauve; 04 68 98 07 16).*

Port-Vendres

Port-Vendres grew up around a cove that offered convenient shelter for galleys, and its development as a naval port and stronghold really took off in 1679, under the influence of Louis XIV's military architect and strategist Vauban. It is today the busiest fishing port on the Roussillon coast.

As you continue along the N 114, be sure to stop off at the **Clos de Paulilles** estate, which not only produces good Banyuls and Collioures, but is also a farm inn *(see the Address Book and Shopping Guide).*

Banyuls-sur-Mer

This charming town is France's most southerly seaside resort. It stretches out around a pretty bay, overlooked by terraced vineyards which produce the fortified wines of the AOC Banyuls, and also Collioure wines.

The youngest and most fruity Banyuls are called "Rimage". When they have matured in tuns for at least thirty months, they become Banyuls Grand Cru. The bunches of grapes are left to macerate with an added grape spirit which causes the fermentation to stop (this is called *mutage*) and encourages the development of aromas.

After being left to age for a long time in oak vats or in glass demijohns that are exposed to sunshine, Banyuls is drunk as an aperitif or with dessert. The **Domaine du Mas Blanc** is one of the leading producers *(see Shopping Guide).*

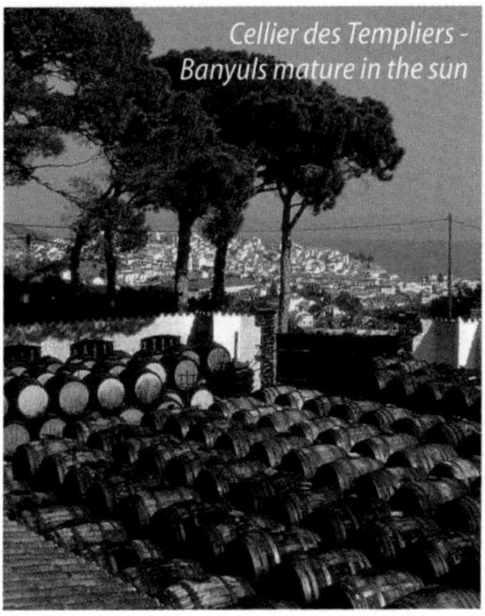

Cellier des Templiers - Banyuls mature in the sun

J. Malburet/MICHELIN

The **Grande Cave** shows a video on the history of Banyuls and organises a guided tour of the place where the oak vats are kept, where the wines are left to age in the sun, and the cellars with their ancient casks *(visit by guided tour Apr–Oct 10am–7.30pm; Nov–Mar Mon–Sat 10am–1pm & 2.30–6.30pm; 04 68 98 36 92; www.banyuls.com).*

Take the little D 86 SW out of Banyuls.

The picturesque road with its endless views of the slopes passes in front of the underground cellar of Mas Reig, set in the oldest wine-growing estate of the Banyuls terroir. The **Cellier des Templiers-Cave du Mas Reig** dates from the days of the Knights Templar (13C), whose feudal castle and sub-commandery (Mas Reig) are nearby *(visit by 45min guided tour Apr–Oct 10.15am–7.30pm; Nov–Mar 10am–1pm & 2.30–6.30pm; closed Dec 5–Jan 1; 04 68 98 36 70; www.banyuls.com).*

Continue along the D 86 to Collioure. If you wish to return to Perpignan, cross the plain of Roussillon on the N 114.

Canal du Midi

M.-H. Carcanague/MICHELIN

Waterside

Cruising the Canal du Midi★

See Itineraries 3 and 4.

The waters of the canal flow peacefully between its beautiful banks, crossing Languedoc from one end to the other through bucolic landscapes and cities full of history and interesting monuments.

Croisières du Midi (Luc Lines)

See Itineraries 3 and 4.

35 quai des Tonneliers, 11200 Homps. Early-Apr–Nov. Reservations required. 10.70€ (children 5.90€). 04 68 91 33 00.

Cruises with commentaries aboard traditional gabares (barges) on the Canal du Midi (2hr), starting from Homps.

Castel Nautique

See Itineraries 3 and 4.

Port de Bram, 11150 Bram. Late Mar–early Nov. 04 68 76 73 34. www.castelnautique.com.

You don't have to hire a live-on boat to explore the Canal du Midi. This company hires out electric boats by the hour or half-day (no licence required).

Beaches

See Itinerary 8.

The sea is never very far from the vineyards in Languedoc-Roussillon. At Banyuls and Collioure, the vines tumble right down to the seashore.

The beaches generally have lifeguards and offer all the services and activities related to water sports. Water quality control tests take place from June onwards. **From La Grande-Motte to Argelès-Plage**, the seaside resorts of the Golfe du Lion offer miles of sandy beaches. **From Collioure to Cerbère**, the sand gives way to the rocky coast of the Côte Vermeille; the beaches are smaller, but full of charm.

Kids

Parc de loisirs historique du château de Chalabre

See Itinerary 5. 25km SW of Limoux via the D 620. Open Easter Sunday–end Aug, school holidays, public holidays and long weekends daily noon–6.30pm. Closed Sat Jul–Aug. 12.50€ (4–12 8€). 04 68 69 37 85. www.chateau-chalabre.com.

In a Cathar-country castle the Chevaliers du Kercorb will give you a taste of medieval life with demonstrations of horseback jousts, weapons exercises and trick riding, and invite you to don a knight's cape and sword for a fun journey into the Middle Ages. Workshops (including calligraphy, mosaic and heraldry) and guided tours of the castle.

Musée des Dinosaures d'Espéraza

See Itinerary 5. 20km S of Limoux via the D 118. Opening times vary. 7€. 04 68 74 26 88. www.dinosauria.org.

Set in the old station, the museum houses a reconstruction of one of the local digs, bone fragments (mostly remoulds) and semi-fossilised eggs in showcases. It explores the extinction of dinosaurs at the end of the secondary era and examines local fossil remains.

War and Religion

Abbaye de Fontfroide★★

See Itinerary [4]. 15km SW of Narbonne, via the N 113, turning left onto the D 613, and then along a tiny little road, keeping left.
The ticket office, bookshop, cellar and restaurant are located in the abbey farm, about one hundred metres below the abbey.
Visit by guided tour (1hr 10min) mid-Jul–end Aug 10am–6pm. Apr–mid-Jul and Sept–Oct 10am–12.15pm & 1–5.30pm. Nov–Mar 10am–noon & 2–4pm. 9€. 04 68 45 11 08. www.fontfroide.com.
This old Cistercian abbey lies tucked almost out of sight deep in a little valley in a peaceful setting surrounded by cypress trees.
The fine flame-coloured shades of ochre and pink in the Corbières sandstone used to build the abbey enhance the serenity of the sight, particularly at sunset.
Most of the abbey buildings date back to the 12C and 13C. The conventual buildings were restored in the 17C and 18C. The setting is delightful, with rose-filled courtyards and superb terraced gardens. Various footpaths enable visitors to walk around the abbey and fully appreciate the charms of its setting.

Ancient cathedral of Maguelone★

See Itinerary [1]. 16km S of Montpellier via the D 986, then along a minor road heading W from Palavas-les-Flots. Open daily 9am–7pm. From mid-May to early Sept you must park in the car park and take the little train. No charge. 04 67 50 63 63. www.espace-maguelone.com.
The cathedral of Maguelone, which stands on an island surrounded by lagoons, is framed by umbrella pines, cedars and eucalyptus.

Abbaye de Fontfroide

B. Kaufmann/MICHELIN

This Romanesque cathedral was extensively fortified, as witnessed by the high, very thick walls with their narrow asymmetric loopholes. A remarkable sculpted doorway leads into the church: on the tympanum is the figure of Christ surrounded by St Mark (represented by a lion), St Matthew (a winged man), St John (an eagle) and St Luke (a bull).

Fort de Salses★★

See Itinerary [8]. 16km N of Perpignan on the N 9. Open Jun–Sept 9.30am–7pm (last admission 1hr before closing). Oct–May Mon–Sat 10am–12.15pm & 2–5pm; Sun 11.30am–4.30pm. Guided tours available (for the upper parts, 45min) by prior arrangement 15 days in advance. Closed Jan 1, May 1, Nov 1 & 11, Dec 25. 7€ (free for under 25s) (Oct–Mar). 04 68 38 60 13.
Rising above the surrounding vineyards, this half-buried fortress is surprisingly big. Today, the weathered pink sandstone and red patina of the brickwork add a softness to its massive severity. Salses fortress, built in the 15C, is a unique example in France of Spanish medieval military architecture; it was adapted by Vauban to meet the demands of modern artillery, only for the Franco-Spanish frontier to be moved south to the Pyrenees.

WINE BUYING GUIDE

INFORMATION

Conseil interprofessionnel des vins du Languedoc – *6 pl. des Jacobins, BP 221, 11102 Narbonne Cedex. ℘04 68 90 38 30, www.languedoc-wines.com.*

Maison des vins du Languedoc – *Mas de Saporta, 34970 Lattes. ℘04 67 06 04 44. www.coteaux-languedoc.com – Open Mon 2–6pm, Tue–Fri 10am–7pm, Sat 10am–1pm & 3–7pm.*

Syndicat des vignerons du Pic St-Loup – *Mairie de Valflaunés, 34270 Valflaunés. ℘04 67 55 97 47. www.pic-saint-loup.com.*

Syndicat de défense du picpoul-de-pinet – *1 ave. de picpoul, 34850 Pinet. ℘04 67 77 03 10. www.picpoul-de-pinet.com.*

Maison des vins de St-Chinian – *Ave. de la Promenade, 34360 St-Chinian. ℘04 67 38 11 69. www.saint-chinian.com.*

Syndicat des vins AOC Faugères – *4 rue de la Poste, 34600 Faugères. ℘04 67 23 47 42. www.faugeres.com.*

Syndicat du cru minervois – *Château de Siran, ave. du Château, 34210 Siran. ℘04 68 27 80 00, www.minervois.com.*

Syndicat des vins AOC Limoux – *20 ave. du Pont de France, 11300 Limoux. ℘04 68 31 12 83. www.limoux-aoc.com.*

Maison des terroirs en Corbières – *Le Château, 11200 Boutenac. ℘04 68 27 73 00. www.aoc-corbieres.com.*

Maison des vignerons du Fitou – *RN 9, 11480 La Palme. ℘04 68 40 42 70. www.cru-fitou.com.*

Les vignerons de la Clape – *ZAC Bonne Source, BP 40527, 11105 Narbonne Cedex. ℘04 68 90 22 22. www.clape.net.*

Conseil interprofessionnel des vins du Roussillon – *19 ave. de Grande-Bretagne, 66006 Perpignan. ℘04 68 51 21 22. www.vins-du-roussillon.com.*

CHARACTERISTICS

Red wines – Crimson to deep purple when young; dark ruby to rich mahogany with age. Aromas of black or red berries, liquorice, fennel and spices during the first years. Hints of truffle, game and chocolate with age. They are generally smooth to the taste, and sometimes very tannic when young, quickly becoming supple with age.

Dry white wines – Pale golden when young, more or less dark straw-coloured with age. Aromas of citrus fruit, exotic fruit, ripe grapes and pear when young, and of spices and currants with age.

Fortified wines – The Muscats have hints of lemon or menthol; Rivesaltes, Maurys and Banyuls have hints of cocoa and cherry when young, then develop aromas and flavours of grilled almonds, kirsch, honey and incense.

Rosé wines – Generally deep colours. Fruity, with hints of raspberry and redcurrant.

STORAGE

Red wines – Ageing varies greatly depending on the *appellation*. Most wines can be kept for at least 5 years, rarely more than 10.

Dry white wines and rosé wines – Most should be drunk within 5 years.

Fortified wines – Most Maurys, Rivesaltes and Banyuls can easily be kept for 10 to 20 years. Most Muscats should be drunk young.

PRICES

Red wines – Vins de pays between 5 to 20€; AOCs bring more *Pic-St-Loup* can fetch 45€; *Costières-de-Nimes* 5 to15€.

Dry white wines – Generally between 5 and 20€; AOC *Costières-de-Nimes* and *Côtes-du-Rousillon* from 10 to 15€.

Fortified and sparkling wines – 5 to 20€; AOC *Maury* from 10 to 30€; *Blanquette-de-Limoux* from 15 to 20€.

Rosé wines – From 5 to 8€; AOC *Faugères* from 10 to 15€.

WINE COOPERATIVES

Cave coopérative du Muscat-de-Frontignan – *14 ave. du Muscat, 34110 Frontignan. ℘04 67 48 12 26 or 04 67 48 93 20. www.frontignan-cooperative.fr. Guided tours (20min): Jun–Sept 10am, 11am, 3.30pm, 4.30pm. Shop: Jun–Sept 9.30am–12.30pm & 3–7.30pm; Oct–May 9.30am–12.30pm & 2.30pm–6.30pm; Closed Jan 1, Dec 25.*

ESTATES

Mas de Daumas Gassac – *Daumas Gassac, 34150 Aniane. ℘04 67 57 71 28. contact@daumas-gassac.com. Open in summer Mon–Sat 10am-6pm, winter 10am-noon & 2-6pm.* Aimé Guibert understood the extraordinary qualitative potential of the subsoils of Languedoc long before anyone else. His 100ha estate contains 45ha of vines grown according to traditional methods, using ploughs and "not the slightest chemical product". Since 2003 the estate has produced the Émile Paynaud vintage, made entirely from Cabernet-Sauvignon. Vin de Pays de l'Hérault.

Domaine du Mas Blanc – *66650 Banyuls-sur-Mer, 04 68 88 32 12, www.domainedumasblanc.com, Open Mon-Sat by appt.* Rightfully considered one of the leading estates in Banyuls, the 21 hectares of vines are carefully tended to by Jean-Michel Parcé. He makes three different cuvées of Collioure from three separate vineyards, and several cuvées of Banyuls. Try his Collioure Cuvée Les Junquets Banyuls, Collioure.

Chateau de Caladroy – *66720 Bélesta. 04 68 57 10 25. www.caladroy.com. Open Mon 8am-noon & 1.30-5.30pm, Tues-Fri 8am-7pm, Sat 9am-1pm & 2-7pm.* Purchased in 1999 by Michel Mézerette, this 130ha estate lies at an altitude of 350m, on pebbly schist soil. Environmentally sensitive methods include working of the land and limitation of chemicals. Traditional vinification occurs over 18 to 21 days, followed by maturation in stainless tanks or oak barrels. Côtes-du-Roussillon, Côtes-du-Roussillon-Villages, Muscat-de-Rivesaltes, Rivesaltes, Vin de Pays de la Côte Catalane.

Château La Voulte Gasparets – *11200 Boutenac – 04 68 27 07 86. chateaulavoulte@wanadoo.fr. Open 9am–noon & 2-6pm.* A great defender of Carignan, Patrick Reverdy runs one of the appellation's leading estates. Located on a terrace of ancient alluvium, the 60ha vineyard is planted with Grenache, Carignan, Syrah, Mourvèdre and Rolle vines. The vines are pruned into a goblet shape and the grapes picked by hand before vinification in concrete and stainless steel vats, followed by ageing in barrels. Corbières.

Château de la Liquière – *34480 Cabrerolles. 04 67 90 29 20. www.chateaulaliquiere.com. Open Mon–Fri 9am-noon & 3-6.30pm, Sat by appt.* One of the oldest properties in the Faugères area, this 60ha estate grows Grenache, Syrah, Cargnan, Mourvedre and Cinsault for its reds; white Grenache, Roussanne, Terret and Clairette for its whites. The vines, planted on hillsides and terraces, thrive in the pebbly schist soil. Ecologically responsible methods include manual harvesting. The older of the estate's two cellars employs gravity in the winemaking process; the newer one is equipped with modern installations. Coteaux-du-Languedoc, Faugères.

Château de Jau – *66600 Cases-de-Pène, 04 68 38 90 10. www.chateaudejau.com. Open summer daily 10am–7pm; winter Mon–Fri 8am–5pm.* The château's vineyards cover 134ha in the communes of Cases-de-Pène, Tautavel and Estagel. The vineyards planted with Syrah, Mourvèdre, Grenache, Carignan, Muscat, Vermentino, Maccabeu are rooted in limestone plateaux, schistose marl and gravelly and clayey limestone soils. The vines are still grown according to traditional methods, and the grapes are picked both manually and mechanically. Cotes-du-Roussillon, Cotes-du-Roussillon-Villages, Muscat-de-Rivesaltes.

SCEA Domaine de Cazal Viel – *Château Cazal Viel, Hameau Cazal Viel, 34460 Cessenon-sur-Orb. 04 67 89 63 15. www.cazal-viel.com. Open 10am–noon & 2–6pm; weekends by appt.* This 150ha estate has belonged to the Miquel family since 1791. The vineyard of clayey limestone soil is particularly well suited to viticulture. Specialties of this estate are wines made from Viognier and Syrah. The storehouse today containes nearly 1 000 oak barrels. Saint-Chinian.

Domaine Jean-Michel Alquier – *34600 Faugères. 04 67 23 07 89. jmalquier@yahoo.fr. Open by appt.* Jean-Michel Alquier runs this 12ha estate, 11ha of which are dedicated to the production of red wine and 1ha to white wine. The Syrah, Grenache Noir, Mourvèdre, Marsanne, Grenache Blanc and Viognier grape varieties are planted in schistose soil, 80% of them on southeast facing slopes. The grapes are picked by hand,

L. Campion / MICHELIN

partially destemmed for traditional vinification, and fermentation times are long. The wines mature in barrels. Faugères.

Domaine Borie de Maurel – *34210 Félines-Minervois. 04 68 91 68 58. www.boriedemaurel.fr. Open Mon–Sat 9am–noon & 2–7pm.* This 33ha property was acquired in 1989 by Sylvie and Michel Escande, joined later by their son Gabriel. Syrah, Grenache and Mourvèdre vines flourish at the foot of the Montagne Noire, in small parcels surrounded by the garrigue. Some parts of the cultivation and winemaking operations are conducted according to the phases of the moon, i.e. planting, bottling, etc. The estate produces a light red "Vin de Café" best drunk chilled. Minervois, Minervois-la-Livinière.

Chateau Pech-Latt – *11220 Lagrasse. 04 68 58 11 40. Open Mon-Thu 8am-noon & 2–5pm, Fri 811am; weekends by appt.* This 100ha estate lies within a cirque of hills at the foot of the Montagne d'Alaric. Lime and red marl compose the soil of the vineyards, planted with Carignan, black Grenach, Syrah and Mourvèdre for the reds, and Marsanne and Vermentino for the whites. The organically farmed estate has been certified Écocert since 1990; no chemical fertilisers or herbicides are used. Corbières.

Domaine Les Mille Vignes – *24 ave. de St-Pancrace, 11480 Lapalme. 04 68 48 57 14 and 06 07 75 58 68. Open daily in summer by appt. 9am–7pm.* Formerly a professor of viticulture in the Rhone Valley, Jacques Guérin took over this estate in Lapalme in 1980. Respect for the environment and the vine holds sway in the cultivation of the 7.5ha vineyard, planted with Grenach and Carignan: no chemical fertlisers, aggressive pruning, limited yield (9–25hl//ha) and green harvesting. Maceration periods extend up to 33 days in small tanks, with frequent pumping and punching down the cap. Fitou, Muscat-de-Rivesaltes, Rivesaltes, Vin de Pays de L'Aude.

Château des Estanilles – *34480 Lenthéric, 04 67 90 29 25. Open by appt. Mon–Fri 9-11.45am & 4-6pm.* Michel Louison left his native Savoie and in 1976 took over 20ha of abandoned vineyards in Lenthéric. In 1996 he was joined by his daughter Sophie, with whom he runs a 32ha vineyard planted on hillsides in schistose soils, applying ecologically responsible principles. The very modern cellar contains thermo-regulated stainless steel vats. Coteaux-du-Languedoc, Faugères.

L'Oustal Blanc – *Chem. des Condomines, 34210 La Livinière. 04 64 93 68 47. Open daily by appt; www.oustal-blanc.com.* A native of this region, winegrower Claude Fonquerle has returned to his roots, joining Philippe Cambie in ownership of this 10ha estate in 2002 after spending twelve years in the Rhone Valley. The old vines (white and black Grenache, Cargnan, Syrah) are cultivated without herbicides or systemic products. Grapes are individually sorted, then fermented sixty days in concrete tanks. The estate also produces red and white vins de table. Minervois, Minervois-la-Livinière.

Domaine Pouderoux – *2 r. Émile-Zola, 66460 Maury. 04 68 57 22 02. 123Pou@wanadoo.fr. Open by appt.* This 15ha estate established on schist and clayey-limestone soil, cultivates Grenache, Syrah, Mourvèdre, Carignan and Muscat, all of which are fermented separately. There are two storehouse areas for aging. Côtes-du-Roussillon-Villages, Maury, Muscat-de-Rivesaltes, Vin de Pays de la Côte Catalane.

Domaine Força-Réal – *Mas de la Garrigue, 66170 Millas. 04 68 85 06 07. www.forcareall.com. Open Mon-Fri 8am-noon & 1-4pm, weekends by appt.* Old drought-resistant vines have taken deep root in this 40ha vineyard, and the yield is low (30 hl/ha on average). Traditional methods hold sway in the vineyard, which is harvested by hand. Wines are made in stainless-steel tanks. The 12-year-old Rivesaltes and the Les Hauts de Força-Réal of the Cotes-du-Roussillon-Villages appellation are aged for 12 months in oak. An underground storehouse for ageing the wines and a small wine-tasting cellar were built in 2002. Côtes-du-Roussillon, Côtes-du-Roussillon-Villages, Muscat-de-Rivesaltes.

Domaine Mas Renée – *Boulevard des Aresquiers, 34110 Vic la Gardiole, 09 79 52 88 01; www.domainemasrenee.fr. Open Jun-Sept 9am-12.30pm & 5-7.30pm, Sun 9.30am-12.30pm, Oct-May Tue, Fri, Sat 9am-12.30pm, Sun 9.30am-12.30pm* This organic estate covers 8ha of almost entirely Muscat a Petit Grains. The clay-limestone slopes overlook the sea at this very attractive place, and the welcome is warm and genuine. Muscat-de-Mireval, Vin de Pays d'Oc.

Domaine l'Aiguelière – *2, Place du Square, 34150 Montpeyroux 04 67 96 61 43.* This 25 hectares estate was created in 1987 by Aimé Commeyras and his winemaker Pierre-Louis Teissedre. Relatively cool climate for the area, Syrah and Grenache make wonderful wines here. All harvesting done by hand, with aging in new oak barrels. Coteaux-du-Languedoc-Montpeyroux, Vin de Pays de l'Hérault, Vin de Pays du Mont Baudile.

Domaine des Deux Ânes – *Rte de Sainte-Eugénie, 11440 Peyriac-de-Mer. 04 68 41 67 79. www.domainedes2anes.com. Open Mon-Sat by appt.* Winegrowers Magali and Dominique have run vineyards in the Jura and the Mâconnais and Beaujolais regions. This unusual career path led these wine enthusiasts to discover the great potential of the terroirs of the Languedoc region, and in 2000 they purchased around twenty hectares on hillsides overlooking the Étangs de Bages and the sea. The vineyard benefits from a considerable amount of sunshine and little rainfall. The soils, consisting of soft rocks and a rather chalky red-brown earth, enable the vines to resist drought. The vineyard produces mainly red wines from four grape varieties: Grenache Noir, Carignan, Mourvèdre and Syrah. The grapes are harvested by hand over a period of one month. The cellar is particularly functional, equipped with stainless steel vats, a thermoregulation system and barrels for maturing the wines. Organic farming methods were adopted in 2002. Corbières.

Prieuré de Saint-Jean de Bébian – *Rte. de Nizas, 34120 Pézenas. 04 67 98 13 60. bebian@wanadoo.fr. Open Mon–Sat 9am –noon & 3–6pm; by appt. in winter.* Chantal Lecouty and Jean-Claude Le Brun, former directors of the Revue du Vin de France, took over this estate in 1994; their knowledge and passion for winemaking has already garnered the estate renown in the world of wine. The 32ha property, spread among several parcels, is cultivated along ecologically responsible principles, including manual harvesting. 2004 saw the release of the estate's rosé made of grapes from its old Cinsault vines. Coteaux-du-Languedoc.

Château de Pinet – *Vignobles Gaujal de St-Bon, 34850 Pinet. 04 68 32 16 67. chateaudepinet@voila.fr. Open May–Sept; by appt. Oct–Apr.* Passed down from father to son for two hundred and fifty years, the estate is now run by women: in the drivers' seat, Simone Arnaud-Gaujal, assisted by her pharmacist-oenologist daughter. The 50ha vineyard planted with Picpoul, Merlot, Syrah, Cabernet-Sauvignon, Grenache and Cinsault covers clayey limestone soils. The vines face south-southeast and are on average 25 to 50 years old. The Château's production is characterised by low yields. Coteaux-du-Languedoc.

Les Clos de Paulilles – *Baie de Paulilles. 66660 Port-Vendres. 04 68 98 07 58. daure@wanadoo.fr. Open 11am–11pm in summer.* This 90ha estate belonging to the Dauré family – who also own the Château de Jau and Mas Cristine – has proved to be one of the stars of the appellation. Except for the terraced parcels, it is cultivated according to ecologically responsible principles and grapes are harvested by hand. Stainless-steel tanks are used for the vinification;

then the wines are matured for 10 to 11 months in barrels. Banyuls, Collioure.

Domaine Cazes – *4 r. Francisco-Ferrer, BP61, 66600 Rivesaltes. 04 68 64 08 26. www.cazes-rivesaltes.com. Open by appt. Mon–Sat 8am–noon (12.30pm in summer), 2–6pm (7pm in summer).* The vineyard, created in the early 19C, now covers 160ha. Around twelve grape varieties are rooted in its clayey limestone soils and produce about fifteen wines using biodynamic methods. Côtes-du-Roussillon, Côtes-du-Roussillon-Villages, Muscat-de-Rvesaltes, Vin de Pays de la Côte Catalane, Vin de Pays d'Oc.

Domaine Canet Valette, *34370 Cazouls-Les Béziers 04 67 93 60 84 www.canetvalette.com. Open by appt.* Domaine Canet Valette is run by Marc and Sophie Valette. Mark's father began buying vines in this region in the mid 1970s, and gradually handed things over to his son, who has now been running things himself for around ten years. In 1998 he built his own winery and cellar, where winemaking takes place by gravity. The domain now covers 18 hectares just outside the village of Cessenon. Try their traditional blend of five local grapes – the romantically-named Une et Mille Nuits. Coteaux-du-Languedoc.

Domaine Haut-Lirou – *34270 St-Jean-de-Cuculles. 04 67 55 38 50. Domaine.Haut.Lirou@mnet.fr. Open by appt. Mon–Sat (daily in summer).* This estate's 60ha of vines stretch out over the clayey limestone foothills of the Pic-St-Loup. A family-run estate for five generations, it was entirely replanted by current owners Jean-Pierre and Maryse Rambier. The vineyard is planted with Grenache, Syrah, Mourvèdre, Cabernet-Sauvignon and Sauvignon Blanc, with a few parcels of Vieux Carignan and Cinsault, and ecologically responsible principles are applied. The grapes are harvested by hand before traditional vinification (each variety separately), and maceration times are long. The wines age twelve to sixteen months in the barrel. Coteaux-du-Languedoc-Pic-Saint-Loup

Domaine de l'Horizon, 4 Rue des Pyrenees 66600 Calce, teibert.thomas@wanado.fr. 06 23 85 24 59, open by appt. Run by a dynamic young German man, Thomas Teibert, this is an estate to watch. Located around 10km from Rivesaltes, Teibert is producing a minerally white wine and a rich, round red from 15 ha of organic vines. Vins de Pays de Cote Catalan

Domaine de Barroubio – *34360 St-Jean-de-Minervois. 04 67 38 14 06. Open 9am–noon & 3–7pm.* A family-run estate since the 15C, the Domaine de Barroubio covers 27ha on a limestone plateau and is planted with Muscat à Petits Grains, Carignan, Syrah and Grenache. The terroir favours the production of Vin du Pays d'Oc, matured in the traditional way. The red wines are matured in barrels. Minvervois, Muscat-de-Saint-Jean-de-Minervois, Vin de Pays d'Oc.

Domaine Virgile Joly – *22 r. du Portail, 34725 St-Saturnin-de-Lucian. 04 67 44 52 21. virgilejoly@wanadoo.fr. Open by appt. in summer Mon–Sat 3–7pm; rest of the year Wed & Sat 3–7pm.* Magdalena and Virgile Joly created this 8.5ha estate in 2000, planted the clayey-limestone and limestone pebbled vineyard with Syrah, Grenache, Cargnan and Cinsault. Organic methods are used; the estate was certified écocert in 2001. Manual harvesting and traditional vinification are followed by a two years of maturation in concrete tanks and oak casks. Coteaux-du-Languedoc-Saint-Saturnin, Vin de Pays de l'Hérault.

Domaine de l'Hortus – *34270 Valflaunès. 04 67 55 31 20. domaine.hortus@wanadoo.fr. Open Mon–Sat 8am–noon & 3–6pm, Sun by appt.* The estate's vineyards, created in 1978, cover 55ha planted with Mourvèdre, Syrah and Grenache for the red wines; Chardonnay, Viognier, Roussanne and Sauvignon for the whites. They are rooted in clayey limestone soils. One of the two red wines is matured in oak casks for between thirteen and fifteen months, while one of the two white wines ferments in new barrels. The Orliac family runs another estate, Clos du Prieur, which covers 10ha in St-Jean-de-Buèges, at the foot of the Larzac plateau. 🍇Coteaux-du-Languedoc-Pic-Saint-Loup. ·

Mas Bruguière – *Hameau de La Plaine, 34270 Valflaunès. ℘04 67 55 20 97.Open Mon–Sat 10am–noon & 3–7pm, Sun by appt.* Owned by the Brugière family since the Revolution, this 20ha vineyard is planted with Grenache, Syrah, Mourvèdre, Roussanne and Marsanne, all thriving in the clayey-limestone soil and well-drained pebbly scree. The wines mature in vats or oak casks, in an underground storehouse. 🍇Coteaux-du-Languedoc-Pic-Saint-Loup.

Domaine des Chênes – *7 r. du Mar.-Joffre, 66600 Vingrau. ℘04 68 29 40 21. domainedeschenes@wanadoo.fr.* Purchased by the Razungles family in 1919, the estate was given a new lease on life in the late 1980s by Gilbert, Simone and their son Alain. The vineyard's 30ha are planted on exceptional terroirs on the steep foothills of the Hautes Corbières. The yield is intentionally limited and the grapes are picked by hand. Frequent soil cultivation reduces the need for herbicides. 🍇Côtes-du-Roussillon, Côtes-du-Roussillon-Villages, Muscat-de-Rivesaltes, Vin de Pays d'Oc.

🍃 WALKING TOURS OF THE VINEYARDS

De vignes en caves – *Information and booking at CDT des Pyrénées-Orientales (tourist board) – ℘04 68 51 52 53.* Six days' hiking on your own or with a guide in the Côtes-du-Roussillon appellation area. Each day, you'll explore a terroir and its natural and cultural heritage and enjoy a picnic and wine tasting. Accommodation is provided by the producers. A similar itinerary is available in the Collioure and Banyuls areas.

ADDRESSES

🏨 STAY

ITINERARIES ① AND ②

🛏️ **Les Tritons** – *Blvd. Joliot-Curie, 34200 Sète. ℘04 67 53 03 98. www.hotellestritons.com. 40 rooms. ☑7€.* Functional, brightly-coloured rooms; those facing front boast air-conditioning and sea views; at the rear all is cool and quiet. Marine decor.

🛏️🛏️ **Hôtel de la Comédie** – *1 bis r. Baudin, 34000 Montpellier. ℘04 67 58 43 64. 20 rooms. ☑6€.* A few strides from the Place de la Comédie, this recently renovated hotel boasts several modern touches. It has a relaxed atmosphere despite its location in a busy area, and is an ideal base for exploring Montpellier.

🛏️🛏️ **Hôtel du Mimosa** – *10 pl. de la Fontaine, 34725 St-Saturnin-de-Lucian. ℘04 67 88 62 62. Closed Nov 6–Mar 16. 7 rooms. ☑9.50€.*Designer furnishings, stonework and original fireplaces form a harmonious blend at this intriguing spot near the village main square. Spacious rooms. Reception opens at 5pm.

🛏️🛏️ **Hôtel du Parc** – *8 r. Achille-Bège, 34000 Montpellier. ℘04 67 41 16 49. 19 rooms. ☑9.50€.* Although the grounds of this fine 18C residence have been parcelled out, its noble façade has remained intact. The well-appointed rooms have been personalised and gradually renovated with discerning taste. In summer, breakfast is sometimes served on the terrace.

🛏️🛏️ **Hôtel Le Molière** – *Pl. du 14-Juillet, 34120 Pézenas. ℘04 67 98 14 00. www.hotel-le-moliere.com. 21 rooms. ☑8€.* The façade of this charming hotel in the town centre is adorned with sculptures. The comfortable, functional rooms are equipped with modern furniture, and the lounge area, in a superb patio, is decorated with attractive wall frescoes illustrating Molière's plays.

🛏️🛏️ **Hôtel Port Marine** – *Môle St-Louis, 34200 Sète. ℘04 67 74 92 34. www.hotel-port-marine.com. 46 rooms. ☑9€. Restaurant* 🍴🍴. Modern hotel near the yacht harbour and fishing pier, with functional rooms that imitate the cabin of a boat. Six of the rooms overlook the sea. Restaurant features regional cuisine.

🛏️🛏️ **Le Moulin d'Issanka** – *Rte. d'Issanka, 34540 Balaruc-le-Vieux. ℘04 67 53 00 06. http://moulindissanka.*

monsite.wanadoo.fr. 3 rooms, 1 suite. . Rustic charm prevails at this 10C structure. Bathrooms feature hand-painted decor by Madame Cervera, who also displays several of her painted ceramics about the property. Depending on the season you can take your breakfast poolside or fireside. The shade park is lovely, especially on sunny days.

ITINERARY 3

Chambre d'hôte La Bastide Vieille – *La Bastide Vieille, 34310 Capestang, 13km W of Béziers via the D 11. 04 67 93 46 23. Closed Nov 1–Mar 1. 3 rooms.* . Guaranteed peace and quiet in this serene, isolated country house surrounded by vines, whose venerable façade is flanked by a 12C tower. The spacious rooms in the old outbuildings are attractively decorated in Provençal style. Charming lounge-cum-library where you can read at leisure.

Château de Lignan – *Place de l'Église, 34490 Lignan-sur-Orb – 7km NW of Béziers via the D 19. 04 67 37 91 47. 49 rooms. 13€. Restaurant* . A former bishop's residence set in a beautiful 6ha park on the banks of the River Orb. The renovated rooms are modern and well equipped. Jacuzzi, hammam, swimming pool and open-air restaurant on a terrace with a view of the estate and its age-old trees.

La Chamberte – *R. de la Source, 34420 Villeneuve-lès Béziers. 04 67 39 84 83. www.la-chamberte.com. Closed Mar 1–12, Oct 1–15. 5 rooms. 15€.* This former wine cellar is preceded by a Mediterranean garden. Mysterious interior décor combining various exotic influences.

ITINERARIES 4 AND 7

Chambre d'hôte Domaine de St-Jean – *11200 Bizanet, 10km SW of Narbonne via the N 9, N 113, D 613 then D 224. 04 68 45 17 31. didierdelbourg bizanet@yahoo.fr. 4 rooms.* . This large wine-growers' house is ideal for those in search of authenticity and peace and quiet. The walls and furniture of its comfortable rooms are decorated with hand-painted motifs. One of the rooms has its own terrace with a lovely view of the Massif de Fontfroide. Pleasant garden cared for by the owner-cum-nursery gardener.

Chambre d'hôte Nuitées Vigneronne de Beaupré – *Rte. d'Armissan, 11100 Narbonne. 04 68 65 85 57. 4 rooms.* . Wine lovers will enjoy discovering the art of winemaking at this spot in the heart of a 9ha winegrowing estate near the centre of Narbonne. The annex features a large dining room and four guestrooms, each decorated in its own colour scheme.

Hôtel de la Plage – *R. Bernard-l'Hermite, at the beach,11430 Gruissan. 04 68 49 00 75. Closed Nov 6–Mar 31. 17 rooms.* . From the terrace of this hotel set in a small 1960s building you can see the famous houses on stilts immortalised by Jean-Jacques Beineix's film *Betty Blue*. Bright, well-kept, but modestly furnished rooms.

Hôtel Des Deux Golfs – *Sur le port, 11370 Port-Leucate. 04 68 40 99 42. Open Mar 15–Nov 15. 30 rooms. 6€.* Located between the marina and the lagoon, this modern hotel has functional rooms with private loggias facing the yacht harbour.

ITINERARY 5

Le Mauzac – *9 ave. Camille-Bouche, 11300 Limoux, RD 118. 04 68 31 12 77. 21 rooms. 6.50€.* A handy place to stop on the road to Carcassonne, this hillside hotel was recently entirely renovated and offers comfortable, well-soundproofed rooms with pine furniture. The ones at the rear are best.

Chambre d'hôte La Maison sur la Colline – *Lieu-dit Ste-Croix, 11000 Carcassonne, 1km S of the "Cité" via the road to Ste-Croix. 04 68 47 57 94 or 06 85 90 70 58. www.lamaisonsurlacolline.com. Closed late Dec–mid-Feb. Reservations advised in high season. 6 rooms.* . *Restaurant* . Perched on a hilltop, this old restored farmhouse offers an enchanting view of the medieval "*cité*". Its spacious rooms, furnished with objects unearthed in second-hand shops, are each decorated in a different colour.

Château de Cavanac – *11570 Cavanac. 04 68 79 61 04. 24 rooms. 10€. Restaurant* . Relax at this 17C château on a winegrowing estate. Individually decorated rooms overlook vineyards and countryside. The restaurant occupies the former stables, and serves grilled dishes, traditional recipes, and wine from the estate.

ITINERARY 6

Auberge du Vigneron – *2 r. Achille-Mir, 11350 Cucugnan. 04 68 45 03 00. Closed Nov 13–Feb 28, Mon except evenings in Jul–Aug and Sun evenings. 6 rooms. 7€. Restaurant .* The operators of this friendly inn will introduce you to the pleasures of good, simple meals accompanied by Corbières ines, and small but nicely decorated rooms. In summer, the restaurant moves from a wine cellar to the terrace, complete with mountain views.

Chambre d'hôte Domaine Grand Guilhem – *Chemin du Col de la Serre, 11360 Cascastel-des-Corbières. 04 68 45 86 67. 4 rooms. 4€.* This nicely restored 19C house has retained its authenticity; you'll settle right in to the charming, impeccably maintained rooms. Wine tasting in the cellar.

Chambre d'hôte Les Palombières d'Estarac – *SW of Estarac, 11100 Bages. 04 68 42 45 56. 4 rooms. 4€. Restaurant* . Nicely decorated rooms, beautifully kept, await at this recently restored home. The dining room, where you can sample Mediterranean dishes, overlooks a park.

ITINERARY 8

Hôtel Le Catalan – *Rte. Cerbère, 66650 Banyuls. 04 68 88 02 80. Closed Dec–Apr. 23 rooms. 7€.* A practical hotel built in the 1970s, complete with balconies, solarium, even a garage. Enjoy the terraced garden.

Chambre d'hôte Domaine du Mas Boluix – *Chemin du Pou-de-les-Colobres, 66000 Perpignan – 3km S of Perpignan on the road to Argelès, then left toward Cabestany. 04 68 08 17 70. www.domaine-de-boluix.com. 6 rooms including 1 suite.* . A peaceful atmosphere reigns in this 18C *mas* (farmhouse) surrounded by the vineyards of Cabestany. Its rooms, with their pristine walls and superb Catalan fabrics, each bear the name of a local artist. Far-reaching view of Roussillon. Wine-tasting and sale of wines from the estate.

Hôtel Méditerranée – *Ave. Aristide-Maillol, 66190 Collioure. 04 68 82 08 60. www.mediterranee-hotel.com. Closed mid-Nov–Dec, Jan 8–Mar 12. 35 rooms. 11.50€. Restaurant* . Nice hotel in an imposing building dominating the seafront at the foot of a hill. Bright rooms furnished in the Catalan style. Good dining room; terrace with a view of the coast; classical cuisine on the menu.

EAT

ITINERARIES 1 AND 2

Simple Simon – *1 r. des Trésoriers-de-France, 34000 Montpellier. 04 67 66 03 43. www.simple-simon.fr. Closed Sun May–Oct, evenings. Reservations suggested.* Simply British! A patchwork of English pastries, an Indian platter or a sweet-and-savoury plate for lunch, salads in summer, soups in winter… all in a cosy, comfortable atmosphere. For the French touch: Languedoc wines by the glass.

Après le Déluge – *5 ave. du Mar.-Plantavit, 34120 Pézenas. 04 67 98 10 77. www.apres-le-deluge.com. Closed Oct–Mar.* Will you dine at Noah's Table or in Perrault's Room? This restaurant offers its patrons five different decors in which to sample the chef's recipes, taken from old books. You'll also have a unique opportunity to taste one of the Marquis de Sade's more innocent pleasures: his favourite cake! A very entertaining setting, with two flower-filled terraces. Musical evenings.

Hôtellerie de Balajan – *41 rte. de Montpellier, 34110 Frontignan. 04 67 48 13 99. www.hotel-balajan.com. Closed Dec 26–Jan 5, Sun evenings offseason, Mon lunchtime and Sat lunchtime.* A nice place to eat on the N 112, surrounded by the vines that produce the famous Muscat-de-Frontignan. The modern-style building houses a dining room decorated with warm colours where you can enjoy traditional recipes infused with southern flavours.

Le Pastis – *3 r. du Terral, 34000 Montpellier. 04 67 66 37 26. Closed early Jan, Aug, Sat & Sun.* This restaurant is popular with wine connoisseurs on account of its cellar filled with wines from the Languedoc vineyards. But it appeals to all gourmets with its market-fresh dishes that delight the palate: roast sea perch with fennel, scallops and prawns, goat's cheese millefeuille, etc.

⊖⊜ **Le Pré Saint-Jean** – *18 ave. du Mar.-Leclerc, 34120 Pézenas. ☎04 67 98 15 31. leprest.jean@wanadoo.fr. Closed Feb holidays, Nov holidays, Thu evenings, Sun evenings and Mon.* Discreet facade conceals a charming restaurant with a "winter garden" atmosphere. Up-to-date regional dishes, and a good selection of local wines.

⊖⊜ **Mazerand** – *Rte. de Fréjorgues, 34970 Lattes, 5km S of Montpellier by the D 986 and the D 172. ☎04 67 64 82 10. www.le-mazerand.com. Closed Sun evenings offseason, Sat lunchtime and Mon.* The Mazerand brothers welcome their guests to their 19C farmhouse, formerly a winegrowing property. Relax on one of the lovely terraces or in the spacious dining room and sample the delicious contemporary cuisine.

⊖⊜⊜ **Le Bistrot d'Ariane** – *34970 Lattes. ☎04 67 20 01 27.* Ideally located at the yacht harbour, Le Bistrot d'Ariane is continually hopping with locals and tourists alike, attracted to the brasserie atmosphere and the regional cuisine. It's a good idea to reserve.

⊖⊜⊜ **Le Fontenay** – *Rte. du Lac de Salagou, 34800 Clermont-l'Hérault. ☎04 67 88 04 06. www.fontenay.net. Closed Jul 3–16, Sat lunchtime, Sun evenings and Wed evenings.* Located in a residential neighbourhood, this flower-bedecked spot has plenty of charms: a Mediterranean-style facade, a nice interior terrace and a pleasant dining room embellished with local art exhibits. The chef specialises in updated versions of tradtional Languedoc recipes.

⊖⊜⊜ **Lennys** – *266 ave. Louis-Cancel, 34270 St-Mathieu-de-Tréviers. ☎04 67 55 37 97. ludovic-dziewulski@wanadoo.fr.* Pleasant auberge near the Pic-St-Loup, with shaded terrace and appetising contemporary cuisine, all with southern flair.

⊖⊜⊜ **Mimosa** – *34725 St-Guiraud, 7.5km N of Clermont-l'Hérault via the N 9, N 109 then D 130E. ☎04 67 96 67 96. le.mimosa@free.fr. Open mid-Mar–Oct; closed Sun evening except Jul–Aug, lunchtime except Sun and Mon.* This old wine-grower's house is tucked away in the heart of the village. In its charming contemporary dining room you can sample pleasant, market-fresh Mediterranean-style cuisine, accompanied by a good choice of regional wines.

ITINERARY 3

⊖⊜ **La Potinière** – *15 r. Alfred-deMusset, 34500 Béziers. ☎04 67 11 95 25. Closed Jun 19–Jul 19, Mon lunchtime and Sun.* Béziers locals are fond of this restaurant, with its charming dining room and enticing menu designed to pique the appetites of passing gourmands.

⊖⊜ **Le Val d'Héry** – *67 ave. du Prés-Wilson, 34500 Béziers. ☎04 67 76 56 73. www.valdhery.com. Closed Jun 20–Jul 11, Sun and Mon.* A pre-prandial stroll on the Plateau des Poètes, an attractive park in the centre of town, and here you are in this restaurant with its walls decorated with paintings. Don't hesitate to compliment the chef, who painted some of the pictures on display… and also perfectly masters the art of adapting recipes to suit contemporary tastes.

⊖⊜ **Les Antiquaires** – *4 r. Bagatelle, 34500 Béziers. ☎04 67 49 31 10. Closed 2 weeks in Aug during the féria, lunchtime and Mon. Reservations required.* Have a seat amid the antique pottery, black and white photos, paintings, musical instruments and other found objects that make up the décor of this charming little spot. Dishes are concocted from market-fresh ingredients, all washed down with local vintages.

⊖⊜⊜ **Château des Colombiers** – *1 r. du Château, 34440 Colombiers. ☎04 67 37 06 93. www.chateau-colombiers.com. Closed Jan 1–10, Nov 2–8, Sun evenings, Wed evenings and Thu from Nov–May.* Constructed over a 12C vaulted cavern, this château was erected in the 16–17C. Boaters can tie up at the dock on the nearby Canal du Midi. Locals and travellers alike enjoy the fine terrace beneath the chestnut trees and the manorial atmosphere.

ITINERARIES 4 AND 7

⊖⊜ **Bistrot du Chef…en gare** – *1 ave. Carnot, 11100 Narbonne. ☎04 68 32 14 52. media.restauration@wanadoo.fr. Closed Tue evenings and Wed.* This rather extraordinary bistro is outfitted in the former station restaurant. The sprightly decor and music memorialize the French singer and songwriter Charles Trenet, whose boyhood home is nearby.

Cave d'Agnès – *29 r. Gilbert-Salamo, 11510 Fitou. 04 68 45 75 91. Closed Nov 13–Mar 31. Reservations required.* Once you have experienced the relaxed atmosphere of this old barn high up in the village you will not want to leave. In addition to grilled meats prepared in front of you in the rustic dining room, the chef prepares generous regional recipes. A good Fitou makes an ideal accompaniment…

L'Estagnol *(Gruissan)– 12 ave. de Narbonne, 11430 Gruissan. 04 68 49 01 27. Closed Oct–Mar, Sun evening and Mon.* Take a step back in time at this former fisherman's house fronting on the lagoon. Provençal decor, southern hospitality, fish specialities on the menu.

L'Estagnol *(Narbonne)– 5 bis cours Mirabeau, 11100 Narbonne. 04 68 65 09 27. fabricemeynadier@wanadoo.fr. Closed Mon evening and Sun.* A lively brasserie on a small square near the covered market, with a pleasant terrace in fine weather. The locals appreciate its good traditional dishes with their regional flavour.

L'Os à Table – *Rte de Salles-d'Aude, 11110 Coursan, 7km NE of Narbonne in the direction of Béziers via the N 9. 04 68 33 55 72. losatable-coursan@wanadoo.fr. Closed Sun evenings and Mon.* With its two modern dining rooms and its summer terrace facing a little garden, this restaurant provides a pleasant setting in which to sample the chef's flavourful cuisine, which is updated for contemporary tastes and makes use of regional produce whenever possible.

Relais Chantovent – *17 Grand-Rue, 34210 Minerve. 04 68 91 14 18. bertet.relais@wanadoo.fr. Closed Dec 16–Mar 14, Sun evenings and Mon.* This Cathar village stretched out on a rocky promontory is a car-free zone, so you will have to walk there. The Relais Chantovent, a pleasant inn whose terrace offers a clear view of the Gorges du Brian, serves good regional dishes with wines from the Minervois, of course.

ITINERARY 5

Auberge de Dame Carcas – *3 pl. du Chateau, 11000 Carcassonne. 04 68 71 23 23. Closed Jan 29–Feb 19, Jun 5–11, Oct 2–8 and Wed.* A fun spot in the ***cité***. Boisterous, welcoming atmosphere on the two levels of dining rooms. Lengthy menu includes dishes freshly grilled on the ground-floor rotisserie.

La Maison de la Blanquette – *46 bis prom. du Tivoli, 11300 Limoux. 04 68 31 01 63. Closed Wed evenings offseason.* Drinks are included in the set menus here: a good opportunity to discover or rediscover Blanquette-de-Limoux and other local wines, while sampling sparkling local recipes. Before you leave, make a detour via the wine shop.

La Marquière – *13 r. St-Jean, 11000 Carcassonne. 04 68 71 52 00. lamarquiere@wanadoo.fr. Closed Jan 15–Feb 15, Wed and Thu.* Rustic little house near the northern ramparts, where you'll find well-executed traditional-style dishes served either in the quiet dining room or the courtyard.

ITINERARY 6

La Balade Gourmande – *Bd Léon-Castel, RN 113, 11200 Lézignan-Corbières. 04 68 27 22 18. Closed 1 week in Feb, Mon evenings, Tue evenings and Wed evenings. Reservations suggested.* Inside this modern pink house are two dining rooms with southern-style decor (yellow walls and Provençal fabrics). Good regional produce and traditional cuisine – if you like cassoulet, the one here is a must.

Auberge de Cucugnan – *2 pl. de la Fontaine, 11350 Cucugnan. 04 68 45 40 84. Closed Jan 1–Mar 15.* You have to wend your way – on foot rather than by car – through a maze of narrow streets to reach this converted barn. Its authentic setting, rustic atmosphere and wine cellar full of regional wines allow you to fully appreciate the chef's generous local-traditional cuisine.

ITINERARY 8

Casa Bonet – *2 r. du Chevalet, 66000 Perpignan. 04 68 34 19 45. casa.bonet@wanadoo.fr.* This Catalan house in the pedestrian area of Perpignan offers a self-serve buffet, tapas and various grilled skewer dishes.

Le Petit Gris – *66720 Tautavel. ✆04 68 29 42 42.* This simple, pleasant spot at the edge of the village offers tranquil views through the bay windows overlooking the vineyards and the Pyrenees. Grilled dishes emphasizing catalan specialties.

Al Fanal and Hôtel El Llagut – *18 av. du Fontaulé, 66650 Banyuls-sur-Mer. ✆04 68 88 00 81. al.fanal@wanadoo.fr. Closed Feb 1–20 and Dec 1–20.* The dining room's maritime decor, the shaded terrace overlooking the harbour, the comings and goings of the boats, and the silvery reflections all make for a holiday atmosphere. So go with the flow and choose a Banyuls from the establishment's small selection before tucking into the chef's delicious regional dishes. Simple guestrooms.

Auberge du Cellier – *1 r. Ste-Eugénie, 66720 Montner. ✆04 68 29 09 78. Closed Mar 7–22, Nov 14–29, Tue and Wed. 6 rooms.* This spot draws its inspiration from the world of wine: the dining room is outfitted in a former wine cellar, and there's a good selection of Côtes du Roussillon to sample. Updated regional cuisine.

Le Cèdre – *29 rte. Banyuls, 66660 Port-Vendres. ✆04 68 82 01 05. www.hotel-le-cedre.com. Closed Nov 20–Feb 5.* Stylish restaurant and charming terrace with sweeping views over port and sea. The menu features traditional dishes. Fresh, brightly coloured guestrooms.

Les Antiquaires – *Pl. Desprès, 66000 Perpignan. ✆04 68 34 06 58. Closed Jun 19–Jul 9, Sun evenings and Mon.* This family-run restaurant, which recently celebrated its 30th anniversary, is run by a charming couple. The lady of the house decorates the rustic yet well-appointed dining room with objects unearthed at antiques shops, while her husband offers the regulars and other patrons good traditional dishes that are always generous and well-prepared.

Les Clos de Paulilles – *Baie de Paulilles, 66660 Port-Vendres – 3km N of Banyuls via the N 114 – ✆04 68 98 07 58. daure@wanadoo.fr. Open evenings Jun–Sept and Sun lunchtime. Reservations required.* At the heart of a wine-growing estate, this restaurant serves rustic cuisine, each course accompanied by a different wine from the estate. To avoid rapid intoxication, sit on the shaded terrace with its sobering fresh sea breeze!

GOURMET SHOPPING

Cabanel et Cie – *72 allée d'Iéna, 11000 Carcassonne. ✆04 68 25 02 58. Open Mon–Sat 8am–12pm & 2–7pm.* This liqueur store offers a wide choice of original spirits such as Or-Kina, made with plants and spices, Micheline, believed to date back to the Middle Ages, Audoise, known as the liqueur of the Cathars, and homemade grog.

Maison Roque – *17 Rte d'Argelès, 66190 Collioure. ✆04 68 82 22 30. roque.collioure@wanadoo.fr. Open Mon–Sat 8am–7.30pm; Sun 9.30am–12.30pm & 2–7pm. Tour of the workshop Mon–Fri 8am–noon & 2–5pm.* Founded in 1870, the Maison Roque perpetuates the traditional small-scale production of the famous anchovies of Collioure. The boutique is on the ground floor, but you can also go up to the first-floor workshop to see expert hands at work preparing the tasty little fish.

Aux Croquants de Montpellier – *7 r. du Faubourg-du-Courreau, 34000 Montpellier. ✆04 67 58 67 38. Open Tue-Sat 7am–7pm; closed public holidays.* This tiny shop has been catering to biscuit lovers for over a hundred years. The star product is the almond-flavoured *croquants de Montpellier*, the recipe for which dates back to 1880. Around fifteen kinds of shortbread biscuit and some special pastries are also produced.

Accent d'Oc – *56 r. Droite, 11100 Narbonne. ✆04 68 32 24 13. www.accentdoc.fr. Open Tue–Sat 10.30am–12.30pm & 2.30–7pm (Mon–Sat Apr–Sept); Sat 10.30am–12.30pm & 2.30–7pm.* The young owners opened this shop in celebration of the gastronomic wealth of Languedoc. Here you will find an array of products made using recipes of long ago: a surprising olive jam, sweet and sour condiments, flavoured vinegars and oils, wine jellies, milk jams etc.

Dotting the banks of Europe's last untamed river and its tributaries, is a patchwork landscape mirroring the extraordinary range of wines produced in the Loire Valley vineyards. The waterways will lead you to keeps and Renaissance châteaux, gardens and royal abbeys, wine-growing villages and historic towns—all in the several UNESCO's World Heritage Sites that cover Sully-sur-Loire to Chalonnes.

Background

The discovery of the remains of a stone wine press near Azay-le-Rideau attests to the existence of vineyards in the Loire Valley as far back as Roman times. St Martin probably planted the first vines on the Vouvray slopes in the 4C. Monks and princes further expanded the vineyards. When the Comte d'Anjou took the English throne in 1154, as Henry II Plantagenet, he started the tradition of serving Anjou wines at Court. It was the white *moelleux* wines that made the reputation of the Anjou vintages, and their reputation was still high in the 15C, when Good King René of Provence was proud to say: "Of all the wines in my cellar – Anjou, Lorraine and Provence – the first is the best." The presence of the Loire River, an ideal mode of transport, played a crucial role in developing exports to Northern Europe. Demand from Dutch merchants, particularly in the 16C, fuelled the expansion of viticulture in Sèvre-et-Maine, Layon, Saumurois and Vouvray. At about the same time, laws were passed requiring wine merchants to obtain their stock over twenty leagues (around 80km) from the capital, which spurred winegrowing around Blois and Orléans, in the Cher Valley and in Sologne. The Loire Valley vineyards suffered during the French Revolution, and during the terrible, counter-revolutionary Vendée wars which followed, nor were they spared in the phylloxera crisis of the late 19C. But in spite of these problems, the Loire Valley today produces some of the most varied and enjoyable wines in France.

Highlights

1 The **Château de Chambord** (p345)

2 The ceramic workshops of **La Borne** (p339)

3 Napolean's maze at the **Parc de Valençay** (p341)

4 The troglodyte houses of **Forges** (p355)

5 The cathedral Saint Etienne in **Bourges** (p340)

Vineyards in Vouvray

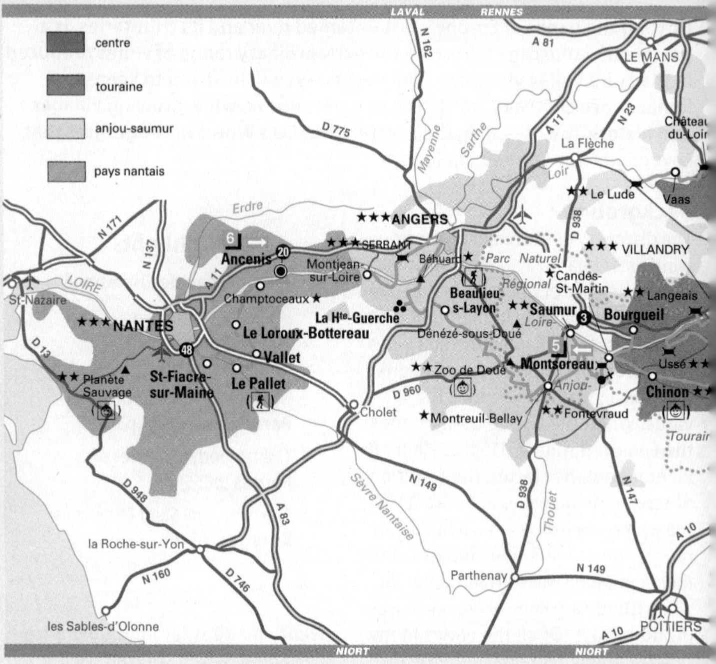

OVERVIEW

The Terroir

See Michelin Local Maps 316, 317, 318 and 323 – Nièvre (58), Cher (18), Loir-et-Cher (41), Indre (36), Indre-et-Loire (37), Maine-et-Loire (49), Loire Atlantique (44).

Vineyards cover more than 70,000ha in the Loire Valley, on a strip of land nearly 600km long, and produces 4 million hl per year. The climate is predominately temperate, ranging from semi-continental in the east to oceanic towards the west. The four main regions are the Central Loire, Touraine, Anjou-Saumur and the Pays Nantais; yet the variety of soils and microclimates has created greatly diverse *terroirs*, reflected in the richness of their wines. In the Central Loire, the **Sancerre** vineyards extend westward on chalky-clay soil, and to the east on flinty ground. The Pouilly vineyards – on the other side of the Loire in Burgundy – are planted on chalky, clay or flinty soil that is predominately Kimmeridgian marl.

In Touraine, the vines planted on the slopes of the Loire, Cher, Indre and Loir Rivers grow on a wide variety of soils ranging from *aubuis* (chalky clay) to *perruches* (flinty clay) as well as sand over clay and light gravel.
Saumur, or "white Anjou", is characterised by chalk tufa, while western Anjou, or "black Anjou", lies on the dark slate of the Massif Armoricain.

Wines

Centre – Sauvignon is the king of white wine grapes, used in AOC Sancerre, **Coteaux-du-Giennois**, **Menetou-Salon**, **Quincy**, **Reuilly**, and **Pouilly-Fumé**. Apart from **Pouilly** and **Quincy**, limited to white wines, these same AOC appellations produce reds from Pinot Noir grapes, as well as rosés. Further south, the **Côtes-Roannaises** and the AOVDQS **Châteaumeillant** (reds and rosés) are worthy of note.

Touraine – AOC **Chinon**, Bourgueil and Saint-Nicolas-de-Bourgueil produce red wines from Cabernet Franc –

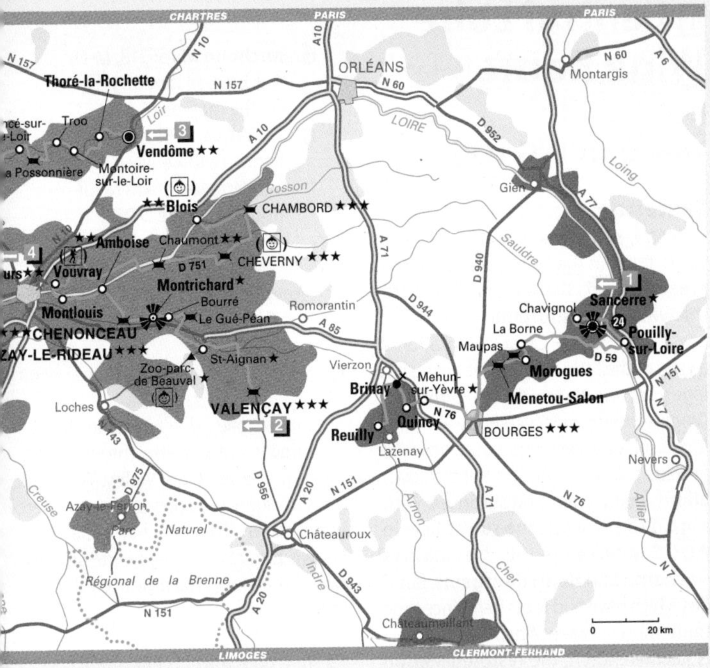

or Breton – grapes, as well as rosés. Some Chinon Blancs also come from Chenin Blanc grapes, or Pineau-de-Loire.

AOC **Vouvray** and **Montlouis**, planted with 100% Chenin Blanc, produce whites with fine bubbles (55%) and still whites (45%) ranging from dry to very sweet. Touraine has many other AOCs, which often produce blends with Gamay as the dominant in reds and Sauvignon in whites, including Touraine (reds, rosés, effervescent whites), Touraine-Azay-le-Rideau (100% Chenin in the whites, predominantly Grolleau in the rosés), **Touraine-Mesland**, **Touraine-Amboise**, **Touraine-Noble-Joué** (*vin gris*, a pale dry rosé, made with three Pinots), Jasnières (whites made with Chenin), and **Coteaux-du-Loir**. Add to that the AOC Valençay, using similar varieties to the Touraines, and the **Cheverny** and **Cour-Cheverny** (whites made with mainly Romorantin grapes) in the Sologne vineyards.

Anjou-Saumur – With their thirty AOCs, the Anjou and Saumur vineyards offer an extraordinary range. The two main varieties are Chenin Blanc for the whites and Cabernet Franc for the reds and rosés. The AOCs include **Saumur** and **Anjou** (reds, whites, and lightly sparkling wines), **Saumur-Champigny** (reds), **Coteaux-de-l'Aubance** (whites), **Coteaux-du-Layon** (very sweet whites), **Bonnezeaux**, **Quarts-de-Chaume** and **Chaume** (very sweet whites), as well as **Savennières** (medium-dry or dry whites, including the famous Coulée-de-Serrant).

Pays Nantais – Muscadet (white) is the main produce here, from Melon-de-Bourgogne in the AOC Muscadet-de-Sèvres et-Maine, Muscadet-de-Coteaux-de-la-Loire. In addition, there are the AOVDQS Gros-Plant du Pays Nantais (white), between Nantes and the ocean, made with Folle Blanche grapes; the **Coteaux-d'Ancenis** (white, red and rosé) east of Nantes.

1 Central Loire Wine Route

Michelin Map: 318, M-O 8, J-L 9. See itinerary 1 on the map p336.
Distance: 140km from Sancerre to Reuilly (Cher). Sancerre lies 46km NE of Bourges by the D 955.

DRIVING TOUR

Sancerre★

Sancerre, perched above a sea of vineyards, takes in the Loire Valley and Nivernais towards the east, and Berry to the west. The **panorama**★★ from the esplanade of porte César (318m) affords a view of the little northern Sancerre villages dotting the route des Vignobles (Wine Route) from St-Satur to St-Gemmes (don't miss the *circuit* that goes down to St-Satur). A walk through the old town affords some charming surprises. With regard to the wine, the surest bets in **AOC Sancerre** are the **Domaines Vacheron** and **Henri Bourgeois**, families which have had roots here since time immemorial *(see Shopping Guide)*.

Near the church, the restored Maison Farnault (14C) houses the **Maison des Sancerre**. This is a wonderful place to inform yourself about wines in general and particularly the Sancerre region via interactive presentations, videos and a relief model. Particularly interesting are interviews with men and women of the profession, which show the human side of the wine industry. This is also a good spot to pick up information about the various cellars and estates in the region. The visit concludes with a tasting *(3 r. du Méridien, 18100 Sancerre; open Jun–Sept 10am–7pm; Mar–May and Oct–Nov 10am–6pm; 02 48 54 11 35; www.maison-des-sancerre.com)*.

SW on D 7, then turn right on D 923.

At the crossroads, don't miss the remarkable **view**★★ of Sancerre, the vineyards, St-Satur and the Loire Valley. The road goes through a sea of grape vines, then winds down the high chalky-clay hills known as *terres blanches* (white ground) where the vineyards produce full-bodied wines.

Turn right towards Chavignol.

The road goes through **Chavignol** which produces the famous *crottin de chavignon* – a goat's cheese that can be soft, hard or extra mature, and goes wonderfully with Sancerre. Local producers are open to see the production process *(www.crottindechavignol.com)*.

D 183 to St-Satur; cross the Loire; right on D 553.

The road runs into the Appellation Pouilly-sur-Loire, made from 50ha of

Sancerre and its vineyards

JACASS/MICHELIN

Chasselais. This area also has 950ha of Sauvignon which produce the famous Pouilly-Fumé.
The **Château de Tracy** (15C-16C) is not open to visitors, but you can taste and purchase wines on the estate and catch a glimpse of the magnificent grounds with cedar trees standing among the vines and a view stretching all the way to Sancerre (*see Shopping Guide*).

At Bois-Gibault, right on D 243 for Les Loges. Watch for the fork to the left for Les Loges under the railway bridge.

Les Loges is a winegrowing hamlet which owes its name to the *loges de vigne*, small buildings used as shelters in the vineyards. Note the typical 19C winemakers' houses with vaulted cellars beneath the staircase.

Pouilly-sur-Loire

To get off to a good start in your exploration of Central Loire wines, go to the **Caves de Pouilly-sur-Loire**, followed by the beautiful **Domaine du Ladoucette** (*see Shopping Guide*).
The **Pavillon du milieu de Loire**, on the banks of the river, has displays of valley wildlife and a room devoted to winegrowing. It also has information about the **reserve naturelle du Val-de-Loire** (nature preserve) and brochures about the **sentiers du Milieu de Loire**, two of which go through vineyards overlooking the Loire (*open Jul–Aug 10am–12.30pm & 2–7pm; Apr–Jun Wed–Mon 10am–12.30pm & 2–6pm; Sept–Oct Wed–Mon 10am–12.30pm & 2–5.30pm; Christmas holidays Wed–Mon 2–5.30pm; closed Jan–Mar, Dec 25; 4.50€; 03 86 39 54 54; www.pavillon-pouilly.com*).

Cross the bridge over the Loire; take D 59; right for Sancerre on D 10 at Vinon.

After 2km, turn left and head up the tiny steep road marked "route des Vignobles" which affords a magnificent **view★** of the Sancerre hills. At the D 955, stop in **Bué** for a tasting at **Domaine Vincent Pinard** (*see Shopping Guide*).

Turn left onto D 955 toward Aix-D'Angillon, then right onto D 22.

La Borne

Known for its stoneware, this village has gained international recognition in the field of contemporary ceramics. Its fifty or so artists and craftsmen come from a variety of countries. Their work can be seen in numerous workshops, at the **Centre de creation céramique** (*open Wed-Mon 2–7pm; daily 2-7pm in school holiday; 02 48 26 96 21; www.ceramiclaborne.org*) and at the **Musée de la Poterie** (*open daily Easter–mid-Nov 3–7pm; s 3€; 02 48 26 73 76;*).

Leave La Borne heading SW on D 46.

Morogues

The vineyards covering the slopes from Morogues to Menetou – the pride and joy of Berry viticulture – were among the most highly valued in France in the days of C15 merchant Jacques Coeur, who did so much to popularise this area. Today they cover more than 400ha and produce fresh and spicy white wines, supple and fragrant reds, and fruity rosés.

Château de Maupas

Visit by guided tour (45min) Easter–late Sept 2–7pm; Sun and public holidays 10am–noon & 2–7pm. 8€. 02 48 64 41 71; www.chateaudemaupas.fr.
The château, in the Maupas family since the time of Louis XV, contains an impressive **plate collection★** and also produces a good red Menetou.

Chateau Menetou-Salon

Visit by guided tour (1hr 30min) May-Sept 10am–7pm (last entry 1hr before closing). 8.50€. 02 48 64 80 54. www.chateau-menetou-salon.com.
Owned for a short time by Jacques Coeur, the **Château de Menetou-Salon** was rebuilt in the 19C. There is an antique car collection in the outbuildings, and beautiful parkland.

To reach Bourges, leave Menetou on the D 59 towards Saint-Martin-d'Auxigny.

Bourges★★★

The Cathédrale St-Étienne and the Palais Jacques Coeur, the heart and soul of Bourges, both benefited from Coeur's love of fine architecture. A successful businessman, he succeeded in amassing a fortune so large that he soon gained the trust of King Charles VII, and became the king's financier in 1439.

The **Cathédrale St-Étienne**★★★, a UNESCO World Heritage site, was built in two stages (1195-1215 and 1225-60). Its **central portal** depicting the Last Judgment is a masterpiece of Gothic sculpture (13C). Don't miss the **stained glass windows**★★★ (mostly early 13C), **crypt**★★ and **astronomical clock**★ dating from 1424. *(open Apr-Sept 8.30am–7.15pm; Oct-Mar 9am-5.45pm)*

The **Palais Jacques Coeur**★★, begun in 1443, is one of the finest civil buildings from the Gothic era. The captivating façade is richly decorated. The master and mistress of the house can be seen in the half-open simulated windows on either side of the festooned loggia, while the central turret is decorated with exotic trees – palms, oranges and dates – evoking countries in the Orient that Coeur travelled to. *(open 9.30am–noon & 2–5.15/6pm; 6.50€; 9.50€ with cathedral; 02 48 24 79 41).*

Other "musts" in Bourges include the **maisons à colombages**★ (half-timbered houses, 15C-16C) in the old section of town north of the cathedral, the **promenade des Remparts**★ (tour of the ramparts) and the **Musée Estève**★★ (abstract art by Berri painter Maurice Estève, born in 1904). The Printemps de Bourges music festival *(3rd week in April)* draws singers from around the world.

N 76 for the Quincy-Reuilly region.

Mehun-sur-Yèvre★

The shady promenade along the Canal du Berry – overlooking the remains of the castle of Jean de Berry and the church – is a lovely place for a walk in this pretty little town. Berry porcelain manufacturers have been established in Foëcy, Noirlac and Mehun since the 19C. The **Pôle de la porcelaine** in Mehun, a pleasant glass building, contains a variety of unusual collector's items *(open May–Sept 10.30am–noon & 2.30–6/6.30pm; Mar–Apr & Oct weekends 2.30–6pm; 4.60€; ; 02 48 57 06 19).*

Quincy

AOC Quincy, stretching between Quincy and Brinay, boasts 200ha planted in Sauvignon grapes which produce a dry, subtle and elegant white wine which is usually at its best within two or three years. During the last weekend in August, Quincy hosts the Fêtes de l'Océan celebrating the marriage of seafood and wine. For an idea of how good this wine can be, try **Domaine Adèle Rouzé Quincy** *(Chemin des Vignes, 18120 Quincy, 02 48 51 35 61; Open by appt.).* This young female winemaker is the daughter of Jacques Rouzé, a well-respected local producer who is also the president of the Quincy wine brotherhood.

Brinay

The little **church** contains a series of 12C **frescoes**★, including a rare calendar of each month's labours (for September – a man trampling grapes in a large vat), and a representation of the Wedding at Cana alluding to the theme of wine.

Left on D 18^E (route du Vignoble) towards Méreau. In Méreau, left on D 918 for Lucy-sur-Arnon and Reuilly.

Reuilly

The **AOC Reuilly** vineyards, spread over both sides of the Arnon, cover 163ha producing remarkable dry and fruity white Sauvignon wines, as well as excellent quality rosés and reds from Pinot Gris and Pinot Noir. And why not visit the little **Musée de la Vigne et du Vin de Reuilly** devoted to winemaking materials *(5, r. Rabelais; open mid-May–mid-Oct Tue–Sun 10am–noon & 3–7pm, open Fri 9am; mid-Oct–mid-May Tue–Sun 10am–noon & 2–6pm, open Fri 9am; 02 54 49 24 94; www.ot-reuilly.fr).*

For an example of the local wine, stop for a visit at **Domaine du Ruilly** *(see Shopping Guide).*

Touraine Wine Routes

More fairytale chateaux, gazing out onto the river Loire and the lovely towns of Ambois and Blois.

- **Population:** 700,000 including Tours.
- **Michelin Map:** 210km. Michelin Local map 323, A-F 1-4. See itinerary 2 on the map on p336.
- **Info:** www.vinsdeloire.fr
- **Location:** Two hours south of Paris near Tours.
- **Timing:** Two days
- **Don't Miss:** Strolling around Blois.
- **Kids:** Aquarium du Val du Loire.

DRIVING TOURS

2 VALENÇAY TO BLOIS

Valençay boasts two AOCs with its name – for its trimmed pyramid-shaped goat's cheese, and for its wines which, like those of Touraine, are made from Sauvignon and Chardonnay grapes.

Château and Parc de Valençay★★★

Open Jul-Aug 9.30am–7pm; Jun 9.30am-6.30pm; May & Sept 10am–6pm; Apr 10.3am–6pm; Oct-mid Nov 10.30am–5.30pm. Château and show 9€. Candlelight evenings late Jul–late Aug Sat 9.30pm 10€. 02 54 00 10 66. www.chateau-valencay.com.

Built around 1540, Valençay is a Renaissance gem. Bonaparte ordered Talleyrand to buy it in 1803 as a place for lavish receptions, and it is also a mecca for Napoleonic history. Sumptuously furnished, the château is surrounded by beautiful **grounds**★. Napoleon's maze, a small farm, a children's castle, picnic area and restaurant make Valençay one of the liveliest châteaux in the Loire Valley. A wine-tasting of Clos du château de Valençay concludes the short play evoking the sumptuous feasts prepared by chef Carême for Talleyrand's guests.

Take the route de Blois (D 956) out of Valençay. After Fontguenand, turn left towards Meusnes on the route des Vignobles Touraine-Val de Loire.

This takes you out of AOC Valençay and into **AOC Touraine**.

With Meusnes to your right, continue on the signposted itinerary (signs show a bunch of grapes) which winds through the vineyards. After crossing the Cher, turn left in Châtillon-sur-Cher and follow the route des Vignobles.

The scenery alternates between vines and woods, then the panorama opens onto a sea of gently sloping vineyards.

Leaving Noyers-sur-Cher, the route des Vignobles forks in opposite directions. Leaving the road to Blois on your right, turn left on road to Saint-Aignan.

Saint-Aignan★

Saint-Aignan, which marks the border of Berry and Touraine, is dominated by a graceful Renaissance château and **collegiate church**★, a gem of Romanesque art (remarkable 12C-15C **frescoes**★★). As the point of departure for the Cher canal to Nitray (37), it is also a hub of river tourism in the region.

Take D 17 along the Cher towards Mareuil-sur-Cher.

A few kilometres after Mareuil, turn left onto the route des Vignobles which leads up to a plateau covered with grape vines; then follow the road down into some winding, wooded valleys. The road takes you through Thésée-la-Romaine (Gallo-Roman site), then offers a superb panorama over the valley as it rises up to the winegrowing slopes of Monthou-sur-Cher. The **Château Gué-Péan** (16C-

Aerial view of Château de Chenonceau

B. Kaufmann/MICHELIN

17C) stands in the little valley. Then head back to the banks of the Cher.

Bourré

At Bourré, the valley narrows. As is often the case in the Touraine and Saumur regions, the hills have been hollowed out by the former tufa quarries turned into troglodyte dwellings, wine cellars or mushroom beds, as here at the **Caves champignonnières des Roches**. The **La Ville Souterraine★** is a lifelike reproduction of a village square carved out of the rock *(both sites visit by guided tour (1hr each) Easter–Nov every hr 10am–5pm; winter holidays 10am, 11am, 3pm & 4pm; 6.50€ for one site or 10.50€ for both;bring warm clothing; 02 54 32 95 33; www.le-champignon.com).*

Montrichard★

Walk to the top of the **castle tower★** in this little medieval town – the best place to appreciate the fine **panorama ★★** over the valley *(open Jun–Aug 10am–6pm; Apr–May & Sept 10am–noon & 2–5pm; sound tours of the dungeon Easter–Sept; 5€; mid-Jul–mid-Aug tours with characters in costume at 4.30pm 10€; 02 54 32 05 10).*
In fine weather you can take a **boat ride** on the *Léonard de Vinci (quai du Cher, 4100 Montrichard; 02 54 75 41 53, ldv.bateau@wanadoo.fr).* The **Caves Monmousseau** run for over 15km: an impressive sequence of underground galleries in which to explore the various stages in making effervescent wine. There is also a large boutique, and a good view over the surrounding valley from the terrace. *71 rte de Vierzon; open daily Apr–mid Nov 10am–7pm; mid-Nov–Mar Mon–Fri 10am–noon & 2–5pm; 02 54 71 66 64; www.monmousseau.com).*

Château de Chenonceau★★★

Open Jul-Aug 9am–8pm; Jun & Sept 9am-7.30pm; Rest of the year times vary. 10€ château, gardens. 13€ with wax museum. 0 820 20 90 90. www.chenonceau.com

A Renaissance treasure built over the Cher River, Chenonceau has been nicknamed "the Ladies' castle" for having nearly always belonged to women, including Catherine de Medici and Diane de Poitiers, the beautiful and insidiously powerful mistress of François I and Henri II. This is an excellent visit with plenty of activities on offer throughout the year. The **gardens★★** and the banks of the Cher provide lovely views of the château. Picnic areas by the moat, restaurants and cafes onsite, and an audio tour for children. The château's vineyards (30ha) produce good wines which can be tasted.

Leave Chenonceaux on D 40 in the direction of Civray-de-Touraine, then towards Amboise (D 31).

3km before Amboise on the left stands the **Pagode de Chanteloup★**. The Duc de Choiseul had this superb *chinoiserie* built here in the 18C – the only vestige of the château. Picnicking allowed on the grounds *(open Jul–Aug 9.30am–7.30pm; Jun 10am–7pm; May & Sept 10am–6.30pm; Apr 10am–noon & 2–6pm, weekends & public holidays 10am–6pm; Oct–Nov weekends & public holidays 10am–5pm; last entrance 30min before closing; 8€ (children: 6€); 02 47 57 20 97; www.pagode-chanteloup.com).*

Amboise★★

This town on the banks of the Loire, which has preserved its ancient feudal structure, is dominated by the most Italian of the Loire châteaux, where François I held extravagant parties, organised by Leonardo da Vinci. But the golden age of Amboise was in the 15C, when Charles VIII brought in artists and craftsmen from Italy to renovate the **château**★★ where he had spent his childhood. The inside contains an exceptional collection of Gothic and Renaissance furniture. There is a splendid **view**★★ from the terrace. Don't miss the **Chapelle St-Hubert**, where Da Vinci is buried. In summer there's a superb sound and light show *(open Jul–Aug 9am–7pm; Apr–Jun 9am–6.30pm; Sept–Nov 9am–6pm; rest of the year hours vary; closed Jan 1, Dec 25; 9.50€; 02 47 57 00 98; www.chateau-amboise.com).*

For a pleasant setting in which to sample Touraine-Amboise wines, try the **Caveau des Vignerons d'Amboise** at the foot of the château *(see Shopping Guide).* The **château du Clos-Lucé**★★ is the house where Leonardo da Vinci spent the last three years of his life. Along with the Master's bedroom, it contains 40 reconstructions of his "fabulous machines".

A magnificent show in the **Parc Léonardo da Vinci** takes you on a discovery of the eclectic genius of this artist-engineer-architect, while videos and thematic displays take you on a deeper journey into the world of this true Renaissance man. There are plans to expand this even further into a "cultural theme park". *(open Jul–Aug 9am–8pm; Feb–Jun & Sep–Oct 9am–7pm; Nov–Dec 9am–6pm; Jan 10am–5pm; 9.50-12.50€ depending on the season; 02 47 57 00 73; www.vinci-closluce.com).*

Leave Amboise on D 751 in the direction of Montlouis.

The road runs along the Loire, providing frequent peeks of the river, its islands and golden sand banks. The pretty little village of **Lussault-sur-Loire** is where the **AOC Montlouis** begins, stretching between the Loire and Cher rivers.

Montlouis -sur-Loire

This little town is built in terraces over the tufa slopes with their hollowed-out cellars. The Maison des vins, on quai Albert-Baillet, is across from the cooperative. The **Domaine de la Taille aux Loups** offers a selection of *moelleux*, dry and fizzy Montlouis wines; the **Domaine François Chidaine** is also worth a stop *(see Shopping Guide).*

The luxury hotel **Château de la Bourdaisière**, set among the vineyards near Montlouis on the route d'Ambois, grows over 400 varieties of tomatoes in its **vegetable garden**★ *(visit by 45min guided tour May–Sept 10am–7pm; Apr & early Oct 10am–noon & 2–6pm; late Oct park only; 7€; free access to grounds and vegetable garden; 02 47 45 16 31; www.chateaulabourdaisiere.com).*

Leave Montlouis on the D 751, which runs alongside the Loire to Vouvray.

Vouvray

Whether sparkling or still, dry, medium or slightly sweet, **Vouvrays** are among the most famous white wines from Touraine. The little town built in terraces on white tufa contains ancient winegrowing houses that are more or less troglodyte caves. Be sure to go around the town on the route des Vignobles, which will take you in particular to the **Caves des Producteurs de Vouvray**, **Clos Naudin** and **Domaine Catherine Champelou** *(see Shopping Guide).*

Follow the GR 33 on two marked trails *(6-18km)* to explore the town's architecture and the panoramas over the Loire and its vineyards. Walk on to **Rochecorbon** where the hillside overlooking the river is dotted with troglodyte caves. The rich houses and palm trees – due to a microclimate – give it an air of the Mediterranean Riviera. This is where the **Marc Brédif** cellars are. Hollowed out between the 8C and 10C, these 2km-long caves contain over a million bottles, the oldest of which date from 1873. Owned by Baron de Ladoucette the tour is well-designed, with an oenological game. Tasting and sales of Vouvray, Chinon, Bourgueil and Saumur-Champigny *(87 quai de la Loire, 37210 Rochecorbon; open Apr–Oct 10.30am–12.30pm & 3–6pm; 5€ 02 47 52 50 07).*

The **Château Moncontour** (late 15C-18C), which Balzac was eager to buy and where he set certain scenes in his story *La Femme de trente ans*, has very old vineyards and a modern *chai* (wine storehouse). Its Musée du Vin contains over 2,000 tools *(Les Patys, 37210 Vouvray; open Apr–Sept daily 9am–7pm, Oct–Mar Mon-Fri 9am–noon & 2–6pm; 4€; 02 47 52 60 77; www.moncontour.com).*

Head E out of Vouvray on the Route touristique de la Vallée de la Brenne (D 46). Go past Vernou-sur-Brenne (many cellars and charming old houses) and continue up to Chançay.

The **Château de Jallanges** is a pretty brick-and-white-stone Renaissance building overlooking vineyards and lovely grounds. A large boutique stocks a range of regional products. *(open Mar–Oct 10am–noon & 2–6pm; 7.50€; 02 47 52 06 66; www.jallanges.com).* After a few kilometres you'll come to the Renaissance gardens of the **Château de Valmer** on a remarkable terraced site overlooking the Brenne. The troglodyte chapel has 16C stained-glass windows, and the château produces its own Vouvray *(open Jul–Aug Tue–Sun 10am–7pm; Jun Tue–Sun 10am–6pm; May weekends 10am–12.30pm & 2–7pm; Sept Tue–Sun 10am–12.30pm & 2–6pm; 8€; 02 47 52 93 12; www.chateau-de-valmer.com).*

Return onD 79; left on D 1.

The road runs along the Vallée de la Cisse and through **AOC Touraine-Amboise**, spread over both banks of the Loire.

In Pocé-sur-Cisse, take a left onto the Route du Vignoble (D 431) and climb up to the beautiful plateaux covered with vineyards, then come back down to Limeray.

After a few kilometres, the road leaves Indre-et-Loire and enters Loir-et-Cher, taking you into **AOC Touraine-Mesland** via the town of Monteaux. The Route du Vignoble rising through the hills to the picturesque village of **Mesland** offers a fine **view** of the Château de Chaumont on the other side of the Loire.

Château de Chaumont-sur-Loire★★

Open Jul-Aug 10am–7pm; Apr–Jun & Sep 10am-6.30pm; Oct-Nov 10am-6pm; rest of year times vary. Last entrance 30min before closing. Closed Jan 1, May 1, Nov 1 & 11, Dec 25. 15 € (8 € for the chateau). 02 54 20 99 22 ; www.domaine-chaumont.fr.

This feudal-looking château, built from 1445-1510, was influenced by the Renaissance. It was first owned by Catherine de Medici and Diane de Poitiers. Later on, Napoleon exiled Madame de Staël here. Since 2008, it has been the property of the regional government, and is becoming a national centre for arts and gardens. Numerous cultural activities and festivals are here, frequently in the magnificent **grounds**. The château's farm houses the **Conservatoire international des parcs et jardins et du paysage** (International Conservatory of parks, gardens and landscaping), where the Festival international des jardins is held from mid-May to mid-October, drawing thousands of visitors Leaving the Loire Valley and its tufa houses with slate roofs at Candé-sur-Beuvron, you head southeast to Valaire and the winegrowing area of Sologne. Asparagus and strawberries are grown here in addition to grapes. **AOC Chev-**

erny extends for more than 2,000ha (but only 610ha in production) on the left bank of the Loire from the Sologne around Blois to the Orléanais border. There are many grape varieties in this mainly sandy terroir. The Cheverny "style" was created from a blend of these.

Château de Cheverny★★★

Open Jul–Aug 9.15am–6.45pm; Apr–Jun & Sept 9.15am–6.15pm; Oct–Mar 9.45am–5pm. 7€ (château and grounds), 11.70€ (château and permanent exhibition), 16.50€ (château and special tour). 02 54 79 96 29. www.chateau-cheverny.com.

The château was built between 1604 and 1634, and the land surrounding it has been in the same family since 1388. Wonderfully furnished and maintained, it is a remarkable example of the classical style. Young visitors and cartoon fans may find something familiar about the building: it was the model for the famous Château de Moulinsart – or Marlinspike in English – in the *Tintin* books: there's a permanent exhibition in the outbuildings about the young hero's adventures. The grounds (100ha) can be visited in an electric car or by boat on the canal. Children are fascinated by feeding time at the **kennel** with its 90 dogs.

The road passes **Cour-Cheverny**, the heart of **AOC Cour-Cheverny**, reserved for white wines made with the Romorantin cépage. Head NE on D 102; then turn left onto D 112 at Bracieux for **Parc de Chambord** and its hunting reserve.

Château de Chambord★★★

Open mid-Jul–late Aug 9am–7.30pm. Early Apr–mid-Jul & Sept 9am–6.15. Oct–Mar 9am–5.15pm. Last entry 30min before closing. Closed Jan 1, May 1, Dec 25. 8.50€ or 9.50€ depending on the season. 02 54 50 40 00. www.chambord.org.

Chambord, built from 1518-45 and probably initially designed by Leonardo da Vinci, has 440 rooms, 365 fireplaces and 83 staircases! Surrounded by 5 000ha of grounds, the château is a UNESCO World Heritage site. Don't miss the superb sound and light show and the equestrian arts show in the Maréchal de Saxe stables in summer. The Chambord estate **grounds** offer a variety of activities from bicycle and horseback rides, roller-skating, horse-drawn carriage rides, boat trips on the Cosson and excursions to hear the calls of the rutting stags.

Blois★★

With its pedestrian streets, winding alleys, townhouses, gardens and terraces, Blois is wonderfully suited to walking tours. The **Maison de la Magie Robert-Houdin**★, takes you into a giant kaleidoscope, an illustrated room and a **Théâtre des Magiciens**★ (Magicians' Theatre). *(open Apr–Aug 10am–12.30pm & 2–6.30pm; Sept Mon-Fri 2-6.30pm; rest of year times vary; 30min shows daily; closed Nov–Mar; 7.50€; 02 54 55 26 26. www.maisondelamagie.fr).*

Some of the names associated with the **Château de Blois**★★★ include Louis XII who brought in the first signs of Italian art in around 1500; Catherine de Medici, who had a cabinet with 237 sculpted panels which, according to Alexandre Dumas, contained secret drawers for poison; Henri III, who had his rival the Duc de Guise assassinated; and Gaston d'Orléans, who commissioned the famous architect Mansart to work there. The **Musée des Beaux-Arts**★ is located on the first floor of the **aile Louis XII** (Louis XII wing) *(open Apr–Sept 9am–6.30pm; Oct–Mar 9am–12.30pm & 2–5.30pm, last entrance 30min before closing; closed Jan 1, Dec 25; 6.50€; 1st Sun Oct–Mar no charge; 02 54 90 33 33. www.ville-blois.fr).*

Regional wines can be tasted and purchased at the **Maison des vins de Loir-et-Cher** on Place du château (*see Shopping Guide*).

"Le pays des châteaux à vélo" (Cycling round château country) offers 300km of safe and well-marked cycling tours around Blois, Chambord and Cheverny, including two through the vineyards. Maps and itineraries are available at regional tourist offices or on the web at *www.chateauxavelo.com.*

3 FROM VENDÔME TO LUDE

95km. Michelin Local Map 317, K-P 2-3.
See itinerary 3 on the map p336.

Vendôme★★

Vendôme, a "little Venice" full of hidden charms, is worth visiting at night. It can even be visited in a boat full of flowers that takes you out on the Loir to explore the Porte d'Eau (Water Gate) and the *chevet* of the abbey-church *(47 r. de la Poterie; Jul–Aug 2.30–7pm; departures from the Embarcadère du Moulin Perrin, off rue du Change; Nightime torchlight tours Aug Thu 9.30pm ihr. 5€; information available across from the landing stage; tourist office 02 54 77 05 07).*

Go W on D 2 out of Vendôme. Turn left onto D 5 in Villiers-sur-Loir, then D 67 towards Thoré and an immediate left after the bridge over the Loir. The road goes through the village of **Rochambeau**, *built partly into the rock.*

Thoré-la-Rochette

The heart of the **appellation Coteaux-du-Vendômois**. The former station – now containing the **Maison du vin et des produits des terroirs vendômois** – is the point of departure for the **Train touristique de la vallée du Loir**; a gently enjoyable trip on a 1950s train which takes you 36km to the troglodyte village of Troo with a number of stops, inclding Montoire station where on 24 October 1940 Pétin met with Hitler to discuss the Vichy regime *(3hr trip with commentary from Thoré to Troo Jun–mid-Sept weekends & public holidays 10€ round-trip; departure 2.25pm from Thore, Jul-Aug three trains each Sunday. 02 54 72 80 82 or 02 54 77 05 07; www.ttvl.fr).*

The road goes through **Lavardin**★, *where the ruins of a feudal castle stand above the town. Leave for Montoire on the pleasant road along the left bank of the Loir.*

Montoire-sur-le-Loir

Montoire would much rather not be remembered for its most "historic" moment – the meeting of Hitler and Pétain – and offers more pleasant sights in the here and now: its old houses, a beautiful bridge over the Loir and the adorable **Chapelle St-Gilles**★ decorated with superbly coloured **frescoes**★★. **Musikenfête**, a museum/show of traditional music, has over 500 instruments that you can listen to on headphones *(Espace de l'Europe, quartier Marescot, 41800 Montoire-sur-Loir; open Mar–Sept Tue-Sun 10am–noon & 2–6pm; Oct–Dec Tue–Sun 2-6pm; closed Jan, Feb, Dec 24–25 & 30–31; 5.80€ 02 54 85 28 95; www.musikenfete.fr).*

Troo

Troo, a troglodyte village overlooking the Loir, is full of terraced houses connected by little streets, stairs and mysterious alleyways. Opposite is the charming **St-Jacques-des-Guérets** church which has preserved some exquisitely fresh Byzantine-looking **murals**★ (12C-13C).

Proceed on D 917 and turn left at Sougé onto the signposted Route Touristique towards Artins. Turn right onto D 10, then right again onto the route de l'Isle Verte; after 100m, turn left onto the road that runs in front of the Château du Pin.

From the bridge opposite the château you can see upstream to **Isle Verte**, at the confluence of the Loir and "its friend the Braye", where Ronsard wanted to be buried. The **church** in **Couture-sur-Loir** (Gothic chancel with Angevin vaulting) contains the tombs of Ronsard's parents.

Manoir de la Possonnière★

Open Jul–Aug 10am–7pm; mid-Mar–Jun & Sept–mid-Nov Fri–mon & public holidays 2–6pm; last entry 1hr before closing; visit by guided tour only afternoons. 6€. 02 54 85 23 30.

This is where the poet Pierre de Ronsard, leader of the Pléiade group, was born in 1524. Every Autumn, a large rose fair is held, where cuttings, plants and flowers are sold.

Go back to Couture and take D 57 N over the Loir. Turn left.

Poncé-sur-le-Loir

Poncé is a town with character. It has a Renaissance château and a remarkable collection of 12C frescoes in its church. The **Centre de Création artisanale "Les Moulins de Paillard"** is a craft centre devoted to pottery and glassblowing *(open May–mid-Sept Tue–Sat 10am–noon & 2–7pm; rest of the year Tue–Sat 2–6pm; closed Jan & public holidays; 02 43 44 45 31.*

The **Château de Poncé**, built in 1542, has a magnificent vaulted **Renaissance staircase**★★ sculpted with a rare sense of whimsy and perspective. The garden is adorned with an arbour and a maze. The dovecote's 1,800 niches and turning ladders have been preserved. The outbuildings contain the Musée du Folklore Sarthois *(open Apr–mid-Nov daily 11.30am-6.30pm; 6.50€; 02 43 44 24 02).*

Follow the route du Vignoble (D 919).

The route takes you to Ruillé-sur-Loir and Lhomme, in the heart of **Appellation Jasnières**. In summer, the **Musée de la Vigne** in **Lhomme** organises walks through the vineyards *(02 43 44 55 38).*

Château-du-Loir

The keep is the only vestige of the feudal castle which gave the town its name. **St-Guingalois Church** contains a 17C Pietà and panels from the Flemish Mannerist School. Stretching out not far from the town is the magnificent forest of Bercé.

Take D 10 out of Château-du-Loir towards Château-la-Vallière. Turn right onto C 2 towards La Bruère-sur-Loir immediately after the bridge at Nogent. Take D 11, then right onto D 30 towards Vaas.

Vaas

Houses, little gardens, the church and washing houses are all next to each other on the banks of the Loir. Don't miss the **Moulin à blé de Rotrou**, a former flour mill, on the left before the bridge. *(visit by 1hr 30min guided tour Jul–Aug 2.30–5.30; Easter–late Jun & Sept–Oct Sun & public holidays 2.30–5.30; 3.20€; 02 43 46 70 22).*

Turn left onto D 305

The route passes the **Cherré archaeological site**. This 1C and 2C AD Gallo-Roman ensemble contains a temple, thermae, two other buildings and an attached reddish sandstone **theatre**.

Château du Lude★★

Grounds accessible Jul–Aug 10am–12.30pm & 2–6pm; 45min guided tours of the château 2–6pm. Grounds accessible Apr–Jun & Sept Thu–Tue 10am–noon & 2–6pm; guided tour Thu–Tue 2.30–6pm. 7 € (4 € for gardens only). 02 43 94 60 09. www.lelude.com.

Le Lude, a magnificent château on the banks of the Loir, has several faces. Its large round towers are Medieval and Gothic, its furnishings, dormer windows and medallions are Italian Renaissance, and its harmonious riverside façade is Louis XVI. The furniture inside is exceptional. In summer there are concerts and jam-making activities. The gardens extend over several levels down to the river.

Château du Lude

A. Cassaigne / MICHELIN

4 FROM TOURS TO ST-NICOLAS-DE-BOURGUEIL

125km. Michelin Local Map 317, J-N 4-6. *See itinerary 4 on the map p336.*

Tours★★

Tours has preserved no less than three old neighbourhoods: **old Tours**★★★ with the Place Plumereau and its Medieval and Renaissance houses, the **quartier Saint-Julien**★ in the centre of town, and the **quartier de la cathédrale**★★ further east with the archbishop's palace. The **Musée des vins de Touraine**, with its tools, stills, wine presses and costumes, is located in the storeroom of St. Julien's church (12C) (*open Wed–Mon 9am–noon & 2–6pm; last entry 30min before closing time; closed Jan 1, May 1, Jul 14, Nov 1 & 11, Dec 25; 3€; 02 47 61 07 93*).

Take D 88 W out of Tours.

The road passes near the **Prieuré de Saint-Cosme**★, where the poet Ronsard is buried (*open May–Aug 10am–7pm; mid-Mar–Apr & Sept–mid-Oct 10am–6pm; midOct–mid-Mar Wed–Mon 10am–12.30pm & 2–5pm; closed Jan 1, Dec 25; 4.50€; 02 47 37 32 70; www.prieure-ronsard.fr*).

Continue on D 88, then turn left at l'Aireau-des-Bergeons.

In **Savonnières** you can visit the amazing petrified caves with their rock formations next to a petrified waterfall, a cemetery, Gallo-Roman remains and objects currently in the process of petrification (*visit by 1hr guided tour Apr–Sept 9am–6.30pm; Feb–Mar & Oct–mid-Dec 9.30–noon & 2–6pm; mid-Nov–mid-Dec Fri–Wed 9.30am–12pm, 2–5.30pm; 5.60€; 02 47 50 00 09; www.grottes-savonnieres.com*).

Place Plumereau, Tours

S. Sauvignier/MICHELIN

Gardens and Château de Villandry★★★

Visit by guided tour (1hr 15min) Jul–Aug 9am–7.30pm. Apr–Jun & Sept 9am–7pm. Rest of year times vary. 6€ gardens; 9€ (château and grounds). 02 47 50 02 09; www.chateauvillandry.com).

The **gardens**★★★ at Villandry are a magnificent recreation of the architectural layout adopted in the Renaissance under the influence of the Italian gardeners brought to France by Charles VIII.

Built in the 16C around the original dungeon, the **château**★★ is decorated with Spanish furniture and an interesting collection of paintings. **Mudéjar ceiling**★ room. There is also a good restaurant with an outside terrace.

Continue on D 7 to Lignières, then cross the bridge towards Langeais.

Château de Langeais★★

Open Jul–Aug 9am–7pm. Apr–Jun & Sept–mid-Nov 9.30am–6.30pm. Mid-Nov–Jan 10am–5pm; Jan-Feb 9.30am-5.30pm. 8.20€. 02 47 96 72 60; www.chateau-de-langeais.com.

The imposing medieval fortress of Langeais has made it through the centuries intact. The richly furnished **apartments**★★★ evoke the atmosphere of seigniorial life in the 15C and early Renaissance.

Head back S over the Loire and take an immediate right onto D 16.

Château d'Ussé★★

Visit by guided tours (45min) Apr–Aug 10am–7pm. Sept-Nov & mid Feb-Mar 10am–6pm. Last entry 1hr before closing. Closed Dec-mid Feb 13€. 02 47 95 54 05; www.chateaudusse.fr.

A. de Valroger/MICHELIN

Built in the 15C at the edge of the Chinon Forest, this château was the inspiration for Charles Perrault's *Sleeping Beauty*. It also has a very interesting **game room**★. Princess Aurora, Carabossa and Prince Charming are all there on display, as you walk down the covered way.

Rivarennes

The village used to have sixty ovens for making *poires tapées* ("beaten pears"). Today you can taste one of these delicious local specialities in a troglodyte cave, **Les Poires Tapée à l'Ancienne** *(R. de Quinçay; open 10am–noon & 2–6pm; Tasting 2.20€ 02 47 95 45 19; www.poirestapees.com).*
This is in **Appellation Touraine-Azay-le-Rideau**, a relatively small vineyard (100ha), but with an original *encépagement*: Chenin for the whites and a Grolleau *assemblage* for the rosés.

Marnay: Musée Maurice-Dufresne★

Open Apr–Sept 9.15–7pm. Feb–Mar & oct–Nov 10am–6pm. 10€. 02 47 45 36 18; www.musee-dufresne.com.
This museum, located in the verdant setting of a former paper mill, has a collection of over 3,000 old machines displayed in a wonderful – almost Surrealist – bric-à-brac manner. Pieces include Blériot's 1909 airplane, a 1792 guillotine, a 1908 Russian sleigh, an 1850 fire engine, a 1912 steam engine, a 1959 Morgan car and military vehicles from the two World Wars turned into farm machinery. A small bar/restaurant has recently opened.

Turn right out of the museum (onto D 120, then D 57) to reach Azay.

Château d'Azay-le-Rideau★★★

Open Jul–Aug 9.30am–7pm. Apr–Jun & Sept 9.30am–6pm; Oct–Mar 10am–12.30pm & 2–5.30pm. Closed 1 Jan, 1 May, 25 Dec. 8.50€ 02 47 45 42 04. http://azay-le-rideau.monuments-nationaux.fr.
A Renaissance gem built in the 16C on an island in the Indre, Azay contains extremely rich decorations and furnishings, in particular its **tapestries**★. But everything here – the trees and the handsome architecture, reflected in the glassy water – is absolutely dazzling.

Go S out of Azay, cross the bridge over the Indre and turn left onto D 17, then right onto D 57

The road goes through **Villaines-les-Rochers**, a picturesque troglodyte village which became the capital of basketry, then **Crissay-sur-Manse**, a postcard-pretty village with old tufa houses – with square (15C) turrets, mullioned windows and hidden gardens – dominated by the imposing ruins of the château (15C).
Continuing west on D 21 takes you into **Appellation Chinon** – Rabelais country. The vineyards, which stretch for over 2,100ha on both sides of the Vienne, take over completely along the road

Château d'Azay-le-Rideau
©José I. Soto/Dreamstime.com

through Panzoult, Cravant-les-Coteaux and Chinon.

Chinon★★

Chinon rises in terraced rows between the Vienne river and chalky slopes crowned by an impressive **medieval fortress**★★ *(Restoration work in progress; parts of the fortress may be closed to visitors; open Apr–Sept 9am–7pm; Oct–Mar 9.30–5pm; closed Jan 1, Dec 25; 3€ during renovations; 02 47 93 13 45; www.forteresse-chinon.fr).*

The "Circuit-Découverte" brochure *(available at the Tourist Office)* is a good guide to **old Chinon**★★.

The **Caves Paintes**, mentioned in Rabelais' tales of Pantagruel, still attract their share of devotees of the vine. Induction ceremonies for the Bons Entonneurs (Rabelaisian singers) take place there several times a year *(Jan, Jun, Sep and Dec)* during a gala evening and show. By booking early enough in advance, you may have a chance to take part in the Rabelaisian festivities *(Secrétariat de la Confrérie, Imp. Des Caves-Painctes, 37500 Chinon, 02 47 93 30 44; www.entonneursrabelaisiens.com).*

The **Musée du Vin et de la Tonnellerie** (Wine and Cooperage Museum) features life-size models of characters such as Rabelais and his disciples who teach you about vineyard work, the winemaking process and making casks *(open Mar–Sept 10am–10pm; 4.50€; 02 47 93 25 63).*

Now it's time for some wine-tasting at **Cave Montplaisir** *(see Shopping Guide)*. The **Maison de la rivière** offers a variety of traditional boat rides, such as cruises at the confluence of the Loire and Vienne rivers, à la carte cruises and planned theme rides *(12 quai Pasteur; call for hours 02 47 93 21 34; www.cpie-val-de-loire.org).*

4.5km W of Chinon *(D 8)*, on the right, is the **Château de Coulaine**, where wine has been made since 1300, is open to visitors *(see Shopping Guide)*. A little further out, in the village of Cravant les Coteaux, is **Domaine Bernard Baudry** *(see Shopping Guide).*

Turn right onto D 749.

By making a slight detour through **Beaumont-en-Véron**, you can taste and buy a wide selection of Chinon wines at estate prices at the **Maison des vins et du tourisme** *(see Shopping Guide)*. Its competent and dynamic guides will provide you with a wealth of information about vineyard tours in the area.

Back on D 8, you will soon come to Savigny-en-Véron and D 7.

As you cross the bridge, there is a view of the superb **site**★ of Candes-St-Martin, at the confluences of the Loire and Vienne, flanking the Plaine du Véron.

Candes-Saint-Martin★

The **collegiate church**★, built in the 12C-13C on the site where St Martin died in 397, was equipped with defences in the 15C. A small path *(to the right of the church)* leads up to the top of the hillside and a beautiful panorama. Rue St-Martin below the church leads to the riverbank.

Leave Candes on D 7, which crosses the Vienne bridge and runs along the Loire. Take the first bridge on the left to reach Bourgueil (D 749).

The **Appellations Bourgueil** and **Saint-Nicolas-de-Bourgueil** are linked by Cabernet Franc, which has different expressions according to the terroir – gravel by the river / tufa on the slopes.

Bourgueil

Bourgueil – famous for its wine, whose ruby-colour and delightful qualities were praised by Rabelais – contains an ancient **winemaking abbey** founded in the late 10C. It was one of the richest in Anjou, possessing vineyards all along its slopes. Today it houses the Musée des Arts et traditions Populaires *(east of town, on the road to Restigné; visit by 1hr guided tour Jul–Aug Wed–Mon 2–6pm; Apr–Jun & Sept–Oct Sun & public holidays 2–6pm; 5.30€; 02 47 97 73 35).*

The **Maison des vins de Bourgueil** has a small selection of wines and provides information on the interesting vineyard walking path which goes through the winegrowing slopes of Benais *(a few kilometres E of Bourgueil)*; you might also try the **Domaine Yannick Amirault** *(see Shopping Guide)*.

Leaving Bourgueil, head for **Chevrette** where the **Cave Touristique du Pays de Bourgueil** and its Wine Museum are located *(open Apr–Oct 9.30am–12.30pm & 2.30–6.30pm; Nov–Mar weekends & public holidays 2–6pm; Apr-Sep: 9.30am–5.30pm. 02 47 58 58 40).*

Saint-Nicolas-de-Bourgueil

Wines are tasted over dinner in the excellent restaurant at the **Caveau des Vignerons** *Le Saint Nicolas Gourmand*, and can be bought in the adjoining cellar which sells all varieties of Saint-Nicolas-de-Bourgueil.

5 Anjou-Saumur Wine Route

This tour takes you through AOCs Saumur, Layon and Savennières.

Michelin Map: 317, D-J 4-5. See itinerary 5 on the map p336.

Distance: About 170km from Montsoreau to Montjean-sur-Loire (Maine-et-Loire).

DRIVING TOUR

Montsoreau

Montsoreau is famous for its (15C) **château** – in a "fortress with comforts" style – which is reflected in the Loire river. Audiovisual exhibition, **"Les Imaginaires de Loire"**★ *(open May–Sept 10am–7pm; Oct–mid-Nov & Feb–Apr 2–6pm; last entrance 45min before closing; 8.10€. 02 41 67 12 60. www.chateau-montsoreau.com).*

Take D 947 S towards Fontevraud.

Abbaye de Fontevraud★★

Open Jun–Sep 9am–6.30pm. Apr–May & Oct 10am–6pm. Nov–Mar 10am–5.30pm. Closed Jan 1, May 1, Nov 1 & 11, Dec 25. 6.90€– 8.50€ depending on season. 02 41 51 71 41. www.abbaye-fontevraud.com).

This royal abbey is one of the greatest monastic complexes in France and the burial place of the Plantagenets. Despite being converted into a prison (1904–1963; writer Jean Genêt was once a prisoner) and undergoing other damage, it has preserved several pure gems of Angevin architecture such as its abbey-church, noted for its light arches, **polychrome effigies**★ and impressive **kitchen**★★. **St Michel's Church**★ (12–15C), in the village, contains exceptional **works of art**★. It retains its literary connections with a number of festivals.

Go back to Montsoreau, turn left onto D 947 towards Saumur.

The slopes along this road are lined with troglodyte dwellings, Renaissance houses, cellars and former quarries, often converted into mushroom-beds. The ones at **Le Saut-aux-Loups** – on the way out of Montsoreau – show the various stages of mushroom culture; they also have delicious *galipettes*, large mushrooms baked in bread ovens, which you can taste in season, and a restaurant (*open Mar-Nov 10am-6pm; 5.50€; 02 41 51 70 30; www.troglo-sautaux-loups.com*).

Turquant

This is where **Appellation Saumur-Champigny** begins, covering 1,550ha in nine town districts. To see the vineyards, you must climb up the hillside. The GR3 and GR36 long-distance hiking routes go right through the vineyards. Stop at **La Grande Vignole** at **Domaine Filliatreau**, a rare example of a seigniorial troglodyte abode with a *fuye* (dovecote) and 16C chapel (*open Apr–Sept 10am–6pm; Oct Thu & Fri 2–6pm, weekends 10am–6pm; 4€; 02 41 38 16 44 or 02 41 52 90 84; www.filliatreau.fr*).

Parnay

The **Romanesque Church** perched on top of the hillside amid the vineyards provides a great opportunity for a lovely walk. There is an ornithological preserve across from the village on a sand bank in the Loire.

Souzay-Champigny

Marguerite d'Anjou's **castle**, connected by a turret to a 13C-14C troglodyte abode, dominates this attractive village. It is also known for its Clos Cristal organic wines (the domaine now belongs to the Hospices de Saumur) with trellised vines climbing over a wall – in order to have their roots facing north and their tops facing south.

Saumur★★

The Château de Saumur, perched atop its tufa hillside, looks like a medieval miniature from the illuminated pages of the *Très Riches Heures du duc de Berry*. Renowned for its famous sparkling wines, the town also has strong connections with France's horse-breeding industry. The winding little streets between the château and the bridge in **old Saumur**★ have kept their medieval layout. Almost unchanged since its reconstruction (late 14C), the **château**★★ conceals a richly ornamented and comfortable abode behind its fortress-like exterior. It contains the **Musée d'Arts décoratifs**★★ and the **Musée du Cheval**★ (Horse Museum) (*museums closed for renovations, although some exhibits on display in the Abbatiale; open Apr–Sept Wed–Mon 10am–1pm & 2–5.30pm; 2€; 02 41 40 24 40*).

The excellent **Maison du vin de Saumur** contains a wealth of information on wine and wine tourism (*see Shopping Guide*).

Don't leave town without visiting one of the many cellars located in Saumur itself where the wines with fine bubbles are slowly talking on their full character. The most curious is probably the **Caves Louis de Grenelle**, a town-beneath-the-town. Guided tours followed by a tasting with commentary. A fun place for learning about wines and wine-growing, with games for children also on offer (*20 r. Marceau, BP 206, 49415 Saumur; open May-Sept daily 9.30am–6.30pm; Oct-Mar Mon–Fri 9.30am–noon & 1.30–6pm; Apr daily 9.30am-noon & 1.30-6pm closed public holidays; 02 41 50 17 63; www.louisdegrenelle.fr*).

Saint-Hilaire-Saint-Florent

The **Caves Bouvet-Ladubay** are more of a cultural centre than a wine store – with cellars hollowed out of the cliff., a wine-tasting school that is open to all wine-lovers, a museum with an exceptional collection of labels, and a contemporary art gallery *(visit by 1hr guided tour Jun–Sept Mon–Fri8.30am–7pm, Sat 9am-7pm, Sun 9.30am–7pm; Oct–May Mon–Fri 8.30am–12.30pm & 2–6pm, Sat-Sun 10am-12.30pm & 2.30–6pm; closed Jan 1, Dec 25; 1€. 02 41 83 83 83. www.bouvet-ladubay.fr).*

Go back to the roundabout across from the Château de Saumur and take the Route Touristique towards Champigny and Fontevraud through the vineyards (D 145).

After the Aunis farm, an important Resistance centre for Saumur cadets during the Second World War, turn right towards Chaintre and **Varrains**, one of the smallest townships in **Appellation Saumur-Champigny**, but the one with the largest number of winemakers. The charmingly-named **Domaine des Roches Neuves** and **Domaine des Sables Verts** merit a stop *(see Shopping Guide).*

In Samoussay, take the first left towards Saint-Cyr-en-Bourg.

The road goes past the **Cave des Vignerons de Saumur**, which has over 10km of underground galleries. Here you can find out about the history of the vineyards, wine-making secrets and a whole range of Saumur wines including Saumur brut, Crémant-de-Loire, Saumur-Champigny and Cabernet-de-Saumur. *(Rte. de Saumoussay, 49260 St-Cyr-en-Bourg; visit by 1hr guided tour Mon–Sat 9.30am–12.30pm & 2–6/6.30pm; closed public holidays; 2.50€; 02 41 53 06 18; www.cavedesaumur.com).*

Château de Brézé★★

Chateau visit by guided tour (1hr) Apr–Sept 10am–6.30pm. Oct–Dec and Feb–Mar Tue–Fri 2–6pm, weekends 10am–6pm. Underground accessible without tour. Closed Nov 1, Dec 24–25. 8.50€ underground; 14€ underground and château. 02 41 51 60 15. www.chateaudebreze.com.

This elegant Renaissance château, remodelled in the 19C, elegantly furnished and surrounded by a sea of vineyards, has a secret – its fabulous **troglodyte complex**★★. Over a kilometre of underground trails with wine cellars, a press for the famous Brézé white wines, cellars – including three which have been turned into a painted "cathedral" **chamber**★, a **bakery**★, and the largest known underground fortress!

Drive towards Montreuil-Bellay, then turn right (D 178) towards St-Just-en-Dive, then left (D 162).

Le Coudray-Macouard – full of little medieval streets lined with 15C-18C houses, a château, church and many cellars – is one of the most picturesque villages in Anjou.

Go S on the little road that runs along the Thouet.

Montreuil-Bellay★

Verdant banks washed by the Thouet, old streets, ancient houses and gardens, fortified surrounding walls and gates all give Montreuil-Bellay true medieval charm. The Medieval kitchen in the **château**★★, a lovely 15C home, has been preserved *(visit by 1hr guided tour Jul–Aug 10am–6.30pm; Apr–Jun & Sept–Oct Wed–Mon 10am–noon & 2–6pm; 8€; 02 41 52 33 06; www.chateau-de-montreuil-bellay.fr).*

Bridge over the Thouet (for Doueé-la-Fontaine); turn left on D 88 for Sanziers, then right on D 178.

Le Puy-Notre-Dame

Throngs of pilgrims came to the 13C **collegiate church**★ during the Middle Ages to venerate the Virgin Mary's belt, brought back from Jerusalem in the 12C. You can learn all about the mysteries of silkworms at the **Musée de la Soie**

Vineyard of Coteaux-du-Layon

S. Sauvignier/MICHELIN

Vivante in this village *(visit by 1hr 15min guided tour May–Nov Tue–Sat 11 10am–noon & 2–6pm; Sun–Mon 2–6pm; rest of the year on request by telephone; 4.50€; 02 41 38 28 25; www.relais-du-bien-etre.com).*

To the west of Le Puy, the D 178 is lined with vineyards as far as the eye can see. It goes through the pretty little village of Argentay, then into **Appellation Coteaux-du-Layon** at Verchers-sur-Layon. Coteaux-du-Layon is a subtle and delicate white wine – *moelleux* or *liquoreux* – produced with the Chenin Blanc or Pineau-de-la-Loire *cépages* harvested in late September when the grapes start to be covered with noble rot. The appellation extends over 1,800ha and 27 townships on the Layon, a small tributary of the Loire. The six local areas with particularly well-exposed soil which can tag the AOC onto their name as a guarantee of quality are Rochefort, St-Aubin-de-Luigé, St-Lambert, Beaulieu, Faye and Rablay. Certain very specific wines from the Butte de Chaume in the Rochefort township have had the right to use the **Appellation Chaume** label since 2003.

From Concourson the road climbs up the steep slopes covered with vine stocks all the way to St-Georges-sur-Layon, a former mining town.

Left on D 84; continue to Tigné, then go N on D 167.

Martigné-Briand

The **château**, ravaged by the Vendée wars, has nevertheless preserved some magnificent remains of its flamboyant 16C splendour. It is best seen when it comes to life on the first Sunday in October, as host to the Vendanges de la Belle Époque.

Turn left onto D 125.

Thouarcé is in the heart of **AOC Bonnezeaux** (90ha). This "divine nectar" blending aromas of candied fruit with undertones of minerals and honey, is only produced on three small, steep slopes with full southern exposure. Gathered in successive pickings to get the best out of the noble rot, this vintage gives full, mellow wines which combine intensity, complexity, freshness and elegance as they age.

Rablay-sur-Layon boasts a 15C Tithing House *(Maison de la Dîme)* in the Grand-Rue and a 17C building which houses artists' workshops.

Beaulieu-sur-Layon

This other small wine-making town, which dominates the Layon slopes (viewpoint indicator), has preserved a few Mansart houses as well as 13C frescoes in the church.

A former railway line has been turned into a hiking path along the Layon for 25km.

The **Château Pierre-Bise** makes an excellent Chaume *premier cru* and affords an exceptional panorama (*see Shopping Guide*).
The road goes down into a valley where cellars and quarries have been dug out of the rock face. In a locality called **Pont-Barré** there is a pretty view over the Layon's narrowing course and the ruins of a Medieval bridge where a violent battle took place in 1793 between the Royalists *(Blancs)* and Revolutionaries *(Bleus)*.

Get back on N 60 and follow it S.

Saint-Lambert-du-Lattay

The **Musée de la Vigne et du Vin d'Anjou**, set up in the Coudraye storerooms, evokes the world of Angevin winemaking, featuring winemaking and cooperage tools, illustrations and a collection of wine presses. In a room called *l'Imaginaire du Vin* you get to use your eyes, nose and taste buds. There is also an observation and exploration game called *Les Clefs du Musée* (The Keys to the Museum) designed especially for children ages 7-14 (*open Jul–Aug: 11am–1pm & 3–7pm; Apr-June and Sept–early Nov weekends & public holiddays 2.30–6.30pm; rest of year by appt. 5.10€; 02 41 78 42 75; www.mvanjou.com).*
As you leave town, try your newfound knowledge at the **Domaine Ogereau** (*see Shopping Guide*). The hilly, winding St-Aubin-de-Luigné road is lined with Butte de Chaume vineyards where the famous **Quarts-de-Chaume** wines are produced on a few rare parcels of land.

Turn left onto D 106 just before St-Aubin, then right.

Château de la Haute-Guerche

Open Jul–Aug 9am–noon & 2–6pm. No charge. 02 41 78 41 48.
This fortress built during the reign of Charles VII and ruined by the Vendée wars, once housed the lords to whom the Chaume lands belonged. They rented them out in return for payment in kind of the best quarter of the vineyard's harvest, which is where the Quarts-de-Chaume appellation's name comes from.

Go back to St-Aubin and take the D 125 to Chaudefonds-sur-Layon.

A visit to **Domaine Patrick Baudouin** makes a pleasant pause; try the excellent liquoreux wines "au naturel" as well as the dry whites (*see Shopping Guide*).

follow the D 121 through Ardenay and take the D 751 to the right to turn right onto the little road that leads to La Haie-Longue.

Going Underground

In Doué and its environs the cellars were dug underground, in the plains, rather than out of the hillside.

Rochemenier Troglodyte Village
In Louresse, 6km N of Doué on D 69 and D 177. Open Apr–Oct 9.30am–7pm. Feb–Mar & Nov weekends & public holidays 2–6pm. 5€. 02 41 59 18 15; www.troglodyte.info. The visit comprises two troglodyte farms (abode and outbuildings) abandoned since about 1930. There is another troglodyte village nearby in **Forges**.

Caverne sculptée de Dénezé-sous-Doué (Sculpted Caves)
31km NW of Beaulieu-sur-Layon on D 83 and D 125. Visit by guided tour (1hr) Jul-Aug 10am-7pm; Apr–Jun & Sept-Oct Tue–Sun 10.30am–1pm & 2–6.30pm. 4€. 02 41 59 15 40. Dress warmly, temperatures are typically about 14°C.
This cave, its walls covered with hundreds of unusual figurines, has long remained a mystery, although It is thought to have housed a secret community of stone carvers whose works illustrate their initiation rites.

Take the **Corniche Angevine**★ (D 751 cliff road) with a view over the entire width of the valley. At **La Haie-Longue** there is a remarkable **view**★★ of the Loire and its *boires*, expanses of water sprawling out lazily under the silvery light. As you leave town, there is a chapel devoted to Notre-Dame-de-Lorette and a monument to René Gasnier, a pioneer of aviation. Further on, **Rochefort-sur-Loire** has preserved a few old houses, but its fame mainly comes from the slopes overlooking the town, a privileged few of which have the Quarts-de-Chaume and Chaume Premier Cru Coteaux-du-Layon Appellations. The **Domaine des Baumard**, 150m from the church, has Quarts-de-Chaume, Savennières and other wines *(see Shopping Guide).*

Béhuard★

The charming island of Béhuard grew up around a rock, on top of which sits the little **Church of Notre-Dame**. Built in the 15C by Louis XI, it became a popular destination for pilgrimages to the Virgin Mary, protector of travellers. Have a walk around the old village with its 15C and 16C houses, and along the wayside cross.

Savennières

The village **church** has a pretty Romanesque *chevet* with sculpted modillions and a southern portal from the same period. Note the herringbone-brick ornamentation on the (10C) shale wall of the nave.

The **AOC Savennières** terroirs, perched atop the steep slopes overlooking the Loire, have very well-exposed soil composed of shale, Volcanic seams and sand. They produce great whites which are mainly converted into dry, full-bodied and rich wines with an invigorating final note and intense, complex aromas. There are two world-class Savennières vintages: Coulée-de-Serrant and Roche-aux-Moines.

Grown with biodynamic methods since 1980, the famous Coulée-de-Serrant stretches over 7ha of steep slopes overlooking the Loire. The **Domaine Vignobles de la Coulée de Serrant** contains a former monastery, the ruins of a former fortified castle and a path with Celtic cypresses *(see Shopping Guide).*

After tasting some of the Savennière and Anjou wines at the **Domaine du Closel**, in the very heart of Savennières, you can visit the English-style gardens (with a picnic area) and vineyards using a map with explanations of the terroir, landscape and growing methods *(1 pl. du Mail, 49170 Savennières; open by appt 9am–12.30pm & 1.30–7pm; 6€; 02 41 72 81 00).*

The road that runs along the Loire towards **Epiré** climbs up through the vineyards over the small but deep valley of a Loire tributary. The **Château de Chambou-reau**, with one of the oldest vineyards in Appellation Savennières, is a lovely 15C home *(see Shopping Guide).*

After La Pointe the road follows the banks of the Maine on to Angers.

Angers★★★

Angers' gigantic medieval fortress is a reminder that it was once the capital of a kingdom comprising England and Sicily. Built by St Louis from 1228-38, the **château**★★★ narrowly escaped destruction during the Religious Wars. Only the tops of its 17 towers were taken off. Its greatest jewel, the **Apocalypse Tapestry**★★★ (14C), originally 133m long and 6m high, is a colourful, grandiose illustration of the Revelations of St John. The royal abode contains a superb collection of 15C and 16C tapestries, including the **Tapestry of the Passion** and **mille-fleurs tapestries**★★ *(open May–Aug 9.30am–6.30pm; Sept–Apr 10am–5.30pm; closed Jan 1, May 1, Nov 1 & 11, Dec 25; 7€; 02 41 87 43 47; www.monum.fr).*

For more glorious tapestries, don't miss the **Musée Jean-Lourçat et de la Tapisserie contemporaine**★★. It occupies the **Hôpital St-Jean**★, founded in 1174, and contains a series of tapestries by Jean-Lourçat (1892-1966) entitled **Le Chant du monde**★★ *(open Jun–Sept 10am–7pm; Oct–Jun Tue–Sun10am–12pm*

& 2–6pm; ⇔4€; ☏02 41 24 18 45; www.angers.fr).
While walking through **old Angers**★ to take in its many monuments – the **Cathédrale Saint-Maurice**★ (12C-13C, 16C), half-timbered 16C houses such as the **Maison d'Adam**★, Église Saint-Serge (13C chancel), **the Galerie David d'Angers**★ and the **Hôtel Pincé**★ – you may want to stop for a break in one of the many gardens in this city known for its flowers and green spaces, including the Jardin des Plantes, the Jardin du Mail and the Arboretum. And to keep up on wines, there's the **Maison du vin de l'Anjou** (*see Shopping Guide*).
The **Académie des vins du Val de Loire** offers training courses, intensive workshops, special appointments, lectures and wine tastings *(Hôtel des Vins La Godeline, 73 r. Plantagenêt, BP 52327, 49023 Angers Cedex 02; ☏02 41 87 62 57; www.interloire.com).*

Take N 23 W out of Angers.

Château de Serrant★★★

Visit by guided tour (1hr) mid-May–Sept daily 9.45am–5.45pm. Oct–mid-Nov & mid-Mar - midMay Wed–Sun 9.45am–noon & 2–5.15pm. ⇔9.50€. ☏02 41 39 13 01; www.chateau-serrant.net.
Begun in 1546, this Renaissance château contains some magnificent **apartments**★★★. The furniture collection is so rich and of such high quality that it has been classified as a historical monument, which is a first.

Take D 961 S out of St-Georges-sur-Loire.

In summer, the **Train touristique Chalonnes par vignes et vallées** takes you down the old streets of **Chalonnes-sur-Loire** and up the vineyards' steep paths, offering superb panoramas of the Layon hills (*open Jul–Aug 4pm; Sun 3.30–5pm; trips lat 1hr 15min. ⇔6.50€; information and reservations ☏02 41 78 25 62).*

Take D 751 W.

The road follows the edge of the plateau, interspersed with little valleys. This is the **Appellation Coteaux-de-la-Loire** area. Perched atop a promontory, **Montjean-sur-Loire** houses a museum evoking former activities in the region such as working with hemp, the Loire as a working river, lime kilns and coal mines.

6 Le Pays Nantais

This tour takes you through the Saumur, Layon and Savennières AOCs.

- **Michelin Map:** 316, G-I 3-5. See itinerary 6 on the map p336.
- **Distance:** About 73km from Ancenis to Nantes (Loire-Atlantique).

DRIVING TOUR

Ancenis

This is the **Appellation Coteaux-d'Ancenis** area, where Ancenis was long an active port for transporting wine. The Vignerons de la Noëlle cultivate 350ha of vineyards and produces Gros-Plant and Coteaux d'Ancenis.

Take D 763 S out of Ancenis.

Liré

Liré is renowned for the poet Joachim du Bellay (1522-60), who sang the praises of his native village in a famous sonnet while on a journey to Rome. The **Musée Joachim-du-Bellay**, in a 16C dwelling, has preserved mementoes relating to the poet (*open Jul–Aug Tues–Fri 10.30–12.30 & 2.30–6pm, Sat-Sun 3.6.30pm; rest of the year hours vary; ⇔4.50€; ☏02 40 09 04 13; www.musee-du-bellay.com).*

Go W on D 751 to reach Liré.

Champtoceaux★

This is a wonderful **site★** perched on top of a peak overlooking the Loire Valley. The **Promenade de Champalud★★**, behind the church, gives a panoramic view of the river divided into branches and vast sandy islands. From there you can visit the ruins of the citadel destroyed in 1420.

Turn left onto D 7 after La Varenne.

Climbing up to the plateau away from the Loire, you enter **AOC Muscadet-Sèvre-et-Maine** country, one of the densest vineyards in the Loire Valley.

Le Loroux-Bottereau

After forming a crack corps during the 1793 insurrection, the inhabitants of this town brought down the wrath of Turreau, who had it destroyed in 1794. Le Loroux has managed to preserve a 13C fresco in the church: there is a fine view of the vineyards from its tower. Get a copy of the free *Bienvenue dans nos caves* brochure at the Tourist Office, which lists the wine-makers in the region who are open.

D 307 (route du Vignoble) for Vallet.

A small road on the left leads to the **Moulin du Pé**; from the top, there is a beautiful view of the Goulaine vineyards and marshes. The **Domaine de l'Écu** at Le Landreau is also open to visitors *(see Shopping Guide).*

Head SE on D 37.

Vallet

This is the capital of Muscadet, so don't miss a visit to the **Maison du Muscadet**. and the **Domaine du Moulin-David** *(see Shopping Guide)*. The **Château de Fromenteau** has a maze and vineyard *(44330 Vallet; open Jul–Aug afternoons; other times by appointment; 02 40 36 23 75; www.chateaudefromenteau.fr).*

The road goes through **Mouzillon**, which celebrates the **Nuit du Muscadet** in early July. It also has a factory making **Petits Mouzillons** biscuits that stopped production in 2007, but has recently been bought and will begin production again in 2010. These are a great accompaniment to Muscadet *(ZA des Quatre-Chemins; 02 40 33 77 77).*

Right, in the direction of Le Pallet.

Le Pallet

At the **Musée du Vignoble Nantais** the "five-senses" room shows the diversity of wine through fun experiments. *(open Mar–Nov; closed Nov 1; 5€; 02 40 80 90 13).* The 7km trail marked by an orange rectangle leaves from the Chapelle Saint-Michel and meanders through the surrounding vineyards.

La Haye-Fouassière

The town's three claims to fame are Muscadet, the LU biscuit factory and *fouace*, a cake shaped like a star with six points, which goes wonderfully with Muscadet and can be found at the **Maison des Vins de Nantes** *(see Shopping Guide).*

Saint-Fiacre-sur-Maine

This township has the highest density of vineyards in France. It is also the birthplace of Sophie Trébuchet, the mother of Victor Hugo who trampled the grapes in his grandfather's wine press.

Nantes★★★

Nantes is the historic capital of the Dukes of Brittany, and the city has retained two major monuments from that magnificent era: the **cathedral★** (begun in 1434 and finished in 1891), with a very pure Gothic **interior★★** containing the **tomb of François II★★**, and the **Château des Ducs de Bretagne★★**, a powerful fortress dating mainly from its reconstruction by François II (1466) *(open 9/10am–6/7pm; closed Tue mid-Sept–mid-May; Jan 1, May 1, Nov 1 & Dec 25; 6€; 02 51 17 49 00.*

The other great architectural era in Nantes was the 18C-19C, when the city derived its wealth from the slave trade, then turned to industry after it was abolished. The former **île Feydeau★** and the **Quartier Graslin★** attest to that prosperity.

Footsteps of famous authors

Du Bellay, Ronsard, Rabelais, Balzac and Julien Gracq are just some of the authors who were born, or lived, in the Loire Valley.

Balzac at the Château de Saché

See Itinerary 4. 7km E of Azay-le-Rideau on D 84. 4.50€. 02 47 26 86 50; www.musee-balzac.fr. Balzac, born in Tours in 1799, loved coming to Saché; at the time it was a 23hr journey from Paris! In the 19C, this 16–18C house belonged to a friend of the writer, Monsieur de Margonne. It is surrounded by beautiful grounds with true romantic charm, which inspired the pages of his *Lily of the Valley.* Several rooms contain manuscripts and mementoes.

Rabelais at La Devinière

See Itinerary 4. 7km SW of Chinon on D 117. 4.50€. 02 47 95 91 18. It was at this charming farm that François Rabelais, the son of a Chinon lawyer, was born in 1494. You can visit the bedroom of the writer who created Gargantua and visit the museum of his work.

Kids

There are more than 50 places in Anjou and Touraine – including castles, museums, animal parks and underground sites – offering activities for kids.

For a complete list of places, ask for the (free) brochure from the Tourist office *(pl. Kennedy, BP 32147, 49021 Angers Cedex 02, 02 41 23 51 51, www.anjou-tourisme.com)* or Touraine *(9 r. Buffon, BP 3217, 37032 Tours Cedex, 02 47 31 47 48, www.tourism-touraine.com).*

Zoo-parc de Beauval★

See Itinerary 2. 4km S of Saint-Aignan on D 675. 20€; 02 54 75 50 00; www.zoobeauval.com. In this 22ha park full of flowers and a variety of environments (Amazonian forests to savannah) live 4,000 animals, including many rare species such as manatees, white tigers with blue eyes, white lions, koalas, black panthers, pumas, hyenas, and orangutans. Shows with birds of prey in free flight, and sea-lions.

Aquarium du Val de Loire★

See Itinerary 2. 8km W of Amboise on D 751. Take D 283 as you leave Lissault-sur-Loire and follow the signs. 0825 08 25 22; 13€ www.aquariumduvaldeloire.com. This handsome aquarium with a highly modern design is noted for its many freshwater fish, including gudgeons and minnows, pike, carp, trout and salmon. It has both little-known local species and astonishing tropical ones. Among the attractions are shark tunnels and an unusual fish petting pool.

Parc des Mini-Châteaux

See Itinerary 2. 08 25 08 25 22; 22€ with aquarium. All the most beautiful châteaux, mansions and homes in the Loire valley are here to see in this 2ha park – reproduced in models on a 1/25 scale. In the evening they are lit up.

Zoo de Doué★★

See Itinerary 5. On the way out of Doué, on the route de Cholet. 16€ (under 10: 9€). 02 41 59 18 58. www.zoodoue.fr. The zoo is located at an exceptional troglodyte **site**★ with former conchiferous stone quarries, cathedral caves and lime kilns. Acacia and bamboo trees, waterfalls and boulders create a natural environment for the 500 often endangered species.

WINE BUYING GUIDE

INFORMATION

Bureau des vins d'Anjou et de Saumur – *Hôtel des Vins La Godeline, 73 r. Plantagenêt, BP 2327, 49023 Angers Cedex 02, ℘02 41 87 62 57. www.interloire.com.*

Conseil interprofessionnel des vins de Nantes – *Maison des Vins de Nantes, Rte. de Bellevue, 44690 La Haye-Fouassière. ℘02 40 36 90 10. www.muscadet.org.*

Syndicat viticole de Pouilly – *2 r. des Écoles, 58150 Pouilly-sur-Loire. ℘03 86 39 06 83.*

Bureau interprofessionnel des vins du Centre – *℘02 48 78 51 07. www.vins-centre-loire.com*

Bureau des vins de la Touraine – *12 r. Étienne-Pallu, 37000 Tours. ℘02 47 60 55 00. www.vinsvaldeloire.fr.*

CHARACTERISTICS

Central Loire Wines – White wines: subtle and crisp Sauvignons with aromas of gunflint, fruit (citrus, blackcurrant, litchi, guava), flowers, plants (broom, rhubarb) and musk. Red wines: full-bodied Pinot Noirs which linger on the palate with distinct aromas of Morello cherries, violets and exotic wood in young wines, maturing with age towards cherries in brandy, game and truffles.

Touraine Wines – White wines: aromatic Sauvignons with aromas of broom, honeysuckle and exotic fruit. Chenin Blanc wines with fine bubbles: aromas of ***brioche***, green apples and honey. Light red wines from Gamay grapes. Vouvrays have aromas of acacia, roses and citrus with undertones of candied apricot, quince and honey. Jasnières and Coteaux-du-Loir have floral and fruity aromas. Chinon, Bourgueil and Saint-Nicolas-de-Bourgueil: on gravelly soil they give light reds which are highly aromatic (red berries); on clay, flint and tufa, they produce full-bodied and well-structured wines maturing with aromas of dark berries, mild spices and game.

Anjou and Saumur Wines – Red wines: aromas of red berries, irises and violets. Fresh and highly aromatic Anjou-Gamays with undertones of fruit drops. White Saumurs with aromas of fruit and white flowers and subtle mineral undertones. Saumur Brut and Crémant-de-Loire have aromas of white fruit, balm, hazelnuts and almonds. White Anjous: aromas ranging from honey and apricots from regions of slate soil to more floral combinations when Sauvignon and/or Chardonnay grapes are present. Coteaux-du-Layons produce strong, complex scents of acacia honey with aromas of citronella and candied fruit. Bonnezeaux, Quarts-de-Chaumes and Savennières: strong, complex scents with aromas of flowers, white and exotic fruit (linden and anise for the Savennières) maturing with undertones of exotic wood, dried or candied fruit, honey and almonds, with a pronounced mineral quality.

Pays Nantais Wines – Muscadet: fresh, with light, ***perlant*** bubbles when they are matured on the lees; scents are discreetly floral and fruity, sometimes minerally. Gros-Plant: a crisp white wine.

STORAGE

The amount of time a Loire wine can be stored varies considerably with the climate. A cool year will produce dry, acidic wines to be consumed rapidly, while a hot summer and autumn will often result in rich wines with a greater ageing potential. Even among Muscadets, which are thought to be for rapid consumption, some vintages may be kept for 10 years. Within the same appellation, the kind of soil may also influence storage time. Regarding the Bourgueil, Saint-Nicolas-de-Bourgueil and Chinon, for example, the wines from gravelly soil are at their best when young, whereas those grown on tufa soils improve with age and may be kept for several decades. Likewise, Sancerres and other wines made with Sauvignon Blanc grapes mature rapidly when grown on chalky soil, while those grown on marly and flinty clay soils take longer to come into their own and have a greater storage potential (2-5 years, and sometimes 10 or more).

Saumur Bruts, Crémants and Mousseux should ordinarily be consumed within 2 or 3 years. Wines with the greatest ageing potential (several decades) include – for the best vintages – Jasnières, Coteaux-du-Layons, Montlouis moelleux, Vouvrays, as well as Bonnezeaux, Quarts-de-Chaumes and Savennières (minimum 8-year storage potential).

PRICES

Very good ***Touraine, Anjou*** and ***Pays Nantais*** white wines can be found for less than 5€.

On average, they range from 8€ to 20€, but certain ***Pouilly-Fumés, Sancerres*** and ***Chinons*** can run over 30-40€.

The best ***Bonnezeaux, Quarts-de-Chaume, Savennières*** and ***Vouvrays*** can reach 45-75€ when already aged. Red wines can be had for 5€ to 10€; ***Chinon*** and ***Bourgeuil*** may reach 20€. ***Saumur*** generally goes for about 15€. Expect to pay 5€ to 8€ for sparkling wines.

WINE MERCHANTS

La Cave de Louis XII – *10 r. Émile-Laurens, 41000 Blois. ℘02 54 74 28 18. Open Tue–Sat 8.30am–12.30pm & 2.30–7pm. Closed public holidays.* Mr. Soyer's cellar possesses some valuable bottles of wine from local producers – Menetou-Salons, Muscadets – as well as a fine selection of wines from Languedoc, the Rhone Valley, Burgundy and Bordeaux. A plus: the selection of gourmet food items and cheeses.

Aux Trésors de Bacchus – *Nouvelle-Place, 18300 Sancerre. ℘02 48 54 17 45. www.fournier-pere-fils.fr. Open daily 10am-7pm.* The owner is extremely knowledgeable; in addition to his own bottles, he offers Sancerres, Pouilly-Fumés and Coteaux-du-Giennois, all estate-bottled and chosen with great care. A fine selection of Burgundies, Bordeaux, Champagnes and wines from the Loire.

Aux Saveurs de la Tonnelle – *4 r. de la Tonnelle, 49400 Saumur. ℘02 41 52 86 62. auxaveursdelatonnelle@cegetel.net. Open Tue-Sat 9.30am-1pm, 2.30-7.30pm; open Sun and Mon in summer. Closed 2 weeks in Feb.* This shop prides itself on its rigorous selection of the best Loire Valley vintages: Chinons, Menetou-Salons, Sancerres, Saulur-Champignys, Rosé-d'Anjou, Vouvrays, Coteaux-du-Layon, etc.

Les Belles Caves – *15 pl. des Halles, 37000 Tours. ℘02 47 38 73 18. Open Tue–Sat 9am–12.30pm & 3–7pm.* This fine cellar has an interesting choice of Loire Valley wines. Many people enjoy his "wine in bulk" corner with Bourgueil, Chinon and Anjou wines. Whisky, spirits and Champagnes are also well-represented among the 1 000 different bottles sold in the shop.

MAISONS DES VINS

Maison du vin de l'Anjou – *5 bis pl. Kennedy, 49000 Angers. ℘02 41 88 81 13. www.vinsvaldeloire.com. Open Apr–Sept Mon afternoon–Sun morning 9am–1pm & 2–7pm; Oct–Mar Tue–Sat 10.30am–12.30pm & 3–6pm. Closed Jan 15–Feb 15, Jan 1, May 1 & Dec 25.*

Maison des vins et du tourisme – *14 r. du 8-Mai-1945, 37420 Beaumont-en-Véron. ℘02 47 58 86 17. Open Mon–Sat 9.30am–12.30pm & 2.30–6.30pm. Closed Jan 1, Dec 25 and public holidays.*

Maison des vins de Bourgueil 'Jean Carmet' – *18 pl. de l'Église, 37140 Bourgueil. ℘02 47 97 92 20. mdv.bourgueil@wanadoo.fr. Open mid-May–mid-Sept Tue–Sat 10am–12.30pm & 3–7pm; mid-Sep–mid-May Fri 2–6pm, Sat 10am–noon & 2–6pm.*

Maison des vins de Loir-et-Cher – *11 pl. du Château, 41000 Blois. ℘02 54 74 76 66. Open Mon–Fri 9am–noon & 2–5pm (6pm in summer). Closed Jan 1, Nov 11 & Dec 25.*

Maison des vins de Nantes – *Bellevue, 44690 La Haye-Fouassière. ℘02 40 36 90 10. Open Mon–Fri 8.30am–12.30pm & 2–6pm (Sat 11am-6pm in Jul-Aug). Closed public holidays.*

Maison du vin de Saumur – *Quai Lucien-Gautier, 49400 Saumur. ℘02 41 38 45 83. mdesvins-saumur@vinsvaldeloire.com. Open Apr–Sept Mon 2–7pm, Tue–Sat 9.30am–1pm & 2–7pm, Sun 9.30am–1pm. Oct–Mar Tue–Sat 10.30am–12.30pm & 3–6.30pm. Closed mid-Jan–mid-Feb, May 1 & 8, Nov 1.*

Maison du Muscadet – *4 rte. d'Ancenis, 44330 Vallet. ℘02 40 36 25 95. Open Apr–Nov daily 10am–noon & 2–pm (7pm n summer); Closed Sun & Wed in Mar & Dec, Jan–Feb 15, Nov 1 & Dec 25.*

WINEGROWING COOPERATIVES

Caveau des vignerons d'Amboise – *Pl. Michel-Debré, 37400 Amboise. ℘02 47 57 23 69. Open mid-Mar–mid-Nov 10am–7pm; www.amboise-valdeloire.com.* Whites, rosés, reds, and traditional, Champagne-style wines from twelve winemakers are presented here. Other local products for sale.

La Cave Montplaisir – *Quai Pasteur, 37500 Chinon. ℘02 47 93 20 75. Open Mar 15–Jun 15 and Sept 15–Nov 15 Thu–Tue 10.30am–12.30pm & 2.30–6pm; Jun 15–Sept 15 daily 10am–7.30pm.* This huge (2 500m²) cellar belongs to 3 winemakers from the area. After visiting the maze of tunnels dug out of the tufa walls – full of bottles, casks and tuns – try a Chinon, Saumur or Touraine rosé at the tasting bar.

Caves de Pouilly-sur-Loire – *39 ave. de la Tuilerie, 58150 Pouilly-sur-Loire. ℘03 86 39 10 99. www.cavespouillysurloire.com. Open Mon–Fri 8am–noon & 1.30–6pm; Sat 9am–noon & 2–5.30pm; Sun in summer10am–12.30pm & 2.30–5.30pm. Closed Jan 1 & Dec 25.* This cellar, created in 1948, now has 100 members and is one of the main producers of Pouilly-Fumé and Coteaux-du-Giennois. The shop has a long bar for tasting their white wines with that typical terroir flavour.

Caves des Producteurs de Vouvray – *"La Vallée Coquette" N 152 betsween Tours and Amboise, 37210 Vouvray. ℘02 47 52 75 03. www.cp-vouvray.com. Open May 15–Sept 15 daily 9am–7ppm; rest of the year 9am–7pm. Closed Jan 1 & Dec 25.* You can see how Explore the tunnel-cellars hollowed out of tufa for a fascinating exploration of the making of Vouvrays – both effervescent and still. Wines from the cooperative and other Loire Valley producers for sale. Tastings.

ESTATES

Château Pierre-Bise – *49750 Beaulieu-sur-Layon. ℘02 41 78 31 44. Open by appt. Mon–Sat 8am–noon & 2–6pm.* This family-owned vineyard covers 54ha planted mainly in Chenin grapes as well as Cabernet Francs and Cabernet-Sauvignons. Yields are low; grapes are harvested manually in successive pickings. A long ageing period follows slow fermentation without yeast or chaptalisation. Anjou, Anjou-Villages, Cabernet-d'Anjou, Chaume 1er Cru, Coteaux-du-Laon, Crémant-de-Loire, Quarts-de-Chaume, Rosé-de-Loire, Savennières.

Château de Coulaine – *2 r. de Coulaine, 37420 Beaumont-en-Véron. ℘02 47 98 44 51. Open by appt.* This château, in the same family for several centuries, has 20ha. The vineyard has been organic since 1997. The vines (Cabernet Franc and Chenin) are rooted in flinty clay, chalky clay or sandy soil. The grapes are treated with a long maceration period, and some vintages are aged in oak barrels. Bourgueil, Chinon, Touraine.

Domaine Yannick Amirault – *5 pavillon du Grand-Clos, 37140 Bourgueil. ℘02 47 97 78 07. Open by appt. Mon–Sat 8am–noon & 2–6pm.* The Cabernet Francs vines get plenty of sunshine due to their southern exposure. The grapes are converted into wine in thermo-regulated vats. Bourgueil, Saint-Nicolas-de-Bourgueil.

Domaine Pinard – *42 r. St-Vincent, 18300 Bué. ℘02 48 54 33 89. Open by appt. Mon–Sat 9am–noon & 2–6.30pm.* This vineyard has been handed down from father to son since 1789. It has 16ha of Sauvignon and Pinot Noir. Standard practise includes manual harvesting, pneumatic pressing, lees pumping, filtering and bottling. Sancerre.

Domaine Patrick Baudouin – *Princé – 49290 Chaudefonds-sur-Layon, ℘02 41 78 66 04. www.patrick-baudouin-layon.com. Open by appt.* Patrick Baudouin took over the family estate created by his great-grandparents in the 1920s. His estate of 10ha includes Chenin, Cabernet Franc and Sauvignon. The esate converted to organic cultivation in 2006. Anjou, Coteaux-du-Layon

Domaine Bernard Baudry – *9 Coteaux de Sonnay, 37500 Cravant les Coteaux; ℘02 47 93 15 79; Tasting cellar next door, open from Tuesday to Friday 8am-noon & 2-6pm. Sat 10am-1pm & 3-5pm.* A well known and quality-driven Chinon producer who has 30ha of Cabernet Franc grapes in the communes of Chinon and Cravant les Coteaux. Father Bernard works alongside his son, Matthieu, who came back to the family estate after stints in Burgundy and California. Bourgueil, Chinon.

Domaine de l'Écu – *La Bretonnière, 44430 Le Landreau. ℘02 40 06 40 91. Open by appt. Mon–Sat 9am–noon & 2–6pm. Closed public holidays.* One of the best producers in the region, this 21ha family vineyard is planted in Melon-de-Bourgogne, Folle Blanche, Cabernet and Chardonnay. The vineyard has been biodynamic since 1996. Wines are aged on the lees for 6 to 12 months depending on the vintage. Gros-Plant du Pays Nantais, Muscadet-Sèvre-et-Maine, Vin de Pays du Jardin de la France.

Domaine François Chidaine – *5 Grande-Rue, Husseau, 37270 Montlouis-sur-Loire. ℘02 47 45 10 20. Open summer daily 10am–noon & 2.30–7pm. Closed Sun in winter.* The estate's Chenin vines are planted on various flinty-clay and chalky plots. The biodynamic vineyard is grown traditionally. In 2002 François and Manuella Chidaine joined in with Nicolas Martin to buy an additional 10ha of vineyards, making a total of 32ha, in the Appellation Vouvray area. Montlouis, Vouvray.

Domaine de la Taille aux Loups – *8 r. des Aîtres, 37270 Montlouis-sur-Loire. ℘02 47 45 11 11. Open daily 9am–7pm.* Established 15 years ago, this winegrowing estate today encompasses 12ha of chenin vines, cultivated on ecologically responsible principles. Manual harvesting occurs in several stages, followed by traditional vinification. Montlouis, Touraine, Vouvray.

Château de Tracy – *Tracy-sur-Loire, 58150 Pouilly-sur-Loire. ℘03 86 26 15 12. www.chateau-de-tracy.com.* This estate has existed since 1396! The 31ha vineyard is planted with Sauvignon and divided into two kinds of soil – chalky Kimmeridgian and flinty clay. The vineyard has been cultivated using environmentally conscious techniques since 1994. The vines – 24 years old on average – are harvested manually. Pouilly-Fumé.

Domaine des Baumard – *La Giraudière, 8 r. de l'Abbaye, 49190 Rochefort-sur-Loire. ℘02 41 78 70 03. www.baumard.fr. Open by appt. Mon–Sat 10am–noon & 2–5.30pm.* The Baumard family has been making wine here since 1634.

S. Sauvignier / MICHELIN

Today Florent proposes a wide range of wines – dry, ***moelleux***, sparkling Crémants-de-Loire and even brandy made from Coteaux-de-Loire. The 40ha of vineyards are grown with a view to preserving the environment. Anjou, Cabernet-d'Anjou, Coteaux-du-Layon, Crémant-de-Loire, Quarts-de-Chaume, Rosé-de-Loire, Savennières

Domaine des Sables Verts – *66, Grand'Rue, 49400 Varrains 02 41 52 91 52, http://domaine-sables-verts.com. Open Mon-Fri by appt.* Among the excellent wines produced by Alain and Dominique Duveau are Cuvee des Sages and Nectar de Chenin Coteaux de Saumur.

Domaine Ogereau – *44 r. de la Belle-Angevine, 49750 Saint-Lambert-du-Lattay. ℘02 41 78 30 53. Open by appt. Mon–Sat 9am–noon & 2–7pm.* The vineyards of this estate cover 24ha, planted in Chenin, Chardonnay, Cabernet Franc, Cabernet-Sauvignon and Groileau. Vincent Ogereau cultivates the vines along traditional methods, using no herbicides. Anjou, Anjou-Villages, Cabernet-d'Anjou, Coteaux-du-Layon, Crémant de-Loire, Rosé-de-Loire, Savennières.

Domaine Henri Bourgeois – *Chavignol, 18300 Sancerre. ℘02 48 78 53 20. www.henribourgeois.com. Open by appt. Mon-Fri 9am-7pm, Sat-Sun 10am–6pm.* The estate, located on the best slopes in Sancerre, has been in the Bourgeois family for ten generations. The vineyard covers 65ha spread over chalky clay, flinty and Kimmeridgian marl soil. Wines are fermented in tanks or barrels, followed by maturation for 3 to 12 months depending on the vintage. The estate acquired a modern wine storehouse and a new tasting cellar in 2004. Coteaux-du-Giennois, Menetou-Salon, Pouilly-Fumé, Quincy, Sancerre.

Domaine Vacheron – *1 r. du Puits-Poulton, 18300 Sancerre. 02 48 54 09 93. Open 10am-noon & 2-6pm.* The 38ha vineyards clustered around the hillock of Sancerre are planted in Pinot Noir for the reds and Sauvignon for the whites. Now farmed organically, the estate is achieving its Biodyvin certification. The reds are aged in oak for about twelve months; the whites age on the lees for 8 months. Sancerre.

Vignoble de la Coulée de Serrant – *Château de La Roche-aux-Moines, 49170 Savennières. 02 41 72 22 32. Open Mon–Sat 8.30am–noon & 2–5.45pm.* This vineyard has 14ha. The Coulée-de-Serrant alone covers an AOC of 7ha, the exclusive property of the Joly family. The vineyard has been grown biodynamically since 1980. Fermentation and maturation take place in casks for 12 months, then in tuns until 18 months of age. Savennières, Savennières-Coulée-de-Serrant, Savennières-Roche-aux-Moines.

Domaine de Ladoucette – *Château du Nozet, 58150 Pouilly-sur-Loire, www.deladoucette.net, 03 86 39 18 33; Open Mon-Fri 10am-noon & 2.30-6pm.* Baron Patrick de Ladoucette continues a long family tradition at this quality estate that produces the renowned Sauvignon of Ladoucette.

Château de Chamboureau – *Épiré, 49170 Savennières. 02 41 77 20 04. Open by appt. Mon–Sat 10am–noon & 2–6pm.* This vineyard has 20ha in production. Winemaking is traditional. Fermentation and ageing are done in barrels for up to twelve months, then in vats up to eighteen months. Anjou, Anjou-Villages, Savennières, Savennières-Roche-aux-Moines.

Château de Villeneuve – *3 r. Jean-Brevet, 49400 Souzay-Champigny. 02 41 51 14 04. Open Mon–Sat 9am–noon & 2–6pm.* The estate has belonged to the Chevallier family since 1969. The 32ha of 30-35-year-old vines with Cabernet Franc and Chenin grapes are rooted in Turonian chalky-clay. The harvest is by hand with rigorous sorting. Wines are aged in wood vats, 500-litre casks and barrels. Saumur, Saumur-Champigny.

Domaine du Moulin David – *104 Les Corbeillères, 44330 Vallet. 02 40 33 91 23. Open by appt Mon–Thur 4-7.30pm, Sat 8,30am-noon.* Didier Blanloeil took charge of this century-old estate in the 1990s. The 30ha vineyard is planted with Cabernet Franc, Cabernet-Sauvignon, Gamay, Merlot, Pinot Noir and Portan for the reds; Melon de Bourgogne, Chardonnay and Sauvignon among others, for the whites. Harvesting is by machine, with rigorous sorting. Muscadet-Sèvre-et-Maine, Vin de Pays du Jardin de la France.

Domaine des Roches Neuves – *56 bd. St-Vincent, 49400 Varrains. 02 41 52 94 02. Open by appt. 8am–noon & 2–6pm.* Wine has been grown on this estate since 1850 with 22ha planted in Cabernet Franc and Chenin. Saumur-Champigny.

Catherine Champalou – *Le Portail, 37210 Vouvray, 02 47 52 64 49.* Didier and Catherine Champalou both graduated from a local agricultural college and went on to establish their own estate in Vouvray in 1984. Today they are making some of the most exciting wines in the region; truly worth seeking out. Vouvray

Domaine de Reuilly, *Chenin des Petites Fontaines, 36260 Reuilly; 02 38 66 16 74.* Denis Jamain works 15 hectares of vines: 11.5 ha of Sauvignon Blanc and Pinot Gris and 3.5 ha of Pinot Noir.

Domaine du Clos Naudin – *14 r. de la Croix-Buisée, 37210 Vouvray. 02 47 52 71 46. Open by appt. Mon–Sat 9am–noon & 2–6pm.* Philippe Foreau has remained faithful to his grandparents' methods of earthing in autumn and unearthing in spring. Chemical weed-killers are prohibited. Grapes are fermented for two months with no yeast or chaptalisation, and are vinified in small barrels. Vouvray.

ADDRESSES

STAY

AROUND ANGERS

Auberge Bienvenue – *104 rte. de Cholet, 49700 Doué-la-Fontaine. 02 41 59 22 44. 10 rooms. 7€. Restaurant* . Spacious rooms in this inviting auberge, along with tasty traditional cooking and a flowered terrace.

Hôtel Le Progrès – *26 r. Denis-Papin, 49000 Angers. 02 41 88 10 14. info@hotelleprogres.com. Closed Aug 7–15, Dec 24–Jan 1. 41 rooms. 7.50€.* Excellently located just a step or two from the station, this welcoming hotel offers modern, bright rooms. The plentiful breakfast buffet will fortify you for your visit to the château.

Chambre d'hôte Le Grand Talon – *3 rte. des Chapelles, 49800 Andard, 11km E of Angers on N 147 towards Saumur then D 4. 02 41 80 42 85. 3 rooms.* An elegant 18C residence covered in Virginia creeper, with a lovely square courtyard in front. The tastefully decorated rooms are very pleasant. In sunny weather, breakfast is served under parasols in the pretty garden. There's no question about it – this is a haven of peace! Delightful welcome.

IN AZAY-LE-RIDEAU

Hôtel de Biencourt – *7 r. Balzac, 37190 Azay-le-Rideau. 02 47 45 20 75. www.hotelbiencourt.com.* Charming little hotel with modern touches just steps from the chateau. Pretty rooms decorated in pastel shades, and generous breakfast served on the verandah.

AROUND BLOIS

Hôtel Anne de Bretagne – *31 ave. J.-Laigret, 41000 Blois. 02 54 78 05 38. 28 rooms. 6€.* Located near the château, this hotel is undergoing gradual renovation of its guestrooms. Rustic furniture, attractive colours. Breakfast is served outdoors in summer.

Chambre d'hôte La Raboullière – *Chemin de Marçon, 41700 Contres, 10km S of Cheverny on D 102 and a smaller road. 02 54 79 05 14. www.larabouillare.com. 5 rooms including 1 suite.* . This pretty Sologne farmhouse was rebuilt with old materials gleaned from neighbouring farms. The richly furnished rooms have ceilings with exposed beams. Breakfast is taken by the fire in winter and in the garden in summer. Lovely walks in the surrounding countryside.

Hôtel St-Hubert – *122 r. Nationale, 41700 Cour-Cheverny. 02 54 79 96 60. www.hotel-sthubert.com. 21 rooms. 8€. Restaurant* .
A pleasantly provincial atmosphere pervades this hotel near the centre of town. The renovated rooms are bright and pleasant, and there's a fireplace in the salon. Large, panelled dining room where you'll enjoy traditional cuisine, including game dishes during the hunting season.

AROUND BOURGES

Chambre d'hôte Domaine de l'Ermitage – *L'Ermitage, 18500 Berry-Bouy, 6km NW of Bourges on D 60. 02 48 26 87 46. domaine-ermitage@wanadoo.fr. Closed Christmas holidays. 5 rooms.* This beautiful house was once priory, and the adjoining paper mill is said to date from 1495. The two buildings now contain quite spacious and well-decorated rooms, which all enjoy the same quiet atmosphere. The grounds are planted with fine mature trees.

Hôtel de la Loire – *2 quai de la Loire, 18300 St-Thibault. 02 48 78 22 22. www. hotel-de-la-loire.com. Closed Dec 21–Jan 7. 11 rooms. 8€.* Georges Simenon, famous for his *Maigret* detective mysteries, was a regular guest at this hotel set on the banks of the Loire. You can sleep in the room he stayed in during the 1930s, decorated in the style of the times. The decor of the other rooms is inspired by different themes, including Africa, Provence and Regency. All rooms have modern comforts.

Le Christina – *5 r. Halle, 18000 Bourges. 02 48 70 56 50. www.le-christina.com. 71 rooms. 7.50€.* This hotel is the perfect headquarters from which to explore the city of Bourges. Well-maintained rooms fall into two categories: comfortable and luxurious, or smaller and functional.

AROUND CHINON

Chambre d'hôte La Milaudière – *5 r. St-Martin, 37500 Ligré, 8km SE of Chinon towards L'île-Bouchard on D 749 then D 29.*

℘02 47 98 37 53. www.milaudiere.com. 7 rooms. This 18C house built with Touraine tufa is a choice stopover in Chinon. The garret rooms are very pleasant and the ground floor room has a great deal of character with its old red-tiled floor and rustic furniture. Kitchen available for guests' use.

Chambre d'hôte La Pilleterie – *8 rte. de Chinon, D 16. 37420 Huismes, 6km N of Chinon on D 16. ℘02 47 95 58 07. 4 rooms.* This estate out in the country is ideal for those in search of peace and quiet. The rustic-style rooms are very pleasant. The quietest are in a separate little house. The estate also has geese and other farm animals kept in a pen – a delight for children.

AROUND FONTEVRAUD-L'ABBAYE

Chambre d'hôte Domaine de Mestré – *49590 Fontevraud-l'Abbaye, 1km N of Fontevraud on D 947 towards Montsoreau. ℘02 41 51 72 32. www.fontevraud.com. Closed Dec 20–Apr 1. 12 rooms. 8€. Meals 24€.* This farm once belonged to the royal abbey of *Fontevraud*. Today it contains rooms with a nice personal touch. Breakfasts and dinners – made with homemade products – are served in the former chapel. The lovely grounds are planted with cedars and lindens.

Hôtel Le Bussy – *4 r. Jeanne-d'Arc, 49730 Montsoreau. ℘02 41 38 11 11. www.hotel-lebussy.fr. Closed Jan, Wed from Nov–Apr. 12 rooms. 8.50€.* The sign for this 18C house evokes the memory of Bussy d'Amboise, the Dame de Montsoreau's lover. The windows in most of the rooms – decorated with Louis-Philippe furniture – give onto the castle and the Loire. Breakfast in the troglodyte room or in the flower garden. Very friendly reception.

AROUND LANGEAIS

Chambre d'hôte La Meulière – *10 r.de la Gare, 37130 Cinq-Mars-la-Pile. 19km NW of Tours on N 152. ℘02 47 96 53 63. lameuliere.free.fr. 3 rooms.* This fine 19C home has the advantage of being located very near the station without experiencing any of its inconveniences. The colourful rooms with soundproofing and period furniture give onto a handsome staircase.

Breakfast is served in a comfortable, attractive dining room. The garden is pleasant.

Chambre d'hôte La Butte de l'Épine – *37340 Continvoir, 2km E of Gizeux on D 15 – ℘02 47 96 62 25. www.labutte-de-lepine.com. Closed mid-Dec–Feb. 3 rooms.* This charming house was inspired by 16C and 17C styles and reconstructed from old building materials. The breakfast/living room has furniture from different periods as well as a large fireplace. The impec-cable rooms are like bijou apartments. The grounds are full of flowers.

NEAR LE LUDE

Le Vedaquais – *Pl. de la Liberté, 72500 Vaas. ℘02 43 46 01 41. 12 rooms. 7€. Restaurant.* The former village town hall and school today offers guestrooms and a prettily decorated restaurant, along with a boutique and internet access. Contemporary flavours reign in the restaurant.

IN MONTLOUIS-SUR-LOIRE

Hôtel le Monarque – *61 r. Porte-Chartraine, 37270 Montlouis-sur-Loire. ℘02 54 78 02 35. lemonarque@free.fr. Closed Dec 4–Jan 8. 22 rooms. 6€. Restaurant.* Thick carpets, quality linens, good soundproofing, neutral colors all contribute to the atmosphere of comfort that pervades this renovated hotel. Lithographs on the walls of the restaurant, where you'll enjoy regional specialities.

Domaine de l'Arbrelle – *Rte. des Ormeaux, by the D 31, 37400 Amboise. ℘02 47 57 57 17. 20 rooms. 9€. Restaurant.* In the heart of a green parc at the edge of a forest, this recently opened hostelry occupies a former farm property. Comfortable salon, and contemporary style guestrooms. Take your meals in the pleasant, rustic dining room or outside on the verandah or terrace.

AROUND MONTRICHARD

Le Moulin de la Renne – *11 rte. de Vierzon, 41140 Thésée, between Montrichard and Noyers-sur-Cher, on D 176, along the Renne. ℘02 54 71 41 56. www.moulindelarenne.com. Closed Jan 10–Feb 10, Mon & Tue noon. 13 rooms. 8.50€. Restaurant.* An old mill surrounded by a shady garden with the Renne running through it. The rooms have all been refurbished in a simple style, and the dining room has been brightened up with cheery colours. The lounge has a fireplace and an aquarium. Children's toys and a terrace overlooking the mill race complete the picture.

AROUND NANTES

Chambre d'hôte l'Orangerie du Parc – *195 r. Grignon, 44115 Basse-Goulaine. ℘02 40 54 91 30. www.gites-de-france-44.fr/lorangerie. 5 rooms.* The greenhouse of this 1850 home, formerly the residence of one of Napoleon's ministers, today offers lovely guestrooms, all on one floor and blending historic and modern touches.

Hôtel des Colonies – *5 r. du Chapeau-Rouge, 44000 Nantes. ℘02 40 48 79 76. www.hoteldescolonies.fr. 38 rooms. 8€.* Temporary art exhibits grace the front hall of this hotel located on a quiet street. The rooms have been updated with contemporary flair.

EAT

IN AMBOISE

L'Épicerie – *46 pl. Michel-Debré, 37400 Amboise. ℘02 47 57 08 94. Closed Oct 26–Dec 18, Mon andTue.* A lovely half-timbered house in old Amboise with a friendly staff, pretty terrace overlooking the château, a pleasant – and tightly packed – dining room, and above all fine, unfussy traditional cuisine: ***confit de canard***, tournedos of duck in pepper sauce and scallops ***en brochette***.

IN ANCENIS

La Toile à Beurre – *82 r. St-Pierre, 44150 Ancenis. ℘02 40 98 89 64. latoileabeurre@wanadoo.fr. Closed Sunday evenings, Wed evenings and Mon.* It's hard to resist Jean-Charles Baron's seasonal – and delicious – traditional dishes. No one could top his ***ventrèche de thon*** (tuna) with a conserve of summer vegetables, fresh asparagus with ***mousseline*** sauce, or veal kidneys in red wine sauce. The house, dating from 1753, has been renovated in excellent taste. Terrace in summer.

IN ANGERS

La Ferme – *2 pl. Freppel, 49000 Angers. ℘02 41 87 09 90. www.la-ferme.fr. Closed Jul 20–Aug 12, Sun evenings and Wed. Reservations required.* Traditional regional cuisine in a clean, simple ambiance at this popular restaurant near the cathedral. Try for a seat on the terrace.

Le Relais – *9 r. de la Gare, 49100 Angers. ℘02 47 57 08 94. le.relais@libertysurf.fr. Closed Aug 6-29, Dec 24–Jan 8, Sun and Mon and public holidays.* A wood-panelled bar, contemporary furnishings and wine-themed frescoes make for a pleasant atmosphere at this restaurant. Updated recipes on the menu, accompanied by a thoughtfully composed wine list.

IN BLOIS

Les Banquettes Rouges – *16 r. des Trois-Marchands, 41000 Blois. ℘02 54 78 74 92. Closed Christmas holidays, Sun and Mon.* This little restaurant in the centre of town offers a daily menu as well as traditional seasonal dishes served à la carte. A warm welcome goes with the colourful decor.

Côté Loire – *2 pl. de la Grève, 41000 Blois. ℘02 54 78 07 86. www.coteloire.com. Closed Jan 5–Feb 6, Aug 27–Sept 4, Sun and Mon.* An inviting 16C inn located near the banks of the Loire. The interior decor was remodelled in very good taste, and the menus of traditional cuisine (pike in butter sauce, ***coq au vin***, veal in white sauce, etc) are changed every day. Cosy rooms and a terrace too.

AROUND BOURGES

Le Bourbonnoux – *44 r. Bourbonnoux, 18000 Bourges. ℘02 48 24 14 76. restaurant.bourbonnoux@wanadoo.fr. Closed Feb 23–Mar 5, Apr 21–May 2, Aug 15–Sept 4, Sat noon, Sun evening and Fri.* Amble down a pretty street dotted with artisans' boutiques and stop at this restaurant near the cathedral.

Les Saisons Gourmandes – *Pl. des Tilleuls, 36260 St-Pierre-de-Jard. ℘02 54 49 37 67. Closed Oct 9–26, Jan 8–Feb 1, Mon evening, Tue evening and Wed except Jul–Aug.* 20C regional-style home converted into a pleasant restaurant. On the terrace or in the dining room beneath the beams, you'll enjoy the chef's take on classical dishes.

AROUND CHINON

La Maison Rouge – *38 r. Voltaire, 37500 Chinon. 02 47 98 43 65. Closed 5 wks in winter.* In the town's medieval district, settle down to the generous "assiettes Rabelaisiennes" (assortment of regional specialities) for a sampling of what the region has to offer. The wine bar offers 16 selections by the glass in addition to an assortment of cheeses.

Le Moulin Bleu – *7 r. du Moulin-Bleu, 37140 Bourgueil. 02 47 97 73 13. www.lemoulinbleu.com. Closed Jun 20–Jul 7, mid-Nov–mid-Mar, Sun evening offseason, Tue evenings and Wed.* Chef Michel Breton's traditional dishes, such as *escargots de Saint-Michel* in walnut butter, pike-perch braised in red wine, or roasted squab in a walnut crust, go deliciously well with a bottle from one of the area's small winemakers. Dine out on the terrace with a panoramic view or inside the 15C mill.

IN LE LUDE

La Renaissance – *2 ave. de la Libération, 72800 Le Lude. 02 43 94 63 10. lelude.renaissance@wanadoo.fr. Closed Feb holidays, Nov holidays, Jul 31–Aug 7, Sun evenings and Mon.* Enjoy a break near the château and sample the contemporary cuisine at this pleasant, modern restaurant. In summer, try the terrace in the adjoining courtyard.

IN MONTRICHARD

Bellevue – *24 quai de la République, 41400 Montrichard. 02 54 32 06 17. 29 rooms.* Fine woodwork in the dining room, along with bay windows overlooking the cheerful valley; traditional cuisine. Most of the guestrooms feature panoramic views of the Cher river.

S. Sauvignier/MICHELIN

IN NANTES

Le Gressin – *40 bis r. Fouré, 44000 Nantes. 02 40 48 26 24. legressin@wanadoo.fr. Closed Aug 1–20, Mon evenings and Sun.* Recently renovated neighbourhood restaurant with attractive stonework, rustic furnishings, rattan accents, and good paintings on the walls. Traditional, seasonal cuisine.

L'Embellie – *14 r. Armand-Brossard, 44000 Nantes. 02 40 48 20 02. Closed Aug 1–21, Sun and Mon.* Thoughtfully prepared dishes and a small but well-selected wine list, all at reasonable prices in welcoming, modern dining room.

AROUND SANCERRE

La Pomme d'Or – *Pl. de la Mairie, 18300 Sancerre. 02 48 54 13 30. Closed Sun evenings Oct–Mar, Tue & Wed. Reservations required.* The tables at this popular restaurant are often booked up for lunch. The *ris de veau* (calf sweetbread) fried in basil, pike-perch baked in white wine, and the *magret de canard* in honey sauce are all delicious and reasonably priced. Bistro-style decor features a Sancerre-inspired fresco.

Côte des Monts Damnés – *18300 Chavignol, 4km W of Sancerre on D183. 02 48 54 01 72. restaurantcmd@wanadoo.fr. Closed Feb, Jun 26–Jul 6, Sun evenings, Mon evenings except Jul–Aug, Tue evenings and Wed.* The famous *côte des Monts Damnés* hillside in Chavignol was thus named because its slopes were so hard to work on. Today, it evokes the tasty regional cuisine served in this pleasant restaurant located on the main street of a winegowing village. The wine list features a very good selection of local crus.

AROUND SAUMUR

Auberge Saint-Pierre – *6 pl. St-Pierre, 49400 Saumur. 02 41 51 26 25. auberge.st.pierre@wanadoo.fr. Closed Sun and Mon.* Enjoy a gastronomic break in the bistro-style setting of this 15C house (next to the église St-Pierre) with its pretty façade blending half-timbering and red brick. The traditional cuisine is very affordable: marrowbone with Guérande salt, *confit de canard*, and rib of beef.

L'Abbaye de Délice – *8 ave. des Roches, 49590 Fontevraud-l'Abbaye. ℘02 41 51 71 04. Closed Feb 4–Mar 10, Jul 2–10, Oct 25–Nov 2, Tue evenings and Wed.* Step back a few decades at this picturesque restaurant along Fontevraud's main street and enjoy the charm of yesteryear. The kitchen emphasises regional products on its menus.

AROUND TOURS

La Crémaillère – *22 r. du Commerce, 37500 Chinon. ℘02 47 98 47 15. Closed Wed.* This little restaurant is nothing if not unique, with its wooded dining room and compartmented seating, with floral-themed painting on the walls. It feels like a Savoyard chalet! On the menu, traditional cuisine and wines by the glass. There's also a nice terrace.

Bistrot de la Tranchée – *103 ave. Tranchée, 37000 Tours. ℘02 47 41 09 08. charles-barrier@yahoo.fr. Closed Aug 3–24, Sun and Mon.* Wooden panelling, wine bottles, comfortable banquettes and an old pizza oven make up the rustic decor of this pleasant spot, where you'll enjoy tasty bistro fare.

La Mère Hamard – *Pl de l'Église, 37360 Semblançay. ℘02 47 56 62 04. reservation@lamerehamard.com. Closed Feb 15–Mar 15, Tue noon from Jun 15–Sept 30, Sun evenings and Mon.* Monique and Pierre Pégué will give you a warm welcome before treating you to their delicious classical cuisine with a regional accent featuring dishes like Racan squab in Szechuan pepper sauce or fried scampi in cream of artichoke sauce, accompanied by a fine wine list from the Loire Valley.

Le Grand Vatel – *8 ave. Brûlé, 37210 Vouvray. ℘02 47 52 70 32. Closed Dec 23–30, Sun evening and Mon.* Frédéric Scicluna's delicious terroir-inspired cooking – braised lettuce stuffed with pigs' feet and herbs, monkfish stew with saffron, three-coloured pike-perch pie – goes wonderfully with the fine selection of still or sparkling white Vouvray. Pleasant terrace.

S. Sauvignier/MICHELIN

Le Vieux Comptoir – *10 r. de la Rôtisserie, 37000 Tours. ℘02 47 64 11 29. Closed Jan, Sun, Mon exc. in summer and public holidays. Reservations suggested.* Pleasant little family bistro tucked away in old Tours. Intimate dining room features a fine wood bar. Traditional cuisine, and a wine list emphasising Loire Valley vintages.

La Tourangelle – *47 quai Albert-Baillet, 37270 Montlouis-sur-Loire. ℘02 47 50 97 35. Closed Feb 7–14, Jun 30–Jul 7, Nov 15–22, Sun evenings and Mon except public holidays.* The tasty contemporary cuisine served here – ***aiguillettes de canettes*** (duck) with mushrooms, turbot poached in liquorice, honey-roasted Touraine grouse – is prepared with fresh market ingredients and goes down very nicely with a glass of Montlouis selected from the excellent wine list.

IN VENDÔME

Le Petit Bilboquet – *Old rte. de Tours, 41100 Vendôme. ℘02 54 77 16 60. Closed Wed evenings, Sun evenings and Mon. Reservations required weekends.* This former officers' dining hall features a 19C wooden façade. On fine days, have a seat on one of the two terraces. Well-prepared selections on the menu and pleasant, unfussy decor.

Provence remains as alluring as ever; cicadas, sunshine, the double-barrelled blue of sea and sky, and a seemingly always-open bottle of rosé. Provence seems to have been specially created for growing vines. The Greeks, who founded ancient Massalia 2,600 years ago, brought with them France's first vines. The transplants flourished, and today, France's oldest vineyards are among the country's finest and most varied, producing not only the famous Provençal rosés but also some renowned reds and whites. Stretching from Les Alpilles just southwest of Avignon to the hills behind Nice, the vineyards offer views of the sea at every turn.

Highlights

1. Taking a boat around the Calanques in **Cassis** (p377)
2. Enjoying a picnic with a glass of rosé in **Massif des Costes** (p375)
3. The unusual rock formations in Les **Baux de Provence** (p373)
4. The vineyards of **Les Iles de Porquerolles** (p383)
5. Exploring the markets of **Aix-en-Provence** (p375)

The cradle of wine

Provence's vines were brought to the area in around 600 BC by the Phoenicians (Greeks from Asia Minor). They have prospered through the ages thanks to support from various quarters, including the Romans – Caesar is believed to have given Provençal wine to his legionnaires on their return from conquering the Gauls – monastic orders, aristocrats and Good King René of Anjou. The latter, who was Count of Provence from 1447 to 1480, so encouraged the growth of the vineyards that he was dubbed the Wine-Grower King. Maybe this long history is partly why Provence has its own vocabulary when it comes to wine. An *avis* is a vine shoot, a *tine* is a vat, and a *crotte* a cellar. One of the grape varieties is known as twisted tail *(pecoui-touar)* or magpie's 'knee' *(ginou d'agasso)* because of the way its bunches of grapes grow on the stalks. But despite the centuries of history, in the early 20C the vineyards suffered from overproduction, and the lower quality of the wines had a lasting impact on their image. Since then the winegrowers have focused on raising quality by reducing yields, concentrating on smoothness, and limiting overexposure to the sun to keep freshness and delicacy in these pale pink wines. A revival is apparent in the recent interest of outside investors, who see financial possibilities here and are increasingly buying and restoring old vineyards - or wanting to develop other building projects. The Provençal wine industry employs more than 20,000 peo-

ple, but is faced with increasing pressure from land-hungry developers.

La Vie en Rose

Rosé is still the major wine produced in Provence, contributing over four-fifths of its yearly bottlings. In France it has long been looked upon as a simple summer barbecue wine, but just as it is experiencing a huge growth in interest worldwide, especially in the UK, the United States and Japan, so are the French beginning to take it more seriously. As the world's leading producer, it is fitting that The Centre for Rosé Research (Centre de Recherche et d'Expérimentation sur le Vin Rosé) was established in 1999 in the village of Vidauban in Provence - currently the only institute of its kind. But Provence rosé remains little exported beyond

S. Sauvignier / MICHELIN

its borders - just 11% is currently sold outside of France, although that figure is rising. And it is worth remembering that Provence makes true rosé - not a mix of red and white grapes, but wine from red varieties that are left in contact with their skins for a short time.

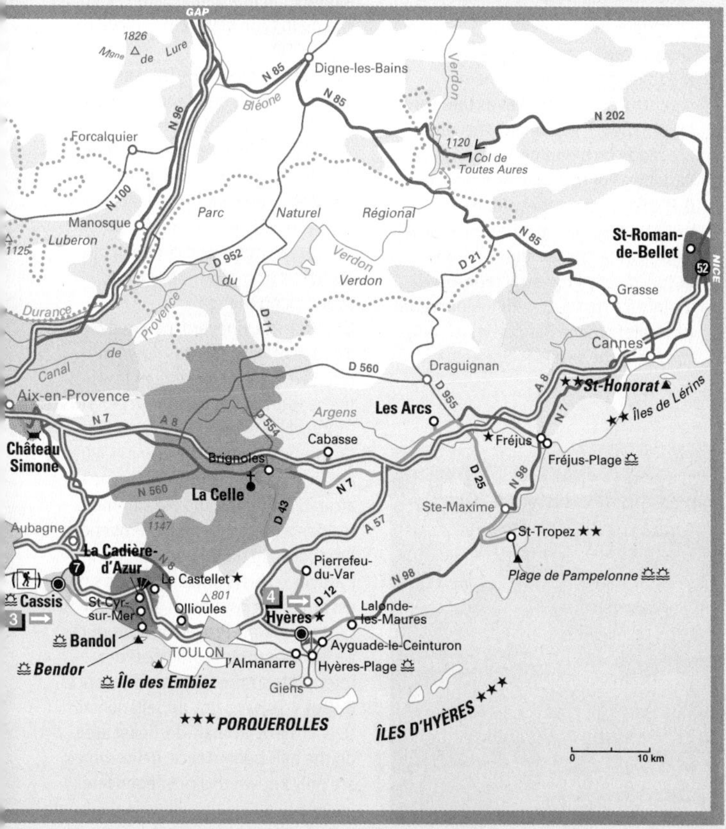

11 - PROVENCE

OVERVIEW

The Terroir

Michelin Local Maps 340 and 341 – Alpes-Maritimes (06), Bouches-du-Rhône (13) and Var (83).
Surface area: 110,000ha.
Production: Five million hectolitres a year.

The wines of Provence owe much of their character to the Mediterranean climate: 3,000 hours of sunshine a year, the *mistral* wind that drains the soil, and very little rain: then there is the varied relief, which gives each appellation a unique character. From east to west, from Les Alpilles to Nice, the soil types are as follows: limestone in Les Alpilles chain and the Aix hills, Cretaceous limestone around Cassis, siliceous limestone in Bandol, siliceous soil in the Massif des Maures, and red sandstone in a strip from Toulon to St-Tropez.

Grape Varieties

In Provence there are as many colourful grape varieties as there are landscapes. Traditionally, the wines are made by blending several grape varieties. For the rosés and reds, there is the Grenache variety (one of the most widespread in Southern France), as well as Syrah, Carignan, Tibouren (a specifically Provençal type, used mainly for rosés), Cinsault, Mourvèdre (the chief type in Bandol, which only thrives at the seaside), Braquet and Folle Noire (only in the Bellet vineyard) and Castet (in the Aix-en-Provence and Palette areas). For the whites, the varieties include Rolle and Vermentino (both of Ligurian origin), Ugni Blanc (an old Provençal type), Sémillon, Clairette, Sauvignon, Marsanne, and Bourboulenc Blanc (for the mellow touch).

Lavender field near Roussillon en Provence

© Crisma/iStockphoto

Appellations

Côtes-de-Provence – With 20,500ha and 900,000hl, this appellation makes up the main vineyard in Provence. It stretches over a third of the Var, extends all the way to Marseille, and has an enclave in Alpes-Maritimes. It is mainly known for its rosés (86% of the production, 11% red and 3% white).
Coteaux-d'Aix-en-Provence – The second largest appellation in Provence at 193,000hl is in the limestone area between the River Durance, Les Alpilles and Montagne Sainte-Victoire. The main type of wine produced is rosé (65%).
Baux-de-Provence – This small appellation has been separated from the AOC Coteaux-d'Aix-en-Provence since 1995, and stretches out below the olive groves of Les Alpilles.
Bandol – The king of Provençal reds is produced in eleven municipalities spread out over a cirque of hills sheltered from the *mistral* wind, overlooking the sea.
Cassis – The vineyard, perched on a cirque of hills, spreads down in terraced fields or *restanques* towards the seaport of Cassis, producing a dry, fruity white wine.
Coteaux-Varois – These wines, 80% are rosé, are only produced in the Var, around Brignoles, the old summer residence of the Counts of Provence. Produces 110,000hl per year.
Palette – This is one of France's smallest appellations. Grown on the outskirts of Aix-en-Provence, it produces a smooth, tannic red, sometimes referred to as the "Claret of Provence".
Bellet – This is a tiny appellation nestled in the St-Roman-de-Bellet area, on the hills behind Nice. Bellet wines are only known to a privileged few.

Hill Wines of Provence

Have picnic essentials in the car at all times, so you can jump out to make the most of the spectacular Alpilles, and the shady olive groves around Aix-en-Provence. Between the chain of Les Alpilles to the west and the massif of La Sainte-Baume to the east, superb vineyards cling to limestone heights, dotted among fields of olives and lavender. This wine trail goes through the AOC areas of **Baux-de-Provence, Coteaux-d'Aix-en-Provence** and the tiny but famous **Palette** appellation.

- **Population:** 135,000 in Aix-en-Provence
- **Michelin Map:** 340.
- **Info:** www.lesbauxdeprovence.com
- **Location:** Inland from the Cote d'Azur
- **Timing:** Two to three lazy days…
- **Don't Miss:** A wander through Baux de Provence.
- **Kids:** Glanum Roman ruins.

DRIVING TOURS

1 LES ALPILLES

43km. Michelin Local Map 340, D-E3.
See itinerary 1 on the map on p370.

The wine-growers of Les Alpilles are a favoured lot: they have earned appellation status for their reds and rosés (which have been classified AOC **Baux-de-Provence** since 1995, while the whites remain AOC Coteaux-d'Aix) and they work in an exceptional setting. Their particular section of timeless Provence consists of blinding white clayey limestone that rises in waves and spreads over the land for about thirty kilometres. Below the crests, a sea of vineyards and olives trembles from the blast of the *mistral* wind. The magnificent wine-growing estates dotted over eight municipalities consist of old family properties that have been handed down from generation to generation.

Saint-Rémy-de-Provence★

Whatever the access road you choose, you pass through vineyards to get to St-Rémy. The small town beautifully symbolises the essence of Provence, with its boulevards shaded by plane trees, its network of winding alleyways and its old houses that have been converted into art galleries. **Place de la République** stands beside the bypass and livens up the centre with outdoor cafés and colourful market days. Take the time to stroll through the alleys to see the impressive **Collegiate church of St-Martin** (which contains a lovely polychrome organ case), **Nostradamus's Birthplace** (with only the façade remaining) and the stylish private mansions.

Leave St-Rémy heading W on D 99, then turn left onto D 27.

Les Baux-de-Provence★★★

Driving along the D 27, a delightful winding secondary road, you'll round a bend and suddenly come upon a spectacular **site**★★★. The bare rock spur of Les Baux stands detached from Les Alpilles, with vertical ravines on either side. The vines have been replaced by a weird landscape (home to the mineral bauxite), where the rock takes on fantastic shapes, as if chiselled by some wild stonecutter. *The village is pedestrianised throughout. Enter on foot through Porte Mage gateway, and then take the street on the left to place Louis-Jou.*

In the offseason, the deserted **alleyways** catapult you back in time. Take a look at the three rooms with pointed vaulting in the former town hall or the **hôtel de ville** dating from the 17C. A street on the right, La Calade, leads to Porte d'Eyguières, which is decorated with coats of arms and used to be the town's only entrance gate. Leading off from the corner of La Calade, rue de l'Église runs to **place St-Vincent**★, where there is a beautiful

Les Beaux-de-Provence

view of the Fontaine valley and the Val d'Enfer. The Romanesque **Church of St-Vincent**★ is flanked on the left by a graceful lantern of the dead. The simple church, which was partly carved out of the bedrock in the 12C, is surprisingly light inside.

Leave SE on D 27; left on D5.

The 17C **Mas de la Dame** comes into view, looking like an island lost in a sea of vines and olives. It stands in a cirque of limestone hills at the foot of Les Baux, The estate, which produces wine and olive oil, is run by the two granddaughters of the original owner, and its organic wine (red, white and rosé) is a success. Go into the cellar and decide for yourself, savouring the site as you do so; it is one of the most beautiful in Les Alpilles *(D 5, 13520 Les Baux-de-Provence; open Mon-Fri 8am–6pm; Sat-Sun 9am-7pm closed Jan 1, Dec 25; 04 90 54 32 24, www.masde-ladame.com).*

Head back along D 5 in the opposite direction. At Maussane-les-Alpilles turn right onto D 17.

At the pretty village of Fontvieille, stop to taste at **Chateau d'Estoublan** *(see Shopping Guide).*

Head back the opposite way along D 17.

Mouriès

With 80,000 olive trees, Mouriès prides itself on having the highest density of olive-growers in the South of France. One only has to pay a visit to the **Moulin à Huile Coopératif du Mas Neuf** to be convinced. Whatever the flavour, subtle or fiery, the AOC olive oil from the Baux-de-Provence valley scoops up the medals in tasting competitions *(13890 Mouriès; open Mon-Fri 9am–12.30pm & 2–7pm, Sat 9am-12.30pm & 3-7pm, Sun 3-7pm; 04 90 54 32 37; www.moulincoop.com).*

Head N on D 24.

In **Destet**, the **Domaine Gourgonnier** makes a worthwhile wine stop *(see Shopping Guide).*

At the end of the D 24, turn right onto D 99. 3km further on, turn left and follow the signs to Château Romanin.

On the northern slopes of Les Alpilles, **Château Romanin** stands isolated in the middle of vines, olives and almond trees (it also produces its own olive oil). The tasting cellar is buried in the rock, under the ruins of a 13C Knights Templars' castle, flanked by a monumental wine-maturing storehouse modelled on a cathedral. Outside, there is a fine view of Mont Ventoux and Les Alpilles. An easy **walking trail** *(25min)*, takes you past 11 instructive panels explaining about vines and the biodynamic methods used in wine-growing. This continues in the cellars, where there is also a boutique and tasting bar. *(Rte. de Cavaillon, 13210 St-Rémy-de-Provence; open Apr–Sept Mon–Fri 9am–7pm, Sat-Sun 11am–7pm; Oct–Mar Mon–Fri 9.30am–1pm & 2–6pm, Sat-Sun 11–7pm; 04 90 92 45 87; www.romanin.com).*

Take D 99 back to St-Rémy-de-Provence.

On the way you can stop at a little place called La Galine to buy wine from **Domaine Hauvette** *(see Shopping Guide).*

2 THE AIX-EN-PROVENCE AREA

About 85km from St-Chamas to Meyreuil. Michelin Local map 340, F-H 3-5. See itinerary 2 on the map p370.

What was once the stronghold of Good King René of Anjou is now that of the noble wine-growing *bastides*. The vineyards stretch out over 4,260ha and 49 municipalities, against the rugged background of Montagne Sainte-Victoire. Many wine-growing estates in the heart of what is now a highly urbanised area have managed to preserve the atmosphere of a much earlier age. The vineyards are bounded to the north by the River Durance and the Trévaresse range, and stretch east to the Salon area and the Étang de Berre. The country to the south of Aix-en-Provence is home to the **Palette** appellation, one of the smallest AOCs in France.

St-Chamas

This curious village is the last fishing port (apart from Martigues) on the **Étang de Berre**★. A few small boats testify to a once-flourishing activity. St-Chamas is also where you will see troglodyte houses *(private)*, right in the middle of the cliff face.

Leave St-Chamas heading SE on D 10.

The vineyards on the north and west shores of the Étang de Berre offer an extraordinary contrast with the gigantic petrochemical installations. Here the wines have AOC **Coteaux-d'Aix-en-Provence** status. You can try them out at **Domaine Calissanne** *(see Shopping Guide).*

After the intersection between D 21 and D 10, you come to **Château Virant**. This estate consists of more than 110ha of vines, about 20ha of olive trees, an enormous cellar, and red, white and rosé wines that have stood the test of time *(Rte. de St-Chamas, 13680 Lançon-Provence; open daily 8am–noon & 1.30–6.30pm; public holidays 8.15am–noon & 2.30–6.30pm; closed Jan 1, Dec 25; 04 90 42 44 47, www.chateauvirant.com).*

Return to crossroads and take D 21 on the right; In Lançon head N on D 15.

Rarely visited except by unusually curious locals, the **Massif des Costes** is a good example of a small, exceptional wine-growing area tucked away from the tourist trail and bursting with Provençal character.

Pélissanne

Every Sunday morning a large market is held on place Roux-de-Brignoles, in front of the town hall. Fruit and vegeta-

Fisherman's hut in St-Chamas

S. Sauvignier/MICHELIN

ble growers, wine-growers and potters abound. Don't leave before stocking up at the **Moulin des Costes**. This beautiful 17C stone mill has recently been put back into action, producing oil and flour. It also sells tapenade, olives, olive wood items and pottery *(445 chemin de St-Pierre, 13330 Pélissanne; open Tue–Fri 3–7pm, Sat 9am–noon & 3–pm; 04 90 55 30 00; www.moulindescostes.com).*

Aurons

From its lookout point, this "doll's village", set in the middle of the massif, which rises to a height of 394m, affords good views of the region's vineyards.

D 22B then winds its way through vineyards, orchards and olive groves to **Vernègues**. The town is in two parts, new and old. The new is below, with dead straight streets. Above, the old town was destroyed by an earthquake in 1909, the worst France has ever known (46 people died and 250 were injured).

D 22 for La Roque-d'Anthéron.

La Roque-d'Anthéron

The village hosts, at the 17C Château de Forbin,an International Piano Festival every summer. One kilometre away, below D 563, **Silvacane Abbey**★★ stands on the banks of the Durance. It is a wonderful example of the plain Cistercian beauty that flourished in Provence in the 13C. The abbey's prosperity declined through the ages to such an extent that it was converted into a farm after the Revolution. The State bought the buildings in 1949. Today the church, cloisters and conventual buildings are open to the public *(open Jun-Sept daily 10am-6pm; Oct-May Wed–Mon 10am–1pm & 2–5pm; closed Jan 1, May 1, Dec 25; 6.50€; 04 42 50 41 69; www.monum.fr).*

D 543 leads to **Rognes**, where the vines and the wine-growers' cooperative greet you as soon as you enter the village, reminding you that most of the inhabitants make a living from wine-making.

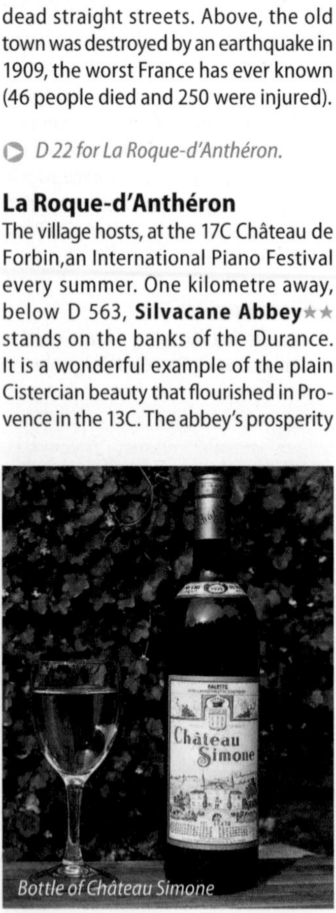

Bottle of Château Simone

S. Sauvignier / MICHELIN

Saint-Cannat

If you can, come here on a Wednesday morning when the market livens up the main square. Plane trees provide shade and the bistros overflow.

As you leave town on the N 7, a small bend and a few hundred yards of gravel track catapult you into another world, **Château de Beaupré**. This graceful 18C Provençal *bastide* has been in the hands of Baron Double's family since 1890 *(see Shopping Guide).*

Continue along N 7 to Aix-en-Provence. Go through town by following the boulevards around the centre, and then head E to Meyreuil, taking N 7 and then D 58H to the right.

Château Simone

13590 Meyreuil. Chateau not open to visitors. Shop: Mon–Sat 9am–noon & 2–6pm. 04 42 66 92 58. www.chateau-simone.fr.

Welcome to the tiny kingdom of a wine sometimes referred to as the "Claret of Provence". Château Simone, the main and oldest producer of one of France's smallest AOC appellations, **Palette**, is worth a special trip (the AOC has 23 ha, and 18 of them are at Chateau Simone). Even if you cannot see the magnificent vaulted cellar or taste the wine, you can still take a look at the elegant estate, set up by Carmelites from Aix-en-Provence in the 16C. It overlooks formal gardens and vines growing on limestone scree.

Seaview Vines Cassis to Nice

The sea dominates in this part of Provence, and many vineyards have a backdrop of blue. Ensure you leave enough time between visits for boat and beach trips.

- **Population:** 1.5 million with Marseille.
- **Michelin Map:** Michelin Local Map 340, I-K 6-7. See itinerary 3 on the map on p370.
- **Info:** www.vinsdeprovence.com.
- **Location:** Eastwards from Marseille along the Cote d'Azur.
- **Timing:** Three to four days
- **Don't Miss:** The Route des Cretes from Cassis to La Ciotat.
- **Kids:** The beaches of Bandol.

DRIVING TOURS

3 FROM CASSIS TO BANDOL

About 52km starting from Cassis.

Cassis

Beyond the vineyards, you see the sea. Cassis is a chic and lively fishing port and renowned wine-producing centre. Its 13 privately owned wine companies are famous for their excellent white wine – dry, delicate and fruity.

Clos Sainte-Magdeleine, **Domaine La Dona Tiga** and the **Maison des Vins** (*see Shopping Guide*) will tell you all you want about AOC Cassis, one of the oldest appellations in France (1936).

The pleasure of the wine is enhanced by Cassis's magnificent **site**★. The summer resort has grown in an amphitheatre between Cap Canaille and the *calanques* (inlets), bathed in a lovely light that inspired artists such as Matisse, Derain, Vlaminck and Dufy.

Before leaving Cassis, try a **boat trip** to see the **Calanques**★★ *(Les Bateliers de Cassis; 45min boat trip to three calanques of Port-Miou, Port-Pin and En-Vau calanques; 13€; 1hr trip to 5 calanques 15€ 1hr 30min trip to 8 calanques 18€; 04 42 01 08 77; www.calanques-cassis.com.*

There's also the sea bed to explore and the beaches to enjoy (*see "Into the Deep Blue Sea" section at the end of the chapter*). When the sun goes down, the ideal place to try the delicious local seafood is along the harbour.

The tourist office provides brochures on walks through the vineyards.

Continue on D 559 towards Bandol. At Les Lecques exit, turn left onto D 66.

Here you enter the Bandol appellation area. The vines cover about 1,400ha between St-Cyr-sur-Mer, Le Castellet and Ollioules, stretching from the Sainte-Baume massif to the sea. The appellation owes its special quality to the regional microclimate: a lot of sunshine (3 000 hours a year), good rainfall, mainly in autumn and winter, and limestone soil with a south-facing prospect that benefits from the gentle sea breeze. Although Bandol produces whites and rosés, its reputation has been made by its reds. The main grape variety, Mourvèdre (not normally grown much in France), produces wonders here.

La Cadière-d'Azur

The 13C Peï Gate, in front of the town hall leads to the old streets that lend the place so much charm. This very old hill town with its ruined ramparts seems to stand guard against its ancient rival, Le Castellet, perched on a hill opposite. From the eastern end of the village there is a fine **view**★ inland over Le Castellet and on to the Sainte-Baume massif.

Leave the village on D 66 and turn immediately right onto a narrow road signposted "Chemin de l'Argile".

This pretty wine road crosses through countryside where the soil type is clay

Cap Lardier, St Tropez Peninsula

Deep Blue Sea

Cassis≘

There are three natural beaches, all fine for children: **Grande-Mer** *(♿, showers, toilet facilites, lockers, pedalo hire)*, **Bestouan** *(showers, toilet facilites, air mattress hire)*, and **Corton** *(small-scale sailing base)*.

Bandol≘

The seaside resort of Bandol is classified as a *Station nautique*, testifying to the variety and quality of the activities on offer (such as the diving centre on Île de Bendor). There are four main sand beaches: Centrale, Casino, Lido to the east, and the well-sheltered Rènecros facing west.

Around Hyères

There are 20km of beaches, all supervised in summer. **Almanarre** stretches along the salt marshes of Étang des Pesquiers. It is a sand beach popular with families.

Hyères-Plage≘ resort lies beside a small forest of umbrella pines. Its beaches include Hippodrome, Capte and Bergerie, stretching all the way to Giens Peninsula. The water is shallow until you get about 60m from the shore.

Ayguade-le-Ceinturon, the old port of Hyères is now a seaside resort. It stands between two sand beaches, one on boulevard du Front-de-Mer, and the other on avenue des Girelles.

St-Tropez

The **beaches around St-Tropez**≘≘ are truly heavenly, with their fine sand and rocky creeks. You are spoilt for choice over a stretch of 10km, and if you feel energetic, can reach the beaches on foot, along the coast path that goes round the peninsula to Cavalaire Bay. There are no traffic jams out to the close and relatively peaceful **Bouillabaisse beach** (ideal for windsurfing when the *mistral* blows), to the west, or the shaded **Graniers beach** *(access via rue Cavaillon)* to the east, on the way to Cannebiers Bay, a well-favoured beach between the citadel and rocks. Further east is **Les Salins beach** *(access via avenue Foch)*.

Fréjus

Be sure to visit **Port-Fréjus**, a waterfront area with architecture and decoration iinspired by ancient Rome. Between Port-Fréjus and Pédégal Bridge, along the seafront promenade, **Fréjus-Plage** extends for more than a kilometre in a lovely wide beach of fine sand. Further west, **Aviation beach** is long and sandy.

(argile), particularly suitable for Mourvèdre vines. The area produces well-known wines that are deep and silky. Take the time to stop at one of the AOC Bandol estates that line the road, for instance **Domaine Bunan-Moulin des Costes** and **Chateau de Pibarnon** (*see Shopping Guide*).

At the end of the road, turn left onto D 559B. 1.5km further on, at a bend, turn right at the sign to "Domaine Ray Jane".

Domaine Ray Jane, Musée de la Tonnellerie et des Outils Vignerons

83330 Le Plan-du-Castellet.
Tour of the museum by appt. Mon–Sat 8am–noon & 2–7pm (6.30pm winter). Closed public holidays.
04 94 98 64 08; www.ray-jane.com.
The Constant family has converted part of the cellar into a private museum. The winegrower himself takes clients on a tour of his collection, to see 19C coopers' instruments, 18C stills, and a reconstruction of a Provençal kitchen.

Return to D 559B, then turn left onto D 226.

Le Castellet★

Several films have been made in this attractive village perched on a wooded hill. The old stronghold has well-preserved ramparts, a carefully restored 12C church and a castle, parts of which date back to the 11C.
Many of the houses were built in the 17C and 18C. From beyond the gate on place de la Mairie there is a fine view of the northern slopes of the wine-growing area, which is protected from the mistral wind by the Sainte-Baume massif. As far as wine is concerned, don't miss **Domaine de l'Olivette** or the **Maison des Vins de Bandol**, offering a broad selection from estates in the Bandol appellation (*see Shopping Guide*).

Head for Le Beausset on D 26.

At Le Beausset, try the wines at **Domaine de l'Ermitage** (*see Shopping Guide*).

Just beyond the roundabout (as you bypass Le Beausset on D 26) turn right.

A narrow road winds its way through olive groves, orchards and vineyards dotted with clumps of broom and cypress trees. It leads to **Chapelle Notre-Dame du Beausset-Vieux**, where the terrace affords a **sweeping panorama**★ that takes in Le Castellet, the Sainte-Baume massif, Gros Cerveau and the coast from Bandol westwards to La Ciotat. From here you can make out the different wine-growing areas, with the AOC Bandol wines on the hills, and the local wines *(vins de pays)* and table wines on the plains.
N 8 heads down to **Ollioules**, which specialises in the cut-flower trade and also in wine-growing.

From Ollioules, take D 11 to Sanary-sur-Mer and then D 559 to Bandol.

Bandol

Bandol developed into a holiday destination in the 19C thanks to the railway. Four beaches of fine sand make it popular today, and seafood restaurants crowdthe lively waterfront. The marina lies in a cove, bordered by **Allée Jean-Moulin**★ and Allée Alfred-Vivien lined with palms and bright flower-beds.

4 BETWEEN THE CÔTES-DE-PROVENCE AND COTEAUX-VAROIS VINEYARDS

Around 175km from Hyères to St-Tropez. Michelin Local Map 340, L-O 5-7. See itinerary 4 on the map p370.

The AOC **Côtes-de-Provence** vineyard is Provence's largest. The appellation covers 84 municipalities, three départements (Bouches-du-Rhône, Var and Alpes-Maritimes) and 19,000ha. The area is right in the heart of Mediterranean Provence, stretching up the valleys of the Arc and the Argens, and running alongside the *calanques* and beaches from Marseille to Nice. Red, white and rosé wines are made here, but rosé accounts for more than 86% of the total production. The AOC Côtes-de-Provence vineyard is cut geographically in half by the **Coteaux-Varois** appellation around Brignoles, which stretches over a limestone area to the foothills of Montagne Sainte-Baume.

Hyères★

Hyères is home to eight Côtes-de-Provence wine-growing estates, including **Château de Mauvanne** (*see Shopping Guide*). The town has charming medieval streets. Go through the **Porte Massillon** gateway and up rue Massillon. Once the main street of the old town, this is now a bustling shopping street with fruit and vegetable stalls and many Renaissance doorways. On place Massillon, the 12C tower, **Tour St-Blaise**, the fortified apse of a Knights Templar commandery, holds temporary exhibitions. *Climb up the steps and go along rue Ste-Catherine.* From the terrace on place St-Paul there is a good **view**★ of the town, the peninsula, and the islands of Porquerolles.
Hyères also boasts some lovely 19C villas as well as lovely parks and gardens. Worth a stop are the **Jardins Olbius-Riquier**, the **Parc St-Bernard** and the **Parc du Château Sainte-Claire**.

The Hyères **vineyards** stretch from the coast south of town, to the foothills of the **Massif des Maures**★★★ north of town. By taking N 98 east, you get to the pleasant seaside resort of **Lalonde-les-Maures**, which is also an important wine centre: its immediate hinterland has no less than 23 estates, including **Château Ste-Marguerite** (*see Shopping Guide*).

Continue on the D 559.

At Bormes les-Mimosas, stop in at **Château Léoube**, the new property of former Domaine d'Ott owner, Romaine Ott.

Turn onto the D 41 N, then the D14.

The road heads north to **Pierrefeu-du-Var**, another wine-growing town with 14 estates and a wine cooperative. Here you can stop at a number of places, such as **Domaine de la Tour des Vidaux**, which also offers accommodation and an evening meal for overnight guests (*see Shopping Guide*).

Head W on D 14, then take D 43 to La Celle, not far from Brignoles.

Abbaye de La Celle

Visit by guided tour (45min) Apr–Sept Mon–Fri 9am–12.30pm & 2–6.30pm; weekends 9am–1pm & 2–5.30pm. Oct–Mar Mon–Fri 9am–noon & 2–5pm, Sat 9am–noon & 2–5.30pm, Sun 10am–noon & 2–5.30pm (last entry 1hr before closing). Closed Jan 1, May 1, Nov 1 & 11, Dec 25. 2.30€. 04 94 59 19 05. www.la-celle.fr.
This 11C-12C Romanesque building was sold during the Revolution and converted into a farm before becoming a luxury hotel. Now under restoration, the abbey church, cloisters and cloister garden, chapterhouse and storeroom, may be visited. Inside the austere, fortress-like Chapel of Ste-Perpétue, there is a Catalan Christ, executed with striking realism, two Baroque altarpieces and the sarcophagus of Garsende de Sabran.
The wine centre, **Maison des vins Coteaux-Varois** is located within the Abbaye de La Celle precinct, in a magnificent 12C building, of which part has been superbly fitted out to display local produce. 80 wine-growers are represented here, and the abbey's own modest production is also on show.
It is a pleasure to stroll through the prestigious site, and see the conservation vineyard with its 88 grape varieties, or the different exhibitions that are put on here.
The centre also offers brochures for three discovery routes of the Coteaux-Varois vineyards that can be done by car (*open Jul–mid-Sept Mon–Sat 10am–noon & 3–7pm, Sun & public holidays 3–7pm; winter Mon–Sat 10am–noon & 2–6pm, closed public holidays; 04 94 69 33 18, coteauxvarois@wanadoo.fr*).

Epic Sunsets

Plateau des Antiques★★ in St-Rémy-de-Provence

Open Apr–Aug 10am–6.30pm; Sept–Mar Tue–Sun 10.30am–7pm. 6.50€. 04 90 91 08 76.
The once prosperous city of Glanum lies amid pine and olive trees 1km south of St-Rémy. It was abandoned after Barbarian invasions at the end of the 3C, but the mausoleum and commemorative arch – remain, together with the archaeological site of **Glanum**★. Apart from the finial that once crowned its dome, the 18m-high **mausoleum**★★, one of the finest of its kind in the Ancient Roman world, has survived virtually intact. The structure was a monument to the memory of the deceased, around 30 BC. The **municipal arch**★ on the main route to the Alps marked the entrance to Glanum. Its perfect proportions and the exceptional quality of its carved decoration show Greek influence.

Musée de Tauroentum in St-Cyr-sur-Mer

131 rte. de la Madrague. 8km W of Bandol on D 559. From St-Cyr-sur-Mer, follow the coast towards La Madrague / Les Lecques port. Open Jun–Sept Wed–Mon 3–7pm. Oct–Mar weekends & pub hols 2–5pm. Apr–May Thu–Sun 2–5pm. 3€. 04 94 26 30 46.
St-Cyr, situated close to the AOC Bandol vineyards, is home to the remains of Tauroentum, the only Roman villa beside the sea on France's Mediterranean coast. The museum stands between Les Lecques and La Madrague on the 1C foundations of a fine mansion.

Fréjus★

33km NE of St-Tropez on N 98.
The tour takes 1.5–2hr as the ruins are scattered over a large area. Leave the car in the car park on place Agricola.
In the 2C the amphitheatre or **Arènes**★ could accommodate approximately 10,000 spectators. Today the original tiered seating has crumbled but the place is still used in summer for shows and bullfights: Picasso came here to watch (*open Tue–Sun; 2€; 04 94 51 34 31; www.ville-frejus.fr*). Walk up to the remains of the theatre on avenue du Theatre-Romain, and then continue up the to the **aqueduct**. The water for Fréjus was collected at Mons, 40km away. The aqueduct reached the city level with the ramparts, and the water was then channelled around the town as far as the water tower *(castellum)* from which the distribution conduits started. This walk ends on the other side of the town centre, at **Porte d'Orée**, a fine archway, most likely some of the remains of the harbour baths. The different vestiges in the immediate area recall that Roman Fréjus was first and foremost a port created by dredging and deepening a lagoon.

Municipal arch at Glanum, Saint-Rémy-de-Provence

S. Sauvignier/MICHELIN

Brignoles

The maze of narrow, twisting streets in old Brignoles now forms the central district of what has become a lively town, set in the heart of the Coteaux-Varois vineyards.

In this appellation area, as in that of Côtes-de-Provence, rosé wine is by far the most common. The vines grow on hillier relief, at an average altitude of 350m (sometimes 500m), where the climate is of a Piedmont type, cold in winter, and hot and dry in summer.

In Brignoles itself, south of place Carami, picturesque old streets lead into the **old town**. It's worth taking a stroll along rue du Grand-Escalier with its arches, rue St-Esprit, and rue des Lanciers, in which there is a **Romanesque house** with twin windows.

The regional museum, **Musée du Pays Brignolais** is housed in a building that dates in part from the 12C, formerly the **Palace of the Counts of Provence**. The tower stands high above the town *(viewing table)*. In the guardroom is the 2C **Gayole tombstone**★, believed to be the oldest Christian monument of ancient Gaul. (○*open Apr–Sept Wed–Sat 9am–noon & 2.30–6pm, Sun 9am–noon & 3–6pm; Oct–Mar Wed–Sat 10am–noon & 2.30–5pm, Sun 10am–noon & 3–5pm;* ○*closed public holidays.* ≈*4€.* ℘*04 94 69 45 18.*

▷ *Head E out of Brignoles on N 7, then turn left onto D 79.*

Lining the road to the village of **Cabasse** are six Coteaux-Varois estates, stretching out along a valley carpeted with vines out of which rise old Provençal buildings. ☞**Domaine Gavoty** makes for an interesting stop (⌂*see Shopping Guide*).

▷ *Head S from Cabasse on D 13, then take N 7 to Les Arcs.*

Les Arcs

The town, nestling in the heart of vineyards that produce excellent wines, vies with Brignoles for the title of capital of the Côtes-de-Provence area. It is dominated by the old Parage quarter and the ruins of Château de Villeneuve, which is the starting point for the Provence wine trail.

The wine centre, ☞**Maison des vins Côtes-de-Provence** is the headquarters of the Côtes-de-Provence appellation. There is a modern tasting area and a gourmet restaurant, Le Bacchus. One Saturday a month an introductory session on wine-tasting is held *(83460 Les Arcs;* ○*open summer daily 10am–7pm, Jul–Aug 10am–8pm; winter daily 10am–6pm;* ○*closed Jan 1, Dec 25; 4hr tasting session* ≈*23€;* ℘*04 94 99 50 20, www.caveaucp.fr).*

☞**Domaine Sainte-Roseline** and the nearby **Chateau d'Esclans** produces prestigious wines(⌂*see Shopping Guide*).

▷ *From Les Arcs, take N 7 for 5.5km towards Fréjus, then turn right onto D 25 to Ste-Maxime. There take N 98 along the coast, then branch off to St-Tropez (41km).*

St-Tropez★★

Everybody is familiar with the jet-set image of "St-Trop", but fewer associate it with the local vineyards spread among umbrella pines and heather.The **harbour**★★ teems with life. On the waterfront and in the neighbouring streets, the traditional pink and yellow houses have been converted into cafés and ice-cream parlours and luxury boutiques.

In the early 20C St-Tropez was painted by great artists whose works are kept in the **Musée de l'Annonciade**★★. The museum is housed in a 16C chapel, a stone's throw from the harbour yet peacefully removed from the bustle of the town. On display are masterpieces of late 19C-early 20C painting by the Pointillists, Fauves and the Nabis group, some of them wonderful interpretations of the area as it was at the time (○*open Jul–Oct Wed–Mon 10am–1pm & 2–7pm; Dec–Jun Wed–Mon 10am–noon & 2–6pm;* ≈*4.50€* ℘*04 94 97 04 01).*

Unusual Vineyards

WINE AND THE ISLANDS

Île de Porquerolles★★★

Departures from Port de la Tour-Fondue, 83400 Giens, on the Giens Peninsula (11km S of Hyères by the D 97). Regular crossings to Porquerolles (20min one way); service year-round except public holidays. 16.50€ round-trip ticket. TLV (Transports Littoral Varois). 04 94 57 44 07. www.tlv-tvm.com.

Off the coast of Hyères are what are known as the Golden Islands (Îles d'Or) – Porquerolles, Port-Cros and Le Levant – forming the southernmost part of Provence. There are three wine-growing estates on Porquerolles, producing red, white and rosé Côtes-de-Provence wine. The most famous, **Domaine de la Courtade**, provides a good opportunity for a ramble *(cars are not allowed on the islands)* among the pine trees and the vines *(see Shopping Guide)*. The Fort St Agathe is also worth a visit *(open May-Sept 10am-noon & 2-6pm)*.

Info: www.porquerolles.com.
Location: Islands off the coast from Hyeres.
Timing: Day trip
Don't Miss: A walk and picnic on the islands
Kids: They will love everything about these day trips.

Île des Embiez

Departures from the Le Brusc landing stage in Six-Fours, 6km SE of Sanary-sur-Mer by the D 559 and the D 616); 14–18 crossings a day (8min). 10€ return ticket. 04 94 05 54 88. www.les-embiez.com.

Opposite Bandol, on Île des Embiez, 10ha of vines planted by the late Paul Ricard, of *pastis* fame, produce 29,000 bottles a year of red, rosé and white.

Île de Bendor

Departures from the landing stage in Bandol, every 30min in summer, from 6.50am. Crossing time 7min. 10€ round trip. 04 94 05 54 88.

On Île de Bendor, formerly owned by the late Paul Ricard, a curious **Exposition des Vins et Spiritueux** displays 8,000 bottles of wine, aperitifs and liqueurs from 52 different countries, as well as a collection of crystal glasses and decanters *(open Jul–Aug; enquire for hours; no charge; 04 94 29 44 34)*.

Îles de Lérins★★

Shuttle service from Cannes (Quai Lauboeuf) May–Sept every hour 8am–noon & 2–4.30pm; return trip 6pm. Winter: no service at 11am. 11€ round trip.Société Planaria, Abbaye de Lérins, Île St-Honorat, 04 92 98 71 38. Book crossing at www.cannes-iles delerins.com

Opposite Cannes, on **Île St-Honorat**★★, the wine is produced by monks, according to age-old tradition. It is sold at the **Boutique de l'Abbaye de Lérins** *(open daily 10.10am–12.15pm & 2–5pm; closed Nov 8–Dec 8; 04 92 99 54 00; www.abbayedelerins.com)*.

BELLET VINEYARD

Michelin Local Map 341, E5. Leave Nice heading W on N 98, then take N 202 to the right. After St-Isidore, turn off to the right and head for St-Roman-du-Bellet.

The tiny (50ha) and extremely old (3C BC) vineyard that makes up the AOC **Bellet** appellation spreads up in terraces or *restanques* on steep slopes of limestone scree in the municipality of Nice, among the Bellet hills looking over the Var plain. The vineyard benefits from a favourable amount of sunshine and its own microclimate, with the *mistral* and *tramontane* winds blowing almost uninterruptedly along the valley. The vineyard's fifteen wine-growers are spread over a residential area in family estates producing reds, rosés and whites. The latter are the best, with notes of lime and honey, but are expensive. Most of the producers are in **St-Roman-de-Bellet**. Château de Bellet is the appellation's flagship wine *(see Shopping Guide)*.

WINE BUYING GUIDE

INFORMATION

Conseil Interprofessionnel des Vins de Provence – *Maison des Vins, N 7, 83460 Les Arcs sur Argens. ℘04 94 99 50 10. www.vinsdeprovence.com.*

Syndicat des Vins des Coteaux d'Aix – *Maison des agriculteurs, 22 ave. Henri-Pontier, 13626 Aix-en-Provence Cedex 1. ℘04 42 23 57 14. www.coteauxaixenprovence.com*

Syndicat des Vignerons de Bellet – *06200 St-Roman-de-Bellet, ℘04 93 37 81 57. www.vinsdebellet.com*

Association des Vins de Bandol – *238 Ch. de la Ferrage, 83330 Le Castellet. ℘04 94 90 29 59. www.vinsdebandol.com.*

Syndicat des Vignerons de Cassis – *Château de Fontcreuse, 13 rte de la Ciotat, 13260 Cassis. ℘04 42 01 71 09.*

Rosé Research Centre – *70 av. Wilson - 83550 Vidauban, ℘04 94 99 74 20 www.centredurose.fr.*

CHARACTERISTICS

The rosés of Provence are fresh and fruity, and can be enjoyed by wine buffs and non-specialists alike. The reds are less well known but are becoming popular. They can be supple with a fruity balance of ripeness and acidity, with red berry flavours. The region also produces reds for storage, which are structured and expressive, matured in tuns and barrels. Provence's whites only make up a small percentage of the overall production but are not to be dismissed: they are complex and aromatic, and sometimes smell of the garrigue or of white fruit, with notes of honey and dried fruit. Two rare appellations complete the range: Palette (near Aix) and Bellet (near Nice), just as small as they are famous.

STORAGE

Baux-de-Provence – Red, 5-10 years, rosé 2-3 years. **Coteaux-d'Aix-en-Provence** – Red, 10-15 years, rosé and white, 2-5 years. **Cassis** – White, up to 10 years. **Palette** – Red, 10-15 years. **Côtes-de-Provence** – Red, 5-10 years; rosé and white should be drunk within a year. **Coteaux-Varois** – Red, up to 10 years; rosé should be drunk young, white, 2-3 years. **Bellet** – Red, 10-15 years, white, 2-10 years.

PRICES

Baux-de-Provence – 10€ to 25€.
Coteaux-d'Aix-en-Provence – 5€ to 20€.
Cassis – 8€ to 20€.
Bandol – 10€ to 30€.
Palette – 20€ to 30€.
Côtes-de-Provence – 5€ to 20€.
Coteaux-Varois – 5€ to 10€.
Bellet – 10€ to 30€.

WINE MERCHANTS AND WINE CENTRES

Le Tonneau de Bacchus – *296 av. du 11-Novembre, 83150 Bandol. ℘04 94 29 01 01. www.tonneau-de-bacchus.com. Open Jul–Aug daily 9.30am–12.30pm & 4–8pm; rest of the year Tue–Sun morning.* The enthusiastic *caviste* (cellarmaster) offers a wide choice of Bandol wines, as well as wines from other parts of France. Ask for the programme on wine courses and the theme evenings organised in the adjoining restaurant, La Table de Bacchus. Tasting sessions for wine or olive oil.

Le Chai Cassidain – *6 r. Séverin-Icard, 13260 Cassis. ℘04 42 01 99 80. Open daily 10am–1pm & 4–8.30pm (10pm in summer).* 13 whites, 2 reds and 5 rosés from the Cassidain vineyard are sold here along with major wines such as Palette, as well as Côtes-du-Rhône, Côtes-de-Provence and wines from other parts of France. This is a friendly shop run by an extremely knowledgeable ***caviste***. On some days, snacks are served with the tastings.

La Maison des Vins - La Maison des Coquillages – *Rte de Marseille, 13260 Cassis. ℘04 42 01 15 61. www.maisondesvinscassis.com. Open Mon–Sat 9am–12.30pm & 2.30–7.30pm; Sun 9am–12.30pm. Closed public holidays in winter.* With their AOC status dating from 1936, the Cassis vineyards cover an area of about 170ha, comprising 14 estates producing mainly white wine (80% of the production). La Maison des Vins sells wines from 11 of them, selected for their quality. Local, regional and national wines are also on sale, as well as local seafood products and platters in the neighbouring boutique.

Maison des Vins de Bandol – *238 Chemin de la Ferrage, 83330 Le Castellet. ✆04 94 90 29 59. www.vinsdebandol.com. Open Mon–Fri 8am–noon & 2–6.30pm.* Home base of the Syndicat des Vignerons de Bandol, this shop organises tastings and other events to educate buyers about the wines of the Bandol AOC.

Petit Village – *At La Foux, near the shopping centre, on the outskirts of Gassin, 83580 Gassin. ✆04 94 56 40 17. www.mavigne.com. Open Jun–Sept 15 Mon–Sat 8.30am–1pm & 2.30–7.30pm; rest of the year Mon–Sat 8.30am–12.30pm & 2.30–7pm.* This large shop is the showcase for the chief wine-growers of the St-Tropez peninsula. It sells wine from a group of eight estates, including the prestigious Château de Pampelonne, and from a cooperative in the Toulon hinterland (Cave St-Roch-les-Vignes in Cuers). Tasting sessions free of charge.

ESTATES

Château Sainte-Roseline – *83460 Les Arcs-sur-Argens. ✆04 94 99 50 30. www.sainte-roseline.com. Open Mon–Fri 9am–7pm. Guided tour at 2.30pm 4€.* Formerly the abbey of La Celle Roubaud, this prestigious vineyard spreads over 100ha, and grows many varieties of grapes. In 2003 a new vinification plant for red wine was installed and has meant wider use of the pigeage technique (pushing down the crust that forms on the fermenting grapes) and the adoption of wooden casks for making their most prestigious products. The Château has been awarded Cru Classé status. Côtes-de-Provence.

Domaine Gavoty – *83340 Cabasse. ✆04 94 69 72 39. domaine.gavoty@wanadoo.fr.* The property has belonged to the Gavoty family since 1806, handed down from generation to generation. Roselyne took over from her father, Pierre, in 1985. Today the vineyard stretches over 53ha and grows Rolle, Grenache, Cinsault, Syrah and Cabernet grapes. There are seven white vintages and several old red ones, all made naturally. Côtes-de-Provence.

Domaine Bunan – *Moulin des Costes, 83740 La Cadière-d'Azur. ✆04 94 98 58 98. www.bunan.com. Open daily Mon–Sat 9am–noon & 2–7pm; Sun 9am–noon & 4–7pm.* This estate in the middle of vines, pines and olive trees produces AOC Bandol and Côtes-de-Provence wines. With its still dating from 1920, it also makes an old marc with stemmed grapes, and a white brandy distilled from marc. Lastly, don't leave without having tried the home-made olive oil, tapenade or honey. Bandol, Côtes-de-Provence.

Vineyard around Brignoles
S. Sauvignier/MICHELIN

Domaine de l'Olivette – *Chemin de l'Olivette, 83330 Le Castellet. ✆04 94 98 58 85. www.domaine-olivette.com.* The property has been in the family since the 18C, expanding over the generations to its present size of 55ha. The vines are mainly planted on the hills around Le Castellet. The property uses the latest techniques and is also advised by a wine laboratory that follows up the wine-making process from the time the grapes are ripe to the time the wine is bottled. Bandol, Côtes-de-Provence.

Clos Sainte-Magdeleine – *Av. du Revestel,13260 Cassis. ✆04 42 01 70 28. jsack@club-internet.fr. Open Mon–Fri 10am–noon & 3–7pm.* The estate was set up at the end of the 19C and has belonged to the Zafiropulo family since 1920. It consists of 9ha of vines for white wine and 3ha for tenant farming. Ecologically responsible farming practices, manual harvesting. Cassis.

Domaine de l'Hermitage – *Chemin de Rouve, 83330 Le Beausset. ✆04 94 98 71 31. www.domainesduffort.com. Open Mon–Fri 9am–noon & 2–6pm (summer 7pm). Closed public holidays.* This family business consists of 70ha of very carefully tended vines, which are pruned back short and treated using ecologically responsible methods. Half of the vineyard produces AOC Bandol wine, aged for at least eighteen months in large oak casks, and the other half is given over to Côtes-de-Provence wine. The star product is a rosé that has won a gold medal. Bandol.

SCA Château de Mauvanne – *2805 rte de Nice, 83400 Hyères. 04 94 66 40 25. chateaudemauvanne@free.fr.*
In 1999 following the advice of Yves Morard, his wine-specialist in Lebanon, who also owns an estate in the Vaucluse, Bassim Rahal bought Château de Mauvanne, thus adding to what he already owned in Lebanon – a vineyard of more than 200ha. Of his 50ha in France, 43 are devoted to vines, with the Grenache, Syrah, Cinsault, Mourvèdre and Tibouren varieties for the reds and rosés, completed by Carignan and Cabernet-Sauvignon; and Rolle, Ugni Blanc and Clairette for the whites. The vineyard is cultivated using ecologically responsible method. The vinification and maturing are carried out traditionally in vats, while the top of the range reds are matured in wood casks. Côtes-de-Provence, Vin de Pays des Maures.

Mas de Gourgonnier – *Le Destet, 13890 Mouriès. 04 90 47 50 45. contact@gourgonnier.com. Open Mon–Sat by appt 9am–noon & 2–6pm. Sun by appt. www.gourgonnier.com.* Owned by the same family for 5 generations, this 46ha estate makes red wines from its Grenache, Syrah, Cinsault, Carignan, Mourvèdre and Cabernet-Sauvignon, and white wines from its Sauvignon, Grenache and Rolle grapes. The vineyard is organically farmed (certified Ecocert since 1975). Traditional winemaking methods are used; the wines are then aged in barrels for 12 months. Baux-de-Provence, Coteaux-d'Aix-en-Provence.

Domaine de la Courtade – *83400 Porquerolles (island). 04 94 58 31 44. www.lacourtade.com. Open Mon–Fri 9am–5pm.* This vineyard was created in 1983, as a result of a meeting between a manufacturer, Henri Vidal, who had been in love with Île de Porquerolles since his childhood, and a wine specialist from Alsace, Richard Auther, passionately fond of scuba diving. After manual harvesting, the wines age in oak tuns, nine months for the whites, 18 months for the reds. Côtes-de-Provence.

Château Calissanne – *13680 Lançon-de-Provence. 04 90 42 63 03. Open daily by appt. 9am–7pm (1pm on Sun).*
Château Calissanne, a property of 1,000ha, has 105ha of vines. Syrah, Cabernet-Sauvignon, Mourvèdre, Grenache, Clairette, Sémillon and Sauvignon are planted on calcareous colluvial deposits at sea level. The vineyard is cultivated using ecologically responsible methods and much of the harvest is done manually. The wines are then matured in oak casks. Baux-de-Provence, Coteaux-d'Aix-en-Provence.

Château Les Valentines – *Quartier Les Jassons, Rte. de Collobrières, 83250 La Londe-les-Maures. 04 94 15 95 50. www.lesvalentines.com. Open Mon–Sat 9am–12.30pm & 2–7pm. Closed public holidays.* The owners of this attractive winery with its Provençal colours have worked relentlessly to give a new lease of life to their 23ha of vines, some of which are over 80 years old. Their first grape harvest dates back to 1997, producing mainly rosés and reds. First and foremost, one should taste the Bagnard wine, AOC Côtes-de-Provence. Côtes-de-Provence.

Château Sainte-Marguerite – *Le Haut-Pansard, 83250 La Londe-les-Maures. 04 94 00 44 44. www.chateausaintemarguerite.com. Open by appt. Mon–Sat 9am–noon & 2–6pm. Closed public holidays.*
This beautiful property lined with palm trees cultivates 50ha that produce some 250 000 bottles a year, 75% of which end up on the tables of great restaurants. On offer are several AOC Côtes-de-Provence wines. Côtes-de-Provence.

Domaine La Tour des Vidaux – *Quartier Les Vidaux, 83390 Pierrefeu-du-Va. 04 94 48 24 01. tourdesvidaux@wanadoo.fr.*
Paul Weindel took over this 24ha property in 1996. He launched into improving the place, installing his own wine-making plant. The vines are grown on schist soil on the southern slopes of the Massif des Maures. The grape varieties are Grenache, Syrah, Cabernet-Sauvignon, Cinsault, Carignan and Tibouren for the reds and

rosés, and Clairette and Ugni Blanc for the whites. The latest techniques are used throughout the property, in combination with traditional methods for the wine-making. Côtes-de-Provence.

Château de Beaupré – *N 7, 13760 St-Cannat. 04 42 57 33 59. www.beaupre.fr. Open daily 9am–noon & 2–6pm.* The property was set up by Christian Double's grandfather in 1890, and consists of 42ha today. For several years now, in conjunction with the regional association of sommeliers, a special wine has been made for red and rosé, called Clos des Sommeliers. Château de Beaupré produces reds, rosés and whites, including a Collection du Château wine, which is fermented in new barrels and then matured in the same barrels for three months before being bottled. Coteaux-d'Aix-en-Provence.

Château Pradeaux – *676 chemin des Pradeaux, 83270 St-Cyr-sur-Mer – 04 94 32 10 21. chateaupradeaux@wanadoo.fr. Open by appt. Mon–Sat 9am–noon & 3–6pm.* Cyrille Portalis and his wife Magali have been running this 26ha property (of which 21ha are used for wine) since 1983. The vines are grown on clayey limestone soil, with Mourvèdre, Grenache and Cinsault grape varieties. The grapes are harvested by hand and the wine-making process is traditional: the grapes are pressed lightly so as not to damage the skins, and the wine is matured in oak casks. Bandol.

Domaine Hauvette – *La Haute-Galine, 13210 St-Rémy-de-Provence. 04 90 92 03 90. Open by appt.* Dominique Hauvette took over here in 1988. The 14ha property, planted with Marsanne, Roussanne, Clairette, Grenache, Syrah, Cabernet-Sauvignon, Cinsault and Carignan, is farmed organically, with the grapes being harvested by hand and the vinification carried out traditionally. 40 000 bottles are produced a year. Baux-de-Provence, Coteaux-d'Aix-en-Provence, Vin de Pays des Bouches-du-Rhône.

Clos Saint-Vincent – *Chemin du Collet-des-Fourniers, St-Roman-de-Bellet, 06200 Nice. 04 92 15 12 69. clos.st.vincent@wanadoo.fr. Open by appt.* The estate's 6.5ha vineyard is planted with Folie Noir and Grenache for its reds, Rolle for the whites and Braquet for the rosés. Founded some 30 years ago, the estate was taken over in 1993 by Joseph Sergi, who makes the most of an exceptional climate and terrain using traditional methods in both farming and winemaking. Bellet.

ADDRESSES

STAY

AROUND AIX-EN-PROVENCE

Château du Petit Sonnailler – *13121 Aurons. 04 90 59 34 47. www.petit-sonnailler.com. 3 rooms.* Located on a winegrowing estate, this spot is hidden in the hills around Aix. There's a crenellated 12C tower which contains a bedroom – our favourite – with medieval wooden panelling. One room is equipped for disabled guests. Wine tasting and sales.

Maison d'hôte La Quinta des Bambous – *Chemin des Ribas, 13100 St-Marc-Jaumegarde. 04 42 24 91 62 http://laquintadesbambous.free.fr. 3 rooms.* This unusual villa faces Montagne Sainte-Victoire. The rooms (each with private bathroom) are decorated with plant motifs and Japanese-inspired artworks. Private terraces, bamboo garden and swimming pool.

BANDOL

Auberge La Cauquière – *Puits d'Isnard, 83330 Le Beausset. 04 94 98 42 75. Closed Jan. 11 rooms. 7€. Restaurant* . Pleasant auberge with garden and pool, just 10 minutes from the beach and on the Bandol wine roue. Nice rooms around a pleasant patio; Provençal cuisine and local wines at table.

Chambre d'hôte Villa Lou Gardian – *646 rte de Bandol, 83110 Sanary-sur-Mer, A 50, Bandol exit. 04 94 88 05 73 or 06 60 88 05 73. www.lou-gardian.com. 4 rooms.* Despite the nearby road, the colourful, air-conditioned rooms in this villa are relatively quiet. Flower garden, swimming pool and tennis.

Les Galets – *49 Montée Voisin, 83150 Bandol. Closed Nov 6–Jan 31. 20 rooms. 7€. Restaurant . 04 94 29 43 46. www.lesgalets-bandol.com.* Splendid sea views from the rooms and balconies of this hillside hotel. Enjoy regional specialities in the dining room, or terrace.

AROUND BRIGNOLES

Chambre d'hôte Château de Vins – *Les Prés du Chateau, 83170 Vins-sur-Caramy, 9km NE of Brignoles on D 24, on the road to Thoronet. 04 94 72 50 40. chateaudevins.com. Closed Dec–Mar. 5 rooms.* This fine 16C building with four turrets has soberly appointed rooms all named after musicians. The place has been renovated by the dedicated and energetic landlord, and hosts cultural events, concerts, music lessons and exhibitions in the summer.

Chambre d'hôte La Cordeline – *14 r. des Cordeliers – 83670 Brignoles. 04 94 59 18 66 or 06 12 99 20 02. www.lacordeline.com. Reservations required. 4 rooms. Restaurant .* This handsome 17C mansion is a haven of peace right in the centre of town. Fine family furniture adorns the huge rooms. As soon as day breaks you can enjoy breakfast with home-made jams on the terrace, in the shade of the climbing vine.

CANNES

Chambre d'hôte Villa L'Églantier – *14 r. Campestra, 06400 Cannes. 04 93 68 22 43. 3 rooms.* In the heights of Cannes, this large white house rises amid palm trees in an exotic garden. Bright, spacious rooms with balcony or terrace.

AROUND HYÈRES

Chambre d'hôte L'Aumônerie – *620 av. de Fontbrun, 83320 Carqueiranne, southeast of town by the D 559 toward Hyères and the road to the right along the sea. 04 94 58 53 56. www.laumoniere.com. Reservations suggested. 4 rooms.* This house, which once belonged to a naval chaplain, is blissfully quiet and likes to keep things that way. The decor in the rooms is restrained. You can have breakfast in bed or on the terrace shaded by maritime pines. Don't miss the garden that leads to the private beach and the sea.

NICE

Chambre d'hôte Castel Enchanté – *61 rte. St-Pierre-de-Féric, 06300 Nice. 04 93 97 02 08. www.castel-enchange.com. 3 rooms, 1 suite.* Follow the narrow path to this handsome 19C house with a garden terrace overlooking a valley. Peaceful, spacious guestrooms.

Villa la Lézardière – *87 blvd. de l'Observatoire, 06000 Nice. 04 93 56 22 86. www.villa-la-lezardiere.com. 5 rooms.* Located on the Grande Corniche, this Provençal-style villa features stunning views of the city and the backdropping Alps. Large garden; swimming pool. Traditional and Thai cuisine.

SALON-DE-PROVENCE

Chambre d'hôte Domaine du Bois Vert – *Quartier Montauban – 13450 Grans – 7km S of Salon on D 16 and then D 19 towards Lançon – 04 90 55 82 98. www.domaineduboisvert.com. 3 rooms.* This drystone *mas*, or farmstead, stands in a park of oak and pine trees beside a river. Its garden-floor rooms are decorated in the Provençal style, with red hexagonal floor tiles, exposed beams and antique furniture.

ST-RÉMY-DE-PROVENCE

Cheval Blanc – *Pl. de l'Église, 13210 St-Rémy-de-Provence. 02 47 30 30 14. www.hotelduchevalblanc.com. Closed Jan 1–Feb 14. 12 rooms. 6.50€. Restaurant .* Spruced-up rooms and dining al fresco make for a very nice experience at this reasonably-priced establishment near old St-Rémy.

Terriciaë – *Rte. de Moussane, 13890 Mouriès. 04 90 97 06 70. www.hotel-terriciae-mouries.com. 27 rooms. 12€.* Bearing the ancient roman name of the town, this hotel offers well-kept rooms decorated à la Provence, some of them overlooking the pool. Others are handicapped-accessible.

PORQUEROLLES

L'Auberge des Glycines – *22 pl. d'Armes, 834000 Porquerolles. 04 94 58 30 36. www.auberge-glycines.com. Closed Jan 1. 11 rooms. 7€. Restaurant .*

This delicious little auberge, with its lavender-blue blinds is all by itself worth a trip to the island. Very nice rooms opening onto a patio shaded by a fig tree, or onto the village square. Provençal cuisine in the restaurant.

IN ST-TROPEZ

Hôtel Lou Cagnard – *18 ave. Paul-Rouseel, 83990 St-Tropez. ℘04 94 97 04 24. hotel-lou-cagnard.com. Closed Nov 6–Dec 27. 19 rooms. 10€.* Older home located near the famous Place des Lices. Recently renovated, impeccably maintained rooms, and breakfast served in the shaded garden, all at a reasonable (for St-Tropez!) price.

EAT

AROUND AIX-EN-PROVENCE

Chez Charlotte – *32 r. des Bernardines, 13100 Aix-en-Provence. ℘04 42 26 77 56. Cosed Dec 25–Jan 1.* Family photos decorate the entry of this nostalgic little spot. The main dining room evokes themes of cinema, present and future. In summer, have a seat on the streetside terrace and enjoy simple, seasonal dishes, prepared with care.

Le Villon – *14 r. du Félibre-Gaut, 13100 Aix-en-Provence. ℘04 42 27 35 27. Closed Sun.* Don't be swayed by the unimpressive facade or the sombre dining room. The plentiful dishes and delicious deserts will win over your taste buds, in a wallet-friendly manner.

Le Craponne – *146 allée de Craponne, 13300 Salon-de-Provence, ℘04 90 53 23 92. Closed Aug 8–31, Dec 26–Jan 2, Sun evenings, Wed evenings and Mon.* This restaurant has a good reputation among the locals and serves traditional fare with a family touch: entrecôte steak *à la bordelaise* (with a red wine sauce), duck in orange sauce, and home-made cakes and pastries.

IN LES ARCS

Logis du Guetteur – *Pl. du Chateau, 83460 Les Arcs. ℘04 94 99 51 10. www.logisduguetteur.com. Closed Feb.* Picturesque restaurant established in an 11C fort, with rustic dining rooms laid out in the medieval cellars and shaded terrace. Contemporary cuisine. Comfortable guestrooms available.

AROUND BANDOL

Le Clocher – *1 r. Paroisse, 83150 Bandol. ℘04 94 32 47 65. le.clocher@wanadoo.fr. Open Jun–Sept.* This friendly little restaurant in old Bandol has a terrace and a dining room which, in style at least, brings to mind one of the local cafés. The delicious local recipes have been updated for contemporary tastes, and make you forget all about the crowds in the pedestrian quarter.

Saint-Pierre - Chez Marcel – *47 r. de la Citadelle, le Brusc, 83410 Six-Fours-les-Plages. ℘4 94 34 02 52. www.lesaintpierre.fr. Closed Mon, Sun lunch Jun–Sep, and all of Jan.* Located near the port, this old fisherman's house serves forth specialities drawn from the region in its pleasant dining room.

AROUND CANNES

Le Comptoir des Vins – *13 bd de la République, 06400 Cannes. ℘04 93 68 13 26. comptoirdesvins@cegetel.net. Closed Jan, Mon (year-round) and Sun lunch Jun–Sept.* There's a wine shop at the front; then you can step back to enjoy simple, generous dishes in the little restaurant at the back. You can have a glass of wine with each dish or choose a bottle directly from the shop shelves.

CASSIS

Le Bonaparte – *14 r. du Gén-Bonaparte, 13260 Cassis. ℘04 42 01 80 84. In Dec closed Mon, and Sun evenings. Reservations required.* This is the place to come for fish dishes (be sure to order the bouillabaisse the day before). The french tricolour scheme of blue, white and red is displayed in the table linens. Local clientele.

La Vieille Auberge – *14 quai Jean-Jacques-Barthélemy, 13260 Cassis. ℘04 42 01 73 54. Closed Sun eve Oct–Apr. Reservations suggested.* Pleasant little auberge serving traditional French and Provençal recipes handed down over generations. Decoration inspired by the sea. Try the veranda facing the port, or the terrace in summer.

AROUND HYÈRES

Le Val Bohème – *3 p. du 4-Septembre, 83143 Le Val. ℘04 94 86 46 20.* Less well-known than its neighbour, this simple little spot makes up for its rather narrow selection by serving dishes made with perfectly fresh ingredients. The daily selection is composed of whatever's available at the market, served on the lovely terrace near the church. Good value.

La Colombe – *663 rte. de Toulon, La Bayarre, 83400 Hyères. 2.5km W of Hyères on the Rte. de Toulon. ℘04 94 35 35 16. www.restaurantlacolombe.com. Call for opening times.* Behind its attractive façade lies an expansive terrace, a great spot to relax in sunny weather. There or in the dining room, decorated in Provençal colours, tuck into well-turned regional specialities.

Le Bistrot à l'Ail – *22 av. Georges-Clemenceau. 83250 La Londe-les-Maures. ℘04 94 66 97 93. Closed Nov 20–Dec 20, lunchtime and Mon evenings in Jul-Aug.* Cédric Gola takes care of the cooking and his wife the guests. They serve beautifully presented Provençal fare made from market-fresh produce. You are sure to enjoy your meal here, whether on the tiny terrace looking onto the street or in the dining room.

Le Jardin Provençal – *18 ave. Georges-Clemenceau, 83250 La Londe-les-Maures. ℘04 94 66 57 34. Closed Dec 15–Jan 20, Mon & Tue lunch Jun–Sept.* It's worth coming here just to see the Provençal garden that surrounds the restaurant's shady terrace. In summer it's advisable to book, so as not to miss out on the local fare and scrumptious desserts.

NICE

Au Rendez-vous des Amis – *176 av. de Rimiez, aire St-Michel, 06000 Nice. ℘04 93 84 49 66. www.rdvdesamis.fr. Closed Feb 26–Mar 14, Oct 23–Nov 22, Tue except in Jul–Aug, Wed.* Isabelle and Thierry welcome you to their restaurant as if they were having you for a meal at home. Not a wide choice – so the ingredients are very fresh – but the fixed menu is reasonably priced.

L'Auberge de la Méditerranée – *21 r. Delille, 06000 Nice. ℘04 93 91 35 65. Closed Aug 14-27, Dec 25–Jan 1, Mon evenings, Tue evenings, Sat lunchtime & Sun.* Welcoming family atmosphere, pleasant decor, tasty regional dishes (the menu changes daily depending on what's available at the market)… a good place to eat.

NEAR ST-RÉMY-DE-PROVENCE

La Pitchoune – *21 pl. de l'Église, 13520 Maussane-les-Alpilles. ℘04 90 54 34 84. Closed mid-Nov–mid-Jan, Fri lunchtime and Mon.* Cute dining rooms in this modest 19C home near the church. In summer you'll enjoy family cooking on the pine-shaded terrace.

Alain Assaud – *13 blvd. Marceau, 13210 St-Rémy-de-Provence. ℘04 90 92 37 11. Closed Nov 15–Dec 15.* St-Rémy gourmands frequently find themselves at this shop-turned-restaurant, tucking into cod with aioli, soupe au pistou, or grilled sea bass.

IN ST-TROPEZ

Le Petit Charron – *6 r. Charrons, 83990 St-Tropez. ℘04 94 97 73 78. c-benoit@wanadoo.fr. Closed Jan 15–30, Mar 1–15, Aug 1–15, Nov 15–Dec 1 and Mon offseason.* Simple, family-style restaurant with bistro decor, serving tasty regional cuisine. Non-smoking.

GOURMET SHOPPING

Gastronomie Provençale – *N 7, Celony, 13090 Aix-en-Provence. ℘04 42 21 14 22. http://darvaux.com.* This small family establishment specialises in potted thrush *(terrine de grive)*, which it has updated for contemporary tastes. It also sells cooked dishes, sauces, oils, and fruit in muscatel.

Le Mas de l'Olivier – *2 r. de la Ciotat, 13260 Cassis. ℘04 42 01 92 41.* This small shop in an alley in the town centre sells herbes de Provence, carefully selected varieties of olive oil, several types of olives, anchovy sauce *(anchoïade)*, tapenade (an olive and caper paste), garlic vinegar and all sorts of delicacies.

Miel de Provence – *Grand-Draille Nord, La Galine, 13210 St-Rémy-de-Provence. ℘04 90 92 28 88.* Brun & Fils have kept bees for five generations. Among their products are honey, pollen, sweets and fabulous home-made *pain d'épices* – a sort of gingerbread.

12 - RHÔNE VALLEY

For the last two thousand years the Rhône's meandering course has been bordered by some of the most renowned and spectacular of France's vineyards. The region is one of the most diverse in France and divides into two distinct geographical areas, stretching over 250 communes and six départements between Vienne and Nîmes. The northern part between Vienne and Valence is striking for its sheer south facing slopes, with a continental climate of cold winters and hot summers. The southern part, from Montélimar to the Luberon, slips into a Mediterranean climate, with vines growing in arid soil between olive groves and lavender fields.

Highlights

1 The Maison Carré in **Nîmes** (p410)
2 A coffee in the leafy central square of **Gigondas** (p402)
3 A hike and picnic up **Mount Ventoux** (p401, 405)
4 Nougat from **Montélimar** (p398)
5 Window shopping in **Ménerbes** (p407)

Making the famous Montélimar nougats

J. Damase / MICHELIN

Cultivated since antiquity, the northern Rhone vineyards have astonishingly steep terraces, with granite hillsides covered by vines from Ampuis (south of Vienne) to Saint-Peray (north of Valence), a 200km ribbon of greenery enveloping the Rhône. Machinery is unsuitable for its terraces which are supported by low stone walls, and virtually all work is done by hand, or sometimes even by helicopter. The combination of geography, poor soil geology and the south and south-east facing slopes make for some rarefied wines with a smoky, spicy character which sought-after by connoisseurs. Beyond Valence, the landscape changes entirely: a vine-free strip of 50km separates the northern Côtes du Rhône from the south. When the vinyeards begin again, a huge plain extends as far as the eye can see, from the Coteaux du Gard to the west to the Luberon and Mont Ventoux to the east. The exceptional sunshine and the richness of the sub-soil (thanks to the alluvial deposits all along the Rhône's banks) help create, among others, the mythical wines of Gigondas and Chateauneuf-du-Pape.

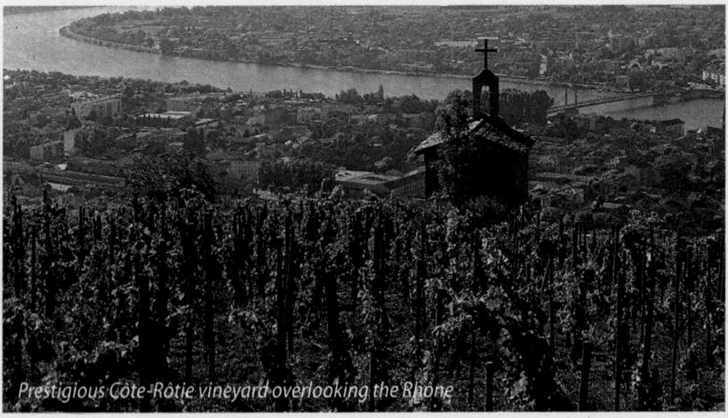
Prestigious Côte-Rôtie vineyard overlooking the Rhône

S. Sauvignier/MICHELIN

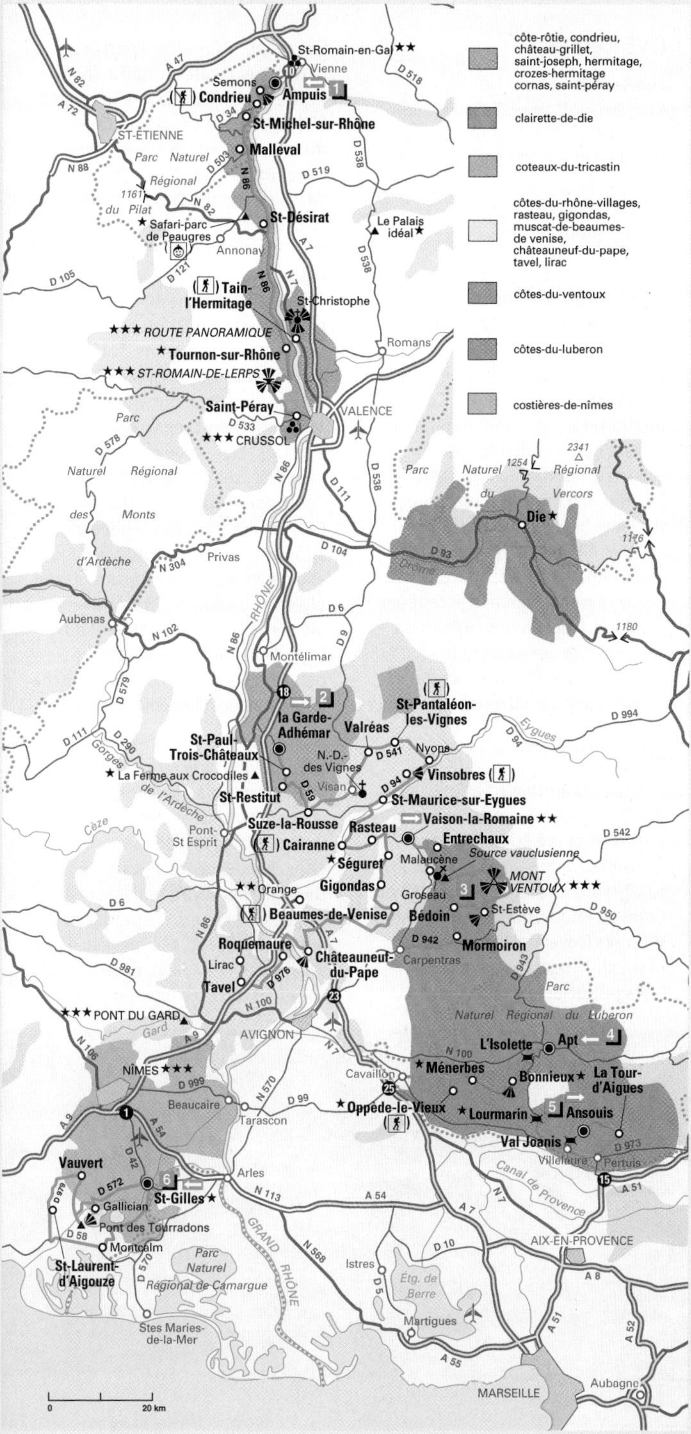
côte-rôtie, condrieu, château-grillet, saint-joseph, hermitage, crozes-hermitage cornas, saint-péray
clairette-de-die
coteaux-du-tricastin
côtes-du-rhône-villages, rasteau, gigondas, muscat-de-beaumes-de venise, châteauneuf-du-pape, tavel, lirac
côtes-du-ventoux
côtes-du-luberon
costières-de-nîmes
St-Romain-en-Gal
Vienne
Semons
Condrieu
Ampuis
St-Michel-sur-Rhône
Malleval
ST-ÉTIENNE
Parc Naturel Régional du Pilat
Safari-parc de Peaugres
St-Désirat
Le Palais idéal
Annonay
Tain-l'Hermitage
St-Christophe
ROUTE PANORAMIQUE
Tournon-sur-Rhône
Romans
ST-ROMAIN-DE-LERPS
Saint-Péray
VALENCE
CRUSSOL
Parc Naturel Régional des Monts d'Ardèche
Parc Naturel Régional du Vercors
Die
Privas
Drôme
Aubenas
RHÔNE
Montélimar
la Garde-Adhémar
St-Pantaléon-les-Vignes
Valréas
St-Paul-Trois-Châteaux
N.-D.-des Vignes
Nyons
Eygues
La Ferme aux Crocodiles
Visan
Vinsobres
St-Restitut
St-Maurice-sur-Eygues
Gorges de l'Ardèche
Suze-la-Rousse
Vaison-la-Romaine
Cèze
Pont-St Esprit
Rasteau
Entrechaux
Cairanne
Séguret
Malaucène
Source vauclusienne
MONT VENTOUX
Orange
Gigondas
Groseau
St-Estève
Beaumes-de-Venise
Bédoin
Mormoiron
Roquemaure
Châteauneuf-du-Pape
Carpentras
Lirac
Tavel
Parc Naturel Régional du Luberon
PONT DU GARD
Gard
AVIGNON
L'Isolette
Apt
NÎMES
Ménerbes
Cavaillon
Bonnieux
La Tour-d'Aigues
Beaucaire
Tarascon
Oppède-le-Vieux
Lourmarin
Ansouis
Val Joanis
Vauvert
Villelaure
Pertuis
Arles
St-Gilles
Canal de Provence
Gallician
Pont des Tourradons
GRAND RHÔNE
AIX-EN-PROVENCE
Montcalm
St-Laurent-d'Aigouze
Parc Naturel Régional de Camargue
Istres
Étg. de Berre
Martigues
Stes Maries-de-la-Mer
MARSEILLE
Aubagne
0
20 km

12 - RHÔNE VALLEY

OVERVIEW

The Terroir

Michelin Local Maps 327, 331, 332 and 339 – Ardèche (07), Drôme (26), Gard (30), Haute-Loire (42), Rhône (69) and Vaucluse (84).

Surface area: 79,045ha.

Production: 3.3 million hl a year; 94% red wines.

Covering over 200km from north to south, the terroirs of the Rhône are astonishingly varied, incorporating a climatic and geological diversity exemplified by the region's **Côtes du Rhône** wines. The Mediterranean climate brings with it the Mistral, a harsh wind that manages to be beneficial to the development of the vines here. Formed by differences in air pressure between north and south, the Mistral brings with it heavy seasonal rains and exceptional sunshine. From Vienne to Avignon and from the Cévennes to the foothills of the Alps, the Rhône Valley has a complex and varied terrain enriched by riverine deposits.

The Wines

As complex and varied as the terroir, the region's wines are predominantly reds (94% of the AOCs, 3% rosés and 3% whites), and split into four main sub-groups: the regional appellation Côtes du Rhône, the **Côtes du Rhône Villages** (covering 90 communes of which 18 bear the appellation "village", including Valréas and Cairanne), 17 Crus (the finest of all, of which eight are located in the northern part), and finally the young Rhône Valley appellations (**Côtes du Luberon**, **Costières de Nîmes**, **Coteaux de Tricastin**, Côtes du Ventoux, and the **Diois** appellations). Two further Crus complete the jigsaw; the sweet Beaumes de Venise and Rasteau wines.

The Côtes du Rhône AOC regulations permit the use of 21 grape varieties, of which eight are white. Some are employed as the principal ingredient (Syrah, Grenache, Mourvèdre, Viognier, Marsanne, Roussanne, Bourboulenc, Clairette), while others play a secondary role (Cinsault, Carignan, Cournoise, Picpoul etc). The northern Côtes du Rhône reds are generally all Syrahs. To the south, the climatic and geological variety means greater diversity: Unusually, 13 grape varieties are permitted in Châteauneuf-du-Pape. Notably, the Muscat blanc à petits grains grape is only used in the naturally sweet Beaumes de Venise.

Buying Note

Here, buying direct from the producer will only mean a small discount. They are reluctant to compete against their wine merchants, who can sometimes offer cheaper prices at wine fairs or through special promotional deals. On the other hand, the producers are the only people to speak to if you really want to find out the details of their methods, terroirs and cellars.

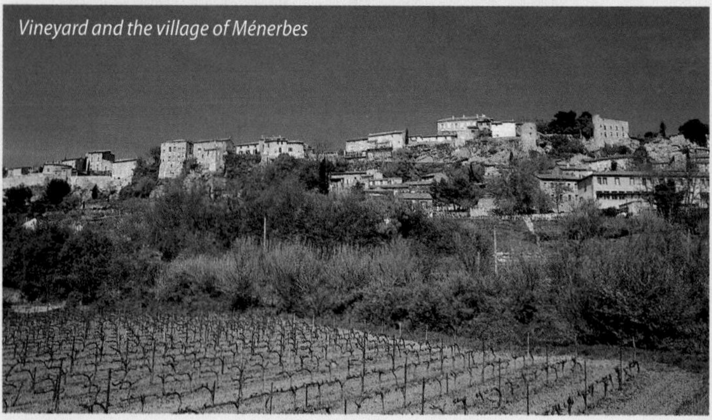

Vineyard and the village of Ménerbes

H. Le Gac/MICHELIN

Northern Côtes du Rhône

The evocatively-named Cote Rotie, 'roasted slopes', gives an idea of the extremity of the landscape here. Excellent walking and driving countryside, always accompanied by the stately Rhone river.

- **Population:** 370,000.
- **Michelin Map:** 327, H-1 7-9 and 331, K-L 3-4. See Itinerary 1 on the map on p393. This route follows the N 86, unless indicated otherwise.
- **Info:** rhone-wines.com.
- **Location:** South of Lyon. Approx. 75km from Ampuis (Rhône) to St-Péray (Ardèche).
- **Timing:** Two days
- **Don't Miss:** The panoramic drive from Tain-l'Hermitage.
- **Kids:** Pierrelatte Croc Farm.

DRIVING TOUR

1 VERTIGINOUS VINEYARDS

Ampuis

The capital of the Côte-Rôtie extends along the right bank of the Rhône, accounting for 90% of production. First recorded in the 1C BC – Pliny the Elder and Plutarch were later to praise **Côte-Rôtie**, "the wine of Vienne" – its vineyards were held to be the oldest in Gaul. They are surrounded by incredibly steep slopes. A backfrop of terraces supported by low stone walls extends away above the rooftops of the village. The **Domaine Etienne Guigal** has a good reputation (*see Shopping Guide*).

From place de l'Église, follow the D 615 towards Les Haies to head up through the Côte-blonde vineyards.

After 3km, every turn provides breathtaking scenery. On the way back down there are fine views of the **château**, now owned by Guigal. Although not open to the public, it has a fine Renaissance façade (16C) on the banks of the Rhône. If you've ever wondered what sort of wine to serve with Christmas or Thanksgiving dinner, this is the place to find out: it was here, in 1553, that the first turkeys were eaten in France!

Condrieu

The Condrieu appellation produces an excellent white wine from the Viognier grape, and is one of the finest Rhone whites. Condrieu blanc is delicious with the local goat's cheese. The paths used by the wine growers of bygone times are known as *coursières* to the townsfolk.

Wine growers or mountaineers?

From Ampuis to l'Hermitage, the northern Côtes du Rhône is distinguished by its steep slopes, sometimes as precipitous as 80% (4 in 5). Laid out in terraces supported by low stone walls, its vineyards seem to defy gravity. The steepness of these granite hillsides precludes any use of machinery, so all work continues to be done by hand. Down in the vineyards on the plain, one man can tend to 10-15ha. In the northern Côtes du Rhône, one man can only work two hectares. The sole concession to modernity is the French wine industry's only monorail, which can be seen at the Ampuis Sud junction (domaines Barge, Gangloff and Montez): of Swiss construction, this transport system has opened up an extremely steep area for cultivation. Thanks to this, equipment, wine harvests and manpower have travelled effortlessly up and down since 2003. Here, there are also many all-terrain vehicles in evidence: far from being a motoring fashion statement, they are essential for reaching the vines along battered tracks.

The tourist office sells a guide to three trails (3km–6km), offering fine views. A less energetic option by car is to follow the *belvédère* signposts on the D 124 uphill towards **Semons** *(parking)* from the Condrieu north exit. From the church (18C) square, the panoramic **view** reveals a loop in the Rhône dominated by vine-covered slopes, and the farmland of the plains where orchards and dairy farming, on the right bank, and cereal crops, on the left, predominate. For a small but good quality local producer, try André Perret *(Verlieu, 42410 Chavanay; t04 74 87 24 74)*.

S on N 86; right on D 34.

Saint-Michel-sur-Rhône

On the banks of the Rhône, the village is home to the **Château Grillet AOC**, one of the rarest in France, made exclusively by **Château Grillet** *(signposted)*, a vineyard of just 3.5ha, producing a sought-after white. Tastings are not available, but the wine is for sale *(see Shopping Guide)* and visitors can admire the turreted chateau beside its vineyard.

Return to N 86; head S before turning right on D 503 towards Malleval.

Malleval

The 16C houses of this village are surrounded by vines and oak s. From the belvédère *(picnic tables and information boards)* there is a fine view over the salt store, *commanderie*, church (11C apse), and the ruins of the keep. Malleval is at the heart of the **Saint-Joseph appellation**: covering 26 communes, these vineyards sit between the Condrieu and Côte-Rôtie AOCs (north) and Cornas (south).

Near the cemetery at the top of the village the vines are especially impressive, rising vertically uphill. The orchards on the village outskirts demonstrate the area's thriving market gardening, set within the Pilat Regional Park.

Stop in **Domaine Pierre Gaillard** for a taste of an excellent Saint-Joseph - ask to try his Condrieu *(see Shopping)*.

Return to the N 86 and head S.

Saint-Desirat

Located in the Distillerie Gauthier, the **Musée de l'Alambic★** traces the history of the mobile distillers. Farmers used to enjoy a special dispensation allowing them to make up to 10 litres of brandy for their personal consumption. In 1960, this loophole was closed and the mobile distillers were replaced by regulated commercial distilleries. Film footage, a fine collection, information boards and reconstructions allow the visitor to understand the processes involved, with a tasting opportunity rounding off the visit in an agreeable fashion. The distillery offers its products for sale, notably its speciality poire Williams eau-de-vie *(open Jul–Aug 8am–7pm, weekends & public holidays 10am–7pm, last admission 1hr before closing; Sept–Jun 8am–noon & 2–6.30pm, weekends & public holidays 10am–noon & 2–6.30pm; 04 75 34 23 11; www.jeangauthier.com)*.

You are still in AOC Saint Joseph here; stop for a tasting at **Domaine Delas Frères** in Saint-Jean-de-Muzols *(see Shopping Guide)*. The **Cave Saint Desirat** also has boutiques in two locations and an interesting exhibition looking at the typical aromas in Rhone wines *(07340 Saint Desirat and 07370 Sarras, 04 75 34 22 05; www.cave-saint-desirat.com)*

Tournon-sur-Rhône★

Situated at the foot of striking granite hills, Tournon is a busy market town. Shady quaysides, the ramparts of the old castle and hilltop ruins make for a quintessential Rhône Valley scene. Built by the lords of Tournon, the **château** dates from the 14C and 15C. The inner courtyard is accessed via a venerable set of double doors. Inside, the **Chateau-Musée Rhodanien** focuses on the Rhône's water traffic and boatmen, as well as local figures such as the sculptor Gimond, a pupil of Maillol, the publisher Charles Forot, and the Ardèche engineer Marc Seguin who in 1825 built the first metal suspension bridge over the river; demolished in 1965, it was subsequently reconstructed using more modern structural techniques. Its revolutionary cabled column system is still in use in America (*open Jul–Aug 10am–noon &, 2–6pm; late Mar–May and Sept–Oct Thu–Tue 2–6pm; Jun daily 2–6pm; 3.50€: 04 75 08 10 30; www.ville-tournon.com)*. On leaving, head to the **terraces**★ for a splendid view over the town and the Rhône.

Cross the Seguin footbridge to Tain-l'Hermitage, leaving behind the slopes of Saint Joseph and entering the **Hermitage** and **Crozes-Hermitage** AOCs, on the hill and on the plain respectively.

Tain-l'Hermitage

Home to the famous Hermitage and Crozes-Hermitage appellations (the latter, extending to some 1,467ha, is the largest vineyard of the northern Côtes du Rhône) this large and peaceful town has a multitude of wine cellars, and a vine covered hillside overlooks its streets. A stone's throw from the river, there are some lovely walks to enjoy – perhaps after a drink at the Café de Nice situated on the banks of the Rhône (t04 75 08 01 56, fine views of the charming town of Tournon, accessibly via a pedestrian bridge over the river). On the right bank heading north, the Promenade Robert-Schumann hugs the river for over 1km with panoramic views of Tournon.

Down in the far left corner of Place du Taurobole, Rue de l'Hermitage opens onto a steep paved pathway (*20mins there and back*) leading to the *belvédère* Pierre Aiguille and the chapelle Saint Christophe; from here there are fine views over the Hermitage vineyards, the river and the Ardèche département. Note the geography, ideally suited to winemaking; shielded from chill north winds, the south facing slopes benefit from a Mediterranean microclimate.

A fine choice of wines is available from the **Cave Coopérative de Tain-l'Hermitage** and from **Paul Jaboulet Ainé** (*Tastings take place at their Vineum boutique; See Shopping Guide)*. One of the Rhone's most famous producers, **Michel Chapoutier**, is also based in Tain l'Hermitage, and you shouldn't leave without taking the opportunity to taste his excellent biodynamic wines *(see Shopping Guide)*.

Head S out of Tournon along Rue du Dr-Cadet and Rue Greffieux towards Saint Romain-de-Lerps.

Panoramic route★★★

Following a ridge, this route offers some extraordinary views. The steep twisting climb is dizzying. Soon the entire Valentinoise plain is visible, the Vercors ridge away to the east. A little further along, the Gorges du Doux open up to the right.

In the village of Plats on the plateau, turn left onto the GR 42 at the war memorial. Note the "tower" of St-Romain-de-Lerps on leaving the village.

Panorama of Saint-Romain-de-Lerps★★★

Two viewing platforms have been sited on either side of a little chapel close to the "tower", surmounted by a transmitter mast. The expansive view takes in 13 *départements* and is one of the most impressive in the Rhône valley.

From St-Romain-de-Lerps, the D 287 leads down to St-Péray and offers some remarkable views of the Valence basin.

In the village of Châteaubourg, the **Domaine Eric and Joel Durand** is worth a visit *(see Shopping Guide)*.

Saint-Péray

Valence's principal suburb, the large town of St-Péray sprawls between housing estates and vineyards. Along with **AOC Cornas** (red wines), 2km north on the N 86 (visit the **Domaine Alain Voge** in the tiny appellation of **Cornas**, the **appellation Saint-Péray** is the last of the vineyards of the northern Côtes du Rhône. The increasingly sought-after **Domaine du Tunnel** is an excellent visit. *See Shopping Guide.*

As a parting gesture, climb to the ruins of the **Château de Crussol**, where the **site**★★★ offers a last chance to see the Valence plain, the Vercors and the Alps.

Valence★

The city is dominated by its Roman-era **cathedral**, rebuilt in the 17C in its original style. Take a stroll through the historic centre with its maze of back streets. On the Grande-Rue, note the **Maison des Têtes**★★, and drink in the lovely **view**★★ of the **Montagne de Crussol** from the **Champ-de-Mars**.

CLAIRETTE DE DIE

150km round trip from Valence. Allow a day. Michelin Map 332, F 5; local p393.

Sited in a hollow surrounded by mountains and high hills, the city is well off the beaten track and most easily approached from the west. Opt instead for the twisting minor roads and head over either the Chaudière, Rousseau or Menée pass to reach the Diois, an attractive landscape of vines, fruit trees and lavender to which Die has given its name.

The city is surrounded by vineyards where Clairette and Muscat make some memorable sparkling wines with low alcohol and a natural sweetness.

Die★

An important crossroads in Antiquity, Die is today a small market town best known for the production of **Clairette-de-Die**; a good example can be obtained from **Cave de Die Jaillance** (*see Shopping Guide*). The other local AOC is **Chatillon-en-Diois**, producing red and white wines from the slopes of the 2,000m Glandasse massif.

The itinerary takes in the **Roman ramparts**, 3m-thick walls which in the 3C stretched for some 2km. Their remains can be followed from the northeast of the town, by the tourist office at **Porte St-Marcel**, to the Cathedral (its wrought iron bell tower is a landmark on approaching Die). The Town Hall is the former bishop's palace. Inside the **Chapelle St-Nicolas**, an 11C private oratory, note the fine 12C mosaic work depicting the Universe (*30min guided tour; ask at tourist office; 2€; 04 75 22 03 03*).

Southern Côtes du Rhône

Olive trees, terraced farming, cypresses... beyond Montélimar one is undoubtedly in Provençe, and no longer in the same Rhône valley as around St-Péray. Gentle villages, plentiful local produce, and frequent markets make this a popular part of France for lazy summer days. The southern Côtes du Rhône has its own distinct identity, its vineyards governed by a Mediterranean climate, chalky soil and the mistral. Even the vines differ from those further north: instead of being trained on vertical supports known as échalas, they are trimmed in a manner which resembles a hand emerging from the soil. It is almost entirely a vast plain on the banks of the Rhône, stretching over four départements (Ardèche, Drôme, Vaucluse and Gard).

- **Population:** 850,000.
- **Info:** rhone-wines.com.
- **Location:** North of Avignon
- **Timing:** Three to four days
- **Don't Miss:** The village of Gigondas
- **Kids:** The Safari Park in Peaugres.

DRIVING TOURS

2 TOUR OF THE VINEYARD VILLAGES

160km from La Garde-Adhémar (Drôme) to Lirac (Gard). Michelin Local Map 332, B-D 7-9. See Itinerary 2 on the map on p393.

Montélimar

This city on the banks of the Rhone is well-known for its nougat, and is the gateway to the Ardèche region. It's pleasant to stroll through the pedestrian-only lanes of the old city, perusing the windows of the small boutiques, or taking a break at a sidewalk café. Don't miss the Place du Marché or the intriguing Musée de la Miniature with its scaled-down collection of furntiure, paintings and sculptures *(19 r. Pierre-Julien; open Jul–Aug 10am–6pm; rest of the year Wed–Sun 2–6pm; closed Jan, Nov 1, Dec 25; 5€; 04 75 53 79 24; www.moureyminiatures.com).*

Drive S from Montélimar by the D 73 toward Donzère.

The route traverses the magnficent **Donzère Pass**★★.

Drive through Donzère and head for La Garde-Adhémar on the D 541.

La Garde-Adhémar

Although not within the Coteaux-du-Tricastin AOC, this village set high above the Tricastin plain is worth a visit for its picturesque limestone houses, vaulted alleyways and winding lanes spanned by arches. An important stronghold of the Adhémar family in the Middle Ages, its **Romanesque church**★ is notable for the attractive silhouette of its two storey octagonal bell tower surmounted by a squat pyramid. Close by, the **Chapelle des Péniténts** has 12C twin west windows, visible from the church square. From the terrace there is a fine **view**★ over the plain, dominated by the Vivarais foothills, most notably the Dent de Rez. Below is the **Jardin des Herbes**, where over 200 species of aromatic and medicinal plants are cultivated.

Rejoin the D 158 and head S.

Saint-Paul-Trois-Châteaux

The village is surrounded by the vineyards of **AOC Côteaux-du-Tricastin**. Comprising five red grape varieties, the appellation takes in 21 communes.
The vines flourish among lavender fields, olive groves and truffle oaks (the truffle is one of the great natural resources of the Tricastin plain). The route leads to the **cathedral**★, built in the 11C and 12C, a fine example of Provençal Romanesque architecture.

Located in the tourist office behind the apse of the cathedral, the **Maison de la Truffe et du Tricastin** is an exhibition of posters, showcases and a video presentation on the cultivation and marketing of truffles. Tricastin's "black diamond" is a highly prized – and very costly – ingredient in many tasty local dishes. In the vaulted cellars below, wines from the Tricastin hills are on display, along with a selection of antique winemaking equipment *(open Jun–Sept Tue–Sat 9.30am–12.30pm & 2.30–6.30pm; Sun 10am–noon & 2.30–6.30pm, Mon 2.30–6.30pm; Oct–Nov & Mar–May Tue–Sat 9am–noon & 2–6pm, Mon 2–6pm; Dec–Feb Tue–Sat 9am-noon & 2–6pm, Mon 2–6pm. Closed public holidays. 3.50€. 04 75 96 61 29).*

Head SE on the D 59 before turning right onto the D 59A.

Beyond Saint-Restitut, the **route des carrières** leads across a limestone plateau, passing truffle oaks and open-cast quarries, worked between the 18C and the 20C.

Return to the D 59 and turn right.

Suze-la-Rousse

The principal town of Medieval Tricastin, the alleyways of Suze wind up the left bank of the Lez. Behind its substantial walls, the town's *calades* (fine Renaissance houses), massive Romanesque church, 17C *halle aux grains*, and old town hall with attractive 15C and 16C façade make this a rewarding place for a stroll.
An imposing **château** sits atop the Colline de la Garenne. This is reached by a path through a 30ha truffle oak plantation. The exterior of the 14C building is a fine example of Medieval military architecture, while its interior was remodelled during the Renaissance, as was the inner courtyard *(visit by 45min guided tour Jul–Aug 9.30–11.30am & 2–6pm; Sept–Jun 9.30–11.30am & 2–5.30pm; closed Tue Nov-Mar; closed Jan 1, Dec 25; 3.50€; 04 75 04 81 44).*

The château is home to the **Université du Vin**; with a range of long and short wine and food courses for amateurs. At the foot of the château, the vine garden is a collection of around 70 grape varieties which allows students and visitors to examine seasonal changes in the plants *(26790 Suze-la-Rousse; introduction to wine tasting weekend 350€, one day combined wine and cookery course 185€, truffle tasting day 200€; 04 75 97 21 30; www-universite-du-vin.com).*

Head E out of Suze towards Visan on the D 251 before joining the D 161. Beyond Visan head SE on the D 20.

Chapelle Notre-Dame-des-Vignes

Open Tue–Sun 10–11.30am & 3–5.30pm. Closed Sun morning. 04 90 41 90 50.

In the chancel of this 13C chapel is a painted wooden statue of the Virgin, the focus of a pilgrimage on 8 September each year. According to legend, it was discovered by a winemaker in a field. Removed to the parish church, the statue miraculously turned up in the same field on three further occasions. The chapel was erected in response to this miracle.

Return to Visan and head N towards Valréas on the D 976.

Valréas

Although well within the Drôme département, this small town producing **Côtes-du-Rhône-Villages** is part of the Vaucluse département, an anomaly which it has shared with the neighbouring villages of Grillon, Richerenches and Visan since 1791. Together they were known as the **"**Enclave des Papes**"**, a reference to their one-time allegiance to the Avignon popes, until 2008, when Chateauneuf-du-Pape took exception and received legal protection for the word 'pope' on French wine bottles. It is still a very pretty place to visit - in the town, the **Tour de Tivoli** is all that remains of the ramparts, today superseded by a ring of shady planted boulevards. At the heart of the alleyways forming the old town are some fine old buildings. The **town hall** has a majestic 15C façade overlooking Place Aristide-Briand. The south door of the church of **Notre-Dame-de-Nazareth** is a good example of Provençal Romanesque architecture. On Place Pie a fine wrought-iron grille opens onto an alley leading to the beautiful 17C **Chapelle des Pénitents-Blancs** *(open Jul–Aug Mon–Fri 10am–noon & 3–5pm; 04 90 35 04 71).*

Also known as the tour de l'Horloge, the tour du château Ripert dominates the garden; from the terrace there is a fine **view** over old Valréas and the Tricastin hills. On the outskirts of Visan, **Domaine la Guintrandy** makes an interesting visit *(see Shopping Guide).*

Head E on the D 541 towards St-Pantaléon-les-Vignes.

St-Pantaléon-les-Vignes

Laid out by the wine makers of the appellation Côtes-du-Rhône-Villages-St-Pantaléon-les-Vignes and **Rousset-les-Vignes**, the **Sentier des Terroirs** has two trails (*2hr30min each, or do both for a 5hr walk*) which wind through pleasant vineyards surrounded by olive groves, lavender fields, pines and oaks. Along the paths are bottle shaped signs, each relating to a chapter in the free guide to the area *(available from the cellars and town halls of the two villages).*

Continue along the D 541, then turn right onto the D 538 to Nyons.

Nyons

Down on the Tricastin plain yet well protected by the mountains, the town sits at the mouth of the Eygues valley. Brought by the Greeks 2,500 years ago, the olive tree thrives here on account of the mild climate. From November to February, the oil mills are operational; some continue to employ traditional methods. The **Musée de l'Olivier** focuses on the history of olive cultivation and oil manufacture *(Pl. Olivier-de-Serres; open*

Jun-Sept Mon-Sat 10-11am & 3–6pm; Oct-May Mon-Sat 3-6pm; 2€; 04 75 26 12 12).

The humpbacked **Pont Roman**★ (or Vieux Pont) was built in the 13-14C. Its 40m arch is one of the most striking in the Midi.

Join the D 94, heading right towards Tulette. Beyond Pont-de-Mirabel, turn right onto the D 190 to reach Vinsobres.

Vinsobres

Perched high above the Eygues valley, this attractive village produces **AOC Vinsobres**. Steep lanes, old stone houses and vaulted passageways are sandwiched between two churches, one Protestant (at the top of the village), one Catholic (at the bottom). From the square in front of the former, there is a fine **view** over the vineyards and the mountains of Garde-Grosse and Ventoux.

There are a number of **signposted routes** starting from the tourist office allowing cyclists and walkers to explore the area's vineyards, olive groves, orchards and lavender fields. Taste both the wines and the excellent estate-produced olive oil at **Domaine Peysson** *(t04 75 26 68 34 ; open 10am-noon & 2-6pm, www.domaine-peysson.com)*. There is also a good boutique at the **Cave de Prieuré**, part of the Cellier des Dauphins, one of the largest cooperatives in the Rhône *(see Shopping Guide)*.

Rejoin the D 94 and continue in the direction of Tulette.

Saint-Maurice-sur-Eygues

At the top of this sleepy Drôme Provençale village beneath plane trees is **Domaine Viret** (signposted), known for its blending of organic and biodynamic winemaking on a 50ha vineyard surrounded by oaks and pines. For the last few years, Alain and Philippe Viret have been busy with an ambitious and unusual project: to construct a cellar using the architectural philosophy of the ancient world and the same methods employed by the builders of medieval cathedrals. *(26110 St-Maurice-sur-Eygues; open 9am–noon & 3–7pm; 04 75 27 62 77; www.domaine-viret.com).*

Continue along the D94 before turning left at the first junction (D 20), before turning right onto the D 51 towards Cairanne.

The route heads through vineyards, leading away from the Baronnies mountains and past the Col du Debat before revealing a panorama over the Dentelles de Montmirail and Mont Ventoux.

Cairanne

Known for its red wine with a powerful bouquet, this old village overlooking vineyards high in the Vaucluse is the capital of the **Côtes-du-Rhône-Villages** appellation. From the lanes between its two chapels dedicated to **St-Roch** (1726) and **Notre-Dame des Excès** (1631), both built in response to plague outbreaks, there are fine **views**★ over vineyards to the Dentelles de Montmirail and Mont Ventoux.

The tourist office provides a free booklet suggesting walks through the old village and the vineyards *(04 90 30 76 53)*.

The **Domaine Brusset** and **l'Oratoire St-Martin** produce some good wines *(see Shopping Guide)*.

The **Parcours Sensoriel de la Cave de Cairanne** is a great way to learn about Rhône wines and appellation Côtes-du-Rhône-Villages-Cairanne in particular. This interactive sensory exhibition (children will not be bored) is located in the cellars of the Cairanne co-operative. Vistors can make their own way round or be guided by a sommelier (who will provide tips on tasting). Combined wine and chocolate events are held in conjunction with the Castelin de Châteauneuf-du-Pape chocolate factory *(Rte.de Bollène, 84290 Cairanne; 1hr 30min guided tour daily 9am-5.30pm 6€; reservation suggested; 04 90 30 82 05, www.cairanne.com).*

The **Écurie du Muzet** gives riders the opportunity to enjoy the vineyard from the saddle (or by horse drawn carriage). Itinerary includes a ride through the

Dentelles de Montmirail in the vicinity of Gigondas, surrounded by vines

vines, a guide to tasting in the Côtes-du-Rhône-Villages-Cairanne cellars and a visit to the Parcours Sensoriel de la Cave de Cairanne *(Quartier le Muzet, 84290 Cairanne; open summer 7–11am & 4.30–7pm; winter 9am–4pm; 04 90 46 12 99, ecuriesdumuzet@aol.com).*

Head E on the D 69 towards Rasteau.

Rasteau

Two attractions draw visitors here: the sweet wine AOC **Rasteau**, produced from vines growing 300m up in the foothills of the Baronnies massif, and the **Musée des Vignerons**, with its collection of antique winemaking tools and bottles *(open Jul–Aug 10am–6pm; mid-Apr–late Jun & Sept 2–6pm; closed early Oct–mid-Apr, Sun and Tue; 3€; 04 90 83 71 79; www.beaurenard.fr).* The **Cave de Rasteau** cooperative cellar has also made great quality strides in recent years, and runs some excellent wine tourism activities from gourmet walks to a large tasting cellar *(t04 90 10 90 14, open Jul-Sept 9am-7pm, Oct-Jun 9am-12.30pm & 2-6pm www.rasteau.com).*

Continue to village of Roaix, then head right towards Séguret on the D 88.

Séguret★

On entering this beautiful village rising in tiers at the foot of a hill, head on from the main street into a vaulted passageway which leads past the attractive 15C Comtadine des Mascarons fountain, the 14C belfry, and the 12C church of St-Denis. From the information board point in the square, there is a good view of the Dentelles and the Comtat plain. A ruined Medieval castle and a network of steep lanes lined with old houses add to the charm of the place and encourage visitors to linger. The vineyards produce **Côtes-du-Rhône-Villages-Séguret**, reds with a hint of almonds and aromatic rosés, which may be sampled at **Domaine du Cabasse** *(see Shopping Guide).*

On leaving Séguret, head left onto the D 23 towards Sablet, then proceed along the D 7 and the D 79.

In Sablet, wines at the **Domaine Piaugier** are carefully and respectfully made *(see Shopping Guide).*

Gigondas

Against the backdrop of the Dentelles de Montmirail, this chic village is well known for **AOC Gigondas**, a full bodied red wine made from the Grenache grape and one of the big names in the lower Rhône valley along with Châteauneuf-du-Pape. There are numerous tasting and direct buying opportunities, notably at **Domaine Les Goubert** *(see Shopping Guide)* and at **Caveau du Gigondas** that has recently opened a wine and food matching bar in the central square called the Caveau des Gourmets *(book-*

ing for wine matching 04 90 36 34 82, plus see Shopping Guide). A climb to the top of the ramparts is rewarded with a sublime **view★** over vineyards and the Cévennes. A short drive from Gigondas, on the road to Beaumes-de-Venise, is the wine-growing village of **Vacqueras**, with less obvious charm than Gigondas but with a number of interesting producers to visit, and a good wine store, Le Taverne de Raimbaut *(t04 90 37 45 20)*, where you can taste and buy wines at domaine prices.

Continue on D 7.

Beaumes-de-Venise

In the southern foothills of the Dentelles de Montmirail, this large village derives its name from the caves overlooking it (*baume* is the Provençal word for cave) and a variant of Venaissin. The subtly aromatic and famous **Muscat-de-Beaumes-de-Venise** hails from here, as visitors arriving along the D 7 will realise: to the right of the first roundabout is the imposing **Cave Cooperative des Vignerons de Beaumes-de-Venise** *(see Shopping Guide)*; adjacent to the shop is an exhibition tracing the history and character of the local AOC. Also worth a visit is **Domaine Vaubelle** *(see Shopping Guide)*.

The Cave des Vignerons and the tourist office provide directions to **two signposted trails** (with explanatory boards on viticulture) which wind around the Dentelles exploring the Trias terroir (one of four geological areas in which Beaumes de Venise grows); a 9km red circuit *(3hr 30min)* and a 4km green circuit *(1hr 40min)*.

Head S on the D 90. Turn right onto the D 55 at Aubignan, then right again onto the D 950. Before reaching the N 7, fork right onto the D 72 which crosses over the motorway. Then turn left onto the D 68 towards Châteauneuf-du-Pape.

Châteauneuf-du-Pape

The Avignon Papacy's involvement in Châteauneuf's vineyards led to the adoption of the town's current name in the 18C. Ruined by the phylloxera outbreak in 1866, the vineyards were subsequently replanted, and in 1923 the local wine growers laid down strict rules to guarantee quality, including territorial limits, grape dimensions, choice of grape varieties (13 permitted, although rarely all used), and production techniques. Today, 300 vineyards grow 3,164 ha of vines. Châteauneuf's bottles proudly display their papal origins, with a tiara and the crossed keys of St Peter chased into the glass.

From the papal fortress, there is a superb **view★★** of the Rhône valley, Roquemaure and the château de l'Hers, Avignon with the Papal Palace rising from the Alpilles; also visible is the Luberon, the Vaucluse plateau, Mont Ventoux, the Dentelles de Montmirail, the Baronnies massif, and the Montagne de la Lance. The town itself is very attractive, filled with small coffee shops, restaurants and a few good hotels.

3km from Châteauneuf on the Sorgues road, **Château La Nerthe** is the appellation's oldest vineyard *(see Shopping)*.

The Pope's favourite tipple

Pliny the Elder referred to Muscat de Beaumes de Venise as early as the 1C, but it was the Avignon Pope Clement V who secured its place in posterity. Such was his liking for Muscat that he had 70ha of vines planted on the hillsides of Beaumes de Venise. After the Papacy's return to Rome the vineyard fell into abeyance. Production did not start again until the end of the 19C and it was not until 1943 that it achieved AOC status. The appellation today covers some 500ha of well established terraces in hilly terrain. Its unusual flavour is derived from the Muscat blanc à petit grain grape, giving an exotic floral bouquet.

The grapes are still hand picked from the trained vines. Used for cooking and a popular aperitif, Muscat is a great accompaniment to foie gras, strong flavoured dishes, puddings and Roquefort.

Emblem of the Holy See on a bottle of Châteauneuf-du-Pape

S. Sauvignier/MICHELIN

Before stopping for a tasting at **Maison des vins Vinadéa** *(see Shopping Guide)*, a visit to the **Musée du Vin Brotte** is a must. The owners of Domaine Barville in Châteauneuf also own this excellent museum looking at everything from soil types to the work of the wine makers (there is an extensive collection of antique winemaking equipment). Visitors will learn that Châteauneuf-du-Pape is the cradle of French AOCs, thanks to Baron Le Roy, a local landowner who, along with the Bordeaux Senator Jean Capus, brought about the 1935 legislation creating the AOC system *(Cave Brotte-Père Anselme; open early Apr–mid-Oct 9am–1pm & 2–7pm; mid Oct–mid-Apr 9am–noon & 2–6pm; closed Jan 1, Dec 25; no charge; 04 90 83 70 07; www.brotte.com.)*

Head out of the village towards Roquemaure on the D 17, before forking right at the "circuit touristique" signpost.

An ideal motoring or biking excursion (be prepared for hils), this 8km circuit winds round the steep minor roads as they weave between the vineyards, giving a rare close up view of the unusual terroir that constitutes **Châteauneuf-du-Pape**, the driest of the Rhône valley. Its reddish soil is strewn with large rounded pebbles. The sun's heat it absorbs by day benefits the vines by night, thereby optimising the ripening grapes. The route takes in numerous domaines where you may stop for a tasting.

Head W out of Châteauneuf-du-Pape on the D 17. Turn left onto the D 976 which crosses over the Rhone.

Roquemaure

This large winemaking town retains some old houses, including that of Cardinal Bertrand near the church. The Tour des Princes de Soubise is the most important remnant of the château where Clement V, the first Avignon pope, died on 20 April 1320. On the opposite bank, the château de l'Hers with its machicolated tower seems to guard over its vineyard.

Every year, the weekend nearest to 14 February witnesses festivities, including a commemoration of the arrival of the relics of St Valentine in the village. These were purchased in Rome by a winemaker in 1868 and offered to the parish to protect the local vines against the phylloxera outbreak.

Located in Château de Clary, the **Académie du Vin et du Goût** was revived in 2003 by wine and olive oil enthusiasts and has become a cultural centre dedicated to wine and gastronomy. The traditional interior has been retained, making an attractive setting for tasting courses, cookery lessons and gastronomic events *(Château de Clary, 30150 Roquemaure; open May–Sept daily 9am–7pm; Oct–Apr daily 9am–6pm; closed Dec 23–Jan 3; 04 66 33 04 86; www.academie-du-vin.com)*.

Head SW on the D 976.

Tavel

Sited on the left bank of the Rhône, this Côtes du Rhône Gardoises village is renowned for its long-established rosé. Fuller-bodied and darker than the wines of Provence, it became the first rosé to be accorded **AOC status** in 1936. Its 952ha of vineyards are all within the *commune*, a striking terroir composed of rounded pebbles, sand and chalky soil. Quite apart from its viticulture, Tavel has another claim to fame: its quarries, now exhausted, supplied the stones used for the Statue of Liberty's foundations. Good wine tastings are on offer at **Domaine de la Mordorée** and **Chateau d'Aqueria** (*see Shopping Guide*). The **circuit des Vignobles**, pleasant by car or on a bike, is punctuated by milestones hewn from the local rocks, with a viewing point (picnic area) from where a fine **panorama** of the vines and village may be enjoyed. North of Tavel on the D 26 is **Lirac**, the centre of an **AOC** which produces robust reds and rosés. The Medieval village of **St Lauren des Arbres**, just to the north of Lirac, is also worth a visit.

3 CÔTES DU VENTOUX

75km from Vaison-la-Romaine to Carpentras (Vaucluse). Michelin Local Map 332, D-E 8-9. *See Itinerary 3 on the map p393.*

At a height of 1,909m, the "Giant of Provence" is classified by UNESCO as a biosphere reserve, with its eponymous vineyard below it. Encompassing some 51 communes (7,450ha) from Vaison-la-Romaine in the north to Apt in the south, it produces fruity wines witha pleasant balance.

From Vaison-la-Romaine head SE on D 938; left on D 54 after 3.5km.

Entrechaux

Once property of the bishops of Vaison, the village is dominated by the hilltop ruins of its château. There are also two estates here where **appellation Côtes-du-Ventoux** wines may be tasted.

Return to Malaucène road via D 13

Malaucène

The 14C fortified church replaced a Roman building; inside there is a Provençal Romanesque nave and carved musical instruments in the 18C organ loft. Adjacent to the church, Porte Soubeyran leads to the **old town**: its fountains, wash-houses, oratories, and at its centre an old belfry crowned by a wrought iron bell tower make this an atmospheric spot. To the left of the church, a path leads to the Calvary, from where there are fine views of the Drôme mountains and Mont Ventoux.

Turn left onto the D 974.

Chapelle Notre-Dame-du Groseau

This chapel is all that remains of a Benedictine abbey. The square building *(closed to the public)* is the chancel of the 12C abbey.

Source Vauclusienne du Groseau

To the left of the road, water pours forth from several fissures at the foot of a steep slope (over 100m) to form a clear pool beneath fine trees. The Romans built an aqueduct to carry water from here to Vaison-la-Romaine.

The route climbs northwards up the steepest face of Mont Ventoux, passing pastureland and pine woods near the Mont Serein refuge. From the viewing point beyond the Ramayettes hut, there is a fine **view**★ of the Baronnies massif and the summit of La Plate.

The panorama becomes broader as the route climbs, revealing the Dentelles de Montmirail and the heights of the western Rhône and the Alps.

Summit of Mont Ventoux★★★

The peak is the site of a military radar station and to the north a radio mast. From the platform on the south side, there is a vast **view**★★★ (information board) from the Pelvoux massif to the Cévennes via the Luberon, the Ste-Victoire peak, the Estaques hills, Marseille, the Étang de Berre, the Alpilles, the Rhône valley and (in good weather) the Canigou.

The descent is down the south face; constructed in 1885, the original hairpin route drops from 1,909m to 310m at Bédoin in just 22km.

Bédoin

Home to four winemaking *domaines*, the picturesque streets in this hilltop village lead to a Jesuit-style church.

D 974 S, then D 14 to Mormoiron.

Perched on a hillside, Bonnieux is a typical Luberon village

G. Magnin/MICHELIN

Mormoiron

The **Moulin à Musique Mécanique** has an interesting collection of items, allowing visitors to see and more importantly hear a serinette dating to 1740, a grand orchestrion from 1900 (nine instruments), a carousel organ and several barrel organs *(Rte. de Carpentras, visit by 1hr guided tour May-Oct Wed 3pm; 5€; 04 90 61 75 91).*

Head W on the D 942 to Carpentras.

CÔTES DU LUBERON

On the left bank of the Rhône and halfway between the Alps and the Mediterranean is the mountainous barrier of the Luberon. Between Calavon and Durance, some 2,530ha of north and south-facing slopes are given over to **AOC Côtes du Luberon**, producing an annual average of 98,000hl, 60% of which is red. The alpine influence on the climate explains why a significant proportion (22%) of its output is white. The Luberon's wines are full-bodied and characterful with a wild and fruity bouquet.

4 THE PETIT LUBERON

41km from Apt to Cavaillon (Vaucluse). Michelin Local Map 332, E-F 10-11. *See Itinerary 4 on the map on p393.*

Apt

Known for its ochre and crystallised fruit, Apt is a pleasant backwater. The quiet charm of its alleyways and its busy Saturday morning market, its stalls laden with fruit and vegetables, Provençal fabrics, infinite varieties of honey and craftware, invite the visitor to linger far longer than planned.

Head W out of Apt on the D 3 towards Bonnieux and continue for 6km.

Chateau de l'Isolette

Rte. de Bonnieux, 84400 Apt. Open Mon-Sat 8.30–11.30am & 2–5.30pm. Closed Dec 25–Jan 1 & public holidays. 04 90 74 16 70.
Against this magnificent backdrop, visitors can indulge in some tasting and direct buying in the cellars before visiting the little winemaking museum.

Bonnieux★

Perched on a hillside, the village dominates the valley where the Petit Luberon gives way to the Grand Luberon. **Haut-Bonnieux** is approached along the vaulted Rue de la Mairie from Place de la Liberté, a steep climb leading to a terrace below the old church. From this point, there is a delightful **view**★ of the Calavon valley, with the precipitous village of Lacoste to the left, while to the right Gordes and Roussillon stand out from red rocks in the direction of the Vaucluse plain.
On rejoining the D 36, a visit can be paid to the **Musée de la Boulangerie**, an interesting exhibit exploring the baker's trade and what bread has meant through the ages *(open Jul–Aug 10am–1pm & 2–6pm; Apr–Jun & Sept–Oct 10am–12.30pm & 2.30–6pm; closed Tue, early Nov–late Mar, May 1 & Dec 25; 3.50€. 04 90 75 88 34).*
A short way outside of Bonnieux **Château la Canourgue** was the location for the 2006 film *A Good Year* (*see Shopping Guide*).

Head S out of Bonnieux on the D 3 before turning left onto the D 109.

The road winds up the side of the Petit Luberon with Bonnieux to the rear before

Lacoste looms into view; the jagged walls of its imposing ruined castle have been partially rebuilt; it once belonged to the Sade family. Imprisoned on numerous occasions and condemned to death in his absence, the infamous Marquis de Sade sought refuge here in 1774.

Ménerbes★

Also perched on a rocky outcrop, Ménerbes is largely responsible for the Luberon's ever increasing popularity. It is an architectural gem, with narrow alleys, imposing residences and attractive squares. Tucked away behind high walls, the houses built by the merchant class now belong to film stars and millionaires, and many have hosted writers and artists including Picasso, Nicolas de Staël, Albert Camus and Peter Mayle. Through such famous names Ménerbes has acquired an international reputation but, unlike some of its neighbours, it has not succumbed to the commercial pressures of tourism. Here, an atmosphere of lively conviviality prevails, perhaps best experienced in the café Le Progrès in Place Albert-Roule.

Located in the **Domaine de la Citadelle**, the **Musée du Tire-Bouchon** has a collection of over 1,000 corkscrews from around the world (*on the way out of Ménerbes, 2.5km on the D 3 towards Cavaillon; Domaine de la Citadelle; open Apr–Oct daily10am–noon & 2–7pm; Nov–Mar Mon–Fri 9am–noon & 2–6pm, Sat 10am–noon; closed public holidays; 4€; 04 90 72 41 58; www.domainedelacitadelle.com).*

Head S on the D 3 before joining the D 188.

Oppède-le-Vieux★

Park in the car park just beyond the village before exploring on foot.

Occupying an impressive **site**★ on a spur, this village hewn into the rock was until recently partly in ruins, but has experienced a revival in its fortunes thanks to the efforts of artists and literary figures who have striven to restore it without detracting from its authenticity. Park your car at the base of the village and then walk from the ancient Place du Bourg to the upper village, with its collegiate church and the ruins of its château. From the terrace in front of the church, there is a fine **view**★ of the Coulon valley, the Vaucluse plateau and Ménerbes.

Created with the assistance of the Parc Naturel Regional du Luberon, the **Sentier des Vignerons d'Oppède** is an excellent way to get to know the local terroir. The route, marked by signs depicting a bunch of grapes, heads through the vineyards, olive groves and cherry orchards at the foot of Oppède. Along the way are five explanatory boards detailing the grape varieties and winemaking techniques. Pleasant at any time of year, but most interesting during harvest time in September and October *(1hr 30min of easy walking departure point close to the oratoire St-Joseph in Oppède; guidebook available from tourist office and Maison du Parc).*

Head NW on the D 176 and the D 3 and D 2 to the left to reach Cavaillon.

After walking through the vines, the **Cave du Luberon** offers a chance to taste many of the wines *(229, Route de Cavaillon, 84660 Maubec; t04 90 76 91 02; Open May-Aug Mon-Sat 8am-1pm & 2-7pm; www.caveduluberon.com).*

5 THE BASSE DURANCE

42km from Ansouis to Lourmarin (Vaucluse). Michelin Local Map 332, F-G 11.
See Itinerary 5 on the map on p393.

Ansouis

Both a fortress and a residence, the 13C **château**★ is no longer open to the public, but is still an attractive site overlooking this atmospheric country town.

After wandering the alleyways, visitors can conclude with a tasting at **Château Turcan** (*see Shopping Guide*).

Those in search of the unusual should visit the **Musée Extraordinaire**, created by diver Georges Mazoyer. Visitors here will discover an underwater cave that has been recreated with finds during Mazoyer's nearly 50 years of deep-sea diving, complete with corals bathed in a blueish light; a curious find in wine-growing country, the cave reflects the fact that the Luberon region was once beneath the oceans *(r. du Vieux Moulin, open Apr–Sept Wed–Mon 2–7pm; Mar & Oct–Dec Wed–Mon 2–6pm; closed Jn 1, Dec 25; 3.50€; 04 90 09 82 64).*

Head NE out of Ansouis on the D 37 before turning right onto the D 135 towards La Tour-d'Aigues.

La Tour-d'Aigues

Destroyed in an accidental fire in 1780 and sacked by revolutionaries in 1792, the ruined château at the centre of the village makes for a scenic backdrop. What remains of the exterior, notably the monumental gateway and richly decorated façade, shows the splendour of this 16C Renaissance residence. Inside there is a keep and a small chapel, while the cellars house two interesting **museums**, one dedicated to Faïence, the other to rural life *(open Jul–mid-Aug daily 10am-1pm, 2.30-6pm; Apr–Jun & mid-Aug–mid-Oct 10am–1pm & 2.30–6pm (closed Sun, Mon morning & Tue afternoon) ; rest of year times vary; 4.50€; 04 90 07 50 33; www.chateaulatourdaigues.com).*

Given that la Tour d'Aigues is at the heart of the appellation Côtes-du-Luberon, wine buffs might wish to visit **Bastide de Rafinel** *(see Shopping Guide).* Or you can combine winetasting with some exercise at the **Chateau de la Dorgonne**, where walking and hiking paths are marked out through the vineyard *(open daily 9am–7pm; 04 90 07 50 18; www.chateauladorgonne.com).*

Take the D 956 to Pertuis then head W on the D 973. Before reaching Villelaure, turn right following the signs for Château Val Joanis.

Pertuis: Val Joanis

84120 Pertuis. Open Apr–Oct 10am–7pm. Mar Mon–Sat 2–6pm. Dec 10am–7pm. (Christmas market). 04 90 79 20 77. www.val-joanis.com.

Behind the cellars of this winemaking estate are fine terraced gardens laid out on three levels, the first a kitchen garden, the second a flower garden, and the third given over to ornamental trees. Running along its left hand side is a rose arbour, while to the right is an olive grove. Exuding peace and tranquillity, this garden is an island of colour among a sea of vines. A relaxed brunch is available every weekend from mid-May to mid-September.

Rejoin the D 973.

In **Cadenet**, wickerwork is the subject matter of the **Musée de la Vannerie**: on the Durance, the village was once renowned for this activity, harvesting willow trees which grew on the banks of the river *(open 10am–noon & 2.30–6.30pm; closed Sun morning, Tue, Wed afternoon. Closed 1 May. 3.50€. 04 90 68 24 44.*

Lourmarin★

In an exceptional location, Lourmarin is known for its **château**★, built during the 15C and the Renaissance. If you only plan to visit one château in the region, it should be this one, with its fine wood panelled and stone galleries in the old wing, and superb rooms richly decorated with Renaissance style furniture. The grand staircase, ending dramatically with a slender pillar supporting a stone cupola, is another architectural highlight *(open Jun–Aug 10am–6pm; May & Sept 10–11.30am & 2.30-5.30pm; Mar–Apr & Oct 10.30–11.30am & 2.30–4.30pm; Nov–Dec & Feb 10.30–11.30am & 2.30–4pm; Jan weekends 2.30–4pm; closed Jan 1; 5.50€; 04 90 68 15 23; www.chateau-de-lourmarin.com).*

Round off with a tasting at **Château Constantin-Chevalier** *(see Shopping Guide).*

A worthwhile final stop in the Côtes du Luberon is **Château St-Pierre de Méjans** at **Puyvert**, not far from Lourmarin *(2km to the SW on the D 27; see Shopping Guide).*

6 THE COSTIÈRES DE NIMES

60km from St-Gilles (Gard). Michelin Local Map 339, K-L 6-7. *See Itinerary 6 on the map on p393.*

St-Gilles★

Gateway to the Camargue, this important winemaking centre is well known for its **St-Gilles Abbey**, a Unesco masterpiece whose façade includes some of the finest examples of Provençal Romanesque statuary. It is difficult today to fully appreciate the significance of this abbey at its peak; imagine the chancel of the former abbey church extending beyond the existing chancel and, to the south, the cloisters with their courtyard surrounded by the chapterhouse, refectory, kitchens and basement storerooms. This great medieval monument fell victim to the Wars of Religion; what remains is its fine **façade**★★ (including some of the best Romenesque sculpture in the South of France), vestiges of the chancel and the **crypt**★ *(ancient chancel, staircase and crypt: open Jul–Aug Tue–Sun 9am–12.30pm & 3-7pm; Apr–Jun & Sept–Oct Tue–Sun 9am–12.30pm & 2–6pm; Nov-Mar Mon–Fri 8.30am–noon & 1.30–5.30pm, Sat Mar–Nov 9am–noon & 2–5pm; Sat Dec-Feb 10am–noon & 2–6pm; 4€; 04 66 87 41 31).*

Head SW out of St Gilles on the N 572 towards Montpellier.

Flanked by slopes, the route cuts through **AOC Costières-de-Nimes** country; to the left are the Scamandre and Charnier, where reeds are harvested.

Turn left onto the D 779.

At **Gallician**, a classic winemaking town, **Château Mas Neuf** *(see Shopping Guide)* is worth a visit.

In Gallician, turn right onto the minor D 381, then left onto the D 104 to the Canal du Rhône at Sète.

Pont des Tourradons

There is an interesting **view**★ from this marshland bridge, taking in typical Petite Camargue landscape; the dead-straight canal, lakes and reed beds, a marriage of land and sky in silence and solitude. Long horned black bulls graze peacefully in the landscape near **Cailar**; one of the best places to experience the true atmosphere of the Camargue.

Head back along the D 104 then turn right onto the D 352.

Vauvert

Today a suburb of Nîmes, this large winemaking village retains its historic centre, its covered market having been converted into an exhibition centre.

Head W on the N 572. Before Aimargues, turn left onto the D 979 towards Aigues-Mortes.

Saint-Laurent-d'Aigouze

Worth a visit in this large winemaking village is its bullfighting arena erected under the shade of plane trees in the square by the church (the sacristy seems to serve as an enclosure for bulls), where traditional contests take place to mark its feast day *(late Aug).*

Continue along the D 979 before turning left onto the D 58.

The route heads through the sandy-earthed fields of wine and asparagus country. Here and there are large farmhouses under shady pine trees.

After 9.5km, turn left onto the minor D 179 towards Montcalm and St-Gilles

In **Montcalm** are the ruins of a huge 18C residence and, out among the vineyards, a farmhouse chapel dating from the same era.

Return to St-Gilles on the D 179 crossing the marshland of the Camargue Gardoise.

Roman Rhône

Nîmes★★★

When Roman legionaries established a colony here in 31 BC, they built 16km of imposing perimeter walls. Situated on the Domitian Way, the settlement was embellished by fine buildings; a forum with the Maison Carrée to the south, an amphitheatre, a circus, baths and fountains fed by an aqueduct (the Pont du Gard is the most impressive remain). The town reached its height in the 2C, with a population of 25,000 and a building programme including Plotinius' basilica and the Fontaine district.

Nîmes' **amphitheatre**★★★ (late 1C-early 2C) differs from its counterpart at Arles in its detail. The best preserved Roman amphitheatre anywhere, it is a two storey limestone structure of 60 arcades. Inside, an ingenious system of corridors, stairways, galleries and vomitoria allowed spectators to exit the amphitheatre within a few minutes (*open Jun–Aug 9am–8pm; Apr–May & Sept 9am–6.30pm; Nov–Feb 9.30am–4.30pm; closed performance days; 7.70€; 04 66 76 72 77; www.arenes-nimes.com).*

The best preserved of Roman temples, the **Maison Carrée**★★★ dates from the reign of Augustus (late 1C BC). The purity of line, proportions and fluted columns suggest a Greek influence; above all, it owes its charm to its almost fragile character, in keeping with the city's other monuments. *(open Jun–Aug 9am–7pm; Apr–May & Sept 9am–6.30pm; Mar & Oct 9.30am–5.30pm; Nov–Feb 9.30am–4.30pm; 4.50€).*

In Gallo-Roman times, the area now covered by the **Jardin de la Fontaine**★★ was the site of baths, a theatre and a temple. Laid out by an 18C military engineer, the garden follows the plan of the ancient Nemausus fountain. To the left of the fountain is the temple of Diana, destroyed in 1577 during the Wars of Religion; surrounded by greenery, it makes for a romantic backdrop. The verdant Mont Cavalier is crowned by the symbol of the city, the **Tour Magne**★, the most imposing vestige of the Roman perimeter walls. This three storey polygonal tower is 34m high (*open Jun–Aug 9am–7pm; Apr–May & Sept 9am–6pm; Feb & Oct 9am–5.30pm; Jan-Mar 9.30am–4.30pm; 2.70€; combined ticket for "Roman Nîmes" including amphitheatre, Maison Carrée and Tour Magne 9.80€; 04 66 67 65 56).*

Gallo-Roman city of Saint-Romain-en Gal★★

In Vienne, 31km S of Lyon by the N7.
Open Tue-Sun 10am–6pm.
Closed Jan 1, May 1, Nov 1, Dec 25.
3.80€. 04 74 53 74 02.

On the right bank of the Rhone, excavations of the site have unearthed a built up area with opulent villas, shops, artisans' workshops and baths. The most impressive finds are on show in the **Museum**★, including the **Dieux Oceans mosaic**★; the mosaics are the principal feature of this site. These floor decorations, often inspired by mythology, give an insight into the tastes of their original owners. Thus, the Orpheus mosaic affirms the triumph of culture over nature. The exceptional **Échassiers wall painting**★ demonstrates the refinement of the interior decoration.

Orange★★

Literally the gateway to this bustling, attractive city, the **triumphal arch**★★ marks the northern approach to Orange, situated on the Via Agrippa, the road linking Lyon and Arles *(on entering the town along the N 7; free parking at the crossroads)*. Remarkable for its size (the third largest surviving arch at 19.21m high, 19.57m wide and 8.40m deep), it is also the best preserved of its kind; the north side is particularly complete in its decoration. Built around 20 BC and subsequently dedicated to Tiberius, it commemorates the exploits of the veterans of the Second Legion. Composed of three archways flanked by columns, and originally surmounted by a bronze chariot and two trophies, it has two peculiarities; the triangular pediment above the central archway and the two attic storeys.

Théâtre Antique★★★

Rue Madeleine Roch. Open 9am. Closes 4.30–7pm depending on season. 7.90€. 04 90 51 17 60. www.theatre-antique.com.

Built during the reign of Augustus (sometimes known as Octavian) this is the only Roman theatre to retain its stage wall intact, an imposing structure some 103m long and 36m high. Its upper storey is composed of two rows of corbels with holes which held the poles supporting the *velum*, an awning to shelter spectators from the sun. The semicircular cavea could accommodate up to 7 000 people, ranged in accordance with their status. Below, the orchestra had rows of movable seats for high ranking spectators. The stage, fitted with wooden flooring under which the machinery was kept, is 61m wide and 9m deep.

The stage wall had a rich decorative scheme composed of marble facing, stucco, mosaics, several tiers of columns, and niches for statues including that of Augustus, now returned to its original position. The wall has three doors: at the centre the royal door (for the principal actors), and two side doors (for minor actors).

Vaison la Romaine★★

Opening times vary; closed Jan 1, Dec 25, Village closed Tue morning; 7€, ticket also admits to other monuments; 04 90 36 50 48; www.vaison-la-romaine.com).

Spread over 15ha, this vast expanse of Roman ruins allows the visitor to get a real understanding of daily life in the ancient settlement of Vasio. The excavated area covers the outskirts of the Gallo-Roman city, while its centre (the Forum and immediate vicinity) lies under the modern town. Presently, the excavations are progressing towards the cathedral in La Villasse district and around the Puymin hill, where a shopping quarter and a sumptuous house **(Peacock villa)** with mosaic decoration have been unearthed. On the northern side of the ancient city are the ruins of the baths (*not open to the public),* in use until the late 3C.

Pont du Gard★★★

24km NE of Nîmes on the N 86 and then the D 19. Free access to the bridge. Parking on either side 7-1am. 5€ (no time limit), no charge if you purchase a day pass which includes entrance to the cinema, museum and kids activities (10€).

One of the wonders of Roman architecture, this 1C masterpiece has bronzed stonework, a backdrop of hills covered in verdant Mediterranean flora, and the green waters of the Gardon, all of which combine to create a vision of splendour. The Romans attached great importance to the quality of the water supplied to their cities; the Pont du Gard formed part of the 50km Nîmes aqueduct, channelling water from its source near Uzès with an average drop of 34cm per kilometre and provided 20,000m^3 to the city per day. Constructed of massive blocks weighing six to eight tonnes which were hauled over 40m up into position, the structure is composed of three storeys of arches resting on top of each other.

Parc Naturel Régional du Pilat

Location: South of Givors and west of Saint-Romain-en-Gal.

Created in 1974, the park covers 65,000ha of beech forest, fir plantations, open plateau, pasture, hills and streams lining deep valleys.

DRIVING TOUR

Off N68 at Chavanay; D7 W to Pélussin.

Pélussin

Park on place Abbé-Vincent in front of the hospital. Walk down rue Dr-Soubeyran; left on rue de la Halle.
The old covered market provides a view of the Rhône plain and the town. Go through a fortified gatehouse and turn left. Note the ancient chapel and castle.

Maison du Parc

Moulin de Virieu, 2 r. Benaÿ. Open Easter–mid-Nov Mon–Fri 9.30am–12.30pm & 2–6pm; weekends & public holidays 9.30am–12.30pm & 2–6.30pm. Rest of the year Mon & Wed–Fri 10am–12.30pm & 2–6pm (Fri 5pm); Sat 9.30am–12.30pm. 04 74 87 52 00. www.parc-naturel-pilat.fr.
In addition to exhibitions and events, the park's main information centre gives full details of its three nature trails, each forming a 3-4km loop, and eight themed hikes, to be followed over the course of a day or two. Of these, the Jean-Jacques Rousseau trail, linking Condrieu and La Jasserie, traces the philosopher's links with the area and his botanical interests. A 22km floral trail takes the rambler from the Mediterranean vegetation of the Malleval region to the subalpine formation of the Crêt de Perdrix. The ornithological trail, running from St-Chabin to St-Pierre-de-Bœuf, is best attempted mid-May to mid-June, when many of the 90 featured bird species can be seen; ranging from mallard on St-Pierre Lake to crossbills in the fir forests and rock bunting out on the gorse heath.

Follow D63 W, then S.

From Faucharat viewpoint there are lovely views of the Régrillon Valley, the Rhone Valley and Pélussin.

Crêt d'Œillon★★★

15min on foot there and back. At the Croix de l'Œillon pass, take the road on the right leading to the turn-off to a private road, ending at the television relay station. Park in the car park. At the top, walk to the left around the fence: the viewing table is on the eastern end of the promontory, at the foot of a monumental cross.
The panorama, from a height of 1,370m, is one of the Rhône's most spectacular. In the foreground, beyond the rocks of the Pic des Trois Dents, there is a bird's-eye view of the Rhône, from Vienne to Serrières. In the distance, to the east, the view stretches right to the beginning of the Alps, south-east to Mont Ventoux and north-east to the Jura.

Return to D63, continue for 11km. The road meanders to and fro through lines of fir trees and broom-covered moorland. Continue E as D63 joins D8A, then turn right on to D8, towards La Jasserie.

Le Crêt de la Perdrix★

15min on foot there and back. At the top of the climb, park near the path leading to the ridge.
The grass-covered summits of the Crêt de la Perdrix and the Crêt de l'OEillon both bristle with strangely eroded granitic rocks, known locally as *chirats*. The view from this second crest, which is less breathtaking though slightly higher at 1 432m, takes in the peaks of Mézenc, Lizieux, Meygal and Gerbier-le-Jonc.

Return by the same route.

WINE BUYING GUIDE

INFORMATION

Inter Rhône, interprofession des vins AOC Côtes du Rhône et vallee du Rhône – *6 Rue des Trois-Faucons – 84000 Avignon. ℘04 90 27 24 00. www.vins-rhone.com.*

Syndicat des Côtes du Ventoux – *Route de Velleron, 84975 Carpentras Cedex. ℘04 90 63 36 50.*

Syndicat des Côtes du Luberon – *90 blvd. St-Roch, BP12, 84240 La Tour d'Aigues. ℘04 90 07 34 40. www.vins-cotes-luberon.com.*

CHARACTERISTICS

With complex bouquets, the wines from the northern part are more refined (Côte Rôtie, Condrieu, Hermitage). The southern wines are simpler and more quaffable, the reds often heady (Côtes du Rhône Villages Cairanne is a good example), the rosés lively and fresh (Tavel), and the whites fruity and smooth (Cairanne). The five southern Crus include the complex, strong and velvety red Châteauneuf du Pape. Further south, the reds of Costières de Nîmes are light country wines, the reds of Côtes du Luberon full bodied (the whites have a floral bouquet), and the Côtes du Ventoux reds fine and quaffable. Low in alcohol, the sparkling, slightly sweet Clairette de Die is a gem.

STORAGE

Wines of the northern Côtes du Rhône – **Côte-Rôtie**: 5-15 years; **Condrieu blanc**: drink young, no more than 2-3 years. **Château Grillet:** white best drunk young, but can develop a certain class when aged (2-10 years). **St Joseph**: whites or reds are best drunk fairly young. **Hermitage**: well suited to laying down.

Southern Côtes du Rhône – All fairly young drinking wines: good news for those without cellars. **Châteauneuf du Pape**: red 5-20 years, white 1-10 years. **Costières de Nîmes**: red 4-5 years, white and rosé best drunk young. **Côtes du Luberon:** red 5 years, rosé 2 years, white 3 years. **Clairette de Die**: ready for immediate drinking.

PRICES

Northern Côtes du Rhône

Prices reflect the effort required to successfully grow vines on the steep northern slopes, where the grapes are harvested by hand. Croze-Hermitage from the plain costs between 5€ and 11€.

Côte-Rôtie: 15-40€
Condrieu: 15-25€
Château Grillet: 30-40€
St Joseph: 10-15€
Hermitage: 35-40€

Southern Côtes du Rhône

Simpler and more quaffable, southern wines start around 5€.

Châteauneuf du Pape: 11-25€
Tavel: 5-8€
Costières de Nîmes: 3-8€
Côtes du Luberon: 5-11€
Côtes du Ventoux: 5-8€
Clairette de Die: 5-8€.

WINE MERCHANTS

La Bouteillerie – *43 r. Nationale, 69420 Condrieu. ℘04 74 59 84 96. www.labouteillerie.com. Open Tue–Sat 9am–noon & 2–7pm, Sun 10am–12.30pm – closed first week in Jan.* A vast range of wines, all of which the boss, M. Gérin, knows like the back of his hand. In layman's terms he explains the great local names like Côte-Rôtie and Condrieu, as well as lesser wines.

Caveau St-Vincent – *Place du Seigneur, 30126 Tavel. ℘04 66 50 24 10. sainte.vincent.tavel@laposte.net. Open Mar–Sept 10am-12.30pm & 2.30-7pm. Closed Jan–Feb and May 1.* An air conditioned cellar in the centre of the village, the ideal spot to get acquainted with France's premier rosé. Local produce for sale.

COOPERATIVES

Cave Coopérative des Vignerons – *Quartier Ravel, 84190 Beaumes de Venise. ℘04 90 12 41 00. Open daily 8.30am–12.30pm (noon in winter) & 2–7pm (6pm in winter); www.beaumes-de-venise.com.* Plenty of Muscat and also the lesser known reds, rosés and whites of the Côtes du Rhône Villages Beaumes de Venise. The cooperative has over 200 members producing 55,000 hl per year.

"Vinadéa" Maison des Vins – *8 Rue du Mar. Foch, 84230 Châteauneuf du Pape. ☏04 90 83 70 69. www.vinadea.com. Open May–Jun 10am–1pm & 2–7pm; Jul–Aug 10am–7pm; Nov–Feb 10am–12.30pm & 2–6pm; closed 1 week late Jan, 25 Dec and 1 Jan.* Founded in 2000, this extremely successful winegrowers' association occupies a former stable with attractive stonework and beams, offering wines from 90 Châteauneuf du Pape vineyards; tastings with advice on offer. Books and gifts.

Cave de Die Jaillance – *Avenue de la Clairette, 26150 Die. ☏04 75 22 30 15. www.jaillance.com. Open 9am–noon & 2–7pm. Closed Jan 1, Dec 25.* The choice and quality on offer takes in not only Clairette de Die, but also Crémant de Die and Châtillon en Diois wines. The guided cellar tour, followed by a tasting, is an ideal introduction for wine beginners.

Caveau Gigondas – *Place du Portail, 84190 Gigondas. ☏04 90 65 82 29. Open 10am–12pm & 2–6.30pm, closed Jan 1, Dec 25; Caveau des Gourmets daily 10am-6pm; www.cave-gigondas.fr.* Open all year and run by an association of around 50 winemakers with 150 ha, this is an opportunity to taste a wide variety of Crus without feeling obliged to buy. Each bottle is the product of a single winemaker; advice available from the staff. In the nearby village of Gigondas, the cooperative has opened a boutique and bar, where visitors can sample tasting plates of food and wine.

Cave de Tain l'Hermitage – *22 rte. de Larnage, 26601 Tain l'Hermitage. ☏04 75 08 91 86. Open Jul-Aug Mon-Sat 9am-7pm, Sun 10am-1pm & 2.30-6.30pm; Aept-Jun Mon-Sat 9am-6.30pm, Sun 10am-1pm & 2.30-6.30pm www.cavedetain.com.* With 400 members producing 55,000hl annually from 1,100ha, this is one of the region's most important cooperatives, covering five appellations and a vin de pays; some rare vintages available which no wine merchant could obtain. Founded in 1933, since when it has continuously strived to improve quality and today has an excellent boutique for tasting.

Cave du Prieuré, *26110 Vinsobres, Open Mon-Fri 9am-12.30pm & 2-6.30 pm Weekends and Bank Holidays 9am-noon & 2-6pm; t: 04 75 27 60 11, www.cellier-des-dauphins.com.* This cooperative, with a good boutique and attractive underground cellars, is part of Cellier des Dauphins, one of the largest winemaking groups in the Rhone. The name comes from a nearby priory dating from the 12C, which is today an attractive Protestant church.

DOMAINES

Domaine Étienne Guigal – *N 86, 69420 Ampuis. ☏04 74 56 10 22. www.guigal.com. Open by appt. Mon–Fri 8am–noon & 2–6pm.* Guigal is one of Côte-Rôtie's best-known names and rightly enjoys international renown. The wines are made to allow grape variety and terroir to shine through., and include iconic labels such as 'La Mouline', 'La Turque' and 'Ex-Voto', produced only in great vintages. Châteauneuf-du-Pape, Condrieu, Côte-Rôtie, Côtes-du-Rhône, Crozes-Hermitage, Gigondas, Hermitage, Saint-Joseph, Tavel.

Domaine du Château Turcan – *Rte. de Pertuis, 2km from Ansouis on the D 56, 84690 Ansouis. ☏04 90 09 83 33. www.chateau-turcan.com. Open Mon–Sat 9.30am–12.30pm & 2-6.30pm; Sun by appt.; closed public holidays.* Covering 25ha in the lower Luberon, Château Turcan not only produces red, rosé and white Crus from 6 different grape varieties, but also has its own museum with over 2 000 winemaking utensils from the 16C to the present day, plus one of the oldest presses in France. Côtes-du-Luberon.

Domaine Vaubelle – *84190 Beaumes de Venise. ☏04 90 65 86 28. Open by appt. Mon-Sat 9am–noon & 2–6pm.* This small family run estate is located in beautiful setting, very close to the hotel Montmirail but a tiny haven of peace. The Lesbros family are more than happy to offer tastings - just phone ahead as they may be out in the vines. Côtes-du-Rhône-Villages, Beaumes-de-Venise Rouge, Beaumes de Venise Rosé.

Château La Canorgue – *Rte. du Pont Julien, 84480 Bonnieux. ☏04 90 75 81 01. Open Jun-Sept Mon–Sat 9am–7pm, Oct-May 9am-noon & 2.30–6.30pm.*

The owner of this small, family owned vineyard operates on strictly organic principles, resulting in a low yield. The wines are aged in oak barrels and bottled at the château. Côtes-du-Luberon, Vin de Pays du Vaucluse.

Domaine de l'Oratoire Saint-Martin – *Rte. de St-Roman, 84290 Cairanne, 04 90 30 82 07. Open Mon–Sat except public holidays 8am–non & 2–6.30pm; www.oratoiresaintmartin.fr.* The Alary family has been involved in winemaking since 1692. Since 1982, Frédéric and Francois have cultivated these 25ha on the hillsides of St-Martin; the vines, some of which are over a century old, are harvested by hand. Open vats are used for their Côtes du Rhône Villages, closed vats for their Côtes du Rhône. The cellars with oak barrels have been in operation for over 150 years. Côtes-du-Rhône, Côtes-du-Rhône-Villages.

Domaine Brusset – *84290 Cairanne. 04 90 30 82 16.www.domainebrusset.fr. Open by appt. Mon–Sat 9am–noon & 2–6pm.* The Brusset family makes some excellent quality Gigondas wines, particularly Les Hauts de Montmirail, from some of the highest plots of vines in the appellation. They are vinified here in Cairanne, along with a number of other appellations. The family have been making wine in the area since 1947, but the arrival of Daniel's son Laurent has made them increasingly a name to watch. Gigondas, Cairanne, Cotes du Ventoux.

Eric and Joel Durand – *Imp. de la Fontaine, 07130 Châteaubourg, 04 75 40 46 78 Open Mon–Fri by appt 9am–noon & 2–6pm,* Eric and Joel are brothers, and are making exciting Saint Joseph and Cornas wines that are starting to be noticed further afield. The tasting room of this 12 ha estate is located in the centre of the old village; a lovely stone house covered in ivy. Cornas, Saint-Joseph.

Domaine la Guintrandy – *Quartier le Deves, 84820 Visan, 04 90 41 91 12, www.vins-cuilleras.com.* Owned by Olivier Cuilleras, all the wines here, including the rosé, are unfiltered to preserve the complexity, and SO2 use is kept to an absolute minimum. The property is located on the outskirts of the former Enclave des Papes in the commune of Visan, and has been a family estate since 1850. Cotes du Rhone Villages

Château La Nerthe – *Rte. de Sorgues, 84230 Châteauneuf-du-Pape. 04 90 83 70 11. www.chateau-la-nerthe.com. Open Mon–Sat 9am–noon & 2–6pm; closed public holidays.* This château has Châteauneuf-du-Pape's oldest cellars. Its wines are highly esteemed and the prices reflect this, although visitors should not be put off. A real treat, worthy of a detour. Châteauneuf-du-Pape.

Domaine Alain Voge – *4 Impasse de l'Équerre – 07130 Cornas – 04 75 40 32 04 – Mon-Fri 9am–12.30pm & 2–6.30pm.* The fourth generation of his family to be engaged in winemaking, Alain Voge has 12ha of hillsides planted with well-established vines, some of which are 70 years old. Eco-friendliness underlies the production. The grapes are harvested by hand; the wines are aged in barrels from Bordeaux and Burgundy. In 2004, Alain Voge was joined by Albéric Mazoyer. Cornas, Saint-Joseph, Saint-Péray.

Château Mas Neuf – *30600 Gallician, 04 66 73 33 23. Open Mon-Fri 9am-12.30pm & 1.30-6pm. www.chateau masneuf.com.* Luc Baudet's 62ha vineyard grows Syrah, Carignan, Grenache Noir, Mourvèdre and Roussanne grapes (he also grows 1ha of olives). Some of his wines are then aged for six to nine months in barrels. The vines grow in sandy, silt-laden "microterroirs", Costières-de-Nîmes, Vin de Pays d'Oc.

Domaine Les Goubert – *84190 Gigondas, 04 90 65 86 38. jpcartier@ terrre-net.fr.* 23ha split over five communes, all farmed using traditional techniques. Red wines are made in concrete tanks; the whites are done in stainless steel. Beaumes-de-Venise, Côtes-du-Rhône, Côtes-du-Rhône-Villages, Gigondas.

Château Constantin-Chevalier – *84160 Lourmarin. 04 90 68 38 99. Open Mon-Sat by appt.* Growing Syrah, Grenache and Carignan for reds and rosés, and Clairette, Ugni Blanc and Vermentino for whites, the château extends over 20ha. Harvested by hand, the grapes are processed in temperature controlled vats using carbonic maceration; the wine is aged in vats and mature timber barrels. Côtes-du-Luberon.

Domaine Pierre Gaillard – *Chez Favier, 42320 Malleval. 04 74 87 13 10. www.domainespierregaillard.com.* Pierre Gaillard has farmed this 22ha estate since 1981. The various vineyard plots of the estate are scattered over a 40km stretch of the Rhone, making for unusual diversity of the terroirs. Each plot is vinified separately, followed by maturation in oak barrels with reintroduction of the lees. Condrieu.

Chateau Saint-Pierre de Mejans – *84160 Puyvert. 04 90 08 50 51; www.saintpierredemejans.com. Open 9.30am–noon & 2.30–7pm (5.30pm in winter). 3€.* The estate's vineyards, extending over 12.5ha of pebbly clay-limestone soil, are planted with Syrah, Carignan, Cinsault, Clairette and white and red Grenache. Farming is done along ecologically responsible methods, so as to bring out the unique characteristics of the terroir. Traditional vinification, at low temperatures, is followed by maturation. The estate's cellar opened in 1993. Côtes-du-Luberon.

Domaine de Piaugier – *3 rte. de Gigondas, 84110 Sablet. 04 90 46 96 49. piaugier@wanadoo.fr. Open by appt. Mon–Fri 9am–noon & 2–6pm.* The latest in a long line of winemakers, Jean-Marc Autran has been in charge here since 1985. Today, the 30ha vineyard includes a wide variety of terroirs. The grapes are processed in bunches and aged in concrete vats and barrels. Côtes-du-Rhône, Côtes-du-Rhône-Villages, Gigondas.

Domaine de Cabasse – *Rte. de Sablet, 84110 Séguret. 04 90 46 91 12. www.domaine-de-cabasse.fr. Open by appt. Mon–Fri (daily Apr–Oct) 8am–noon & 2–6pm.* The estate produces appellation Côtes du Rhône Villages (Sablet and Séguret) and Gigondas reds, rosés and whites on its 20ha vineyard. The grapes are hand picked and graded before processing and ageing in vats and barrels for between eight months and two years depending on vintage and grape variety. Côtes-du-Rhône-Villages, Gigondas.

Domaine Delas Frères – *ZA de l'Olivet – 07300 St-Jean-de-Muzols – 04 75 08 92 97. www.delas.com. Open June-Sept 9am-12.15pm & 2-7pm. Oct-May Mon–Fri 9.30–noon & 2.30–6.30pm.* Founded in 1835, the estate today comprises vineyards in Hermitage, Saint-Joseph and Crozes-Hermitage appellations. On its granite slopes, the estate grows Syrah, Marsanne and Roussanne. The vineyards are farmed entirely by hand. Châteauneuf-du-Pape, Condrieu, Cornas, Côteaux-du-Tricastin, Côte-Rôtie, Côtes-du-Rhône, Crozes-Hermitage, Côtes-du-Ventoux, Gigondas, Hermitage, Saint-Joseph, Tavel, Vacqueyras.

Domaine du Tunnel – *20 Rue de la République – 07130 St-Péray – 04 75 80 04 66. Open daily by appt. 8am-1pm & 2-8pm.* Covering 5.5ha, the vineyard flourishes in a mix of limestone, clay and granite soil. The ***"lutte raisonnée"*** approach taken by Stephane and Sandrine Robert has seen herbicides banished. The grapes are hand picked. The reds are aged in barrels, the whites in a combination of stainless steel vats and barrels. These wines sell out pretty much as soon as they are bottled, so coming to the property is an excellent opportunity to do some serious tasting. Cornas, Saint-Joseph, Saint-Péray.

Paul Jaboulet / Vineum – *Route des Beaumes, 26300 Châteauneuf sur Isère. 04 75 47 35 55. Open Tues-Sat 10am-noon & 2-6pm. www.jaboulet.com.* Founded in 1834, this winery is now owned by the Swiss Frey family who also own Chateau La Lagune in Bordeaux. The estate covers 100ha and also includes a wine merchants, dealing not only in some of the best known names in the northern Côtes du Rhône, but also southern wines like Châteauneuf-du-Pape and Gigondas. Today, all visits and tastings take place in the cellars located in the Roman mines at Châteauneuf-sur-Isère, and there are films, tours and tastings on offer. Châteauneuf-du-Pape, Condrieu, Cornas, Côteaux-du-Tricastin, Côte-Rôtie, Côtes-du-Rhône, Crozes-Hermitage, Côtes-du-Ventoux, Gigondas, Hermitage, Muscat-de-Baumes-de-Venise, Saint-Joseph, Tavel, Vacqueyras

Michel Chapoutier – *18 Avenue du Docteur-Paul-Durand, 26600 Tain l'Hermitage; 04 75 08 28 65, Open daily 9am-7pm; www.chapoutier.com.* Chapoutier makes renowned wine across the Rhone, and also has joint ventures in Australia, South Africa and Portugal, but is most famous for his Hermitage wines. Among his many excellent bottlings, try his white Hermitage, including the cuvée Chante Allouette. His tasting rooms are always open, and offer a wide range of bottles. Côte-Rôtie, Côtes-du-Rhône, Crozes-Hermitage, Hermitage.

Domaine de la Mordorée – *Chemin des Oliviers, 30126 Tavel. 04 66 50 00 75. Open by appt. Mon-Fri 8am–noon & 1.30–5.30pm; Sat-Sun 10am-noon & 3-6pm; www.domaine-modoree.com.* Christophe Delorme manages 38 parcels of land in eight communes totalling 55ha. In 2001 a new tasting cellar was opened, and 2004 saw the planting of Condrieu vines. There is also an excellent estate honey on sale. Châteauneuf-du-Pape, Côtes-du-Rhône, Lirac, Tavel

Château d'Aqueria, *rte. de Roquemaure, 30126 Tavel. t04 66 50 04 56 ; www.aqueria.com.* Vincent and Bruno de Bez have 66 has of vines in Tavel and Lirac, making around 24,000 cases annually. Since coming to work on the property with their father in the 1980s, they have renovated the vinification facilities and added stainless steel tanks. Lirac, Tavel.

Bastide de Rafinel – *84240 La Tour d'Aigues. 04 90 07 48 61. Open by appt.* The 5ha estate sits on the southern slopes of the Luberon at an altitude of 300m, planted with. Grenache, Roussanne, Vermentino, Ugni Blanc, Syrah and Carignan. The estate is presently converting to organic farming. Côtes-du-Luberon.

Château Grillet – *42410 Verin. 04 74 59 51 56.* Founded by her Neyret-Gachet ancestors, Isabelle Baratin-Canet runs this 3.5ha exclusively Viognier vineyard, planted in granitic sand on steep terraces. The wines are aged in vats and oak barrels. This vineyard is unique in France for being an appellation in its own right. Château-Grillet.

ADDRESSES

STAY

IN ANSOUIS

Chambre d'Hôte un Patio en Luberon – *R. du Grand-Four, 84690 Ansouis. 04 90 09 94 25. 5 rooms.* . *Restaurant* . Right in the heart of the medieval village, this 16C auberge has maintained its charm of yesteryear through a careful renovation. Individually decorated rooms harmonise historic and modern styles. Vaulted dining room and a lovely patio with a fountain.

Chambre d'Hôte La Lombarde – *Puyvert, 84160 Lourmarin. 04 90 08 40 60. www.lalombarde.fr. Closed Nov–Feb. 4 rooms, 2 self-catering apts.* . Amid a peaceful 10ha wine estate, this ancient house welcomes you to its 4 rooms and 2 *gîtes*, each with its own entrance. Small private terraces and well-kept swimming pool. They also offer airplane rides!

AROUND BONNIEUX

Chambre d'Hôte Domaine de la Carraire – *Chemin de la Carraire, 84360 Lauris. 04 90 08 36 89. www.lacarraire.com. Closed Nov 15–Apr 1. 5 rooms. 7€.* Quintessential Provençal hostelry surrounded by vines, a pool and mature plane trees, all at very affordable prices, even in high season.

La Bastide de Soubeyras – *Rte. des Beaumettes, 84560 Ménerbes. 04 90 72 94 14. www.bastidesoubeyras.com. Closed Feb. 6 rooms.* . Absolutely charming drystone residence perched on a hillside overlooking the village. Provençal-style rooms, garden and swimming pool. Three evenings a week the owner invites her guests to a meal featuring the flavors of the Luberon.

AROUND CONDRIEU

Hôtel La Domaine de Claire fontaine – *Chemin des Fontanettes, 38121 Chonas-l'Amballan. 04 74 58 81 52. www.domaine-de-clairefontaine.fr. Closed Dec 16–Jan 15. 28 rooms. 14€. Restaurant* . Once a retreat for the bishops of Lyon, this old building (1766) has characterful accommodation and sophisticated cuisine. Delightful annex and terrace overlooking beautiful parkland planted with ancient trees.

DIE

Hôtel des Alpes – *87 r. Camille-Buffardel, 26150 Die. 04 75 22 15 83. www.hotelalpes.fr. 24 rooms. 6€.* Those seeking to experience the home of Clairette need look no further than this 14C coaching inn. Spacious accommodation, which has been gradually restored; the ideal base from which to explore the streets of Die.

AROUND NÎMES

Chambre d'Hôte Le Mas de Plisset – *Rte. de Nimes, 30900 St-Gilles. 04 66 87 18 91. Closed Nov holidays. 4 rooms.* This house on a still-operating farm features a hardworking country atmosphere. Guestrooms are simple and functional, yet comfortable. Organic jams on the breakfast table.

Hôtel Passiflore – *1 r. Neuve, 30310 Vergeze. 04 66 35 00 00. 11 rooms. 7.50€.* Run by an English couple, this 18C farmhouse has a cosy lounge area, and attractive restaurant and breakfast room decorated in Provençal style. The quiet rooms overlook a verdant inner courtyard.

NYONS

Hôtel Picholine – *Promenade Perrière, 26110 Nyons, 1km N of Nyons on Promenade des Anglais. 04 75 26 06 21. www.picholine26.com. Closed Feb 4–28 and Oct 15–Nov 7. 16 rooms. 7.50€. Restaurant .* A tranquil spot in the Nyons hills, this large edifice on a private road has a garden with swimming pool shaded by olive trees and a pleasant terrace likely to induce apathy. Functional rooms, some with balconies.

ORANGE

Mas des Aigras – *Chemin des Aigras, 84100 Orange. 04 90 34 81 01. masdesaigras@free.fr. Closed Oct 23–Nov 9, Dec 18–Jan 11, Mon evenings, Tue & Wed from Oct–Mar. 12 rooms. 12€. Restaurant .* An attractive farmhouse in pale stone among vines and fields not far from Orange.

Its charming young owners have improved the accommodation's decor and introduced air conditioning. The kitchen uses organic produce.

AROUND ST-PAUL-TROIS-CHÂTEAUX

Gite du Val des Nymphes – *Domaine de Magne, 26700 La Garde-Adhémar, 1km along the Chapelle-du-Val-des-Nymphes road. 04 75 04 44 54. val.des.nymphes@wanadoo.fr.* 5 rooms, 2 self-catering apts. *Restaurant .* Surrounded by its own land, this Tricastin fruit farm is a delight. Rooms overlook the orchards. Meals are served in a fine vaulted dining room decorated with antique tools.

AROUND VAISON LA ROMAINE

Chambre d'Hôte La Farigoule – *Le Plan-de Dieu, 84150 Violès, 7km W of Gigondas on the D 80 towards Orange and then the D 8 and the D 997 towards Violès. 04 90 70 91 78. www.la-farigoule.com. Closed Nov–Mar. 5 rooms.* This 18C winemaking estate has retained its original charm. The rooms, reached via a fine staircase and decorated with antique furniture, are individually named after famous Provençal authors. Breakfast is served in an attractive vaulted room. Garden.

Chambre d'Hôte Mas de la Lause – *Chemin de Geysset, rte. de Suzette, 84330 Le Barroux. 04 90 62 33 33. www.provence-gites.com. Closed late Oct–Mar 15. 5 rooms. . Restaurant .* Built in 1883, this farmhouse is tucked away among vines and apricot trees. Restored in contemporary style, its rooms retain their Provençal colour scheme. Prepared using local produce, the robust cuisine is served in the dining room or outside under an awning, overlooking the château.

Hôtel du Domaine des Tilleuls – *Rte. du Mont Ventoux, 84340 Maloucene, 04 90 65 22 31. www.hotel-domaine destilleuls.com. 20 rooms. 9€.* This former silkworm farm now offers Provençal style accommodation in pastel tones with tiled floors and shimmering fabrics. Air conditioning is not necessary, the 18C stone walls ensuring a cool ambience. Ask for a room overlooking the park.

⊜⊜ **Hôtel La Garance** – *Ste-Colombe, 84410 Bédoin, 4km E of Bédoin on the Mont Ventoux road. ℘04 90 12 81 00. www.lagarance.fr. Closed Nov 14–Mar 31. 13 rooms. ☕7.50€.* A restored farmhouse at the heart of a small village surrounded by vines and orchards. The rooms have Mediterranean colour schemes and original flooring. Those at the back have views of Mont Ventoux. Breakfast served on the terrace in summer. Swimming pool.

⊜⊜ **Hôtel Les Géraniums** – *Place de la Croix, 84330 Le Barroux. ℘04 90 62 41 08. www.avignon-et-provence.com/hotel/les-geraniums. Closed Jan 3–Mar 19. 22 rooms. ☕10€. Restaurant ⊜⊜.* This imposing stone house sits at the heart of a fortified village dominating the Comtat plain. Rustic, impeccably kept rooms. Generous local cuisine served on the large terrace or in the dining room, decorated with pictures painted by an appreciative guest.

AROUND VALENCE

⊜ **Hôtel de l'Europe** – *15 ave. Félix-Faure, 26000 Valence. ℘04 75 82 62 65. www.hotels-valence.com. 26 rooms. ☕6€.* Located along a busy avenue, this renovated hotel features brightly coloured rooms and double windows for soundproofing.

⊜⊜ **Hôtel de France** – *16 blvd. du Gén-de-Gaulle, 26000 Valence. ℘04 75 43 00 87. www.hotel-valence.com. 34 rooms. ☕6€.* Renovated inside and out, this hotel is in a perfect location from which to explore the historic town centre.

EAT

AROUND ANSOUIS

⊜ **Auberge de la Tour** – *51 r. Antoine-de-Très, 84240 La Tour-d'Aigues. ℘04 90 07 34 64. Closed Jan 2–15, Oct 23–Nov 1, Sun evenings and Mon.* Laid-back atmosphere at this spot, tucked away in the heart of the village. The menu features Provence-style cuisine.

⊜⊜ **La Récréation** – *15 ave. Philippe-de-Girard, 84160 Lourmarin. ℘04 90 68 23 73. Closed Wed.* No need to look further… just two steps from the tourist office, this charming Provençal restaurant is open all day, serving specialities of the region and Luberon wines. A good spot for an afternoon break over pastries.

AROUND BONNIEUX

⊜⊜ **La Flambée** – *Place du 4-Septembre, 84480 Bonnieux. ℘04 90 75 82 20. Closed 3 wks in Jan, Mon in winter. 4 rooms ⊜. ☕5€.* Grilled meats, pizzas from a wood oven and other specialities – ***daube provençale, pain de chèvre***, truffles, game – are served in this family restaurant which remains impervious to the fads of fashion. Rustic dining room and terrace with view over the Cavalon valley. Reasonably priced.

⊜⊜ **Les Gérardies** – *140 Cours Gambetta, 84300 Cavillon. ℘04 90 71 35 55. www.lesgerardies.com. Closed Thus lunchtime and Wed.* Despite its location along a busy boulevard, this restaurant is calm and quiet, thanks to its interior patio. Updated Provençal dishes on the menu incorporate market-fresh ingredients.

AROUND CONDRIEU

⊜⊜ **Bistrot à Vins de Serine** – *Place de l'Église, 69420 Ampuis. ℘04 74 56 15 19. Closed Sept 1–15, Sun and Tue–Thu evenings.* As the name implies, this is an opportunity to taste some interesting wines as well as having a meal. In summer, guests are served on the terrace with a vineyard view.

⊜⊜ **La Reclusière** – *39 Grande-Rue, 69420 Condrieu. ℘04 74 56 67 27. www.lareclusiere.free.fr. Closed Feb 12–25.* On entering this merchant's house, guests find themselves in bright dining rooms decorated with pictures. Traditional cuisine with a modern twist courtesy of the chef and his team.

⊜⊜ **Alain Charles** – *Rte. Nationale, 42410 Chavanay. ℘04 74 87 23 02. www.hotel-restaurant-charles.com. Closed Jan 2–10, Aug 16–Sept 7, Sun evening and Mon except public holidays 4 rooms ⊜ ☕7.60€.* A good stopping point for gourmets following the Côtes du Rhône route. Behind its welcoming façade awaits a friendly team of staff who ensure their guests have a pleasant meal. Elegant and rather original decor is the backdrop for classic cuisine dictated by seasonal availability.

S. Sauvignier / MICHELIN

IN DIE

⊖⊖ **Les Bâtets** – *Rte. de Chamaloc, 26150 Die, 3.5km from town by the D 518 toward Chamaloc. ✆04 75 22 11 45.* The chef at this rustic farmhouse in a peaceful valley serves forth well-executed specialties of the region. Portions are generous. For dessert, try the poached pear in dandelion sauce. It's best to call ahead… the restaurant closes at irregular times.

AROUND NÎIMES

⊖ **Le Bistrot au Chapon Fin** – *3 pl. du Chateau-Fadaise, 30900 Nîmes. ✆04 66 67 34 73. auchaonfin@cegetel.net. Closed Sat lunchtime & Sun.* A nice little bistro behind the Église St-Paul. Check the sign outside to see the specials of the day, created from whatever's fresh at the market. Good list of wines from the region. There's a wine bar, and an outdoor terrace.

⊖ **Le Clément IV** – *36 quai du Canal, 30900 St-Gilles. ✆04 66 87 00 66. Closed Sun evenings and Mon.* Seafood and Camargue specialities are served on the veranda or terrace. Picture-postcard views over the yacht harbour along the canal through the marsh.

⊖⊖ **Aux Plaisir des Halles** – *4 r. Littré, 30900 Nîmes. ✆04 66 36 01 02. Closed Feb 10–26, Oct 28–Nov 13, Sun and Mon.* The talk of the town; beyond its discreet façade the ambience is one of contemporary chic, both on the terrace and in the fine cuisine itself. The excellent wine list offers an interesting regional selection.

AROUND NYONS

⊖⊖ **Au Délice de Provence** – *6 La Placette, 84600 Valréas. ✆04 90 28 16 91. Closed Tue & Wed.* A stone built house with two recently renovated dining rooms, where guests can savour regional cuisine carefully prepared from the freshest ingredients: ***gigot de lotte, filet de canette, agneau à la provençale, rillettes de truite de mer, savarin aux pruneaux…***

⊖⊖ **La Charrette Bleue** – *Route du Gap, 26110 Nyons. ✆04 75 27 72 33. Closed Dec 18–Feb 3, Tue from Sept–Jun, Sun evenings Oct–March, Wed.* The sign of this pretty stone farmhouse with tiled roof is evocative of the autobiographical works of local writer René Barjavel. Tasty regional dishes may be enjoyed out on the terrace or in the dining room with exposed beams.

AROUND ORANGE

⊖ **Le Yaca** – *24 Place Silvain, 84100 Orange. ✆04 90 34 70 03. Closed Oct 28–Nov 24, Tue evenings & Wed.* The owner will stop at nothing to keep his clients happy. Generous portions of fresh, simple cuisine at reasonable prices. Terrace in summer.

⊖⊖ **La Garbure** – *3 r. Joseph-Ducas, 84230 Chateauneuf-du-Pape. ✆04 90 83 75 08. www.la-garbure.com. Closed Jan, Nov 15–30, Sat lunchtime, Sun lunchtime, Mon lunchtime in high season, Sun and Mon off season. 8 rooms ⊖⊖. ☕8€.* Let your appetite guide you through the regional dishes on offer at this attractive spot, with a small dining room painted in bright colours. Several guestrooms if you wish to stay the night.

⊖⊖ **Le Pistou** – *15 Rue Joseph-Ducos, 84230 Châteauneuf-du-Pape. ✆04 90 83 71 75. charlotte.ledoux@tiscali.fr. Closed Jan, Sun evening & Mon.* A small establishment in the centre of town, on an alley leading to the Papal fortress. The menu includes local specialities: try ***paupiette d'agneau au basilic*** or monkfish in bouillabaisse sauce.

ST-PAUL-TROIS-CHÂTEAUX

⊖⊖ **L'Esplan** – *Place de l'Esplan, 26130 St-Paul-Trois-Châteaux. ℘04 75 96 64 46. www.esplan.provence.com. Closd Dec 15–Jan 15, Sun evening from Sept 30–Apr 30, and lunchtime*. Behind the fine façade is a dining room in pastel tones and an inner courtyard shaded by an old palm tree. A mouth-watering menu reveals the chef's passionate approach; cuisine incorporating herbs, vegetables and seasonal produce from his garden.

AROUND VAISON LA ROMAINE

⊖ **Saint-Hubert** – *Le Village, 84340 Entrechaux. ℘04 90 46 00 05. Closed Jan 29–Mar 10, Sept 25–Oct 7, Tue & Wed.* Run by the same family since 1929, this spot focuses on traditional cuisine; nearly every dish has a classic quality to it, from the ***terrines maison*** to the ***filet de perche à la provençale***, served under an arbour in summer.

⊖⊖ **Auberge d'Anais** – *Le Péreyras, 84340 Entrechaux, 5km SE of Vaison towards St-Marcellin on the D 54 and then the D 938. ℘04 90 36 20 06. Closed Nov 15–Mar 1, Mon from Mar–Sept, Sat from Oct–mid-Nov. 7 rooms.* Surrounded by vines and olive trees, this establishment has many regulars who value its appetising cuisine, own wine, and good service. The chef uses local produce and has a seasonal truffle menu. A few guest rooms and a swimming pool.

⊖⊖ **Auberge de la Bartavelle** – *12 Place Sus-Auze, 84110 Vaison-la-Romaine. ℘04 90 36 02 16, Closed Jan 2–Feb 8, Nov 12–19, Mon.* Inside, this centrally located establishment has the air of a private residence: wood floors, summer holiday photos, etc.
The menu is composed of traditional dishes with a southern influence including aubergine tart and ***pieds et paquets*** – a local speciality of tripe and sheep's trotters which is an acquired taste, to say the least!

⊖⊖ **Le Mesclun** – *R. de la Poterne, 84110 Séguret. ℘04 90 46 93 43. www.lemesclun.com. Closed Jan, Tue offseason and Mon.* Good restaurant in the heart of a charming hillside village. Small, yellow-painted rooms, shaded terrace and cuisine marked with the stamp of the south.

⊖⊖ **Les Florets** – *Route des Dentelles, 84190 Gigondas. ℘04 90 65 85 01. www.hotel-lesflorets.com. Closed Jan 1–Mar 20, Mon evenings & Tue fromNov–Apr, Wed.* Deep in the countryside at the foot of the Dentelles de Montmirail, this pleasant establishment has been run by the same family for three generations. Tasty local cuisine accompanied by their own wines, namely Gigondas, Vacqueyras and Côtes du Rhône. Delightful terrace.

⊖⊖ **Mas de Bouvau** – *Rte. de Cairanne, 84150 Violes. ℘04 90 70 94 08. henri.hertzog@wanadoo.fr.* A traditional Provençal farmhouse transformed into a restaurant. Although the decor is only vaguely in keeping with local tastes, the menu has plenty of regional specialities such as ***croustillant de chèvre chaud à la tapenade*** and ***tranche de gigot d'agneau aux herbes*** and home-made pâtisseries.

IN VALENCE

⊖⊖ **La Petite Auberge** – *1 r. Athènes, 26000 Valence. ℘04 75 43 20 30. www.lapetiteauberge.net. Closed Jul 28 – Aug 23, Wed evening and Sun except public holidays.* Behind a rather sober exterior lie two rustic dining rooms welcome you to relax and tuck into lightly updated regional fare. Family atmosphere.

SHOPPING

A. Blachère – *Route des Sorgues, 84230 Châteauneuf-du-Pape. ℘04 90 83 53 81.* Founded by the Blachère family in 1835, this is one of Provençe's oldest artisan distilleries. It specialises in making beverages from the local scrubland flora; Élixir du Mont Ventoux, Comtadine, Vieux Marc de Provençe and aperitif Lou Gardian are among its creations. Enjoyable stuff, but proceed with caution!

Le Moulin Autrand-Dozol – *Promenade de la Digue, le Pont-Roman, 26110 Nyons. ℘04 75 26 02 52. www.moulin-dozol.com.* This shop and museum, visitors can acquire the local AOC olive oil (traditionally cold pressed), as well as soaps, tapenades, honey, spices and other local produce.

13 - SAVOIE AND BUGEY

Savoie and Bugey are home to the sunniest slopes of the Alpine foothills. The area between lakes Geneva and du Bourget, and the river valleys of the Ain and Isère, is chequered with small vineyards. In the Ain region, the Bugey wine-growing district nestles in a deep bend of the Rhône on the southernmost fringe of the Jura. In Savoie, the vineyards only survive through the income generated by the annual masses of winter-sports tourists. However, the wines of Savoie are more than a mere accompaniment to fondues and raclettes. The wide range of grape varieties ensures the production of quality wines, which are well worth seeking out in a region famed for its magnificent scenery.

Highlights

1 A boat ride on the stunning **Lake Geneva** (p424,)
2 A trip to a spa in **Thonon-les-Bains** (p424)
3 A walk through the **Forest de Ripaille** (p425)
4 The Resistance Museum in **Nantua** (p430)
5 River trout with a glass of sparkling rosé from **Cerdon** (p429)

The vineyards of Savoie (also known as Savoy) and Bugey date back to the Romans, but only really developed due to the influence of monks during the 12C from a number of important local abbeys.

At their height, the vineyards of Bugey covered 14,000 ha, where today they are only 500 ha, and those of Savoie today cover 2,000 ha. The areas were badly affected by Phylloxerra but the winemakers that remain are justly proud of the variety of their grapes and wines, and these are fascinating areas to explore, covering the beautiful scenery from the Swiss border to the Upper Rhone.

Wines from these areas are usually best drunk when young and fresh, although some producers are making wines to drink after a longer ageing in oak. They are not, as commonly thought, true cold-climate wines, despite the association with the skiing mountains of the French Alps. In fact, the steep sunny exposure of the grapes during the growing season means it is easy for them to achieve a good ripeness each year, and at the altitude of the vineyards (almost entirely below 500m) there is very little snowfall even in winter.

Bugey is even greener and more gentle than the Savoie, full of lakes and rivers for fresh water fishing and swimming, and a lovely part of France for invigorating walks through the vineyards.

Vineyards at the foot of Mont Granier, to the west of Montmélian

B. Kaufmann/MICHELIN

OVERVIEW

The Terroir

Michelin Local Map 328 and 333 – Haute-Savoie (74), Savoie (73) and Ain (01).
Area: 2,000ha of vineyards in Savoie, 500ha in the Bugey district.
Production: 130,000hl, both areas combined. The vines are in most cases grown on scree from glacial moraines. The climate is of continental/mountain type, with cold winters and mild to hot summers. It rains in spring and autumn, but there is plenty of sunshine all the year round.

Wines

The general **Vin-de-Savoie** appellation (AOC) is also home to 17 crus: Ripaille, Marin and Marignan (Lake Léman sector), Ayze (Bonneville sector), Chautagne and Jongieux (Rhône Valley and Lake Bourget sector), St-Jeoire-Prieuré, Montmélian, Cruet, Chignin-Bergeron, Arbin, Abymes and Apremont, St-Jean-de-la-Porte (Montmélian sector). The white wines, which represent 70% of the region, are produced from the Altesse, Chardonnay and Jacquère grape varieties, the reds and rosés from Gamay, Mondeuse and Pinot Noir.

The **Ayze Mousseux** appellation is given to a sparkling white wine produced from the Gringet and Roussette-d'ayze varieties. The **Crépy** appellation applies to white wines. The **Roussette-de-Savoie** appellation applies to dry white wines. The **Seyssel** appellation produces another white made from Altesse grapes. The **Vin-du-Bugey** appellation (AOVDQS) applies mainly to white wines. They include Cerdon, Montagnieu and Manicle, and are made from the Altesse, Chardonnay and Molette grapevarieties.

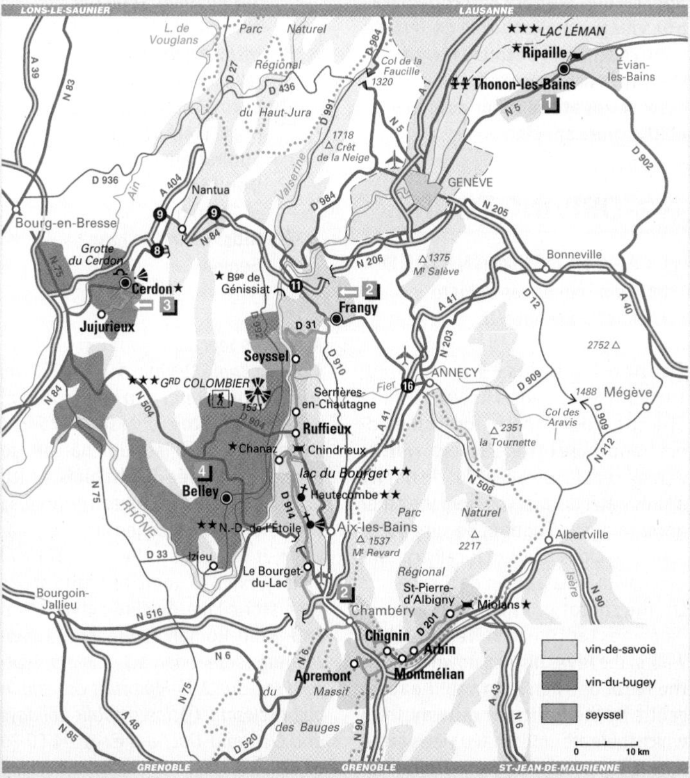

Lake Geneva

Savoie Wine Route

Spectacular scenery and chocolate-box villages make this an enjoyable wine route. And because few of the wines are exported, the discoveries at the cellar door are all the more special.

- **Population:** 960,000.
- **Michelin Map:** Michelin Local Map 328, K-L 2-3. See itinerary 1 on the map on p423.
- **Info:** www.vin-de-savoie.org
- **Location:** The foothills of the French Alps
- **Timing:** Two days
- **Don't Miss:** The village of Chignin
- **Kids:** Sailing on Lake Geneva.

DRIVING TOURS

1 LAKE GENEVA VINEYARDS

16km from Thonon-les-Bains to Douvaine (Haute-Savoie).

Thonon-les-Bains

Thonon is renowned for its waters: those of its spa, reputed to be good for the kidneys, and those of Lake Geneva, with its magnificent landscapes. But do not let all this water distract you from the other good things in Thonon. Be sure to try some delicious fillets of locally caught perch with a glass of vin de ripaille.

On the shores of **Lake Geneva★★★** (known as Lac Léman in French), take a walk in the **Rives** district, down towards the harbour. Then return to the town centre by the **funicular railway**, from which there are unrestricted views of the area (*open Jul–Aug 8am–11pm; mid-Apr–Jun & Sept 8am–9pm; Oct–mid-Apr Mon-Sat 8am–12.30pm & 1.30–6.30pm, Sun 2–6pm; 3min trip every 15min; 1.80€ round trip; 04 50 71 21 54).*

On reaching the Place du Château, go and see the **Musée du Chablais**, which occupies part of the Château de Sonnaz (17C): Recently reopened after renovations, it houses a collection of local history exhibits, remains of the area's prehistoric lake-dwelling civilisation and Gallo-Roman artefacts (*open Jul–Aug 10am–noon & 3–6.30pm; Sept-Jun Wed–Sun 2.30–6pm; last visit 30min before closing; closed public holidays and Oct–mid-Dec; 2€; 04 50 70 69 49).*

Return to Rives by car and follow the Quai de Ripaille, at the end of which you can turn left into the driveway leading to the château.

Fondation Ripaille★

The buildings of the **Château de Ripaille**, their roofs clad in bright-coloured tiles, rise above serried ranks of vines which produce a highly regarded white Chasselas. The building complex, such a distinctive sign of this region, evokes the most brilliant period of the House of Savoy. The interior is decorated in neo-Gothic style. After crossing the mulberry courtyard, you can visit first the wine press then the 17C kitchen (*visit by 1hr guided tour Jul–Aug 11am, 2.30pm, 3.15pm, 5pm; Apr–Jun & Sept 11am, 2.30pm, 4pm; Feb–Mar & Oct–Nov 3pm; 6€; 04 50 26 64 44; www.ripaille.fr*).

The **Forest** of Ripaille covers an area of 53ha. From its waymarked paths you can watch roe deer. The trees in the **arboretum** were planted between 1930 and 1934 with over 30 different species of oak tree. Nearby, in a clearing, stands a national monument to the Righteous, erected in homage to the men and women of Savoie who risked their lives escorting Jews to Switzerland during the Second World War (*open May–Sept Tue–Sun 10am–7pm; Oct–Apr Tue–Sun 10am–4.30pm; closed Dec; no charge; 04 50 26 28 22*).

Travel E from Ripaille, taking the D 32 to Marin.

Marin

There is a small vineyard in the village growing Chasselas grapes. Marin maintains memories of the old tradition of growing vines against the trunks of hollowed-out chestnut trees 6 to 8m high, known as crosses.

Return to Thonon by the N 5 and continue on the same road to Douvaine.

As you go through **Sciez**, you will see vineyards laid out on the steep banks of Lake Geneva. These produce Marignan

Château de Ripaille and its vineyard

M.-H. Carcanague/MICHELIN

wines – nothing to do with the famous French defeat of the Swiss at Marignano (1515).

The **Abbey of Filly** (11C), west of Sciez, has the oldest wine cellar in Savoie, still producing a good white wine.

The vineyards of **Crépy** produce white Chasselas wines. They are covered by a small AOC which also applies to the small area south of Douvaine around Loisin, Massongy and Baillason. The monks of Notre-Dame de Filly are said to have perfected the technique of making these *perlant* (gently sparkling) wines. Fruity and light in character, they go well with fried fish from the lake.

2 FOLLOWING THE RHÔNE

Approximately 150km from Frangy (Haute-Savoie) to Miolans (Savoie). Michelin Local Map 328, H-J 4-7.

See itinerary 2 on the map p423.

A good part of the Savoie wine-growing district stretches along the valley of the upper Rhône in a landscape which is undulating but not yet mountainous. The vineyards are generally scattered, but more densely packed around the charming villages, many of which boast their own particular Cru.

Frangy

"I found the wine of Frangy so excellent that I would have been ashamed to remain tight-lipped in such fine company", wrote Jean-Jacques Rousseau in his *Confessions* concerning a tipple that has been produced here since the 11C. You are in the heart of **Roussette** country.

Leave Frangy and travel S on the D 910 for 3km then turn right onto the D 31 towards Desingy, continue via Usinens, then Challonges, reaching Seyssel by the D 14 and D 992.

Vineyards are more in evidence around Desingy. The countryside becomes hillier in the vicinity of Usinens and Challonges, pretty wine-growing villages where Roussette is grown. From the church at Bassy, there is a fine view of the Seyssel dam.

Seyssel

Cut in half by the Rhône, Seyssel is unusual in straddling two départements: Ain and Haute-Savoie. The town has given its name to the **Seyssel AOC** appellation, the oldest in Savoie, though there is no mention of its vineyards before the 11C. Seyssel is renowned for this sparkling wine made from Altesse and Molette grapes. The best wine-growing areas are north of the town, around Corbonod. Try the Caves de Seyssels Lambert, for their sparkling Royal Seyssel Brut *(2 rue de Montauban, 74910 Seyssel; t04 50 56 21 59; Open Tues-Sat 9am-noon & 2-7pm; www.lambert-de-seyssel.com).*

The environment and history of the region are very well illustrated at the **Maison du Haut Rhône**, which shows films and stages temporary exhibitions *(quai Gallatin, 74910 Seyssel; open Jul–Aug Mon-Fri 9am–noon & 2–6pm (Thur 8pm); Sat 9am-noon & 1-4pm; rest of year times vary; no charge; 04 50 56 77 04; www.maison-du-haut-rhone.org).*

Travel S on the D 991. After Châteaufort, turn left and climb the hill to Motz, then come back on the D 56, a pleasant road with fine views of the Chautagne and the Lac du Bourget.

The western part of the Chautagne is marshland planted with poplars, while the eastern part consists of sunny slopes planted mainly with Gamay. Producing almost a quarter of the wine covered by the AOC Vin-de-Savoie appellation, the vineyards stretch from Motz, in the north, to Chindrieux, in the south.

Serrières-en-Chautagne

Distinctive of this area are a number of fortified houses and castles.

Take time to walk the Châtaignier footpath *(2hr 30min there and back, starting from Serrières, difference in level 250m).* This detour takes in the curious neo-Gothic château of Lapeyrouse and reveals some fine views.

Ruffieux

Among the vineyards rises the **Château de Mécoras** (12C-16C), a fine specimen of medieval architecture. The **Cave de Chautagne** sells a score of different wines and houses a small museum of wine-making tools and equipment *(73310 Ruffieux; open Apr–Oct Mon-Sat 9am–noon & 2–7pm, Sun 10am-noon & 2-6pm; Nov–Mar Mon-Sat 9am–noon & 2–6pm; closed Jan 1, Apr 29–30, Dec 25; 04 79 54 27 12; www.cave-de-chautagne.com).*

Chindrieux

The **Château de Châtillon** stands on a site which controlled the main routes of Roman Gaul. The walls date from the 13C *(visit by 30min guided tour Easter Sunday–Nov 1 Wed 2–5.30pm; 3€; 04 79 54 28 15).*

While in Chindrieux, visit the **Rucher de Chautagne** a bee-keeping establishment selling delicious mountain honeys, often infused with lavender, acacia, or chestnut *(Francoise Guichon, 2233 rte. du Sapenay, 73310 Chindrieux; 04 79 54 20 68; Open Mon-Fri 4-8pm, Sat-Sun 9am-6pm, or by appt.).*

Continue on the D 991, then turn right onto the D 914, before taking the D 18.

The road wends its way through the reed-beds and poplars of the Chautagne marshlands, with views of vineyards on the hillsides.

Savières Canal

4km long, this canal provides a natural overflow for the waters of the Lac du Bourget, channelling them into the Rhône, and a safety valve for the "raging bull" floods of Provence. It is unusual in that at times its water flows in the opposite direction: when the snows melt in the spring, and during heavy rainfall in autumn, the rising waters of the Rhône flow back into the lake.

Chanaz★

This charming village was a popular stopping place when working boats still plied the Savières Canal: inns which once served the bargees have revived the old tradition. Do not miss the rare walnut-oil mill, still in operation.

Continue on the D18 to Hautecombe Abbey.

The road follows the banks of the **Lac du Bourget**★★, with splendid views of the eastern shoreline and Aix-les-Bains.

Royal abbey of Hautecombe★★

It was here in this romantic setting that the sovereigns of the House of Savoy chose to be buried. The exuberantly decorated **church** was restored in the 19C in the troubadour Gothic style. The interior is a profusion of marble, stuccowork and illusionist painting (trompe-l'oeil). The thirty or so tombs of the princes of Savoy are adorned with 300 statues. Down below, beside the lake, is a huge boat-storage shed (12C) projecting into the water. It is said to be the only one in France.

Return the way you came and, when you reach the D 914, turn left.

Chapelle Notre-Dame-de-l'Étoile

15min on foot there and back.

The signposted driveway leading to the chapel is on a wide bend in the D914.

From the platform in front of the building there is a **view**★★ of the lake – looking out towards the charming curve of the Bay of Grésine – and also its mountain setting, with the Grand Colombier to the north and the Allevard massif to the south.

Le Bourget-du-Lac

Le Bourget was the main port of Savoie until 1859. A steam-boat service connected it with Lyon via the Savières Canal and the Rhône.

The **church** was built over a crypt which may date from the Carolingian era. Inside, the **frieze**★ from the former *jubé* (rood screen), now set into the walls of the apse, is regarded as the masterpiece of 13C sculpture in Savoie (*open year-round; guided tour available Jul–Aug 10am–6pm; enquire at the tourist office;. 04 79 25 01 99).*

The **Château Thomas II** *(near the mouth of the Leysse)* was a simple hunting lodge belonging to the counts of Savoy. Meetings were held there to make and break family and diplomatic alliances (*visit by 1hr 30min guided tour Jul–Aug; enquire at the tourist office; 04 79 25 01 99).*

Continue toward Chambéry via the N 504 (exit 15).

Chambéry★★

At the foot of the Bauges massif, this attractive city was the capital of the Savoie earldom from 1232 to 1559. You can take a pleasant stroll through the **old town**★★ by starting from the Curial area and following Rue Ducis, which leads to the Charles Dullin theatre and the **cathedral of St-François-de-Sales**★ (15–16C). Continuing on, you'll pass the famous Fountain of Elephants, the city's most popular monument. Rue de Boigne leads to the **château**★, former residence of the counts of Savoie; its elegant **Sainte-Chapelle**★ houses a 70-bell carillon (*visit by guided tour only; enquire at the tourist office).*

Leave Chambéry to the SE toward Montmélian. After Challes-les-Eaux, turn left onto the D 5, then right onto the D 21.

Chignin

This attractive village, with its dramatic ruined towers and beautiful views, lends its name to Chignin wines, mainly whites made with the Jacquère grape. The name should not be confused with **Chignin-Bergeron**, which applies only to white wines made with Roussanne grapes, the Savoie whites most suitable for ageing. There are plenty of wineries in this area, including the **André and Michel Quénard** estate *(see Shopping Guide).*

Travel S on one of the roads which joins the N 6, turn left for a short distance then immediately left again towards Apremont.

Apremont

Apremont makes white wines made principally from the Jacquère grape. The name of the local Abymes (abysses) wines recalls an earthquake which killed thousands of people in the 13C. These wines are very similar to Apremont, but with slightly more pronounced citrus flavours. You can buy them at the **Vigneron Savoyard** cooperative *(see Shopping Guide).*

Follow the D 12 southward towards Marches.

This area also produces some good wines from the Mondeuse grape, for instance those grown on the **Jean Perrier et Fils estate**, in the hamlet of Saint-André near **Marches** *(see Shopping Guide).*

Montmélian

Though the former fortress was demolished in 1706, Montmélian still has some fine tall houses, with courtyards linked by covered passageways. The city is in the centre of a wine-growing region, whose scattered vineyards produce Savoie's most highly regarded wines. The **Musée régional de la Vigne et du Vin** provides an excellent introduction to the subject *(46 r. Jean-Pierre-Veyrat; open Jul–Sept daily 10am–noon & 2–6.30pm, closed Sun morning, Mon morning and public holidays; Oct–Jun Wed & Fri 2–5.30pm; 4€; 04 79 84 42 23; www.montmelian.com).*

Arbin

Some powerful Mondeuse wines with a well-justified reputation are produced around this small village, somewhat spoilt by creeping development. Try the wines of the **Chais du Moulin** or **Domaine de Prieuré St-Christophe** estates *(see Shopping Guide).*

Near Arbin, the village of **Cruet** is better known for its white Jacquère wines, but it also produces some good red Arbin. The **Combe de Savoie**, the northern section of the "Alpine furrow", is the name given to the valley of the Isère between Albertville and the Chambéry, where it is crossed by another valley.

Saint-Pierre-d'Albigny

Historic gateway to the **Bauges** massif, St-Pierre-d'Albigny occupies a superb elevated position overlooking the coomb. There are many fine old buildings, including family mansions and fortified houses.

Join the D 911 for 800m, then turn right onto the D 101. Leave your car in the car park at Miolans, 100m out of the village.

Château de Miolans★

Open Jul–Aug 10am–7pm. May–Jun & Sept Mon–Sat 10am–noon & 1.30–6.30pm, Sun 1.30pm–7pm. Apr weekends & public holidays 1.30–7pm. Nov school holidays 1.30–7pm. 6€. 04 79 28 57 04.

Standing proudly on its platform of rock, 200m above the Combe de Savoie, the castle, with its four lateral turrets, was used to keep watch over the routes of the Bauges, the Tarentaise and the Maurienne regions from 923 to 1523. It was then converted into a state prison (1559-1792). There is an unusual defensive **covered way**★; its embrasures covered the approach to the castle for 200m.

Afterward, take the D 201 to Fréterive for a taste of the wines of Savoie at the **Domaine Jean-Pierre and Philippe Grisard** *(see Shopping Guide).*

Bugey Wine Route

One of the least explored wine regions in France, and yet one of its most picturesque. Wines here are almost entirely sold direct from the producers, and are the perfect match for local foods such as the Bresse chicken.
The Bugey district is an attractive part of France, nestling in a deep bend in the upper Rhône in the southern part of the Ain ***département*****. Bugey's cuisine makes the most of the region's dairy products, freshwater fish, fruits, truffles and, of course, wines.**
The area was the home of Jean-Anthelme Brillat-Savarin, author of the witty compendium of culinary anecdotes ***La Physiologie du goût*** **(The Physiology of Taste). He was born in Belley. To the north of his home town is one of three fairly scattered areas of vineyards; the other two are to be found around Cerdon and Montagnieu.**

- **Population:** 100,000.
- **Info:** www.vins-dubugey.net.
- **Location:** The gateway to the Rhone
- **Timing:** Two days
- **Don't Miss:** The Cerdon caves
- **Kids:** The Lavours nature reserve.

DRIVING TOURS

3 THE CERDON AREA

20km from Cerdon to Jujurieux (Ain). Michelin Local Map 328, F4.
See itinerary 3 on the map on p423.

Cerdon★

In a magnificent setting of caves, narrow gorges and stunning viewpoints, Cerdon has lent its name to a unique sparkling rosé. One of the most interesting producers is found at **Domaine Renardat-Fâche** *(see Shopping Guide)*. Visit the village on foot; its narrow streets are set off by fountains and stone bridges. A copper workshop, **La Cuivrerie de Cerdon**, established on the site of a former mill continues to work sheet-copper using 19C techniques and sells a range of beautiful copper pans and household objects, as well as explaining the history and techniques behind the process (*visit by 1hr guided tour Mon-Fri 9am–noon & 1.30–6.30, Sat-Sun 9.30am–noon & 2–6.30pm; guided tours in the afternoon by appt. closed Jan 1, Dec 25; 5€; 04 74 39 96 44; www.cuivreriedecerdon.com).*

Take the N 84 east out of Cerdon in the direction of Nantua.

Grotte du Cerdon (Cerdon cave)

At Labalme-sur-Cerdon. Visit by guided tour (1hr 30min Jul–Aug 10am–6pm (last entry 5pm); Apr–Jun & Sept- Oct Mon-Sat 1.45pm & 3.45pm; Sun afternoon departures every 30min 12.30-5pm 6.50€. Picnic area. 04 74 37 36 79; www.grotte-cerdon.com.
The tour follows the course of a dried-up underground river. The tunnel, featuring fine rock formations, leads to a cavern with a 30m arch opening onto the outside world.

Old copper workshop in Cerdon
G. Magnin/ MICHELIN

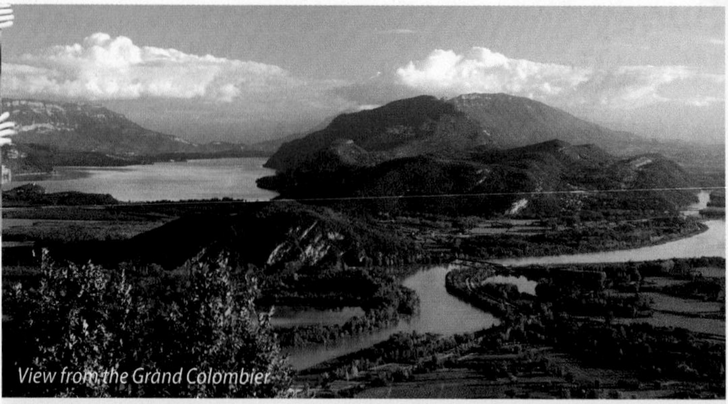

View from the Grand Colombier

Man-made Wonders

Grand Colombier★★★

35km SW of Frangy via the N 508, then the D 992 and the D 120A from Anglefort. Rising to a height of 1,531m, the Grand Colombier is the highest mountain in the Bugey. Two summits are easily accessible on foot: to the north, a rounded vantage point on which there is a cross *(20min on foot there and back)*; to the south, a summit, with a sharp drop on the west side *(45 min on foot there and back)*. Magnificent views.

Génissiat Dam★

10km NW of Frangy via the D 314, then the D 14 and the D 214.
This dam, commissioned in 1948, created an artificial lake 23 km long.

Heroes

Resistance fighters were in the heart of the Bugey in 1943. Their headquarters in the **Valromey**, was attacked by German forces in February 1944. After it had re-formed, the Resistance was again the object of an enemy sweep in July.
The *maquisards* then broke up into small groups and withdrew to the remotest mountain hide-outs.

Ain and Haut-Jura Museum of Resistance and Deportation★

In Nantua, 58km N of Belley. Open May–Sept Tue–Sun 10am–1pm & 2–6pm; rest of year by appt. Guided tours (30min–1hr) available. 4€. 04 74 75 07 50. www.ain.fr.
The old prison in Nantua, where resistance fighters were held, houses this effective museum. Skilfully illustrated by **tableaux**★, with audioguide commentary by former *maquisards* and a British soldier, the collections evoke the atmosphere of the 1940s, the Occupation, the Resistance and its organisation, and the Deportation. The visit ends with a montage of films from the period.

Izieu

21km SW of Belley via the D 992, then the D 19D.
The name of this village is associated with one of the most heart-rending tragedies of the Second World War. A colony of Jewish children had found refuge in a hamlet about 800m beyond the village.
On 6 April 1944 the Gestapo from Lyon arrested the 44 children, and their 7 teachers, because they were Jews. One person escaped in the course of the raid, and only one survived concentration camp.
In 1987, after Klaus Barbie was sentenced for this crime against humanity, a **Memorial Museum**★ (*open summer 10am–6.30pm; rest of year times vary; 5€; 04 79 87 21 05; www.izieu.alma.fr*) devoted to the Izieu children was founded.
The main house illustrates daily life in this place of refuge. The barn houses a hsitory exhibition.

Return to Cerdon and take the D 63 SW towards Jujurieux.

The little village of **Mérignat** is home to some welcoming and talented wine-growers such as **Raphael Bartucci**, with 1.8 ha of vines *(Chemin du Paradis, 01450 Merignat; 04 74 39 95 94, by appt.).*

Jujurieux

This village with its thirteen châteaux still has some reminders of its silk-weaving heritage, in particular the **Bonnet Silkworks**: you can visit the collections and workshops of this former silk mill *(visit by 1hr guided tour mid-Jun–mid-Sept Wed–Mon 10am–noon & 2–6pm, weekends 2.30–6.30pm; 4.50€; 04 74 37 23 14).*

4 THE BELLEY WINE-GROWING AREA

10km from Belley to Lavours (Ain). Michelin Local Map 328, H6. See itinerary 4 on the map on p423.

North of Belley, the last of the eastern slopes rising from the Lavours marshlands are home to some of the best Bugey wines.

Belley

The chief town of the Bugey district preserves the memory of its most famous son, the jurist and philosopher of taste Jean-Anthelme Brillat-Savarin (1755-1826). There is a sculpted bust of him at the north end of the Promenoir. His family home is at 62 Grande-Rue.

D 69 NE out of Belley, then the D 69C

All along this road are wineries where you will receive a warm welcome, such as the **Maison Angelot** at **Marignieu** *(see Shopping Guide).*

Continue on D 69C; left on D 37.

Vongnes is the main village in this area, where the **Caveau Bugiste** is worth visiting *(see Shopping Guide).*

Drive N to Ceyzérieu, then turn right towards Aignoz.

Lavours Marshland Nature Reserve

A raised walkway 2,400m long *(open year round)* takes you right into the heart of the marsh, a world of its own.

At the **Maison du marais**, you can learn all about this aquatic environment and its biological diversity *(open Apr-Sep: weekends & public holidays 10am–12.30pm & 2–6.30pm; spring holidays and Jul–Aug daily 10am–12.30pm & 2–7pm; closed Oct–Mar; 3€; 04 79 87 90 39, www.reserve-lavours.com).*

WINE BUYING GUIDE

CHARACTERISTICS

Reds – Gamay wines are generally fairly light in colour, while those made from Mondeuse are darker. Berry fruit and fresh pepper notes in the bouquet.

Dry whites – The Jacquère and Chardonnay wines are paler with greenish highlights, Chasselas wines yellower. They have an aroma of citrus and exotic fruits, with a hint of mint when young. Some are gently sparkling *(perlant)*.

Sparkling wines – Pale in colour with yellow highlights, not aggressively sparkling, with toasted brioche and hazelnut flavours. Cerdon is sweet and fruity.

STORING

Reds – Rarely keep for more than three years, with the exception of good Mondeuse vintages. **Dry whites** – Drink young. Some Chasselas and Chardonnay wines will last for 3 to 5 years. Chignin-Bergeron will keep for 10 years.

PRICES

From 5 to 15€.

COOPERATIVE WINERIES

Le Vigneron Savoyard – *Rte. du Crozet, 73190 Apremont. 04 79 28 33 23. vigneron.savoyard@wanadoo.fr. Open Mon–Sat 8am–noon & 2–6pm. Closed 2 wks in May & public holidays.*

This cooperative sells a full selection of regional wines.

Caveau Bugiste – *Chef-Lieu, 01350 Vongnes. ✆04 79 87 92 32; www.caveau-bugiste.fr. Open 9am–noon & 2–7pm.* The speciality of this venerable but welcoming institution is a red Manicle, Brillat-Savarin's favourite *Cru*. There is also a museum with traditional winemaking tools, and art exhibitions.

ESTATES

Le Chai des Moulins – *Chemin des Moulins, 73800 Arbin. ✆04 79 84 30 99. Open Mon-Fri by appt.* Having taken over from their father in 2002, Louis and Joseph Trosset became the fourth generation of winegrowers on this family estate. The 4ha vineyard, planted only with Mondeuse on its clayey limestone soil, faces south. The vines, an average age of 25 years, are cultivated with the environment in mind, and are harvested manually. Vin-de-Savoie

Domaine de Prieuré St-Christophe *73250 Fréterive, ✆ 04 79 28 62 10; Open Mon-Fri by appt.* This biodynamic estate is run by Michel Grisard, who created it himself and has pretty much single-handedly revived the fortunes of the Mondeuse grape, a distant cousin of Syrah. Vin-de-Savoie

André et Michel Quénard – *Torméry, 73800 Chignin, ✆04 79 28 12 75. Open Mon-Tues, Thur-Fri 8.30-11.45am & 1.30-4.45pm. Wed & Sat by appt. 1.30-4.45pm.* There seems to be a never-ending supply of winemakers called Quénard in Chignin, but this stony, steeply sloping Torméry hillside undoubtedly produces one of the best local wines. Its 20ha of vines benefit from a privileged sunny position. This unusual terroir produces a white Chignin from Jacquère grapes whose reputation dates back to the 11C, as well as a Chignin-Bergeron made from Roussane. Pétillant-de-Savoie, Roussette-de-Savoie, Vins-de-Savoie.

Domaine Renardat-Fâche – *Merignat ✆04 74 39 97 19; Open by appt. Mon-Sat 9-noon & 2-5.* Alain and his son Elie make an excellent sparkling wine from Poulsard and Gamay grapes. They work 2.5 ha of vines, and are one of the few Buguey producers who are known widely outside of the region. Roussette-de-Savoie, Vin-de-Savoie

Domaine Jean-Pierre et Philippe Grisard – *Chef-Lieu, 733250 Fréterive. ✆04 79 28 54 09; Open Mon-Fri 8am-noon & 1.30-6.30pm, Sat 8am-noon & 1.30-5pm; www.domainegrisard.com.* In the same family for 170 years, this 15ha estate links traditional with modern methods in its winemaking practices - for example the wines are aged in oak barrels but vinification takes place at low temperatures. The same family also runs a 'pépinière' growing young vines. Roussette-de-Savoie, Vin-de-Savoie

Domaine Noël Dupasquier – *Aimavigne, 73170 Jongieux. ✆04 79 44 02 23. Open by appt. Mon–Sat 9am-noon & 2.30-7pm.* This welcoming estate is located in a tucked-away village. Benefiting from the area's microclimate and varied soils, the regional grape varieties thrive on arid slopes. They are grown using chemically non-interventionist methods and vinified in the traditional manner, without added yeast. Wines are aged in oak for 12 months. Roussette-de-Savoie, Vins-de-Savoie.

Domaine Jean Perrier et Fils – *ZA Plan du Cumin, 73800 Les Marches, ✆04 79 28 11 45. www.vins-perrier.com. Open Mon–Fri 8am–noon & 2–5pm.* A major wine-grower and merchant, Gilbert Perrier heads this estate, which has been in his family for one hundred and fifty years. Assisted by his three sons, he runs a 37ha vineyard producing Apremont, Abymes, Chignin, Chignin-Bergeron and Arbin. Pétillant-de-Savoie, Roussette-de-Savoie, Vins-de-Savoie.

Maison Angelot – *01300 Marignieu, ✆04 79 42 18 84. Open by appt. Mon-Sat 9am–noon & 2–7pm, Sun 9am-noon & 3-7pm; www.maison-angelot.com.* In the family since the beginning of the 20th century, the estate was taken over in 1987 by Philippe Angelot, who was joined by his brother that same year. Managed in an eco-friendly way, the vineyard consists of 25ha, 60% planted with white grape varieties (Chardonnay, Roussette, Aligoté) and 40% with vines producing reds and rosés (Gamay, Pinot, Mondeuse). The plots are south-southeast facing, at altitudes of between 200 and 350m. Roussette-de-Bugey, Vin-du-Bugey

ADDRESSES

STAY

AROUND BELLEY

Chambre d'hôte Les Charmettes – *La Vellaz, 01510 Virieu-le-Grand, 11km N of Belley by N 504 to Chazey-Bons then D 31C. 04 79 87 32 18. 3 rooms.* You can be assured of a pleasant stay in the magnificently restored former stables of this delightful farmhouse. The bedrooms are charming and comfortable; one is equipped for the disabled. Cooking facilities available. Peaceful country.

AROUND CERDON

Chambre d'hôte de Bosseron – *325 rte. de Genève, 01160 Neuville-sur-Ain, 8km NE of Pont-d'Ain on N 84 – 04 74 37 77 06. Closed Nov–Mar. 4 rooms.* This property is set in a fine 2ha park on the banks of the Ain. The house has character and individually designed bedrooms. The outbuildings have been renovated to house a fitness centre, billiard room and kitchen.

AROUND MONTMÉLIAN

Hôtel La Croix du Sud – *3 r. du Dr-Duvernay, 73100 Aix-les-Bains. 04 79 35 05 87. www.hotel-lacroixdusud.com. Closed end Oct–Mar. 16 rooms. 6€.* The owner of this rose-coloured hotel enjoys pampering the clients. Modest but very clean rooms with nice decorative touches.

Auberge Au Pas de l'Alpette – *Bellecombe, 38530 Chapareillan, 7km SW of Montmélian by N 6 and N 90. 04 76 45 22 65. www.alpette.com. Closed end Nov, Sun evenings and Wed. 13 rooms. 7€. Restaurant.* This isolated mountain inn in the heart of the Chartreuse massif offers an exceptional view of Mont Blanc. Simple, clean attic rooms. At table, feast on raclettes, fondues and young goat with morels.

AROUND THONON-LES-BAINS

L'Ombre des Marronniers – *17 pl. de Crête – 74200 Thonon-les-Bains – 04 50 71 26 18. Closed Apr 28–May 8, Dec 22–Jan 8. 17 rooms. 6.50€. Restaurant.* In this picturesque chalet surrounded by a delightful garden, ask for one of the four Savoyard-style rooms, real little bijou apartments. The others are well maintained but a little old-fashioned.

EAT

IN BELLEY

Auberge La Fine Fourchette – *N 504, 01300 Belley. 04 79 81 59 33. Closed Aug 22–31, Sun evenings and Mon.* The large windows of the restaurant, tastefully decorated in a classical/rustic style, look out onto the Rhône Canal and open countryside. If weather permits, eat out on the terrace, which has fine views. Good, traditional, generous food.

AROUND CERDON

Bernard Charpy – *1 r. Croix-Chalon, 01460 Brion. 04 74 76 24 15. Closed May 18–24, Aug 7–30, Dec 26–Jan 3, Sun and Mon.* A charming chalet-style building just outside Nantua. Bernard Charpy presents an attractive traditional cuisine, with a good choice of fish which changes with the seasons. A bonus: affordable prices.

AROUND LE BOURGET-DU-LAC

Atmosphères – *618 rte. des Tournelles, 73370 Les Catons, 2.5km NW of Le Bourget-du-Lac via the D 42. 04 79 25 01 29. www.atmospheres-hotel.com. Closed Feb 19–28, Nov. holidays, Wed except evenings Jul–Aug and Tue.* Surronded by greenery, this peaceful chalet overlooks the lake, with lovely mountain views and inventive cooking.

AROUND SEYSSEL

Auberge de la Cave de la Ferme – *R. du Grand-Pont, 74270 Frangy, exit 11 of the A 40. 04 50 44 75 04. Closed Sun and Mon.* The owners of this inn produce Savoie wines (Roussette, Mondeuse) and marc brandy. Cuisine has a regional emphasis with delicious cheese and pork-meat.

AROUND MONTMÉLIAN

St-Vincent – *Le Gaz, 73800 Montmélian. 04 79 28 21 85. Closed Feb holidays, June 28–Jul 8, Nov. holidays, Sun evenings, Mon evenings and Wed.* A friendly restaurant on the main street of the village. The owners serve appetising dishes. In their delightful vaulted dining room or on the vineyard view terrace.

Auberge Bessannaise – *28 Pl. Monge, 73000 Chambéry. 04 79 33 40 37. Closed Thu evenings in winter, Mon.* Recognisable by its flower decked facade and terrace, this restaurant occupies a regional-style house where clients flock for the fondue, house foie gras, and fresh fish from lake Bourget.

14 - THE SOUTH WEST

This is D'Artagnan and Cyrano country, where rebellion and nobility go hand in hand, and good living is an art performed with refinement and inspired by a sure sense of identity. From the Pyrenean foothills to the Rouergue region, and from the Dordogne Valley to the Toulouse area, people display their local character with pride. As you travel you will discover the gentle hills of Périgord Pourpre; the fertile hillsides of Gascony; the River Lot meandering round the Cahors vineyards; the medieval cities of the Gaillac region; the mountains of Béarn and of the Basque country; and the dales of Rouergue. Vineyards are less prominent here than in other regions; yet the orchards, pastures, farmyards and cereal fields of this land of plenty offer a wide choice of delicacies to accompany fine wines.

Background

Historically, the mosaic of vineyards scattered across the southwest quarter of France have at least one thing in common: for centuries, all were excluded from the market place by Bordeaux. Anxious to preserve their special trade agreements with northern Europe, the Bordeaux wine-growers invented all kinds of cunning taxes and regulations to avoid competition from inland wines. For instance, wines from Bergerac, Cahors,

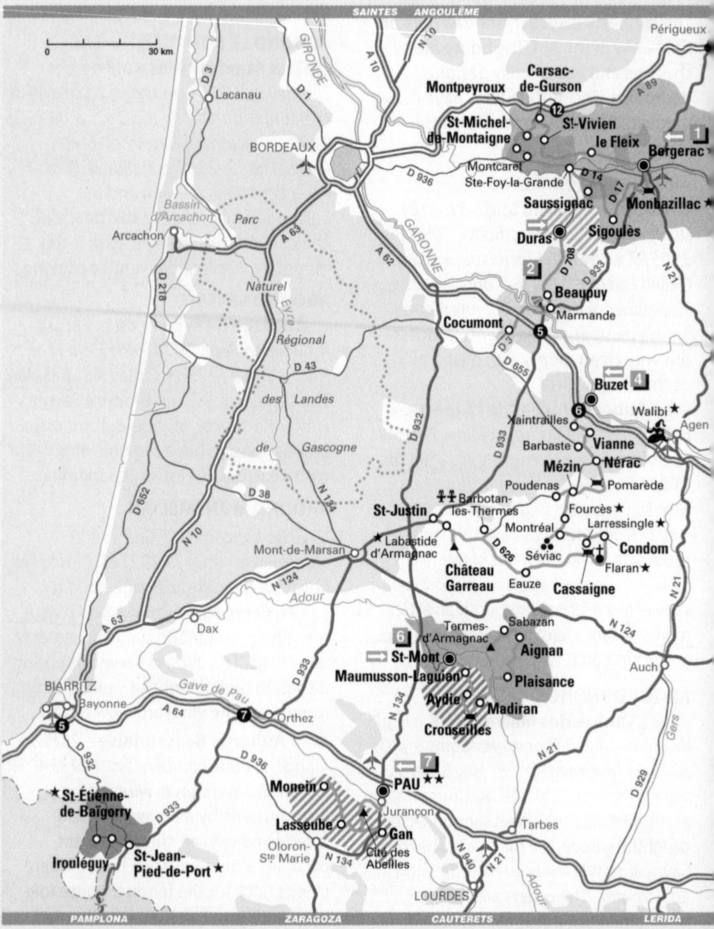

Gaillac and Agen were only allowed into the port of La Lune in Bordeaux once Bordeaux wines had been sold and shipped. Fortunately, the development of the railway and road networks enabled wines from the Southwest to break free without losing their identity in the process: the region has preserved a number of ancient grape varieties, some of which were probably already being cultivated long before the arrival of the Romans. It is thought that many varieties that are grown all over France - such as Cabernet Franc that is so prized in the Loire and in Bordeaux - have their origins growing as wild grapes in the foothills of the Pyrenées.

Highlights

1. Take a gabare boat from the old port of **Bergerac** (p437)
2. Admire the view while driving across the **Millau Viaduct** (p443)
3. Indulge a sweet tooth at the Musee de l'Art et du Sucre in **Cordes-sur-Ciel** (p449)
4. Visit an Armagnac distillery in **Gascony** (p445)
5. Explore the Citadel in **Saint-Jean Pied-de-Port** (p453)

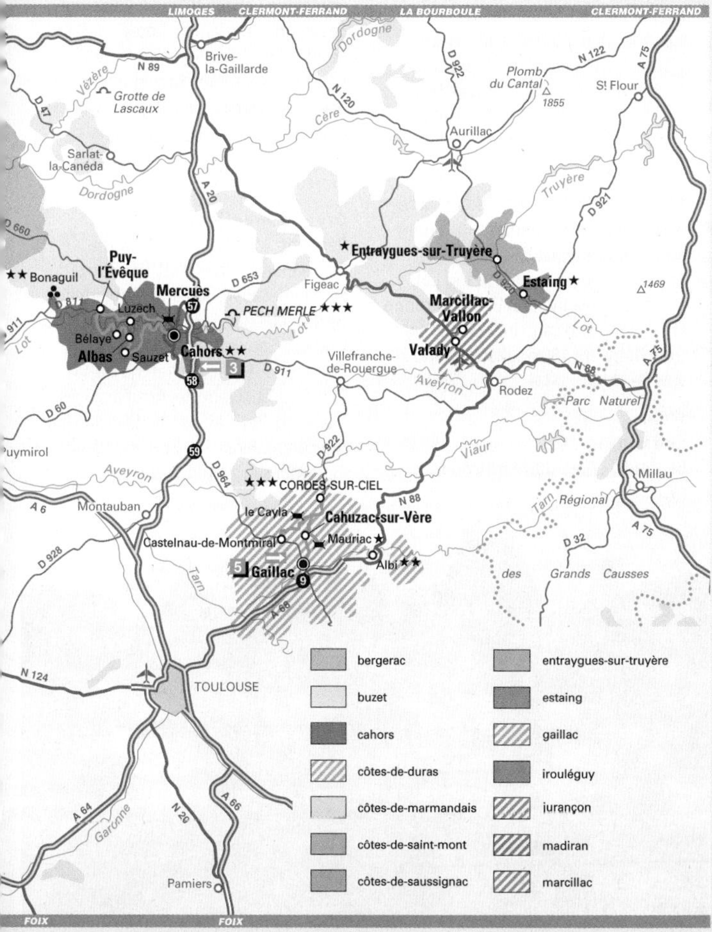

14 - THE SOUTH WEST

OVERVIEW

The Terroir

Michelin Local Maps 329, 336, 337, 338 and 342 – Aveyron (12), Dordogne (24), Gers (32), Lot (46), Lot-et-Garonne (47), Pyrénées-Atlantiques (64), Tarn (81).

Areas and production:
Bergerac 12,200ha, yield 650,000hl; **Buzet** 2,000ha, yield 73,000hl; **Cahors** 4,200ha, yield 200,300hl; **Côtes-de-Duras** 2,000ha, yield 114,000hl; **Côtes-du-Frontonnais** 2,400ha, yield 82,000hl; **Côtes-du-Marmandais** 1,650ha, yield 85,600hl; **Côtes-de-St-Mont** 850ha, yield 48,000hl; **Entraygues et Fel** 20ha, yield 550hl; **Estaing** 19ha, yield 700hl; **Gaillac** 3,850ha, yield 180,000hl; **Irouléguy** 210ha, yield 55,000hl; **Jurançon** 1,050ha, yield 40,000hl; **Madiran** 1,300ha, yield 65,000hl; **Marcillac** 170ha, yield 7,400hl; **Monbazillac** 2,000ha, yield 48,000hl; **Pacherenc-du-Vic-Bilh** 250ha, yield 9,000hl.

Over such a large area there is no consistent climate, but mild winters, wet springs, hot summers and sunny autumns are typical. Soils consist of clay near the Dordogne and Lot, gravel or gravelly sand in the Garonne area, stone and sand in Gascony. In total there are 18 appellations and 22 vins de pays.

Wines

Red wines
Bergerac, Côtes-du-Marmandais, Côtes-de-Duras, Buzet: Cabernet Franc, Cabernet-Sauvignon, Merlot and Malbec. Cahors: Malbec. Gaillac: Braucol, Syrah, Merlot, Négrette, Gamay and Cabernet-Sauvignon. Madiran: Tannat. Irouléguy: Cabernet Franc, Cabernet-Sauvignon and Tannat. Côtes-de-St-Mont: Tannat, Fer-Servadou, Cabernet Franc and Cabernet-Sauvignon. Marcillac: Gamay, Jurançon Noir and Merlot. Côtes-du-Frontonnais: Cabernet Franc, Cabernet-Sauvignon, Cinsault Noir and Gamay.

Vineyards of Cahors

J. Damase / MICHELIN

Dry and sweet white wines
Bergerac, Monbazillac, Côtes-du-Marmandais, Côtes-de-Duras, Buzet: Sémillon, Sauvignon and Muscadelle. Gaillac: Mauzac, Loin de l'Oeil, Ondenc, Sauvignon and Muscadelle. Côtes-de-St-Mont, Pacherenc-du-Vic-Bilh: Courbu, Clairette, Arrufiac, Gros-Manseng, Petit-Manseng, Sémillon and Sauvignon. Jurançon: Gros-Manseng, Petit-Manseng and Courbu.

Château de Monbazillac

S. Sauvignier/MICHELIN

1 Bergerac Country

The Guyenne region was dominated by the English crown during the height of the Middle Ages. Outside the fortified walls of the its medieval towns, or *bastides*, vineyards alternate with orchards of plum trees, pastures and woods, where there always seems to be a good place to enjoy a meal and a fine bottle. The Bergerac vineyards are the most extensive of the whole southwest, both in volume and area. They stretch some 50km from west to east along the north bank of the Dordogne, briefly crossing over to the hillsides on the opposite bank, south of the town of Bergerac. Sweet white wines long dominated production but, today production is 60% red and 40% white. All 93 municipalities in the Bergerac area are entitled to the Bergerac AOC. There are also six main sub-appellations.

- **Michelin Map:** 329 B-E 6-7. See round trip 1 on the map on p434.
- **Info:** www.vins-bergerac.fr
- **Location:** 130km drive. East of the Bordeaux region, on the hills and slopes of the Dordogne Valley.
- **Don't Miss:** Wandering through the atmospheric old town, with its Medieval houses.

DRIVING TOUR

Bergerac★

The historic capital of the middle Dordogne Valley is the link between Bordeaux and the inland areas. Bergerac owes a lot to Edmond Rostand who chose it as the birthplace of his voluble hero Cyrano.

Old Bergerac★★ is situated next to the **old harbour** where the trading boats, known as *gabares*, used to moor to unload wood from the upper valley and load wine casks bound for Bordeaux. Strolling along the narrow streets, you will discover old timber-framed houses. One of these has been turned into the **Musée regional du Vin et de la Batellerie★: cooperage**. This ancient craft, which played an important role in the economy, is illustrated here and inland water transport comes to life through various models of *gabares* (*open10am–noon & 2–5.30pm, Sat 10am–noon, Sun 2.30–6.30pm; 2€*; 5 rue des Conférences; *05 53 63 04 13)*.

A Renaissance building houses the **Musée du Tabac★★**, which reveals the rather un-PC story of tobacco: Once extensively cultivated in the Bergerac region, it has now almost disappeared. *10 rue de l'Ancinne Pont. Open mid-Mar–mid-Nov Tue–Fri 10am–noon & 2–6pm, Sat 10am–noon & 2–5pm, Sun 2.30–6.30pm; mid-Nov–mid-Mar Tue–Fri 10am–noon & 2–6pm; Sat 10am-noon; 5€; 05 53 63 04 13; www.france-tabac.com/musee.htm.*

The former **Cloître des Récollets** *(access via quai Salvette)* today houses the **Maison des vins de Bergerac**: exhibitions about wine (*see Shopping Guide)* are held in the **cloister building** (12C-17C).

Drive NE out of Bergerac along N 21.

On the outskirts of Bergerac, the **Pécharmant** vineyards, exclusively devoted to the production of rich red wines, climb up the hillsides framing the Caudau Valley.

Return to Bergerac and follow D 933 S.

This is the beginning of the **Monbazillac** appellation, reserved for sweet white wines. It covers a hillside area extending over 2,500ha on the south bank of the Dordogne and includes the region's oldest vineyards, appreciated by the Dutch as early as the 17C because the wines travelled well. Monbazillac wines are

made from grapes affected by what is called "noble rot" and collected manually through successive harvests. The process is the same as at Sauternes (*see BORDEAUX*).
The building of **Monbazillac cooperative** is about 4km from Bergerac.

Left on D 14; then right on D 13.

Château de Monbazillac★

Open Apr–Oct 10am–7.30pm; 6.30€. 05 53 61 52 52; www.chateau-monbazillac.com

The architectural style of this building erected circa 1550 is a blend of military austerity and Renaissance elegance. Inside, the **Great Hall** is adorned with a monumental fireplace and 17C Flemish furniture and tapestries. The wine storehouse, giving on to the main courtyard, has been turned into a restaurant and boutique. The **Musée du Vin** contains, among other exhibits, ancient winemaking and harvesting implements. Even when it is closed in winter, this makes a good stopping point for the view. Several renowned estates are west of the château, among them **Clos l'Envège** (*see Shopping Guide*).

At Monbazillac, right on D 14E.

On the site of the 15C **Moulin de Malfourat**, a viewing table, perched on top of a 180m-high hill, provides details of the **panorama**★.

D 14E joins D 933; turn right then immediately left onto D 17.

The road runs through **Pomport**, a small municipality of the Monbazillac area, which produces some of the best Monbazillacs such as those of **Domaine de L'Ancienne Cure**(*see Shopping Guide*).

Drive to Sigoulès via D 17.

Sigoulès boasts a 16C church as well as one of the largest **cooperatives** in the Bergerac region (*see Shopping Guide*).

Drive NW out of Sigoulès along D 15 then turn left onto D 14 and left again onto D 4 to Saussignac.

Saussignac

This village, camped on a hillside, is surrounded by vineyards of the same name. The Côtes-de-Saussignac vines produce only sweet and extra sweet white wines. The **Côtes-de-Saussignac** AOC was "revived" by a handful of Britons among the many who have settled in the region.

Return on D 4; left on D 14.

Sainte-Foy-la-Grande

Briefly dip back into the Bordeaux region at this point. This attractive town lies at the border between the Gironde and the Dordogne.

Leave Ste-Foy W on D 936. Drive to a place called Tête Noire and turn right.

Montcaret

The site beneath the fine Romanesque church was occupied in Gallo-Roman times by a large **villa** with a peristyle, an atrium and its own **baths**. Particularly remarkable is the heating system, which worked by means of draughts, and the well-preserved 4C **mosaics**★, which comprise sixteen squares decorated with aquatic motifs (*open late May–late Sept 9.45am–12.30pm & 2–6.30pm, last admission 1hr before closing; Oct–May Sun–Fri 10am–12.30pm & 2–5.30pm; closed Jan 1, May 1, Nov 1 & 11, Dec 25; 3€; 05 53 58 50 18*).

Leave to the north.

Château de Montaigne

Visit of the tower by guided tour (45min) Jul–Aug 10am–6.30pm; May–Jun & Sept–Oct Wed–Sun 10am–noon & 2–6.30pm; Feb–Apr & Nov–Dec Wed–Sun 10am–noon & 2–5.30pm. Closed Dec 25. 6€. 05 53 58 63 93. www.chateau-montaigne.com.

Memories of **Michel Eyquem**, lord of Montaigne (1533-92), still haunt the **tower-library** where he dictated the

Essays to his secretary. The beams are engraved with Greek and Latin maxims selected by the philosopher.
The present château, a fine late-19C, neo-Renaissance building, has replaced Montaigne's former residence, destroyed by fire. Walk round the edifice to admire the charming landscape of vineyards and woodland. The wines produced by the vineyards of the estate are on sale at the reception.

NW on D 9; right on D 21 and right again onto D 10 to Montpeyroux.

Between St-Michel-de-Montaigne and Fougueyrolles in the east, the hillsides produce dry white **Montravel** wines as well as sweet white wines classified as **Haut-Montravel** and **Côtes-de-Montravel**. Of particular interest in the Montravel appellation is Chateau Le Raz, where densely-planted vines produce high quality wines. Try cuvée Les Filles and Grand Chene *(24240 Monestier; 05 53 82 48 41; Open Mon–Fri, Sat by appt; www.le-raz.com.*

Montpeyroux

There is a fine view of the area from this isolated hilltop village. Note the west front of the Romanesque **church**, surrounded by the churchyard: its lower parts feature modillions with unusual bawdy motifs. Nearby, an elegant 17C-18C **castle** comprises a main building with two pavilions at right angles flanked by round towers.

Leave Montpeyroux NE.

The road leads to the **Gurson recreation area**, offering opportunities for fishing, canoeing and other sporting activities on the beach that runs alongside Gurson lake. Above are the ruins of **Gurson castle** (11C-14C) camped on a hill planted with vines.

Carsac-de-Gurson

This village, surrounded by vineyards, boasts a fine Romanesque church. **La Grappe de Gurson Cooperative** offers a selection of Bergerac wines *(see Shopping Guide).*

Leave Carsac E on D 32; 2km on, right on a minor road to St-Vivien.

Saint-Vivien

You can buy wine from the **St-Vivien et Bonneville Cooperative**, housed in an unusual neo-medieval building *(see Shopping Guide).*

Turn left just before Vélines, then right past the gymnasium.

Les jardins de Sardy★

Open Easter–mid-Nov 10am–6pm. *6€. 05 53 27 51 45.*
Italian and English in influence, these splendid gardens, where colours blend and fragrances mingle, were intended to increase people's sense of smell as well as visual awareness through a wide variety of flowers and herbs. Château de Sardy overlooks 5ha of hillside vineyards. A good-quality Bergerac produced in small quantity *(visit of the wine cellars on request).*

Drive to Vélines; left on D 32E2 towards Fougueyrolles and Le Fleix.

Running on top of the plateau, the small road winds through vineyards, past some of the finest estates in Bergerac country, such as **Château Roque-Peyre** *(See accommodation)* in **Fougueyrolles and Chateau Tour des Gendres in Ribagnac**. *(see Shopping Guide).*

Le Fleix

In this small town on the banks of the Dordogne, historically linked to the Protestant faith, the treaty ending the seventh War of Religion was signed in 1580. The Protestant church is housed in a former castle in the town centre.

Drive E to Prigonrieux along D 32.

In spite of its name, the tiny **Rosette** appellation, located on the hillsides overlooking **Prigonrieux**, only produces sweet white wines with a strong bouquet.

2 Côtes de Duras & Marmande

The Côtes-de-Duras AOC covers around 2,000ha following on the from the Entre-Deux-Mers appellation (*see Bordeaux*). These wines use similar grapes to those of Bordeaux and make dry and sweet styles. The road runs through undulating countryside and orchards of plum trees; once dried, these become the delicious Agen prunes.

Michelin Map: 336 C-D 1-3. See itinerary 2 on the map on p434.

Location: 40km from Duras to Cocumont (Lot-et-Garonne).

Don't Miss: A walk through the vineyards around Cocumont.

DRIVING TOUR

Duras

The dukes of Duras inspired Marguerite Donadieu, whose father was a native of nearby Pardaillan, to take Duras as her pen name. In her book *Les Impudents*, the Duras castle is mentioned, but under the name of Ostel. Built in 1308, the original **castle** had eight towers. In 1680 it was remodelled into a country residence then suffered during the Revolution.

A tour of the castle includes the guardroom, the kitchen, the bakery, the well, the dungeons and the whispering room. A **museum** provides information on wine-growing and wines, cereals, arts and crafts and daily life (*last admission 1hr before closing; open Apr–Sept 10am–6pm/7pm; Nov–Mar weekends & school holidays 2–6pm; 6€; 05 53 83 77 32; www.chateau-de-duras.com).*

The **Maison des Vins**, which houses the Association of Côtes-de-Duras winegrowers, provides information about the estates which are open to the public and has 160 different wines for sale; the nearby **Cave Berticot** cooperative sells a fine Sauvignon made from grapes of old vines (*see Shopping Guide).*

End your visit to Duras on a sweet note by calling at **Éts Guinguet**, where all kinds of prune and chocolate specialities are made by traditional methods (*Route de Monségur, 47120 Duras, 05 53 83 72 47; www.maisonguinguet.com).*

South on D 708 for Marmande.

The **Côtes-du-Marmandais** AOC extends on both sides of the Garonne, around Marmande, and covers an area of 1,600ha. The bulk of the production comes from local cooperatives.

Beaupuy

There is a superb view of the Garonne Valley from this village which boasts a lovely 13C church.

Marmande

The rather dowdy town of Marmande is renowned for its plums, peaches, melons, tobacco and above all its tomatoes. The **Église Notre-Dame** (13C-16C) contains a 17C Entombment on the left near the entrance. On the south side of the church, there is a Renaissance cloister with French-style gardens.

Leave Marmande S via the bridge across the Garonne, turn right onto D 116 then left onto D 3 and drive 14.5km to Cocumont.

Cocumont

The municipality of Cocumont offers a **discovery trail** across the vineyards. This walk, which affords magnificent viewpoints, will also offer you an insight into the mysteries of the wine-grower's craft. The Cave du Marmandais cooperative sells a selection of local wines. (*see Shopping Guide*). The area used to produce white wines, but today the Cocumont vineyards are mainly devoted to reds. The **Élian Da Ros estate** is worth a visit to understand the potential of these vineyards (*see Shopping*).

3 Cahors Wine Road

The vineyards of the Cahors AOC follow the meanders of the Lot and climb up on terraces to the plateaux stretching along the river between Cahors and Soturac. Explore both banks of the Lot and discover historic villages, impressive castles and magnificent views of one of France's most beautiful valleys. Cahors wines are exclusively red, and almost entirely made from Malbec grapes.

- **Michelin Map:** 337 C-E 4-5. See round trip 3 on the map on p434.
- **Location:** 90km starting from Cahors (Lot).
- **Don't Miss:** Wandering through the medieval streets of Cahors.

DRIVING TOUR

Cahors★★

The monuments of Cahors reveal a great deal about its past. It was historically a successful city, and its wines among the most celebrated in Europe, but it was the most badly affected region in France by the phyloxerra outbreak, and has only really begun to recover its reputation in the last decade. But even while the region was more famous for its truffles than its wine, there were always reminders of its past glories.

Spanning the Lot, **Pont Valentré**★★ is a kind of fortress guarding the river crossing and is regarded as the emblem of Cahors. Built in 1308, it was considerably remodelled when Viollet-de-Duc undertook its restoration in 1879. As for the **Cathédrale St-Étienne**★★, its construction began in the 11C and it owes its fortress-like appearance to the work commissioned by its successive bishops. The **north doorway**★★, depicting the Ascension, is the former Romanesque doorway of the west front; erected in 1135. Inside the Cathedral, there is a marked contrast between the well-lit nave and the chancel decorated with stained glass and paintings.

The **Cathedral district**★ is the most picturesque part of town with its narrow streets and old houses. The 13C **Église St-Barthélemy**, situated in the upper part of the old town, features a fine rectangular belfry-porch. From the nearby terrace, there is a lovely view of the Lot Valley. Follow rue de la Barre to the **Barbican** and **Tour St-Jean**★ (also known, rather grimly, as the Tower of the Hanged Men), the finest fortified buildings in Cahors.

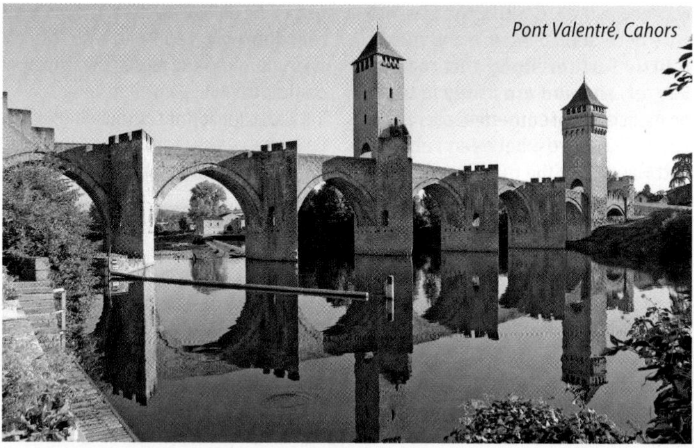

Pont Valentré, Cahors

R. Mattès/MICHELIN

NW on D 8 towards Luzech.

The **Cap Nature** Site in **Pradines** organises recreational activities up in the trees, suitable for everyone from the age of three *(Chemin de l'Isle, 46090 Pradines; open mid-Jun–mid-Sept 9am–7pm; Mar–mid-Jun & mid-Sept–mid-Nov Wed & weekends 1–6pm; reservations required; 05 65 22 25 12; www.capnature.eu).*
A short drive away is **Douelle**, a former stopover for inland water transport, where staves used for making barrels, known as *douelles*, were unloaded. Fine view of the Lot.

Turn right in Largueil.

The **Côtes d'Olt cooperative** in **Parnac** initiated the revival of Cahors wines after the severe frosts of 1956. The Château Saint-Didier, home of the **Domaine Franck et Jacques Rigal**, is also well worth a visit *(see Shopping Guide).*

Rejoin D 8 and turn right then left onto D 23. Drive through St-Vincent-Rivière-d'Olt and continue to Cambayrac.

Cambayrac lies beyond the hamlet of Cournou, in a pleasant landscape of vineyards and arid plateaux.

Cambayrac

The **church** features a Romanesque apse adorned in the 17C with a rare Classical-style decoration of marble and stucco.
A little further along this road, at Sauzet, and you are firmly in truffle country, on the southern border of the Cahors vineyards. Between February and March, visit the truffle market held in the market at Lalbenque, not far from Sauzet.

Drive N to Albas along D 37.

Albas

This small town, which used to be the seat of the bishops of Cahors, has retained the remains of the Episcopal castle and narrow streets lined with old houses.

Follow D 8 to Bélaye.

Bélaye

This village stands on top of a high cliff towering over the Lot. From the upper square, there is a panoramic **view★** of the valley. Elegant houses recall the times when Bélaye formed part of the fief of the bishops of Cahors. An increasingly important cello festival takes place in the church during the first week in August.

Grézels

The bishops of Cahors owned the Lot Valley between Cahors and Puy-l'Évêque and Grézels marked one of the boundaries of their fief. In the 12C, they therefore built the **Château de la Coste** to guard the entrance to their land. A small **Wine Museum** is housed inside *(open mid-Jul–Aug 3–6pm; 4€; 05 65 21 38 28).*

Continue along D 8.

The Pont de Courbenac offers the best overall **view** of the town of Puy-l'Évêque.

Puy-l'Évêque

This small town is built on terraces on the north bank of the Lot; the old ochre-coloured stone houses nestle round the keep and the **Église St-Sauveur**, once part of the defence system. The magnificent **doorway** is adorned with statues. The only remaining part of the Episcopal castle is the 13C, 23m-high **keep** towering above the former outbuildings of the Episcopal palace. Admire the panoramic **view** of the valley from the **Esplanade de la Truffière**, next to the keep.
Clos Triguedina is one of the fine wines of the area *(see Shopping Guide).*
If you follow the Lot Valley, west of Puy-l'Évêque, you will come across some of the famous estates of the Cahors region, such as **Château de Chambert** in Floressas and the **Château du Cèdre** in **Bru** *(see Shopping Guide).*

Going Back in Time

Pech-Merle Cave★★★

32km E of Cahors along D 663, D 662 and D 41. Visit by guided tour (1hr) only; ticket office open 9.30am–noon & 1.30–5pm. Closed Jan 1–Mar 31 & Nov–Dec. Visit limited to 700 visitors per day (reservations suggested 4 days in advance in Jul–Aug). 7.50€. 05 65 31 27 05. www.pechmerle.com.

During the tour of the cave, you can admire stalactites and stalagmites as well as rock carvings and paintings between 16,000 and 20,000 years old. The **Chapelle des Mammouths** is decorated with drawings of bison and mammoth. In the lower part of the prehistoric gallery, a panel is decorated with the silhouettes of two horses, patterned all over and around with dots and hand prints.

Bonaguil Castle★★

50km NW of Cahors; drive along D 911 to Duravel then follow the signs. Open Jun–Aug 10am–7pm. Mar–May & Sept–Oct 10.30am–1pm & 2.30–5.30pm. Nov–Feb weekends, school & public holidys 11am–1pm & 2.30–5pm. Closed Jan, Dec 25 & 31. 6€. 05 53 71 90 33. www.bonaguil.org.

This splendid medieval fortress, on the borders of Quercy and Périgord Noir, is one of the most perfect specimens of 15C-16C military architecture. Enter the castle through the barbican, a huge bastion which represented the first line of defence. The second line of defence comprised the Grosse Tour (Great Tower), one of the largest of its kind ever built in France. Towering over both lines of defence, the keep was the watch and command station. The complex included shops and facilities which granted the castle complete autonomy in the event of a siege… but the castle was never put to the test.

Millau Viaduct

The 'Pont du Gard of the 21st century should not be missed when in this part of France. Designed by Lord Norman Forster, the viaduct crosses the Tarn valley to connect the Causse du Larzac to the Causse Rouge.

Musée Toulouse-Lautrec★★

In Albi, 23km E of Gaillac via D 988 and N 88. Open Jul–Aug 9am–6pm. Jun & Sept 9am–noon & 2–6pm. Apr–May 10am–noon & 2–6pm. Mar–Oct Wed–Mon 10am–noon & 2–5.30pm. Jan–Feb & Nov–Dec Wed–Mon 10am–noon & 2–5pm. Closed Jan 1, May 1, Nov 1, Dec 25. 5.50€. 05 63 49 48 70. www.musee-toulouse-lautrec.com. Henri de Toulouse-Lautrec was born into a wealthy aristocratic family in Albi in 1864. His childhood was marred by two accidents which left him deformed and he left Albi for Montmartre in 1882. Over one thousand works bequeathed by the artist's parents are exhibited here.

Prehistoric painting in Grotte du Pech-Merle

E. Larribère/MICHELIN

KIDS

Walibi Aquitaine★
4km SW of Agen along D 656. Open June 15–late Aug 10am–6pm. Apr-May & Sept-Nov 10am–5pm; 10am–6pm; 22.50€ (children 3-11 17€). 05 53 96 58 32. www.walibi.com. This amusement park offers something for visitors of all ages. You can whirl round in giant coffee cups, go down the raging Radja River or watch the musical fountains (650 moving fountains) and the trained seals performing acrobatics.

Cite de l'Espace
Just outside of Toulouse, this is the leading family attraction in the southwest. Interactive exhibits, a planetarium, life-size replicats of the Mir Space Station and Ariane Five space rocket and plenty of chidlren's space-themed play areas *(Avenue Jean Gonord, 31500 Toulouse, 05 62 71 56 21; Open 9.30am-5pm (until 7pm Jul-Aug); 21€; www.cite-espace.com).*

Leave Puy-l'Évêque E along D 811.

Prayssac

Lively in summer, with many open air markets, this small town lying beneath Calvayrac castle overlooks one of the tighter meanders of the Lot, enclosing the **Domaine Cosse-Maisonneuve** vineyards which produce good wines *(see Shopping Guide).*

The **Dolmens discovery trail** to the north-east leads to many megaliths dating back to 3BC *(itinerary available from the tourist office).*

Drive to Luzech along D 9.

Luzech

Crowned by its castle keep, Luzech occupies a magnificent site tucked inside a loop of the Lot, with the remains of the Roman Oppidum of Impernal to the north and the Pistoule promontory to the south, from where you can do parachute jumping and hiking.

It's worth heading up to the top of Impernal Hill, from where there is a beautiful view over the town below and surrounding vineyards. Equally impressive is the view from the terrace of the 12C **keep**. Stroll through the **old town** and explore the district around place des Consuls which has retained its medieval look. Housed in the fine vaulted cellar of the 13C Consuls' residence *(tourist office)*, the **Musée Archéologique Armand-Viré** retraces the rich past of the site. Some items dating back to Roman times. *Open Jul-Aug Mon–Sat 10-am–1pm & 2–6pm; Sept-June Mon-Sat 10am-1pm & 2-5pm; 3€; 05 65 20 17 27; www.ville-luzech.fr.*

Drive on to Cahors along D 9 and D 145.

The narrow road follows the meanders of the Lot and goes through **Caix** with its splendid water sports centre offering swimming, sailing and windsurfing. **Domaine de Lagrézette**, a handsome Renaissance building in **Caillac**, produces some of the finest Cahors wines, owned by Alain Dominique Perrin, former director of luxury goods Richemont Group. The underground cellars and the barrel storehouse, can be visited *(46140 Caillac; open by appt. 10am–5pm; 05 65 20 07 42; www.chateau-lagrezette.tm.fr).*

Rejoin D 145 and drive on to Mercuès.

Château de Mercuès

05 65 20 00 01; www.chateaudemercues.com.
The château occupies a remarkable site overlooking the north bank of the Lot. Mentioned as early as 1212, extended in the 14C and 15C, the fortress became a country residence in the 16C and later the seat of the bishops of Cahors: it was restored in the 19C. Today it is a hotel-restaurant. The vineyard of the château is renowned, but the cellars can currently only be visited by hotel guests.

4 Gascony

DRIVING TOUR

- **Michelin Map:** Michelin Local Map 336 A-E 4-6. See itinerary 4 on the map on p434.
- **Location:** 215km from Buzet-sur-Baïse to Labastide-d'Armagnac.
- **Don't Miss:** Fields of sunflowers in summer.

Buzet-sur-Baïse

The Buzet vineyards lie along both banks of the river Garonne, between Marmande and Agen. Revived in the 1960s thanks to **Les Vignerons de Buzet** cooperative, the vineyards produce red, white and rosé wines mainly from Bordeaux grape varieties. The Vignerons de Buzet produces all the varieties of wines qualifying for the **Buzet** AOC and accounts for around 97% of the entire appellation's production. It offers a tour of the maturing cellars which contain 4, 000 barrels, and has an informative slide show. A visit to the cooperage reveals the fascinating subtleties of the barrel-makers craft *(Saubouère; open daily in summer 9am–12.30pm & 2–7pm; winter by appt.; 05 53 84 74 30; www.vignerons-buzet.fr).*

Follow D 108 S to Xaintrailles.

South of the Garonne Valley, between the Gers and the Baïse, vineyards have been devoted to the production of **Armagnac** for centuries.

The production of Armagnac extends over three specific areas: Bas-Armagnac in the west, where soils are acid and sandy; Haut-Armagnac in the east and the north, where chalky soils prevail; Ténarèze in the centre where soils are a mixture of clay, chalk and sand.

In the land of musketeers, of good food and of rugby, people know how to enjoy themselves. The Festival de Jazz in Marciac, Festival des Bandas in Condom and the Tempo Latino in Vic-Fezensac are essential summer entertainment.

E to Vianne on D 141.

Vianne

The fortifications of this former English *bastide*, founded in 1284, are almost intact and it has retained its distinctive chequerboard plan. Glassmaking is the traditional activity and there are glass-blowers and glass-cutters still working here.

D 642 south, cross the Baïse; drive on to Barbaste, then D 930 to Nérac.

Nérac

Jeanne d'Albret, Henri IV's mother, set up in Nérac an important centre for

Armagnac and Floc-de-Gascogne

Armagnac is distilled from white wines made from Colombard, Ugni Blanc, Baco and Folle Blanche grapes. The process takes place no later than 30 March, following the harvest. The white eau-de-vie (spirit) is then stored in oak casks where it acquires its colour and is matured for varying lengths of time. There are three main categories according to age: the "3 Stars" or "VS" have spent at least eighteen months maturing in casks; the "VO" (Very Old) or "VSOP" (Very Superior Old Pale) have matured for at least four and a half years; the "XO", "Napoléon", are at least five and a half years old. Since 2005, a white Armagnac known as Blanche has been a separate AOC.

Floc-de-Gascogne, produced in Armagnac country, is a fortified wine made from a mixture of fresh grape juice - containing at least 170g of sugar per litre - with young Armagnac. The alcohol stops the fermentation of the must, which thus retains its sugar. Floc can be either white or rosé. www.floc-de-gascogne.fr.

the promotion of humanist ideas and the Protestant faith. The poet Clément Marot described the place as "a refuge more pleasant than freedom". A tour of the **old town**★ includes the **Maison de Sully** (second half of the 16C), **Pont Vieux**, old houses with typical loggias and **Pont Neuf** affording a fine view of the river banks.

The **Promenade de la Garenne**, along the Baïse, offers a very pleasant walk beneath one-hundred-year-old oak trees. Jeanne d'Albret's Renaissance **castle** has a small **museum** houseing archaeological collections *open June-Sept 10am–6pm; Oct–May Tue–Thur, Sat-Sun 2–6pm; 4€; 05 53 65 21 11).*

Château du Frandat produces Buzet wine, Armagnac and Floc *(see Shopping Guide).*

Leave Nérac S along the Condom road (D 930). 6.5km further on, behind a screen of greenery on the right, stands Pomarède castle.

Château de Pomarède

47600 Moncrabeau. Visit by guided tour (30min) mid-Jul–mid-Sept 9am–noon & 3–6pm; rest of the year, enquire. 4€. 05 53 65 43 01.

This 17C-18C Gascon-style manor features a dovecot, a wine cellar, stables and a saddlery.

Rejoin the road and turn right onto D 149 1km further on.

Mézin

This hilltop place is a centre of winegrowing and cork-making. The 11C **Église St-Jean-Baptiste** features a composite style. The **Musée du Liège et du Bouchon** illustrates the times when Mézin was one of the capitals of cork-making (*open Jul–Aug Tue–Sun 10am–12.30pm & 2–6.30pm; Apr–Jun & Sept-Oct Tue–Sat 2–6pm, Sun 3–5.30pm; closed public holidays except Jul 14 & Aug 15; 4€; 05 53 65 68 16).*

Drive W out of Mézin along D 656. As you leave, note on your left a Gascon dovecot perched on pillars.

Poudenas

This village, crisscrossed by steep streets, is dominated by a 16C-17C **castle** featuring a fine Italian-style façade (*visit by guided tour on request with mimimum of 10 people; 5; 05 53 65 70 53).*

From the old bridge, there is a lovely view of the castle, the church tower and the Hôtellerie du Roy Henry with its wooden gallery.

Return to Mézin and turn right onto D 5 running into D 29.

Fourcès★

This attractive circular *bastide*, one of the most charming villages of the Gers area, is popular with artists and craftsmen. The lofty 15C-16C **castle** stands alongside the Auzoue where water lilies grow in summer. Today it is a renowned hotel and restaurant. An array of colours brightens up the small town on the last weekend in April, when the springflower market and festival is on.

Montréal

This *bastide*, founded in 1256, has retained its fortified Gothic church and its central square lined with arcaded houses; one of these has been turned into an interesting **Musée archéologique** displaying finds from the Séviac site *(access via the tourist office; open Jul–Aug Mon 10am-12.30pm & 2-6pm, Tue–Sat 10am–12.30pm & 2–7pm; Mar–Jun & Sept–Nov Tue–Sat 10am–12.30pm & 2–6pm; Dec–Feb Tue–Sat 10am–12.30pm & 2–5.30pm; 05 62 29 42 85).*

Follow the signs to the Séviac site, west of Montréal.

Villa gallo-romaine de Séviac

Open Jul–Aug, 10am–7pm. Mar–Jun & Sept–Nov 10am–noon & 2–6pm. Guided tours (1hr) available. 4€, combined ticket to the Musée archéologique in Montréal. 05 62 29 48 57; www.seviac-villa.com.

Excavations have revealed the foundations of a luxury 4C Gallo-Roman villa, as well as various remains testifying to a permanent occupation of the site from the 2C to the 7C. The extensive baths of the villa include rooms heated by hypocaust (an underfloor heating system), a swimming pool and several pools lined with marble and decorated with exceptionally fine mosaics.

Follow D 15 towards Condom as far as Larressingle.

Larressingle★

This walled-in 13C gem is the favourite haunt of artists and craftsmen. A spiral staircase links the three storeys of the ruined **keep**. The fortified Romanesque **church** has been reduced to two adjoining chancels.

Walk round the fortifications along the path running outside the walls. You'll also discover the **Cité des Machines du Moyen-Âge**, a 13C siege camp, realistically reconstructed at the foot of the fortifications (*visit by guided tour (1–2hr) Jul-Aug 10am–7pm; Sept-Jun 2-6pm; 8€; 05 62 68 33 88).*

A shop, situated opposite the main entrance to the village, sells regional products, local wines and Armagnac from nearby farms.

Condom

The historic capital of the Armagnac and Ténarèze areas is a handsome, well restored city that is always pleasantly bustling with activity. Its name may be a source of stifled amusement for English-speaking visitors but the name in fact comes from a Gallo-Roman word meaning 'old market town'. Every summer, Condom enthusiastically livens up to the sound of brass bands during the Festival des bandas, and there are lively markets throughout the year.

The **Cathédrale St-Pierre**★, with its impressive square tower, dates from the early 16C and is one of the last great Gothic buildings to be erected in the Gers region. Adjoining the eastern gallery of the **cloisters**★, St Catherine's Chapel, now a public passageway, has attractive polychrome keystones.

Those who appreciate Armagnac and Floc are spoilt for choice. By way of an introduction to the subject, visit the **Musée de l'Armagnac** *(rue Jules-Ferry)* which displays a rare collection of implements, an array of cooperage tools, bottles made by Gascon glassmakers and various stills (*open Apr–Oct Wed–Mon 10am–noon & 3-6pm; Nov-Mar Wed–Sun 2–5pm; closed public holidays; 2.20€. 05 62 28 47 17).*

For a more practical approach, call at **Maison Ryst-Dupeyron**, housed in the fine 18C Hôtel de Cugnac. This establishment offers a visit of the 18C wine cellar. The tour includes audio-visual presentations and a free tasting *(1 r. Daunou; visit by 1hr guided tour Jul–Aug Mon–Fri 9am–noon & 2–5pm, weekends & public holidays 2.30–6.30pm; Sept–Jun 9am–noon & 2–5.30pm; closed Jan 1; no charge; 05 62 28 08 08).*

Leave Condom S along D 930.

Abbaye de Flaran★

Open Jul–Aug 9.30am–7pm. Feb–Jun & Sept–Dec 9.30am–12.30pm & 2–6pm. Closed last fortnight in Jan, May 1 & Dec 25. 5€, no charge 1st Sun of the month (Nov-Mar). 05 62 28 50 19.

Admire the simplicity and austerity of this beautiful Cistercian abbey: owned by the Gers *département*, it holds first-class art exhibitions.

Built between 1180 and 1210, the **church** features interior columns with very simple ornamentation. The **cloister** is reached via the church. The west gallery alone is original (late 14C); it is covered with timberwork. The **gardens** are in two sections: one is laid out in the French style and the other, near the old mill, grows herbs and medicinal plants.

Drive NW to Cassaigne along D 142.

Château de Cassaigne

Open Jul-Aug 9am–noon & 2–6pm, Sept-Jun Tues-Sat 9am-noon & 2-6pm, Sun 2-6pm. 05 62 28 04 02. www.chateaudecassaigne.com.

The former country residence of the bishops of Condom dates from the 13C. The visit includes a tour of the wine cellar and a slide show relating the history of the château, wine-growing and the origins of Armagnac. There are interesting 16C kitchens. Don't forget to taste the local product after admiring the vineyards.

D 208 and D 931 lead to Gondrin and Eauze.

The fine Romanesque church in **Mouchan** is worth a visit. **Gondrin** is an attractive *bastide* surrounded by vineyards. Gourmets will want to call at the **Ferme du Cassou**, where they can find just about all the delicacies of the Gers from foie gras to local goats' cheese (*open in season Sun afternoon–Sat 9am–7pm; 05 62 29 15 22; www.fermeducassou.com).*

Eauze

The capital of Bas-Armagnac is the ancient Elusa, the region's main city in Gallo-Roman times, which have left their mark. The sandy soils of Bas-Armagnac are reckoned to produce the best wines for distillation. Wine-growers, who have signposts along the roads, also sell Côtes-de-Gascogne local wines. **Château du Tariquet** makes a popuar, good quality white wine, and is one of the largest wine-growing estates in France (*see Shopping Guide).*

Place d'Armagnac is a picturesque square lined with arcaded houses. The 15C **Cathédrale St-Luperc** is a typical example of southern Gothic architecture.

The prime exhibit of the **Musée archéologique** is the **Gallo-Roman treasury** of Eauze: coins and jewellery encrusted with precious stones (*open Jun–Sept Wed–Mon 10am–12.30pm, 2–6pm; Feb–May & Oct–Dec Wed–Mon 2–5pm, mornings by request; closed 1st weekend in July & public holidays; 4€; no charge 1st Sun of the month Nov-Mar; 05 62 09 71 38).*

Another excellent dry white Cotes de Gascogne in Gondrin, just east of Eauze, is Domaine de Cassagnoles. A little further afield, try Domaine San de Guilhem (see Shopping Guide.)

Continue to Barbotan-les-Thermes along D 626 and D 656.

Barbotan-les-Thermes♆♆

The hot underground springs, renowned for the treatment of leg complaints, have encouraged the growth of exotic plants in the **park** surrounding the spa establishment: a pleasant place for a stroll before visiting the 12C **church**.

In summer, **Uby Lake**, situated south of the town, offers its shores, laid out as a recreation area, to anyone wishing to take a dip.

Continue to Labastide-d'Armagnac along D 626.

On the right before reaching Labastide, a path leads to **Notre-Dame-des-Cyclistes** Chapel, dedicated to cycling enthusiasts who, in the words of the prayer to protect them, "travel all across the Lord's beautiful Creation". It's a charming spot and makes a perfect stop for a picnic.

Labastide-d'Armagnac★

Lovely *bastide* founded in 1291. Place Royale is surrounded by old timber-framed houses surmounting a row of arcades bedecked with climbing roses. Impressive 15C bell-tower.

Saint-Justin

This is the oldest *bastide* in the Landes region (1280). It already existed at the time of Henri IV.

Return to Labastide-d'Armagnac, follow D 626 towards Cazaubon then turn right and drive 3.5km along D 209.

Écomusée de l'Armagnac – Château Garreau

Open Apr–mid-Nov Mon–Fri 9am–noon & 2–6pm; weekends 3–6pm, mid-Nov–Mar Mon–Fri 9am–noon & 2–6pm. 5€. 05 58 44 88 38.

This important estate has set up a winegrowers' museum displaying implements and old stills. A pleasant trail will enable you to discover the local aquatic fauna and an experimental wood where ceps are cultivated. A shop sells produce from the estate.

5 Gaillac Area

The hillsides of the Gaillac area, dotted with fairy-tale villages, are reminiscent of Tuscany and offer a gentle transition from the Atlantic to the Mediterranean influence. Gaillac, extending over 3,850ha west of Albi, has been a wine-growing region since Roman times. There is a wide variety of grape types, which explains why just about every kind of wine is produced here: sparkling, dry and sweet white wines, red and rosé wines, all under Gaillac AOC.

- **Michelin Map:** Local Map 338 C-D 6-7. See tour 5 on the map on p434.
- **Location:** 80km starting from Gaillac (Tarn).
- **Don't Miss:** The hilltop town of Cordes sur Ciel.

DRIVING TOUR

Gaillac

Gaillac istelf is a beautiful town that rewards a few days exploration. Stroll through the network of narrow winding streets lined with old houses that form a harmonious blend of brick and wood. The Hauts de Gaillac hike *(5hr, 18km medium difficulty)* offers the opportunity of discovering the surrounding vineyards *(map available at the tourist office)*. Construction work on the **abbey church of St-Michel** began in the 11C and lasted until the 14C. The former abbey buildings house the **Maison des vins de Gaillac** which provides information on the vineyards, as well as tastings and sales *(see Shopping Guide)*.

The **Musée de l'Abbaye St-Michel**, housed in the same building, displays illustrates the crafts connected with wine-growing *(open Jul-Aug 9.30-1pm & 2-7pm, Sept-Jun 10am–noon & 2–6.30pm; closed Jan 1, May 1, Nov 1, Dec 25; 2.50€; 05 63 57 14 65). Also in Gaillac, the Musée des Beaux Arts is housed in the Italian-style summer villa, Château de Foucaud. Open Jun-Sept Tues-Sept, 10am-noon & 2-6pm. Rest of year Fri-Sun 10am-noon & 2-6pm; 2.50P.*

The **René Rieux and Domaine Rotier** estates are renowned for their good quality *(see Shopping Guide)*.

Leave Gaillac N along D 922 towards Cahuzac-sur-Vère.

Cahuzac-sur-Vère

This former stronghold has some of the most renowned estates of the Gaillac area, in particular **Domaine des Tres Cantous**, famous for its remarkable Vin d'Autan and Vin de Voile. Robert Plageoles, an erudite enthusiast, speaks very poetically about his wines and the old grape varieties that he has revived *(81140 Cahuzac-sur-Vère; open Mon–Sat 8am–noon & 2–6pm; Sun by appt; 05 63 33 90 40; www.vins-plageoles.com)*.

D 21 leads SE to Mauriac castle.

Château de Mauriac★

Visit by 1hr guided tour May–Oct 3–6pm. Rest of the year Sun & public holidays 3–6pm. 6€. 05 63 41 71 18 www.bistes.com.

Partly dating from the 14C, this castle has a fine harmonious façade. The tour includes several ground-floor rooms displaying paintings by artist Bernard Bistes, the owner of the castle. The first-floor rooms have all been restored and furnished in different styles and colour schemes.

Follow D 21 then turn left onto D 30.

The road runs through vineyards to **Cestayrols** where **Domaine de Lacroux** produces an excellent red *(see Shopping Guide)*. The 15C church in **Noailles** boasts a fine vaulted chancel.

North on D 30; right on D 922.

Cordes-sur-Ciel★★★

This medieval town occupies a splendid **site**★★ on a height overlooking the Cérou Valley. Sometimes called the "town with a hundred Gothic arches", Cordes is a timeless city, made all the more beautiful by the sunlight playing on the pink and grey hues of its sandstone façades. Visiting Cordes means breathing in the atmosphere of this old city, strolling through the narrow cobbled streets among exceptionally fine 13C-14C **Gothic houses**★★, admiring the carved ornamentation of their façades and the often highly original window displays made by craftsmen!

Maison Prunet, located in the centre of the fortified town, houses the **Musée de l'Art et du sucre**; a mini-paradise – or a trial of temptation – for anyone with a real sweet tooth! Mostly displayed in glass cases are works of art made entirely of sugar and chocolate (*open Jun 15–Sept 15 10.30am-12.30pm & 1.30-7pm; rest of the year Tues pm-Sun 10.30am–12.30pm & 1.30–6pm; 3€; 05 63 56 02 40).*

Drive S along D 922 towards Gaillac, then, 8km further on, turn right to Le Cayla castle.

Chateau-Musée du Cayla

This typical Languedoc manor house was the family home of **Eugénie de Guérin** (1805-48) and her brother **Maurice** (1810-39), both romantic poets and writers; the **Musée Maurice-et-Eugénie-de-Guérin** is devoted to them. The peaceful surroundings and the faithfully reconstructed living quarters are a moving commemoration of the writers, and exhibitions are regularly held by visiting writers and artists (*visit by 1hr guided tour Jul-Aug 10am–12.30 & 2–7pm; rest of year times vary 2€, no charge on the 1st Sun of the month Oct–Apr; 05 63 33 90 30; http://musee-cayla.tarn.fr).*

Continue along the same road until you join up with D 1; turn right then left onto D 4.

The road runs through landscapes where vineyards give way to woodland. The 14C church in **Vieux** contains beautiful frescoes.

Castelnau-de-Montmiral

This picturesque village is an ancient 13C *bastide*, perched on a rocky spur. It is easy to imagine what an important look-out position this must have been: the name Montmiral derives in part from *mirer*, meaning "to see" in Occitan. From its rich past, the *bastide* has retained some old houses, skilfully restored. On the west and south sides of **place des Arcades**, surrounded by arcades, there are two 17C houses. In the 15C parish **church**, note the **gem-encrusted cross-reliquary**★ of the counts of Armagnac, known as the "Montmiral Cross", a fine example of 13C religious gold and silver work. **Château de Mayragues** produces fine Gaillac wines (*see Shopping Guide).*

Return to Gaillac along D 964.

6 Rivière-Basse Area

This undulating region heralds the Pyrenées. Situated southwest of the Gers and encroaching on the Hautes-Pyrénées, the vineyards of Madiran AOC produce renowned red wines. Pacherenc-du-Vic-Bilh, grown around the same area, is a usually sweet and occasionally dry white wine.

Michelin Map: Michelin Local Map 336 B-C 7-8. See round trip 6 on the map on p434.

Location: 75km starting from St-Mont (Gers).

DRIVING TOUR

Saint-Mont

This village, with its picturesque narrow streets, is dominated by an 11C-13C abbey church. However, its main attraction is the **Cave des Producteurs Plaimont**. This important cooperative is one of the most dynamic in France *(see Shopping Guide)*.

Drive S along D 946 then turn left onto D 262 towards Viella.

The road overlooks the vineyards and offers superb views extending as far as the Pyrenees. The village of **Viella** is known for its fine 18C **Château de Viella** *(see Shopping Guide)*.

Continue E along D 136 towards Maumusson-Laguian.

Maumusson-Laguian

Château Lafitte-Teston is worth a visit: the splendid winery of the estate is built over an impressive underground barrel cellar *(32400 Maumusson-Laguian; open Mon–Sat 9am-noon & 1.30–7pm; 05 62 69 74 58; www.chateau-laffitte-teston.com)*.

Follow a minor road S onto D 317 towards Aydie.

Aydie

Aydie is the largest municipality of the Madiran AOC.

The **Château d'Aydie-Vignobles Laplace** is well-known for the quality of its wines and its friendly welcome *(see Shopping Guide)*.

Continue along D 317.

Crouseilles

The **Château de Crouseilles**, a fine 18C building, typical of Béarn, belongs to the local cooperative and its 250 members *(see Shopping Guide)*.

Madiran

The Madiran AOC vineyards were established in the 11C by Benedictine monks, near the village which gave them its name. The vast 12C **abbey church**, built over a remarkable crypt, is still standing. The **Maison des vins du Pacherenc et du Madiran** has been set up in the former priory, next to the church. It offers information about the vineyards as well as a wine tasting and the sale of locally produced wine in rotation *(65700 Madiran; (open Jul–Aug Mon–Sat 10.30am–6pm, Sun 11am–12.30pm & 2–6pm; Sept-Jun Tue–Fri 9am–12.30pm & 2–5.30pm, Sat 10.30am–5.30pm; closed week of Christmas, Jul 14, Aug 15; 05 62 31 90 67; www.civso.com)*.

Drive NE along D 58, turn left onto D 935, then right onto D 946 to Plaisance, then north via D 3 and turn right onto D 20.

Aignan

Situated on the fringe of a vast forest, Aignan castle, famous for its production of Armagnac, has retained a few traces of its medieval past: a square surrounded by covered galleries resting on wooden pillars, half-timbered houses and a Romanesque church with a carved doorway. The castle and its park are privately-owned, but visitors are allowed to enter the courtyard and enjoy the view.

Termes-d'Armagnac

The fortress of Thibaut de Termes (1405-67), one of Joan of Arc's comrades-in-arms, has lost its keep and part of the main building. On the south platform, reached via a dark, steep spiral staircase, you will see the wax figures of the **Musée du Panache gascon**: Gascon musketeers (starting with D'Artagnan), Henri IV, and Thibaut's departure are the prize exhibits *(open Jun–Sept 10am–7.30pm (closed Tues morn); rest of the year Wed–Mon 2–6pm; closed Jan 1; Dec 25; 5€; 05 62 69 25 12; www.toursdetermes.fr)*.

Return to St-Mont via Riscle.

7 Jurançon

The name of Henri IV has been linked with Jurançon and its vineyards ever since the lips of the future king were moistened with a drop of southern wine at his christening.

Michelin Map: Michelin Local Map 342 J-K 3. See itinerary 7 on the map on p434.

Location: 55km from Pau to Monein – (Pyrénées-Atlantiques).

DRIVING TOUR

Pau★★

This is Henri IV's elegant native town. A funicular *(no charge)* links the upper town (Place Royale) and the lower town (railway station). From the **boulevard des Pyrénées**★★, a magnificent **panorama**★★★ extends over the Pyrenees range, from the Pic du Midi de Bigorre to the Pic d'Anie. Plaques fixed to the balustrade show the summits directly opposite and their respective heights. The 14C **castle**★★ was built on the orders of Gaston Phoebus, Count of Foix, a hot-tempered but cultured man best remembered for his treatise on hunting, the *Livre de la Chasse*. The fortress was remodelled into a Renaissance palace by Marguerite d'Angoulême, and houses a superb collection of **tapestries**★★★. The **King's bedroom** contains Henri IV's cradle: a turtle shell from the Galapagos Islands *(visit by 1hr 15min tour mid-Jun–mid-Sept 9.30am–12.30pm & 1.30–6.45pm; mid-Sept–mid-Apr 9.30–11.45am & 2–5pm; 5€, no charge 1st Sun of the month; 05 59 82 38 07. www.musee-chateau-pau.fr)*. East of the castle lies the old town, where a network of picturesque streets lined with antique shops and restaurants offers a stroll.

Leave Pau S along N 134. Drive NW from Jurancson along D 2.

In **Laroin**, you could visit the renowned **Domaine de Souch** *(see Shopping Guide)*.

Turn left onto the winding D 502.

La Cité des Abeilles

Open Jul–Aug 2–7pm (last admission 1hr before closing); rest of year varies; 5€; 05 59 83 10 31. www.citedes abeilles.com.

Devoted to bees, this educational open-air museum offers a nature trail on a hill-side abounding in melliferous plants.

Left onto a minor road running into D 217; turn left then right onto D 230.

The **Chapelle-de-Rousse** area is one of the main centres of Jurançon wine. **Clos Lapeyre** is a good quality estate that has a small musuem in its cellars. A thematic trail offers a pleasant stroll through the vineyard *(La Chapelle-de-Rousse, 64110 Jurançon; Mon–Sat 2–6pm; 05 59 21 50 80; www.jurancon-lapeyre.fr)*.

South towards Gan, then D 24 west to Lasseube, then D 34 towards Monein.

The road runs through the vineyards between Lacommande and Monein. The imposing **Église St-Blaise** (12C-18C) in **Lacommande** features an amazing number of different styles; **Clos Bellevue** in **Cuqueron** produces good wines *(05 59 21 34 82)*.

Monein

Monein is proud of having one of the best Jurançon vineyards; you will be able to judge for yourself at the **Confrérie du Jurançon** *(30min guided tours Juk–Sept by appt in advance; 05 59 21 34 58)*.

It is in the Monein area that you are likely to find the finest sweet Jurançons, often harvested at the beginning of winter, as is the case in the **Cauhapé**, **Bru-Baché**and **Clos Uroulat estates** *(see Shopping Guide)*.

Irouléguy

Irouléguy is the only appellation on the French side of the Basque country, with Spain just a short drive away.

Michelin Map: See map on p434 and Michelin Local Map 342 D-E 3-4.
Location: One of the smallest appellations in southwest France, Irouléguy rises between 200 and 400 metres up into the Pyrénées mountains.
Don't Miss: Matching some mountain Brébis cheese with the local dry white wine.

Saint-Jean-Pied-de-Port★

This very attractive town makes a great base for exploring the region. It is marked by the citadel, restored by Vauban, which guards the town with its red sandstone walls.

Rue de la citadelle, running down to the Nive river, is lined with 16C and 17C houses. N°41, known as the **bishops' prison (Prison des Eveques)**, houses an exhibition devoted to the St Jacques de Compostelle pilgramage route that passes through the area. *(open Jul–Aug 10am–7pm; mid-Apr–Jun & Sept–Oct Wed–Mon 11am-12.30pm & 2–6.30pm; 3€; 05 59 37 00 92).*

Situated in rue de l'Église, the Gothic **Église Notre-Dame** features fine sandstone pillars.

The bastion of the **citadel** offers a panorama of the whole Saint-Jean Valley and its lovely villages (viewing table).

A dramatic *tower*, of Navarre-influenced design, stands in the middle of the vineyards of the **Brana estate**, one of the rare independent producers in this area. Try the Cabernet Franc Irouléguy wine, and don't leave without a bottle of the remarkable pear eau-de-vie *(open Jul–mid-Sept 10am–noon & 2.30–6.30pm; 8€; 05 59 37 00 44).*

In **Ispoure**, as you leave S-Jean-Pied-de-Port to the north, stop in at the **Ferme Abiota** to sample their excellent wines.

In the village of **Irouléguy** *(on D 15, between St-Jean-Pied-de-Port and St-Étienne-de-Baïgorry)*, the **Arretxea estate** is another good place to visit *(see Shopping Guide).*

Saint-Étienne-de-Baïgorry★

11km W of St-Jean-Pied-de-Port along D 15. This typical Basque village is at the very centre of the Irouléguy appellation, as you'll see during a visit to the **Cave coopérative des Vignerons du Pays Basque** *(see Shopping Guide).*

Built in the 18C over a remodelled Romanesque base, the **Église St-Étienne**★ is a good example of typical Basque architecture.

Aveyron Region

Marcillac, Estaing, Entraigues-le-Fel, Côtes-de-Millau… the Aveyron vineyards are a patchwork of small appellations which kept on going in spite of the onslaught of phylloxera, economic ups and downs, and the difficulty of making wine on "faisses"; arid terraces cultivated by a handful of tough wine-growers. These vineyards are all the more interesting since they are located in magnificent surroundings, in the Tarn Gorges and Lot Valley. Make sure your car is fully loaded up with petrol, and take a camera.

Michelin Map: See the map on p434 and Michelin Local Map 338 G4 H3.
Location: Beautifully located vineyards on steep slopes in the Tarn Gorge
Don't Miss: Millau Viaduct

Marcillac vineyards on the red soil of Rouergue

J. Malburet/MICHELIN

MARCILLAC

The small **Marcillac** AOC covers a mere 160ha planted with the Fer-Servadou variety, known here as Mansois, which produces red wines only.

The **Domaine du Cros estate** in **Goutrens** *(12.5km SW of Marcillac along D 962 and D 43)* is one of the main producers *(see Shopping Guide)*.

Marcillac-Vallon

17km NW of Rodez along D 901.

Lying at the bottom of a sheltered valley, the village has fine old houses with cellars. Here, wine was once kept in goatskins rather than barrels, and used to be carried by mules.

Every year at Whitsuntide, the feast of Saint-Bourrou is celebrated in the chapel of **Notre-Dame-de-Foncourieu** *(1km N of the town)*; during this amazing feast, wine-growers welcome the appearance of the first buds on the vines.

Valady

6km southwest of Marcillac along D 962.

The **Vignerons du Vallon** cooperative is located here, in the very heart of the Marcillac appellation *(see Shopping Guide)*. The manor, an old 13C building with a stone-slab roof, houses a small museum of local arts, crafts and daily life.

ESTAING AND ENTRAYGUES-LE-FEL WINES (VDQS)

Estaing★

40km NE of Rodez along D 988 to Espalion, then D 920.

Nestling inside a loop of the Lot, the **castle**, dominated by its 14C-15C keep, guards a group of old houses with stone-slab roofs. It is home to a religious community. The 15C **church** facing the castle boasts a superb bell tower.

The **Vignerons d'Olt** grow the entire production of this small appellation (14ha) consisting of special red and white wines made from a combination of chenin and Mauzac varieties *(L'Escaillou, 12190 Coubiscou; open Jun–Sept Tue–Sat 10am–12.30pm & 3–6.30pm; Oct–May Tue–Wed & Fri 10am–12.30pm, Sat 10am–12.30pm & 3–6.30pm; 05 65 30 71 86; cave.vignerons@wanadoo.fr)*.

Entraygues-sur-Truyère★

17km NW of Estaing along D 920.

Situated at the exit of the splendid Gorges de la Truyère, Entraygues is a small picturesque city and a sports and leisure resort (canoeing-kayaking, rambling). The 20ha vineyard produces fruity white and red wines. It extends over sunny terraced hillsides bordering the River Lot.

WINE BUYING GUIDE

INFORMATION

Comité interprofessionnel des Vins du Sud-Ouest – *BP 92123, 31321 Castanet-Tolosan. ℘05 61 73 87 06. www.vins-du-sud-ouest.com.*

Conseil Interprofessionnel des Vins de la Région de Bergerac – *1 r. des Récollets, 24104 Bergerac. ℘05 53 63 57 57. www.vins-bergerac.fr.*

Union Interprofessionnelle du Vin de Cahors – *430 av. Jean-Jaurès, BP 61, 46002 Cahors Cedex 9. ℘05 65 23 22 24. www.vindecahors.fr.*

Union Interprofessionnelle des Vins des Côtes de Duras – *Maison des Vins, D 668, 47120 Duras. ℘05 53 94 13 48. www.cotesdeduras.com.*

Bureau national interprofessionnel de L'Armagnac AOC – *Place de la Liberté, 32800 Eauze. ℘05 62 08 11 00, www.armagnac.fr.*

Syndicat des Vins de Pays des Côtes de Gascogne – *℘05 62 09 82 19. www.vins-cotes-gascogne.fr.*

Comission Interprofessionnelle desVins de Madiran et du Pacherenc du Vic Bilh – *Le Prieuré, pl. de l'Église, 65700 Madiran. ℘05 62 31 90 67. www.civso.com.*

Syndicat de Défense des Vins d'Entraygues et du Fel – *Le Buis, 12140 Entraygues. ℘05 65 44 50 45. www.civso.com.*

Syndicat des Vins VDQS Estaing – *3 r. Flandres-Dunkerque, 12190 Estaing. ℘05 65 44 75 38. www.civso.com.*

Commission Interprofessionnelle du Vin de Gaillac – *Aabbaye St-Michel, 81600 Gaillac. ℘05 63 57 70 60. www.vins-gaillac.com.*

CHARACTERISTICS

Bergerac, Côtes-de-Duras, Côtes-du-Marmandais, red Buzet – Light ruby to dark purple. Aromas: red berries, blackcurrant, green pepper developing into prune and truffle.

Dry white Bergerac – Light straw to golden green. Aromas: almond and citrus fruit developing into coffee.

Sweet Bergerac – Light straw to golden copper. Aromas: iodine, roasted almond, wild strawberry.

Cahors – Dark purple. Aromas: blackberry, black berries, spices, maturing into truffle and prune. Very tannic when young, becoming more supple with age.

Red Gaillac – Carmine to purple red. Aromas: red berries, pepper and spices.

Sweet Gaillac – Straw-coloured when young, turning to caramel when very old. Aromas: exotic fruit, pear, candied fruit maturing into iodised and spicy flavours.

Dry Jurançon – Light straw to golden green. Aromas: citrus fruit, lime and exotic fruit developing into honey.

Sweet Jurançon – Straw to golden yellow. Aromas: candied citrus fruit, honey and roasted almond.

Red Irouléguy – Vermilion to dark ruby. Aromas: white pepper and red berries.

STORAGE

Red wines – 5 to 10 years depending on quality. Longer for Madiran, Côtes-de-Bergerac and Cahors wines.

Dry white wines – 3 to 5 years for most wines. Montravel wines and some of the Gaillacs keep longer.

Sweet and extra sweet white wines – Monbazillac, Haut-Montravel and some sweet Gaillacs keep very well for over 10 years.

PRICE

Red wines – *Côtes-de-Duras, Côtes-du-Marmandais, Gaillace, Marcillac, Montravel*: 5 to 15€. *Bergerac, Buzet, Côtes-du-Frontonnais*: 5 to 20€. *Cahors, Madiran*: 5 to 25€ (a few go for 76€. *Irouléguy*: 8 to 20€ *Pécharmant*: 5 to 30€.

White wines – Bergerac sec: 10 to 25€. *Côtes-de-Duras, Saussignac*: 8 to 23€. *Jurançon Moeilleux*: 10 to 30€; some at 76€; *dry whites* 10 to 20€. *Monbazillac:* 8 to 10€.
Montravel Sec: 5 to 15€;
Pacherenc-du-Vic-Bilh: 8 to 15€.

WINE MERCHANTS

Atrium – *Route de Toulouse, 46000 Cahors. ℘05 65 20 80 80. www.atrium-online.fr. Open Mon–Sat 8am–12.30pm & 2–7.30pm. Jul–Aug daily 8am–8pm.* This is the headquarters of the Atrium chain, whose concept of storehouse-shop entirely dedicated to wine and to the promotion of the vineyards of

Southwest France is most original. The shop offers a selection from each region and, in particular, a good choice of Cahors, Madiran, Gaillac and Buzet wines.

COOPERATIVES

Cave du Marmandais– *47200 Cocumont. ℘05 53 794 50 21. Open Mon–Sat 9am–noon & 2.30–6pm. Closed public holidays; www.origine-marmandais.com.* Good selection of Côtes-du-Marmandais red wines.

La Grappe de Gurson – *24610 Carsac-de-Gurson. ℘05 53 82 81 50. Open Mon–Fri 10am–noon & 2–6pm. Sat 9am-noon &2-7pm; www.pays-de-bergerac.com.* This cooperative provides a good insight into Bergerac wines and offers very good value for money.

Les Vignerons de Landerrouat-Duras – *Rte. de Ste-Foy-la-Grande, 47120 Duras. ℘05 53 83 75 47. berticot@wanadoo.fr. Open Jul-Aug 8am–12.30 & 2–7pm. Jun, Sept 8am-noon & 2-6pm, rest of year Mon-Fri 8am-noon & 2-6pm.*
Cooperative of 150 winemaker, nearly 35% of whom employ ecologically responsible practices. Wines are aged in oak barrels for 6 to 12 months, or in stainless-steel tanks for 18 months. Whites age on the lees for 3 to 9 months. Côtes-de-Duras.

Cave des Producteurs de Jurançon – *53 ave. Henri-IV, 64290 Gan. ℘05 59 21 57 03. www.cavedejurancon.com. Open Jun–Aug daily 8am–12.30 & 1.30–7pm. Sept–May Mon–Sat 8am–12.30 & 1.30–7pm; www.cavedejurancon.com.*
Grain Sauvage with powerful grape flavours; Château de Navailles made with handpicked grapes; Pyre d'Or, a superb dry Jurançon, Château Les Astous or Croix du Prince, perfect as an apéritif…all these treasures of the Jurançon region are on offer here, at reasonable prices.

Cave de Monbazillac – *Rte. d'Eymet, 24240 Monbazillac. ℘05 53 63 65 06. www.chateau-monbazillac.com. Open Jul–Aug 10am–7.30pm; Sept 10am-7pm, rest of year times vary. Closed public holidays.* The cooperative, which also houses the Musée du Vin offers the best wines of this appellation. A corner is set aside for tasting, allowing visitors to test their nose, and, in the area devoted to the discovery of the terroir, a few wine-making secrets are revealed.

Côtes d'Olt – *Caunezil, 46140 Parnac. ℘05 65 30 71 86. www.vinovalis.com.* These wines are made from 25-year-old vines situated in an exceptionally fine terroir. The cooperative, which includes 250 wine-growers, was set up in 1947 and is now part of the Vinovalis group. For an area covering 1,000ha, there are as many as 1,300 maturing barrels and between one and a half and two million bottles going through the ageing process. Quality controls meet ISO 9000 standards at every stage of the winemaking process. The cellar produces nearly a quarter of the total Cahors output. Cahors.

Cave Cooperative des Vignerons du Pays Basque – *Rte. de St-Jean-Pied-de-Port, 64430 St-Étienne-de-Baïgorry. ℘05 59 37 41 33. Open daily 9am–noon & 2–6.30pm. Closed Sun Oct–May. Guided tours on request (3€).* The cooperative produces most of the Irouléguy AOC and sells many first-rate wines.

Les Producteurs Plaimont – *Rte. d'Orthez, 32400 St-Mont. ℘05 62 69 62 87. Open by appt. Tues–Fri 9am–noon & 2–6pm, Sat 9-noon & 2-5pm, www.plaimont.com.* Today, the cooperative has 1,000 members and vineyards covering 5,300ha. Harvesting is done largely by hand, but what really sets this place apart is the sense of working as a team, and meticulous attention to detail. The cooperative owns more than 5,000 barrels one third of which is renewed every year. Côtes-de-Saint-Mont, Madiran, Pacherenc-du-Vic-Bilh, Vin de Pays des Côtes du Condomois, Vin de Pays des Côtes de Gascogne.

Les Viticulteurs Réunis de St-Vivien et Bonneville – *La Reynaudie, 24230 St-Vivien. ℘05 53 27 52 22. Open Mon–Fri 9am–12.30pm & 2.30–6pm, Sat 9am-noon & 2-5pm. Closed public holidays.* This cooperative has a choice of red and white Bergeracs, at good price.s.

Cave de *Sigoulès – 24240 Sigoulès. ℘05 53 61 55 00. Open May–Sept 9.30am –12.30pm & 2.30–6.30pm; Oct–Apr Mon–Sat 9.30am–12.30pm & 2–5.30pm. Closed public holidays.* Almost all the appellations of the Bergerac region can be found here.

Caves des Vignerons du Vallon – *RN 140, 12330 Valady. ℘05 65 72 70 21 Open Mon–Sat 9am–noon & 2–6pm. Closed public holidays.* This cooperative, which includes some forty wine-growers from Valady and the surrounding area, only sells Marcillac AOC wine. Made from the Fer-Servadou grapes, locally known as mansois, this wine has a fine red colour, raspberry, blackcurrant or bilberry aromas and is both smooth and rich.

WINE CENTRES

Maison des vins de Bergerac – *2 pl. Cayla, quai Salvette, 24100 Bergerac. ℘05 53 63 57 55. www.vins-bergerac.fr. Open Jul–Aug 10am–7pm; Sept Tue–Sat 10am–12.30pm, 2–6pm. Rest of year times vary; www.vins-bergerac.fr.*

La Maison des Vins des Côtes de Duras – *Rte. de Marmande, 47120 Duras. ℘05 53 20 20 70. www.cotesdeduras.com. Open Jun–Sept 10am–noon & 1–6.30pm. Oct-May Mon–Fri 9am–noon & 2–5.30pm.*

Maison des vins de Gaillac - Caveau St-Michel – *Abbaye St-Michel, 81600 Gaillac. ℘05 63 57 15 40. www.vins-gaillac.com. Open Jul–Aug 10am–1pm & 2–7pm ; rest of the year, 10am–noon & 2–6pm. Closed Jan 1, May 1, Nov 1 & Dec 25.* 90 producers and 3 cooperative cellars from the Gaillac AOC are represented here. Tastings, sales, introduction to tasting courses.

Maison des Vins et du Terroir du Jurançon – *64360 Lacommande. ℘05 59 82 70 30. Open mid-Jun–mid-Sept Mon–Sat 10am–noon & 3–7pm, Sun & public holidays 3–7pm. Mid-Sept–mid-Jun Wed–Sun 2–6pm.*

ESTATES

Domaine des Cailloutis – *81140 Andillac. ℘05 63 33 97 63. Open May–Oct daily by appt. 1–7pm.* Having taught oenology in Burgundy for seven years, Bernard Fabre took over the management of this estate in 1998. Some of the vines in the 7ha vineyard are more than 50 years old, and include Braucol, Duras, Mauzac, Jurançon Noir, Ondec and Len de Lel. Organic principles hold sway here; wines are made without yeast, chaptalisation. The red Gaillac Prestige wine is aged for a year in oak barrels. Gaillac, Gaillac Doux, Vin de Pays du Tarn.

Château d'Aydie – Vignobles Laplace – *64330 Aydie, ℘05 59 04 08 00. Open daily 9am–12.30pm & 2–7pm; www.famille laplace.com.* In 1961, the Laplace family pioneered estate-bottling in this part of France, and developed new techniques for taming the often fierce tannins of the local Tannat grape. Today, this excellent-quality property includes 55ha of vineyards planted on mixed soils composed either of chalk and clay or silica and clay. Madiran wines are matured in barrels for eighteen months. Madiran, Pacherenc-du-Vic-Bilh, Vin de Pays des Côtes de Gascogne.

Château de Mayragues – *12km NE of Gaillac along D 964 then D 15, 81140 Castelnau-de-Montmiral. ℘05 63 33 94 08. www.chateau-de-mayragues.com. Open Mon–Sat 9am–12.30 & 2-7pm. Closed Dec 25.* There are many reasons why one should visit this château: its fortified architectural style (14C and 16C), its hilly surroundings, its vineyards (biodynamic wine growing) and its Gaillac wines: red, rosé, white, sparkling and slightly sparkling wines. Two guest rooms and a self-catering cottage available. Gaillac, Gaillac Doux, Vin de Pays du Tarn.

Domaine Élian Da Ros – *Laclotte – 47250 Cocumont – ℘05 53 20 75 22. Open by appt.* This family estate was taken over in 1997 by Élian Da Ros who, one year later, built his own cellars and left the cooperative. Today the vineyard covers 18ha planted with Merlot, Cabernet-Sauvignon, Cabernet Franc, Malbec and Syrah varieties for red wines and with Sauvignon Blanc, Sauvignon Gris and Sémillon for white wines, with an average of 30 years of age. Da Ros worked with Zind Humbrecht in Alsace,

Bottles of Gaillac

S. Sauvignier / MICHELIN

Bottles of Bergerac

S. Sauvignier/MICHELIN

before returning to his family estate and introducing biodynamic practices, no fining or racking. Wines are matured in large casks and barrels for twelve to twenty months depending on the vintage and the year. Côtes-du-Marmandais.

Cave de Crouseilles – *64350 Crouseilles, 05 59 68 10 93. Open for tasting and sales May–Sept Mon–Sat 9am–1pm & 2–7pm, Sun 10am–7pm. Oct–Apr Mon–Sat 9.30am–12.30pm & 2–6pm, Sun 1 –6pm. Chateau open May-Sept 9.30-12.30 & 2-6pm; Cellar tour by appt.* In less than 50 years, the Crouseilles cellar, established in the château of the same name, has acquired a good reputation. In the shop and tasting area, you will discover the red Madiran and the dry or sweet Pacherenc-du-Vic-Bilh which are the prize appellations of this estate.

Château du Tariquet – *32800 Eauze, 05 62 09 87 82. Open Mon-Sat 12a,-noon & 2-6pm; www.tariquet.com.* Today, the estate is not only renowned for its Bas-Armagnac and Floc-de-Gascogne, but also for its Côtes-de-Gascogne white wine. One of the biggest estates in Gascony at 700 hectares, owner Yves Grassa rightly deserves his reputation as a trailblazer, and a visit here is impressive not only for the size of the cellars, but for their cleanliness and attention to detail. The Colombard-Ugni Blanc blend is the classic wine, and very good value. Vin de Pays des Côtes de Gascogne

Domaine de Cassagnoles - *32330 Gondrin. 05 62 28 40 57. Open Mon-Fri 9am-12.30 & 2-6pm (Sat 5.30). www.domainedecassagnoles.com.* Another good quality Cotes de Gascogne, where Janine and Gilles Baumann use low temperature vinification to coax a fruity, crisp expression of the Colombard grape. A good boutique also sells regional products from honey to foie gras.

Domaine San de Guilhem, *05 62 06 57 02; www.armagnac-cadeaux.com. Open Mon-Fri 8am-noon &1.30-5.30pm.* Alan Lalanne cultivates 60ha of vines into both Armagnac and Cotes de Gascogne wines that are very well regarded. The whites are fresh and crisp, while the reds are round, fruity and easy to love.

Château Roque-Peyre – *33220 Fougueyrolles. 05 53 24 77 98. Open 8am–noon & 2–5pm. Tasting fee.* Managed by the Vallette family since 1888, this estate's 45ha vineyard is planted with Cabernet-Sauvignon, Merlot, Cabernet Franc, Sauvignon, Sémillon and Muscadelle, all farmed with ecologically responsible methods. Micro-oxygenation is employed in the maturation process; some wines age in barrels for 12 to 24 months depending on the type. Bergerac, Montravel.

Domaine René Rieux – *1495 rte. de Cordes, 81600 Gaillac. 05 63 57 29 29. Open Mon–Fri 9am–12.30pm & 1.30-6pm; www.domainererenerieux.com.* The estate comprises a 27ha hillside vineyard planted on chalky-clay soil. The cultivation methods are largely organic. Harvesting is done by hand and the grapes lightly pressed while still whole. Harmonie wines are fermented in vats, whereas Concerto wines are fermented and matured in casks. Lastly, sparkling Symphonie wines are made according to the Méthode Gaillacoise with natural yeast and without addition of liqueur. Gaillac, Gaillac Doux, Gaillac Mousseux.

Domaine Rotier – *Petit Nareye, 81600 Cadalen. 05 63 41 75 14. Open Mon–Sat 9am–noon & 2–7pm; www.domaine-rotier.com.* One of the most dynamic names in the region, Alain Rotier makes a variety of good quality wines from 35

ha of vines, planted at over 6,000 plants per hectare. No chemical fertilisers have been used at this estate since 1985. Gaillac.

Domaine du Cros – *12390 Goutrens, 05 65 72 71 77. www.domaine-du-cros.com. Open by appt. Mon–Sat 8am–noon & 2–6pm.* The estate, which, in 1984 covered only 3ha, now extends over 26ha exclusively planted with Mansoi, the local name of the Fer-Servadou grape variety. Vinification, lasting twenty to twenty-five days, takes place in stainless-steel, thermo-regulated vats. The wine is matured in barrels for eighteen months before being bottled. Marcillac.

Domaine Arretxea – *64220 Irouléguy. 05 59 37 33 67. Open by appt.* This terraced mountain vineyard is cultivated by organic methods certified by Écocert: no chemical fertilizer is used; organic insecticides are used and compost freely added. Irouléguy.

Domaine de Souch – *805 ch. de Souch, 64110 Laroin-Jurançon. 05 59 06 27 22. Open Mon–Sat 9am–noon & 2–6pm, Sun by appt.* Managed today by Yvonne Hegoburu in memory of her late husband, this biodynamic estate raises Courbu, Petit and Gros Mansengs without pesticides or other chemical interference. Jurançon, Jurançon Sec.

Clos l'Envège – *24240 Monbazillac. 05 53 07 10 31. Open by appt Mon–Sat.* Headed by Julien de Savignac since 1998, this 8ha estate grows Sémillon, Muscadelle and Sauvignon. Hand-harvested grapes are carefully sorted, and fermentation occurs in stainless-steel tanks with temperature control and gentle pressing. Wines are aged 18 months in barrels. Monbazillac.

Domaine Bru-Baché – *R. Barada, 64360 Monein. 05 59 21 36 34. Open by appt. Mon–Fri 8.30am–noon & 1.30–6pm. Sat by appt.* The 8ha vineyard of this estate, extending on the Casterasses hillsides overlooking the village of Monein, thrives on sedimentary clay. Claude Loustalot respects the terroir and uses natural cultivation and vinification methods. Harvesting is done by hand. Wines are matured in oak casks for sixteen to eighteen months. Jurançon, Jurançon Sec.

Clos Uroulat – *Quartier Trouilh, 64360 Monein. 05 59 21 46 19. Open by appt. Mon–Sat.* Charles Hours is an oenologist who created this estate in 1983 with the help of his daughter Marie. The vineyard, extending over 15ha, is planted with Gros and Petit Manseng varieties thriving on chalky pudding-stone. Following the manual harvest, the grapes are fermented and the wine is then matured in oak casks. Some wines are made from sun-dried grapes. Jurançon, Jurançon Sec.

Domaine Cauhapé – *Quartier Castet, 64360 Monein. 05 59 21 33 02. Open Mon-Fri 8am-12.30pm & 1.30-6pm, Sat 10am-6pm; www.cauhape.com.* Henri Ramonteu is a top Jurançon wine-grower whose hillside vineyard extends over 40ha. Gros and Petit Manseng are grown on gravelly and stony soils consisting of clay and silica. The late harvest coincides with the first snowfalls. Béarn, Jurançon, Jurançon Sec.

Château du Frandat – *Rte. d'Agen, D 7 2km E of Nérac, 47600 Nérac. 05 53 65 23 83. Open Mon–Sat 9am–noon & 2–6pm. Closed Nov–Mar except by appt and Sun.* This estate is proud to make three different products all classified as AOC: red, rosé and white Buzet wines, rosé and white Floc-de-Gascogne and Armagnac. Tour of the storehouse and free tasting. Buzet.

Domaine Franck et Jacques Rigal – *Château St-Didier, 46140 Parnac. 05 65 30 70 10. Open Mon–Sat 9am–noon & 2–6pm.* The Rigal family manages three major châteaux: St-Didier-Parnac, le Prieuré de Cénac and Grézels. This one is the largest in the appellation, with 70ha of vines planted on soils of varous types. Ecologically responsible cultivation methods, with manual and mechanical harvesting. Vinification takes place in stainless-steel tanks; wines are then barrel-aged for 18 monts. Some very good value branded Cahors wines also, under the Rigal label. Cahors.

Domaine de L'Ancienne Cure – *24560 Colombier. 05 53 58 27 90. Mon-Sat 9am-6pm; www.domaine-anciennecure.fr.* One of the best renowned Bergerac estates, covering 50 hectares and run by Christian Roche. Try the Cuvee de

Bottles of Cahors

S. Sauvignier/MICHELIN

l'Abbaye for an excellent example of a sweet wine from this area, and the L'Extase for a similarly excellent red. Monbazillac, Saussignac, Bergerac.

Chateau Le Raz, *Open Mon-fri 8.30-12.15 & 2-6.30, Sat by appt. ✆05 53 82 48 41; le-raz.com.* Crisp and lively whites, from vines planted at 6,200 per hectare; very high for Bergerac. 62 hectares in total, 45% white and 55% red.

Tour des Gendres, *24240 Ribagnac, ✆05 53 57 12 43,* Tour des Gendres is home to Luc de Conti, who runs the estate with his brother Jean and cousin, Francis on organic lines.

Domaine Cosse-Maisonneuve – *Lacapelle Cabernac, 46700 Les Beraudies. ✆05 65 24 22 37. Open by appt. Mon-Fri 9–11am & 2–6pm.* Catherine Maisonneuve and Matthieu Cosse took over the estate in 2001, and today grow Malbec, Merlot and Tannat in iron-rich soil of the 14ha vineyard with organic farming. Winemaking is done with whole grapes; the wine are aged in barrels, half of which are new. Cahors.

Clos Triguedina – *Jean-Luc-Baldès, 46700 Puy-l'Évêque. ✆05 65 21 30 81. Open Mon–Sat 9am–noon & 2–6pm; Sun by appt. Closed Jan 1, Dec 25.* The Baldès family has been in the wine-growing business for eight generations and continues to run this 60ha estate with passion and know-how. Clos Triguedina, which the estate produces, is one of the top names of the Cahors AOC and one of the most award-winning wines in Quercy. Tour of the cellar, storehouse and family museum. Cahors, Vin de Pays du Comté Tolosan.

Ferme Abotia – *Ispoure, 64220 St-Jean-Pied-de-Port. ✆05 59 37 03 99. www.abotia.com. Open Mon–Sat 9am–noon & 2–7pm, Sun & public holidays by appt.* This estate has been run by the Errecart family for several generations; the present owners use their know-how to perfect two top products of the Basque gastronomy: an excellent Irouléguy AOC, and prime farmhouse pork sold as sausages, paté and hams. Irouléguy.

Château de Chambert – *Les Haut Coteaux, 46700 Floressas – ✆0870 407 818. Open Mon-Sat 8.30am-12.30pm & 2-6.30p, Sat 10am-12.30pm & 3-6.30pm; www.chambert.com.* Recently restored by owner Philippe Lejeune, this is a rising star in the Cahors appellation, located high on a plateau overlooking the surrounding area. Cahors.

Château de Viella – *Rte. de Maumusson, 32400 Viella. ✆05 62 69 75 81. Open Mon–Sat 8.30am–7pm.* Situated within the boundaries of the municipality of Viella, this hillside vineyard extends over 25ha of pebbly-clay soil planted with Petit Manseng, Tannat and Arrufiac grape varieties enjoying plenty of sunshine. Harvesting is done by hand; the grapes then spend a long time in the vats before being left to mature in new casks. Madiran, Pacherenc-du-Vic-Bilh.

Château du Cèdre – *Bru, 46700 Vire-sur-Lot. ✆05 65 36 53 87. Open Mon–Sat 9am–noon & 2–6pm; www.chateaudu cedre.com.* Pascal and Jean-Marc Verhaeghe, who combine their desire for quality with their wish to respect the terroir, cultivate the 25ha vineyard without using weedkillers. The wine-making process includes picking, sorting and de-stemming the whole harvest by hand. The estate has a small boutique. Cahors.

ADDRESSES

STAY

IN BEAUMARCHÉS

Relais du Bastidou – *À Cayron, 32160 Beaumarchés. 05 62 69 19 94. www.le-relais-du-bastidou.com. Closed Feb 10–20 & Oct 20–Nov 30. 8 rooms. 8€.* Calm reigns at this former farm in the countryside. Rustic chic rooms in the old farmhouse. Sauna and jacuzzi. Country-style dining room with a fine brick chimney.

AROUND BERGERAC

Europ Hôtel – *20 r. du Petit-Sol, 244100 Bergerac. 05 53 57 06 54. www.europ-hotel-bergerac.com. 22 rooms. 7€.* You'll think you've landed in the country when you settle down beneath the tree-shaded pool. This hotel is located near the station, away from the centre of town. Rooms are dated but very clean; modest prices.

Hôtel l'Escapade – *La Grâce, 33220 Port-Ste-Foy-et-Ponchapt. 05 53 24 22 79. www.escapade-dordogne.com. Closed Oct 20–Feb 1, Sun evenings and Mon Feb–Easter Sunday. 7€. Restaurant.* Lovely country retreat on a former tobacco farm near an equestrian centre. Peaceful, rustic-style rooms. Bucolic dining room and terrace with nature view.

Hôtel Verotel – *Rte. d'Agen, Domaine de l'Espinassat, 24100 Bergerac. 05 53 24 89 76. www.hotelverotel.fr. 50 rooms. 6.50€. Restaurant.* A large, classical-style building at the Bergerac exit comprises 50 guestrooms of varying sizes, some suitable for families. Bay windows overlook terrace and pool.

Manoir Grand Vignoble – *Le Grand-Vignoble, 24140 St-Julien-de-Crempse. 05 53 24 23 18. grand.vignoble@wanadoo.fr. Closed Nov 12–Mar 24. 44 rooms. 9€. Restaurant.* This 17C manor house is surrounded by a vast 43ha. The main building houses the dining room (regional cuisine and local wines: Pécharmant, Bergerac) as well as about ten rooms, some with four-poster beds. Larger, contemporary rooms are located in the outbuildings.

AROUND CAHORS

Hôtel Bellevue – *Pl. Truffière, 46700 Puy-l'Évêque. 05 65 36 06 60. hotelbellevue.puyleveque@wanadoo.fr. Closed Jan 10–Feb 6 and Nov 13–28. 11 rooms. 9€.* This hotel, built on a spur overlooking the Lot, is appropriately named. The spacious rooms boast a contemporary style with distinctive features. Inventive cuisine and splendid view of the valley from the Côté Lot restaurant. Regional dishes at L'Aganit.

Hôtel Jean XXII – *5 blvd. Gambetta, 46000 Cahors. 05 65 35 07 66. www.hotel-escargot.com. Closed Feb school hols, Nov 5–20 and Sun in offseason. 9 rooms. 7€.* This hotel (formerly the Hôtel l'Escargot), situated near the Tour Jean-XXII (named after Jacques Duèze, a native of Cahors, elected Pope in 1322), is housed in the former palace erected by the Pope's family. It contains functional rooms with colourful furniture and a refurbished breakfast room.

Hôtel Source Bleue – *Le Bourg, 46700 Touzac, 8km west of Puy-l'Évêque along D 811. 05 65 36 52 01. source bleue@wanadoo.fr. Closed mid-Nov–mid-Apr. 17 rooms. 7€. Restaurant.* The "blue stream", which sprang up on the south bank of the Lot, mysteriously moved, around 1950, to the north bank among these ancient paper mills later turned into a hotel and restaurant. Elegant rooms with distinctive features. Traditional cuisine served in a 17C outbuilding set up as a dining room.

AROUND CONDOM

Hôtel Continental – *20 r. du Mar.-Foch, 32100 Condom. 05 62 68 37 00. www.lecontinental.net. Closed Dec 23–Jan 17. 25 rooms. 10€. Restaurant.* The Baise river runs past this nicely renovated hotel. Comfortable rooms with old engravings; most overlook a small garden. Chic yellow and orange dining room; summer terrace. Regional dishes.

Hôtel Logis des Cordeliers – *R. de la Paix, 32100 Condom. 05 62 28 03 68. www.logisdescordeliers.com. Closed Jan 2–Feb 7. 21 rooms. 7€.* This recent building situated in a peaceful district away from the town centre has functional rooms. Those with a balcony overlooking the swimming pool are more pleasant. Friendly welcome.

Hôtel de la Paix – *24 ave. des Thermes, 32150 Barbotan-les-Thermes. 05 62 69 52 06. hotel.paix@wanadoo.fr. Closed Nov 12–Mar 15.32 rooms. 7€. Restaurant*. Recent building close to the church and the spa centre. The attractive, well-kept rooms are furnished in a functional style. Plain decor and family-hotel atmosphere in the restaurant offering a selection of traditional dishes (dietary menus on request).

AROUND DURAS

Les Rives de l'Avance – *Moulin-de-Trivail, 47430 Ste-Marthe. 05 53 20 60 22. 16 rooms. 6€.* This hotel, built in peaceful, green surroundings, on the edge of the small River Avance and close to a water-mill, offers an unexpected pastoral stopover near the motorway. Functional, colourful rooms.

Hôtel Le Capricorne – *1 r. Paul-Valéry, 47200 Marmande – 05 53 64 16 14. www.lecapricorne-hotel.com. Closed Dec 22–Jan 7. 34 rooms. 7.50€.* This modern building camped on the edge of the main road houses bright soundproofed rooms, which were recently refurbished. In the dining room decorated in a contemporary style and extended by a small terrace, you will be offered a choice of traditional dishes served with a local Marmandais wine.

AROUND GAILLAC

Chambre d'hôte Aurifat – *81170 Cordes-sur-Ciel. 05 63 56 07 03. www.aurifat.com. Closed mid-Dec–mid-Feb. 4 rooms.* A delightful place within walking distance Cordes. This former 13C brick watchtower with adjacent dovecot has been beautifully restored: the rooms (all non-smoking) are pretty and the terraced garden overlooks the nearby fields. Lovely pool.

Hôtel Verrerie – *R. de l'Égalité, 81600 Gaillac. 05 63 57 32 77. www.la-verrerie.com. 14 rooms. 9€. Restaurant*. A tiny museum illustrates the history of this 200-year-old building, which was a glassworks – as the name suggests – and then a pasta factory before becoming a hotel. Of its modern, practical rooms, the best are those overlooking the park, which has a fine bamboo plantation. The dining room leads to a pleasant terrace.

AROUND MARCILLAC

Hôtel à la Route d'Argent – *on the D 988, 12340 Bozouls. 05 65 44 92 27. Closed Jan 2–Feb 24, Mon except evenings Jul–Aug and Sun evenings. 21 rooms. 6€. Restaurant*. Huge building, typical of the region, completely modernised. Comfortable, bright rooms, contemporary dining room serving traditional dishes made from market-fresh ingredients.

Chambre d'hôte Cervel – *Rte. de Vinnac, 12190 Estaing. 05 65 44 09 89. Closed Nov 15–Mar 30. 4 rooms. Restaurant*. This hillside farmhouse belongs to a friendly couple in love with their region. The rooms are extremely comfortable and the menu offers imaginative regional dishes. You'll love the resident goats, and the highly scented Aubrac tea.

IN NÉRAC

Chambre d'hôte Le Domaine du Cauze – *47600 Nérac, 2.5km east of Nérac along D 656 towards Agen. 05 53 65 54 44. www.domaineducauze.com. 4 rooms and 1 suite. Reservations required. Restaurant*. Convivial farmhouse perched on a green hilltop which, when the weather is clear, affords a glimpse of the edge of the Landes forest. The rooms vary in décor; some have antique furniture, others have family items or modern, functional units. Meals served in the arbour, weather permitting.

AROUND PAU

Hôtel Central – *15 r. L.-Daran, 64000 Pau. 05 59 27 72 75. www.hotelcentralpau.com. Closed Dec 18–Jan 3. 28 rooms. 6.50€.* You'll feel welcome in this small hotel in the town centre. The size and comfort of the rooms vary; they are gradually being refurbished; all are well-kept. Some offer wireless Internet; good soundproofing.

Hôtel de Gramont – *3 pl. Gramont, 64000 Pau. 05 59 27 84 04. www.hotelgramont.com. ClosedDec 20–Jan 5. 33 rooms. 8.50€.* This lodge is dates back to the 17C and is thought to be the oldest hotel in Pau. The rooms have distinctive features; some antiques. Top floor rooms are less spacious but recently refurbished.

AROUND ST-JEAN-PIED-DE-PORT

⊜⊜ **Hôtel Central** – *Pl. Charles-de-Gaulle – 64220 St-Jean-Pied-de-Port – ℘ 05 59 37 00 22. Closed Dec 1–Mar 1, Tue from Mar–Jun. 12 rooms. ☕8€. Restaurant* ⊜⊜. This hotel is well situated in the lively part of town. A 200-year-old staircase leads to slightly old-fashioned or recently brightened-up rooms, all of them soundproofed.

EAT

AROUND BERGERAC

⊜⊜ **Au Fil de l'Eau** – *3 r. de la Rouquette, 33220 Port-Ste-Foy-et-Ponchapt, 2km N of Ste-Foy-la-Grande via the D 708. ℘05 53 24 72 60. Closed Feb 26–Mar 15, Nov 5–30, Sun evenings except Jul–Aug and Mon.* A young and dynamic chef has recently taken over this spot, updating the menu every three months with traditional recipes using market ingredients. Have a seat in the dining room or on the lovely terrace overlooking the Dordogne.

⊜⊜ **La Flambée** – *153 ave. Pasteur, 24100 Bergerac. ℘05 53 57 52 33. 21. www.laflambee.com.* This old house features two tastefully decorated dining rooms that mix rustic and contemporary styles. Beams, a stone fireplace and intimate atmosphere in one; the other opens onto the terrace and grounds. Excellent regional cuisine.

⊜⊜ **La Tour des Vents** – *Au Moulin-de-Malfourat, 24240 Monbazillac, 3km W of Monbazillac along D 14E. ℘05 53 58 30 10. moulin.malfourat@wanadoo.fr. Closed Jan 2–Feb 9, Oct 23–27, Sun evenings and Tue lunchtime except Jul–Aug, Mon.* This is a haven of peace built beneath a ruined windmill. The dining room and terrace offer a fine view of the Bergerac vineyards. The tasty and plentiful cuisine, accompanied when appropriate by a very pleasant Monbazillac, is the other strong point of the establishment.

⊜⊜⊜ **L'Imparfait** – *8 r. des Fontaines, 24100 Bergerac. ℘05 53 57 47 92. Closed Nov 16–Feb 14.* A strange name for this excellent restaurant in the heart of the old city. Medieval building with characterful dining room (stonework, open beams), market-fresh cuisine and grilled dishes.

Celebrated cassoulet toulousain

É. Larribère / MICHELIN

AROUND CAHORS

⊜⊜ **Au Fil des Douceurs** – *90 quai de la Verrerie, 46000 Cahors. ℘05 65 22 13 04. Closed Jan 1–21, Jun 26–Jul 9, Sun and Mon.* Feel the river current lapping away as you dine aboard this *gabare*, which formerly carried wood to Bordeaux. Today solidly moored near the Cabessut Bridge, the boat is a restaurant serving traditional fare.

⊜⊜ **La Garenne** – *Route de Brive, St-Henri, 46000 Cahors. ℘05 65 35 40 67. michel.carrendier@wanadoo.fr. Closed Feb 1–Mar 15, Mon evenings, Tue evenings, Wed.* This building in typical Quercy style was once used as stables. Stone walls, exposed timberwork, fine furniture in local style and old rural objects make up a pleasant rustic decor. However, La Garenne's strong point is its tasty cuisine which offers a wide choice of regional specialities.

⊜⊜ **Le Vinois** – *Le bourg, 46140 Caillac. ℘05 65 30 53 60. www.levinois.com. Closed Nov 17–Mar 8, Tue & Wed except evenings mid-Jul–Aug.* Tempting restaurant near the village church. Refnined contemporary décor, designer furnishings, jazz music and modern cuisine.

⊜⊜⊜ **Claudel Loup** – *Métairie Haute, 46140 Anglars-Juillac. ℘05 65 36 76 20. www.claudelloup.com. Closed Tue evenings & Wed except Jul–Sept. 5 rooms* ⊜⊜⊜. ☕9€. Handsome 19C building in a tree-filled garden. Contemporary cuisine served in a lovely dining room or on the terrace beneath the mature plane trees. Comfortable guestrooms.

AROUND CONDOM

La Table des Cordeliers – *1 r. des Cordeliers, 32100 Condom. ✆05 62 68 43 82. www.latabledescordeliers.fr. Closed Jan 15–Feb 5, Mon except evenings Jul–Sept, Wed evenings in summer; Sun evenings.* Near the Logis des Cordeliers, this restaurant occupies a 14C chapel. One dining room is set out beneath the majestic Gothic vaults, and there's a second, more rustic room for winter. Market-fresh cuisine.

Chez Simone – *Pl. des Champions-de-France, 32250 Montréal. ✆05 62 29 44 40. Closed Feb 19–26, Sun evenings, Mon.* M. Daubin, the jovial owner of this village inn since 1992, extends a particularly friendly welcome to the numerous gourmets who come to enjoy his typically regional cuisine. The elegant dining room brightened up by colourful murals offers conviviality with its authentic family atmosphere.

AROUND DURAS

Auberge du Moulin d'Ané – *Rte. de Gontaud, 47200 Virazeil, 7km east of Marmande along D 933 then D 267. ✆05 53 20 18 25. Closed Tue evenings, Sun evenings except Jul–Aug, Wed. Reservations suggested.* This 17C stone mill in the heart of the countryside welcomes its guests on its veranda, offering a view of the tumbling waters of a cascade, or in its rustic-style dining room and delights them with regional specialities or traditional dishes which change with the seasons and the availability of fresh produce.

Hostellerie des Ducs – *Blvd. Jean-Brisseau, 47120 Duras, 21km S. of Ste-Foy-la-Grande by the D 708. ✆05 53 83 74 58. hostellerie.des.ducs@wanadoo.fr. Closed Sun evenings and Mon Oct–Jun, Sat lunchtime and Mon lunchtime. 15 rooms . ☕9€.* This former presbytery near the château draws locals and tourists alike for its regional fare. Functional rooms, garden and swimming pool.

AROUND GAILLAC

La Table du Sommelier – *34 pl. du Griffoul, 81600 Gaillac. ✆05 63 81 20 10. Closed Sun & Mon except Jul–Aug.* With its rich convivial setting combining rustic tables, wooden chests and wine-growing tools, La Table du Sommelier has definitively won over those who love good wine and thoroughly enjoy good food. The key to success? A clever choice of imaginative dishes and a highly appealing wine list.

Hostellerie du Vieux Cordes – *21 r. St-Michel, Haut-de-la-Cité, 81170 Cordes-sur-Ciel. ✆05 63 53 79 20. www.thuries.fr. Closed Jan. 18 rooms . ☕8.50€.* An old monastery in the heart of the splendid medieval city crowning the Puech de Mordagne makes a stopover of undeniable character. Take a table on the terrace or in the attractive patio and enjoy the regional cuisine in which salmon and duck are prominent.

La Falaise – *Rte. de Cordes, 81140 Cahuzac-sur-Vère, 11km N of Gaillac along D 922. ✆05 63 33 96 31. www.lafalaiserestaurant.com. Closed Sun evenings, Tue lunchtime, Mon.* On the way out of the village, a small ordinary façade hides two particularly pleasant dining rooms, extending onto a charming terrace shaded by willows. Here you can enjoy mouth-watering traditional dishes accompanied by generous, ruby-coloured Gaillacs.

AROUND GASCONY

Le Café Gascon – *5 r. Lamartine, 32000 Auch. ✆05 62 61 88 08. cafe.gascon@wanadoo.fr. Closed Jan–Mar, Wed. Reservations required.* An old wooden staircase separates the two dining rooms of this restaurant. Prepare to wait a bit as your meal is carefully prepared to order. Afterward, treat yourself to a local favourite: Café Gascon, made at table.

AROUND MARCILLAC

Auberge du Fel – *Au Fel, 12140 Entraygues-sur-Truyère. ✆05 65 44 52 30. www.auberge-du-fel.com. Closed Nov 6–Apr 7.* The view of the surrounding countryside from this old house overlooking the River Lot will enhance your discovery of the gourmet dishes, often flavoured with herbs: even the homemade ice creams include not just mint but also basil and thyme flavours.

Le Méjane – *R. Méjane, 12500 Espalion. ✆05 65 48 22 37. Closed Mar 6–30, Jun 26–30, Mon except evenings offseason, Wed except Jul–Aug, Sun evenings.* Food-lovers won't forget this restaurant located in the lovely town of Espalion. Regulars frequent this dining room, with its light woodwork and mirros, eagerly awaiting the expertly prepared creations of the chef, who is particularly adept at updated versions of traditional recipes.

NÉRAC

Aux Délices du Roy – *7 r. du Château, 47600 Nérac. ℘05 53 65 81 12. Closed Sun evenings offseason, Wed.* Nestling beneath the castle of the House of Albret, this convivial family restaurant offers a small rustic dining room, recently painted in blue and yellow and enhanced by colourful furnishings. In the kitchen, M Sarthou, the owner-chef, skilfully blends seafood and traditional recipes.

AROUND PAU

La Michodière – *34 r. Pasteur, 64000 Pau. ℘ 05 59 27 53 85. Closed Jul 25–Aug 20, Sun, public holidays.* From the ground-floor dining room, there is a view of the kitchen where the chef is busy preparing delicious dishes selected according to the availability of fresh produce. Lobster *sauce corail* and duck's liver escalope Michodière-style are reliable and popular choices.

Arcé – *Route du Col-d'Ispéguy, 64430 St-Étienne-de-Baïgorry. ℘ 05 59 37 40 14. www.hotel-arce.com. Closed mid-Nov–mid-Mar, Wed lunchtime and Mon Sept 15–Jul 15 except public holidays.* The greenery surrounding the house, the typical white façade highlighted by red shutters, the pretty terrace shaded by plane trees, the rippling water of the river, the warm family welcome… the food? You won't want to leave once you've experienced the chef's tasty and copious cuisine!

La Chaumière de Bidouze – *Bidouze, 32400 Riscle, 3km rte. de Pau, then to the right. ℘05 62 69 86 56. www.chaumieredebidouze.com. Closed Dec 24–Jan 1. 14 rooms. ☕6€.* Welcoming ambiance, peace and quiet, plus local products at the lovely cottage in the Gers countryside. Divine Gascony cuisine. A variety of guestrooms available.

La Table d'Hôte – *1 r. du Hédas, 64000 Pau. ℘05 59 27 56 06. la-table-dhote@wanadoo.fr. Closed Dec holidays, Mon except evenings in Jul-Aug, and Sun.* The chef's cuisine, served in an attractive rustic dining room, is mainly based on regional recipes and products, revealing the finer aspects of the Béarn tradition. On the wine list, Jurançons and Madirans are prominent, as they blend admirably well with regional dishes.

AROUND ST-JEAN-PIED-DE-PORT

Pecoïtz – *Rte. d'Iraty, 64220 Aincille. 7km SE of St-Jean-Pied-de-Port along D 933 and D 18. ℘05 59 37 11 88. pecoitz@wanadoo.fr. Closed Jan 1–Mar 15, Fri Oct–May. 14 rooms. ☕5€.* Convivial restaurant promoting the fine specialities of Basque cuisine, including ham piperade and chicken basquaise, cooked with tomatoes and sweet peppers. Prepared with dedication, these regional dishes release their full flavour when they are accompanied by a special bottle of Irouléguy. A few plain but clean bedrooms.

GOURMET DELIGHTS

In an area which is so rich in gastronomic specialities, you may want to try your hand at a cookery course.

Loisirs-Accueil Gers

The Gers Loisirs-Accueil service offers several ways to discover the local gastronomy: a package including the visit of wine storehouses, a market tour and a day's cooking practice; a foie gras weekend in a farm including an introduction to the art of carving a goose and preparing foie gras; a course with a top chef of the Ronde des Mousquetaires *(Maison de l'agriculture, Route de Tarbes, BP 178, 32003 Auch Cedex; ℘05 62 61 79 00; www.gers-tourisme.com).*

Hôtel de la Reine Jeanne (Pyrenées-Atlantique)

41 km NW of Pau by the N 117. 44 r. du Bourg-Vieux, 64300 Orthez.Course offered mid-Oct–Aug. ℘05 59 67 00 76 or 05 59 65 03 06. www.reine-jeanne.fr.
This course offers an introduction to traditional farm cooking.

INDEX

MAPS AND PLANS

MAPS OF THE WINE REGIONS

ROAD MAPS

All Michelin publications are cross-referenced and the reference for each French wine region is given at the start of the chapter. From our range of products we recommend the following:

Local Maps, on a scale of 1:150 000 or 1:180 000, with detailed information on a small scale for those who want to fully discover all that one or two départements have to offer. Michelin local maps have an alphabetical index of places and plans of principal towns and are numbered from 301 to 345 (see map below).

Regional Maps, on a scale of 1:250 000 to 1:300 000, cover the regions of France and show the primary and secondary road networks, together with tourist information. They are useful when covering a large area or travelling longer distances between towns and have an alphabetical index of places and plans of principal towns.

Internet users can access personalised route plans, Michelin maps and town plans, and addresses of hotels and restaurants featured in the Michelin Guide France through the website at **www.ViaMichelin.com**

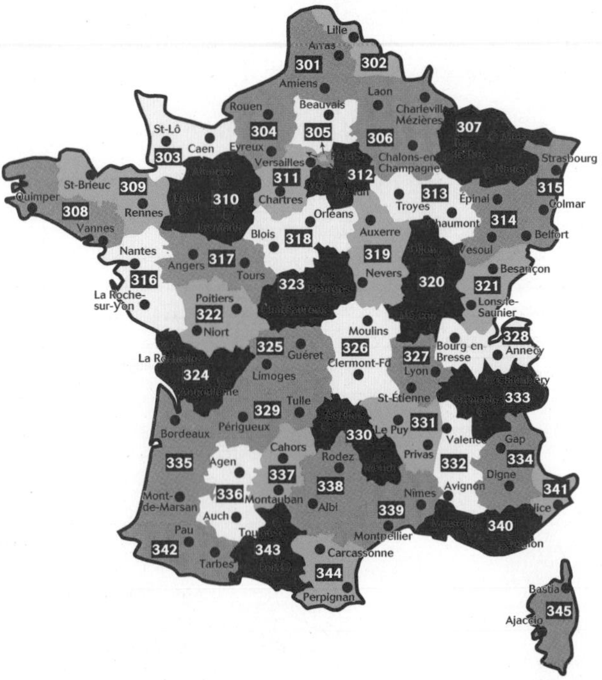

MAP LEGEND

Selected monuments and sights

- Tour - Departure point
- Catholic church
- Protestant church, other temple
- Synagogue - Mosque
- Building
- Statue, small building
- Calvary, wayside cross
- Fountain
- Rampart - Tower - Gate
- Château, castle, historic house
- Ruins
- Dam
- Factory, power plant
- Fort
- Cave
- Troglodyte site
- Prehistoric site
- Viewing table
- Viewpoint
- Other place of interest

Sports and recreation

- Racecourse
- Skating ring
- Outdoor, indoor swimming pool
- Multiplex Cinema
- Marina, sailing centre
- Trail refuge hut
- Cable cars, gondolas
- Funicular, rack railway
- Tourist train
- Recreation area, park
- Theme, amusement park
- Wildlife park, zoo
- Gardens, park, arboretum
- Bird sanctuary, aviary
- Walking tour, footpath
- Of special interest to children

Special symbols

- Beach
- Cycling tours
- Pony trekking
- Vineyard

Abbreviations

A	Agricultural office (Chambre d'agriculture)
C	Chamber of Commerce (Chambre de commerce)
H	Town hall (Hôtel de ville)
J	Law courts (Palais de justice)
M	Museum (Musée)
P	Local authority offices (Préfecture, sous-préfecture)
POL.	Police station (Police)
	Police station (Gendarmerie)
T	Theatre (Théâtre)
U	University (Université)

Additional symbols

- Tourist information
- Motorway or other primary route
- Junction: complete, limited
- Pedestrian street
- Unsuitable for traffic, street subject to restrictions
- Steps – Footpath
- Train station – Auto-train station
- Coach (bus) station
- Tram
- Metro, underground
- Park-and-Ride
- Access for the disabled
- Covered market
- Barracks
- Drawbridge
- Quarry
- Mine
- Car ferry (river or lake)
- Ferry service: cars and passengers
- Foot passengers only
- Access route number common to Michelin maps and town plans

Bert (R.)...	Main shopping street
AZ B	Map co-ordinates
►►	Visit if time permits

Michelin Apa Publications Ltd

A joint venture between Michelin and Langenscheidt

58 Borough High Street, London SE1 1XF, United Kingdom

ISBN 978-1-906261-81-8
Printed: November 2009
Printed and bound In Germany

Vintages

	1994	1995	1996	1997	1998	1999	2000	2001	2002	2003	2004	2005	2006	2007	2008
Alsace															
Bordeaux (white)															
Bordeaux (red)															
Burgundy (white)															
Burgundy (red)															
Beaujolais															
Champagne															
Côtes du Rhône North															
Côtes du Rhône South															
Provence															
Languedoc-Roussillon															
Loire Valley (Muscadet)															
Loire Valley (Anjou Touraine)															
Loire Valley (Pouilly Sancerre)															

VINTAGE: GOOD: AVERAGE: